16.95 ✓

✓

D0549633

Retail Marketing

WITHDRAWN FROM
ST HELENS COLLEGE LIBRARY

damage to cover

LENS COLLEGE LIBRARY

19

WITHDRAWN FROM
the CMU LIBRARY

Retail Marketing

Peter J. McGoldrick

School of Management
UMIST

McGRAW-HILL BOOK COMPANY

London · New York · St Louis · San Francisco · Auckland
Bogotá · Caracas · Lisbon · Madrid · Mexico · Milan
Montreal · New Delhi · Panama · Paris · San Juan · São Paulo
Singapore · Sydney · Tokyo · Toronto

Published by
McGRAW-HILL Book Company Europe
Shoppenhangers Road, Maidenhead, Berkshire, England SL6 2QL
Telephone 0628 23432
Fax 0628 770224

British Library Cataloguing in Publication Data

McGoldrick, Peter J.
  Retail marketing.
  1. Retailing. Marketing
  I. Title

  658.8'7

ISBN 0-07-084159-4

Library of Congress Cataloging-in-Publication Data

McGoldrick, Peter J.
  Retail marketing/Peter McGoldrick.
    p. cm.
  Includes bibliographical references.
  ISBN 0-07-084159-4
  1. Retail trade. 2. Marketing research. I. Title.
HF5429.M355 1990
658.8'7--dc20   89-13735

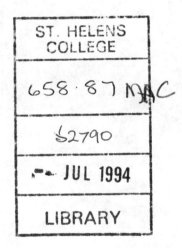

ST. HELENS
COLLEGE

658·87 MAC

£2790

JUL 1994

LIBRARY

Copyright © 1990 McGraw-Hill International (UK) Limited. All rights reserved. No part of this publication may be reproduced, stored in a retrieval system, or transmitted, in any form or by any means, electronic, mechanical, photocopying, recording, or otherwise, without the prior permission of McGraw-Hill International (UK) Limited.

67 CL 93

Typeset by Computape (Pickering) Limited, North Yorkshire
and printed and bound in Great Britain by Clays Ltd, St Ives plc

CONTENTS

PREFACE

The last twenty years have seen a dramatic metamorphosis within the retailing industry, as retailers have ceased to play the subordinate role in the marketing of consumer goods. Now the power and influence of many major retailers greatly exceeds that of their manufacturer-suppliers. This change has created the need for a far more rigorous and systematic approach to retail marketing. It has also created more exciting career opportunities within the industry, as retailers have realized the need to recruit, develop and motivate this new and sophisticated breed of retail managers.

This book has been written for all serious students of retailing, whether they be practising managers or members of undergraduate/postgraduate courses in universities or polytechnics. An orientation has been maintained towards the functions and problems of retail marketing management, but the subject-matter is also relevant to those in closely related areas, such as manufacturer sales, shopping centre development, consumer research, consultancy and advertising. While most of the examples and cases quoted relate to national or international retail companies, many of the concepts and strategies explored within this text could also be exploited by smaller retail businesses.

This book also sets out to dispel any illusion that retail marketing is a less rigorous or demanding discipline than product marketing. In addition to the problems faced by any marketer, most retailers must also manage a very large product assortment, deal with the complexities and risks of selecting new locations and successfully manage a constant and direct interface with their customers. To the manager, student or researcher, the challenges of retail marketing are very great indeed.

While acknowledging the necessary creative inputs, a scientific approach to the strategies and functions of retail marketing is advocated. Current and emerging techniques are analysed, but it is not the intention to provide simple answers; the approach is rather to develop a framework and guidelines for the effective analysis of management problems. What theory is available and relevant is presented but certainly not exalted; every effort has been made to present material, at times complex, in a style that is clear and free of excessive jargon.

The content of this text has been derived from a very wide range of sources and evolved through twelve years of teaching retail marketing to undergraduates, postgraduates and management courses. Insights have been provided by numerous retail managers with whom I have worked in a research, consultancy or teaching capacity. The research base of the text has been derived mainly from the retailing and marketing literature, but contributions from the disciplines of geography, economics and psychology are also presented.

Having introduced the function of retail marketing in Chapter 1, Part One of the text follows a progression through the logical stages of planning marketing strategy. Chapter 2 examines the changing environment and structure of retailing, both nationally and internationally. In Chapter 3, the importance of correctly identifying consumer needs and wants is emphasized and various methods of segmenting markets are considered. Chapter 4 presents some of the planning frameworks that can assist in formulating retail strategy, assessing strategic alternatives and positioning the retail offering. Chapter 5 is concerned with evaluating retail performance, both in terms of the 'image value' produced and in terms of more conventional financial measures.

Part Two examines seven major elements of the retail marketing mix, starting in Chapter 6 with store location decisions and techniques. Chapter 7 looks at the buying function, approaches to product selection and the negotiation of buying terms. The many facets of retail pricing are analysed in Chapter 8 within a new multi-dimensional framework. Chapter 9 examines trends and strategies in the development of retailers' own brands, an important topic largely ignored in many retail texts. The types, trends and stages of retail advertising and promotion provide the subject-matter of Chapter 10. Chapter 11 considers the in-store selling environment, from its overall design and atmosphere, through to the detail of space allocation and display. In the final chapter, personal, financial and other elements of the retail service mix are discussed.

It is recognized that some elements of retail marketing, such as retail location, have developed a massive research base that cannot be fully acknowledged within the context of a wide ranging text. On the other hand, functions such as retail buying have attracted rather less research attention but are no less amenable to an analytical approach. In all chapters, a detailed bibliography is provided to encourage and facilitate further study in depth. Review questions are also provided as the basis for group discussion and to help individual readers to apply the concepts encountered within each chapter.

Peter McGoldrick

ACKNOWLEDGEMENTS

I would like to thank all the people who have helped me in researching and writing this book. In particular, I am grateful for the encouragement provided at the outset and throughout this project by Professors Martin Christopher, John Dawson and Bert Rosenbloom. I am also indebted to Professors Roland Smith and Malcolm Cunningham for providing me with the opportunity and the space to develop the subject of retail marketing within the School of Management at UMIST.

It is not possible to individually acknowledge the many retail managers who have helped me in my research and course development; their influence upon this book has however been considerable. Researching the literature base required the extensive help and co-operation of some excellent libraries. I would like to thank John French, Rita Olive, and their colleagues in the UMIST Library Service, and the librarians of the Manchester Business School. I am also particularly grateful to Bernard Howcroft, Bob Hilton, Fiona Swailes and Linda Duckworth of the C.W.S. Library and Information Service.

The material for this book is drawn from many sources which, whenever possible, are individually acknowledged within the text. I am grateful to all the publishers and authors who gave their permission, usually freely, to quote extracts and exhibits. I am especially grateful to Professor Jerker Nilsson for his permission to cite his work on retail buying in Chapter 7, and to my colleague Stuart Eliot for his advice on retail structure in Chapter 2. I am greatly indebted to Euromonitor for agreeing to provide a large proportion of the industry data quoted within this book.

This project has benefited from the professionalism and perseverance of the editorial team at McGraw-Hill, especially Julie Ganner, Business and Economics Editor. I am grateful to the anonymous reviewers of the initial proposal and of the final manuscript for their invaluable comments and advice. I would like to give a special thank you to Mary O'Mahony for all her hard work and patience in typing all the drafts and the manuscript.

INTRODUCTION TO RETAIL MARKETING

Retailing is an activity of enormous economic significance in every Western European country. In Britain, over two million people are employed in retailing, representing nearly 10 per cent of all employees. A further 1.2 million are employed in wholesaling activities, which means that the distributive trades account for over 15 per cent of the employed population. Retail sales exceeded £75,000 million by 1987, over 44 per cent of total expenditure by consumers (Institute for Retail Studies 1989). Retailing is also a very visible form of economic activity, and one that exerts a major influence upon the lives of consumers.

In spite of its scale and importance, the retailing industry was not initially at the forefront in embracing the marketing concept. In the 1960s this could be attributed to the fragmented nature of the industry, characterized by a very large number of small organizations. The industry became rapidly more concentrated, and major retailers wielded their new-found power through aggressive buying, high-budget advertising campaigns or elaborate store designs. The use of marketing weapons, however, does not always indicate that the marketing concept is being applied. It is only in relatively recent years that many retailers have taken an enlightened and integrative view of their marketing activities.

The marketing concept may be simply expressed as the identification and satisfaction of consumer needs and wants, at a profit. The application of this concept is not a simple matter; neither is it a problem that can be solved just by appointing a marketing department. It involves the development of a philosophy that must pervade all sections of the organization, from chief executive to the most junior member of the store staff. Systems must be established for monitoring consumers' perceptions and motivations and for assessing changes in the marketing environment. Internally, an integrative structure must be developed which delivers a co-ordinated response to these opportunities and challenges, at a suitable rate of return. This is the scope of retail marketing and the subject matter of this text.

1.1 THE EVOLUTION OF RETAIL MARKETING

This section examines the development and characteristics of the retail marketing function. First, the role of retailing within the total distribution channel is considered; this is followed by an examination of the ways in which retailers have increased their power *vis-à-vis* other members of the channel. Of particular relevance here is the extent to which retailers have taken increased control in the marketing of consumer goods. The emergence and format of the marketing function within retailing organizations is then considered.

1.1.1 Channels of distribution

Marketing texts originating in the USA, which for many years have provided the backbone of marketing education, tended to present a view of the manufacturer–retailer relationship that does not entirely reflect the situation in the UK or some other European countries. Being based upon a different economic and legislative environment, they usually portray a dynamic but more regulated interaction. US retailers have grown in size and influence, but the effect of the Robinson–Patman Act (see Office of Fair Trading 1985, ch. 6) has been to limit their scope for negotiation of superior terms. US writers have contributed a great deal to the understanding of distribution channels, but the important environmental differences should not be overlooked.

A review of the vast volume of literature pertaining to distribution channels would be beyond the scope of this section. It is important to appreciate, however, that there are many inter-relationships and interdependencies between product marketing and retail marketing. Unfortunately, much of the literature fails to convey the true nature of these interrelationships, tending to depict distribution channels as a subordinate element of the manufacturer's marketing mix. This manufacturer-centred view of channels has seriously understated the power, scope and importance of retail marketing. Indeed, it is equally realistic now to talk of 'channels of supply' within a retailer-centred view of the marketing process.

Reviews of the conceptual and empirical contributions to the study of distribution channels have usually identified several alternative schools of thought. Gattorna (1978) categorized the microeconomic, institutional, functional, organizational systems and behavioural approaches to the study of channels. While it could be perceived as counter-productive to review literature relating to a common topic under such diverse headings, it cannot be denied that there has been relatively little integration of these various approaches.

After an extensive review of literature relating to distribution channels, Gattorna (1978) concluded:

Despite its volume and apparent comprehensiveness, therefore, the channels literature is curiously deficient; it is mainly descriptive in nature, lacks explanatory power and has virtually no predicative value.

Introducing a new framework for the comparative analysis of distribution channels, Stern and Reve (1980) were also critical of the fragmented way in which channel theory had evolved:

Published studies related to distribution channels present, collectively, a rather disjointed collage. This is due, in part, to the absence of a framework which can accommodate the various paradigms and orientations employed.

The dangers of regarding distribution channels as passive and orderly adjuncts to the manufacturer's marketing activities were recognized at an early stage by McVey (1960):

It may be that the 'channel of distribution' is a concept that is primarily academic in usage and unfamiliar to many firms selling to and through these channels.

The middleman is not a hired link in a chain forged by a manufacturer but rather an independent market, the focus of a large group of customers for whom he buys.

As he grows and builds a following, he may find that his prestige in his market is greater than that of the suppliers whose goods he sells.

These early insights proved to be highly accurate, ironically, especially in terms of the subsequent developments in retailing in the UK.

These few extracts clearly cannot do justice to a vast area of literature; they also paint a rather negative picture of its contribution. They do however alert readers to some of the potential

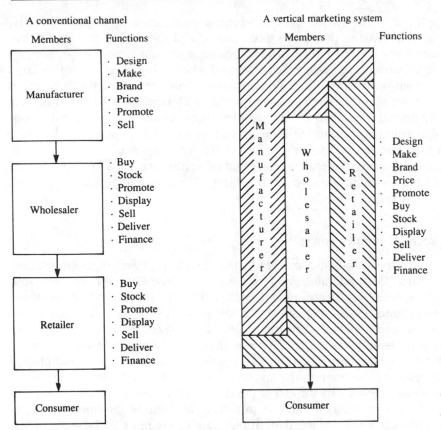

Figure 1.1   The shifting of functions within the channel
Source: Walters (1979, p. 215).

pitfalls of the manufacturer-oriented view of distribution and marketing channels. It is accepted that some of the more recent behavioural approaches to the topic, notably studies of conflict and power within the channel (e.g. Gaski 1984), come closer to providing a realistic background for the analysis of retailer–manufacturer relationships.

In discussing channels of distribution, it is also essential to recognize the extent to which the conventional barriers between manufacturing, wholesaling and retailing have broken down. Figure 1.1 compares the 'conventional channel' with the 'vertical marketing system', the latter being defined by McCammon (1970) as 'rationalized and capital intensive networks designed to achieve technological, managerial and promotional economies through the integration, coordination of synchronization of marketing flows from points of production to points of ultimate use'. To achieve such a system, some manufacturers have bought their way into retailing, while others, such as Benetton, have pursued similar results through franchising (see Section 2.2.4). Still others have sought to maximize their influence over the point of purchase by willingly taking over many of the retailer's traditional roles. For example, the major packers of herbs and spices frequently attend to the merchandising of their own supermarket displays.

On the other side of the coin, major retailers have increasingly subsumed the wholesaling role and many have also taken over the tasks of physical distribution. Alternatively, transportation and warehousing may be subcontracted to specialist agencies, such as Cory or Lowfied (Whimster 1981). The manufacturer's exclusive hold over the design and production functions has also been eroded. Although few retailers have chosen to acquire manufacturing facilities directly, they can be very closely involved in the design specifications and the quality control process. Indeed, Marks & Spencer has been described as a manufacturer without factories.

These changes have effectively eliminated the traditional wholesaling function from a large proportion of the distribution channel. In response to these pressures, there has been much rationalization and regrouping within the wholesaling sector, with large groups such as Booker McConnell developing extensive interests in retailing. Another response has been the development of wholesaler-led voluntary groups of retailers (see Section 2.2.3). Some of the more aggressive cash-and-carry operators, such as Makro, have also expanded to fill the void, following the decline of traditional wholesaling (Key Note 1986); these have used buying, pricing and promotional techniques more akin to those of large-scale retailing than traditional wholesaling.

1.1.2 The development of retailer power

The last thirty years has seen a dramatic increase in the scale and power of major retailing organizations. In the early 1960s manufacturers exercised considerable power over retailers, helped by the ability to enforce resale price maintenance and by the fragmented nature of the retailing industry. McClelland (1961) complained that 'the power of the manufacturers in my judgement is now not only excessive but overweening'. Within six years, he was citing instances of retailers exercising considerable power over their suppliers in order to obtain superior terms (McClelland 1967). Power in a specific negotiation was seen to depend upon the turnover offered to a supplier and the retailer's 'freedom, in the last resort, not to buy or to buy in very small quantities from a particular supplier'. By the end of the 1970s, the balance of power had shifted from the manufacturers to the retailers in most sectors. The chairman of the Food Manufacturers' Federation complained of the retailers that, 'If they continue to press for large discounts, some manufacturing firms will go out of business or be taken over' (Financial Times 1979).

An overview of the retailer–manufacturer relationship in several European countries was provided by Pommerening (1979), a principal in McKinsey's Hamburg office. He set the changes within a time-scale of three decades:

- 1950s: 'Manufacturer is King'—postwar shortages and a fragmented distribution system place the primary emphasis upon manufacturing and supply.
- 1960s: 'Consumer is King'—increasing competition brought more emphasis upon marketing and the development of manufacturer brands.
- 1970s: 'Trade is King'—the more concentrated and powerful retailing industry increasingly took over the functions of marketing.

Gabor (1977) listed three major reasons for the transfer of power:

1. The abolition of resale price maintenance (RPM), in 1964 in the UK, in most product sectors. This represented a significant landmark in the shift of power, although pressures for change existed well before the legislation. The arguments for and against RPM were subject to detailed analysis by Pickering (1966) and Yamey (1966).
2. The spread of private brands, which accounted for nearly 22 per cent of retail sales and 25 per cent of food sales by 1986 (Euromonitor 1987). The importance of this component of retail marketing merited the inclusion of Chapter 9 on this topic.
3. Increased concentration, which is both an effect and a cause of further retail power. By 1986, large multiple chains (with ten or more outlets) held 58.6 per cent of retail trade in Britain

Table 1.1 Concentration in grocery retailing

Organization/type	Share of grocery market (%) 1986	1988
Tesco	12.5	14.2
J. Sainsbury	12.8	14.1
Gateway	12.2	11.4
Argyll	9.3	10.2
Asda	7.5	7.7
Kwik Save	2.8	2.9
Waitrose	2.3	2.6
Bejam	1.8	2.3
Morrisons	1.4	1.7
Other multiples	8.3	5.8
Co-operatives	12.4	11.9
Independents	16.7	15.4

Source: Institute of Grocery Distribution (1989, p. 2).

(British Business 1988). The grocery sector is particularly highly concentrated, as Table 1.1 illustrates. By 1988, the top five organizations held 57.6 per cent of the grocery market, an increase from 54.3 per cent just two years earlier. The position of multiples in the UK and other European countries is discussed in Section 2.2.1.

The relative sizes of major retailers and major manufacturers were compared in terms of market capitalization by Grant (1987). In the food sector, this represented £2,452 million in the case of Sainsbury, compared with Unilever's £1,922 million. The imbalance was far greater in some other sectors, such as clothing, where Marks & Spencer at £4,495 million was compared with Vantona Viyella at £437 million.

The debate as to the desirability of large retailer buying power culminated in a reference to the Monopolies and Mergers Commission in 1977. After an extensive enquiry, the Commission report was published in 1981. Under Section 78(1) of the Fair Trading Act 1973, the Secretary of State required the Commission to submit a report on:

the general effect on the public interest of the following practice, which appears to him to be a practice within section 78(1)(b), that is to say—the practice of the acquisition by or the supply to some retailers of goods—

(a) at prices less than those charged to other retailers by the supplier, whether the reduction is by way of a discount, rebate or allowance or by means of prices specially negotiated, or
(b) on terms which involve the provision of any special benefit in money or money's worth by the supplier to those retailers in connection with the supply of the goods by or to the retailers, not being a benefit provided to other retailers, where the reduction or the value of the benefit cannot be attributed to savings in the supplier's costs. (Monopolies and Mergers Commission 1981)

The Commission consulted widely with all sectors of the industry; it also conducted limited surveys of supply terms, margins and retail prices of a few selected products. Pressure was clearly exerted by many manufacturers and smaller retailers to recommend some form of restriction upon the effects of large retailer buying power, possibly along the lines of Robinson–Patman in the USA. The multiple retailers for their part presented a convincing argument, best summarized by reference to the evidence given by the Multiple Shops Federation:

Interference with the present well-established commercial arrangements would:

i)   be detrimental to suppliers and, if buying on competitive terms were prevented, could result in an increase in buying from foreign suppliers with serious consequences for the balance of payments and home employment;

ii) disrupt the operation of the retail trade, preventing expansion, development and efficient operation as the result of competition; and

iii) be against the interests of the consumer, since it would inevitably result in higher prices and a reduction in service.

The latter view generally prevailed, and the Commission concluded that the general effect of the practice on the public interest had not been harmful. This conclusion was extended to a comment that the practice had actually been 'part and parcel' of developments beneficial to competition and the consumer. The case was re-examined a few years later by the Office of Fair Trading (1985), and it was concluded that there had been no 'material change' to the factors that had led the Monopolies and Mergers Commission to its conclusion in 1981. Some of the data from these two studies are presented in Chapter 7 to illustrate the terms of trade negotiated by retail buyers.

The process of retailer concentration seems likely to continue, until a point is reached when government intervention is inevitable. Such a point may be a merger proposal which would significantly reduce competition nationally or regionally. If the retailing industry avoids provoking such intervention, then the power of major retailers may grow still further. There are however some economic forces which could begin to undermine retailer power, noted by O'Reilly (1984), president of H. J. Heinz, USA:

1. Surplus floorspace capacity arising from rapid geographical expansion, causing space productivity to fall

2. The intensification of competition as retailers' strategies converge in terms of locations, retail formats, assortments and private brands

3. A possible serious decline in High Street property values, especially as new technology reduces the financial institutions' reliance on large networks of branches

4. The sheer scale of retailers' investment in stores, distribution systems, information systems, etc., which could make them less flexible and more vulnerable to those offering new formats, improved economies and superior systems to the market

These factors should not be dismissed as wishful thinking on the part of a major food manufacturer. In that the power of major retailers has continued to grow for over twenty-five years, it is too easy to form the myopic view that the process could never be halted or reversed.

1.1.3 Control of the retail marketing mix

The concept of the retailing mix has developed alongside that of the marketing mix, although the degree of control that retailers could exert has been a function of the manufacturer–retailer power balance. In an early treatment of the topic, Lazer and Kelley (1961) defined the retail mix as 'the total package of goods and services that a store offers for sale to the public. The retail mix, then, is the composite of all effort which was programmed by management and which embodies the adjustment of the retail store to its market environment'.

This early definition rightly emphasized that retailing is not just about offering products for sale, but a complex product/service proposition. It also stressed the importance of co-ordinating the mix with a programmed effort, appropriately attuned to the needs and opportunities within the market.

Lazer and Kelley classified the retailing mix under three major headings, each element being focused towards the consumer through the utilization of market information:

1. Goods and service mix
2. Physical distribution mix
3. Communications mix

While manufacturers could exert extensive control over pricing and other elements of the mix, the scope for producing a co-ordinated and carefully attuned retail marketing mix was somewhat limited. The shift of power, described in the previous section, has given retailers far more scope to utilize the full range of marketing mix elements in pursuit of their strategic objectives. This has not only had a profound effect upon the quality of retail marketing, but has also changed the general nature of consumer goods marketing. Figure 1.2 illustrates the extent to which the control of marketing mix variables has shifted from manufacturers to retailers. In that this was based upon an overview of consumer goods marketing in Europe by Pommerening (1979), the extent and pace of the changes naturally varies between countries. Let us take each element in turn:

1. *Product range* Retailers have become increasingly adept at assembling a product mix oriented towards their target market(s). They are rather less concerned about stocking a manufacturer's full range, unless the incentives to do so are very large.
2. *Product image* In order to position a product carefully and to cultivate a consistent brand image, a manufacturer would wish to exert influence over the pricing and merchandising of the product. A retailer, on the other hand, may regard a top brand as a suitable focus for special offers. Considerable controversy arose between Hotpoint and Comet because of heavy discounting of the former's branded products.
3. *Consumer franchise* As retailers have developed their store names as major brands, customer loyalty has tended to shift from products to stores. Retailer's own-brand products have played a significant part in the reinforcement of retailer brand images (see Chapter 9).
4. *Shelf price* Following the abolition of resale price maintenance in most areas, this element of the mix saw a more drastic shift of control than any other. Individual product profit maximization has therefore given way to assortment pricing and to the optimization of overall store price image and profitability (see Chapter 8).
5. *Distribution* Manufacturers require maximum distribution to launch a new product or achieve economies of scale on existing products. Unimpressed by such arguments, the buyer applies the retailer's own assortment and profitability criteria in deciding whether or not to list the product and, if so, how much of it to take into stock (see Chapter 7).
6. *Shelving* The average size of stores has increased, but the demands upon selling space have increased even faster. Retailers have therefore become far more scientific in their approaches to allocating shelf space in order to maximize the effectiveness of the available display space (see Chapter 11).
7. *Advertising* Retailers have been able to utilize larger advertising budgets than most manufacturers, assisted by advertising allowances from manufacturers. They have also now become more sophisticated in their communications strategies and in building better differentiated images (see Chapter 10).

Allied to the shift of power, therefore, there have also been major changes in the way in which retailers have utilized the elements of the marketing mix. The competitive and legislative

Elements of marketing mix	Past ▼ manufacturer control	Present ▼ trade control	Examples
Product range			Dependent on trade stocking policies
Product image			Devalued by trade preoccupation with price
Consumer franchise			Store franchise eroding brand franchise
Shelf price			Subject to loss-leading by trade
Distribution			Governed by trade inventory policies
Shelving			Controlled by trade store schematic
Advertising			Trade outspending manufacturers

Figure 1.2 Control of the marketing mix
Source: Pommerening (1979, p. 8).

environment of the UK has been especially conducive to these developments, but parallel changes have occurred in many other countries. In the USA, manufacturers have retained more power *vis-à-vis* retailers but the latter have considerably improved their skills in strategic marketing:

a quiet revolution has been occurring among retailers, who, faced with increasingly saturated markets, are now taking up the methods and tools that used to be the exclusive province of the brand marketer. Retailers are becoming more sophisticated strategists, developing distinctive approaches to a particular market segment. (Cohen and Jones 1978)

1.1.4 Development of the retail marketing function

Retailers have therefore ceased to be subordinate members of the marketing channel; their power has grown considerably, and a great deal of control can now be exercised over the key elements of the mix. This power has not always been translated into a truly co-ordinated marketing function. Many retailers have utilized the weapons of marketing without necessarily adopting an integrative and strategic approach to their marketing activities. Blackwell and Talarzyk (1983) observed:

In retailing, however, implementation of the marketing concept appeared to be mostly at the firm's operational, rather than strategic, levels. Certain policies, such as customer service, refund policies, hours of operation, and other areas of tactical importance, seemed to be more affected by the marketing concept than were truly strategic levels of management.

To a large extent, this problem arose through the lack of a strong marketing function within the organization. Some retail organizations have been 'marketing-led' for many years; MacNeary (1981) described the extensive scale and scope of the marketing department within J. Sainsbury. For many organizations, the marketing department is a relatively new arrival; for some others, it is yet to arrive.

Piercy (1984) has traced the transfer of the marketing function from manufacturers to retailers during the 1980s. He suggested a number of criteria that a retail company should apply in assessing the need for a retail marketing department:

1. Are there signs that the marketing side of the business is underperforming?
2. Have we reached point where a marketing specialization is needed?

3. Are there problems of co-ordination in the marketing area?
4. Are there problems of integration in the marketing area?
5. What are the competitors doing?

Based upon these criteria, few retailers of any size can justify not establishing a co-ordinated marketing function. Unfortunately, the response of a number of medium-sized companies to the marketing challenge has been to simply bestow the title 'marketing' upon an existing group or individual within the organization. While this may serve to signal a new orientation, it is unlikely to bring the full potential of the retail marketing approach. Piercy (1986) subsequently offered suggestions as to how a retailer should approach the task of organizing its marketing function.

There have been few studies of the role and organization of marketing departments within UK retail companies. A survey by Piercy (1987a, 1987b) provided insights into 70 companies and led to a number of important conclusions:

1. The majority of marketing departments had been established in the 1980s.
2. Most marketing departments were small in size but, in most cases, were growing.
3. The head of marketing was usually seen as having a status equal to or higher than that of other department heads.
4. The power of the marketing department, *vis-à-vis* the buying and finance departments, varied considerably between companies.
5. Marketing was usually represented on the board of directors, although this was not so in 17 per cent of cases.
6. Two-thirds of the companies saw themselves as marketing-oriented, most of the rest being sales-oriented.

These conclusions depict a situation in which the marketing function is growing rapidly in size and status; it was accepted, however, that marketing was probably less well represented in many of the companies that did not respond to the survey.

Further analyses were undertaken to classify the responsibilities and the orientations of the marketing departments. Figure 1.3 summarizes these results and illustrates the emphases within different types of marketing department. The 'high-integration' marketing department takes a high level of responsibility for all areas of marketing. The 'merchandising-oriented' marketing department, on the other hand, tends to concentrate its responsibilities in the traditional areas of the merchandising/buying department, although some input to corporate strategy is likely. The 'services-oriented' department, as the term suggests, tends to deal with specific functions, such as market research and advertising, with low involvement in other areas. This typology effectively illustrates that the existence of a marketing department does not necessarily signal the arrival of an integrated marketing function within the company.

1.2 DEVELOPMENTS IN INFORMATION SYSTEMS

It is difficult to dispute that decision-making in retail marketing, or indeed in any other form of business, can be only as good as the information upon which the decisions are based. The rapid progress that is being made in the technology and applications of computers for retailers is therefore highly pertinent to the development of retail marketing. According to Ody (1987):

At the highest levels, retail executives have realised the need for help in these areas for some time—but they are only beginning to appreciate that computer-literate marketing staff manipulating sophisticated data-bases can provide them with the answers.

Responsibility for:	High-integration marketing department	Merchandising-oriented marketing department	Services-oriented marketing department
Product and pricing policy	HI	Medium	LO
Marketing services	HI	LO	Medium
Marketing communications	HI	LO	Medium
Corporate strategy	HI	Medium	LO
Total	HI	Medium	LO

Figure 1.3 Types of retailer marketing department
Source: Piercy (1987, p. 59).

Piercy (1980) had earlier identified the main requirements of a marketing information system; he also illustrated how the possession of superior information can further increase the power of retailers (Piercy 1983).

The widespread use of computers for basic accounting, personnel, warehousing and transport functions was firmly established by the early 1970s. From the retail marketing viewpoint, the most relevant area of development has been the more recent growth in point-of-sale (PoS) computers. The use of computers or terminals at individual store level has become viable as they have become smaller, faster, more reliable and (in relative terms) cheaper. Closely allied to this progress has been the development of product codes which are standardized between manufacturers, retailers and other distributors. Readers will find many accounts of these developments within the trade magazines and journals. This section will very briefly examine the main developments of point-of-sale computers and coding systems, and will then summarize the implications and benefits of adopting this form of information technology.

1.2.1 Codes and computers

Product codes are by no means an innovation in retailing; companies have for many years used codes in the place of product descriptions to simplify ordering and invoicing systems. Codes have also been used in a limited way to record the sales of fast-moving lines at the checkout, a facility available even on some electro-mechanical checkout registers. Such systems are usually described as 'velocity coding', short codes being allocated to the very fast-moving lines and slightly longer codes being allocated to some other fast-moving lines (Marketing Trends 1979). One store using this system found that the top 100 lines represented 3 per cent of the assortment but 34 per cent of the turnover. Such a coding system has three major limitations:

1. Sales of all the uncoded items cannot be directly recorded at the checkouts.
2. Codes are retailer-specific and therefore must be encoded by the retailer.
3. The codes are of limited or no benefit in assisting communication between retailer and supplier.

In order to overcome these limitations, associations were formed during the 1970s in both Europe and the USA in order to agree upon standard product numbering systems. Like many computer-related developments, this has become 'rich' in jargon and abbreviations; the following are commonly used:

SPNS Standard Product Numbering System
ANA Article Number Association (UK)
EAN European Article Number
UPC Universal Product Code (USA)
DNB Distribution Number Bank (USA)

In January 1972, the Distribution Number Bank was set up in Washington to issue the Universal Product Code (UPC). This is an 11-digit code, the first five denoting the manufacturer, the next five the exact item (Bol and Speh 1986). It was 1978 before an agreed system was established in Europe, this being the European Article Number (EAN), which has since gained acceptance in other parts of the world and is compatible with the UPC. This system uses 13 digits, ten as in the UPC system, two for country of origin, and one check digit (Marketing Trends 1979).

In that 13 digits are an unrealistic number for manual entry at the checkout, the UPC and EAN systems utilize an agreed system of 'bar codes' to enable the codes to be machine-'read' by laser scanners at the checkout. These symbols, representing the codes by a series of black lines of varying thickness, started to appear on retailers' own label ranges from 1978 and on manufacturers' labels from 1979. Clearly, the proportion of items carrying a bar code is a major determinant of the viability of laser scanning systems in stores.

There is a wide range of electronic point-of-sale (EPoS) systems available to retailers. At the lower levels of investment there are the relatively modest electronic cash registers, with manual code entry, limited price look-up facility and cassette storage of transactions. At the highest levels there are checkout terminals directly coupled to a store or chain computer, incorporating machine reading of codes, full price look-up, detailed receipts, and all the information and control benefits discussed later. Some of the most fundamental system alternatives are:

Velocity codes	*v.*	all product codes
Retailer's own codes	*v.*	universal code, e.g. EAN
Manual code entry	*v.*	machine-read symbol
Bar code	*v.*	magnetic tag
Data stored at checkout (e.g. on cassettes)	*v.*	checkout on-line to computer
Computer in store	*v.*	computer at regional or head office
Direct data transmission	*v.*	data sent by post or road

Within the UK grocery sector, there were 873 stores with full-scale scanning installations at the start of 1989 (IGD News 1989). Over 200 of these were Sainsbury stores; among the non-food retailers, Boots had 180 scanning stores (Retail Review 1989). EPoS systems are by no means limited to larger stores. Marks & Spencer acquired around 2,500 'stand-alone point-of-sale' systems, which need neither power nor communications cables, for its smaller stores (Retail 1988). Euromonitor (1989) reported that the UK ranked third in Europe in terms of scanning stores, behind France and West Germany. A number of interesting innovations in scanning arrangements are being tried, including a 'self-scanning' store in Tilburg (Netherlands), where customers use a portable scanning unit to scan items as they are placed in the shopping trolley (Hughes 1989).

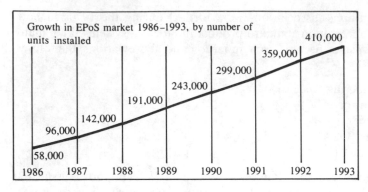

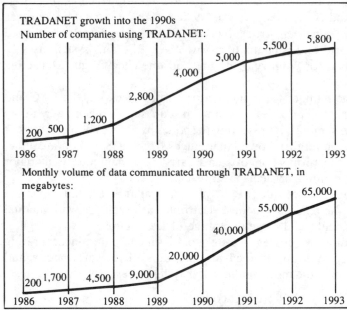

Figure 1.4 The growth of EPoS and Tradanet
Source: Retail (1988, p. 39).

In order to achieve the full benefits of inter-company data flows, there have been parallel developments in communications networks and formats. In the USA, retailers and manufacturers have co-operated in a system called Electronic Data Interchange (EDI) (Achabal and McIntyre 1987). In the UK, the dominant service is Tradanet, launched in 1985 by the Article Number Association and the computer manufacturer, ICL (Retail & Distribution Management 1985, 1988). Figure 1.4 shows how the number of EPoS units and participation in the Tradanet system are expected to increase up to 1993.

1.2.2 Benefits of EPoS systems

One problem in evaluating the costs and benefits of installing an EPoS system is that the potential benefits are so diverse and, in some cases, difficult to quantify. A major report by McKinsey (1974) analysed 'hard' benefits and 'soft' benefits, although this distinction is difficult to sustain. All the benefits contribute to the better performance of retail marketing, either directly or indirectly. The major benefits are summarized below:

1. Logistical benefits
   (a) The rapid flow of information and the immediate recording of sales allows stockholding to be reduced; in the grocery sector, the typical holding of 2.5 weeks' sales has been reduced to 1.4 in some cases (Robson 1987).
   (b) Orders to suppliers can be automatically triggered or suggested.
   (c) Deliveries can be scheduled to reduce congestion in the loading area, thereby improving vehicle utilization.

2. Productivity benefits
   (a) Faster checkouts mean better utilization of store labour.
   (b) Detailed records of transaction flows facilitate better labour scheduling (Dawson et al. 1987).
   (c) There is less need for 'front-end' supervision, and cash management is facilitated.
   (d) No/less item price marking is required, although more care is required in shelf-edge marking.
   (e) Better stock control and faster checkouts allow more productive use of space.

3. Buying benefits
   (a) Buyers have a constantly updated record of sales trends by product and by store.
   (b) It is not necessary to accept manufacturer's generalized or selective reports of sales trends.
   (c) Demand forecasts can be based upon detailed knowledge of seasonal and local trends.

4. Customer service
   (a) Faster checkouts and better labour scheduling reduce queues.
   (b) Itemized receipt provides a detailed record of purchases.
   (c) There should be fewer checkout errors, although cases have been reported of stores failing to harmonize the prices on the shelf markers with those in the computer file.
   (d) Further time saving is achieved if the EPoS system is linked to automatic cheque printing, credit authorization or electronic funds transfer systems (EFTPoS; see Chapter 12).

5. Marketing strategy
   (a) Immediate feedback can be obtained after adjustments in pricing, product range, display allocations or advertising.
   (b) Experiments involving the manipulation of marketing variables can be more easily and rapidly analysed.
   (c) Store layouts can be improved through the analysis of product purchase patterns, i.e. which products tend to be bought within the same transaction.
   (d) Analysis of transaction numbers and sizes by time of day/day of week can provide guidelines for policies regarding hours of opening and customer service levels.
   (e) If some form of customer identification is linked to the transaction record, for example if a store card is used, then many additional opportunities are available. The success of each commodity group in attracting specific customer segments can be analysed. Communications can be sent to certain customers to increase their loyalty to the store and/or to encourage them to use different sections of the store (see Chapter 12).

The information that can be captured at the point of sale is naturally of interest to manufacturers and data agencies too. Such systems clearly offer scope greatly to improve the quality and efficiency of retail audits and marketing experiments. In the USA a few agencies have developed 'instrumented markets' to serve as marketing research laboratories. Little (1987) described the characteristics of an instrumented market:

1. Small to medium-sized city
2. Scanners in all supermarkets
3. Voluntary panel of 3,000 households
4. Identification of panellists at stores
5. Controllable (cable) television advertisements to homes
6. Observation of in-store conditions
7. Store and panel data relating to purchases, prices, promotions, advertising, coupons and displays

By 1987, the Behavior Scan service of Information Resources Inc. operated ten markets of this type, providing powerful laboratories for testing new products, advertising and other marketing activities.

From the retailer's viewpoint, it is obviously essential that the benefits of EPoS systems are not outweighed by adverse consumer reactions. From the USA there was evidence that a major consumer lobby had formed against the elimination of item price marking. Harris and Mills (1980) found that 20 per cent of shoppers in non-scanning stores said that they would switch stores if price marking ceased, although it seems unlikely that the switch would actually be that large. Pommer *et al.* (1980) reported that users of scanning stores could recognize some benefits, but generally disliked the lack of item prices and also felt that cost savings were not leading to lower prices. From a longitudinal analysis of shoppers' attitudes to scanners, Jackson *et al.* (1987) concluded:

It may be apparent to marketers how scanners help them. It may even be apparent to marketers how scanners help the shopper. The results of this investigation suggest, however, that it is only moderately apparent to shoppers how scanners help them.

An implication from this study was that the retailers involved had not effectively communicated the benefits to consumers.

The evidence available in the UK would indicate that customers are more favourably disposed to scanning, possibly because more care was taken to educate and inform customers in the scanning stores. Walman (1981) surveyed shoppers at five scanning stores and found some appreciation of the better layout, wider stock range, faster checkouts and the itemized receipts. The Office of Fair Trading (1982) investigated the likely effects of item price removal on price awareness and generally concluded that awareness would not be adversely affected, given the itemized receipts and provided that price marking on shelves was maintained with a high standard of clarity. Clarke (1982) suggested that electronic displays, as used at some banks and petrol stations, could be used to display prices in supermarkets efficiently.

Another potential hazard of EPoS systems is the production of a huge data glut, of little use to decision-makers if not effectively organized. To illustrate the dimension of this problem, Little (1987) cited the following example of a supermarket chain:

    2,000 stores
  10,000 items/store
  10 measures/item
   5 bytes/measure
                = 1,000,000,000 bytes/week.

This is by no means an extreme example, as many stores carry more than 10,000 bar-coded items and 10 measures per item would include price, display characteristics, advertising features, etc. It is clearly necessary to develop a management information system (MIS) which delivers appropriate, timely and digestible information to decision-makers. As Bendall (1985) pointed out:

Also important is the need for MIS to break away from historic tendencies to report everything to everybody; so there should be much more selectivity in the information presented to individuals, matched to their needs and highlighting differences or variances from that expected.

The investment in hardware to produce EPoS data is partly wasted, unless the systems exist to harness these data and integrate EPoS within an overall information system. As Jones (1987) observed:

EPoS is beginning to be seen—rightly—as merely the starting point in the whole retail information system cycle and a whole string of further application areas are beginning to emerge and be successfully applied.

Some of these further applications are considered in the subsequent chapters; the analysis of individual item profitability in Chapter 5, the analysis of shelf space/display response in Chapter 11, and the utilization of customer transaction data in Chapter 12.

1.3   RETAIL MARKETING CYCLES

As a final perspective upon the development of retail marketing, this section will briefly examine two of the hypotheses that have attempted to explain changes over time in retail institutions, companies and stores. A detail review of these and other 'theories' was provided by Brown (1987), who observed: 'theory is a rather generous term for what have been described as little more than inductively derived generalisations'.

In spite of their limitations, these hypotheses have attracted a large volume of literature, and it cannot be denied that they provide some insights into cyclical tendencies within retailing. The most widely quoted are the 'wheel of retailing' and the 'retail life-cycle'. A further generalization, the 'retail accordion', is discussed in Chapter 4 in relation to retailers' choices between strategies of diversification and generalization.

1.3.1   The wheel of retailing

The concept was suggested by McNair (1958) and subsequently analysed by Hollander (1960):

This hypothesis holds that new types of retailers usually enter the market as low-status, low-margin, low-price operators. Gradually they acquire more elaborate establishments and facilities, with both increased investments and higher operating costs. Finally they mature as higher-cost, high-price merchants, vulnerable to newer types who, in turn, go through the same pattern.

Figure 1.5 illustrates the phases of the 'wheel' with the marketing mix and characteristics that would be associated with each of these phases. It is possible to identify several conforming examples. For example, department stores, which started mainly as low-cost competitors to the smaller retailers, then were severely undercut by supermarkets and discount warehouses (McNair 1958). It has more recently been suggested that the challenge to the discounters presented by 'off-price' retailers in the USA also adheres well to the 'wheel' hypothesis (Kaikati 1985).

In both the USA and Europe, extensive evidence is available showing how supermarkets tended to elaborate their trading style. Several writers have noted how depressed profits and severe price competition led US supermarkets to turn to various forms of non-price competition, including more services and longer hours. Bucklin (1972) explained the dilemma of the supermarket operators, who found themselves in practice unable to compete on price because other

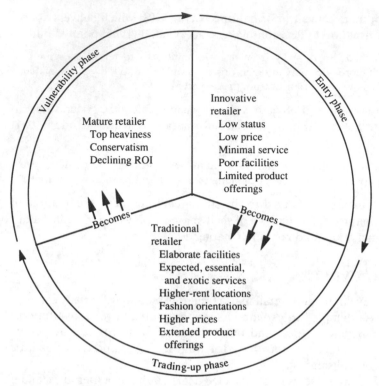

Figure 1.5 The wheel of retailing
          Source: Brown (1988, p. 17).

suppliers immediately retaliated. The result was a form of 'ratchet effect' as prices were gradually edged higher to finance increasingly elaborate non-price competitive devices.

A substantial elaboration of reaffirmation of the 'wheel' concept was provided by McNair and May (1978), who pointed out that the process was tending both to quicken and to affect an increasing number of retail sectors, at least in the USA. Added to the food and department store sectors, which have experienced such change for a considerable time, now are clothing stores, leisure outlets and other specialist retail sectors.

Many explanations of the 'wheel' process have been suggested. One, put forward by Converse (1959), is that the personality of management becomes less cost-conscious and aggressive as the original entrepreneurs either grow older or hand over control to their successors. Another, proposed by Levy (1947), is that retailers are frequently subject to 'misguidance' by various supplies of equipment and other store factors, encouraging them to invest in more elaborate facilities. Although Hollander (1960) found this latter explanation to be 'implausible', examples are cited elsewhere in this book of retailers being urged to invest in expensive design refits, advertising and other services.

The process of 'trading up' was examined in some detail by Goldman (1975), who, among other writers, pointed to the danger of generalizing the 'wheel' hypothesis too widely. He also differentiated between different types of 'trading up', namely, routine, where more of existing services are added; non-routine, where new services are added; and innovative, where a totally new price–service combination is introduced. Kaynak (1979) also noted major exceptions to the 'wheel' pattern, notably in less highly developed countries where retail institutions tended to be copied from those already existing in North America or Western Europe. In such cases, the institution may well adopt an up-market trading position initially and subsequently 'trade down'. Following an analysis of the products offered by the electrical goods discounter Comet over a ten-year period, Savitt (1984) observed:

The 'wheel of retailing' pervades the marketing literature as if it were a law rather than an untested hypothesis.

Retail evolution must be considered in a wider context than it is normally found. In general, retail change theories must be brought from their general level to a more specific one. In doing this, their validity must be more firmly established.

1.3.2 The retail life-cycle

The retail life-cycle concept, expounded by Davidson *et al.* (1976), attempted to overcome two of the most distinct limitations of the 'wheel'. These are, first, the emphasis upon changing costs and margins, which does little to explain change in retail forms that enter the market at a high margin position, and second, the fact that the rate and diversity of retail innovation is becoming increasingly difficult to explain within the 'wheel' framework.

The product life-cycle, from which the retail life-cycle is derived, is a concept very familiar to marketing practitioners and theorists alike (e.g. Levitt 1965). The idea that the retail institutions themselves, like the product that they sell, could be considered to have a life-cycle was formalized somewhat later. The life-cycle may be divided broadly into four phases: innovation, accelerated development, maturity, and decline.

According to the generalizations of Davidson *et al.* (1976), organizations at the innovation stage are characterized as having few competitors, rapid sales growth, and low-moderate profitability. As development accelerates, profitability is usually high so competition starts to increase. At the maturity stage there are many direct and some indirect competitors, so profitability would typically moderate. As more, and innovatory, indirect competitors develop, sales and profits typically fall, placing the institution clearly in the 'decline' phase.

It was also observed that the life-cycle of retail institutions is tending to become shorter. Table 1.2 illustrates that the department store in the USA enjoyed an eighty-year period of growth before its market share peaked. More recent innovations have demonstrated far shorter life-cycles, the discount department store peaking in just twenty years. If life-cycles are becoming much shorter, long-term investments in expensive property assets must clearly be viewed with caution. The table also points to the need to achieve satisfactory return on investment within a short time-scale, and to the possible attractions of leasing rather than owning certain stores.

A further theoretical extension was provided by Davidson and Johnson (1981), in which the retail life-cycle was combined with portfolio theory to suggest ways in which a retail company or store could protect itself from overall decline. In this way a retail chain could be viewed as an assortment of stores, each of which typically will be at a different stage of the life-cycle; similarly, a store may be seen as a collection of departments, each of which may demonstrate life-cycle tendencies. This concept clearly suggests guidelines for store rationalization, merger and acquisition activity and strategic repositioning.

This analytical framework could well help to highlight the problem of organizations such as the co-operatives in the United Kingdom. Although a significant superstore operator, the Co-operative Movement has in its 'portfolio' far too many stores that have been in decline for many years. Multiples such as Sainsbury and Tesco have also had many outmoded outlets but have been more successful in rejuvenating and rationalizing their stock of outlets. The framework

Table 1.2   Life-cycles of five retail institutions

Institution	Approx. date of innovation	Approx. date of max. market share	Approx. no. of years required to reach maturity	Est. max. market share	Est. 1975 market share
Downtown department store	1860	1940	80	8.5%	1.1% of total retail sales
Variety store	1910	1955	45	16.5%	9.5% of general merchandise sales
Supermarket	1930	1965	35	70.0%	64.5% of grocery store sales
Discount department store	1950	1970	20	6.5%	5.7% of total retail sales
Home improvement center	1965	1980 (est.)	15	35.0%	25.3% of hardware and building material sales

Source: Reprinted by permission of *Harvard Business Review*. An exhibit from 'The retail life cycle', by W. R. Davidson, A. D. Bates and S. J. Bass, **54**(6), 1976. Copyright © 1976 by the President and Fellows of Harvard College; all rights reserved.

could prove to have useful predictive capabilities, even for relatively 'young' multiples. In that most of their outlets have been opened in recent years, a high proportion will still be within their growth or maturity phases; in the future, however, such companies could face the problem of almost simultaneous decline of all their outlets, unless a vigorous replacement or repositioning programme is maintained.

In common with most other theories or generalizations, it is easy to find exceptions to the general rule. These concepts do however serve as reminders that retail marketing operates in a dynamic and rapidly changing environment. Change cannot be averted and, by failing to respond to changes in the competitive environment, the company or institution will quickly drift into a weaker position. These concepts underline the need to develop a strong marketing planning function to initiate positive strategic moves, rather than succumb to these cyclical tendencies.

SUMMARY

In spite of its enormous scale and economic significance, the retailing industry in general did not adopt the marketing concept at an early stage. For many years there was a tendency to regard retailers as subordinate, even passive, elements of manufacturer-led marketing channels. The rapid shift of power from manufacturers to retailers has forced a change in this view. From being a highly fragmented industry, retailing is now highly concentrated in many areas, with some major retailers having grown larger than their largest suppliers. The possibility of using legislation to limit the buying power of large UK retailers was investigated but rejected.

The more powerful retailers have taken an increasing degree of control over the elements of the retail marketing mix. With the abolition of resale price maintenance, the shift of control was most rapid in the case of retail pricing, but every other element of the mix has also become increasingly retailer-led. Initially there was a tendency for retailers to wield their marketing power at the tactical, rather than the strategic, level. The last decade has seen the development of more co-ordinated marketing functions within some retail companies, although in others the role of marketing is still mainly at the operational level.

Well informed and appropriate retail marketing decisions require the availability of comprehensive, timely and accurate information. The development of electronic point-of-sale (EPoS) systems represents a major step towards better information for operational and marketing decisions. Internationally agreed product coding systems have developed alongside the technology for capturing data at the point of sale. Scanning systems can provide a wealth of data to assist distribution, buying, store management and many marketing decisions, provided that these data are assimilated into an effective information system. Aspects of customer service can also be enhanced, but care must be taken to avoid adverse customer reactions.

Retailing is a dynamic industry, subject to constant change brought about by economic, demographic, legislative, technological and competitive forces. Some writers have observed cyclical tendencies in the life and trading styles of retail companies and institutions. The 'wheel of retailing' hypothesis suggests that retail innovators tend progressively to trade up, leaving themselves eventually vulnerable to new innovators. The concept of the life-cycle has also been applied to retailing institutions, and retail life-cycles appear to be getting shorter. Although these generalizations obviously cannot be applied in every case, they do help to underline the need for positive, long-term marketing planning.

REVIEW QUESTIONS

1. 'The middleman is not a hired link in a chain forged by a manufacturer.' Discuss.
2. Identify the main differences between a 'conventional channel' and a 'vertical marketing system'. Give an example of a vertical marketing system.
3. How do you explain the shift of power from manufacturers to retailers in many countries?
4. Do you believe that the power of retailers will continue to grow? Justify your answer.
5. Taking a retail sector of your choice, illustrate how the control of marketing mix elements has shifted from manufacturers to retailers.
6. 'In retailing, implementation of the marketing concept appeared to be mostly at the firm's operational, rather than strategic, levels.' Discuss.
7. Compare the usefulness and the functions typically performed by the following types of retail marketing department:

   (a) high-integration;
   (b) merchandising-oriented;
   (c) services-oriented.

8. Show how the information capable of being provided by a point-of-sale computer system can assist in the development and refinement of retail marketing strategy.
9. What are the advantages of using standard product numbering rather than velocity codes in an EPoS system?
10. What are the main hazards of introducing point-of-sale scanners, in terms of adverse customer reactions? How would you suggest that a retailer should avoid these hazards?

11. Explain McNair's 'wheel of retailing' hypothesis, giving examples of retail companies or institutions that have (a) complied and (b) not complied with this hypothesis.
12. Is there any evidence that retail life-cycles are becoming shorter? Discuss the implications of your answer for retail marketing strategy.

REFERENCES

Achabal, D. D. and S. H. McIntyre (1987), 'Information technology is reshaping retailing', *Journal of Retailing*, **63**(4), 321–5.

Bendall, A. (1985), 'More sophisticated hi-tech to underpin high street revolution', *Retail*, **3**(3), 6–7.

Blackwell, R. D. and W. W. Talarzyk (1983), 'Life-style retailing: competitive strategies for the 1980s', *Journal of Retailing*, **59**(4), 7–27.

Bol, J. P. W. and T. W. Speh (1986), 'How retailers can profit from scanners—an investigation into the uses of scanner data', in ESOMAR (ed.), *Retail Strategies for Profit and Growth*, ESOMAR, Amsterdam, pp. 225–45.

British Business (1988), 'DTI retailing inquiry for 1986', *British Business*, 18 March 29–30.

Brown, S. (1987), 'Institutional change in retailing: a review and synthesis', *European Journal of Marketing*, **21**(6), 5–36.

Brown, S. (1988), 'The wheel of the wheel of retailing', *International Journal of Retailing*, **3**(1), 16–37.

Bucklin, L. P. (1972), *Competition and Evolution in the Distributive Trades*, Prentice Hall, Englewood Cliffs, NJ.

Clarke, B. (1982), 'PoS developments', *IGD News*, **7**, 15–18.

Cohen, A. I. and A. L. Jones (1978), 'Brand marketing in the new retail environment', *Harvard Business Review*, **56**(5), 141–8.

Converse, P. D. (1959), 'Mediocrity in retailing', *Journal of Marketing*, **23**(2), 419–20.

Davidson, W. R., A. D. Bates and S. J. Bass (1976), 'The retail life cycle', *Harvard Business Review*, **54**(6), 89–96.

Davidson, W. R. and N. E. Johnson (1981), 'Portfolio theory and the retailing life cycle', in R. W. Stampfl and E. C. Hirschman (eds.), *Theory in Retailing: Traditional and Non-Traditional Sources*, American Marketing Association, Chicago, pp. 51–63.

Dawson, J. A., A. M. Findlay and L. Sparks (1987), 'The impact of scanning on employment in UK food stores: a preliminary analysis', *Journal of Marketing Management*, **2**(3), 285–300.

Euromonitor (1987), *Retail Trade in the United Kingdom*, Euromonitor, London.

Euromonitor (1989), *Retail Trade International 1989/90*, Vol. 1, Euromonitor, London.

Financial Times (1979), 'Food manufacturers in the doldrums', *Financial Times*, 30 April, 39.

Gabor, A. (1977), *Pricing, Principles and Practices*, Heinemann, London.

Gaski, J. F. (1984), 'The theory of power and conflict in channels of distribution', *Journal of Marketing*, **48**(3), 9–29.

Gattorna, J. (1978), 'Channels of distribution conceptualisations: a state-of-the-art review', *European Journal of Marketing*, **12**(7), 471–512.

Goldman, A. (1975), 'The role of trading up in the development of the retailing system', *Journal of Marketing*, **39**(1), 54–62.

Grant, R. M. (1987), 'Manufacturer–retailer relations: the shifting balance of power', in G. Johnson (ed.), *Business Strategy and Retailing*, John Wiley, Chichester, pp. 43–58.

Harris, B. F. and M. K. Mills (1980), 'The impact of item price removal on grocery shopping behaviour', *Journal of Retailing*, **56**(4), 73–93.

Hollander, S. C. (1960), 'The wheel of retailing', *Journal of Marketing*, **24**(3), 37–42.

Hughes, C. (1989), 'The store where the customer does the scanning', *Retail & Distribution Management*, **17**(2), 10–11.

IGD News (1989), 'Food retailing 1988', *IGD News*, **71**, 1–2.

Institute of Grocery Distribution (1989), *Food Industry Statistics Digest*, IGD, Watford.

Institute for Retail Studies (1989), *Distributive Trades Profile 1988: A Statistical Digest*, IRS, University of Stirling.

Jackson, G. B., R. W. Jackson and C. E. Newmiller (1987), 'A longitudinal examination of shopper attitudes towards scanners', *International Journal of Retailing*, **2**(3), 49–58.

Jones, G. (1987), 'EPoS and the retailer's information needs', in E. McFadyen (ed.), *The Changing Face of British Retailing*, Newman, London, pp. 22–32.

Kaikati, J. D. (1985), 'Don't discount off-price retailers', *Harvard Business Review*, **63**(3), 85–92.

Kaynak, E. (1979), 'A refined approach to the wheel of retailing', *European Journal of Marketing*, **13**(7), 237–45.

Key Note (1986), *Cash and Carry Outlets*, Key Note Publications, London.

Lazer, W. and E. J. Kelley (1961), 'The retailing mix: planning and management', *Journal of Retailing*, **37**(1), 34–41.

Levitt, T. (1965), 'Exploit the product life cycle', *Harvard Business Review*, **43**(6), 81–94.

Levy, H. (1947), *The Shops of Britain*, Kegan Paul, London.

Little, J. D. C. (1987), 'Information technology in marketing', Working Paper 1860–87, Massachusetts Institute of Technology, Cambridge, Mass.

MacNeary, A. (1981), *J. Sainsbury: An Investment Review*, Capel-Cure Myers, London.

Marketing Trends (1979), 'Marketing research at the checkout', *Marketing Trends*, **1**, 1–3.

McCammon, B. C. (1970), 'Perspectives for distribution programming', in L. P. Bucklin (ed.), *Vertical Marketing Systems*, Scott, Foresman, Glenview, Ill.

McClelland, W. G. (1961), 'Address to the British Association' in P. J. Barker *et al.* (eds.), *Case Studies in the Competitive Process*, Heinemann, London.

McClelland, W. G. (1967), *Costs and Competition in Retailing*, Macmillan, London.

McKinsey (1974), *Evaluating Feasibility of SPNS in the UK Grocery Industry*, Institute of Grocery Distribution, Watford.

McNair, M. P. (1958), 'Significant trends and developments in the post war period', in A. B. Smith (ed.), *Competitive Distribution in a Free High Level Economy and its Implications for the University*, University of Pittsburg Press, Pittsburg, pp. 1–25.

McNair, M. P. and E. G. May (1978), 'The next revolution of the retailing wheel', *Harvard Business Review*, **56**(5), 89–91.

McVey, P. (1960), 'Are channels of distribution what the text books say?' *Journal of Marketing*, **24**(3), 61–5.

Monopolies and Mergers Commission (1981), *Discounts to Retailers*, HMSO, London.

Ody, P. (1987), 'Creating long term strategy for retailing', *Retail & Distribution Management*, **15**(6), 8–11.

Office of Fair Trading (1982), *Micro-electronics and Retailing*, OFT, London.

Office of Fair Trading (1985), *Competition and Retailing*, OFT, London.

O'Reilly, A. (1984), 'Manufacturers versus retailers: the long-term winners?' *Retail & Distribution Management*, **12**(3), 40–1.

Pickering, J. F. (1966), *Resale Price Maintenance in Practice*, Allen & Unwin, London.

Piercy, N. (1980), 'Evaluating marketing information', *Retail & Distribution Management*, **8**(2), 55–8.

Piercy, N. (1983), 'Retailer information power—the channel marketing information system', *Marketing Intelligence & Planning*, **1**(1), 40–55.

Piercy, N. (1984), 'Is marketing moving from the manufacturer to the retailer?' *Retail & Distribution Management*, **12**(5), 25–8.

Piercy, N. (1986), 'Organising for marketing in retailing', *Retail & Distribution Management*, **14**(3), 21–3.

Piercy, N. (1987a), 'Marketing in UK retailing, part 1', *Retail & Distribution Management*, **15**(2), 52–5.

Piercy, N. (1987b), 'Marketing in UK retailing, part 2', *Retail & Distribution Management*, **15**(3), 58–60.

Pommer, M. D., E. N. Berkowitz and J. R. Walton (1980), 'UPC scanning: an assessment of shopper response to technological change', *Journal of Retailing*, **56**(2), 25–44.

Pommerening, D. J. (1979), 'Brand marketing: fresh thinking needed', *Marketing Trends*, **1**, 7–9.

Retail (1988), 'Retail technology', *Retail*, **6**(1), 38–9.

Retail & Distribution Management (1985), 'Tradanet launched by ANA and ICL', *Retail & Distribution Management*, **13**(3), 42–3.

Retail & Distribution Management (1988), 'Using information systems for decision making', *Retail & Distribution Management*, **16**(4), 22–5.

Retail Review (1989), 'Retail giants extol EPoS power', *Retail Review*, no. 151, 2.

Robson (1987), 'Professional trade management—the American perspective', *IGD News*, **52**, 1–2.

Savitt, R. (1984), 'The "wheel of retailing" and retail product management', *European Journal of Marketing*, **18**(6/7), 43–54.

Stern, L. W. and T. Reve (1980), 'Distribution channels as political economies: a framework for comparative analysis', *Journal of Marketing*, **44**(3), 52–64.

Walman, B. (1981), 'What shoppers think about scanning', *Retail & Distribution Management*, **9**(4), 27–8.

Walters, D. (1979), 'Manufacturer/retailer relationships', *European Journal of Marketing*, **13**(7), 179–222.

Whimster, C. (1981), 'The operation of an independent distribution system', *Retail & Distribution Management*, **9**(4), 59–63.

Yamey, B. S. (1966), *Resale Price Maintenance*, Wiedenfeld & Nicolson, London.

NATIONAL AND INTERNATIONAL ENVIRONMENTS

INTRODUCTION

A prerequisite for successful strategic planning is a clear understanding of the major elements and trends within the environment of retail marketing. Without this, major opportunities are likely to be missed and threats to the company may well go undetected, until its position has already been undermined. For many years the retail environment has been subject to major changes in terms of competition and store types. Now the changes are becoming both more rapid and more diverse, with increasingly mobile, demanding consumers and with growing competition between retail formats, across national boundaries, and between different retailing channels. A full review of these changes would be beyond the scope of this chapter and, indeed, would become rapidly outdated. The purpose of the chapter is to draw attention to some of the most salient elements and to identify major sources of current information on these trends.

The first section considers changes in consumers' expenditure and shopping patterns, examining some of the underlying influences upon these changes and prospects for the years ahead. Attention then turns to the structure of the retailing industry, starting with an overview of the main types of retailing organization, i.e. multiples, independents, co-operative societies, symbol groups and franchises. Changes in the number of types of retail outlet are then considered, including small stores, convenience stores, superstores, hypermarkets, shopping centres and retail parks.

The final sections of the chapter consider two important extensions to the traditional boundaries of the retailing environment. The arrival of the Single European Market has focused the minds of retail planners upon the opportunities and threats of increased international retail competition. This is by no means limited to Europe; most 'transnational' retailing involving British companies has in fact been transatlantic retailing. The prospects for further increases in non-store retailing are also evaluated, including the growth of a more dynamic mail order sector and the development of teleshopping systems.

2.1 EXPENDITURE AND SHOPPING PATTERNS

This section takes a very brief overview of some key indicators of economic, demographic and behavioural change within the retailing environment. Changes in the value and the volume of retail sales are first assessed, with comparisons offered between European countries and between the major product sectors. Projected shifts in consumer expenditure patterns through the 1990s

Table 2.1   Value of retail sales: European comparisons, 1982 and 1987

	Value of retail sales 1987 ($ b)	Retail sales per capita 1987 ($000)	Retail sales as % of consumer expenditure	
			1982 (%)	1987 (%)
West Germany	260	4.3	41.9	41.6
Italy	250	4.4	58.5	53.5
France	225	4.1	44.6	43.0
UK	186	3.2	41.4	40.5
Spain	101	2.6	55.0	52.0
Netherlands	55	3.0	44.4	40.7
Switzerland	42	6.5	43.6	41.8
Belgium	40	4.1	44.8	44.0
Sweden	39	4.3	48.2	45.5
Finland	23	4.7	50.6	47.0
Austria	23	3.1	39.1	35.1
Denmark	20	4.0	40.0	38.0
Greece	18	1.8	62.0	62.0
Norway	16	3.9	41.9	38.0
Portugal	13	1.3	59.0	55.5
Ireland	8	2.2	—	—
Luxemburg	3	4.3	—	—
Total/average	1,322	3.7	44.7	42.4

Source: derived from Euromonitor (1989, pp. 14–16).

are considered. Attention then turns to the changing consumer, starting with basic demographic trends in population and age structures. Less tangible changes in attitudes and life-styles are also considered. Finally, indications of changing shopping patterns are evaluated, notably the increased mobility of shoppers, the reductions in shopping frequency for basic commodities, and the demand for more pleasurable shopping experiences.

2.1.1   Expenditure and retail sales

The total value of consumer expenditure in retail stores within Europe was estimated at $1,322 billion in 1987. This represented an increase, in volume terms, of 7 per cent over the preceding period of four years. There were however very significant differences between the 17 countries within the analysis. The UK had shown the highest increase, of around 16 per cent over that period, whereas Ireland had seen no growth and Austria a slight fall (Euromonitor 1989). Unfortunately, this boom in UK retail sales had been funded in part by a very significant fall in the savings ratio, which expresses personal savings as a percentage of total personal disposable income. The UK savings ratio had fallen from 11.9 in 1982 to 4.1 in 1988; much of the sales growth had resulted from reduced savings and increased consumer credit (Central Statistical Office 1989).

Table 2.1 shows retail sales levels within the European market; in value terms, the UK market

Table 2.2 Increases in sales volume by UK sectors, 1977–1987

Sector	Retail sales volume		Volume growth 1977–1987 (%)
	1977	1987	
	(1980 = 100)		
Food retailers	91.2	118.8	30.3
Clothing and footwear retailers	85.0	148.0	74.1
Household goods retailers	86.0	162.0	88.4
Other non-food retailers	101.0	113.0	11.9
Mixed retail businesses	90.9	131.1	44.2
All retailers	91.5	129.8	41.9

Source: derived from Central Statistical Office *Annual Abstract of Statistics* (1989, p. 212). Reproduced with the permission of the Controller of HMSO.

is smaller than that of West Germany, Italy and France. Adjusting these figures to take into account the very different population levels of these countries produces the estimates of retail sales per capita. Here the UK is significantly below average, with annual per capital retail expenditure of $3,200 compared with the average of $3,700. Highest by far on this measure is Switzerland, with the UK at rank 11 out of the 17 countries. These comparisons help to explain the interest of UK retailers in expanding overseas, a topic considered in Section 2.4.

Retail sales are of course only one element of consumers' expenditure, and a declining element in most cases. Between 1982 and 1987, retail expenditure fell on (unweighted) average from 44.7 to 42.4 per cent of consumers' expenditure. To a greater or lesser extent, this fall was experienced in all the 15 countries in this analysis, with the exception of Greece. Noticeably, retail expenditure tends to be a lower proportion of consumer expenditure in the more affluent countries. This general fall in the proportion of expenditure going through retail channels has prompted many retailers to diversify into the provision of financial and other services (see Chapter 12).

Looking in greater detail at the UK retail market, Table 2.2 shows how retail sales volumes changed in five major product sectors over the ten-year period 1977–87. The overall growth of 41.9 per cent was not shared equally between the sectors, with retailers of household goods, clothing and footwear enjoying the best of the spending boom. These commodity groups are of course also the most susceptible to downturns in consumers' disposable incomes, as many of the products are non-essential or their purchase can be postponed. This factor makes economic forecasts a particularly important element of marketing planning in these sectors. The definition of 'mixed retail businesses' is as follows:

Large and small mixed businesses (department stores, variety stores etc.), general mail order houses. They have less than 80% of turnover in any one sector. In the case of food retailers and hire shops, the proportion is taken at 50%. (Institute for Retail Studies 1989)

There are many problems associated with the forecasting of consumer expenditure, especially in the longer term. Significant changes in economic or fiscal policy, or changes in the government itself, can exert major influences upon future expenditure trends. Retailers do however require such forecasts as a basis for their medium- and long-term planning.

Table 2.3 presents a summary of recent changes in expenditure and of forecasts to the turn of the century. Some forecasters would regard these as optimistic in terms of continued volume growth. Sales volumes are predicted to continue reasonably strong growth, especially in the

Table 2.3   Recent and forecast changes in expenditure, 1981–2000

	Average annual volume change (%)		
Product category	*1981–86*	*1987–92*	*1992–2000*
Durables			
Cars	6.8	5.6	4.6
Furniture etc.	1.1	3.2	2.7
Radio, television, etc.	12.0	4.8	4.3
Non-durables			
Food	0.9	0.5	0.3
Beer	− 0.4	1.5	0.7
Wines & spirits	2.8	4.2	3.3
Tobacco	− 3.6	− 0.1	− 0.5
Clothing	6.3	3.6	3.3
Footwear	5.5	2.8	3.0
Energy products	2.3	0.6	0.6
Other goods	4.2	5.0	3.9
Rent, rates, etc.	1.3	1.1	1.0
Other services	4.3	5.6	3.9
Total	3.1	3.5	2.8
Total durables	6.9	5.3	4.2
Total non-durables	2.7	3.2	2.6

Source: Retail Business (1989, p. 9).

durable product sectors. Strong, long-term growth is also anticipated in the 'other goods' and 'other services' categories, the former including such items as toys and sports goods.

Food will continue to be a major proportion of consumer spending, but its relative significance is likely to decline, from 12 per cent in 1990 to 9.3 per cent in the year 2000. Consumption of most meats, milks, fats and sugar is declining, although demand continues to grow for fish, fruit, vegetables and soft drinks. Belay (1986) predicted a continued switch from quantity to quality in food consumption, resulting in an overall increase in the value of food expenditures. This was attributed to four main areas of influence:

1. Nutritional adaptation—the switch to enriched, healthier and/or slimming products (e.g. Webster 1987)
2. Food taste improvements—by using better or more natural ingredients, or by using more adventurous fruits, aromas or spices
3. Incorporation of a service—notably, convenience in preparation or sizes
4. Image improvements—achieved through packaging and other forms of communication

This illustrates the importance of looking in detail at the prospects for each product sector, rather than just 'jumping on the bandwagon' and diversifying into categories with the highest overall growth prospect. Examples of successful and not so successful diversification will be considered in Chapter 4.

2.1.2   The changing consumer

Although sales and expenditure data provide essential indicators of market sizes and market trends, they do little to explain why these changes occur. They do even less to pick out consumer needs and desires that are currently not being fulfilled. For this purpose, a close understanding of the consumer is required, and ways of achieving this are the subject of the following chapter. Here we will look briefly at some of the most significant aspects of consumer change affecting retailers; more extensive treatments of this topic have been provided by Lucas (1986) and Poynor (1987).

Major changes are occurring within the demographic structure of the market-place, which includes the dimensions of population, age, households and occupations. Table 2.4 summarizes the overall trends in UK population growth and the changes within specific age bands. The projections for the 30-year period to 1991 showed an overall growth in population of 7.4 per cent, compared with 14.5 per cent over the preceding 30-year period. Taking the most recent 10-year period for which data were available at the time of writing, the population grew by only 1.3 per cent between 1977 and 1987 (Central Statistical Office 1989). Retailers can therefore no longer assume that the market will grow around them; increased trade must usually be won from a competitor and/or by the intelligent targeting of specific market segments.

Recent population growth is partly the result of increased life expectancy, which has tended to counteract the effects of a generally falling birth rate. The age structure of the population is therefore changing radically, with a decline of 12.9 per cent in the number of people under 18 years of age between 1977 and 1987. At the other end of the age scale, those aged 60 or over are expected to represent 18 per cent of males and 23 per cent of females in 1991. A group of particular significance, in terms of its size and spending power, is the 45–54 age range, which is projected to grow by 19 per cent by 1995 (Marketing Business 1989).

Table 2.4   Changes in the UK population structure

Year	0–14	15–29	30–44	45–59	60 +	Total population (m)
			Millions within each age band (percentages in brackets)			*Total population (m)*
Males						
1931	6.0	5.4	4.5	3.8	2.4	22.1
	(27)	(24)	(20)	(17)	(11)	
1961	6.3	5.2	5.2	5.1	3.6	25.5
	(25)	(20)	(20)	(20)	(14)	
1991	5.6	6.5	6.0	4.7	4.9	27.6
	(20)	(24)	(22)	(17)	(18)	
Females						
1931	5.9	5.7	5.2	4.2	3.0	24.0
	(25)	(24)	(22)	(18)	(13)	
1961	6.0	5.1	5.3	5.5	5.3	27.3
	(22)	(19)	(19)	(20)	(19)	
1991	5.3	6.2	6.0	4.8	6.8	29.1
	(18)	(21)	(21)	(16)	(23)	

Source: adapted from 'The retail environment in the UK' by S. Segal-Horn in G. Johnson (ed.), *Business Strategy and Retailing*, Copyright © 1987 John Wiley & Sons Ltd. Reprinted by permission of John Wiley & Sons Ltd.

These demographic shifts mean that retailers operating within the youth market are under particular pressure to consider alternative segments or to focus upon specific elements of that market. As the Henley Centre has pointed out, it would be risky to base a market strategy on demographic projections alone. Attitudes towards marriage, births outside marriage, contraception and abortion are all subject to change, as are mortality rates with the appearance of a disease such as Aids:

Demographics should not be ignored; they have an important impact on the size of consumer markets as well as influencing attitudinal shifts.

The prominence of youth culture is about to fade—marketers should consider what is likely to come next. (Marketing Business 1989)

The size and composition of households has also been subject to rapid change. Between 1971 and 1982 the proportion of households with four or more people fell from 33 to 27 per cent; over the same period, the one- or two-person households grew from 48 to 56 per cent (Lucas 1986). In the USA, the 'traditional' arrangement of two adults and two children has now declined to just 7 per cent of all households (Segal-Horn 1987). This trend towards more, smaller, households can be attributed to rising divorce rates, more people living alone, more childless couples and more single people. Even within the more traditional households, the Henley Centre has reported a trend towards the 'cellular household', in which the ownership of duplicate televisions, audio equipment and other durables allows different members of the household to 'do their own thing' as and when they choose (Poynor 1987). These changes in household structure affect both the demand for specific products and the shopping patterns adopted to obtain them.

The sharp division between the 'haves' and the 'have-nots' is becoming an unfortunate and seemingly long-term feature of the market in the UK, reflecting the situation in the USA, which has been described as 'disruptive socially and economically' (May *et al.* 1988). In the UK virtually all the wealth is owned by 50 per cent of the population, with the top 10 per cent owning about half (Poynor 1987). A high level of unemployment is coupled with an even higher level of underemployment, with many people obliged to take low-grade, low-paid employment. This important characteristic of the market often appears forgotten when commentators generalize about rising incomes, rising living standards and increased demand for services and quality, rather than low prices. It follows that even a fairly modest redistribution of wealth, possibly following a shift towards centre–left government, could have major effects upon the characteristics and priorities of the market.

Not surprisingly, much attention has been given to the especially affluent consumer groups, some of which have acquired acronyms of their own. For example, 'dinkies' (dual income, no kids) were estimated to represent 4.3 million couples, with average annual *disposable* incomes of over £15,000 (Poynor 1987). Reliable estimates of the number of 'yuppies' (young, urban, upwardly mobile professionals) are harder to come by, in part because the label also depicts an emerging attitude:

profit and money are no longer dirty words in most circles and 'Going for it' has become the Yuppy motto par excellence! (Poynor 1987)

These changing attitudes were also summarized by Bob Tyrell of the Henley Centre:

it's the filofax generation with almost more money than sense. Like it or not, morally and socially, consumption is increasingly the measure of status and the means of asserting identity.

It's not indiscriminate consumerism, albeit at times it looks somewhat foolish. Today's and tomorrow's consumers are looking for variety, stimulation and individuality: the objective now is to keep away from the Jones, not keep up with them. (Alexander 1988)

These changes in life-style have created new challenges to the retail marketer to define accurately and effectively satisfy these needs. Some of the life-style trends of the 1980s and 1990s were summarized by Lucas (1986):

more casual;
flexibility of roles/women's liberation;
instant gratification;
new theology of pleasure;
changing morality;
concern about appearance and health;
novelty, change and escape;
naturalism;
personal creativity;
changing attitudes towards credit;
new work ethics;
self-help versus institutional reliance;
consumerism;
ecology orientation;
time conservation;
convenience.

May *et al.* (1988) observed that life-styles can no longer be predicted from such factors as class, type of employment or income. While some retailers have adapted to these life-style trends, 'others are struggling to fit these new customers into the stereotypes of the past'. Some of the traditional and less traditional approaches to segmenting markets are considered in Chapter 3.

2.1.3 Shopping patterns

The development of large stores and major retail chains has been assisted by many changes in shoppers' habits, preferences and resources. In particular, increased access to cars for the purpose of shopping has widened the competitive arena, from immediate localities to larger geographical areas. The impact of this upon retail marketing has been considerable; as shoppers become willing and able to select from the retail outlets over a wide area, there are two main effects:

1. Less attractive outlets, no longer enjoying a spatial monopoly, are forced to either compete more vigorously or go out of business.
2. Large outlets can enjoy greater economies of scale by drawing trade from a very wide catchment area, if their 'retail mix' is sufficiently attractive to shoppers.

Table 2.5 shows the growth that has occurred in the ownership of private vehicles in Great Britain since 1961; over that period there has been a three-fold increase in the number of private vehicles. Of course, car ownership data do not represent all relevant aspects of mobility. The ability to shop by car has also increased as a result of shorter working hours, more women drivers and more two-car households. The Henley Centre has predicted that by the year 2000, 72 per cent of households will have access to at least one car, 32 per cent will have access to two (Alexander 1988).

Increased shopper mobility had an early impact upon the retail grocery trade but by now all sectors have been affected, to a greater or lesser extent, by this change. In an early study of shopping patterns at two superstores, Thorpe and McGoldrick (1974) found that 76 and 92 per cent of shoppers came by car, compared with 35 per cent at a nearby town centre. Shopping

Table 2.5 Cars and private vans in Great Britain, 1961–1988

Year	Cars and private vans ('000)	Cars per person
1961	6,114	0.115
1971	12,361	0.222
1981	14,943	0.264
1988	18,432	0.323

Source: derived from Central Statistical Office, *Monthly Digests of Statistics*, HMSO, London.

Table 2.6 Frequency of major grocery shopping in Britain, 1986 (%)*

	More than weekly	Weekly	Less than weekly
All shoppers	17.5	65.0	17.5
Age range			
16–34	13.2	66.5	20.2
35–54	14.9	66.3	18.8
55 or over	24.5	61.9	13.7
Social class			
AB	16.0	57.9	26.1
C1	15.4	62.9	21.7
C2	14.9	70.4	14.7
DE	22.0	65.1	12.8
Occupation			
Full-time	10.7	68.0	21.3
Part-time	14.7	68.2	17.1
Not employed	22.5	62.2	15.4

*Base: 3,000 adults who do the major grocery shopping for themselves or for their household.
Source: adapted from Euromonitor (1986).

patterns at the superstores were also characterized by greater travel distance, lower shopping frequencies and a higher propensity to shop in the company of family or friends. More recent indicators suggest that 62 per cent of people undertake their major grocery shopping trips by car (Euromonitor 1986).

The weekly major shopping trip for groceries is now the norm, although a growing proportion of shoppers try to extend this shopping cycle to two weeks or longer. Table 2.6 illustrates some differences between major demographic segments in terms of shopping frequencies. The under-35s, the up-market shoppers and those in full-time employment are the groups least prone to shop frequently for major grocery items. The lengthening of the grocery shopping cycle, especially among the more affluent shoppers, does create interesting opportunities for convenience stores to supply fresh foods and other 'top-up shopping' requirements (see Section 2.3.2).

Reduced shopping frequencies can be related to several demand and supply side-factors. For food shopping, the increased ownership of adequate refrigeration equipment and freezers has increased the storage cycle, especially for the smaller households. Higher shopper mobility and lower shopping frequencies have contributed to a reduction in the number of shops, which in turn has further perpetuated these trends. Shoppers have become more selective and more demanding in their choice of store and are therefore willing to consolidate their shopping into fewer but longer trips to get to the standard of shop required.

The increased number of women in paid employment (Walters 1986) has also reduced the time available to shop frequently, while at the same time contributing to an increased role for men in shopping. From a situation where women undertook most of the shopping for a household, we moved to a situation of the male partner acting as driver/porter; now, increasingly, he is likely to shop independently or as a more equal partner in the shopping process. Longer opening hours have also contributed to the trend towards joint or family shopping trips. Some retailers have presented an effective response to these changing shopping patterns, providing ample car parking, pleasant and spacious environments, wide product assortments, efficient checkout arrangements and a choice of payment modes (see Chapter 12).

The trend towards 'one-stop' shopping patterns is not limited to the grocery sector (Euromonitor 1987a). As electrical goods, furniture, carpets, DIY items, car accessories and even shoes come to be sold in larger, less centrally situated outlets (see Section 2.3), shopping patterns inevitably change. Even if few outlets truly provide the facility for 'one-stop' shopping, clusters of large stores on the edge of town cater for major, multi-purpose shopping trips.

Shopping patterns have therefore become more time-efficient for many shoppers, but at the same time retail environments are being developed to make shopping a more pleasurable activity (see Chapter 11). A greater polarization has been predicted (MacNulty 1989) between fun shopping and functional or chore-type shopping, with the former becoming a real leisure activity and the latter being undertaken with as little input of time and effort as possible. It cannot however be assumed that food shopping is invariably regarded as a chore, any more than it can be assumed that clothes shopping is regarded as fun; the problem will be to tailor the shopping experience to suit the preferred shopping patterns of the target market in each commodity area.

2.2 TYPES OF RETAILING ORGANIZATION

This section now looks at one important element of the competitive structure of retailing, namely, the main types of retailing organization. As noted in the introductory chapter, the increased power of retailers within the marketing channel could not have come about without the rapid growth of the larger retailers. The shift of trade between multiples and independents is considered first, with the position of multiples in Great Britain compared with those in Europe. Attention is then given to co-operative societies and symbol groups, both of which are especially significant within the grocery sector. Finally, the growth of franchising, both nationally and internationally, is considered.

2.2.1   Multiples v. independents

One of the most significant changes in retailing structure has been the increasing proportion of trade taken by the multiple retailers at the expense of other types of organization. Multiples are usually referred to as 'corporate chains' in the USA. In Europe, different sources have variously defined a multiple as a retailer with at least two, five or ten outlets; such differences create problems in comparing data. The 'ten-plus' definition was most commonly used in the UK and is still widely used in the grocery sector. The all-sector retailing enquiries, however, use the 'two-plus' definition but facilitate comparisons by isolating a category of 'small multiples' with between two and nine outlets (British Business 1988).

Based upon the retailing enquiries for 1982, 1984 and 1986, Table 2.7 compares independents with small and large multiples over those years. The retail enquiries offer the most comprehensive analysis of industry data, but unfortunately, the full results for 1986 were still awaited in spring 1989. Changes in criteria and methodology can also introduce some elements of unreliability into comparisons over time. The percentages calculated in Table 2.7 are however reliable estimates of the share of retail trade as a whole taken by each type of organization. It may be noted that the number of independent retail businesses had remained fairly stable over that period, with a decline of only 1.4 per cent; the number of persons employed showed a similar rate

Table 2.7   Multiples and independents in the UK, 1982–1986

	Single-outlet retailers	Small multiples (2–9 outlets)	Large multiples (10 + outlets)
1982			
No. of businesses	220,219	27,744	987
No. of outlets	220,219	73,163	63,208
Persons engaged ('000)	850	339	1,069
Retail turnover (£m)	20,906	8,975	38,021
Share of retail trade (%)	30.8	13.2	56.0
1984			
No. of businesses	218,700	27,399	832
No. of outlets	218,700	70,235	60,793
Persons engaged ('000)	840	331	1,146
Retail turnover (£m)	24,028	9,935	46,165
Share of retail trade (%)	30.0	12.4	57.6
1986			
No. of businesses	217,050	26,331	904
No. of outlets	217,050	66,765	60,144
Persons engaged ('000)	838	328	1,169
Retail turnover (£m)	27,935	11,950	56,540
Share of retail trade (%)	29.0	12.4	58.6
Change in turnover, 1982–6 (%)	+ 33.6	+ 33.1	+ 48.7
Change in share 1982–6 (%)	− 5.8	− 6.1	+ 4.6

Source: adapted from Central Statistical Office (1989, p. 211); British Business (1988, p. 29).

Table 2.8 Structure of the British grocery sector by region, 1970–1986

| | % share of grocery turnover | | |
	Multiples	Independents	Co-operatives
Year (all regions)			
1970	42.0	43.0	15.0
1980	60.9	24.9	14.2
1986	71.0	18.0	11.0
Region (1985)			
Scotland	64.2	20.3	15.5
Tyne Tees	70.2	16.3	13.5
Yorkshire	68.5	19.1	12.4
Lancashire	66.9	18.1	15.0
Midlands	65.5	21.1	13.4
Anglia	66.0	16.7	17.3
London	80.2	15.2	4.6
Southern	74.0	16.3	9.7
Wales & West	64.6	22.2	13.2

Source: based upon Nielsen data, quoted in Nielsen (1988); Beaumont (1987, p. 56).

of decline. The independents' share of retail trade, however, had declined by 5.8 per cent. The proportional loss of trade by the small multiples was in fact slightly larger, which may appear surprising. Some of this category grew to enter the next category; others were absorbed into larger multiples through acquisition. The significance of mergers and acquisitions is considered in Chapter 4. The problems with these definitions were illustrated by the Carrefour chain; having fewer than ten outlets for many years in the UK, albeit very large outlets indeed, Carrefour was variously classified as an independent or a small multiple; the Carrefour stores in the UK were then absorbed by acquisition into the Gateway chain, which was subsequently the target of international acquisition.

It should be noted that the categories within Table 2.7 cover all retailers, including co-operatives, most of which fall within the 'large multiples' category. It is advantageous for many purposes to identify the co-operatives separately, as in the analysis of the grocery sector in Table 2.8. This shows that the penetration of the multiples has been particularly strong in this sector, growing from 42 per cent in 1970 to 71 per cent in 1986. By 1988 the top two grocery retailers, Tesco and J. Sainsbury, held 28.3 per cent; the top five, which includes Gateway, Argyll and Asda, held 57.6 per cent (Institute of Grocery Distribution 1989). A survey of expert opinions by Killen and Lees (1988) suggested that by 1996 multiples would hold around 77 per cent of grocery turnover, with independents holding 13 per cent and co-operatives 9 per cent. The buying implications of this high level of penetration are considered in Chapter 7.

There are some important differences between regions with regard to the penetration of the multiples. In part, this reflects the balance of conurbations and more remote areas within the different regions. The multiples' penetration varies between 80.2 per cent in London and 64.2 per cent in Scotland. Conversely, the share of grocery trade held by independents varies from 22.2 per cent in Wales and the West to 15.2 per cent in London. This clearly could raise the issue of local oligopolies, which could eventually prompt legislation to curb the power of the multiples. A review of such legislation in other countries is provided by the Office of Fair Trading (1985).

Table 2.9 Multiples in Europe, 1982–1995

	% retail market share		
	1982	1988	1995 (f)
Austria	21	31	36
Denmark	13	16	22
Finland	n.a.	11	11
France	17	18	20
Netherlands	26	28	32
Norway (incl. franchising)	24	34	38
Spain	n.a.	14	18
Sweden	21	20	23
Switzerland	15	19	23
West Germany	22	24	30

Source: Euromonitor (1989, p. 24).

Largely because of more restrictive legislation, the multiples hold rather smaller relative shares in other European countries. With few exceptions, however, their shares are growing, in some cases very rapidly (see Table 2.9). For example, Euromonitor (1989) forecast a growth from 21 to 36 per cent between 1982 and 1995 in Austria. Over the same period, the multiples' share of food turnover is expected to grow from 36 to 47 per cent in Austria and in the Netherlands from 40 to 55 per cent. In most cases, however, the multiples hold less than 30 per cent of retail trade, illustrating that the retail structure of Britain is far from typical of Europe as a whole.

2.2.2 Co-operative societies

The co-operative societies in the UK still collectively represent the largest retailer in the country. On current projections, however, this position may soon be usurped by J. Sainsbury, Marks & Spencer and/or Tesco, each of which had achieved a turnover equal to around 75 per cent of the co-operatives by 1988. The major problem is that the Co-op comprises a large number of largely autonomous societies; it is not a single, fully integrated retailing organization.

Table 2.10 illustrates how the number of societies decreased dramatically between 1977 and 1987, although 91 was still clearly far too many. As early as 1968, a regional plan for the co-operative movement in the UK called for 50 societies (Bamfield 1978a); by 1973 the target had been moved to just 26 large, regional societies (Bamfield 1978b). Unfortunately, autonomous regional societies often resist mergers until they are left with no option, by which time the society has typically lost its hold upon its trading area and is in an enfeebled financial state. The pace of mergers has increased but, as the Co-operative Union pointed out:

this was due more to economic necessity than to enlightened foresight on the part of most of the societies concerned.

Continued resistance to mergers by societies whose results indicate an urgent need for such action could well result in the disappearance of the society for all time. (Brown 1982)

The growth of turnover shown in Table 2.10 is more than compensated by price increases. The Co-op's share of retail trade slipped from 5.67 per cent in 1982 to 4.32 per cent in 1986 (Central Statistical Office 1989). More recent figures indicated some measure of recovery, with an 8 per cent

Table 2.10 Turnover of UK co-operative societies, 1977–1987

Year	No. of societies	Retail turnover (£m)	Membership (m)
1977	231	2,713	10.62
1979	216	3,430	10.38
1981	187	4,098	9.53
1983	129	4,300	8.69
1985	103	4,768	8.16
1987	91	5,258	9.25

Source: derived from Institute for Retail Studies (1989, p. 22).

improvement in sales in 1988 (Retail Business 1989b). The Co-operative Wholesale Society also reported a 25 per cent increase in its trading profit over that year. The Co-op has traditionally held its strongest position in the grocery sector, although this share slipped from 15 to 11 per cent between 1970 and 1986. Table 2.8 illustrated major regional differences, with its strongest positions being in Anglia, Scotland and Lancashire, the weakest in London and the South.

The problems and prospects of the co-operatives in the UK have been reviewed in detail by Eliot (1982, 1983, 1985). Many problems were identified, in particular the following.

1. *Failure to keep pace with retail developments* For example, the Co-op has retained an emphasis upon food, a sector of little volume growth (see Section 2.1.1). It also has far too many small shops and too few large ones, in spite of many openings and closures in recent years. Accordingly, the societies are unable to enjoy the economies of scale of larger stores, and many customers have been lost to the larger, more attractive stores of competitors.
2. *A fragmented organizational structure in the UK* The reluctance to merge societies results in many boards of directors, with different objectives and policies. Expensive duplication of administrative and buying skills occurs, yet many societies are too small to recruit the skills required in retailing today. Similarly, sufficient finance and management resources may not be available for the development of large, modern stores. Different societies adopt different policies with regard to pricing, range and layout; several different trading names have been used, such as Domus, Leo's, KK and Shopping Giant. As a result, the movement lacks a coherent trading image (Eliot 1983).

This second point was further analysed by Bamfield (1987), who reviewed the positioning problems of the UK co-operatives. Although many cost-cutting programmes have occurred, the co-operatives do not enjoy the economies of scale required to 'play the low-cost game' with the largest multiples. Neither, for the most part, have they been able effectively to differentiate themselves on other dimensions. They have therefore encountered the classic positioning problem of being 'stuck in the middle' (see Chapter 4). There are of course major differences in the levels of success achieved by the different societies, depending largely upon their size, levels of regional competition, and the willingness of society managers to move with the times.

Table 2.11   Co-operatives in Europe, 1988

Country	Major co-ops	Share of all retail trade 1982 (%)	Share of all retail trade 1988 (%)	Share of food trade 1988 (%)
Switzerland	Co-op Migros	27	27	38
Denmark	FDB Co-op Soc.	19	20	39
Finland	S-Group EKA	n.a.	20	30
Sweden	KF/Konsum	16	16	21
Norway	NKL	14	15	23
Italy	—	n.a.	13	13
Austria	Konsum	9	8	13
UK	Co-op Socs.	6	5	12
W. Germany	Co-op AG	5	5	14
France	—	3	2	3
Netherlands	—	0.5	0.3	1

Source: adapted from Euromonitor (1989, pp. 20–1).

There are even more significant differences when comparisons are made between European countries. Table 2.11 compares the position of co-operatives in the UK with those of ten other countries. In the Netherlands, as in Belgium, co-operatives have all but disappeared (Euromonitor 1989). In contrast, the co-operatives in the Scandinavian countries are either holding or improving their shares. This could not be achieved without major shifts towards the operating style of the multiples. Individual profit centres have been established within KF/Konsum in Sweden, and NKL in Norway has had to review its policy of keeping open unviable shops in small villages. In West Germany, the Co-op AG took a step further, now being quoted on the stock exchange.

These international comparisons provide a sharp reminder that the co-operatives can choose between extinction, survival and growth. The more favourable outcomes, however, require a willingness to abandon their cherished autonomy and to change, quickly. The co-operative movement as a whole still has some considerable strengths and resources; even its image contains elements of membership/customer orientation, which could become powerful weapons if backed up with the right product/service offering. These resources and opportunities could very soon be lost, however, if the movement does not quickly become fully integrated and cost-efficient.

2.2.3   Voluntary groups

One response of independent retailers and wholesalers to the growth of the multiples has been the formation of 'voluntary', 'symbol' or 'affiliation' groups. Within this form of contractual chain, a group name is utilized and the retailers normally are required to obtain a certain proportion of their goods from the group wholesalers. The organization typically provides buying and other marketing services, including special promotions, advertising and frequently also own labels. Member retailers normally pay a modest levy towards the cost of these services, which averaged £12.50 per week with the Spar voluntary group. Euromonitor (1988) identified several advantages of group membership for the retailers:

1. Turnover is increased through promotions, lower prices and application of group marketing expertise.
2. Selling costs as a percentage of turnover are therefore reduced.
3. Better labour productivity is achieved through higher turnover and better administrative systems.
4. Space productivity improves through specialist advice on space allocation, merchandising and display.
5. Group buying power brings lower buying prices.
6. Profitability and thus return on capital is improved.
7. Benefits are gained through own-branding and the image of the group.
8. Loans and financial support are available to develop units.

In spite of these potential advantages, some retailers elect not to join a group and others leave or switch groups. Livesey and Nagy (1980, 1981) examined the reasons behind these decisions. Dissatisfaction with high membership or delivery charges, or with high prices, were the main reasons for leaving a group; a preference for complete independence was the main reason given for not joining a group. In recent years the major groups have become more selective in their recruitment of member retailers, and some weaker or non-compliant members have been weeded out. This has been part of a drive to raise standards and increase consistency within the groups.

Despite intensive efforts, the share of retail trade held by the voluntary groups is expected to continue to fall, from 7.3 per cent in 1986 to 6.2 per cent in 1991 (Euromonitor 1988). In that they were introduced essentially as a defensive measure, voluntary groups tend to exist in sectors that are under pressure from the multiples. Table 2.12 shows the sectors and sub-sectors within which they have a significant presence. In volume terms, the grocery groups are the most significant. Spar, Mace, Londis, VG and Nisa each serves over 1,000 outlets. In terms of market share, the chemists sector has the most powerful voluntary group presence. Numark, Vantage, Vestric and Unichem each serves over 2,000 chemists; 75 per cent of chemist's shops are within one or more voluntary group.

The strength of voluntary groups varies enormously between the different countries of Europe. Table 2.13 presents a compilation by Euromonitor (1989) of trends in total retail and food market shares, with projections to 1995. The gaps indicate that reliable comparative data were not available; they do not suggest an absence of voluntary groups. The European view is clearly very mixed, with the voluntary groups holding strong shares in most of the Scandinavian countries. This type of affiliation appears especially well suited to areas with low population densities. In Finland the voluntary groups command around two-thirds of the retail food market. They have also retained considerable strength in West Germany, where Rewe serves around 7,000 outlets and Edeka serves 15,000. There, as in Norway and the Netherlands, the voluntary groups are expected to be under increasing pressure from the multiples in the 1990s.

2.2.4 Franchising

Franchising, in various forms, has a long history in both the UK (Ayling 1988) and the USA (Kaynak 1988). Only relatively recently, however, has it emerged as a major element of UK retail structure. Seaman (1988) estimated that franchising held 10 per cent of the UK retail market in 1988, compared with 2 per cent in 1983. Over the same period, the number of franchisees in

Table 2.12 UK market share of voluntary groups, 1986

Sector	Turnover of group members (£m)	Share of sector (%)
Small grocers	2,265	55
Food specialists	350	5
Total food	2,615	7
CTN	1,000	14
Footwear	25	1
Furnishers	150	3
Electricals	375	7
DIY hardware	450	12
Total DIY hardware	975	7
Chemists	1,800	57
Jewellers	55	4
Toys, sports goods	90	8
Mixed businesses	515	3
Total	7,075	7

Source: Euromonitor (1988, p. 15).

Table 2.13 Voluntary groups: European trends, 1982–1995

Country	Percentage market share (value)					
	1982		1988		1995 (f)	
	Total	Food	Total	Food	Total	Food
Austria	—	36	—	36	—	35
Belgium	—	—	11	—	13	—
Denmark	33	—	33	36	36	35
Finland	—	58	40	66	42	67
Italy	—	19	—	21	—	25
Netherlands	33	—	32	30	30	25
Norway	27	25	24	25	20	25
Spain	2	—	4	—	4	—
Sweden	35	40	36	44	39	47
Switzerland	—	—	—	12	—	10
West Germany	40	58	39	57	35	52

Source: Euromonitor (1988, pp. 29–30).

Western Europe was estimated to have grown from 9,000 to 90,000, with every likelihood that the growth rate would further accelerate. Given the differences in definitions and the proportions of non-retail franchises, it is difficult to obtain reliable comparative data; what is clear is that the growth rate has been phenomenal.

Definitions of what comprises a franchise arrangement differ considerably, and there are some very different forms of franchise. Using a classification suggested by Vaughn (1979), Stern and Stanworth (1988) identified four main types:

1. *The manufacturer–retailer franchise*   Within this arrangement, the manufacturer is the franchisor and the franchisee sells direct to the public. Many such franchises are to be found in the retailing of cars and petrol.
2. *The manufacturer–wholesaler franchise*   The most notable examples are Coca-Cola and Pepsi-Cola, who franchise the independent bottlers which, in turn, serve retail outlets.
3. *The wholesaler–retailer franchise*   The voluntary groups discussed in the previous section could be classified as this type of franchise.
4. *The trademark, trade-name, licensor–retailer franchise*   This is the type that has grown most rapidly and is often referred to simply as 'business format' franchising. This type usually includes a high service element, such as fast food, car-hire and print service franchises.

A detailed definition of a franchise, which explains the roles of the two parties involved, was presented by Euromonitor (1987b). It is defined as a contractual licence granted by one person (the franchisor) to another (the franchisee), which:

a) permits or requires the franchisee to carry on, during the period of the franchise, a particular business under or using a specific name belonging to or associated with the franchisor, and
b) entitles the franchisor to exercise continuing control during the period of the franchise over the manner in which the franchisee carries on the business which is the subject of the franchise, and
c) obliges the franchisor to provide the franchisee with assistance in carrying on the business which is the subject of the franchise (in relation to the organisation of the franchisee's business, the training of staff, merchandising, management or otherwise) and
d) requires the franchisee periodically, during the period of the franchise, to pay to the franchisor sums of money in consideration for the franchise, or for the goods or services provided by the franchisor to the franchisee and
e) which is not a transaction between a holding company and its subsidiary or between subsidiaries of the same holding company, or between an individual and a company controlled by him. (Euromonitor 1987b)

Estimates of the number of franchised outlets in the UK suggest a growth from 2,600 in 1980 to 15,000 in 1987 (Euromonitor 1987a; Retail 1988). Table 2.14 illustrates this increase through the 1980s. Franchising has also developed rapidly in many other European countries. In 1985 there were more franchisees, relative to numbers in the population, in the Netherlands, France and Belgium than there were in the UK (Euromonitor 1987b). Kaynak (1988) reviewed the process of globalization of franchise systems. The role of franchising in multinational retailing is considered in Section 2.4.

Particular success stories of franchising in the UK include the Body Shop, Benetton and Tie Rack, although many others made less distinguished progress (Retail 1988). In general, franchised outlets are far less likely to fail than are independently operated ones (Ayling 1988); Seaman (1988) estimated that 25 per cent of independent business start-ups fail in year 1, whereas 90 per cent of franchised businesses succeed. There are of course some notable instances of failure, such as the bankruptcy of Young's Dresswear and Pronuptia in 1985; this company was rescued from receivership and is now making good progress again.

Table 2.14   Franchised outlets in the
UK, 1980–1987

Year	Franchised outlets	% change
1980	2,600	—
1981	3,500	34.6
1982	5,000	42.9
1983	7,000	40.0
1984	8,600	22.9
1985	10,200	18.6
1986	12,500	22.5
1987	15,000	20.0

Source: Euromonitor (1987a, p. 233);
Retail (1988, p. 40).

The rapid growth of franchising in the 1980s has been linked with the high levels of unemployment during that period, including the unemployment of many competent, potential franchisees with some capital from redundancy payments. This is of course not the only reason why franchising has grown; there are many positive benefits for the franchisees. These were summarized by Hunt (1977):

1. The trade name of the franchise—all the goodwill associated with the franchisor's trade name can be transferred to the franchisee's business.
2. Pre-opening assistance—site selection, building plans, training programmes, operating manuals, assistance in finding suppliers and supervision of the store opening.
3. Post-opening assistance—advertising, bookkeeping, supplies, field supervision and advice services.

In theory, and very often in practice too, franchising achieves the best of both worlds in business, combining the power and sophistication of a large organization with the energy and commitment of the independent owner–manager.

Unfortunately, franchising also developed a rather poor image, which in some cases was entirely deserved. While introducing their 'Good Franchise Guide', Attwood and Hough (1988) alerted readers to the sharp practices that may be encountered in some franchise advertisements and contracts. There is a tendency to obscure important details and to present very optimistic projections of likely profits, tendencies noted earlier in the USA by Hunt (1977). Some franchisees also find themselves contracted to obtain supplies from the franchisor at prices far in excess of those obtainable elsewhere. The arrangements for selling the business can also be unfavourable for the franchisee under some contracts. Caution and a great deal of attention to the legal details is therefore urged, before entering a franchise agreement.

2.3   SHOP TYPES AND NUMBERS

This section examines changes in the retailing environment in terms of the retailing outlets themselves. The physical structure of retailing has evolved rapidly in recent years through a combination of economic forces, consumer trends, competitive initiatives and the relaxation of certain planning constraints. An understanding of these changes is a vital first step towards major strategic decisions on where, how and within what format to compete. To begin with, the long-term decline and more recent levelling out of shop numbers is analysed and comparisons are made with shop densities in other parts of Europe. The problems of the traditional small store and the merits of the convenience store concept are then discussed. Attention then turns to the larger individual outlets, the superstores and hypermarkets. Finally, the recent shopping centre development boom is examined, notably the out-of-town developments of retail parks and large, regional centres.

2.3.1 Number of shops

There was a dramatic decline in the number of shops in Britain through the 1970s, with numbers falling from 509,818 in 1971 to 362,500 in 1980 (Schiller and Boucke 1989). This represented a loss of over 16,000 outlets per year, around 45 per day, during those years. This rate of decline slowed considerably in the 1980s, as Table 2.15 illustrates, with the overall loss averaging 8–9 outlets per day between 1980 and 1986. This has not been distributed evenly between the different types of business, with food outlets declining most rapidly but with some levelling out or growth in other sectors. The strongest growth has been in the 'other non-food' and 'mixed retail business' categories.

The reduction of grocery and other foodshops has by no means been limited to the independent sector. Regular analyses of grocery outlet numbers are published by the Institute of Grocery Distribution. These showed a 38.8 per cent fall, from 7,000 to 4,280 multiple grocery outlets, between 1977 and 1987 (defining a multiple as an organization with ten or more outlets). Over the same period, co-operative grocery outlets declined by 36.3 per cent and independent grocery outlets by 36.8 per cent (IGD News 1989). This reflects the continued weeding out of smaller, uneconomic branches by the grocery multiples and co-operatives, a process that now includes the closure of many 'medium-sized' supermarkets. Openings and closures by the grocery multiples in 1987 were summarized in the following terms:

Average sales area for multiple grocery store	11,926 sq. ft
Average size of newly opened store in 1987	22,238 sq. ft
Average size of stores closed in 1987	5,309 sq. ft

Even in the grocery sector, however, there is some evidence of a slowing down in the rate of decline in shop numbers. The reduction between 1986 and 1987 was only 530, compared with an average of over 3,000 per year since 1977 (IGD News 1989).

If a far broader definition of retail outlet were adopted, to include the financial and catering service outlets, then a rather different picture emerges. This would suggest that the decline in the number of retail outlets ceased by 1982, since when there has been a steady growth overall (Schiller and Boucke 1989). There are some arguments in favour of including cafés, restaurants, banks, estate agents, etc., as retail outlets; from the viewpoint of the developer, town planner or, indeed, the consumer, they are all a part of the attraction of a particular centre. There is also an increasing tendency for product retailers to diversify into services (see Chapter 12), and for financial and other service providers to adopt the retail marketing perspective.

Table 2.15 Number of retail outlets in the UK by kind of business, 1980–1986

Broad kind of business	No. of outlets ('000; % share of total in brackets)				% change 1980–86
	1980	1982	1984	1986	
Food	122.8 (34)	114.8 (33)	106.8 (31)	99.8 (29)	− 18.7
Drink, tobacco & confectionery	57.4 (16)	57.2 (16)	57.3 (17)	56.5 (16)	− 1.6
Clothing, footwear & leather goods	59.4 (16)	55.7 (16)	56.0 (16)	59.3 (17)	− 0.2
Household goods	61.7 (17)	59.1 (17)	57.1 (17)	60.7 (18)	− 1.6
Other non-food	45.5 (13)	45.5 (13)	48.0 (14)	50.9 (15)	12.1
Mixed retail business	9.8 (3)	11.0 (3)	10.9 (3)	10.4 (3)	6.1
Hire & repair business	6.2 (2)	6.5 (2)	6.9 (2)	5.9 (2)	− 4.8
Total retail	362.5 (100)	349.7 (100)	343.2 (100)	343.4 (100)	− 5.3

Source: Institute for Retail Studies (1989, p. 20).

The problem of differing definitions and survey dates makes European comparisons of shop numbers a difficult task. Table 2.16 was compiled by Euromonitor (1989) in relation to 16 European countries. This illustrates that the UK is by no means 'a nation of shopkeepers', in terms of outlets per 1,000 members of the population. In general, the highest 'densities' of shops per head persist in countries with less developed retail infrastructures and/or with a higher proportion of rural areas. The tradition of small, family-run shops has also prevailed more strongly in some countries, such as France and Belgium.

2.3.2 Small shops and c-stores

The rapid decline in shop numbers in Britain has been most strongly reflected in the thinning out of the traditional small stores, many of which were independent, family firms. Dawson (1983) traced the fall in the independent shop numbers, from 445,000 in 1961 to 390,000 in 1971, then down to 230,000 by 1981. It is more difficult for a small shop to achieve the economies of scale in buying, management expertise and labour that can be achieved by larger outlets. Referring to the 'ousting of smallness', Nooteboom *et al.* (1986) described some of the economic forces that have tended to press smaller, independent stores out of the market in many European countries. They also noted that periodic downturns in national economies, causing general pressure on retail margins, have had an especially adverse effect upon small independent stores.

While economies of scale represent the main underlying cause of falling numbers, many more specific reasons have caused small, independent retailers to cease trading. Because of the adverse

Table 2.16 Number of outlets: European comparisons

Country	Outlets (*'000*)	Outlets per 1,000 population
Spain	739.9	19.2
Greece	185.0	18.7
Belgium	114.0	11.5
Netherlands	158.0	10.8
France	590.0	10.5
Denmark	48.7	9.5
Italy[b]	533.4	9.3
Norway	38.1	9.2
Ireland[a]	31.3	9.2
Portugal[a]	81.0	9.0
Switzerland	52.3	8.1
Finland	36.3	7.4
UK	343.2	6.1
Sweden[c]	48.0	5.7
West Germany	310.0	5.1
Austria[a]	38.0	5.0

[a] Based upon pre-1984 data.
[b] Fixed outlets only.
[c] Excludes state-controlled pharmacies and off-licences (liquor stores).

Source: Euromonitor (1989, p. 17).

implications of this trend, especially in terms of the welfare of more isolated, poorer and/or less mobile consumers, a number of studies have examined its causes in some detail (e.g. Bechhofer *et al.* 1974; Bates 1976; Dawson and Kirby 1979; Kirby and Law 1981). Dawson (1983) summarized the reasons for the decline of independent traders:

a) broad economic and social change (inflation, recession, buying behaviour);
b) competition from multiples and co-operatives;
c) increased operating costs (rates, electricity etc.);
d) lack of capital for investment;
e) availability of supplies of goods (price, quantity, delivery, etc.);
f) urban renewal;
g) age of entrepreneur (approaching retirement);
h) poor locations;
i) inflexible management attitudes.

The problem of obtaining required quantities of supplies at reasonable prices reflects a vicious circle, whereby the decline of the independents has contributed to a decline in the delivered wholesale trade and an increase in the minimum sizes of delivered orders. Unaffiliated independents have therefore been obliged to make more use of cash-and-carry wholesalers, thereby further lengthening their working days and increasing an already very high workload.

Table 2.17   C-store operators in the UK, 1987

	Outlets	No. on forecourts	Ave. sq. ft. selling area
Symbol groups			
8 till late (Spar)	1,550	70	1,000
Late Stop (VG)	340	20	1,000
Convenience Express (Mace Line)	82	11	980
Londis	900	10	800
Costcutter	83	1	1,000
Total Symbols	2,955	112	
Specialists			
Circle K	138	10	2,000
7-Eleven	48	1	1,600
M & W	56	—	2,000
Cullens	51	—	1,600
Circle C	24	1	—
Lateshopper	25	—	—
Total Specialists	342	12	
CTNs			
Dillons	24	—	1,300
One Stop	18	—	1,800
Preedy	3	—	—
Star News Shops	130	—	—
Forbuoys	25	—	—
Total CTNs	200	—	—
Co-operatives			
Stop & Shops (CRS)	150	—	—
All House (Leicestershire)	46	—	—
8 til 8 (North East)	116	—	—
Late Shop (United)	32	—	—
Open Later (Norwest)	15	1	—
Late Late Supershop (CWS)	13	1	1,800
Total Co-operatives	372	2	
Other			
Rusts	15	—	1,800
AM–PM Ltd	7	—	—
Apollo	7	—	—
Augustus Barnett Plus	8	—	—
Total Other	37	—	—
Grand total	3,906		

Source: derived from Euromonitor (1988, pp. 13–16).

In spite of all these problems, the decline of the small shops now seems to be levelling out, if not actually reversing in some sectors. One factor in many urban areas has been the influence of Asian and other ethnic groups in retailing (Ward 1987). They have proved to be more resilient to the pressures upon small retailers, and the survival rates of their stores are relatively high (McEvoy and Aldrich 1986). In part, this has been achieved by lowering the financial barriers to entry and to survival, in particular, by attributing low labour costs. Many have also proved adept at assembling a product and service mix well attuned to the needs of their local communities.

Clearly, there is a future for small shops, provided they fulfil a role complementary to that of the larger stores which now dominate most sectors. Many of the reasons for small-store closures relate to problems of management expertise and supply chains, rather than to their smallness *per se*. The 'convenience store' (c-store) is an expression of this new role for smaller outlets, and the concept has been adopted extensively in several sectors. Many independents have adopted, arguably pioneered, elements of the c-store concept, notably long opening hours and assortments geared to high frequency and/or 'top-up' shopping needs. The more widespread c-store developments, however, have been made by the symbol groups, co-operatives, franchises and specialist chains. A number of definitions of c-stores have been suggested, the following by the Economist Intelligence Unit (1986):

The essential elements of a convenience store are that its product range is a mix of commodities and services frequently required by customers at short notice, and made available to them through the expedient of trading within and outside of normal shopping hours on a seven-day-a-week basis. Products most regularly stocked include traditional CTN items, groceries, stationery and cards, proprietary medicines, toiletries and household goods. Stores tend to be located in residential communities or within easy reach of them by car. The catchment areas are therefore limited.

Table 2.17 summarizes the main types of c-stores operating under group names in the UK. The impact of the symbol groups is clearly illustrated, in particular Spar. The first Spar conversion of the c-store format was in 1981, but the excellent results achieved soon brought many more converts (Retail 1987). Typical trading hours in a Spar '8 till late' are between 9am and 10pm, seven days a week. Most of the petrol companies have at least experimented with c-stores at filling stations. With over 20,000 filling stations in the UK, it could be that the 'convenience store with pumps' will become as common as it is in some other countries (Kirby 1987). Many co-operative societies have also found the c-store concept to be a better alternative to closing still more small stores. A particularly interesting development has been the formation of a franchising subsidiary by the Co-operative Wholesale Society under the 'Late Late Supershop' banner.

Every store experiences a shift in clientele and demand at different times of day (see Chapter 12), but this is especially true of c-stores. Mintel (1986) noted the following pattern experienced by many c-stores:

Before 9.00am	Workers buying CTN products and schoolchildren buying snack foods
9.00am–noon	Housewives buying food and household items
Noon–2.00pm	Workers/schoolchildren buying sandwiches, snacks, drinks, ice cream, CTN products
2.00pm–4.00pm	Housewives buying food and household items
4.00pm–6.00pm	Schoolchildren buying snack foods and comics, workers buying CTN products and some 'top-up' (or emergency) items

After 6.00pm	Workers buying main meal food items and top-up items; adults (male-biased) buying alcohol, cigarettes and confectionary

This pattern obviously varies according to the proximity of main roads, bus stops, schools and places of work. Many c-stores, both on and off forecourts, have provided an extra incentive to visit the store by introducing video hire facilities.

The development of c-stores has complied strongly with the theory of retail polarization, expounded by D. A. Kirby:

According to the theory, the retail systems of most 'high level economies' will polarise. At the end of the spectrum, the large retail operation will dominate the market, satisfying those consumer segments (the majority) which are highly mobile and able and prepared to shop in bulk. At the other extreme will be the small, efficient retail operation which satisfies the majority shopping needs of a consumer minority (ie, those unable or unwilling to buy in bulk), plus the minority needs of the consumer majority. For this latter group, the small, local store is used for 'topping up'—for the purchase of forgotten or out-of-stock items, for perishables or for 'emergency' items. (Kirby 1986)

This theory suggests an important future role for the c-store, provided that the essential criteria of convenience and efficiency are met. It must be recognized, however, that the viability of c-stores rests in part upon the inconvenience of using larger stores. As larger stores become more easily accessible to more people, if/when their hours are further extended, and as their checkout facilities become faster and better suited to secondary (as well as primary) shopping trips, it will become considerably harder for c-stores to offer significant competitive advantage.

2.3.3 Superstores and hypermarkets

At the other end of the retailing spectrum, the number of very large stores has increased steadily over the last twenty years. The term 'superstore' is used to describe stores with over 25,000 sq. ft of single-level selling area, a high proportion of which is devoted to the selling of groceries. Stores meeting this description but with over 50,000 sq. ft of selling area are often referred to as 'hypermarkets' (Euromonitor 1987c). The Unit for Retail Planning Information (URPI) uses slightly higher definition thresholds, based upon metric measures:

Superstores are defined as single-level self-service stores selling a wide range of food, or food and non-food goods with at least 2,500 square metres (27,000 sq. ft.) trading floorspace and supported by car parking. Stores selling only non-food goods are excluded. Stores with 5,000 square metres (54,000 sq. ft.) or more are commonly referred to as Hypermarkets. (Unit for Retail Planning Information 1988)

In fact, the two terms are frequently used interchangeably. Some UK grocery multiples do not use the term 'hypermarket' at all, in spite of the fact that some of their stores fall within the category. The view has been expressed that the term 'superstore' tends to be less intimidating to local residents and more acceptable to planning authorities. In comparisons between European countries, on the other hand, readers are likely to encounter the term 'hypermarket' used to describe both categories. These inconsistencies in the use of the terms can cause confusion when comparing sources. The exclusive prerogative of the grocery trade to the terms has also been greatly eroded; 'superstore' is now used to describe some large (and some not so large) outlets in the electrical, furniture, DIY, clothing, footwear and other sectors. Their development in the non-grocery sectors has not been as closely documented.

URPI data trace the development of superstores and hypermarkets in the UK from the first openings in 1967; by 1977 there were 100 and 17, respectively, by 1987 there were 373 and 44

Table 2.18 Penetration of grocery superstores and hypermarkets in Great Britain, 1982 and 1988

Standard region	No. of stores 1982	No. of stores 1988	% change 1982–88	Population per store ('000)
North	19	35	84	88.0
Wales	18	32	78	88.2
E. Midlands	26	43	65	91.2
North East	52	69	37	92.4
Yorks & Humberside	36	53	47	92.4
W. Midlands	34	50	47	103.6
East Anglia	7	18	157	110.7
South West	16	38	138	119.6
Scotland	42	41	− 2	124.9
South East	55	86	56	142.7
Greater London	11	35	218	193.6
Total GB	316	500	45	110.4

Source: based upon IGD data, derived from Institute for Retail Studies (1989, p. 27); Institute of Grocery Distribution (1988, p. 40).

(Unit for Retail Planning Information 1988). Noticeably, the pace at which hypermarkets have developed has not matched that of the superstores. To an extent, this reflects the problems of obtaining sites of that magnitude. It also reflects a decision by some major multiples to concentrate developments at or, in some cases, below superstore size. As noted in Section 2.3.1, the average size of newly opened grocery stores in 1987 was 22,238 sq. ft, i.e. just below superstore size. Apart from problems of site availability and costs, some grocery retailers have decided to specialize more in the selling of food and to limit the proliferation of their non-food assortments; these decisions are discussed in Section 4.2.

The penetration of grocery superstores and hypermarkets differs very considerably between the regions of Great Britain. Based upon the 25,000 sq. ft definition, Table 2.18 shows 500 such stores in 1988, with high penetration in many areas of the North but low penetration in London and the South East. These regional differences relate largely to the geographical spread of companies (notably Asda) which took the lead in the development of superstores. They also reflect the significant differences that existed between the planning attitudes in different regions; these are discussed further in Section 6.2.

In European comparisons, the share of food sales held by hypermarkets and superstores is very similar in the UK, France and West Germany, at 20–21 per cent. In Belgium the share is 17 per cent, in Denmark 10 per cent and in the Netherlands 7 per cent (Corporate Intelligence Group 1989). It should be noted, however, that the penetration of supermarkets is considerably higher in the UK than in France or West Germany, representing a high level of concentration of food retailing through medium–large-sized, self-service outlets.

As superstores increasingly start to compete with each other, the possibility of superstore saturation must be considered seriously (e.g. Jones 1982). This applied not only to grocery superstores but also to the DIY sector, where their development has also been prolific. There are however still many opportunities for the development of large stores in regions and local areas of low penetration. It is inevitable that some of the older, less attractive and/or badly located superstores will eventually be superseded by newer outlets (Retail 1989).

2.3.4 Shopping centre developments

In parallel to the development of (mainly) free-standing superstores and hypermarkets, there has also been vigorous development of shopping centres over the last two decades. Until the mid-1970s, these were concentrated within existing or new town centres; from 1976, the out-of-town shopping centre started to make an impact. Both 1976 and 1988 were peak years for shopping centre openings. In 1976 over 85 per cent of shopping centre floorspace was in a town centre; by 1988 the proportion had fallen to around 28 per cent, the remainder comprising out-of-town (or edge-of-town) centres and retail parks (Hillier Parker 1989a).

Schiller (1987) described three waves of such out-of-town development. The first wave involved food, the second bulky goods, and the third comparison shopping. The 'first wave' was led by the superstore groups, discussed in the previous section. Their attempts to sell non-food ranges alongside groceries were largely unsuccessful, so little threat was seen to the major role of the town centres. The 'second wave' of decentralization involved bulky goods, such as DIY, carpets, furniture, larger electrical items and garden centres. These did comprise a threat to the town centres but provoked less opposition from planners than the first wave, largely because the out-of-town locations seemed manifestly more suitable for the retailing of bulky items.

The 'third wave' presented an even more direct threat to the town centres as it involved clothing and other comparison shopping. The decision by Marks & Spencer to open out-of-town stores, announced in 1984, was identified as a major element in this third wave. A detailed study of one of Marks & Spencer's out-of-town developments was undertaken by Brown (1988).

The appeal of out-of-town centres can be summarized mainly in terms of greater car-borne accessibility and lower land costs. Planning restrictions have been the main inhibiting factor (see Section 6.2). Schiller (1987) has identified four main types of out-of-town shopping centre:

1. *Speciality centres* These consist mainly of a cluster of small, independent units selling items of appeal to tourists and visitors, such as Liverpool's Albert Dock or London's Covent Garden.
2. *District centres* These are usually of between 100,000 and 300,000 sq. ft, with a superstore as the 'anchor'. These centres typically offer an even mix of food and routine durable goods.
3. *Retail parks* These started in the early 1980s as rather utilitarian groupings of retail warehouses; more recently, the trend has been towards more integration and more attractive, park-like designs. From just one retail park in 1982, development accelerated in the late 1980s, and there were 90 by 1988 (Hillier Parker 1989b). By 1989 over 55 per cent of shopping centre proposals were for retail parks (Hillier Parker 1989c).
4. *Regional centres* These comprise at least 500,000 sq. ft of comparison retailing. The first in Britain was at Brent Cross, followed by Milton Keynes. The third, and the biggest in Europe, is the 2 million sq. ft Metro Centre, three miles outside Newcastle (Sands 1986; Davies and Howard 1987). The main mall of the Metro Centre is half a mile long and the ends are anchored by a Carrefour superstore and a large Marks & Spencer store (see Section 6.1).

Considerable interest has naturally been shown in the last of these categories, which comes the closest to offering a complete alternative to town centre shopping. Such centres are far more common in North America; it would require 340 such regional centres in Britain to provide the same number per head of population as in the USA (Rogers 1987). To attract shoppers from the

Table 2.19 UK shopping centre schemes in the pipeline, 1980–1989

| Year | Proposed | Floorspace (m sq. ft) of schemes 50,000 sq. ft + | | Total |
		With planning consent	Under construction	
1980	10.0	10.0	8.9	28.9
1981	12.0	10.2	9.2	31.4
1982	14.0	12.5	6.5	33.0
1983	13.5	11.2	7.1	31.8
1984	15.0	10.8	5.8	31.6
1985	21.4	12.1	7.2	40.7
1986	31.8	20.1	11.1	63.0
1987	52.2	28.8	14.9	95.9
1988	89.8	32.6	20.2	142.0
1989	79.5	48.0	28.3	155.8

Source: Hillier Parker (1989c).

traditional centres, these malls must offer a blend of comparison shopping, leisure and catering facilities. Food courts have become a major focal point and facility for shoppers in many new centres (e.g. Worthington 1988).

The progress of shopping centre developments has been carefully traced through the 1980s by Hillier Parker. Table 2.19 shows their analysis of 'schemes in the pipeline', i.e. those proposed, those with planning consent and those under construction. Given the long lead times of shopping centre developments, this provides a more sensitive analysis of trends than measures of floorspace actually opened. Development pressure grew very rapidly in the second half of the 1980s, but by 1989 there were signs of nervousness, with some proposals being withdrawn and others being reduced in scale.

An assessment of the future of large-scale shopping centre developments in Europe should include an analysis of trends in North America. Canada's West Edmonton Mall, with 5 million sq. ft, is the world's largest and probably best known shopping centre development (Johnson 1987; Hallsworth 1988). This centre has proved to be a massive tourist attraction, but doubts have been expressed as to whether the two-mile long concourses provide the ideal basis for convenient shopping. Indeed, the major department stores in the centre of Edmonton are grouped more closely than those in the West Edmonton Mall. More general concerns have also been expressed about the appeal of large shopping malls to North American consumers. A firm of consultants with the modest title 'Brain Reserves' has pointed to an American consumer sated with consumer goods, with more interests at home, and increasingly bored and weary of the typical three-mile walk when visiting a mall (Mundow 1989). The wider problems of the malls were summarized by Rogers (1987):

1. their principal department store tenants are in decline;
2. many were not designed in a manner that can provide the space and visibility required by the new generation of large speciality stores;
3. they are usually expensive operating environments;
4. many have become inconvenient, boring and stereotyped, not unlike many of Britain's High Streets;
5. as regional shopping centres encroach upon each others' catchment areas, only the best and the best located can continue to prosper.

While there are many important differences between North American and European retail markets, these trends should provide important warning signals to retailers and developers in Europe.

2.4   THE INTERNATIONAL DIMENSION

The discussion so far has been concerned mostly with domestic trading environments. Some would argue that retailing in more than one country is only a logical extension of the general principles of retail marketing, i.e. the identification and satisfaction of consumer needs, at a profit. The most distinctive element of multinational retailing, of course, is that the international differences in consumer needs, customs, styles and tastes are likely to be far greater than those existing between the regions of one country. Add to this the differences between the economic, competitive and legislative environments, and it is clear that the structural and strategic elements of multinational retailing merit separate attention. A particular difficulty, of course, is in obtaining reliable and truly comparable data with which to assess other national retailing environments; the problems of such comparisons were discussed in detail by Tordjman (1986).

It should be acknowledged that multinational retailing is not a new phenomenon. Over twenty years ago, Hollander (1969) commented:

Retailers used to talk of local, regional and national chains. In today's merchandising world, however, the retail organisation that doesn't reach across national boundaries may seem almost parochial.

Woolworth was an early example of the trend, opening its first UK Woolworth store in Liverpool in 1909 (Mitton 1987). From this small beginning, the UK subsidiary developed over 1,000 stores by the end of the 1970s, to the extent that many shoppers were unaware that it was American-owned. Since then, of course, the chain has become British-owned and has shifted strategic emphasis from variety stores to more focused trading formats (see Chapter 4). Overall, however, the history of multinational retailing has been chequered, with periods of grandiose expansion and periods of hurried withdrawals (Jefferys 1985).

2.4.1   International retailers

The arrival of the Single European Market (SEM) has caused retailers to look far more closely at the opportunities and threats offered by increased international competition. The highly concentrated and generally efficient UK retailing industry may view the fragmented retailing in some other parts of Europe as an opportunity (Retail & Distribution Management 1988). It would be dangerous, however, to assume that this fragmentation exists simply because of a lack of capital or appropriate expertise within the country concerned; local and national planning attitudes usually have played a major part. On the other side of the coin, retailing in the UK may be more attractive to other Europeans because of more relaxed planning attitudes, good transportation, a concentrated industry structure and, during most of the 1980s, relatively high profitability. This could make underperforming multiples vulnerable to international acquisition. It has in fact been suggested that there may be more attractions for foreign investment in UK retailing than vice versa (Corporate Intelligence Group 1988, 1989). Table 2.20 compares post-tax profits of some major European retailers. It illustrates that lower margins and higher tax rates are characteristic of most retailing in Europe outside the UK, even when allowance is made for the fact that 1986/7 was a very good year for the margins of many UK retailers.

A large proportion of the international expansion by UK retailers has so far been towards the USA and Canada, rather than Europe. The flow of European retail investment into North

Table 2.20 Post-tax net profits of selected European retailers, 1984/5–1986/7

Retailer	Country	Net profits (%) 1984/5	Net profits (%) 1986/7
Storehouse	UK	6.2	7.9
Next	UK	9.5	7.5
Burtons	UK	n.a.	7.3
Dixons	UK	4.1	7.0
Boots	UK	6.6	7.0
Marks & Spencer	UK	5.7	6.5
Sears	UK	5.4	5.7
Harris Queensway	UK	4.3	5.6
Ward White	UK	4.5	5.3
Asda MFI	UK	3.9	4.9
Darty	France	3.0	4.5
Sainsbury	UK	3.6	4.1
Woolworth	UK	5.2	3.8
Tesco	UK	2.0	3.3
W.H. Smith	UK	2.4	2.8
KBijenkorf Beheer	Netherlands	1.1	2.6
Argyll	UK	1.7	2.5
Dee Corporation	UK	1.8	2.1
Nouvelles Galeries	France	0.7	1.6
Carrefour	France	1.2	1.3
Arhold	Netherlands	1.0	1.2
Casino	France	0.8	1.1
GB-Inno-BM	Belgium	1.4	1.1
Printemps	France	0.6	0.9
Euromarche	France	n.a.	0.9
Delhaize	Belgium	0.5	0.8
Promodes	France	0.7	0.7
Galeries Lafayette	France	0.6	0.1

Source: Paribas Quilter, quoted in: Corporate Intelligence Group (1989, p. 65).

America has been around $5.55 billion, compared with only $2.5 billion flowing in the opposite direction, mostly in fast food operations. A number of reasons have been cited for the relative disinclination of North American retailers to expand into Europe (Ody 1989):

1. an unsaturated domestic market;
2. legislative restraints elsewhere;
3. high land prices in Europe;
4. previous failure of foreign investment.

Table 2.21 Retailing activities abroad: selected UK companies, 1986/7

Rank	British company	Overseas sales 1986/7 (£ '000)	% of total 1986/7 retail sales of co.	Sectors involved in overseas	Trading names overseas	USA	Canada	Europe	Total
1	BAT Industries	4,260,000	89.4	Department Stores	Ivey/Marshall Field				
					Saks/Horten	94		58	
					Brueners	57			
				Furniture	Thimbles	46			
				Variety stores	People's/Shoppers Drug Market	830	540		
									(1625)
2	J. Sainsbury	746,500	16.2	Grocery	Shaws	49			49
3	Dee Corporation	502,000	12.3	Grocery	Compre Bien			132	
				Sporting goods	Hermans	200			
									(332)
4	Dixons Group	490,000	32.1	Electricals	Tipton/Silo	145			
				DIY	Busy Beaver	11			
									(156)
5	Great Universal Stores	415,000	22.2	Mail order	(Various—				X
				Clothing	Burberrys	X			X
				Mixed retailing	Woodhouse/Legare/Cherney/GUS/Lewis Dan Hands)			X	
6	Mountleigh Group	400,000	100.0	Department stores	Galerias Preciados			29	29
7	Marks & Spencer	330,100	8.0	Mixed retailing	M & S D'Alliards	4	262		
					Marks & Spencer			10	
									(276)
8	Thorn EMI	303,700	35.3	Electricals	Fona/HMV Music Studios			19	
				TV rental	Rent A Centre	270			
					(Various)				X
9	Sears	250,400	16.1	Footwear	Manfield/Invito			56	
					Butler	500			
				Clothing	Wallis			X	
				Sports goods	Olympus			2	
				Jewellery	Mappin & Webb			4	
									(580)
10	Boots	205,000	8.7	Mixed retailing/ chemists	Sephora			29	
					Boots Drug Store		182		
					Boots the Chemist				
									(225)

Source: Corporate Intelligence Group (1988, pp. 279–80).   X Data unavailable

Table 2.21 illustrates the significance of North America within the international expansions of ten UK companies. The numbers of outlets abroad do not necessarily reflect the sales or profit contributions of these outlets. It may be noted that Marks & Spencer has a similar number of outlets in the UK and in Canada, yet overseas sales represent only 8 per cent of company sales. Many companies are obliged to regard their initial overseas expansions as learning experiences and/or long-term investments. Companies with current/recent involvement in Europe include BAT in West Germany, Dee and Mountleigh in Spain, Thorn in Sweden, Sears in the Netherlands, Boots and Marks & Spencer in France.

The significance of the USA as a springboard for UK retailers' expansions abroad is illustrated by the fact that 65 per cent of their overseas outlets are in that country (Corporate Intelligence Group 1988). English-speaking countries collectively account for 83 per cent of (identified) overseas retail outlets owned by British firms. Kacker (1985) identified several reasons why European retailers in general have been keen to invest in the USA:

1. Environmental or macro-level factors
   (a) The fall of the dollar in the 1970s made US stock cheap to acquire and European bids attractive to US companies.
   (b) The legislative framework in the USA was relatively favourable towards foreign acquisitions.
   (c) Public policy in Europe has done much to restrict the growth of organizations and the development of large outlets, owing to stricter planning and zoning regulations.
   (d) Low or zero population growth in many European countries, coupled with recession in the 1970s, offered poor domestic prospects.
2. Organizational or micro-level factors
   (a) Because of the above factors, many companies were anxious to develop new investment portfolios to reduce the financial and political risks of retailing in one country.
   (b) Retailers who had become dominant at home could see little prospect of further penetration into the domestic market.
   (c) Many retailers were keen to learn new skills by entry to the USA; some invested in extensive management training within the USA.

Kacker refers to some of these as 'push factors', causing retailers to look outside their domestic markets, others as 'pull factors', representing particular attractions of investment in the USA. Kerin and Variaya (1985) further noted the attractions of the favourable labour climate in the USA to foreign investors. Retail property and other assets also tended to be valued more highly by foreign than by US investors, making the acquisition package more attractive to the former. Tordjman (1988) warns however that, in spite of its many attractions to European retailers, the USA is a highly competitive and difficult market in which to succeed. New entrants can rarely achieve the economies of scale or cost advantages enjoyed in their home market, and large US retailers are very quick to react to any innovation that could threaten their market shares.

2.4.2 Approaches to internationalization

The objective of developing outlets in other countries can be pursued in several different ways. Which way is most appropriate depends upon several factors, including the availability of capital, the availability of management skills in international operations, the level of understanding of market needs within the target country, and the compatibility of the domestic trading format(s) with those needs. It is clear from recent history that companies have sometimes adopted the wrong approach, and there are a number of examples of leading retailers at home running into difficulties abroad (Rogers 1986). Mitton (1987) has identified and evaluated four main entry strategies:

1. *Self-start entry* In other words, the chain is built up from scratch, as in the case of Woolworth within the UK. A variation upon this approach is to make relatively modest acquisitions to gain a foothold and local management expertise, then actively to pursue organic growth within the country concerned. This is broadly the approach adopted by Laura Ashley, which by 1988 had nearly 200 overseas outlets, over half in the USA. Unlike

some earlier entrants, Laura Ashley has given considerable autonomy to local administrations:

This philosophy probably owes much to the failure of Marks & Spencer, brilliantly successful in the UK market, to repeat its performance in Canada, where it sought to impose British formats and methods on unreceptive customers. There are also other such examples which have fuelled the assertion that retailing cannot be exported, a tenet which more recent emigrants are endeavouring to disprove through investing in going concerns and adapting cautiously to indigenous working and selling conditions. (Corporate Intelligence Group 1988)

2. *Quick entry by acquisition*   This is the approach used in the majority of instances of UK retailers developing abroad. Notable acquisitions include Kings supermarkets and the Brooks Brothers menswear chain in the USA by Marks & Spencer. In some cases the overseas retailing interests are largely unrelated to the company's activities at home. For example, BAT owns over 1,600 department, variety and drug stores, mostly in North America, but at home now limits its retailing interests to Argos catalogue showrooms and the Jewellers Guild (Corporate Intelligence Group 1988). A major problem of entry by acquisition is that the companies available for purchase are often in financial difficulty; considerable time and financial support is therefore required to restore such firms (Mitton 1987). The cost of buying into more successful companies with strong management teams can be extremely high.

3. *Franchising*   Where a retailing concept can be readily exported, franchising can avoid much of the risk and demands upon capital of direct acquisition. The Italian-based Benetton trades from over 4,000 shops worldwide, as well as being the largest manufacturer of woollen garments in the world (Treadgold 1988). The UK-based Body Shop has also largely followed this route, with around 200 outlets in many parts of the world. A major problem, of course, is that many people with the capital to open a franchised outlet may lack retailing expertise. Many of the Tandy Corporation's outlets in the UK reverted to company ownership for this reason (Mitton 1987). For a comprehensive discussion of global franchising, see Kaynak (1988).

4. *Joint venture*   The cost and risks of entry may be reduced by partnership developments with organizations already familiar with the country's market and trading conditions. This approach can also reduce the time-scale of overseas development. Rogers (1986) specified two main requirements of successful expansion into North America:

First, a commitment to invest the time, research and money to become fully familiar with a very different culture and marketplace. Secondly, an ability to keep or attract good, motivated, 'native' management that knows the competitive milieu and is in touch with the rapidly changing demographics, needs and preferences of the North American consumer. To achieve the latter often makes part ownership more attractive than full ownership, despite the lesser ego rewards and public relations benefits!

Whatever their benefits at the outset, many joint ventures and partnerships have been terminated, often because both parties hoped to gain more from the deal than they put in (Mitton 1987). Burt (1986) described how Carrefour has progressively divested itself of many of its minority shareholdings, including its 10 per cent share of Hypermarket Holdings in the UK. The company has chosen to concentrate growth in those ventures where it holds a majority interest and/or controls the management of the subsidiary.

Differences in entry approaches, management styles and positioning strategies have led to some very different formats of international retailing. A number of typologies of international, transnational or cross-frontier retailing have been suggested (e.g. Treadgold 1988). One of the most fundamental distinctions is between global and multinational retailing.

Global retailing   The offer varies little across national boundaries, and the global retailer is targeting essentially the same group of customers in each country. Andre Tordjman has identified three typical characteristics of global retailers (Ody 1989):

1. Classic or 'fashionably classic' merchandise
2. A unique merchandise offer
3. Own-label merchandise

Many global retailers are also manufacturers or designers, such as Benetton, Ikea, Laura Ashley and Habitat/Conran. In some cases, a major motivation for manufacturers expanding their vertical integration to outlets abroad is to secure outlets for their vast manufacturing plants (Mitton 1987), for example the Canadian-based Bata footwear chain.

A benefit of truly global style retailing is that enormous economies of scale can be achieved in manufacturing and/or buying. Strong central control of merchandise, trading format and image is required, and managements are not encouraged to be critical of the operation. Local management will typically have control of the day-to-day running of the outlets, but the effectiveness of this will be closely monitored through the central chain's information systems. Toys R Us is an example of a global retailer that uses a very uniform style; each store is around 45,000 sq. ft, carries 18,000 lines and offers 400–500 parking spaces:

As well as offering the same product assortment internationally, Toys R Us is also moving towards a worldwide pricing policy with common pricepoints in all its outlets. (Ody 1989)

Joseph Baczko, president of the company's international division, claims that Toys R Us have not internationalized because of saturation in the USA market. Indeed, they see scope for 250 more stores in their home market; but:

There are 50 million kids in Europe and they have converging lifestyles in music, designer labels and Big Macs. The international market is a reality and consumers are becoming more similar globally. This is going to be even more true of children, so retailing has to become international as well.

The problems of global style retailing are vulnerability to consumer change and to competition. What does the originator of a winning formula do when imitators copy or improve upon the format within certain countries? Tordjman (Ody 1989) concluded that global retailing can be highly successful, but is most suitable for very specialized niche retailers.

Multinational retailing   Rather more of the retailers with an international presence could better be described as multinational, rather than global. This suggests the use of marketing styles more adjusted to the needs and market gaps within the countries concerned. Usually, local management is given more control over product selection, pricing and store ambience. International retailers within this category tend to learn from the other countries, rather than just imposing a standard formula upon them. Figure 2.1 suggests a matrix of marketing and management styles for international retailing; it illustrates that many companies pursue an adjusted marketing approach while maintaining a fairly high degree of centralized management.

The term 'multinational', strictly speaking, covers companies operating in just two or more countries. De Somogyi (1986) pointed out that many such retailers do in fact trade in no more than three countries. Treadgold (1988) has suggested alternative terminologies to describe these approaches. 'Concentrated internationalization' is used to describe 'border-hopping' into adjacent countries or into a small number of similar and familiar markets. The initial expansions of Ikea from Sweden into other Scandinavian countries could be thus described. The term 'dispersed internationalization' was applied to the expansion into markets more geographically

Styles of management and marketing	Decentralized management	Centralized management
Standardized marketing	C & A	Benetton Laura Ashley
Adjusted marketing	Carrefour Auchan	Habitat/Conran Ikea M & S

Figure 2.1   International retailing matrix
    Source: Andre Tordjman; quoted in Ody (1989, p. 7).

and culturally remote from the home market. Such typologies serve to draw attention to the very different approaches that may be used, and also provide a framework for assessing international retailing opportunities.

2.5   NON-STORE RETAILING

The vast majority of consumer purchases are made through retail outlets; the proportion of items reaching customers through non-store channels is still relatively small. However, some of these alternative channels are demonstrating significant growth and potential, which merits separate attention within this final section. Non-store channels include traditional, catalogue-based mail order systems and an increasing volume of direct response selling by manufacturers, specialist agencies or retailers. More recently, various forms of home shopping by teleshopping (or electronic shopping) have been launched. This section examines the trends in catalogue mail order in the UK and in Europe, and looks at the problems and prospects for teleshopping systems.

2.5.1   Mail order retailing

Mail order retailing, mainly using networks of local agents to circulate catalogues and collect payments, grew steadily from the 1950s. Between 1950 and 1970, its share of retail sales increased from 0.9 to 4.2 per cent, then declined slightly to 3.9 per cent by 1980. By 1987 the share of all retail sales was down to 3.4 per cent, although this represented 5.5 per cent of non-food sales (Euromonitor 1988c). Mail order penetration was significantly higher in certain product areas, notably soft furnishings (16.2 per cent) and womenswear/infantswear (12.2 per cent).

The traditional stronghold of mail order has been in the lower social classes, a major attraction being the extended credit terms. This feature tended to be less of an attraction to more wealthy consumers, who had less need for credit for minor purchases and, in any event, were more able to obtain credit elsewhere. This down-market bias was still apparent by 1981, when over 50 per cent of adults in the C2 and D categories were mail order users, compared with 37 per cent in the AB categories. This customer bias partially explained the loss of share experienced by mail order in the 1970s and 1980s. Rising unemployment and recessions increased the number of bad debts and the returns rate. Returns have always been a major problem, and cost factor, in mail order retailing; it is estimated that 45–50 per cent of clothing sales are returned (Euromonitor 1988c).

The effectiveness of the agent network has also declined, to the detriment of traditional forms of mail order retailing. In the early 1970s the typical ratio of agents to clients was 1:10. By 1987

Table 2.22 Mail order: European comparisons, 1982 and 1987

Country	% share of retail sales 1982	1987	% share non-food	Per-capita sales ($)
Austria	2.7	3.2	5.5	100
Belgium	1.3	1.4	2.3	59
Denmark	1.6	2.0	4.0	82
Finland	0.8	1.2	2.2	58
France	2.3	2.7	5.1	108
Ireland	—	0.5	1.0	10
Italy	0.4	0.4	0.7	18
Netherlands	1.3	1.7	3.5	62
Norway	1.7	2.9	5.6	115
Spain	—	0.2	0.3	5
Sweden	1.4	2.9	5.5	133
Switzerland	2.1	2.5	4.5	163
UK	3.5	3.4	5.5	110
West Germany	5.7	5.7	8.7	240

Source: derived from Euromonitor (1989, pp. 26–7).

this had fallen to just 1:2, with many 'agents' simply using the catalogue for their own purchases (Key Note 1988). Competitive pressures also contributed to the decline of the mail order share. Until relatively recently, the mail order companies had not kept pace with the marketing innovations of the High Street retailers. Mail order catalogues, and the products therein, had come to acquire a rather dull image. Possibly the greatest loss of competitive advantage for mail order retailers was the vast increase in credit systems available at most retail stores (see Chapter 12).

The penetration of mail order retailing across Europe is fairly limited; only in West Germany does it have a higher share than in the UK (Table 2.22). The pattern in most countries, however, has been one of increasing shares, especially in Norway and Sweden. In general, mail order appears to be strongest in the countries that already have a well developed retail structure (Euromonitor 1989). The extent of population dispersion would also appear to be linked to the success of mail order. At sub-regional level, many mail order companies derive a high proportion of their sales from the rural areas, more remote from major shopping centres.

The structure of the mail order industry in the UK is far more concentrated than the proliferation of catalogue names would suggest. Table 2.23 shows the major operators and some of the catalogue names used. Great Universal Stores (GUS) holds 35 per cent of this market, followed by Littlewoods with 24 per cent. Both have several different, full-range catalogues; in some cases little differs other than the front cover. In addition, most companies are now introducing 'specialogues', catalogues targeted to specific needs of specific customer segments. The use of increasingly sophisticated databases has made this a feasible strategy in recent years, although results so far are mixed. Among the specialogues introduced by Grattan, 'Streets of London' offers working girls' fashion and 'Young Additions' cater for the needs of mothers and children.

Table 2.23   UK mail order companies, 1987

Company and catalogue name	Users ('000)	Market share (%)
GUS	11,971	35.4
GUS	1,997	
Kays	4,525	
Trafford	992	
John Noble	506	
John Myers	446	
John England	783	
Family Album	940	
Marshall Ward	1,782	
Littlewoods	7,138	23.8
Littlewoods	2,738	
Brian Mills	1,453	
Burlington	735	
Janet Frazer	790	
John Moores	735	
Peter Craig	677	
Freemans	3,052	12.3
Empire Stores	2,127	4.8
Grattan/Next	2,058	8.5
You and Yours	358	
N. Brown		2.0
JD Williams	482	
Ambrose Wilson	459	
Others	—	13.2
Total	19,298	100

Source: derived from Euromonitor (1988c, pp. 28, 42).

There have recently been interesting signs of a revival in mail order retailing, coupled with a blurring of the distinctions between mail order, direct response selling and traditional retailing. Marks & Spencer established a deal with N. Brown to assist its entry to mail order, via the medium of mini-catalogues of around 12 pages (Retail 1986). The rapidly growing database generated through the development of the Marks & Spencer charge card has provided the basis for customer targeting. Many other High Street retailers have also used the opportunity presented by charge cards and other customer information to initiate mail order/direct response activities.

The most notable entry to catalogue mail order retailing in recent years was the Next Directory, product of a merger between Next and Grattan. With production costs of £9.00 per copy, this catalogue brought new standards of design to mail order retailing (Market Place 1988). The catalogue uses high-quality photography, graphics and paper, as well as incorporating fabric swatches. Orders can be placed by telephone and all calls are charged at local rates; most orders are delivered in just 48 hours.

The proposition of the Next Directory has produced a customer profile very different from that of most mail order companies, with around 40 per cent of customers in the AB social class. The Next Directory has also made a major breakthrough by reducing returns to under 20 per cent, far below the industry average. It was estimated that every 1 per cent reduction in returns adds £1 million to profits (Euromonitor 1988c). Not surprisingly, other companies have responded by improving catalogue designs, reducing delivery times and encouraging telephone ordering with credit card payment.

2.5.2 Teleshopping

The terms 'teleshopping' and 'electronic shopping' have been used to describe a very wide range of home shopping services. What distinguishes them from traditional mail order is that some form of electronic communications technology is used at the offering, ordering and/or payment stage. Teleshopping may involve the use of telephone, cable television, radio, satellite or other communication technologies. It is helpful to classify different types of teleshopping, according to their level of technological sophistication.

1. Telephone ordering in response to posted or collected catalogues; the debit or credit transaction is also likely to be completed by telephone. As noted in the previous section, the major mail order companies are increasingly moving towards this system to help reduce the delays between making the purchase decision, placing the order, and receiving the goods.
2. As above, but in response to published or broadcast advertisements. This form of direct response selling has been used by some retailers to expand their geographical markets. For example, Harrods generated an excellent response by placing an advertisement in the *New York Times*; customers ordered through Telecom's international 0800 freephone service.
3. Computerized product information, order transmission and transaction systems, using home computers or responding to telephone enquiries from consumers. For example, Comp-U-Card offers a 'Discount Hotline' to subscribers, who pay a subscription of £20 for the service. This claims to offer the lowest prices in Britain on a range of over 20,000 brand name products. The service has been highly successful in many countries. Comp-U-Card has established links with a network of retailers but does not actually handle the merchandise.
4. Localized, computer-linked selection and ordering systems, typically situated in local community centres for the benefit of less mobile shoppers. An early and notable example is the Gateshead Shopping and Information Service (SIS), launched in 1980 through the collaboration of Tesco and the local authority (Davies 1985). Subsequently, Bradford Centrepoint was launched with the co-operation of Morrisons superstores (Retail & Distribution Management 1986).
5. Public videotex-based systems, which allow the shopper to examine the available 'pages' of information and to order via the network. A major pilot scheme, 'Club 403', was launched with government support in 1981, but it closed at the end of the funding period in 1986 (Euromonitor 1988c). The commercial Prestel-based systems in the UK include Littlewood's 'Shop TV', using a catalogue closely aligned with that of the company's 'Index' catalogue showrooms.
6. Cable or satellite television networks with dedicated shopping channels, providing high-quality picture and sound presentations but usually requiring separate telephone ordering. An early example was a shopping cable station launched in Tampa, Florida, in 1982; within the first few years, 70 per cent of those receiving the station had bought a TV-sold item (Harris 1987).

7. Interactive cable television-based systems, allowing the customer access to more detailed videodisc information about specific products or services and encouraging more immediate, interactive ordering. J. C. Penney's 'Teleaction' claims to be the world's first commercial, truly interactive, television retail system (Chain Store Age Executive 1988).

Systems that are regarded as technologically advanced do not necessarily achieve the required market penetration; several schemes and experiments have now been terminated. Some successful schemes, such as Comp-U-Card, shifted towards less advanced communications technology in order to widen its market. Within some organizations, it is apparent that teleshopping developments are motivated by a desire to apply available technology, rather than to develop technology appropriate to identified market needs.

A few studies have set out to assess customer attitudes towards teleshopping; McKay and Fletcher (1988) summarized the advantages and disadvantages perceived by customers:

1. Advantages
   (a) Avoids the drudgery of queuing at stores
   (b) Quick and convenient
   (c) Delivery eliminates bag-carrying
   (d) Allows easy price comparisons
   (e) Offers more choice
   (f) Relieves High Street congestion
   (g) Relieves transport/parking problems
   (h) Removes personal transport costs
   (i) Increases leisure time
2. Disadvantages
   (a) Television not available for ordinary viewing
   (b) Telephone not available for ordinary use
   (c) Risk of unauthorized use by children, guests or helpers
   (d) Risk of errors when ordering
   (e) Difficulty of establishing responsibility for errors

The more technologically sophisticated types of teleshopping have made very little impact so far in the UK. The unavailability of the relevant communications equipment has greatly inhibited the spread of such systems. By 1986 only 1 per cent of homes in the UK with a television were connected to a cable system. This contrasts with 49.4 per cent in the USA and even higher levels in Belgium, the Netherlands, Switzerland and Denmark (Euromonitor 1988c). The Prestel system also failed to achieve the level of penetration that was anticipated, mainly because of its high cost. By 1987 there were 77,000 registered users of Prestel, only 37 per cent of whom were domestic users.

The UK experience contrasts with that of France, where the government decided to fund the installation of 'Minitel' terminals through the national telephone network. By the end of 1988, 4.7 million terminals had been given away and 95 per cent of these are actually used (Alexander 1989). The original purpose of the terminals was to provide an electronic telephone directory, but no less than 8,800 other services are available through the system. La Redoute is France's largest mail order and teleshopping company, and by the end of 1987 it accounted for 32 per cent of the turnover through Minitel.

The failure or limited penetration of many teleshopping systems in the UK should not cause complacency among store-based retailers. The chairman of Tesco offered this prediction:

Upper income groups will do an increasing amount of their convenience shopping via T.V.

By the early 21st century, teleshopping could well account for a fifth of this affluent market, and, once established, the practice will spread. (Mintel 1987)

As the technologies of teleshopping improve and become more widely available, the effects of teleshopping upon store-based retailing could be extensive (Dawson and Sparks 1986). By creating direct or alternative linkages between suppliers and consumers, the current power of retailers in the marketing channel could be reduced (Goldstucker *et al.* 1986). The diversion of retail sales, especially of high-value durables, from traditional stores could also reduce the viability and property value of many existing sites (Guy 1985). Ultimately, if teleshopping channels become more powerful and stable, the barriers to entry could become higher than those of retailing in its present form (Rosenberg and Hirschman 1980).

Faced with this threat, store-based retailers may choose between a number of possible strategic responses. If we exclude the option to capitulate, these may be classified as follows:

1. *Hesitate and evaluate* This may be a sensible option in some circumstances, avoiding the costs of false starts or of investing in the wrong technology. The danger is that it may not be possible to acquire the necessary expertise quickly when the time is right.
2. *Imitate* Simply copy the developments of competitors. This is all too common as a strategic reaction, but is unlikely to lead to competitive advantage.
3. *Innovate* Develop a teleshopping system that offers distinctive advantages to the target market, advantages that may or may not arise through a particular technological development.
4. *Retaliate* Develop the particular benefits of store-based shopping that are absent from teleshopping; as is discussed in the next chapter, shopping offers many forms of social and psychological satisfaction beyond that of simply obtaining products.

SUMMARY

The 1980s were characterized by considerable growth in consumer expenditure, although much of this growth was fuelled by reduced savings and increased credit. In terms of per capita retail expenditure, the UK is still some way behind most of its European partners. The demographics of the market are shifting significantly, with an ageing population structure and a trend towards more smaller households. Consumer life-styles are changing at a rather faster rate, with new life-style priorities bringing greater demand for individuality. Shopping patterns have also changed, with increased access to cars bringing a shift towards fewer, larger shopping trips and a greater willingness to travel some distance to preferred shops. The rise in the number of working women has increased male participation in shopping and increased the demand for longer opening hours.

The structure of retailing has also experienced major changes, the most significant being the continued growth of the multiples (corporate chains). The share held by the multiples in the UK is far higher than that of the multiples in any other European country. This share has been gained mostly at the expense of independent retailers, but the smaller multiples and co-operatives have also lost ground. The co-operatives have continued to operate as many autonomous societies, thereby failing to realize the full buying and marketing potential of the co-operative movement. Symbol groups, such as Spar in the grocery sector and Numark in the chemists sector, have offered a valuable lifeline to many independent retailers. Franchising is growing rapidly as a retail business format, offering an attractive blend of large-scale professionalism and individual enterprise.

There was a very rapid decline in the number of shops in Britain until the mid-1980s; some argue that numbers are now increasing again, if service outlets are taken into account. Britain has considerably fewer shops per capita than most other European countries. The vast majority of closures have been small shops, but the emergence of the convenience store format has helped to arrest this trend. Large, new stores, including superstores and hypermarkets, are taking an increasing share in most retail sectors; there is evidence of polarization in consumers' regular shopping habits, with major trips to large stores and intermediary 'topping-up' in small, local stores. There has been a vigorous phase of shopping centre developments, and most retail sectors have now established a presence in out-of-town centres or retail parks.

The saturation of domestic markets and the arrival of the Single European Market have motivated many retailers to develop outlets in other countries. However, European countries, characterized by low retail profitability and severe planning restrictions, have generally been less popular targets than North America for British retailers. Many overseas expansions have produced disappointing results, often through a failure properly to assess the needs and opportunities within the new market. Approaches to internationalization have included self-start, entry by acquisition, franchising, and joint ventures. A few international retailers have developed a truly global style of retailing; most could be better described as multinational, with a variety of different formats.

Non-store retailing still has a fairly limited presence in most European countries. Traditional mail order systems, based upon large catalogues and using a vast network of agents, lost ground as credit became widely available elsewhere. A more aggressive and focused approach has been taken by new entrants to mail order retailing, which is producing a more dynamic sector. The more sophisticated forms of electronic shopping are still in their infancy in the UK, although significant progress has been made in France and in the USA. The more straightforward forms of telephone ordering, in response to catalogues or advertisements, have expanded rapidly. The possible future growth of teleshopping could pose a significant threat to store-based retailers.

REVIEW QUESTIONS

1. Giving relevant examples, show how forecasts of consumer expenditure are essential to retailers' medium- and long-term planning.
2. Taking a retail company of your choice, how should that company respond to the long-term changes in the population age structure and in the structure of households?
3. What have been the most significant changes in consumers' shopping patterns? Identify retail companies that have been particularly successful in exploiting these changes.
4. Do you expect that the share of the market held by multiple retailers will continue to grow? Give reasons for your answer.
5. Why have the co-operatives tended to lose market share? What steps should be taken to reverse this trend?
6. What are the main functions of a symbol (or voluntary) group? Why do some retailers choose to leave these groups or not to join one at all?
7. Give examples to illustrate the main types of franchising arrangement. Why has franchising grown rapidly in recent years?
8. How do you account for the fact that shop numbers are no longer declining sharply?
9. What are the essential characteristics of the convenience store (c-store) format? What do you see as the major threats to the long-term future of c-stores?
10. Explain the theory of retail polarization.
11. What factors have retarded the development of superstores and hypermarkets? How do you assess the potential for this type of outlet in non-food retail sectors?

12. Describe the 'three waves' of retail development out of town. Give examples to illustrate each of these three waves.
13. What factors motivate retailers to develop outlets in more than one country? What additional problems face the retailer seeking international expansion?
14. Outline the alternative approaches to international expansion that are available to retailers. What are the benefits and problems of each of these approaches?
15. Giving examples, illustrate the differences between global and multinational retailing. What operational styles are characteristic of each?
16. How do you account for the decline in traditional forms of mail order? What strategies have been adopted by recent new entrants to mail order retailing?
17. What factors have retarded the development of teleshopping, and what factors may ultimately stimulate its growth?
18. Do you envisage the prospect of 'retailing without stores'? Justify your answer.

REFERENCES

Alexander, J. (1988), 'Tomorrow's shopper—a profile', *Retail & Distribution Management*, **16**(2), 19–21.
Alexander, J. (1989), 'Shopping the electronic way', *Retail & Distribution Management*, **17** (2), 13–15.
Attwood, T. and L. Hough (1988), *The Good Franchise Guide*, Kogan Page, London.
Ayling, D. (1988), 'Franchising in the UK', *Quarterly Review of Marketing*, **13**(4), 19–24.
Bamfield, J. A. N. (1978a), 'The revival of the Co-ops', *Retail & Distribution Management*, **6**(2), 18–23.
Bamfield, J. A. N. (1978b), 'What future for the Co-op?' *Retail & Distribution Management*, **6**(3), 14–18.
Bamfield, J. A. N. (1987), 'Rationalization and the problems of repositioning: UK co-operatives caught in the middle', in G. Johnson (ed.), *Business Strategy and Retailing*, John Wiley, Chichester, pp. 153–70.
Bates, P. (1976), *The Independent Grocery Retailer: Characteristics and Problems—a Report of a Survey*, Report 23, RORU, Manchester Business School.
Beaumont, J. A. (1987), 'Trends in food retailing', in E. McFadyen (ed.), *The Changing Face of British Retailing*, Newman, London, pp. 52–63.
Bechhofer, F., B. Elliott, M. Rushforth and R. Bland (1974), 'Small shopkeepers: matters of money and meaning', *Sociological Review*, **22**(4), 465–82.
Belay, J. (1986), 'Trends in the consumption environment in Europe', in ESOMAR (ed.), *Retail Strategies for Profit and Growth*, ESOMAR, Amsterdam, pp. 1–10.
British Business (1988), 'DTI retailing inquiry for 1986', *British Business*, 18 March, 29–30.
Brown, M. (1982), 'The democrats' dilemma', *Marketing*, **10**(4), 19–20.
Brown, S. (1988), 'Marks out of town', *Retail & Distribution Management*, **16**(2), 13–18.
Burt, S. (1986), 'The Carrefour group—the first 25 years', *International Journal of Retailing*, **1**(3), 54–78.
Central Statistical Office (1989), *Annual Abstract of Statistics*, HMSO, London.
Chain Store Age Executive (1988), 'Electronic shopping', *Chain Store Age Executive*, July, 15–24.
Corporate Intelligence Group (1988), *The Retail Rankings*, Corporate Intelligence Research Publications, London.
Corporate Intelligence Group (1989), *Retailing and 1992: the Impact and Opportunities*, Corporate Intelligence Research Publications, London.
Davies, R. L. (1985), 'The Gateshead Shopping and Information Service', *Environment and Planning B*, **12**, 209–20.
Davies, R. L. and E. B. Howard (1987), 'New centres, new choices', *Retail*, **4**(4), 41–4.
Dawson, J. A. (1983), 'Independent retailing in Great Britain: dinosaur or chameleon?' *Retail & Distribution Management*, **11**(3), 29–32.
Dawson, J. A. and D. A. Kirby (1979), *Small Scale Retailing in the UK*, Saxon House, Farnborough.
Dawson, J. A. and L. Sparks (1986), 'New technology in UK retailing: issues and responses', *Journal of Marketing Management*, **2**(1), 7–29.
De Somogyi, J. (1986), 'Retail planning for the next ten years', *Retail & Distribution Management*, **14**(5), 9–13.
Economist Intelligence Unit (1986), *Retailing in Britain*, EIU, London.
Eliot, S. J. (1982), 'Small shops and the consumer co-operative movement', *Journal of Consumer Studies and Home Economics*, **6**(1), 29–38.
Eliot, S. J. (1983), 'The crisis in the co-operative movement', *Retail & Distribution Management*, **11**(4), 8–14.
Eliot, S. J. (1985), 'The Co-ops' road to recovery', *Retail & Distribution Management*, **13**(4), 9–13.
Euromonitor (1986), *Changing Face of Grocery Retailing*, Euromonitor, London.

Euromonitor (1987a), *Retail Trade in the United Kingdom*, Euromonitor, London.

Euromonitor (1987b), *Franchising in the European Economy: Trends and Forecasts 1980–1990*, Euromonitor, London.

Euromonitor (1987c), *Hypermarket and Superstore Retailing in the UK*, Euromonitor, London.

Euromonitor (1988a), *Voluntary Chains and Buying Groups*, Euromonitor, London.

Euromonitor (1988b), *Convenience Stores in the UK 1980–1990*, Euromonitor, London.

Euromonitor (1988c), *Home Shopping in the UK*, Euromonitor, London.

Euromonitor (1989), *Retail Trade International 1989/90, Vol. 1*, Euromonitor, London.

Goldstucker, J. L., G. P. Moschis and T. J. Stanley (1986), 'Possible effects of electronic shopping on restructuring of distribution channels', *International Journal of Retailing*, **1**(1), 20–32.

Guy, C. M. (1985), 'Some speculations on the retailing and planning implications of "push-button shopping" in Britain', *Environment and Planning B*, **12**, 193–208.

Hallsworth, A. (1988), 'West Edmonton: Canada's shopping fantasy-land', *Retail & Distribution Management*, **16**(1), 26–9.

Harris, T. (1987), 'TV hard sell hits home', *Marketing*, 11 June, 17–18.

Hillier Parker (1989a), *British Shopping Developments 1988 Supplement*, Hillier Parker May & Rowden May, London.

Hillier Parker (1989b), *Retail Parks*, Hillier Parker May & Rowden May, London.

Hillier Parker (1989c), *Shopping Schemes in the Pipeline*, Hillier Parker May & Rowden May, London.

Hollander, S. C. (1969), 'The international shopkeepers', *MSU Business Topics*, **17**(2), 13–28.

Hunt, S. D. (1977), 'Franchising: promises, problems, prospects', *Journal of Retailing*, **53**(3), 71–84.

IGD News (1989), 'Food retailing 1988', *IGD News*, **71**, 1–3.

Institute for Retail Studies (1989), *Distributive Trades Profile 1988: a Statistical Digest*, IRS, University of Stirling.

Institute of Grocery Distribution (1988), *Grocery Store Directory: 25,000 sq. ft. and Above 1988*, IGD, Watford.

Institute of Grocery Distribution (1989), *Food Industry Statistics Digest*, IGD, Watford.

Jefferys, J. B. (1985), 'Multinational retailing: are the food chains different?', in M. P. Kacker, *Transatlantic Trends in Retailing: Takeovers and Flow of Know-How*, Quorum Books, Westport, Conn., pp. 141–4.

Johnson, D. B. (1987), 'The West Edmonton Mall—from super-regional to mega-regional shopping centre', *International Journal of Retailing*, **2**(2), 53–69.

Jones, P. M. (1982), 'Hypermarkets and superstores—saturation or future growth', *Retail & Distribution Management*, **10**(4), 20–7.

Kacker, M. P. (1985), *Transatlantic Trends in Retailing: Takeovers and Flow of Know-How*, Quorum Books, Westport, Conn.

Kaynak, E. (1988), *Transnational Retailing*, Walter de Gruyter, Berlin.

Kerin, R. A. and N. Varaiya (1985), 'Mergers and acquisitions in retailing: a review and critical analysis', *Journal of Retailing*, **61**(1), 9–34.

Key Note (1988), *Mail Order*, Key Note Publications, London.

Killen, V. and R. Lees (1988), 'The future of grocery retailing in the UK', *Retail & Distribution Management*, **16**(4), 8–12.

Kirby, D. A. (1976), 'The convenience store phenomenon: the rebirth of America's small shop', *Retail & Distribution Management*, **4**(3), 31–3.

Kirby, D. A. (1986), 'Convenience stores: the polarisation of British retailing', *Retail & Distribution Management*, **14**(2), 7–12.

Kirby, D. A. (1987), 'Convenience stores', in E. McFadyen (ed.), *The Changing Face of British Retailing*, Newman Books, London, pp. 94–102.

Kirby, D. A. and D. C. Law (1981), 'The birth and death of small retail units in Britain', *Retail & Distribution Management*, **9**(1), 16–19.

Livesey, F. and E. A. Nagy (1980), 'Voluntary groups: why do retailers leave them?' *Retail & Distribution Management*, **8**(1), 55–6.

Livesey, F. and E. A. Nagy (1981), 'Independents versus affiliation: what factors motivate retailers?' *Retail & Distribution Management*, **9**(3), 26–8.

Lucas, M. D. (1986), 'Changing stores to suit the changing customer', in ESOMAR (ed.), *Retail Strategies for Profit and Growth*, ESOMAR, Amsterdam, pp. 59–77.

MacNulty, C. (1989), 'The future of the UK', *Retail*, **6**(4), 39–41.

Marketing Business (1989), 'Counting heads, the age-old market problem', *Marketing Business*, **4**, 6–7.

Market Place (1988), 'Mail order', *Market Place*, **4**(2), 2–12.

May, E. G., C. W. Ress and W. J. Salmon (1988), 'Future trends in retailing: merchandise line trends and store trends 1980–1990', in E. Kaynak (ed.), *Transnational Retailing*, Walter de Gruyter, Berlin, pp. 333–48.

McEvoy, D. and H. Aldrich (1986), 'Survival rates of Asian and white retailers', *International Small Business Journal*, **4**(3), 28–37.

McKay, J. and K. Fletcher (1988), 'Consumers' attitudes towards teleshopping', *Quarterly Review of Marketing*, **13**(3), 1–7.

Mintel (1986), 'Neighbourhood retailing', *Retail Intelligence*, Autumn, 16–60.

Mintel (1987), 'Home shopping', *Retail Intelligence*, **1**, 165–72.

Mitton, A. E. (1987), 'Foreign retail companies operating in the UK: strategy and performance', *Retail & Distribution Management*, **15**(1), 29–31.

Mundow, A. (1989), 'Decline and fall of the mall', *Guardian*, 13 May, 9.

Nielsen (1988), *Grocery Industry Trade Statistics*, A. C. Nielsen, Oxford.

Nooteboom, B., R. Thurik and S. Vollebregt (1986), 'Cases and causes of structural change in retailing', in ESOMAR (ed.), *Retail Strategies for Profit and Growth*, ESOMAR, Amsterdam, pp. 177–98.

Ody, P. (1989), 'Internationalism: the route to growth', *Retail & Distribution Management*, **17**(2), 6–9.

Office of Fair Trading (1985), *Competition and Retailing*, Office of Fair Trading, London.

Poynor, M. (1987), 'The changing consumer', in E. McFadyen (ed.), *The Changing Face of British Retailing*, Newman Books, London, pp. 103–13.

Retail (1986), 'Marks moves into mail order', *Retail*, **4**(2), 4.

Retail (1987), 'Convenience stores', *Retail*, **5**(1), 22–3.

Retail (1988), 'Retail franchising', *Retail*, **6**(1), 40–1.

Retail (1989), 'The fallacy of retail saturation', *Retail*, **6**(4), 42–4.

Retail Business (1989a), 'Consumer spending prospects to 2000', *Retail Business*, Market Report, no. 372, 4–12.

Retail Business (1989b), 'Annual review of retailing', *Retail Business*, Trade Reviews, **10**, 3–15.

Retail & Distribution Management (1986), 'Bradford's new teleshopping service', *Retail & Distribution Management*, **14**(1), 35–6.

Retail & Distribution Management (1988), 'Europe 1992: the opportunities and the threats', *Retail & Distribution Management*, **16**(6), 4–7.

Rogers, D. (1986), 'American reflections', *Retail & Distribution Management*, **14**(6), 48–9.

Rogers, D. (1987), 'America's shopping centres: a mid-life crisis?', *Retail & Distribution Management*, **15**(6), 21–5.

Rosenberg, L. J. and E.C. Hirschman (1980), 'Retailing without stores', *Harvard Business Review*, **58**(4), 103–12.

Sands, D. (1986), 'The Metro Centre opens at Gateshead', *Retail & Distribution Management*, **14**(6), 13–17.

Schiller, R. (1987), 'Out of town exodus', in E. McFadyen (ed.), *The Changing Face of British Retailing*, Newman Books, London, pp. 64–73.

Schiller, R. and O. Boucke (1989), 'Are shop numbers rising or falling?' *Retail & Distribution Management*, **17**(2), 16–19.

Seaman, R. (1988), 'Franchising: the new marketing tool of British business', *MBA Review*, October, 6–9.

Segal-Horn, S. (1987), 'The retail environment in the UK', in G. Johnson (ed.), *Business Strategy and Retailing*, John Wiley, Chichester, pp. 13–33.

Stern, P. and J. Stanworth (1988), 'The development of franchising in Britain', *The Natwest Bank Review*, May, 38–48.

Thorpe, D. and P. J. McGoldrick (1974), *Superstores, Discounters and a Covered Centre: a Study of Competition in North Manchester*, Manchester Business School.

Tordjman, A. (1986), 'A comparative study of distribution in six European countries: methodological problems and results', in ESOMAR (ed.), *Retail Strategies for Profit and Growth*, ESOMAR, Amsterdam, pp. 13–56.

Tordjman, A. (1988), 'The French hypermarket: could it be developed in the States?' *Retail & Distribution Management*, **16**(4), 14–16.

Treadgold, A. (1988), 'Retailing without frontiers', *Retail & Distribution Management*, **16**(6), 8–12.

Unit for Retail Planning Information (1988), *1988 List of UK Hypermarkets and Superstores*, URPI, Reading.

Vaughn, C. L. (1979), *Franchising—its Nature, Scope, Advantages and Development*, Lexington Books, Lexington, Mass.

Walters, D. (1986), 'International consumer trends', *Retail*, **4**(3), 41–4.

Ward, R. (1987), 'Small retailers in inner urban areas', in G. Johnson (ed.), *Business Strategy and Retailing*, John Wiley, Chichester, pp. 275–87.

Webster, S. (1987), *Food Retailing 1987*, Institute of Grocery Distribution, Watford.

Worthington, S. (1988), 'A tale of two speciality shopping centres', *Retail & Distribution Management*, **16**(3), 8–12.

THREE
IDENTIFICATION OF MARKET NEEDS

INTRODUCTION

Fundamental to the formulation of retail marketing strategy is a clear understanding of consumer needs, motives and patronage decision processes. It is also easy to forget that every shopper is an individual with a set of needs and motives that differ, at least slightly, from those of other shoppers. In an increasingly competitive trading environment, the best rewards go to retailers who can profitably assemble a product and service mix that is carefully attuned to the requirements of clearly defined consumer segments.

The successful identification of needs does not in itself guarantee a successful marketing strategy, although it is a very logical first step. Without this step, there is a tendency for strategy formulation to dwell upon the range of existing solutions, rather than developing formats to satisfy specific sets of consumer requirements. Insufficient attention to real needs can lead to the copying or continuation of formats that should in fact be evolved or completely superseded. It can also lead to a failure to anticipate or to effectively diagnose declining demand for a particular product–service mix.

Most retailers would claim to be customer-oriented and may also point to the constant interface with shoppers as indicative of an understanding of consumer needs. Although much insight could be gained through the interactions between customers and staff, in reality, the full potential is rarely realized. Formal feedback channels between sales staff and senior management are often weak; customer complaints and enquiries tend to be regarded as something to be dealt with rather than as a valuable information source. This situation is starting to change, and in some enlightened companies senior managers maintain close contact with customers by spending time working on the shop floor or by attending discussion groups of actual/potential customers.

'Internal' channels of communication can provide much insight into consumer needs, but obviously these must be supplemented with 'external' information. The retailer is confronted with a rapidly growing range of secondary sources, presenting research and analysis of various customer, product and store types. The commercial secondary sources tend to be fairly expensive but cost far less than the equivalent primary research. Their main drawbacks, however, are that the information quickly becomes dated, it is available to all competitors, and neither the questions asked nor the samples drawn may be entirely appropriate to a specific retailer's strategic decisions. Most major retailers therefore undertake or commission primary research to try to maintain a competitive edge in monitoring needs, motives and attitudes. Many of the research techniques employed will be considered here and in Chapter 5.

This chapter begins by considering shoppers' needs and motives at the most fundamental level, and then some of the specific motives associated with the shopping activity. The criteria employed in selecting between shopping centres or individual stores are next examined, drawing upon examples from different sectors and countries. Some alternative explanations of the consumer's patronage decision process are then discussed. In the penultimate section of the chapter, attention turns to the techniques of market segmentation; approaches are compared and some typologies of shopping orientations examined.

3.1 MOTIVES FOR SHOPPING

'Motives, predispositions to behave in a certain way, give direction to needs and identify goals to achieve' (Arnold *et al.* 1983a). It is in the interest of the retail strategist to go 'back to basics' in attempting to understand consumer motives; otherwise there is a tendency to confuse needs and solutions. For example, the statement that 'our customers need better service at the checkout' may be perfectly true, but the solution of better checkout service should be carefully appraised in terms of the fundamental needs that it satisfies. The service may satisfy a physical need for greater ease at the checkout, or it may satisfy needs for more human interaction, more security or more prestige. A strategic solution can therefore satisfy several different needs, but it must also be recognized that such needs may be satisfied by several different solutions.

3.1.1 Needs and motives

One of the most influential theories of human needs has been that of Maslow (1970), which was initially developed in the 1940s. He suggested a hierarchy of needs, from the most basic or primitive through to the most civilized or mature:

1. Physiological needs
2. Safety needs
3. Belongingness needs
4. Esteem needs
5. Self-actualization needs

The theory suggests that people seek to progress through this hierarchy, and, as needs at one level are satisfied, those at the next level tend to take over. Inevitably, the theory has been criticized, mainly for the lack of empirical support for the number of categories or the hierarchical order. McClelland (1967), for example, theorized that human needs can be grouped into three broad categories:

1. Affiliation needs
2. Power needs
3. Achievement needs

Basic classifications of this type can however help to understand the underlying structure of human needs. For example, in developing an in-house credit card, a retailer may appeal to the need for safety (less cash handling), as well as needs for belongingness ('club' membership), esteem (prestige) or power (additional entitlements). Similarly, the appeal of a very high-status store may be geared to reflect the achievement and self-actualization of customers able to shop there.

The 'dual factor' theory of Herzberg (1966), although developed in relation to job satisfaction/ dissatisfaction, has also been applied to the understanding of consumer motivations. Herzberg suggested that a distinction should be made between factors causing satisfaction and those causing dissatisfaction. The removal of a 'dissatisfier' would not necessarily produce satisfaction; it would simply overcome one area of dissatisfaction. For example, a retailer with an awkward returns procedure may not produce a significant attraction by improving this, but may overcome a factor that was inhibiting sales. On the other hand, intensification of 'satisfiers', such as a better selling environment or special offers, would be unlikely to alleviate the blockage to sales caused by the returns procedure. Although essentially a very simple concept, this dual factor theory offers some important insights into the patronage decision process, which is considered in Section 3.3.

3.1.2 The shopping activity

Studies of shoppers' motivations have tended to emphasize the need for the actual products or, alternatively, the reasons for selecting one store/centre as opposed to others. Tauber (1972) made a notable departure from previous patronage research by asking the most basic question, 'Why do people shop?' He encouraged strategists and researchers to address their attention to the primary motivations that determine the *shopping activity*, rather than simply to assume that the need to purchase products is the only, or even the main, reason for shopping. Tauber hypothesized that:

peoples' motives for shopping are a function of many variables, some of which are unrelated to the actual buying of products. It is maintained that an understanding of the shopping motives requires the consideration of satisfactions which shopping activities provide, as well as the utility obtained from the merchandise that may be purchased.

Based upon in-depth interviews with both male and female shoppers, Tauber suggested several types of *personal* motive for shopping, classified as follows:

1. *Role playing*   Shopping may be a learned and expected behaviour pattern which, for some, becomes an integral part of their role.
2. *Diversion*   Shopping may provide a break from the daily routine, a form of recreation; it can provide a diversionary pastime for individuals or free entertainment for the family.
3. *Self gratification*   The shopping trip may represent an antidote to loneliness or boredom; the act of purchasing may be an attempt to alleviate depression.
4. *Learning about new trends*   Many people enjoy shopping as an opportunity to see new things and get new ideas.
5. *Physical activity*   The exercise provided by shopping is an attraction to some, especially those whose work and travel modes provide little opportunity for exercise.
6. *Sensory stimulation*   The shopping environment can provide many forms of stimulation, through light, colours, sounds, scents and through handling the products.

In addition to these personal motives, a number of *social* motives were also hypothesized:

1. *Social experiences outside the home*   Like the traditional market, the shopping area can provide the opportunity for social interaction, meeting friends or simply 'people-watching'.
2. *Communication with others having a similar interest*   Hobby, sports and even DIY shops provide the opportunity for interaction with staff and customers with similar interests.
3. *Peer group attraction*   Using a particular store may reflect a desire to be among the group to which one chooses or aspires to belong; this may be particularly significant in patronizing a high-status or a 'trend' store.

4. *Status and authority*   In that stores seek to serve the customer, especially when contemplating high-cost, comparison purchases, some shoppers enjoy being 'waited on' while in the store.
5. *Pleasure of bargaining*   Some derive satisfaction from the process of haggling or from shopping around to obtain the best bargains.

This extended typology of motives underlying the shopping activity represents an important development from the view of shopping as simply a process of economic exchange. Many consumers do not overtly acknowledge these personal and social motives, preferring to justify their shopping behaviour in more 'rational' terms. Many surveys have therefore failed to detect the strength of these factors within the consumer's patronage decision process. An exception was a study published by Mintel (1986), which examined shopping within the context of leisure activities. Table 3.1 illustrates that many consider shopping for clothes to be fun, creative, active, social and/or a form of relaxation. Food shopping was regarded by most as an essential chore but also by many as an obligation undertaken for the family, possibly a form of role-playing. Research studies clearly must give more attention to the actual shopping activity, in order to provide guidelines in designing the competitive mix and in promoting the store(s) to the target customer group.

3.2   STORE CHOICE

A clear understanding of why consumers patronize one store and not another has become a major objective of retail strategists and researchers. Indeed, this knowledge could be likened to the 'pot of gold' of the research rainbow, although at times it is almost as elusive. As retailers have become more quickly responsive to the actions of competitors, retail formats in some sectors have tended to converge. In these situations, the precise components of the patronage decision become decreasingly obvious.

Retailers have long been criticized for not being well informed as to their customers' patronage motives. For example, Watkins and Vandemark (1971) claimed that 'most [retail] managers speak in generalities, quoting opinions and individual biases which may or may not have validity in their trading area'. Subsequently, Jolson and Spath (1973) found that retailers in some sectors achieved very little success in ranking the factors of most importance to their customers. This situation improved somewhat in the 1980s, with a stronger retail marketing orientation and a flood of new information sources, both internal and external. In particular, the range of published market studies has grown rapidly. As noted earlier, however, these usually represent broad generalizations across whole sectors, types of store and/or localities. Retailers that depend entirely upon standard sources therefore may be led towards standard or follower strategies.

3.2.1   Store selection criteria

There is considerable evidence that store selection criteria tend to be situation-specific and that they tend to shift over time. For example, Kenny-Levick (1969) illustrated very significant contrasts between the motivations of Liverpool shoppers and those of Chicago shoppers, studied by Stone (1954). In this comparison, however, there were major differences between the methodologies of the two studies. Table 3.2 shows some of the results of two closely matched studies of grocery store selection criteria, 17 years apart (Bates and Gabor 1987). In that co-op shoppers comprised over one third of each sample, the criteria of dividend, principle, etc.,

Table 3.1   Attitudes to shopping in Britain, 1986

	For groceries (%)	For clothes (%)	For household items (%)
Family obligation	38	23	37
Essential chore	78	53	34
Educational	2	1	4
Creative	1	9	2
Active	7	5	4
Relaxing	1	11	5
Social	4	7	5
Fun	4	29	23
None of these	2	3	6

Source: Mintel (1986, pp. 45–75).

Table 3.2   Main reasons for selecting a grocery shop, 1967 and 1984

Reasons	1967 (%)	1984 (%)
Cheap prices, fair prices, good value, bargains	25.6	19.6
Convenience; nearest to home, workplace, etc.	25.3	45.2
Cleanliness, good layout, etc.	13.8	6.0
Good quality, variety, choice, satisfaction	13.7	20.1
Dividend, principle, member, employee, habit	9.7	6.6
Delivery service	7.2	—
Trading stamps	1.1	—
Other reasons	3.6	2.5
Samples (N =)	1,294	1,000

Source: derived from Bates and Gabor (1987, pp. 183–207).

appear in both 1967 and 1984. A shift towards quality, choice and convenience as major criteria is implied, accompanied by a reduced emphasis upon cheap prices.

Table 3.2 illustrates very broad groupings of patronage reasons, which was necessary to summarize the longitudinal comparison. Given the opportunity and research resources, it is of course advisable to study reasons for selecting the main shop at the most disaggregate level possible. Table 3.3 is based upon a sample of nearly 3,000 shoppers, allowing many individual reasons to be identified and breakdowns to occur between segments. In this analysis, differences between age and social class groups are illustrated; not included within this table but available from the study are breakdowns between the patrons of individual retailers.

Table 3.2 and 3.3 illustrate two of the many different approaches to researching patronage criteria. In the latter case, shoppers were asked what they liked about the store that they use most frequently. This approach has a number of implications, as follows:

Table 3.3 Things liked about main grocery store

Factor	Total	Age group 16–34	Age group 35–54	Age group 55 +	Social class AB	Social class C1	Social class C2	Social class DE
				(% citing factor)				
Clean and hygienic	51	48	52	52	58	52	47	50
Extensive range	45	44	47	45	53	48	46	39
Know the layout	44	48	45	39	46	45	45	42
Good value	43	44	43	42	15	27	27	31
Good parking	42	42	46	37	56	48	42	30
Quality of foods	36	35	37	37	45	41	33	32
Cheap/low prices	34	40	32	31	25	31	37	39
Opens late	33	41	36	21	39	36	34	26
Good fresh fruit/veg.	33	35	31	32	37	34	31	31
Spacious	31	30	33	30	36	36	29	26
Easy walking distance	31	31	26	35	20	30	28	39
Convenient for transport	28	25	29	30	28	29	30	26
Good fresh meat	28	27	27	28	30	28	29	26
Selection of frozen food	27	26	30	27	30	27	28	26
Efficient checkout service	24	21	23	29	25	25	23	25
In-store bakery	20	25	21	14	21	25	22	14
Own label products	19	21	19	18	22	22	18	17
Chilled/ready foods	12	13	12	11	15	13	12	11
Range of non-foods	12	13	13	9	16	15	12	8
Good fresh fish	11	12	11	11	12	12	11	11
Carry out service	4	5	5	4	5	4	5	4
Other factor	6	7	6	6	5	6	7	6

Source: derived from Euromonitor (1986).

1. Many more criteria are likely to be cited as the question is not limited to the main reason; thus the columns add to far more than 100 as respondents mentioned about six factors on average.
2. A large number of mentions does not necessarily indicate that a factor is a major determinant of patronage, i.e. whether improvements in that factor would quickly trigger a change in the store used. For example, cleanliness received the most mentions but is probably part of the minimum requirement for a store to be used. Efficient checkout service received about half as many mentions, but for some shoppers is a major issue in selecting between two or more alternative grocery stores. Whether or not a factor is a major determinant depends very largely upon the competitive context in a respondent's local area.
3. In that responses are limited to attributes of stores currently used, the frequency of mentions is strongly affected by the availability of particular stores/products/services. For example, carry-out service received relatively few mentions mainly because it is often not readily available.

4. This type of question finds out much about what is liked; it does not indicate what would be liked that is not currently available. This may lead to an emphasis upon existing solutions, if considered in isolation.

Provided that the above issues are clearly recognized, results of the type illustrated in Table 3.3 can be a very valuable input to retail strategy formulation. Unfortunately, it is not uncommon to find managers using research findings that are sound but out of context, in order to prove/ disprove a particular case. 'Omnibus surveys', covering many shoppers and stores, are best used as a starting point for more specific research, not as a general statement of shoppers motives that can be applied to every competitive situaton.

3.2.2 Influences upon selection criteria

Differences in time, retail sector, place, sample, methodology and research orientation represent just six of the major difficulties in combining or comparing studies of shoppers' motives. Even when most of these factors are held fairly constant, studies have illustrated significant differences between the patronage motives of shoppers in different geographical regions or countries. For example, 35 per cent of the primary motivations of middle-class Anglo-Americans in Oklahoma were classified as 'economic', compared with 54 per cent of those of a similar class of Mexican-Americans in Texas (Boone *et al.* 1974). Such differences between areas can offer a basis for geographical price differentiation, which will be examined in Chapter 8. Conversely, the extent of such differentials may largely determine the importance of prices as a patronage motive in the area.

Tigert (1983), comparing food store patronage motives and price differentials within 14 cities, illustrated that 'low prices' increased and 'locational convenience' decreased in importance as the price differentials widened. Within the same set of studies, certain comparisons over time were also drawn. For example, in the year that one store launched a range of generic products, the number of shoppers quoting 'low prices' as a major reason for using the store increased considerably. This underlines the point that shoppers' motives both influence, and are influenced by, retailers' marketing strategies.

Using part of the same data set, Arnold *et al.* (1983b) illustrated differences between the most important attributes for shoppers in four different countries. Locational convenience emerged as the primary attribute for shoppers in Toronto and Cleveland (USA), followed by 'lowest overall prices'. In Birmingham (UK) prices were indicated to be the primary factor, whereas in Amsterdam it appeared to be 'shopping environment'. Some of these contrasts can be attributed to major differences in population densities, geographical dispersions and standards of living. The studies were however separated in time by up to four years, and there were also some differences between the methodologies used. In any case, the results do provide a warning of the dangers of generalizing shopping motives across national boundaries or even within relatively confined geographical areas.

Shoppers' motivations to use a specific store are also in part a function of their motives for patronizing the shopping centre within which the store lies, and vice versa (e.g. Gentry and Burns 1977). The viability of major shopping centres is usually dependent upon the developer's ability to attract major 'anchor tenants', such as department/variety stores or a superstore. Although these are usually assumed to be the main magnets to the centre, customers are actually often drawn there by the availability of smaller, specialist stores. In some cases, no specific shop provides the single main attraction, customers being motivated by the sheer choice of stores or characteristics of the centre itself. The motivational structure of a multi-store

Table 3.4 Attribute importance in store selection

Attributes	Grocery store (rank)	Department store (rank)
Dependable products	1	1
Store is clean	2	10
Easy to find items you want	3	5
Fast checkouts	4	6
High-quality products	5	4
High value for money	6	3
Fully stocked	7	—
Helpful store personnel	8	7
Easy to move through store	9	—
Adequate number of personnel	10	—
Fair on adjustments	—	2
Easy to return purchases	—	8
Easy to exchange purchases	—	9

Source: derived from Hansen and Deutscher (1977/8, pp. 59–72, 95).

shopping trip is clearly likely to be very different from that of a single store trip, making it inappropriate to generalize about customers' patronage motives across dissimilar location types.

It is fairly obvious that different criteria will dominate in the selection of stores within different sectors. Hansen and Deutscher (1977/8) obtained ratings of the importance of 41 attributes in the selection of grocery and department stores. Table 3.4 summarizes the ten attributes that were rated as most important in each case. In that particular study, 'dependable products' received the highest importance ratings in both cases and six other attributes appear in both listings. Only in the case of the department stores do the 'risk reduction' attributes of returns/exchange policies emerge as highly important in the store choice process.

The perceived risks associated with the products to be purchased clearly influence patronage motives and behaviour. Mason and Mayer (1972) observed that the propensity to shop around is closely related to the level of perceived risk in the purchase. Korgaonkar (1982) concluded that the reduction of perceived risk, through the selling of known brands at reasonable prices, gave catalogue showrooms a distinct advantage over some competitors. Over many years, Marks & Spencer have successfully reduced perceived risks through their well-known product reliability and returns policies.

The level of perceived risk is a function both of the purchase type and of the shopper characteristics. Relationships with socioeconomic variables were established by Prasad (1975), who also pointed to the dangers of stores sensitizing customers to the 'social risks' of patronizing them. This could occur, for example, if low prices or other attributes are over-promoted, which may make customers worry that their status may be demeaned by using the store. Measures of self-confidence have also been investigated as possible explanations of differing levels of perceived risk (e.g. Hisrich *et al*. 1972; Dash *et al*. 1976). In the latter study, it was found that department store customers tended to perceive higher levels of perceived risk in the purchase of audio products than did those patronizing speciality stores for these items.

It is hoped that this brief discussion of store selection criteria will have illustrated some of the many contextual and methodological influences upon the findings of specific studies. A warning is being sounded against over generalization of results and against accepting results at face value, without adequate knowledge of the study context and methods. There is also a tendency to blur the distinction between motives and store attributes; sometimes they are discussed as though synonymous. This can actually deflect attention from the fundamental needs and motives that the attribute(s) may help to satisfy, which in turn may suppress the search for better/cheaper/ more innovative solutions to those needs.

3.3 THE PATRONAGE DECISION PROCESS

The study of the consumer's patronage decision process and the development of store choice models holds out the prospect of being able to influence this process more precisely, rapidly and/or economically. In the general field of consumer behaviour, significant advances have been made in the construction and refinement of comprehensive models, notably those of Nicosia (1966), Howard and Sheth (1969) and Engel *et al.* (1986). These offer helpful insights into the patronage decision process, especially in relation to single-item, major purchases. There are however important differences between the processes of selecting a store and selecting a product. With regard to the former, Rosenbloom and Schiffman (1981) noted:

The amount of work addressing the interfaces between consumer behaviour and retailing has been great. Unfortunately, this extensive body of theory and research has yet to be synthesized into general or even middle-range theories of consumer shopping behaviour in the retail setting. What exists presently are some customer-segmentation taxonomies and a small 'glossary' of concepts relating consumer behaviour and retailing.

One problem has been the very considerable diversity of perspectives and approaches. At one extreme, arising from the interface between marketing and urban geography, there has been the development of models emphasizing the location factor, generally depicting patronage behaviour at the most aggregate level. These spatial models are considered in Chapter 6 in relation to store location decisions. In contrast, behavioural models have been developed which focus upon the decision process of individual shoppers. Some are essentially descriptive, while others are of a stochastic nature, with detailed formulations attempting to predict probable behavioural outcomes. A few models attempt to provide an overall view, while the majority focus upon a particular element of the decision process. Some relate primarily to the choice of a centre, others to the choice of a specific retailer. So disparate have been the approaches and orientations that it is not difficult to understand why an integrated framework has been slow to develop.

It would be beyond the scope and purpose of this section to provide a full review of these various modelling approaches or of the extensive body of work on retail patronage behaviour. To explore these areas in greater depth, readers may wish to consult the volumes edited by Darden and Lusch (e.g. 1983) as an excellent starting point. Here it is sufficient to draw from these different approaches some of the specific insights they provide into how consumers process and evaluate marketing cues in order to arrive at a patronage decision.

3.3.1 Models of store choice

Flow charts can be a helpful aid to understanding the elements, their sequence, and the factors affecting the store choice process. For example, Monroe and Guiltinan (1975) set out to establish

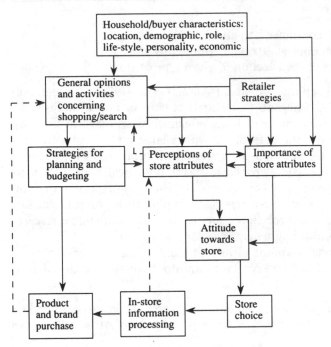

Figure 3.1   Sequence of effects in store choice
Source: derived from Monroe and Guiltinan (1975, p. 21).

the sequence of effects leading to store choice, using time-path analysis: Figure 3.1 depicts this model. Although less elaborate than some of the general consumer behaviour models, it points to the many household and buyer characteristics that influence both perceptions of attributes and the importance attached to these attributes. It also establishes the important distinction between the store decision and the product choice decisions. Efforts to influence store choice effectively and then to maximize sales within the store represent related but different elements of retail marketing strategy, a distinction that many models fail to convey. The figure also stresses the important intervening role of attitude between the marketing mix variables and the store choice decision (e.g. Korgaonkar *et al.* 1985).

An element of the overall decision that has received considerable attention is the process by which attitude towards the store is formed, given a range of perceptions relating to individual attributes. The approach of Fishbein (1967) has been widely applied to the modelling and measurement of overall attitude; this holds that 'an individual's attitude towards any object is a function of his beliefs about the object and the evaluative aspects of those beliefs'. The overall attitudes towards the object (store) could therefore be expressed as a uni-dimensional construct, representing a function of the individual evaluations (A-scales) weighted according to their salience (B-scales). The Fishbein model was adapted slightly by Bass and Talarzyk (1972) to relate more specifically to attitudes towards stores. Termed a 'multi-attribute attitude model', this involved the summation of attribute ratings, each weighted according to its importance as rated by consumers. Expressed more formally:

$$A_{jk} = \sum_{i=1}^{n} W_{ik} B_{ijk}$$

A_{jk} = consumer k's attitude score for store j
W_{ik} = importance weight assigned by consumer k to attribute i
B_{ijk} = consumer k's belief as to the amount of attribute i offered by store j
n = number of important attributes in the selection of given type of store.

A more detailed exposition of the approach was provided by James *et al.* (1976), although only six attributes were rated in their study. Sampson and Harris (1970), in line with Fishbein, claimed that about twelve attributes were capable of being effectively researched in this way. Given the problem of handling multi-attribute judgements with a large number of attributes, Louviere and Gaeth (1987) suggested the solution of 'hierarchical information integration'. Using this approach, individual attributes (e.g. parking, travel time, width of aisles) are combined to form higher-order constructs (e.g. convenience). The authors claim that the procedure could offer an explanation of how consumers may simplify their complex decision tasks; they warn against such simplification procedures simply to produce tractable research designs or to satisfy the preconceived notions of management or researchers.

The appeal of the multi-attribute model, in terms of its face validity and ease of implementation, was discussed by Howell (1981). He did however cast some doubt on the practice of using respondent-stated importance weights:

In general, subjects have been found to overstate (when compared with regression-derived estimates) the importance attached to minor dimensions, and understate the importance attached to a few major dimensions.

A major drawback of the multi-attribute model is the unrealistic implication that consumers make an almost simultaneous evaluation of the many attributes in arriving at their store choice. Fotheringham (1987) noted that such decisions are more likely to involve a hierarchical evaluation of alternatives. If stores are eliminated progressively from the active choice set, then the importance or weightings of attributes used to distinguish between the remaining stores will change at each stage in the decision. As Meyer and Eagle (1982) observed:

there is evidence that consumers are not likely to make choices simply by noting how good various alternatives are with respect to a multiattribute utility function. Rather, choices often appear to be made hierarchically; that is, the attributes used to discriminate among alternatives (the parameters and elements of the utility function) change as various candidates are eliminated from consideration.

From the viewpoint of the model-builder, this presents serious problems in estimating the large number of parameters involved, although various attempts to do so have been reported (e.g. Gensch and Svestka 1979). Meyer and Eagle (1982) addressed the 'context effect', whereby the salience of attributes varies according to the amount of variability across the remaining alternative choices on that attribute. They proposed a 'bilinear differences model', which takes into account the shifting importance weights and also assumes that choices are made on a 'paired' basis, even when several alternative stores are available:

the model implies a choices process whereby an individual's 'focus of attention' may shift to minor attributes (such as subtle aspects of appearance) as alternatives become increasingly similar on major attributes (such as price).

As noted in the previous section, this warns against adopting a simplistic or generalized view of attribute importance. For example, I observed consumer food store choices in a UK town which was not directly exposed to superstores competition until the mid-1980s. When the first one opened, store choices were dominated by the superior prices and choice offered by that store, relative to existing supermarket competition. When the second superstore opened, range and prices appeared evenly matched, so factors such as store atmosphere or the perceived status of using one of the stores became more significant elements within the choice process. Expressed simply, choice and prices had not ceased to be important, but they had started to be taken for granted, as many shoppers narrowed their choice to the two superstores.

Another unrealistic assumption within the conventional multi-attribute attitude model is that consumer attitude responses to attribute differences are linear or consistent across the whole range. As is discussed in the chapters of Part Two, there is considerable evidence of nonlinear responses to price, display or other changes/differences. It may be reasonably assumed that consumers have certain 'thresholds' of acceptable prices, location, range, services, etc. Within these thresholds, there are likely to be 'zones of indifference' in relation to specific attributes. Some evidence of response thresholds was provided by Malhotra (1983) in relation to the patronage of record shops by students. The stores' images for variety, service, price, location and facilities were found to be salient, but a threshold, rather than a linear, function was indicated.

If one adopts the assumption of thresholds of acceptability within the patronage decision process, then the task of modelling should be reduced to the subset of stores that comprise the actual choice set. This concept has been applied in relation to spatial models, where distance or lack of information may limit the consumer's choice set (e.g. Black 1984). The concept may be extended further to exclude stores that are not within the choice set of a particular consumer or segment for reasons other than distance; for example, some stores may be regarded as too small, too dirty, too difficult for parking, etc. Malhotra (1986) suggested that store choice models should be based upon 'censored preference data', excluding stores that are declared unacceptable by consumers. Not only does this procedure slightly simplify the modelling process, it also reduces errors introduced by including stores that are irrelevant to the consumers' patronage decision.

If the first stage of the patronage decision is, in effect, the rejection of unacceptable alternatives, the 'dual factor' theory of motivation may be applicable to an extent (see Section 3.1.1). Some factors may be particularly instrumental in a store being rejected from the choice set, whereas others may serve to establish competitive advantage within the choice set. Within spatial interaction models, distance or time needed to get to the store were traditionally regarded as the 'deterrence' factors'; clearly, other factors, such as adverse prices or service, also serve to deter patronage and possibly to exclude a store from the choice set.

One problem in applying the Herzberg (1966) dual factor theory literally in this context is that many store attributes can serve either to deter or to attract. An interesting classification of store patronage factors into 'attractions' and 'costs' was provided by Brown (1978). The latter included not only the monetary costs but also the time, physical and psychological costs of shopping.

Even the same intensity/quantity of an attribute may have opposite effects for different customer segments. High prices would deter many but could attract those seeking status; large stores may signal choice and ease to some but may intimidate others. The shopper's psychological interpretations or images of stores may therefore provide greater insights into the decision process than direct ratings, rankings and combinations of attitudes towards major attributes. Studies of store images are considered in Chapter 5, and models of the choice process are considered further in Chapter 7, in relation to retailers' product selection and buying decisions.

3.4 SEGMENTING RETAIL MARKETS

The previous sections have illustrated the wide range of needs and wants that can motivate product purchases and the shopping activity. Every customer has a different set of needs, wants and motives, but in very few consumer goods markets is it feasible to really tailor the marketing mix to the level of the individual customer. Hence the need to identify reasonably homogeneous groupings, or segments, of shoppers to be the target(s) of retail marketing efforts. There are many different ways in which a retailer can define market segments, based upon consumer characteristics and/or their shopping orientations; examples of each are considered in this section.

The need for more systematic forms of market segmentation has increased with the intensification of retail competition and with the growth of the multiple chains. Meeting the competition 'head on' in a very broadly defined market, such as electrical goods, is usually a viable strategy only for the retailer(s) that enjoy the greatest economies of scale and cost advantages; even for them, it may well not be the most profitable strategy. Ironically, as the multiples grew rapidly, there was an intensive phase of standardization, both in product ranges and in outlet formats. The likelihood of the same mix being appropriate in all areas is however remote, a realization that has brought a phase of greater adaptation, either within an overall format or by developing various clearly differentiated formats designed to appeal to different market segments.

3.4.1 Approaches to market segmentation

There are numerous possible bases for market segmentation, including demographics, geographical location, life-styles and psychographics. The most important characteristic of the segmentation variables is that they should be indicative, directly or indirectly, of relevant need, preference, consumption or behaviour patterns. The segments must also be:

1. *Measurable*—for this reason, variables that can be easily identified and measured, such as age or residential area, may be preferred to variables or attributes requiring more elaborate measurement techniques;
2. *Economically viable*—the segment must be capable of producing the profit contribution to justify the effort and cost of target marketing and possible repositioning;
3. *Accessible*—even a segment that is clearly identified and obviously viable may not be accessible, either geographically or in terms of cost/effective media communications.

Some examples of retail market segmentation bases and variables are listed in Table 3.5; some of these are relatively simple variables, while others represent more complex clusters of attributes. Some categories are entirely discrete, whereas others, such as ownership categories or life-style orientations, can overlap considerably.

Following a study of some 37 characteristics that may correlate with store selection, Bellenger *et al.* (1976) concluded that the relatively simple variables, such as education, age and income, provide the most useful and manageable bases for market segmentation. The most appropriate variables differed between six merchandise categories studied, indicating the dangers of generalizing across retail sectors. They also concluded that some of the more 'methodologically awkward' factors, such as social class and life-style, are less promising as segmentation variables. It should be noted however that the AB/C1/C2/DE occupation classifications (see Monk 1978) are very widely used in the UK. There has been much debate in the marketing literature as to the relative efficiency of social class and income as predictors of consumer behaviour; Hisrich and Peters (1974) concluded that the most appropriate variable depends upon the product class and the aspect of behaviour under consideration.

Although most of the demographic variables score highly on the criteria of being easily identified and easily measured, it has long been asserted that psychographic segmentation can improve our ability to predict and understand consumer behaviour. Chotin (1969) defined

Table 3.5 Examples of segmentation bases

Bases/variables	Typical categories
Demographic	
Age	Under 3; 3–4, 5–8, 9–11; 12–15; 16–18; 19–24; 25–34; 35–44; 45–54; 55–64; 65 +
Sex	Male; female
Education	Minimum; O-levels; A-levels; degree or equivalent; postgraduate
Occupation	AB; C1; C2; DE
Family	1–2; 3–4; 5 +
Family life-cycle	Young single; young married without children; young married with children; older married without children; older married with children; older single
Income	Under £5,000; £5,000–£10,000; £10,000–£15,000; £15,000–£20,000; £20,000–£25,000; £25,000–£30,000; Over £30,000
Ownership of durables	Car; 2 + cars; freezer; video recorder; microwave
House ownership	Fully owned; mortgaged; renting
Geographic	
Area type	Metropolitan area; small city; town; village
Area density	Urban; suburban; rural
Neighbourhood type	ACORN classifications (see Table 3.6)
House type	Detached; semi-detached; terrace; flat
Standard region	Scotland; North East; Yorkshire & Humberside; North West; Midlands; Wales; South West; South East; Anglia; London
Behavioural	
User status	Non-user; less than £50 per year; £50–£100; £100–£200; £200–£500; £500–£750; £750–£1,000; £1,000–£2,000; over £2,000
User frequency	4 + times weekly; 2–3 times weekly; weekly; fortnightly; monthly; 5–10 times yearly; yearly; non-user
Store loyalty	Absolute; high; medium; low; none
Psychographic	
Life-style orientations	Instant gratification; time-poor; health-conscious; individualistic; concern for environment
Fashion orientations	Leader; follower; independent; neutral; uninvolved; negative; rejector
Benefits sought	Convenience; lowest price; value for money; highest quality; style and design; choice; enjoyment
Values and attitudes	Survivors; sustainers; belongers; emulators; achievers; I-am-me; experientials; societally conscious; integrateds

psychographics as 'the consumer's psychological and emotional reactions'. Yankelovich (1964) had already noted the need for segmentation bases that relate more to attitudes and opinions than to demographic characteristics:

We should discard the old, unquestioned assumption that demography is always the best way of looking at markets.

Markets should be scrutinised for important differences in buyer attitudes, motivations, values, usage patterns, aesthetic preferences or degrees of susceptibility.

It is becoming increasingly difficult to predict behaviour patterns on the basis of demographic alone. As Huie (1985) pointed out:

There is a blurring of the behavioural patterns into which we used to neatly pigeon-hole people. Rich–poor, old–young, boy–girl—they are not the predictable labelling they used to be.

Some of the recent life-style trends (see Chapter 2) cut across traditional classifications. For example, the health-conscious or the environmentally concerned consumer may be 21 or 60 years of age, may earn £8,000 a year or £30,000. Although the age and income level will inevitably influence the level and type of consumption, it may be the life-style characteristic that forms the most suitable focus for the retailer.

The techniques of factor analysis and cluster analysis (e.g. Punj and Stewart 1983) can be applied to reduce large numbers of potential predictor variables and derive new or sector-specific typologies of shoppers. For example, based upon 17 attitude/opinion statements from department store customers, May (1971) identified three major clusters: these were labelled 'price', 'fun' and 'self-confidence'. Gutman and Mills (1982) analysed 67 life-style items and identified seven fashion life-style segments, which could be useful in predicting the patronage and requirements of clothing shoppers; these are shown in Table 3.5. The values and attitude categories within the table are based upon the 'VALS' value life-style groups, classified by Mitchell (1983).

A segmentation system that incorporates various demographic, geographic and life-style characteristics is ACORN (A Classification of Residential Neighbourhoods). Using published census statistics and taking 40 variables into account, ACORN classifies areas of around 150 households into 38 neighbourhood types or 11 aggregated groupings; these are shown in Table 3.6. Obviously, some of these neighbourhood types are more homogeneous than others (Rogers 1986) and therefore are better predictors of the residents' purchasing and shopping behaviour. The segments are however extremely measurable and accessible; with geocoding, lists of addresses within specified ACORN groups can be produced for promotional or research purposes. Further applications of geocoded data are discussed in Chapter 6.

3.4.2 Typologies of shopping orientations

Having looked at some of the segmentation approaches based upon characteristics of the consumer, this section turns to segmentation by shopping orientations. This approach involves the definition of customer groups according to their shopping behaviour, motives and attitudes. Various psychographic measures are now typically used to assist in defining the segments. The concept of a typology based upon shopping orientations has a fairly long history. Stone (1954) defined four distinct shopper types, based upon 124 depth interviews:

1. The economic consumer (33%)
2. The personalizing consumer (28%)
3. The ethical consumer (18%)
4. The apathetic consumer (17%)
   (Indeterminate 4%)

Table 3.6 ACORN groups and types

Groups and types		% UK*
A	AGRICULTURAL AREAS	3.4
1	Agricultural villages	2.6
2	Areas of farms and smallholdings	0.8
B	MODERN FAMILY HOUSING, HIGHER INCOMES	17.4
3	Cheap modern private housing	4.3
4	Recent private housing, young families	3.6
5	Modern private housing, older children	6.0
6	New detached houses, young families	2.9
7	Military bases	0.7
C	OLDER HOUSING OF INTERMEDIATE STATUS	17.9
8	Mixed owner-occupied and council estates	3.5
9	Small town centres and flats above shops	4.1
10	Villages with non-farm employment	4.8
11	Older private housing skilled workers	5.5
D	POOR-QUALITY OLDER TERRACED HOUSING	4.2
12	Unimproved terraces with old people	2.5
13	Pre-1914 terraces, low-income families	1.4
14	Tenement flats lacking amenities	0.4
E	BETTER-OFF COUNCIL ESTATES	13.1
15	Council estates, well-off older workers	3.4
16	Recent council estates	2.8
17	Council estates, well-off young workers	5.0
18	Small council houses, often Scottish	1.9
F	LESS WELL-OFF COUNCIL ESTATES	8.8
19	Low-rise estates in industrial towns	4.6
20	Interwar council estates, older people	2.9
21	Council housing for the elderly	1.4
G	POOREST COUNCIL ESTATES	7.0
22	New council estates in inner cities	2.0
23	Overspill estates, high unemployment	3.0
24	Council estates with overcrowding	1.5
25	Council estates with worst poverty	0.6
H	MULTI-RACIAL AREAS	3.8
26	Multi-occupied terraces, poor Asians	0.4
27	Owner-occupied terraces with Asians	1.0
28	Multi-let housing with Afro-Caribbeans	0.7
29	Better-off multi-ethnic areas	1.7
I	HIGH-STATUS NON-FAMILY AREAS	4.2
30	High-status areas, few children	2.1
31	Multi-let big old houses and flats	1.5
32	Furnished flats, mostly single people	0.5
J	AFFLUENT SUBURBAN HOUSING	15.8
33	Interwar semis, white-collar workers	5.7
34	Spacious interwar semis, big gardens	5.0
35	Villages with wealthy older commuters	2.9
36	Detached houses, exclusive suburbs	2.3
K	BETTER-OFF RETIREMENT AREAS	3.8
37	Private houses, well-off elderly	2.3
38	Private flats with single pensioners	1.6
U	UNCLASSIFIED	0.5

Source: © CACI Limited 1989.　　　　　　　　　　　　　　　*1990 projection

The approach of developing motivation-based typologies has been adopted in several sub-sequent studies, some of which were reviewed by Westbrook and Black (1985) and Lesser and Hughes (1986a, 1986b). Inevitably, the classifications differ somewhat between studies, partly because of differences in time, store type, sector and methodology. The value of segmentation based upon shopping orientations is that it relates most directly to the retail patronage activity; the drawback is that segments defined in this way may be more difficult to measure and reach. Considerable attention has however been given to four orientation segments in particular, which were defined by Stephenson and Willett (1969) as follows:

1. The convenience shopper
2. The recreational shopper
3. The price-bargain shopper
4. The store-loyal shopper

The *convenience-oriented* segment has been the subject of several studies. Anderson (1971, 1972) found that, in relation to food shopping, this orientation was highest among households at the intermediate stage in the life-cycle. Bearden *et al.* (1978) found convenience shoppers to be less traditional, more outgoing and more socially conscious; they also tended to be younger, better educated and better paid. Williams *et al.* (1978) formed a distinction between 'apathetic' shoppers, who rate most store attributes adversely, and 'convenience' shoppers, who demonstrate a more positive acceptance of the price–convenience trade-off.

An additional perspective on the 'convenience' segment is that of shoppers' 'disposable time' (e.g. MacKay 1973). The concept of the 'time-buying consumer' was further developed by Berry (1979), who observed that time scarcity was on the increase, partly because more women work, partly because of more demand for 'me time'. Whether this time scarcity is real or perceived, enforced or self-inflicted, it amounts to a growing pressure both for convenience products and for convenient shopping. Indeed, in-home shoppers may be regarded as a form of 'ultra-convenience' segment.

Time was also cited as a major explanation for shopping preferences by Holman and Wilson (1982), who considered that most consumers sought to restore one of two types of 'time disequilibrium'. Some suffer too much obligatory time (time scarcity), while others have too much discretionary time. The *recreational shopper* is likely to be in the latter category, and shopping offers a way of filling time, both in the number of shopping trips undertaken and the ways in which these are conducted; more browsing and pre-search activity is likely to be undertaken.

Bellenger *et al.* (1977) found that recreational shoppers tend to seek a high-quality shopping environment, with extensive variety and a large number of related services, such as restaurants. They also tend to be less well educated, with slightly less than average household income. Bellenger and Korgaonkar (1980) concluded that the recreational shoppers represent a significant percentage of consumers and a disproportionate number of women. Their particular importance in retail marketing terms lies in their lower levels of purchase planning and their greater tendency to make impulse purchases.

Various different types of *price-bargain* orientation have been identified, ranging from the more balanced motivations of the 'economic shopper' (e.g. Darden and Reynolds 1971) through to the more extreme bargain orientation of the 'deal-prone' segment (e.g. Blattberg *et al.* 1978). 'Price' shoppers were found by Williams *et al.* (1978) to account for 27 per cent of their sample. Noticeably, this group perceived advertising favourably, presumably because they tended to use and trust it as a source of price information. Of six shopper types defined by Moschis (1976), the 'specials shoppers' were found to attach high credibility to advertisements in newspapers and magazines as a source of information.

In an early study of 'deal-prone' consumers, Webster (1965) found that older housewives tended to be more deal-prone, possibly reflecting more traditional shopping patterns and their greater expertise in searching the market-place. Blattberg *et al.* (1978) found low levels of deal-proneness among those from upper-income households, house-owners, car-owners and non-working women. A distinction must however be drawn between the deal-prone shopper and the discount store patron. Bearden *et al.* (1978) illustrated that discount store customers tend to be younger and better educated, not the usual profile of the deal-prone shopper. This contrast is indicative of some important differences between those who seek 'deals' and those who seek lower prices 'across the board', a distinction that is further developed in Chapter 8.

Attempts to define the *store-loyal* customer have used a variety of loyalty measures, such as the proportion of budget allocated to a store, the number of stores patronized, the number of switches between stores, or an index of these measures (e.g. Enis and Paul 1970). They concluded that loyalty is a worth-while segmentation criterion and that loyal customers are a potentially profitable segment, confirming an earlier finding of Massy (1966).

Several attempts have been made to identify characteristics of store-loyal customers. Enis and Paul (1970) found that customers with less education and in low-skill, manual employment tend to be the most store-loyal. Reynolds *et al.* (1974) found the 'generalised store-loyal housewife' to be older, with less educational attainment and lower family income. They also found that the store-loyal customers tended not to be opinion leaders, and were less gregarious and less venturesome. Goldman (1977) identified relationships between shopping styles and loyalty, store loyalty being associated with low levels of store search, low knowledge about the store system and low utilization of the set of stores known.

Miller and Granzin (1979) pointed out that loyalty should be seen to arise through the success of a store in satisfying customers with certain characteristics, not just as a direct outcome of these characteristics. To a lesser extent, this problem of identifying causes and effects also applies to most other segments defined according to shopping behaviour and orientations. Another problem is the diversity of labels attached to the segments by different researchers, making comparisons betwen studies difficult. Such a comparison was however undertaken by Lesser and Hughes (1986a, 1986b) across 21 other studies, providing a comprehensive summary of identified typologies. In spite of the problems, shopping orientations do provide a basis for segmentation and target marketing which is very directly rooted in shoppers' motives and behaviour.

SUMMARY

An understanding of consumers' needs and motives is an essential prerequisite of successful retail marketing strategy. The identification and satisfaction of consumer needs is one of the most fundamental principles of retail marketing; without this focus, strategic planning can easily become dominated by the actions of competitors or internal influences. The most successful examples of innovation and evolution in retail formats represent accurate and profitable responses to previously unsatisfied needs. The constant interface with customers does not necessarily lead to a clear understanding of their needs, or of those of potential target groups. Effective research procedures and information systems, both internal and external, are required.

A common flaw in strategic planning is a failure to distinguish between solutions and needs. Sometimes overlooked is the fact that most strategic solutions satisfy more than one underlying need, which in turn may be satisfied by alternative or better solutions. Some of the basic classifications of human needs could provide frameworks for understanding why shoppers act and react in certain ways. The shopping activity itself, for example, may satisfy many personal and social motives, some not related to the buying of products. These may include the need for diversion, physical activity, sensory stimulation or social experiences. While some regard shopping as an essential chore, many see it as satisfying other more diverse needs.

There have been numerous studies of consumers' store choice criteria, as retailers and researchers seek to identify the store attributes that are most instrumental in store choice decisions. There is some evidence of shifting priorities over time, shifts that have been both reflected in and influenced by changes in retailers' strategic emphasis. It is however dangerous to generalize from the findings of studies based upon a diversity of methodologies, locations and sectors. The choice of a store is also in part a function of the choice of a shopping centre. The perceived risks associated with the intended product purchases also influence store choice.

An understanding of the process by which attitudes are formed and patronage decisions are made is an important but elusive goal of retail strategists and researchers. It is clear that attitudes are influenced not only by shopping experiences and retailer strategies but also by the economic, demographic, psychographic and life-style characteristics of the shopper. Various simple formulations, such as the multi-attribute attitude model, have been suggested as ways in which individual attribute evaluations may be combined. There is evidence however that consumers have certain thresholds of acceptability and zones of indifference in evaluating store attributes. The salience of particular attributes may also be highly specific to a competitive situation, depending upon the elements of differentiation between the stores within the consumers' active choice set.

In most retail sectors it is appropriate to target marketing efforts at groupings, or segments, of shoppers who are likely to share some common characteristics, in terms of their needs, motives and patronage criteria. There are many different possible bases for market segmentation; in practice, the defined segments must be measurable, economically viable and accessible, both in logistical and in communications terms. A great deal of segmentation uses relatively simple demographic variables, such as age or income, and geographical variables, such as region or area type.

Increased use is now being made of psychographic segmentation bases, such as values, attitudes or life-style orientations. With the rapid development of geographical information systems in recent years, detailed classifications and databases of residential neighbourhoods have also become available for segmentation purposes. Another approach is to use typologies of shopping orientations, for example convenience, recreational, price-bargain and store-loyal shoppers.

REVIEW QUESTIONS

1. Discuss, with examples, the major pitfalls in developing retail strategy without an adequate understanding of consumer needs.
2. What are the principal research approaches and information systems that could be utilized by a large retail organization to maintain contact with consumer needs?
3. Identify the underlying needs that may be satisfied by the introduction of a counter service delicatessen into a supermarket. Suggest some of the possible alternative solutions to these needs.
4. How can the shopping activity itself satisfy personal and social motives that are not necessarily related to the actual buying of products?
5. Why is it dangerous to assume that store selection criteria identified in previous studies can be applied to similar store choice situations?
6. Illustrate how the choice of a store may be influenced by the perceived risks of buying:

   (a) a video recorder;
   (b) a dress for an important occasion.

What steps could a retailer take to reduce these perceived risks?
7. Taking an actual store choice situation within your recent experience, try to depict the major influences and the sequences of effects in your patronage decision.
8. Outline the basic principles of the multi-attribute attitude model. What are the main limitations of this concept as a model of the consumer's patronage decision?
9. What factors should be considered in selecting a basis for retail market segmentation?
10. What is the basis of the ACORN classification system? Explain how you could use this system to help in establishing and launching new outlets for a financial services agency.
11. Explain what is meant by psychographic segmentation. Give examples of psychographic segments that would be relevant to a clothing retailer.
12. Evaluate the advantages and problems of segmenting retail markets on the basis of consumers' shopping orientations.

REFERENCES

Anderson, W. T. (1971), 'Identifying the convenience-oriented consumer', *Journal of Marketing Research*, **8**(2), 179–83.
Anderson, W. T. (1972), 'Convenience orientation and consumption behavior', *Journal of Retailing*, **48**(3), 49–71, 127.
Arnold, D. R., L. M. Capella and G. D. Smith (1983a), *Strategic Retail Management*, Addison-Wesley, Reading, Mass.
Arnold, S. J., T. H. Oum and D. J. Tigert (1983b), 'Determinant attributes in retail patronage: seasonal, temporal, regional and international comparisons', *Journal of Marketing Research*, **20**(2), 149–57.
Bass, F. M. and W. W. Talarzyk (1972), 'An attitude model for the study of brand preference', *Journal of Marketing Research*, **9**(1), 93–96.
Bates, J. M. and A. Gabor (1987), 'Changes in subjective welfare and purchasing behaviour: report on an enquiry', *Journal of the Market Research Society*, **29**(2), 183–207.
Bearden, W. O., J. E. Teel and R. M. Durand (1978), 'Media usage, psychographic, and demographic dimensions of retail shoppers', *Journal of Retailing*, **54**(1), 65–74.
Bellenger, D. N. and P. K. Korgaonkar (1980), 'Profiling the recreational shopper', *Journal of Retailing*, **56**(3), 77–92.
Bellenger, D. N., D. H. Robertson and B. A. Greenberg (1977), 'Shopping centre patronage motives', *Journal of Retailing*, **53**(2), 29–38.
Bellenger, D. N., D. H. Robertson and E. C. Hirschman (1976), 'Age and education as key correlates of store selection for female shoppers', *Journal of Retailing*, **52**(4), 71–8.
Berry, L. L. (1979), 'The time-buying consumer', *Journal of Retailing*, **55**(4), 58–69.
Black, W. C. (1984), 'Choice-set definition in patronage modeling', *Journal of Retailing*, **60**(2), 63–85.
Blattberg, R., T. Buesing, P. Peacock and S. Sen (1978), 'Identifying the deal prone segment', *Journal of Marketing Research*, **15**(3), 369–77.
Boone, L. E., D. L. Kurtz, J. C. Johnson and J. A. Bonno (1974), '"City shoppers and urban identification" revisited', *Journal of Marketing*, **38**(3), 67–9.
Brown, D. J. (1978), 'Assessing retail trade: a review of the consumer behaviour literature,' *International Journal of Physical Distribution and Materials Management*, **9**(3), 115–147.
CACI (1989), *ACORN User's Guide*, CACI Market Analysis, London.
Chotin, M. (1969), 'The psychologist looks at market segmentation', *The Analyst*, **1**(4), 22–7.
Darden, W. R. and R. F. Lusch (1983), *Patronage Behavior and Retail Management*, Elsevier–North Holland, New York.
Darden, W. R. and F. D. Reynolds (1971), 'Shopping orientations and product usage rates', *Journal of Marketing Research*, **8**(4), 505–8.
Dash, J. F., L. G. Schiffman and C. Berenson (1976), 'Risk- and personality-related dimensions of store choice', *Journal of Marketing*, **40**(1), 32–9.
Engel, J. F., R. D. Blackwell and P. W. Miniard (1986), *Consumer Behavior*, Holt, Rinehart & Winston, New York.
Enis, B. M. and G. W. Paul (1970), '"Store loyalty" as a basis for market segmentation', *Journal of Retailing*, **46**(3), 42–56.
Euromonitor (1986), *The Changing Face of Grocery Retailing*, Euromonitor, London.
Fishbein, M. (1967), *Attitude Theory and Measurement*, John Wiley, New York.
Fotheringham, A. S. (1987), 'Consumer store choice and retail competition', *Fourth International Conference on Distribution*, CESCOM, Milan.
Gensch, D. H. and J. A. Svestka (1979), 'An exact hierarchical algorithm for determining aggregate statistics from individual choice data', *Management Science*, **25**, 939–52.

Gentry, J. W. and A. C. Burns (1977), 'How "important" are evaluative criteria in shopping centre patronage?' *Journal of Retailing*, **53**(4), 73–86, 94.

Goldman, A. (1977), 'The shopping style explanation for store loyalty', *Journal of Retailing*, **53**(4), 33–46, 94.

Gutman, J. and M. K. Mills (1982), 'Fashion life-style, self-concept, shopping orientation, and store patronage: an integrative analysis', *Journal of Retailing*, **58**(2), 64–86.

Hansen, R. A. and T. Deutscher (1977/8), 'An empirical investigation of attribute importance in retail store selection', *Journal of Retailing*, **53**(4), 59–72, 95.

Herzberg, F. (1966), *Work and the Nature of Man*, Staples Press, London.

Hisrich, R. D., R. J. Dornoff and J. B. Kernan (1972), 'Perceived risk in store selection', *Journal of Marketing Research*, **9**(4), 435–9.

Hisrich, R. D. and M. P. Peters (1974), 'Selecting the superior segmentation correlate', *Journal of Marketing*, **38**(3), 60–3.

Holman, R. H. and R. D. Wilson (1982), 'Temporal equilibrium as a basis for retail shopping behavior', *Journal of Retailing*, **58**(1), 58–81.

Howard, J. A. and J. N. Sheth (1969), *The Theory of Buyer Behavior*, John Wiley, New York.

Howell, R. (1981), 'Issues in multiattribute modeling of consumer patronage', in R. F. Lusch and W. R. Darden (eds.), *Retail Patronage Theory 1981 Workshop Proceedings*, University of Oklahoma, pp. 229–34.

Huie, J. (1985), 'Understanding the new breed of consumer', in J. Gattorna (ed.), *Insights in Strategic Retail Management*, MCB, Bradford, pp. 45–8.

James, D. L., R. M. Durand and R. A. Dreves (1976), 'The use of a multiattribute attitude model in a store image study', *Journal of Retailing*, **52**(2), 23–32.

Jolson, M. A. and W. F. Spath (1973), 'Understanding and fulfilling shoppers' requirements: an anomaly in retail?' *Journal of Retailing*, **49**(2), 38–40.

Kenny-Levick, C. (1969), 'Customer motivations: examples from the grocery trade', *British Journal of Marketing*, **3**, 2–8.

Korgaonkar, P. K. (1982), 'Consumer preferences for catalog showrooms and discount stores: the moderating role of product risk', *Journal of Retailing*, **58**(3), 76–88.

Korgaonkar, P. K., D. Lund and B. Price (1985), 'A structural equations approach toward examination of store attitude and store patronage behavior', *Journal of Retailing*, **61**(2), 39–60.

Lesser, J. A. and M. A. Hughes (1986a), 'Towards a typology of shoppers', *Business Horizons*, **29**(6), 56–62.

Lesser, J. A. and M. A. Hughes (1986b), 'The generalizability of psychographic market segments across geographic locations', *Journal of Marketing*, **50**(1), 18–27.

Louviere, J. J. and G. J. Gaeth (1987), 'Decomposing the determinants of retail facility choice using the method of hierarchical information integration: a supermarket illustration', *Journal of Retailing*, **63**(1), 25–48.

MacKay, D. B. (1973), 'A spectral analysis of the frequency of supermarket visits', *Journal of Marketing Research*, **10**(1), 84–90.

Malhotra, N. K. (1983), 'A threshold model of store choice', *Journal of Retailing*, **59**(2), 3–21.

Malhotra, N. K. (1986), 'Modeling store choice based on censored preference data', *Journal of Retailing*, **62**(2), 128–44.

Maslow, A. H. (1970), *Motivation and Personality*, Harper & Row, New York.

Mason, J. B. and M. L. Mayer (1972), 'Empirical observations of consumer behavior as related to goods classification and retail strategy', *Journal of Retailing*, **48**(3), 17–31.

Massy, W. F. (1966), 'Brand and store loyalty as bases for market segmentation', in J. E. Newman (ed.), *On Knowing the Consumer*, John Wiley, New York, pp. 169–72.

May, E. G. (1971), 'Psychographics in department store imagery', Report No. 71–131, Marketing Science Institute, Cambridge, Mass.

McClelland, D. C. (1967), *The Achieving Society*, Free Press, New York.

Meyer, R. J. and T. C. Eagle (1982), 'Context-induced parameter instability in a disaggregate—stochastic model of store choice', *Journal of Marketing Research*, **19**(1), 62–71.

Miller, K. E. and K. L. Granzin (1979), 'Simultaneous loyalty and benefit segmentation of retail store customers', *Journal of Retailing*, **55**(1), 47–60.

Mintel (1986), 'Is shopping fun?' *Mintel Leisure Intelligence*, **16**, 45–75.

Mitchell, A. (1983), *The Nine American Life Styles: Who We Are and Where We're Going*, Macmillan, New York.

Monk, D. (1978), *Social Grading on the National Readership Survey*, JICNARS, London.

Monroe, K. B. and J. P. Guiltinan (1975), 'A path-analytic exploration of retail patronage influences', *Journal of Consumer Research*, **2**, 21.

Moschis, G. P. (1976), 'Shopping orientations and consumer uses of information', *Journal of Retailing*, **52**(2), 61–70, 93.

Nicosia, F. M. (1966), *Consumer Decision Processes*, Prentice-Hall, Englewood Cliffs, NJ.

Prasad, V. K. (1975), 'Socioeconomic product risk and patronage preferences of retail shoppers', *Journal of Marketing*, **39**(3), 42–7.

Punj, G. and D. W. Stewart (1983), 'Cluster analysis in marketing research: review and suggestions for application', *Journal of Marketing Research*, **20**(2), 134–48.

Reynolds, F. D., W. R. Darden and W. S. Martin (1974), 'Developing an image of the store-loyal customer', *Journal of Retailing*, **50**(4), 73–84.

Rogers, D. (1986), 'Demographic data reports', *Retail & Distribution Management*, **14**(5), 23–6.

Rosenbloom, B. and L. G. Schiffman (1981), 'Retailing theory: perspectives and approaches', in R. W. Stampfl and E. C. Hirschman (eds.), *Theory in Retailing: Traditional and Nontraditional Sources*, American Marketing Association, Chicago, pp. 168–79.

Sampson, P. and P. Harris (1970), 'A user's guide to Fishbein', *Journal of the Market Research Society*, **12**(3), 145–66.

Stephenson, D. and R. P. Willett (1969), 'Analysis of consumers' retail patronage strategies', in P. R. MacDonald (ed.), *Marketing Involvement in Society and Economy*, AMA, Chicago, pp. 316–22.

Stone, G. P. (1954), 'City shoppers and urban identification: observations on the social psychology of city life', *American Journal of Sociology*, **60**, 36–45.

Tauber, E. M. (1972), 'Why do people shop?' *Journal of Marketing*, **36**(4), 46–9.

Tigert, D. J. (1983), 'Pushing the hot buttons for a successful retailing strategy', in W. R. Dearden and R. F. Lusch (eds.), *Patronage Behavior and Retail Management*, Elsevier–North Holland, New York.

Watkins, E. P. and V. A. Vandemark (1971), 'Customer information systems', *Journal of Retailing*, **47**(1), 50–4.

Webster, F. E. (1965), 'The "deal-prone" consumer', *Journal of Marketing Research*, **2**(2), 186–9.

Westbrook, R. A. and W. C. Black (1985), 'A motivation-based shopper typology', *Journal of Retailing*, **61**(1), 78–103.

Williams, R. H., J. J. Painter and H. R. Nicholas (1978), 'A policy-oriented typology of grocery shoppers', *Journal of Retailing*, **54**(1), 27–42.

Wilson, B. L. (1984), 'Modern methods of sales forecasting: regression models', in R. L. Davies and D. S. Rogers (eds.), *Store Location and Store Assessment Research*, John Wiley, Chichester, pp. 301–18.

Yankelovich, D. (1964), 'New criteria for market segmentation', *Harvard Business Review*, **42**(2), 83–90.

FOUR
FORMULATING RETAIL STRATEGY

INTRODUCTION

Formal structures and processes for strategic planning have a very short history in most retail companies. The more widespread recognition of the need for a marketing orientation was not initially coupled with a propensity for long-term strategic planning. As Rosenbloom (1980) aptly observed:

retailing executives by tradition and experience tend to be oriented to the very short term. They are used to reacting quickly and decisively to meet the problems of operating their business in a rapidly changing and highly competitive environment. They like to think of themselves as 'quick on their feet' and take pride in being so. Strategic planning however requires a longer range and a more sober posture if it is to be done effectively.

The problems caused by a reactive rather than a strategic style of management are, in retrospect, easy to see. In the 1970s, virtually all supermarket operators became engaged in similar price-cutting programmes, which did little to establish their identity or to maximize their return on investment. More recently, many retailers have spent millions of pounds on design refits, often doing little more than imitating those of more successful and innovatory competitors. While pricing and design can be very powerful strategic weapons, they are no substitutes for a strategic plan. From a review of the state of strategic planning in retailing, Gilligan and Sutton (1987) observed: 'much retail management has been reactive and dedicated more to crisis firefighting than to long-term analysis and planning'.

So what should be the scope of strategic planning in a retail organization? Johnson (1987) suggested a number of areas with which strategy should be concerned:

1. The scope of an organization's activities
2. Matching an organization's activities to its business environment
3. Matching the activities of a business to its resource capability
4. Usually, the major allocation or reallocation of resources
5. The long-term direction of the business

Consequently, strategic decisions are likely to have implications throughout the organization and to be complex in nature. For this reason, strategic planning must occur at the highest management level. Pennington (1985) notes that strategic planning is the only function among the chief executive's responsibilities that cannot be delegated. In many retail companies strategic planning groups have been formed, but this should be an input into, not a substitute for, top-level planning. Without strong leadership, the planning and implementation can be greatly hampered by inter-functional rivalries, vested interests and lack of vision (e.g. Green 1987; Pennington 1985).

This chapter first examines some of the logical steps in formulating retail strategy. The retailer must take stock of its own strengths and weaknesses, and of the opportunities and threats within the competitive environment. A mission statement may be formulated, which is designed to crystallize and to communicate the company's strategic objectives. The concept of product strategy is a useful framework to help determine the markets within which, and the assortments with which, to compete. The retailer must also determine the overall approach to gaining or sustaining competitive advantage, possibly through differentiation, cost leadership and/or focus strategies.

Some major areas of decision-making are then considered in greater detail. First, the relative merits of specialization and diversification are examined—essentially, the choice between assortment depth and assortment width. Diversification or expansion strategies may also be pursued at the corporate level through acquisitions or mergers; some of the benefits and risks of this approach are assessed. Various types of collaborative arrangements may offer an alternative; these can take the form of partnership agreements, joint development programmes or concessionaires, usually termed 'shops within shops'. Finally, the chapter turns to the closely linked processes of targeting and positioning. Having established the segment(s) within which to compete, alternative approaches to positioning strategy are considered.

4.1   RETAIL STRATEGY FRAMEWORKS

Following the work of Ansoff (1965), there has been a great deal of development within the business strategy literature, notably the work of Porter (1980, 1985). Frameworks have been developed to assist in the strategic planning process, although only within relatively recent years have these been extensively applied to retailing (e.g. Knee and Walters 1985). Some of the concepts and frameworks that have emerged are presented within this section. First, the problems of defining corporate mission are considered; then the use of a strategic audit is illustrated. The concept of product market strategy is next explored and some applications to retailing are presented. Finally, alternative approaches to gaining competitive advantage are considered, based upon Porter's 'generic strategies' of cost leadership, differentiation or focus.

In that these concepts and frameworks played an important role in the development of strategic thinking within the 1980s, it is considered appropriate to summarize their main characteristics and their applications to retailing. They are not however intended as a substitute for management creativity and innovation (e.g. Wickstrom 1988). Rather, they should be seen as systematic approaches to the analysis of market opportunities, competitive conditions, company capabilities and alternative strategic actions.

4.1.1   Corporate mission and the strategic audit

Before a company can move to the stage of defining its strategic objectives in detail, it is essential to establish firmly the overall role or mission of the organization. Mason and Mayer (1987) defined the mission as 'what the firm plans to accomplish in the markets in which it will compete for the customers it wants to serve'.

The components of a mission statement are likely to include overall aspirations for sales growth, market share, net profit, return on investment and/or cash flow (Rosenbloom 1980). Although mission statements tend to be concerned mostly with economic aspects, increasing numbers of companies are including social or moral elements, in terms of service either to the customers or to the wider community. Marks & Spencer have backed up this type of commitment with a range of community projects, and several firms are now engaged in various forms of sponsorships (see Chapter 13). Some companies are very guarded about revealing their corporate mission, whereas others use it to inspire confidence, create shared values, and generate goodwill. For example, the large and diversified Dayton Hudson corporation in the USA expresses its commitment to the four 'constituencies' that it sees as essential to the success of its business:

1. customers, by serving as their purchasing agent;
2. employees, by providing jobs and contributing to their personal and professional development;
3. shareholders, by providing an attractive return on their investment;
4. communities, by contributing to their health and vitality an amount equal to 5% of the company's federally taxable income for worthwhile community projects. (Macke 1983)

In the UK, the J. Sainsbury company has long extolled its commitment to the concept of excellence, a corporate value which it also instils into a fifth 'constituency', the many producers of its large own-brand range.

The definition of corporate mission requires finding answers to some very basic but none the less difficult questions, such as:

- Where are we?
- How did we get here?
- Where could we be?
- Where should we be?
- How would we get there?

These questions require the consideration of a range of complex factors, some of which can be evaluated only in a qualitative way (Piercy 1983):

- The history of the company
- The preference of managers and owners
- Who the company is and what the customer values
- What the firm is good at
- The changing competitive environment
- The market potential

Even the first of the questions above requires a careful definition of the business within which the company operates, which may be less obvious than it first appears. As an example, Piercy (1983) suggested a progression of possible business definitions for a retailer operating garden centres:

1. Horticulture—selling plants and related products
2. Providing a comprehensive gardening service
3. Making gardening easier
4. Filling people's disposable time
5. Entertainment/leisure
6. Fulfilling people's dreams

Each of these possible business definitions says something different about the consumer needs that may be satisfied by the garden centre. More importantly, they help to avoid the classic pitfalls of 'marketing myopia' (Levitt 1960) and also to provide alternative insights into where the company could be. In his analysis of strategies in American retailing, Savitt (1987) referred to an emerging 'production orientation', whereby retailers produce a far more complete and integrated product/service offering, to become in effect a part of their customers' consumption system. Thus, a supplier of hardware products offering some advice could progress to become an integral part of the consumer's home maintenance operation. This could include not only the supplying of the required products but also a full range of gardening and household repair/ maintenance services. This involves moving away from a perception of being a store supplying merchandise, with a few additional services, to being a complete system for satisfying the particular set of customer needs.

Having defined the fundamental purpose of the company, a form of strategic audit may assist in formulating specific objectives and plans. One approach to this is 'SWOT' analysis, which involves producing a systematic evaluation of the company's strengths and weaknesses, plus the opportunities and threats within the competitive environment. Table 4.1 illustrates some of the items that should be appraised, although this list is designed to be illustrative, not exhaustive. The most relevant external issues, generally representing the opportunities or threats, were discussed in the preceding chapters. The internal aspects of the company, upon which the evaluation of strengths and weaknesses is mainly based, are considered in the chapters that follow.

Although in essence a very simple concept, SWOT analysis or a similar approach to a strategic audit can be developed to a high degree of sophistication, involving an extensive network of internal and external information systems. While some attributes can be quantified to a reasonable degree of precision, others require essentially qualitative judgements. Another problem in appraising strengths and weaknesses is to maintain the necessary objectivity in evaluating the company's capabilities, aspects that are sometimes ignored in the pursuit of opportunistic ventures (e.g. Mintzberg and Waters 1982). Some of the attempts by UK grocery chains to diversify into wider ranges of non-foods, for example, were defeated largely by a lack of buying and marketing capability in those areas. A framework similar to that used for assessing the company's strengths and weaknesses can also be usefully applied to the assessment of competitors' capabilities (Porter 1980).

4.1.2 Product-market strategy

One way of viewing strategic options is in terms of a product–mission matrix, advocated by Ansoff (1965). No firm can afford to stand still for long in terms of product and/or market development, given competitive pressures and ever shortening product and retail life-cycles (see Chapter 2). This being the case, a company must constantly evaluate opportunities for expansion or diversification if it wishes to progress, or even simply to avert decline. Ansoff referred to the 'sales gap' (or 'planning gap'), which represents the increasing difference between what is likely to be achieved without significant strategic actions and what could be achieved through expansion and/or diversification.

Figure 4.1 represents Ansoff's original product–mission matrix, which has been very widely quoted and revised within the strategic planning literature. Ansoff (1965) defined strategic change as a realignment of the firm's product-market environment, which does not necessarily involve diversification. The alternatives include various forms of expansion, i.e. market penetration, market development and/or product development. The matrix illustrates the main 'growth vectors' available to a company, expressed in the most general of terms. These major alternative directions for growth will be considered in greater detail in Section 4.2.

An adaptation of Ansoff's matrix to strategic planning in retailing is shown in Figure 4.2. Here the assortment is substituted for the product dimension, given that most retailers are concerned

Table 4.1 Typical components of a strategic audit

Components	Examples of issues
STRENGTHS/WEAKNESSES	(Internal)
Stores	Size profile
	Locations
	Design characteristics
	Development potential
Buying	Buying power
	Product sector experience
	Breadth of buying expertise
	Outside agents and networks
Product range	Width of range
	Depth of assortment
	Distinctive/innovatory products
	Own-brand penetration
Management	Skills and expertise
	Leadership and vision
	Organization structure
	Cohesiveness of organization
Marketing	Advertising effectiveness
	Pricing policies
	Merchandising skills
	Customer service levels
	Marketing research
Personnel	Numbers and age structure
	Union strength
	Skill levels
	Training resources
Systems	Order/payment systems
	POS information
	Reporting/communication
	Returns/complaints procedures
	Financial accounting
Distribution	Warehouse location/capacity/type
	Transportation systems
	Goods receiving facilities
	Third-party contracts
Finance	Cost structures
	Gross/net margins
	Return on investment
	Working capital
	Total assets

Table 4.1   (*cont.*)

OPPORTUNITIES/THREATS	(External)
Economic changes	Unemployment levels
	Distribution of wealth
	Interest rates
	Disposable incomes
Social changes	Ageing population
	More, smaller households
	Two-career families
	Changing life-styles
Consumer changes	Different needs and wants
	Beliefs and attitudes
	Perceptions (images) of company
	Loyalty and patronage patterns
Suppliers	Bargaining power
	Production capacity
	Reliability
	R & D capability
Market structure	Relative market shares
	Leader/follower roles
	Oligopoly/monopolistic competition
	Mergers and acquisitions
Competitors	Existing/new competition
	Direct/indirect competition
	Strengths and weaknesses of competitors
	Competitor strategies
	Likely competitor reactions
Legislation	Competition policy
	Restrictions on trading hours/days
	Bargain offer regulations
	Land use policy
	Credit restrictions

with very large numbers of product assortment decisions. The mission (or market) dimension is expressed in terms of old or new segments, which draws attention to the fact that market expansion opportunities for a retailer may well exist within the existing general markets. Kristenson (1983) forms a further useful distinction between geographic segments and those based upon other criteria. Clearly, the retail strategies required to develop new geographic markets are somewhat distinct from those required to capture new segments within existing trading areas. Figure 4.2 retains an essential feature of Ansoff's original matrix; as one moves from the upper left corner towards the lower right corner, the alternatives involve increased risk because of diminishing knowledge of circumstances and prospects.

The general strategic framework has been subject to extensive development and elaboration. For example, Omura (1986) presented the 20-cell matrix illustrated in Figure 4.3. Within both the major dimensions, further distinctions are drawn. Rather than just two categories of market, mission or segment, four are suggested; these are based upon a sub-matrix of markets and needs,

Mission Product	Present	New
Present	Expansion (market penetration)	Expansion (product development)
New	Expansion (market development)	Diversification

Figure 4.1   Ansoff's product–mission matrix
Source: Ansoff (1988, p. 128).

Segments Assortment	Existing assortment	New assortment
Existing segments	Increased share of market	Expansion, product development
New segments	Expansion, market development	Diversification

Figure 4.2   An assortment–market segment matrix
Source: derived from Kristenson (1983, p. 47).

present and different. The previous chapter has emphasized the importance of trying to identify the precise needs, not just the general market or segment, that the retail offering is designed to satisfy. The lowest level of risk is normally incurred when focusing upon the present needs of the present market segment(s); the highest is incurred when attempting to satisfy different needs within different markets. Between these two extremes there are the options of addressing more or different needs of the present market, or of concentrating upon the same needs but in different markets.

On the other dimension, Omura distinguished between changes in the merchandising mix and in the service package associated with it. Moving from the present merchandise mix, the first suggested alternative is to alter the 'delivery' of this mix. For example, a store-based retailer may decide to offer some or all of its merchandise through a mail order catalogue or through teleshopping. This may better cater for the convenience needs of existing customers and/or may permit extension into a new market. Conversely, a catalogue retailer, such as Argos, develops superstores to cater for the need to browse or to attract purchasers who wish to see and handle products before purchase.

Market/needs	Present merchandise mix	Alter delivery of present merchandise mix	New merchandise with related service requirements		New merchandise with unrelated service requirements
			Assortment manipulation	Merchandise line extension	
Present market Present needs	(1)	(2)	(3)	(4)	(5)
Present market Different needs	(6)	(7)	(8)	(9)	(10)
Different market Present needs	(11)	(12)	(13)	(14)	(15)
Different market Different needs	(16)	(17)	(18)	(19)	(20)

Figure 4.3 Product–market strategy alternatives
Source: Omura (1986, p. 26).

Alternatives to the merchandise mix within the existing service format can take many different forms, but two general categories are suggested. The assortment may be manipulated to establish more strength and depth in growing or more profitable product areas, while phasing out less profitable lines or categories. Many department stores, facing a loss of trade to the carpet specialists, phased their carpet departments down or completely out, devoting more selling space to high-margin cosmetics or fashion goods. The recent strategic moves of Woolworths included an extreme version of assortment manipulation, with a decision to concentrate just upon the key areas of opportunity and trading strength. Alternatively, a company may decide to extend into new merchandise lines, such as the rapid diversifications of Next or the more gradual range development of Marks & Spencer.

The highest risk is naturally associated with new merchandise sold with service requirements unrelated to those of existing merchandise. One fairly extreme example was the move of food retailer Asda into selling cars, which has since been abandoned. This type of alternative is the most difficult to achieve through the internal development of the retailer's capabilities. A more rapid route may be found through acquisitions or partnership arrangements, drawing upon the merchandise and service experience/capability of another company. With more extreme forms of product/service diversification, however, there is a danger that the 'common thread', the relationship between the present and future directions of the firm, may be lost or non-existent. Instances of acquisition and partnership arrangements will be considered in Section 4.2.

4.1.3 Competitive advantage and differentiation

The frameworks presented so far are helpful in assessing where to compete, in terms of the target markets or segments and in terms of the assortments appropriate to them. Further insights into the question of how best to compete can be derived from the concepts of competitive advantage and differentiation, and from the frameworks that have evolved around these concepts.

Porter (1985) observed that 'sustainable competitive advantage' is the key to long-term

Competitive advantage

	Lower cost	Differentiation	
Competitive scope	1. Cost leadership	2. Differentiation	Broad target
	3(a) Cost focus	3(b) Differentiation focus	Narrow focus

Figure 4.4   The generic strategies
Source: Reprinted with permission of The Free Press, a division of Macmillan Inc. from *Competitive advantage: creating and sustaining superior performance* by Michael E. Porter. Copyright © 1985 by Michael E. Porter.

above-average performance. Although a company may have numerous specific strengths and weaknesses compared with its competitors, he maintained that there are in essence two basic types of competitive advantage: low cost and differentiation. Placing these on a matrix with the competitive scope of the firm produces Porter's three 'generic strategies':

1. Overall cost leadership
2. Differentiation
3. Focus

The third of these may be subdivided into cost focus and differentiation focus. This basic framework is illustrated in Figure 4.4.

In developing the concept of the generic strategies, Porter (1980) specified some of the skills, resources and organizational requirements commonly associated with each. Although presented initially in relation to manufacturing industries, these have been adopted and applied to the retailing industry. The overall cost leadership position is typically associated with sustained investment and access to capital, intense supervision of labour, low-cost distribution and tight control systems. In the case of retailing, the required attributes would also be likely to include strong buying, merchandising expertise and highly efficient store management systems. This 'productivity-led' form of competitive advantage may be translated into strict range control and a price leadership position. Competitive advantage through differentiation is likely to be associated with strong marketing abilities, creative flair and a good reputation for quality and/or innovation. In retailing, this may translate into particular advantages in terms of product range, locations, store design/ambiance, services and/or promotion. A focus strategy is likely to involve some of the cost leadership or differentiation attributes, but directed at a particular target market segment. Approaches to target marketing are considered in Section 4.3.

The strategic approach of differentiation in retailing received early attention from Davidson and Doody (1966), who defined it as 'an attempt on the part of the retailer to adapt his offer to the differences that exist in the needs and wants of consumers'.

The concept of the 'value chain' is helpful in assessing potential sources of differentiation. Porter (1985) held that:

every firm is a collection of activities that are performed to design, produce, market, deliver and support its product.

An analysis of the value chain, rather than value added, is the appropriate way to examine competitive advantage.

There have been a number of adaptations of the value chain concept to the retailing context.

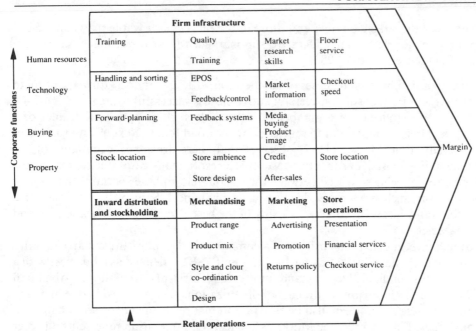

Figure 4.5 The value chain—possible sources of differentiation
Source: 'Retailer strategies in the UK' by J. McGee in G. Johnson (ed.), *Business Strategy and Retailing*, Copyright © 1987 John Wiley & Sons Ltd. Reprinted by permission of John Wiley & Sons Ltd.

Figure 4.5 presents a matrix comprising operational elements and the major corporate functions. Each of the many elements of the value chain can serve to increase value, real or perceived, and therefore can contribute to differentiation. A particular merit of the value chain concept is in helping to highlight the specific components of differentiation, their relative contributions to the process and their relative costs. It also emphasizes that the elements must not be in conflict but must combine to produce effective differentiation.

Porter maintained that a company must usually decide between the alternative generic strategies; otherwise it is likely to become 'stuck in the middle'. Few companies are able profitably to pursue more than one of these strategies within the same division or business unit. The costs associated with effective differentiation usually shift the business to a relatively high-cost position *vis-à-vis* the competition.

There are naturally some potential risks associated with long-term adhesion to one of the generic strategies (Porter 1980). A cost leadership position can be lost, for example, if inflation, competitors' innovations or technological change reduce the cost advantage. A cost emphasis may also make the company less sensitive to required changes in the assortment or the marketing approach. In contrast, the main risks associated with a differentiation strategy may be summarized as follows:

1. The need for the differentiating factor(s) may diminish.
2. The price differential *vis-à-vis* low-cost competitors could become too great to retain customer loyalty.
3. Imitation, real or superficial, tends to reduce perceptions of differentials over time.

Focus strategies too have their potential risks:

1. The relative costs of the focuser may increase and offset the cost advantages or differentiation achieved.

2. The requirements of the strategic target and those of the market as a whole may converge.
3. Competitors may invade particularly lucrative sub-markets within the strategic target, i.e. may 'outfocus the focuser' (Porter 1980).

   This framework greatly simplifies the bases of competition, although it does draw attention to the fundamental characteristics of some successful and some less successful strategies. Figure 4.6 classified the competitive strategies of a number of UK retailers within this basic framework. Harrods is seen as a classic example of differentiation with broad focus, Next as an example of narrow-focus differentiation. McGee (1987) observes that there are many occupants of the central position, including most department and variety stores. In many cases this represents the uncomfortable position of being squeezed between the discounters and the speciality stores. For market leaders, however, such as Marks & Spencer in clothing and J. Sainsbury in grocery, this central position illustrates success in combining many of the best elements of cost leadership and differentiation strategies.

   It is important to appreciate that the position of a company on the competitive map can differ considerably between each individual 'strategic business unit' (SBU), defined as a business with a 'clear market focus, an identifiable strategy and an identifiable set of competitors' (Abell and Hammond 1979). While this is obvious in the case of organizations such as Ward White or Sears, with quite distinct business units, it can also be true of different departments or sections within certain retail companies. For example, the Marks & Spencer food operation represents a higher level of differentiation and a far more narrow focus than the company's clothing operation. It should also be recognized that strategic positions shift over time, both as a result of strategic moves and as a result of cyclical tendencies. For discussions of the relationships between Porter's framework and some of the theories of retail change, see Omura (1986) or Brown (1988).

4.2 MAJOR STRATEGIC ALTERNATIVES

Having examined some of the frameworks available to assist in the formulation of retail marketing strategies, we will now turn our attention to some of the ways in which these strategies may be implemented. The concept of product market strategy suggests various directions in which the company may consider moving in order to increase or sustain growth. Some of these 'growth vectors' involve the development or diversification of the product assortment, whereas others involve concentration upon the existing assortment. These most fundamental of assortment decisions are the main theme of this section; the more specific tasks of selecting and buying the assortment are considered in Chapter 7.

   Attention is first given to the overall decision between increased diversification and greater specialization. The alternatives in essence are to provide consumers with choice in breadth or in depth, unless the retailer is in the unusual position of being able to offer both. Of course, retailers are not limited to internal expansion or diversification; acquisitions and mergers have played a significant part in helping some companies to accomplish these objectives. Finally, various collaborative arrangements are considered, including partnership companies, joint development agreements and concessions.

4.2.1 Diversification or specialization

The 'retail accordion theory' suggests that the pattern of retail evolution has tended to alternate between domination by wide-assortment retailers and domination by narrow-line, specialized retailers (Hower 1943; Hollander 1966). This wide–narrow–wide pattern gave the theory its

Lower cost   Differentiation

Broad target	Comet Debenhams BHS M & S	Harrods
Narrow target	Our Price Independent grocer	Burtons Next

Figure 4.6 Examples of generic strategies
Source: Retailer strategies in the UK by J. McGee in G. Johnson (ed.), *Business Strategy and Retailing*, Copyright © 1987 John Wiley & Sons Ltd. Reprinted by permission of John Wiley & Sons Ltd.

name. Most support has been given to this theory by the pattern of evolution of retailing in the USA. In early settlements the general store stocked a very diverse range, but as settlements grew and developed, so did more specialized stores. Department stores subsequently emerged, offering wide assortments, but these then lost ground to more specialized chains. From the 1950s, many of the specialists started to proliferate their product ranges, notably the supermarkets and drug stores. The term 'scrambled merchandising' described the practice of selling product lines not traditional in the type of outlet. This form of merchandising sought to satisfy the demand for one-stop shopping. More recently, as consumers have become more demanding of choice, some of the more specialist stores have proved best able to meet the demand for choice in depth.

The retail accordion certainly should not be viewed as a predictive tool or a precise explanatory model (Rosenbloom 1981). It does however draw attention to this curious facet of retail evolution, and also serves to emphasize that both diversification and specialization strategies have succeeded under certain sets of circumstances. As major assortment decisions become part of more positively defined product–market strategies, it will become increasingly difficult to identify clearly which phase of the retail accordion applies. During the 1980s we saw many retailers moving towards diversification and many other examples of greater specialization. In both cases it is possible to identify successful and unsuccessful examples.

It is possible to classify at least three forms of specialization (Poynor 1986):

1. Narrow product range–narrow target market, for example Tie Rack
2. Narrow product range–broad target market, for example Virgin Records
3. Broad product range–narrow target markets, for example Harvey Nichols

In other words, the form of specialization, or concentration, can relate to the product range and/or the target market. Many successful examples of deep specialization can be observed. In New York City, Barney's has developed one of the world's largest men's stores, offering a vast variety of suits and other menswear and attracting customers from a very wide catchment area (Rosenbloom 1976). In Willowbrook, New Jersey, Fortunoffs has a store with 125,000 sq. ft of trading area, specializing in housewares and domestic items (Gattorna 1985). Once attracted to the store, it is most unlikely that the consumer's needs would not be satisfied within these product categories. On a smaller scale, the Poster Shop in the UK has specialized intensively, not even selling calendars or postcards (Market Place 1986a). A range of over 1,500 posters is offered, along with a profitable poster framing service. Extolling the virtues of speciality stores and centres, Milligan (1987) observed:

Throughout the world people are seeking to counteract the uniformity of supermarkets and shopping malls with the vitality and organised chaos of the bazaar.

After a period in which retail growth has been led by the big variety stores and multiple chains, we are seeing the emergence of a new breed of specialist retailer catering to very particular styles and interest, or concentrating on a narrow range of goods.

The variety stores have not always pursued greater diversification. Recounting the history of Marks & Spencer, Turner (1971) observed that the company sold toys, music and records, jewellery, books and sports equipment in the 1920s. By the early 1930s, over 70 per cent of the product range had been dropped.

Simon Marks had decided that it was foolish to try to serve the whole market, and sought instead to make a unique contribution in his chosen fields of clothing and food.

In contrast, Woolworth continued to support a very diverse product range, until relatively recently. Ironically, Marks & Spencer is now diversifying, for example into ranges of furniture (Retail 1987c). Woolworth, on the other hand, has become increasingly specialized with its 'Operation Focus'. This reduced the number of merchandise departments from 62 to 6, the number of lines from 50,000 to 20,000, and the number of suppliers from 8,000 to around 1,000 (Brown 1988). In Woolworths case, specialization was one of the few options that would enable the variety store chain to survive. Marks & Spencer, on the other hand, had achieved a dominant position within their traditional product categories; diversification, along with internationalization (see Chapter 2), was therefore one of few available options for growth.

The grocery sector has also illustrated somewhat varied strategies with regard to specialization or diversification. The late 1970s saw a general movement towards greater diversification, with the development of superstores. Virtually all the multiples' stores in excess of 25,000 sq. ft sold clothing, electrical tools and garden sundries; 73 per cent also sold footwear and 38 per cent sold furniture (Beaumont 1980). Although the movement towards larger outlets has continued, many of the chains have chosen to specialize increasingly upon their core area of food. Morrison's have reduced their clothing ranges to frequently purchased items, while devoting more space to specialist food sections. Safeway too has limited its non-food merchandise to rapid-turnover items and concentrated upon the development of health foods, salad bars, etc. Tesco has dropped many non-food ranges and is emphasizing fresh foods; 10 per cent of space in a new 60,000 sq. ft store at Brookfield was given to a fresh produce 'market' (Retail 1988a).

Asda too has been developing its fresh food sections but has also maintained a more diverse range of non-foods. Within a typical Asda superstore of around 40,000 sq. ft, around 40 per cent of the space is usually devoted to non-grocery items. One of Asda's most dramatic, and well publicized, diversifications was to start selling cars through franchised 'Asdadrive' outlets at a few of their superstores (Retail & Distribution Management 1986). Within a year, however, the company decided to withdraw from this venture:

when you realise your managers' energies are being diverted from the hardcore of the business, what else can you do but bite the bullet? (Super Marketing 1987)

Other fundamental diversifications include the retailing of financial services (Bendall and Hayes 1987) by many major retailers, including Marks & Spencer. These developments are further considered in Chapter 12.

The examples outlined above will have illustrated that there are no simple rules to guide strategic decisions regarding the width, or the depth, of the product assortment. Clearly, a retailer must consider a range of environmental, market and internal factors when evaluating a diversification opportunity (Omura 1986). Some of the diversifications that may be deemed to have 'failed' do have certain characteristics in common, including some or all of the following:

1. The image of the retailer was not compatible with the new product range(s), in terms of status or the reduction of perceived risks.
2. The buyer behaviour associated with the purchase of the new ranges was significantly different from that associated with the traditional ranges, in terms of shopping frequency, pre-purchase search behaviour, group decision-making, etc.
3. Economies of scale in buying, distribution and marketing did not carry over into the new ranges.
4. The depth of the new ranges could not compete with those of specialist retailers.

The unsuccessful ventures into the sale of 'white goods' (washing machines, refrigerators, etc.) by some grocery superstore operators met with all these problems. Hirschman and Wallendorf (1982) also noted a 'cultural continuum', which restricts retailers of 'high-culture' items from entering 'popular-culture' markets, and vice versa. The introduction of a small range of lead crystal glassware into a discount furniture warehouse provides a recent illustration of this problem.

An approach to overcoming some of these problems of product and/or market incompatibility is to develop, or acquire, separate business units. The attractiveness of the retail market under consideration must first be evaluated most carefully, and a number of frameworks must exist to assist in this task (e.g. Finn 1987). The option of acquisition is considered in the following section. One recent example of an internally developed, separate chain is Childrens World, by Boots (Retail 1987d). Tweddell (1986) terms this process 'intrapreneurialism', and commented that:

Despite the difficulties, I believe that the rewards for 'intrapreneurialism' are often greater than those gained by going down the acquisition route, but it does impose tough disciplines on the mother company.

4.2.2 Acquisitions or mergers

Probably the most rapid route towards diversification at the corporate level is that of acquisition or merger. In Chapter 2 it was noted that the UK retailing sector experienced a vast volume of acquisition and merger activity during the 1980s. Much of this activity, however, was motivated more by the desire to achieve rapid expansion, increased market share and greater economies of scale within existing or related product-markets. It is appropriate at this stage to look at the options of acquisition or merger and to assess some of the strategic goals that can be accomplished by such means.

As a means to diversify, acquisition is not without considerable risks. Porter (1987) studied the diversification records of 33 prestigious companies in the USA and found that most had divested themselves of many more acquisitions than they had retained. He presented some explanations for why so many corporate diversification strategies fail:

1. It is the individual *business units* that compete, not the diversified company. The strategy will therefore fail unless the success of each unit is carefully nurtured.
2. Diversification adds *costs* and *constraints* to the business units. These costs may include the corporate overhead and many more hidden costs/constraints, such as the need to comply with corporate planning, control or personnel systems/policies.
3. *Shareholders* can diversify themselves, adapting their portfolios to their own preferences. In

Table 4.2 Examples of major acquisitions and mergers

Bidder	Company acquired	Date	Value (£m)
British Home Stores/Habitat	Mothercare (merger)	1985	1,520*
Dee Corporation	Fine Fare	1986	686
Argyll	Safeway	1987	681
Asda	MFI	1985	570
Burton	Debenhams	1985	566
Paternoster	Woolworth's	1982	310
Next	Grattan	1986	300
Dixons	Currys	1984	248
Dee Corporation	International	1984	180
Woolworths	Comet	1984	177
Ratners	H. Samuel	1986	150
Harris Queensway	Times Furnishing, Home Charm	1986	146
Habitat/Mothercare	(merger)	1981	118*
Sears	Foster Brothers	1985	115
Argyll	Allied Suppliers	1982	101
Ward White	Payless	1986	94
Ward White	Halfords	1984	52
Ward White	Owen Owen	1985	51

Combined value of the merged company.
Source: derived from Euromonitor (1987a. pp. 272–4).

that they can buy shares at the market price, they can often diversify more cheaply than the corporation, which typically incurs a sizeable acquisition premium.

Given these basic premises, Porter (1987) concluded that corporate diversification strategies can succeed only if they truly add value. This added value must be sufficient to offset the costs and constraints, and it must offer to shareholders diversification benefits that they could not achieve themselves. Most of the companies studied by Porter had diversified between industries, which inevitably involves higher risk than acquisitions within the same industry. The question remains whether it is appropriate, in operational terms, to regard such disparate activities as food retailing, furniture retailing and car retailing as being parts of the same industry.

The spate of retail takeovers in the 1980s has been attributed in many cases to a recession following a period of high inflation. The inflation of the 1970s masked the inefficiencies of many retailers, which could easily pass on their higher costs in the form of price rises. The combination of a recession and reduced inflation left such companies in a weak position and vulnerable to take-over. This coincided with a rapid growth of interest in the retail sector within the stock market (Euromonitor 1987a). A new breed of high-profile retailing entrepreneurs had also emerged, such as Ralph Halpern at Burton, Alec Monk at Dee Corporation and Terence Conran at Storehouse. Their highly rated shares and confidence in their business formulae left them well placed to acquire the less efficiently run and undervalued companies.

Table 4.2 shows some of the major acquisitions and mergers within the UK retailing industry between 1980 and 1987. A number of different strategic objectives have been illustrated, including the following:

Diversification/defensive   The acquisition of MFI by Asda was largely a response to the latter's concern about the predicted saturation of the grocery market with superstores (Cox 1987). The two companies had some attributes in common, notably large edge-of-town sites and an emphasis upon promotional price advertising. The performance of MFI following acquisition, however, was disappointing, and the Asda–MFI combination seemed to achieve very little (Shamoon 1986). In 1987 the decision was made to concentrate on the core business of grocery retailing, and Asda divested itself of MFI, at somewhat of a loss.

Since its acquisition from its US parent in 1982, Woolworths has vigorously diversified through acquisitions, notably the discount electrical retailer Comet, the DIY chain B&Q and the discount chemist Superdrug. In that most of the group's profits flowed from the acquired businesses, doubts continued to be expressed about the core variety store business. In 1986, a bid for the group by Dixons was narrowly defeated. Since that time, 'Operation Focus' has been launched to improve the performance of the variety stores.

Market share/economies of scale   Many acquisitions have been motivated more by the desire to expand than to diversify. For example, the acquisitions of International, Fine Fare and Carrefour by the Dee Corporation may be regarded more as new store openings than diversifications. Faced with trying to compete with chains of the stature of Tesco and J. Sainsbury, acquisition was the only route by which Dee could establish a nationwide grocery chain, with all the attendant economies of scale in buying, operations and marketing. Unlike the largely organically grown Tesco and J. Sainsbury, however, Dee has faced the additional costs of combining operations and of attempting to create a new image under the Gateway name.

The Argyll group has also grown by acquisition and has applied a 'profit enhancement programme' to the acquired businesses (Retail & Distribution Management 1987). The acquisition of the UK Safeway chain from its US parent was of particular interest in that Safeway enjoyed a considerably higher sales density and better image than Argyll. The larger Argyll (Presto) stores have been progressively integrated under the Safeway name (Retail 1987a), although it is yet to be seen whether Safeway's competitive advantage may be diluted by the application of some of Argyll's buying and control systems.

Synergy/skills transfer   In theory, most acquisitions/mergers are supposed to create synergy, i.e. to produce benefits over and above those that could have been produced by the business units operating independently. In reality, the synergistic benefits are often less than apparent. A notable exception was the merging of Habitat and Mothercare, forming the Storehouse group. According to Knee and Walters (1985):

If Habitat's competitive advantage was based upon design and marketing skills, then Mothercare's was the cost-effective operations organisation based upon a revolutionary computerised stock control system.

Each of the two partners in this merger was therefore able to contribute skills to assist the other in overcoming a major area of weakness.

Alternative channel development   In Chapter 2 we observed that retailing can comprise different channels of distribution to the end users, including convenience stores, superstores, catalogue stores, mail order and teleshopping. The acquisition of the Grattan mail order business by Next preceded the launch of the 'Next Directory', generally seen as a new and stylish approach to mail order retailing. This fuelled speculation that other major retailers might buy their way into alternative channels, although the initial profit performance of Next Directory was not encouraging. If the demand for non-store retailing grows, this could become a more common strategic objective for acquisition.

It is therefore inappropriate to regard acquisitions/mergers as single strategy alternatives; rather, they should be seen as possible ways of pursuing various strategic objectives. It is also clear that many acquisitions have failed to comply with one or more of the basic premises suggested by Porter (1987) and discussed earlier. It is certainly worth noting that the retail acquisitions phase in the UK contrasted somewhat with the sell-offs in the USA (Retail 1987b). Although there are many reasons for this contrast, the failure of many acquisitions/mergers is one of them. It has also been noted that some of the most successful retailers, such as J. Sainsbury and Marks & Spencer, have developed in the UK mainly by organic growth (e.g. Cox 1987).

4.2.3 Partnerships or concessions

The preceding sections have illustrated that either diversification strategies or acquisitions can bring problems and risks, especially when the latter is used as a route to enter new product-markets. Yet many major retailers are meeting a growing consumer demand for choice in depth, requiring specialist assortments, while at the same time wishing to diversify and escape the constraints of their existing product-markets. The possible solutions to this dilemma include partnership arrangements, wherein two relatively specialist retailers agree to work together in some locations to provide both depth and width of assortment, while also hopefully creating a form of synergy in terms of joint attraction.

Two of the most notable partnership agreements have included J. Sainsbury, which otherwise has been the most consistent of the major grocery chains in its policy of specialization on its core area of food. Six SavaCentres, averaging 72,000 sq. ft were developed jointly with the British Home Stores variety chain (Euromonitor 1987a). This joint development enabled Sainsbury to gain merchandise knowledge, especially in textiles, quickly and relatively cheaply (Cox 1987). Since this agreement was formed, British Home Stores was merged into the Storehouse group, which in 1989 sold its 50 per cent stake in SavaCentres to J. Sainsbury. The end of this partnership was attributed largely to moves by Storehouse to eliminate debts and defend against possible hostile acquisition bids. In selling its stake to Sainsbury, it was agreed that British Home Stores would continue as the main suppliers of clothing, textiles and lighting to SavaCentre for at least five-and-a-half more years. Another Sainsbury subsidiary, Homebase (home improvement and garden centres), also found its origins in a joint agreement, this time with the Belgian retailer Gb-Inno-BM in 1979. By 1987, 34 Homebase stores had been developed to capture a share of the buoyant DIY, home and garden market.

Joint developments do not necessarily involve the development of a joint company. Marks & Spencer and Tesco signed a joint venture agreement to develop side by side in new edge/out-of-town centres. In this case it was felt that joint planning applications from two premier retailers would help to win sites in key locations (Cox 1987). There is rather more product range overlap between these two companies than between J. Sainsbury and British Home Stores, but Marks & Spencer have emphatically stated that they will be selling food in these locations (Poynor 1985). The first of these joint developments was the Brookfield Centre in Hertfordshire, although other prime sites are being vigorously pursued. At Brookfield it is notable that the partners compete, particularly in the areas of convenience foods, wines, toiletries, cosmetics and babycare items (Retail 1988b). Far from being a deficit, these areas of competition may contribute to the cumulative attraction of this type of joint development.

Another possible solution to the problems of offering specialization within diversity is to utilize concessionaires, often referred to as 'shops within shops'. According to the definition of Mintel (1985):

a shop within shop is taken to mean a space which a host retailer lets to another retailer, wholesaler or manufacturer so that the hirer of the space may sell goods under his own name.

The term 'leased departments' tends to be used for similar arrangements in the USA (e.g. *Davidson et al.* 1970). The terms 'concession' and 'shop within shop' are generally considered interchangeable, although the latter is often preferred when an established retailer, rather than a manufacturer, runs the shop within shop. In such cases, a range of products and brands is likely to be sold, rather than the single brand or range of the specific manufacturer.

A wide variety of agreements exist between concessions and host retailers, and payments for space usually take one of the following forms:

1. A percentage of the concessionaire's sales
2. As above, but with a minimum level of payment
3. A fixed rental for the space occupied
4. A fixed rental plus a percentage of sales
5. A rental proportional to the *host* retailer's sales

The first concession in the UK was probably a Jaegar ladies fashion concession opened in Selfridges in 1935 (Worthington 1984). By 1987 there were estimated to be 301 companies operating over 28,000 concession units in the UK (Mintel 1987). These ranged from relatively small units, such as the Edward Mann hat concessions, to major department concessions, such as Comet electricals in Debenhams department stores or Laura Ashley home furnishings within Homebase DIY superstores. Concessions have been especially prominent in the department store sector, accounting for around 20 per cent of sector sales (Euromonitor 1987b).

A large number of possible advantages and possible problems must be considered in evaluating the strategy of concessions. Table 4.3 summarizes these, from the viewpoint of the host retailer. Clearly, not all these issues apply in all cases, and neither does the order within the table signify relative importance. For a small host retailer, the main benefit of using a well-known concession may be its superior buying power and reputation. For a larger retailer, the use of concessions may be primarily to develop into new product areas, without incurring the usual risks and set-up costs. Usually a major advantage of concessions is the short-term nature of the agreement, which maintains pressure upon the concessions and gives the host retailer considerable flexibility.

The potential problems of the concessions strategy were illustrated in a number of cases in the 1980s. One of the most prolific users of concessions, Bourne's department store in London's Oxford Street, failed; most commentators attributed this failure to the blurred image and lower profit margins from using concessions. In its hostile bid for Debenhams, the Burton group was highly critical of the excessive use previously made of concessions:

the company had forgotten retailing, becoming instead landlords and credit card operators dependent on the retailing skills of others.

we will end, however, Debenham's hotch potch of shops-in-shops with conflicting marketing images and confusion merchandising and floor layouts. (Mintel 1985)

Table 4.3 Possible advantages and problems of using concessions

Possible advantages

Flexibility through short-term contracts
Use of specialist expertise in buying and merchandising
Ability to learn from concession's expertise
Provide specialization with diversity
Tactical response to life-style retailing by specialist multiples
Opportunities for clearer segmentation and positioning
Well-known names provide an attraction to the store
Add further interest and excitement to the store
Benefits from concession's advertising and promotion
Lower prices through greater buying power or vertical integration
Superior quality of displays and promotions
Better-quality staff
Additional staff motivation through rivalry
Constant pressure upon concession to perform
Reduction in staff wage and training costs to retailer
Reduction in fixture and fittings costs to retailer
Reduced risk of unsold stock
Guaranteed income for store
More productive use of excess or 'dead' space
Higher profit/sq. metre than own department

Possible problems

More difficult to establish/maintain coherent image for store
Excessive diversity of design formats in store
Bad concession can seriously damage reputation
Mismatch between concession merchandise and store
Increased confusion in store layout
May become a substitute for real innovation
Diversion of sales from own departments to concessions
Less control over stock levels and prices
Staff less/not loyal to store
Antagonism between concession and store staff
Increased administration for store management
Reduction in realized gross margin may lead to lower net profit

Source: McGoldrick (1989, pp. 287–310).

These harsh criticisms certainly have not signalled the end for concessions, but they have warned against using them simply as the easy solution to buying or merchandising problems. Concessions are now being used in a variety of retail settings, including superstores and other out-of-town outlets. Concessions providing services, such as hairdressing, eye care or financial services, are also expanding their operations in many sectors. For a partnership arrangement to be successful, the combination must provide a greater attraction than that achieved by the two companies operating separately. For a concession to be successfully used, it must provide a stronger attraction to the store and/or superior profitability than the host retailer could itself achieve in that product category.

4.3   TARGETING AND POSITIONING

In the previous chapter, many of the approaches to segmenting retail markets were discussed. Market segmentation can certainly assist in the understanding and satisfaction of consumer needs; it can also serve as a first step in the process of deciding upon the areas of the market in which to compete. It has long since been realized that very few retailers can, in reality, regard the whole market as 'their oyster'. Quoting from one retailer well over thirty years ago, Martineau (1958) stressed this aspect of retail marketing:

It is high time we retailers realised that we cannot be all things to all people. When we try to do that, we end up with no particular appeal for anybody. Each of us has his own individual niche in the market place. It is up to us to decide where we fit, who comprises our customer body, and then to fulfill, as completely and satisfactorily as possible, the expectations of our particular group and our logical market.

In this section, two key elements of retail strategy formulation are considered: first, ways of defining the target market(s) for which the company is to compete; second, strategies for positioning the retail offering to gain maximum competitive advantage within those markets.

4.3.1   Target marketing

An essential prerequisite for target marketing is an understanding of the needs of viable market segments (see Section 3.4). The selection of the most appropriate target segments should include the evaluation of a number of criteria (Mason and Mayer 1987), including:

1. Ability to meet the needs of the segment
2. Present size of the segment
3. Future growth potential
4. Strength of present and anticipated competition
5. Investment required
6. Profit potential

It is sometimes argued that stores with a necessarily broad appeal, notably supermarkets, need be less concerned with target marketing. Sharples (1986) quoted the marketing director of Fine Fare:

this almost certainly comes down to being all things to all [people]. As every consultant in this room knows, that's wrong. But as every shopkeeper in this room also knows, that's exactly what we do.

In that a major grocery store must usually attract at least a third of the food business within its geographical catchment area, this argument can be supported to an extent. It is not however true to suggest that the grocery chains do not have distinctive customer profiles, whether this be the outcome of careful target marketing or the outcome of ill-defined strategies in the past. Table 4.4 illustrates these profiles on just one dimension, social class. The contrasts between the profiles of Waitrose or Sainsbury and those of Gateway or Kwik Save are very clear (Verdict 1987). Some but not all of the differences arise because of different regional strengths; for example, Gateway is especially strong in the North East and Scotland, Waitrose in the prosperous South East. Differences also emerge from age-based profiles, for example the bias towards older shoppers at the Co-op and younger shoppers at Asda (e.g. Waters 1986).

Some clothing retailers have focused upon relatively narrow target markets in their quest for

Table 4.4   UK grocers' sales by class of customer, 1987 (%)

	A or B	C1, C2	D or E
Waitrose	35	45	20
Sainsbury	21	55	24
Tesco	19	54	27
Presto-Safeway	19	50	30
Asda	18	56	26
Gateway	15	54	33
Kwik Save	8	43	49
All	16	48	36
(Base = 7,805 adults)			

Source: Verdict (1987, p. 9).

Table 4.5   Sears group—target markets

Trading name	Outlets	Target age	Class
Fosters	320	24–40	C1, C2, D
Your Price	110	16 +	C2, D, E
Hornes	44	25–45	B, C
Esq	15	25–45	A, B, C1
Jargon	14	16–25	C1, C2
Zy	13	16–25	B, C
Bradleys	11	30 +	C, D, E
Millets	167	16 +	C, D, E
Dormie	24	25 +	A, B, C
Adams	120	0–8	C1, C2

Source: Retail (1987e, pp. 20–1).

competitive advantage. Table 4.5 shows the several trading names used at one stage by the diverse Sears group, with the target market in each case. These range from Jargon, with a high fashion emphasis, to Your Price, oriented towards the cost-conscious consumer. Millets sells very casual clothing and camping equipment to a fairly wide market, up-market Dormie specializes in the hire of evening wear, and Adams sells childrenswear (Retail 1987e).

The British Shoe Corporation, also part of the Sear group, has defined the target markets in its various divisions along the following lines:

Volume	—	Curtess
Family	—	Freeman, Hardy & Willis
		Trueform
Fashion	—	Dolcis
		Tiptoe
Quality	—	Saxone
		Manfield

In this case, the establishment of these targets represented a much needed departure from the uniformity and lack of clear positioning of the group's 3,500 footwear outlets.

The examples cited above are targets defined primarily in terms of age, social class and/or merchandise appeal. The technique of life-style segmentation has also been applied to the definition of target markets, producing the concept of 'life-style retailing'. This has been defined by Blackwell and Talarzyk (1983):

Life-style retailing may be explained as the policy of tailoring a retail offering closely to the life-styles of specific target-market segments.

A life-style retail organization is one that bases its strategy and operations on unique living patterns of its target customers rather than on demographics or merchandise strength.

Blackwell and Talarzyk contrasted life-style retailing with what they term 'supplier-style retailing', with its emphasis upon homogeneity in retail operations. An example of a highly successful life-style retailer in the USA is The Limited. This company described its life-style target in the following terms:

The Limited's target market is the 16 to 35 year old female. She is educated, affluent, gregarious, fashion-oriented, and more often than not, she is a working woman who lives in or near a major metropolitan area. The Limited is her favourite place to shop because of our fashion and quality.

Some British retailers have become increasingly conscious of the opportunities presented by life-style targeting. For example, Anita Roddick of the Body Shop describes her target as the 'new consumers', people in their twenties and thirties who are socially aware, caring and concerned about the environment (Ody 1987). Various major retail organizations have also used life-style criteria for more specifically focused outlets. For example, the target for Littlewood's Inside Story outlets have been described as 'younger people who would rather like designer sheets but can't really afford them' (Market Place 1986a). Most of the customers of Champion Sport, one of many examples of 'nichemanship' by the Burton group, were described by one commentator (Market Place 1986c) in the following terms:

the real volume in sportswear is to be found in selling to the poseurs. The tracksuits that never see the turf or track, the training shoes for those whose training is confined to the bar.

Some other retailers have fairly obvious target markets, based upon phases in the family life-cycle, rather than upon life-style as such. For example: 'Mothercare didn't invent babies—people have been having them for a long time—but the stores offered a new approach which, like all good ideas, seems obvious in retrospect' (Sharples 1984). Toys 'R' Us, a notable success in the USA, now operates in the UK, seeking to provide 'truly classless stores where all socio-economic groups feel equally at home' (Sharples 1986). These stores offer a vast choice, in terms of both depth and width, and offer parents a form of one-stop shopping for all their children's needs.

The above should not be taken to indicate that target marketing is free of pitfalls. The demise of the Now chain illustrated some of these. Now had been targeted at the 8- to 16-year-olds, who had received little attention from other specialist retailers. The failure of Now has been attributed to an insufficient recognition of buying needs and habits for children of that age. At this age children's clothes are bought almost exclusively by their parents, and merchandise uniformity, plus the exchange and refund policies of the major chains, are highly valued (Retail 1987e). Another analyst attributed some of the success of Next to the fact that it missed its target:

Narrowcasting can bring its own pitfalls. The genius of Next is that it missed its target market. No criticism here of its cohesive lifestyle product policy but a reference to the fact that Next reaches a far wider age range than was originally planned. (Poynor 1986)

Table 4.6 UK clothing shops' sales, by age of customer, 1987 (%)

	Age group	
Chain	15–44	45+
Burton/Collier	83	17
Dorothy Perkins	89	11
Mothercare	82	18
Next for Men	96	4
Next for Women	86	14
Top Man/Principles for Men	97	3
Top Shop/Principles/Evans	77	23
Wallis/Miss Selfridge	90	10
C & A	64	36
All	53	47
(Base = 7,805 adults)		

Source: Verdict (1987, p. 38).

A major problem in the implementation of target marketing has been the tendency of many retailers to pursue the same targets. Table 4.6 illustrates the general preoccupation of the specialist chains with the 15–44 age group. As noted by Verdict (1987), the whole point of target marketing is lost if everyone shoots at the same target. Stoddart (1987) asks:

Why do the vast majority segment only by demographics, and, worse still, why do so many focus on the same segment?

Retail (1985) referred to the 'infatuation' with the 25–44-year-old market and the neglect of the increasingly wealthy older markets. Those in the 45–64 age band often have higher disposable incomes, especially where children have ceased to be a financial burden, the mortgage is paid off or is negligible and, in some cases, both partners are working again. The retired will also become a larger and increasingly attractive segment as relatively high institutional and/or index-linked pensions progressively replace or supplement meagre state pensions. Until fairly recently, little research had been done to better understand this important 'grey market', although the situation is now changing. Lumpkin *et al.* (1985) set out to investigate the particular elements within the stores patronage decisions of these older shoppers; Tantiwong and Wilton (1985) identified specific segments within the elderly market. It is likely that these potential targets will receive considerably more research and retail management attention in the years to come.

4.3.2 Positioning strategies

Having selected and evaluated the most appropriate target market(s), the retailer is then faced with the task of positioning the retail mix to serve the target customers most effectively and profitably. The concept of positioning found its origins in product marketing:

Positioning is the place a product occupies in a given market, as perceived by the relevant group of customers; that group of customers is known as the target segment of the market. (Wind 1980)

The concept was popularized in the 1970s in a series of articles by Ries and Trout; they subsequently defined it in the following terms, which extended its scope of application:

Positioning starts with a product. A piece of merchandise, a service, a company, an institution or even a person.

But positioning is not what you do to a product. Positioning is what you do to the mind of the prospect. That is, you position the product in the mind of the prospect. (Ries and Trout 1982)

These definitions correctly emphasize the issue of perception in relation to positioning; no amount of manipulation of the retail mix will add up to effective positioning, unless it produces a coherent and favourable image within the minds of the target customers. It must be noted, however, that Ries and Trout were writing from the advertiser's perspective, therefore were primarily concerned with communication strategies. Effective positioning must embrace the total retail marketing effort if the results are to be credible and sustainable.

There have been many cases of retailers attempting to reposition simply by switching advertising messages; unless these messages are reinforced by customers' experiences within the store, the chances are that the retailer has just wasted a great deal of advertising expenditure. Walters (1988) stressed the functional elements that are essential to positioning:

The success of the positioning relies upon identifying not just the major strategy issues, but also the support areas that create the added value for the customer. It requires a clear definition of the functional strategies necessary to achieve marketing and financial objectives.

He depicts positioning as the cumulative effect of four main areas of functional strategy:

1. Merchandise strategy
2. Trading style/format strategy
3. Customer service strategy
4. Customer communications strategy

These functional areas have the potential of adding value, provided of course that the strategies are in accord with the needs and preferences of the target customers. This aspect of positioning was emphasized by Wortzel (1987):

strategic positioning involves providing unique value. The retailer must first identify a specific consumer segment and then gain a thorough understanding of it—including what kinds of goods these people want to buy, how they want to shop for them, and what augmented benefits and services they expect.

The importance of positioning to retailers has now been firmly established; it was described by King and Ring (1980) as 'the most critical strategic problem confronting the retailer'. The relationship between effective positioning and commercial performance has been observed, for example, in the UK menswear sector by Davies and Brooks (1989). Some of the most successful retail companies were identified by Cook and Doyle (1978) as 'premium positioned retailers', such as Marks & Spencer, and 'innovatory positioned retailers', such as DIY superstores. Positioning has also become important to shopping centres; as these proliferate, and as shoppers are increasingly faced with a choice of centres within easy travel distance, it is essential that centres create a distinctive appeal to their target market. As May (1981) observed, 'the positioning issue has moved to a higher level, from product to store to shopping complex'.

Retailers may encounter many different types of problem in their positioning; careful diagnostic research is required (e.g. Davies 1987), and some of the techniques are described in the following chapter. Kotler (1988) classifies three broad types of positioning problem, which can equally be applied to products or to retailers:

1. *Underpositioning*—when buyers see you as 'just another company'. The uniformity of food retailers' price-based advertising for many years actually contributed to underpositioning (see Chapter 10).
2. *Overpositioning*—when buyers perceive the company too narrowly, reducing the opportunities to develop into other products or market segments. Ring (1983) outlined the particular dilemma of some very exclusive, high-fashion appeal stores; to expand their markets they must broaden their appeal, yet in doing this they risk the loss of their valuable core of very high spenders.
3. *Confused positioning*—some department stores lack a coherent or consistent image, having tried to compete at various times on the basis of price, choice, service and fashion appeals. Even sure-footed Marks & Spencer encountered some image problems when it introduced noticeably higher-priced ranges towards the end of 1987. To some customers, this signalled a shift away from a good-value position; the company quickly took steps to remedy this perception. Some of the less well judged attempts at diversification by food retailers (see Section 4.2.1) also led to confused positioning. Knee and Walters (1985) emphasized the need for consistency in positioning and the need to find a 'common thread'.

Various writers have offered suggestions as to how retailers should select their positioning strategies. These often use the device of a 'positioning map', typically comprising two axes representing two important dimensions of product or market differences. Lucas and Gresham (1988) presented a map based upon the high service–low service and high price–low price dimensions. This produced four quadrants:

1. Low price–high service: a strategy leading to poor profit performance
2. High price–high service: a service-oriented retail strategy
3. Low price–low service: a price-oriented strategy
4. High price–low service: a poor value strategy

Examples can be formed of retailers who have entered or moved into each of these quadrants; clearly, only quadrants 2 and 3 offer viable areas of positioning, sustainable in the long term. Wortzel (1987) adopted a somewhat different approach in the positioning map depicted in Figure 4.7. Here a distinction was drawn between high and low gross margins and between functional and symbolic types of merchandise. The latter distinction was argued on the grounds that people use and shop for functional and symbolic goods in rather different ways. He concluded that three broad categories of positioning strategy are available to the retailer:

1. *Product differentiation*—which may be achieved through unusually broad or deep assortments, edited assortments or combinations, unique products or products not widely available elsewhere
2. *Service and personality augmentation*—for which many potential approaches exist, including locational convenience, transaction convenience, longer hours, personal service, credit, easy returns system, delivery, etc.
3. *Price leadership*—which might be established through low prices, good value pricing or 'leader line' pricing on key items (see Chapter 8)

The task of identifying the optimum positioning, or even of effectively depicting existing positioning, is far from simple because of the many dimensions potentially involved. Careful research of consumer perceptions and preferences is required to establish the dimensions most relevant to store choice and to the distinctions drawn between retailers. Berry and Barnes (1987) identified four dimensions which, used in various combinations, appear to offer favourable positioning opportunities:

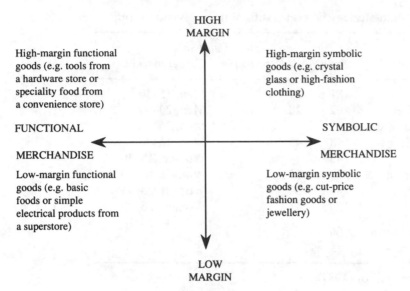

HIGH MARGIN

High-margin functional goods (e.g. tools from a hardware store or speciality food from a convenience store)

High-margin symbolic goods (e.g. crystal glass or high-fashion clothing)

FUNCTIONAL

SYMBOLIC

MERCHANDISE

MERCHANDISE

Low-margin functional goods (e.g. basic foods or simple electrical products from a superstore)

Low-margin symbolic goods (e.g. cut-price fashion goods or jewellery)

LOW MARGIN

Figure 4.7   A retail positioning map

Source: adapted from Wortzel (1987, pp. 45–56).

Reprinted with permission from: *The Journal of Business Strategy*. Volume 7, Issue 4, Copyright © 1987 Warren Gorham & Lamont, Inc. 210 South Street, Boston, MA 02111. All Rights Reserved.

1. *Value retailing*—such as furniture or DIY warehouses or discount stores
2. *Time-efficient retailing*—such as wide-range, fast-service food stores or catalogue showrooms, each of which seeks to cater for the 'time-poor' consumer, or the consumer who simply prefers to shop with ease
3. *High-contact retailing*—such as department stores or speciality stores offering a high level of personal service to advise, personalize, serve and encourage loyalty
4. *Sensory retailing*—designed to make the shopping experience more exciting and more of an enjoyable/stimulating event, usually through the intensive use of 'atmospherics' (see Chapter 11)

In their attempts to avoid the dangers of under- or confused positioning, some retailers have established separate business units, positioned to cater for different target groups. Ralph Halpern, chairman of the Burton group, described this approach as 'multi-strategy market positioning' (McFadyen 1983). The case of the Sears group has already been discussed in the previous section (see Table 4.5), and Table 4.7 shows the different trading names and outlets within the Burton group (Euromonitor 1987b). Figure 4.8 illustrates the positioning objectives of seven trading names within the British Shoe Corporation, expressed in terms of price bands on one axis and age bands on the other. One possible problem of this approach is that the same customers may use the differentially positioned outlets of the same group, possibly encountering equivalent products at different prices. This is sometimes referred to as 'cross-shopping'; Cort and Dominguez (1977) concluded that this was an inevitable feature of multiple positioning and that it could produce incremental business for the retailer, rather than just 'siphoning' trade from one type of outlet to the other.

The need for strategic positioning is very obvious in the case of fashion stores, but grocery retailers too are now paying more attention to the concept. To an extent, this has arisen through a disillusionment with the use of price as the dominant competitive weapon:

Table 4.7   Multi-strategy market positioning: the Burton group

| | No. of outlets | | |
Trading name	Solus	In Debenhams	Target market
Top Man	181	17	Men, 15–30
Burton/Collier	462	28	Men, 20–40
Principles for Men	27	37	Men, 25–45
Champion Sport	18	45	Men, 15–30
Top Shop	143	49	Women, 15–30
Dorothy Perkins	303	55	Women, 18–30
Principles	85	50	Women, 25–45
Evans	120	41	Women, 25–49
Debenhams Stores	66		
Harvey Nichols	1		

Source: Euromonitor (1987b).

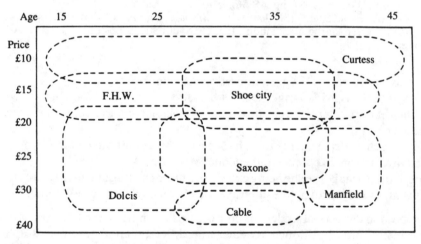

Figure 4.8   Positioning within British Shoe Corporation
Source: Retail (1989, p. 23).

The lowering of prices without consideration of other marketing mix changes may lead many consumers to view supermarkets as commodities, ie., stores with no differentiating characteristics except for the prices. (Bellenger *et al.* 1977)

It becomes even more important then for the retailer to differentiate himself from his competitor by creating a personality or image which is different and which is his own. If people are operating similar kinds of stores, then they are probably operating from similar cost bases, and price in itself is likely to be less of a difference against a competitor. (Davis 1982)

Faced with a mixture of store sizes and locations, many food retailers elected to pursue multiple positioning strategies. For example, Tesco created the 'Victor Value' chain of low-cost discount stores, which were subsequently sold to Bejam. Fine Fare similarly converted some of its smaller outlets to 'Shoppers' Paradise' discount stores. Some co-operative societies have applied the convenience store formula to certain outlets. One outcome of positioning moves is that the grocery trade is becoming fragmented into five main entities, based upon price, location and store size: i.e. superstores, supermarkets, limited-range discount stores, convenience stores and speciality stores (Ellert 1981). Classifications of this type should not however deflect attention from the opportunities for differentiation and effective positioning within each sub-sector.

SUMMARY

Retailers have not been at the forefront of strategic planning until relatively recently. The industry has a tradition of fast and reactive decision-making, which was slow to give way to more formal strategic planning processes. We have therefore seen much 'lemming-like' behaviour, with many retailers pursuing the same markets, with similar assortments, using the same promotional tools. It has now become apparent that expenditures on price cuts, advertising, design refits, etc, are often wasted, unless they form part of a coherent and overall strategy.

At the core of the strategic plan must be a statement of the company's overall direction and what it plans to accomplish. This may be defined and communicated in the form of a mission statement. A strategic audit can help retailers in assessing their competitive environment and their own constraints and capabilities. SWOT analysis is one approach, using a comprehensive checklist to audit strengths/weaknesses within the company and opportunities/threats within the external environment.

Although creativity and innovation still have a major role in strategy formulation, a number of frameworks have evolved to help envisage strategic alternatives. Ansoff's product–mission matrix, and many elaborations upon this, suggest alternative approaches to filling the 'planning gap', the difference between sales with and without significant strategic changes. A retailer may move from present to new assortments and/or market segments. The greater the movement from existing products and markets, the greater the level of risk.

The key to long-term success lies in the creation of sustainable competitive advantage. Porter argued that there are essentially two types, namely, low cost and differentiation. These may be applied to wide or narrow market segments, hence the 'generic strategy' alternatives of cost leadership, differentiation, cost focus and differentiation focus. In its quest for competitive advantage, the retailer should identify the 'value chain', comprising the functions and operations that create value, real or perceived, and therefore contribute to effective differentiation.

One of the major strategic decisions facing the retailer is the choice between specialization and diversification. Specialization can take the form of a narrow range, with choice in depth, or a broader assortment, focused upon the needs of a specialist market segment. Options for diversification include the extension of existing assortments, the addition of new assortments, and the creation of separate business units. It is important that diversification should have some form of 'common thread' with existing markets or activities, and that it is not extended beyond the company's capabilities.

Retailers may also utilize the options of acquisition or merger to pursue their strategic goals at the corporate level. This approach may be used to diversify out of saturated, static or declining markets, to buy market share and increase economies of scale, to share/transfer skills or strengths to create synergistic benefits, or to develop alternative channels of distribution. Many acquisitions have not achieved the intended results, usually because insufficient synergy is achieved to outweigh the additional costs and constraints upon the individual business units. Alternative approaches include two or more separate companies collaborating in jointly owned companies or joint development programmes. Another approach is to utilize concessionaire agreements, whereby space within stores is allocated to other retailers or manufacturers to operate as shops within shops.

A key element of retailing strategy is the decision upon the market segment(s) within which to compete. These may be selected on the basis of segment size, growth potential, competition, company capabilities, required investment and/or profit potential. Many companies express their target markets in terms of age or class characteristics, but there are many opportunities to base target marketing upon life-style, family life-cycle and other segmentation variables. There has been a tendency for many retailers to pursue the same targets, often ignoring strong potential in other segments.

Positioning requires a clear understanding of the needs and motives of the target segments; the retail offering can then be positioned to best match these needs and to create effective differentiation. Many retailers suffer the lack of a strong identity or have created a confused image in the minds of consumers. A positioning map can be a useful planning and diagnostic tool, although the dimensions or axes of the map must be relevant to the sector and the target market. Some retail groups have pursued 'multi-strategy market positioning', developing different trading formats for different market segments.

REVIEW QUESTIONS

1. Select a retail company within the fashion sector or the home furnishing sector. How would you define the corporate mission for that company? To whom would you wish to communicate this mission statement?
2. Draw up a checklist of the factors that a retailer should consider in conducting a strategic audit.
3. How would you adapt Ansoff's product–mission matrix to help a retailer to identify alternative ways of filling its planning gap?
4. Give examples of retailers pursuing each of the following strategies: cost leadership, differentiation, cost focus, differentiation focus. What are the particular risks of pursuing each of these strategies?
5. Taking a grocery retailer of your choice, how would you categorize the value chain for that company? What elements of this value chain particularly contribute to differentiation for that company?
6. Give an example of (a) successful and (b) unsuccessful diversification by retail companies in recent years. For what reasons did one diversification fail and the other succeed?
7. What factors have motivated acquisitions and mergers by retail companies? What are the major drawbacks of this strategic approach?
8. What advantages do partnership agreements offer, compared with acquisition or merger? Why has the partnership approach not been more widely used?
9. What are the main benefits and the main problems for department stores in using concessionaires?
10. You have been called upon to advise a chain of small- to medium-sized menswear shops. How should they determine the target markets within which to compete?
11. Taking any retail sector, construct a positioning map and show, based upon your own judgements, the relative positions of the retailers operating in that sector. Explain the basis of your choice of axes in drawing this map. What alternative axes could have been used?
12. Outline one example of multi-strategy market positioning by a retail group. What are the advantages and the potential pitfalls of this approach?

REFERENCES

Abell, D. and J. Hammond (1979), *Strategic Market Planning*, Prentice-Hall, Englewood Cliffs, NJ.

Ansoff, H. I. (1988), *New Corporate Strategy: An Analytical Approach to Business Policy for Growth and Expansion*, John Wiley, New York.

Ansoff, H. I. (1987), *Corporate Strategy*, Penguin, Harmondsworth.

Beaumont, J. (1980), 'Diversification and growth', *Market Place*, April/May, 15, 30.

Bellenger, D. N., T. J. Stanley and J. W. Allen (1977), 'Food retailing in the 1980s: problems and prospects', *Journal of Retailing*, **53**(3), 59–70, 112.

Bendall, A. and J. Hayes (1987), 'Retailers and the financial services revolution: can retail skills give competitive edge?' *Retail*, **5**(2), 44.

Berry, L. L. and J. A. Barnes (1987), 'Retail positioning strategies in the USA', in G. Johnson (ed.), *Business Strategy and Retailing*, John Wiley, Chichester, pp. 107–15.

Blackwell, R. D. and W. W. Talarzyk (1983), 'Life-style retailing: competitive strategies for the 1980s', *Journal of Retailing*, **59**(4), 7–27.

Brown, S. (1988), 'Retailing change: cycles and strategy', *Quarterly Review of Marketing*, **13**(3), 8–12.

Cook, D. and P. Doyle (1978), 'Retailing in the 80's', *Retail & Distribution Management*, **6**(5), 14–18.

Cort, S. G. and L. V. Dominguez (1977), 'Cross-shopping and retail growth', *Journal of Marketing Research*, **14**(2), 187–92.

Cox, R. (1987), 'Mergers and acquisitions', in E. McFadyen (ed.), *The Changing Face of British Retailing*, Newman Books, London, pp. 126–34.

Davidson, W. R. and A. F. Doody (1966), *Retailing Management*, Ronald Press, New York.

Davidson, W. R., A. F. Doody and J. R. Lowry (1970), 'Leased department as a major force in the growth of discount store retailing', *Journal of Marketing*, **34**(1), 39–46.

Davies, G. (1987), 'Monitoring retailing strategy by measuring customer perception', in G. Johnson (ed.), *Business Strategy and Retailing*, John Wiley, Chichester, pp. 133–52.

Davies, G. J. and J. M. Brooks (1989), *Positioning Strategy in Retailing*, Paul Chapman, London.

Davis, P. (1982), 'The shape of retail trading policies', *Retail & Distribution Management*, **10**(5), 8–13.

Ellert, R. (1981), 'Put pricing in its place', *Marketing*, **4**(3), 22–3.

Euromonitor (1987a), *Retail Trade in the United Kingdom*, Euromonitor, London.

Euromonitor (1987b), *Concessions Retailing in the UK*, Euromonitor, London.

Finn, A. (1987), 'Characterizing the attractiveness of retail markets', *Journal of Retailing*, **63**(2), 129–62.

Gattorna, J.L. (1985), 'Strategic retailing insights', in J. L. Gattorna (ed.), *Insights in Strategic Retail Management*, MCB, Bradford, pp. 5–8.

Gilligan, C. and C. Sutton (1987), 'Strategic planning in grocery and DIY retailing', in G. Johnson (ed.), *Business Strategy and Retailing*, John Wiley, Chichester, pp. 177–91.

Green, S. (1987), 'From riches to rags: the John Collier story: an interpretative study of strategic change', in G. Johnson (ed.), *Business Strategy and Retailing*, John Wiley, Chichester.

Hirschman, E. C. and M. R. Wallendorf (1982), 'Characteristics of the cultural continuum: implications for retailing', *Journal of Retailing*, **58**(1), 5–21.

Hollander, S. C. (1966), 'Notes on the retail accordion', *Journal of Retailing*, **42**(2), 24–40.

Hower, R. (1943), *History of Macy's of New York*, Harvard University Press, Cambridge, Mass.

Johnson, G. (1987), *Business Strategy and Retailing*, John Wiley, Chichester.

King, C. W. and L. J. Ring (1980), 'Market positioning across retail fashion institutions: a comparative analysis of store types', *Journal of Retailing*, **56**(1), 37–55.

Knee, D. and D. Walters (1985), *Strategy in Retailing: Theory and Application*, Philip Allan, Oxford.

Kotler, P. (1988), *Marketing Management: Analysis, Planning, Implementation and Control*, Prentice-Hall, Englewood Cliffs, NJ.

Kristenson, L. (1983), 'Strategic planning in retailing', *European Journal of Marketing*, **17**(2), 43–59.

Levitt, T. (1960), 'Marketing myopia', *Harvard Business Review*, **38**(4), 45–56.

Lucas, G. H. and L. G. Gresham (1988), 'How to position for retail success', *Business*, **38**(2), 3–13.

Lumpkin, J. R., B. A. Greenberg and J. L. Goldstucker (1985), 'Marketplace needs of the elderly: determinant attributes and store choice', *Journal of Retailing*, **61**(2), 75–105.

Macke, K. A. (1983), 'Managing change: how Dayton Hudson meets the challenge', *Journal of Business Strategy*, **4**(1), 78–81.

Market Place (1986a), 'The right image', *Market Place*, **4**, 45.

Market Place (1986b), 'Inside story', *Market Place*, **4**, 15–17.

Market Place (1986c), 'Champion sport', *Market Place*, **4**, 11–12.

Martineau, P. (1958), 'The personality of the retail store', *Harvard Business Review*, **36**(1), 47–55.

Mason, J. B. and M. L. Mayer (1987), *Modern Retailing: Theory and Practice*, Business Publications, Plano, Texas.

May, E. G. (1981), 'Product positioning and segmentation strategy: adaptable to retail stores?' in R. W. Stampfl and E. C. Hirschman (eds.), *Theory in Retailing: Traditional and Non-traditional Sources*, American Marketing Association, Chicago, pp. 144–54.

McFadyen, E. (1983), 'How to achieve successful regeneration', *Retail & Distribution Management*, **11**(6), 8–14.

McGee, J. (1987), 'Retailer strategies in the UK', in G. Johnson (ed.), *Business Strategy and Retailing*, John Wiley, Chichester.

McGoldrick, P. J. (1989), 'Department store concessions—strategic decisions and consumer reactions', in L. Pellegrini and S. K. Reddy (eds.), *Retail and Marketing Channels*, Routledge, London, pp. 287–310.

Milligan, J. (1987), 'Speciality shopping: its effective promotion', *Retail & Distribution Management*, **15**(5), 66–7.

Mintel (1985), 'Shops within shops', *Mintel Retail Intelligence*, 87–100.

Mintel (1987), 'Retail concessions', *Retail Intelligence*, **5**, 4.1–4.70.

Mintzberg, H. and J. A. Waters (1982), 'Tracking strategy in an entrepreneurial firm', *Academy of Management Journal*, **25**(3), 465–99.

Ody, P. (1987), 'Using profit to create jobs and social change: the story of the Body Shop', *Retail & Distribution Management*, **15**(5), 9–12.

Omura, G. S. (1986), 'Developing retail strategy,' *International Journal of Retailing*, **1**(3), 17–32.

Pennington, A. L. (1985), 'The Pennington collection on retail planning', in J. Gattorna (ed.), *Insights into Strategic Retail Management*, MCB, Bradford.

Piercy, N. (1983), 'Analysing corporate mission: improving retail strategy', *Retail & Distribution Management*, **11**(2), 31–5.

Porter, M. E. (1980), *Competitive Strategy: Techniques for Analyzing Industries and Competitors*, Free Press, New York.

Porter, M. E. (1985), *Competitive Advantage: Creating and Sustaining Superior Performance*, Free Press, New York.

Porter, M. E. (1987), 'From competitive advantage to corporate strategy', *Harvard Business Review*, **87**(3), 43–59.

Poynor, M. (1985), 'Finding the right site', *Retail & Distribution Management*, **13**(5), 7–11.

Poynor, M. (1986), 'There's no business like shop business', *Retail & Distribution Management*, **14**(4), 6–9.

Retail (1985), 'The lost tribe', *Retail*, **3**(3), 30–1.

Retail (1987a), 'Integrating winners', *Retail*, **4**(4), 25–6.

Retail (1987b), 'The corporate raider as good guy', *Retail*, **4**(4), 30.

Retail (1987c), 'M & S first choice for furniture', *Retail*, **4**(4), 17.

Retail (1987d), 'Children's World', *Retail*, **4**(4), 7.

Retail (1987e), 'Divided we stand', *Retail*, **5**(2), 20–1.

Retail (1988a), 'Food retailing', *Retail*, **6**(2), 16–44.

Retail (1988b), 'Browser bar', *Retail*, **5**(4), 2.

Retail (1989), 'No fears at Sears', *Retail*, **6**(4), 16–24.

Retail & Distribution Management (1986), 'Asda's move into car sales', *Retail & Distribution Management*, **14**(4), 24.

Retail & Distribution Management (1987), 'How to manage change', *Retail & Distribution Management*, **15**(5), 29–31.

Ries, A. and J. Trout (1982), *The Battle for Your Mind*, Warner Books, New York.

Ring, L. J. (1983), 'High-end fashion positioning', in W. R. Darden and R. F. Lush (eds.), *Patronage Behaviour and Retail Management*, Elsevier–North Holland, New York, pp. 165–78.

Rosenbloom, B. (1976), 'The trade area mix and retailing mix: a retail strategy matrix', *Journal of Marketing*, **40**(4), 58–66.

Rosenbloom, B. (1980), 'Strategic planning in retailing: prospects and problems', *Journal of Retailing*, **56**(1), 107–18.

Rosenbloom, B. (1981), *Retail Marketing*, Random House, New York.

Savitt, R. (1987), 'American retailing strategies and the changing competitive environment', in G. Johnson (ed.), *Business Strategy and Retailing*, John Wiley, Chichester, pp. 117–32.

Shamoon, S. (1986), 'High noon on the high street', *Business*, April, 87–96.

Sharples, S. (1984), 'Retailers' rival strategies for the 1980s', *Retail & Distribution Management*, **12**(4), 10–16.

Sharples, S. (1986), 'Confounding the new conventions', *Retail & Distribution Management*, **14**(3), 13–15.

Stoddart, D. (1987), 'The grey market', *Retail*, **5**(2), 40–1.

Super Marketing (1987), 'Hard road', *Super Marketing*, no. 771 (15 May), 4.

Tantiwong, D. and P. C. Wilton (1985), 'Understanding foodstore preferences among the elderly using hybrid conjoint measurement models', *Journal of Retailing*, **61**(4), 35–64.

Turner, G. (1971), *Business in Britain*, Penguin, London.

Tweddell, C. (1986), 'How to create retail innovation', *Retail*, **4**(2), 20.

Verdict (1987), *Verdict on Retail Market Segmentation*, Verdict Research, London.

Walters, D. W. (1988), *Strategic Retailing Management: a Case Study Approach*, Prentice-Hall, Hemel Hempstead.

Waters, P. (1986), 'Sainsbury's voted most preferred store chain', *Super Marketing*, 14 February, 4.

Wickstrom, B. (1988), 'Retail innovators—a study of attitudes, behaviour and sales success', in E. Kaynak (ed.), *Transnational Retailing*, de Gruyter, Berlin, pp. 63–85.

Wind, Y. (1980), 'Going to market: new twists on some old tricks', *The Wharton Magazine*, **4**, 34–9.

Worthington, S. (1984), 'Shops within shops: a changing strategy for retailers', *Retail & Distribution Management*, **12**(6), 15–17.

Wortzel, L. H. (1987), 'Retailing strategies for today's mature marketplace', *Journal of Business Strategy*, **7**(4), 45–56.

FIVE

EVALUATING RETAIL PERFORMANCE

INTRODUCTION

In Part One so far we have looked at ways of assessing the marketing environment, identifying consumers' needs, and formulating retail strategy. Attention now turns to ways of evaluating the performance of the company, either in its entirety or in terms of its individual elements. This chapter looks at retail performance from two crucial perspectives. First, the assessment of image is examined as a means of evaluating the marketing performance of the company from an all-important perspective, i.e. that of actual and potential customers. Second, means of analysing the financial performance of the company are considered, using more traditional tools of cost and profit analysis.

This blend of performance indicators reflects a growing appreciation of the linkages between marketing and financial outcomes (e.g. Sharma and Mahajan 1980; Cronin and Skinner 1984). Goodman (1985) pointed out:

Target market satisfaction is, after all, the measure of the output of a service industry. Value added in its conventional sense of sales price less costs of inputs acquired from outsiders (usually materials, supplies and purchased services) may be a flawed proxy for consumer satisfaction to the extent that sales are (in part) caused by exogenous factors.

The accumulated image is therefore an indicator of the asset value of the 'retail brand'. This is really a more sophisticated development from the practice of allocating a value for 'goodwill' when a shop was sold. Some manufacturers are now placing a more definite asset value upon their major brands, reflecting an appreciation that brand images represent the (usually) long-term outcome of their marketing activities. This is not to imply that more direct measures of financial performance are any less important; with the spate of acquisition bids in the retail sector (Section 4.2.2), a retailer ignores its balance sheet at its peril! It is important, however, to appreciate that some of the traditional financial criteria provide only a short-term perspective and do little to disaggregate or diagnose elements of marketing performance.

The first section therefore addresses the importance of image monitoring to the evaluation and reformation of retail marketing strategies. Concepts of store image are discussed and a summary is provided of the many components identified within studies of image. Alternative approaches to image analysis are evaluated, followed by examples of the types of image comparison that may be undertaken. The second section starts with an appraisal of the main cost elements within a retail operation. Various measures of retail productivity and profitability are then considered. Finally, attention is given to ways of assessing the financial performance of individual items or categories within the store.

5.1 MONITORING STORE IMAGES

The importance to retailers of effectively monitoring their images has been firmly established and documented over the last three decades. In one of the earliest and most inspirational of the many papers on retail images, Martineau (1958) quoted several case studies, illustrating how the success or failure of stores could often be attributed to undertested or underemphasized elements of their image. One such example was of a grocery chain, which was far more successful than its rivals, in spite of offering essentially the same services, products and prices. Image research showed the successful chain to be distinctive in being perceived as 'clean and white', 'the store where you can see your friends' and 'the store with helpful personnel'. In this case, prices were not the distinctive feature: 'It is significant that not once did any of the shoppers interviewed mention lower prices, better bargains, or greater savings.'

Some of the most substantive justifications for systematically researching image have been provided by May (1973, 1974). Many of her studies relate to department store images, but these serve to illustrate how image monitoring can either dictate immediate actions or direct longer-term marketing programmes. In one case based upon supermarket images, the research had monitored a major change from a mid-price/high-quality/trading-stamps strategy to a low-price/high-quality/no-stamps strategy. The research undertaken indicated the level of awareness and credibility of the promotions, as well as reassuring the company that the high-quality image was surviving the changes (May 1973).

Oxenfeldt (1974) also pointed to the problems and importance of image monitoring, in terms of the strong possibility that a store might have an image other than that which it 'deserves', in terms of relatively objective measures. In particular, he identified five conditions under which images may be better or worse than they deserve:

1. Past circumstances which still exert a strong effect on present images; there seems to be a very long lag of impressions behind store realities
2. Effects of premeditated image-building by rivals; i.e., their failures will help, their successes will hurt
3. Errors or accidents by the retailer itself or by rivals
4. The role of certain influential persons who praise or attack the store
5. Present benefits that are not seen or recognized by potential customers

It may be expected that image monitoring is more important to manufacturers than to retailers, given that retailers are in constant daily contact with their customers. Given, however, that the more senior retail decision-makers do not have a great deal of direct contact with consumers, this is unfortunately not the case. From a comparative study of retailers' and customers' perceptions of the most important criteria in purchasing electrical appliances, McClure and Ryans (1968) concluded that:

Their familiarity and frequency of contact with customers make them the envy of many manufacturers operating from remote corporate offices. Yet this familiarity and frequency of contact do not seem to give retailers a highly accurate understanding of consumers.

From her wide range of retail image studies, May (1974) confirmed that the way in which stores are perceived by managers is often in sharp disagreement with the perceptions of customers. She also noted that there were substantial dissimilarities between the images held by different members of management. Probably the most systematic comparison of management and customer images was undertaken by Pathak *et al.* (1974), who drew the following conclusions:

1. Store managers consistently overrate their stores on all of the store image dimensions.
2. Managers of mass merchandising stores are merchandising-oriented, and the intangible facets of marketing are not properly appreciated.
3. Management of higher-status stores anticipate store images held by customers better than does management of lower-status stores.

Rosenbloom (1981) also observed that many retailers set about the task of image development from altogether the wrong basis. Often it is the internal traditions of the company or trade peer groups that form the basis, rather than a clear understanding of customer attitudes and perceptions. Under these circumstances, it is highly unlikely that the resultant image positioning will be in accord with the needs of preferences of the target segment(s). As retail marketers seek increasingly scientific and reliable bases for their major positioning decisions, a clear understanding of image concepts and components, plus a familiarity with the measurement and comparison techniques, is now essential.

5.1.1 Store image concepts

Definitions of store image have proliferated as the study of the subject has advanced. One of the earliest definitions of image, specifically in relation to retail stores, was that of Martineau (1958):

the way in which the store is defined in the shopper's mind, partly by its functional qualities and partly by an aura of psychological attributes.

This definition emphasizes the need to consider not only the more visible or measurable factors but also the less tangible factors, such as the 'personality' of the store. Martineau continued to explain how architecture, displays, symbols, colours and staff attitudes are all 'key personality variables'. This definition can however be criticized for tending to ascribe a 'mystique' to the concept that is not entirely warranted. As Doyle and Fenwick (1974) pointed out:

many of the examples of successful image creation cited by Martineau and other studies depend upon physical, but non-price aspects of the store.

Thus, rather than classifying image as part of the 'non-logical basis of shopping behaviour,' as Martineau suggests, it is reasonable to view the customer as rationally evaluating the store on a multi-attribute utility function.

The possible nature of such functions was considered in Section 3.3. An element of store image about which writers do not disagree is its complexity, in terms of both the many components involved and the diverse patterns of relationship involved. These factors are summed up in a succinct definition of store image provided by Arons (1961): 'a complex of meanings and relationships serving to characterise the store for people'. Many of the definitions that have emerged could be criticized for implying a stability in store image that is not likely to exist. Images can be changed as a result of relatively minor observations or occurrences which happen to be noticeable and salient to particular shoppers. This limitation was largely overcome by Berry (1969), who, following an in-depth study of department store image, defined image in behavioural terms:

an image is the result of differential reinforcement in the context of a given stimulus or set of stimuli. Specifically, department store image is the result at any one point in time of differential reinforcement, in the context of a department store, previous to that time. Stated differently, department store image is the total conceptualised or expected reinforcement that an individual associates with a particular store.

Berry further explained that the effect of any specific stimulus was largely determined by a number of individual 'state variables' or conditions of deprivation/satiation, and 'societal and sub-cultural norms'. In other words, many personal characteristics and expectations of the society within which the individual lives influence perceptions, reactions and therefore the nature of the images formed.

The limited amount of information upon which images can be formed has been observed by other researchers. Lindquist (1974) found that this characteristic of image has been recognized in other contexts for many years. Drawing upon the early work of Boulding (1956), Lindquist noted that:

the behaviour of a human is not directed by mere knowledge and information but is a product of the images that a man perceives. [Boulding] argues that we function or react not in response to what is true but to what we believe to be true. He asserts further that we use subjective values and knowledge to mediate between ourselves and the world around us.

the human mind can handle only a certain number of complex situations and stimuli; therefore, it attempts to oversimplify circumstances and thus abstracts only a few meanings that appear salient.

This aspect of image is clearly of fundamental significance in retail marketing and will be given further consideration in future chapters, notably in relation to price images in Chapter 8. It has also been noted that, while images are usually formed on the basis of limited information, they none the less assume a greater proportion and significance than the individual contributory components. This characteristic, and the subjective nature of image, was stressed by Oxenfeldt (1974):

What exactly do we mean by the image of a store? I submit that it is more than a factual description of its many characteristics. In many cases, it is less like a photograph than a highly interpretive portrait. In other words, an image is more than a sum of its parts. It represents interaction among characteristics and includes (or is strongly affected by) extraneous elements.

The images held by consumers are thus formed, somewhat selectively, from a combination of factual and emotional material. Sometimes the term 'image' is used in a very limited sense to denote just the less tangible aspects of a store. This does however imply an artificial distinction between the tangible and the intangible components of image which is potentially dangerous for two main reasons:

1. Although consumers could, in theory, obtain precise and objective measures of such tangible attributes as prices and locations, in reality, their images are likely to be formed from more subjective impressions based upon various cues (Mazursky and Jacoby 1986) which signal something about the level of prices or the convenience of the location.
2. The so-called intangible elements, such as store atmosphere, are increasingly being disaggregated and studied as a collection of fairly tangible attributes, such as music, lighting, space, colours, aromas, etc. (see Chapter 11).

5.1.2   Components of store image

Many academic researchers and consultants have attempted to identify and classify the components of store image. Some writers have ascribed more specific meanings to the terms 'attribute', 'components' and 'dimension'. For example, 'attributes (the narrowest, most specific constructs), components (aggregation of similar attributes), and dimensions (the most general

Table 5.1   A classification of store image components

1. Price of merchandise
   (a) Low prices
   (b) Fair or competitive prices
   (c) High or non-competitive prices
   (d) Values, except with specific regard to premiums, such as stamps, or quality of merchandise

2. Quality of merchandise
   (a) Good or poor quality of merchandise
   (b) Good or poor department(s), except with respect to assortment, fashion, etc.
   (c) Stock brand names

3. Assortment of merchandise
   (a) Breadth of merchandise
   (b) Depth of merchandise
   (c) Carries a brand I like

4. Fashion of merchandise

5. Sales personnel
   (a) Attitude of sales personnel
   (b) Knowledgeability of sales personnel
   (c) Number of sales personnel
   (d) Good or poor service

6. Locational convenience
   (a) Location from home
   (b) Location from work
   (c) Access
   (d) Good or poor location

7. Other convenience factors
   (a) Parking
   (b) Hours store is open
   (c) Convenience with regard to other stores
   (d) Store layout with respect to convenience
   (e) Convenience (in general)

8. Services
   (a) Credit
   (b) Delivery
   (c) Restaurant facilities
   (d) Other services (gift consultants, layaway plans, baby strollers, escalators, etc.)

9. Sales promotions
   (a) Special sales, including quality or assortment of sales merchandise
   (b) Stamps and other promotions
   (c) Fashion shows and other special events

10. Advertising
    (a) Style and quality of advertising
    (b) Media and vehicles used
    (c) Reliability of advertising

11. Store atmosphere
    (a) Layout of store without respect to convenience
    (b) External and internal decor of store
    (c) Merchandise display
    (d) Customer type
    (e) Congestion
    (f) Good for gifts, except with respect to quality, assortment or fashion of merchandise
    (g) 'Prestige' store

12. Reputation on adjustments
    (a) Returns
    (b) Exchange
    (c) Reputation for fairness

Source: Kunkel and Berry (1968, p. 26).

constructs)' (Hansen and Deutscher 1977). Unfortunately, these definitions are neither precise nor consistently utilized across the various image studies.

Most writers have chosen to classify image factors in a way that relates to elements of the retail marketing mix. Table 5.1 shows a classification by Kunkel and Berry (1968), used to group open-ended responses by over 700 customers of three department stores; 99 per cent of the 3,737 image responses could be classified using these headings and sub-headings. A detailed breakdown of components draws attention to the dangers of analysing image at the level of the broad categories (dimensions). For example, the 'convenience' dimensions can relate to location *vis-à-vis* home, work or other stores, car parking, accessibility, opening hours, internal layout, etc. Simply knowing that a store rates well or badly on the convenience dimensions would therefore do little to suggest the appropriate management action.

A review of image-related studies enabled Lindquist (1974) to construct a detailed tabulation of the attributes mentioned by some 26 researchers in 19 separate studies; Table 5.2 provides a summary of this tabulation. A distinction is made between the studies that found some empirical support for the attribute and those within which the attribute was simply hypothesized. Naturally, the number of 'scholarly mentions' does not necessarily indicate the relative importance of the attribute; another limitation is that the majority of these studies were based upon department store images.

The listing of image components derived from Lindquist (1974), shown in Table 5.2, is by no means the most comprehensive ever produced. May (1971a) discussed the problems associated with selecting a list of components that avoids redundancy but is sufficiently comprehensive to include the less obvious factors that are salient to some shoppers. In a study of the images of four department stores, May approached this task by subjecting respondents' importance ratings of 52 initial components to a form of cluster analysis. The clusters produced varied between stores, from seven to twelve clusters emerging. This study again highlighted the importance of understanding the individual components that can contribute to an image dimension. Taking, for example, images of prices, these could be based upon some or all of the following components:

budget merchandise;
has good sales;
easy to open a charge account;
merchandise represents good value;
advertises specials;
prices clearly marked;
good markdowns;
high/low prices. (May 1971a)

The relative importance of the various image components can be partially derived from the studies of patronage motives, discussed in Section 3.2. It should be re-emphasized, however, that the importance of components varies considerably between markets, sectors, competitive situations and customer segments. Hirschman *et al.* (1978) asked respondents in seven locations to rate the importance of ten store image dimensions. Although there was some stability in the rank orders of importance, there were significant differences:

the belief that the major dimensions composing these images are consistent from one market to another is not supported by this research. Thus, to assure himself that he is positioning a store on relevant dimensions, a retailer should determine what are the major dimensions within each market the store is operating.

This finding is completely in accord with those of Tigert (1982) and Arnold *et al.* (1983), who, as discussed in Section 3.1.3, noted very considerable differences between geographically separated markets.

Table 5.2 Summary of image attribute evidence

| | Studies in which attribute mentioned (%) | | |
Attribute	Hypothetical	Empirical	Total
Merchandise			
Quality	16	37	53
Assortment	21	37	58
Fashion	5	32	37
Guarantee	5	—	5
Pricing	21	32	53
Service			
General	16	21	37
Staff service	5	32	37
Self-service	—	5	5
Ease of return	—	32	32
Credit	11	21	32
Delivery	5	16	21
Phone orders	—	16	16
Clientele			
Social class	16	11	26
Self-image	5	11	16
Store personnel	5	26	32
Physical			
Facilities	5	5	11
Layout	11	21	32
Shopping ease	11	—	11
Architecture	—	5	5
Convenience			
General	—	11	11
Location	11	37	47
Parking	11	16	26
Promotion			
Sales	—	5	5
Displays	5	16	21
Advertising	11	21	32
Trading stamps	5	11	16
Symbols and colours	—	5	5
Atmosphere			
Congeniality	5	16	21
Institutional			
Conservative/modern	—	5	5
Reputation	—	16	16
Reliability	5	16	21
Post-transaction			
Satisfaction	5	—	5

Source: derived from Lindquist (1974, pp. 33–5).

There are sound reasons why the relative importance of attributes should vary between markets, whether the comparison is on an international, regional or even locality scale. First, in so far as different localities are likely to be dominated by different shopper segments, however these be defined, they will inevitably have some different attitudes, needs and priorities. Second, competition varies within each market. While a relatively homogeneous segment of shoppers may well give similar attribute importance rankings *if* faced with the same competitive situation, in practice this is rarely the case. Case histories reported by Martineau (1958) and May (1973) illustrated vividly that a generalized view of attribute importance may offer little insight into how consumers may react to a specific competitive situation. If consumers perceived few differences between the stores on the attributes that are usually the most salient, they would probably discriminate between the stores on attributes that would usually be given only low rankings.

5.1.3 The measurement of images

Given that image research is concerned with the measurement of attitudes and opinions, rather than with more easily quantifiable factors, it is appropriate to summarize the principal measurement techniques utilized and the issues that have arisen. Clearly, even the most statistically significant set of results cannot be more reliable or valid than the initial measurement system. The range of available techniques for the measurement of consumer images and attitudes is quite large:

A wide range of both structured and unstructured instruments have been used . . . projective techniques, open-end questions, objective questions, word association tests, Osgood's semantic differential, Stephenson's Q-sort technique, adjective check lists, chess board techniques, pictorial techniques, thermometer techniques and critical incident techniques. (Myers 1968)

Only some of these techniques have been commonly applied in retail image research, although all would appear potentially useful in achieving certain research objectives. A succinct discussion of the basic techniques used by social psychologists in the measurement of attitudes was provided by Oppenheim (1976). At the end of the day, the choice of measurement technique, sample design and study focus must attempt to minimize the factors that can confound and distort image measures. Peterson and Kerin (1983) represented these potentially confounding influences in the form of an equation:

$$R = f(SO, SC, MI, M, EN, E)$$

where
   R = image response (in general or in particular)
   SO = stimulus object (retail store) characteristics
   SC = subject (consumer) characteristics
   MI = measurement instrument characteristics
   M = mode of data collection
   EN = data collection environment
   E = extraneous or error (i.e., all other) factors.

Scaling techniques   The semantic differential is probably the most widely used scaling system in retail image research. The device was evolved by Osgood *et al.* (1957) and generally consists of a number of seven- or five-point scales that are bipolar, i.e. with the extremes defined by

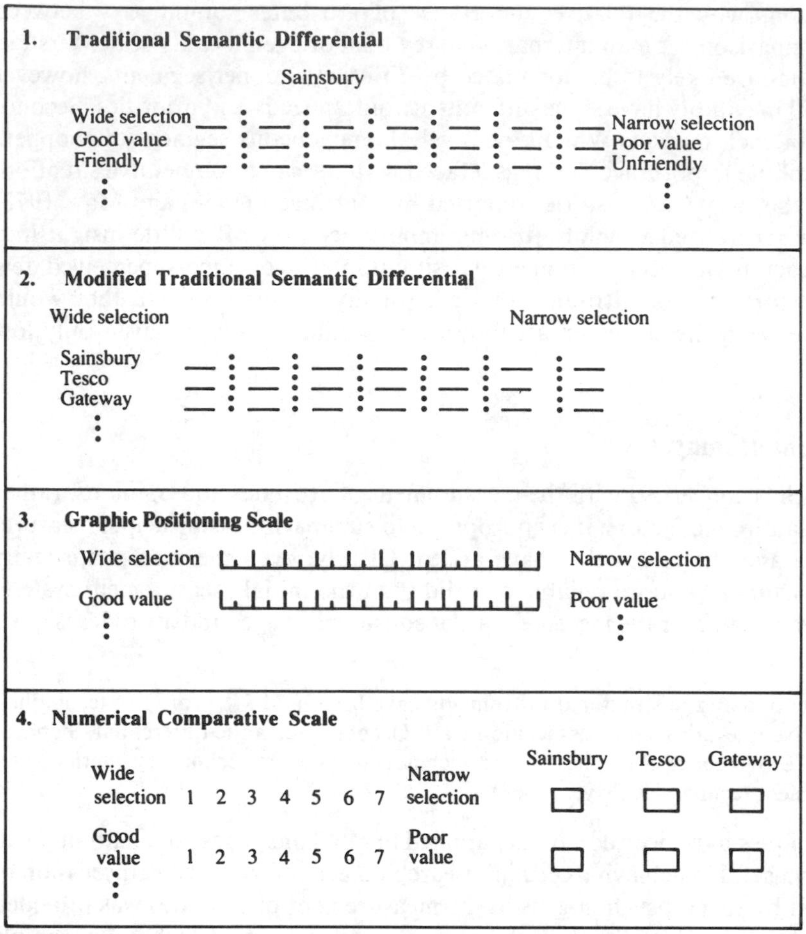

Figure 5.1   Examples of scale formats in image research
Source: adapted from Golden, Albaum and Zimmer (1987, pp. 393–410).

contrasting adjectives, such as 'clean–dirty'. Figure 5.1 shows some of the scale formats that may be applied in store image research. Using the traditional semantic differential, each retailer (or store or department) in turn would be rated on all attributes.

A modification of this approach is to rate each retailer in turn on a single attribute, and then go on to rate each one on the next attribute. The graphic positioning scale uses a slightly different format; respondents place a symbol, typically a letter, to represent their perceptions of each retailer's position on a scale between bipolar adjectives. Compared with traditional scales, this has the particular advantage of saving space on the questionnaire. The main drawbacks, however, are the difficulties of coding the data for computer analysis and the more complex instructions for respondents. A modified technique to overcome these drawbacks is the numerical comparative scale.

Other variations upon this approach include unpopular attitude scales, such as used by James *et al.* (1976), wherein single attributes are rated on a scale, such as 'very good–very bad'. An alternative form of unpopular scale is the 'staple scale', wherein a single adjective is rated on a non-verbal scale, which may run from + 5 to − 5. According to Tull and Hawkins (1987):

Unlike the semantic differential, the scale values are used to indicate how accurately *one* adjective describes the concept in question.

The advantages of this technique lie in the ease of administration and the absence of any need to pretest the adjectives or phrases to ensure true bipolarity.

This approach was tested by Hawkins *et al.* (1976) in the measurement of store images and was found to have high levels of test–retest reliability. It also overcomes the problem that items such as 'high-priced' and 'low-priced', while seemingly direct opposites, may in fact reflect different concepts in consumers' minds. Another structured, and essentially unpopular, technique is the 'agree–disagree' scale, originally evolved by Likert (1932), which is useful for scaling respondents' level of agreement with a given set of sentences.

Semantic differentials and other rating scales have considerable advantages in allowing comparisons between different groups of respondents in relation to common and defined attributes. Osgood *et al.* (1957) presented extensive evidence as to the validity, reliability and sensitivity of semantic differentials. They do, however, have certain conceptual and analytical problems. For example, Oppenheim (1976) questioned: 'are we justified in basing our calculations on the assumption of equality of intervals, both within each scale and between different scales?' The problems of this linear assumption which is implicit within most rating scales, was discussed further in Section 3.3. This particular problem has been ignored by many researchers, or, at least, the linear form has been accepted as a reasonable approximation.

Open-ended techniques   A more widely discussed problem of attitude scales is that they involve forced-choice measures that may not isolate critical image components (e.g. Berry 1969; Kunkel and Berry 1968; McDougall and Fry 1974). Open-ended techniques have therefore been used by some researchers, and the extensive list of components derived by Kunkel and Berry (1968) (Table 5.1) was produced by this approach. Criticizing the use of rigid scales, these researchers pointed out that 'people are encouraged to respond to characteristics that do not necessarily comprise the image they have of the store being studied'.

Cardozo (1974) also noted the problem that factors relevant in the purchase of one type of product may be largely irrelevant to another: 'dimensions may not by any means be the same as those which the consumer considers meaningful in the purchase of a particular product'. In order to overcome some of these problems, he adopted a psycho-linguistic approach. This was essentially open-ended but encouraged respondents to build their own image structures by noting the stores mentioned and the adjectives (dimensions) used to describe them. Using name-tags and a peg-board, respondents were then asked to position the stores on the board according to their level of similarity or difference. This procedure evoked further discussion of why the stores were thus placed. The technique therefore developed some structure and allowed limited quantification of 'mentions', without imposing a structure upon the respondents.

The most significant problem of scale measurements is that they 'force' choices, although open-ended techniques tend to have limitations in quantification and comparison. Various techniques have been adopted to overcome the problems inherent within both of these basic approaches. McDougall and Fry (1974) combined semantic differentials and open-ended questioning, which revealed some unexpected but important dimensions and also showed that respondents are more reluctant to use the negative end of scales, even when this represents their feeling about a store. In this study, the scales were administered before the open-ended discussion, thus possibly conditioning the scale responses. Most commercial studies that now combine these techniques use open-ended questions first, in order to help elicit the most relevant dimensions to be scaled.

Among the problems in classifying open-ended responses to an image survey are the possible subjectivity of the analyst and the possible inconsistencies in the approaches used when more than one analyst is involved. Having obtained open-ended image responses from a sample of nearly 900 mail panel members, Zimmer and Golden (1988) used content analysis largely to overcome these problems:

Content analysis is a research technique for the objective, systematic and quantitative description of the manifest content of communication. (Berelson 1954)

Using a clearly formulated set of rules and procedures, a reasonable level of consistency was found between the categories formed by three different analysts. It is noticeable from this study that many of the responses related to overall, global impressions of stores, although such impressions may well be rooted in perceptions of specific attributes. It led the researchers to conclude:

when the researcher elicits store image in terms of specific attributes, some of the richness of the consumer's own imagery is lost, as consumers do not limit thinking to specific store attributes, nor do they necessarily think of store attributes at all. (Zimmer and Golden 1988)

Multidimensional scaling   An approach which permits some structuring and quantification of images, while avoiding the rigidity of fixed scales, is multi-dimensional scaling (MDS). This has been used in various forms by, for example, Doyle and Fenwick (1974), Singson (1975), Jain and Etgar (1976), Davies (1987) and Green *et al.* (1987). The benefits of this approach were described by Singson:

MDS starts with only one piece of information, namely, judgement of similarities between all pairs of stimuli within the stimulus set under study. From this set of similarities judgements, the researcher attempts to infer the basic attribute(s) that underlie people's perceptions about the set of objects or stimuli. Since the researcher does not start with preselected attributes, he avoids the possibility of superimposing his own perception about the set of stimuli under study upon the respondents. Thus, MDS represents an unobtrusive way of getting at people's perception.

By this approach, a multi-dimensional map can be evolved, indicating the perceived similarities and differences between stores and the most salient dimensions by which these are assessed. The technique has the potential of exposing judgement criteria of which the respondents are not consciously aware or that they are less willing to discuss. Based upon a study of the images of five stores in Manchester city centre, Davies (1987) used MDS to produce the two- and three-dimensional maps shown in Figure 5.2. Maps of this type show the relative positions of the five stores in a form of 'image space' (Doyle 1975).

Ways of collecting the data have varied between the studies that used MDS. Doyle and Fenwick (1974) and Singson (1975) asked respondents to rate the similarities of all possible pairs of stores, then used relatively conventional scaling techniques to help them to identify and label the dimensions upon which store similarities were being evaluated. In common with some other multivariate techniques, such as factor analysis, this final stage requires considerable judgement on the part of the researchers and represents a significant limitation.

One approach to overcoming this limitation is to combine the use of MDS with other analytical techniques. Green *et al.* (1987) noted the display power of MDS but also the difficulty of interpreting axes. They therefore utilized a combination of MDS, conjoint analysis and cluster analysis to achieve greater analytical and predicative capabilities. While such approaches appear to offer the potential for further understanding the ways in which customers differentiate between stores, the view has been expressed that both the administration and the interpretation

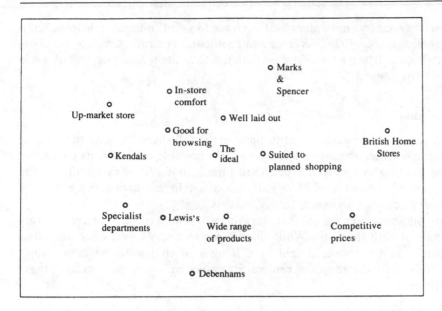

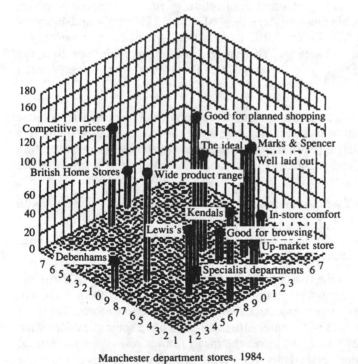

Manchester department stores, 1984.

Figure 5.2   Multi-dimensional scaling maps
Source: 'Monitoring retailing strategy by measuring customer perception' by G. Davies in G. Johnson (ed.), *Business Strategy and Retailing*, Copyright © 1987 John Wiley & Sons Ltd. Reprinted by permission of John Wiley & Sons Ltd.

of multi-dimensional scaling are too unfamiliar and abstract to be of immediate help to retail marketing management (James *et al.* 1976). As large retail companies recruit increasing numbers of managers and research specialists who are familiar with multivariate techniques, this obstacle is likely to be progressively removed.

5.1.4 Image comparisons

However sophisticated or basic the measurement technique, the full value of image monitoring can be realized only through simultaneous comparison and, if possible comparisons over time. The advantages of also tracking images over a period of time is that a 'moving picture' of the store's positioning is created (Pessemier 1980). This can assist in evaluating the effects of strategic moves, marketing activities and competitors' actions.

So far, the impression may have been gained that store image research is concerned exclusively with comparing one retailer with its rivals. While this is true in many cases, there are other important contrasts that can be drawn, notably the images of individual branches, their customers, individual departments or shopping centres. Examples will be given of each of these types of image comparison.

Retailer–retailer comparison   This is the most usual application of image research, of which many case studies may be found within the literature (e.g. Marcus 1972; Doyle and Fenwick 1974; Jain and Etgar 1976; Davis 1987). Figure 5.2 illustrates this type of comparison, based upon the technique of multi-dimensional scaling. Where more basic rating scales are used, the comparisons are usually expressed in terms of the average (mean) values of ratings given to each store on each dimension.

Clientele–clientele comparisons   A different approach to the comparison of images is to focus upon the image of the clientele of various stores, rather than upon the images held by them. It is clear from many studies that particular types of shoppers patronize particular stores, reflecting the association between store image and self-image. This association can be put to effective use by retail management:

Other factors being equal, consumers will seek out those stores whose image most closely correlates with their self-status image. (Weale 1961)

Projecting a store image which is consistent with the target markets' self-image will increase loyalty among those shoppers. (Bellenger, Stanton and Steinberg 1976)

One of the most direct approaches to the comparison of clientele images was that of Burstiner (1974). He developed a 15-scale semantic differential to compare perceptions of the social class, personality and life-styles of shoppers patronizing three New York department stores. Table 5.3 shows the average (mean) rating for each of the three stores on each of 15 semantic differential scales. The ratings were on a scale of 1 to 7; the lower the mean ratings, the closer the ratings were to the word on the left, and vice versa. Thus, for example, shoppers at 'Bloomies' were perceived as being more sophisticated, extravagant and intelligent, especially when contrasted with the shoppers at Korvettes.

Alternative approaches to comparing clienteles, especially in relation to their perceived social class, were demonstrated by Marcus (1972). In one stage of the study, respondents were shown a picture depicting a high-, middle- or low-class shopper; they were asked to indicate the store to which that shopper was going. In another stage, respondents were asked which store six types of women were most likely to use; the 'types of women' were chosen to reflect different social levels

Table 5.3 Impressions of shoppers at three New York stores

| Scale (1–7) | Comparative mean ratings | | |
	Macy's	Bloomingdale's	Korvettes
Modern.........................Old-fashioned	3.50	2.55	3.36
Unfriendly....................Neighbourly	4.20	4.12	4.28
Rugged.........................Delicate	3.93	4.87	3.29
Quality-seekers..............Bargain-hunters	3.76	2.31	5.85
Serious ....Humorous	3.36	3.07	3.93
Plain.............................Sophisticated	3.79	5.48	2.68
High-income ....Low-income	3.78	2.46	5.20
Apartment-dwellers.......Home-owners	3.63	3.64	3.25
Economical ....Extravagant	3.33	5.13	2.13
Mostly married ....Mostly single	2.93	3.77	3.01
Leaders ....Followers	4.39	3.18	5.00
Middle-class..................Lower-class	2.85	2.05	4.51
Dull people ....Intelligent people	4.33	5.09	3.74
Executives ....Workers	4.80	2.89	5.70
Mostly younger.............Mostly older	4.54	3.69	3.63

Source: Burstiner (1974, p. 30).

and ranged from cleaner to bank president's wife (with due apologies to female readers!). The approach of comparing stores' clienteles provides valuable, alternative insights into perceptions of store 'personalities', and also can suggest segmentation criteria. The specific application of this form of image monitoring to the creation of retail advertisements is discussed in Chapter 10.

Store–store comparisons Many comparisons of specific retailer's images have left the impression that the findings can be generalized, to a greater or lesser extent, across all stores within the chain. Marcus (1972) effectively challenged this assumption by showing that image ratings given to three branches of the May Company in various districts of Los Angeles differed significantly. Figure 5.3 shows the positions of the mean ratings of the three stores compared with those of the fairly up-market Robinson's store. The 17 scales were selected to reflect some of the tangible and less tangible image components.

Figure 5.3 shows that the May stores in general received less favourable ratings than the Robinson's store. The most notable exception was in respect of price, although a higher price rating is obviously consistent with the higher-status image of Robinson's. The most important outcome of this comparison, however, is the difference between the individual May stores. For example, the image of May's Arcadia branch was closer to that of Robinson's than it was to that of May's Crenshaw branch, which was the least well perceived store.

There are three main reasons why images can differ very considerably between branches:

1. In spite of the standardization programmes of many retailers, every store differs at least slightly in terms of size, location, layout and/or staff.
2. No two localities are exactly alike in terms of competition mix and strength; shoppers therefore have different expectations and bases for comparison.
3. While most retailers seek out locations with specific customer characteristics in mind (see Chapter 6), there are always some local differences that are likely to influence patronage motives and customer reactions.

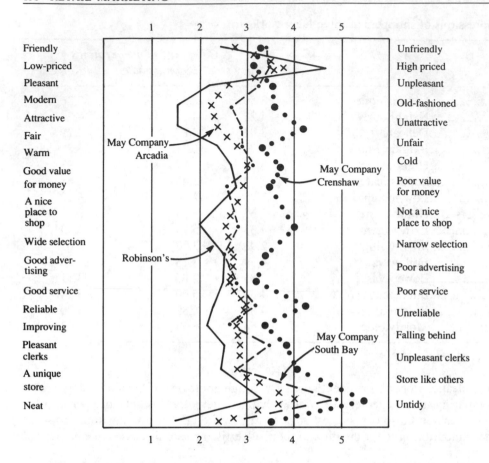

Figure 5.3   Inter-store image comparisons
Source: Marcus (1972, p. 39).

It is important, therefore, to be sensitive to local differences, rather than simply to assume that national marketing leads to a national image. Local image monitoring can also be helpful in suggesting local modifications to the assortment, the communications emphasis or prices. Geographical price differentials are considered in Chapter 8.

Department–department comparisons   As many stores become increasingly diversified, there are sound reasons for believing that both the importance and the ratings of image components will differ by department within a store. May (1971b) illustrated how specific buying situations lead to preferences for particular types of store and, accordingly, how the importance of image dimensions varies by product class. She also noted the likelihood that a store may have not just one image but a composite of many images:

Some of these images may be quite similar to each other and to the image for the store as a whole; other images may show a high degree of differentiation in the customers' minds as among the various areas of the one store. (May 1971c)

This proposition was further explored by Cardozo (1974), who investigated the images of stores in relation to the health and beauty aids and the housewares product groups. For both

Table 5.4 Departmental price and quality ratings

	Price ratings (%)				Quality ratings (%)			
	Lower than ave.	About ave.	Higher than ave.	Don't know	Below ave.	About ave.	Above ave.	Don't know
Ladies' & men's knitwear	9	63	24	4	1	16	80	3
Ladies' nightwear & underwear	12	56	26	6	1	20	74	5
Men's nightwear & underwear	9	50	15	26	1	25	50	24
Other ladies' clothes	9	55	28	8	3	27	62	8
Other men's clothes	8	48	19	25	3	25	49	23
Footwear	13	45	14	28	11	32	33	25
Children's clothes	8	36	27	29	1	18	55	26
Food & drinks	5	33	58	4	1	15	80	4
Household goods	3	43	28	26	2	28	48	22
Cosmetics	4	39	17	40	5	25	31	39
Plants	7	41	17	35	2	24	41	33

Source: McGoldrick (1979, p. 22).

product groups, price was the most frequently mentioned factor (using the psycho-linguistic approach), but there were substantive differences between both the implied importance and the evaluations of image dimensions in respect of the two groups. McGoldrick (1979) compared consumers' ratings of major image dimensions relating to 11 product groups/departments within one Marks & Spencer store. In that Marks & Spencer is highly regarded for its consistency and management skills, this store was considered to be a difficult test for departmental image differences. Table 5.4 summarizes the price and quality ratings given to the various 'departments' of the store. Most of the departmental ratings were broadly consistent with the store's overall image for good quality and good value. There were exceptions, however, notably footwear and cosmetics, which were sufficient to warrant action in these areas.

A subsequent study by Stewart and Hood (1983) extended the study of product category images to include also those of Littlewoods and British Home Stores; again, some differences in the images and competitive positions of individual departments were revealed. Clearly, such intra-store image differences may not necessarily work to the detriment of the retailer. For example, the relatively high-price image of Marks & Spencer's food (Table 5.4) has not prevented them from being highly successful; indeed, it may have actually contributed to that success by positioning the company distinctively on the price–quality dimensions. Adverse image differences can however be most detrimental to a store's overall image; at least occasionally, retailers should disaggregate their image monitoring by product class, especially if they are selling a diverse product assortment. There is also clearly a series of linkages between store images and the brands sold; the positive or negative effects of selling strongly branded manufacturers' products should also be considered (Jacoby and Mazursky 1984).

Centre–centre comparisons   The relative positioning of shopping centres can also be evaluated through image measurement techniques. One of relatively few studies that has focused upon shopping centre images was that of Nevin and Houston (1983), who utilized factor analysis to extract three major dimensions from 16 image rating scales. These image dimensions, labelled 'assortment', 'facilities' and 'market posture', were then added to a model designed to predict consumers' choices of shopping areas (see Chapter 6). In a UMIST study to be completed in 1990, the images of the Metrocentre and Eldon Square centres in Tyneside are being compared, using 27 rating scales. Preliminary results show significant differences on all but one of the 27 attributes, with the newer Metrocentre receiving the better ratings on most but not all attributes.

Although the image of a centre may be somewhat beyond the control of the individual retailer, such an evaluation can assist in location decisions, helping to identify the centres that are compatible with the retailer's image. Knowledge of a centre's image can also help in evaluating or predicting the performance of a store within that centre.

5.2   ANALYSIS OF COSTS AND PROFITABILITY

It is very easy to spend money in the pursuit of increased market share or in the implementation of a new marketing strategy. As will be demonstrated in the following chapters, few of the tools of retail marketing can be utilized without the adjustment of cost structures. Yet the most successful and consistently profitable retail companies are those that have developed a coherent positioning statement, while maintaining constant vigilance in the area of costs and profitability. Financial control is not of course synonymous with cost minimization; many companies that have made this mistake have tended to be mediocre and short-lived.

Two of the most profitable yet contrasting food retailers in the UK are Kwik Save and Marks & Spencer. In the former case, costs are held well below industry norms, enabling the company to offer low prices while realizing consistently healthy profits. In the latter case, the financial emphasis is upon effective cost control, within the primary objective of maintaining a premium position. It is essential, therefore, to be aware of the elements of retail cost and the opportunities that may exist to improve the profitability of a retailing strategy.

5.2.1   Elements of retail cost

Inevitably, details of cost structures are among retailers' most closely guarded secrets, although aggregated and edited cost information can sometimes be gleaned from company reports. Unfortunately, the inter-company figures exchange (e.g. Retail Outlets Research Unit 1974), which provided an invaluable fund of cost/productivity/profit data from the grocery retail sector, no longer operates. Tables 5.5 and 5.6 are based upon a survey of retail costs by the Institute of Fiscal Studies; the primary motive for this survey was to provide a basis for the analysis of the economic effects of possible Sunday trading. Although this survey was not especially large, it was supplemented from other sources and it represents some of the most reliable published information on the subject (Auld 1984).

Table 5.5 has been adapted from its original format to give due emphasis to the importance of the cost of goods sold (COGS). In virtually all retail sectors, this is the major element of retail costs, although its relative importance varies both between and within sectors. COGS tends to represent a very high proportion of costs in the food sector, hence the lowest level of percentage gross margin in this sector (Table 5.6). This illustrates the critical importance to cost control of professional and powerful retail buying units. From a small sample of buying prices, for example, the Monopolies and Mergers Commission (1981) found that the four largest grocery

Table 5.5   Breakdown of UK retail costs by sector

| Retail sector | Major cost elements as % of turnover | | | | | |
	Cost of goods	Labour	Premises	Services, transport	Energy	Stock holding
Food	79.3	9.9	5.9	3.9	0.9	0.1
Clothing & footwear	60.2	18.3	14.1	8.2	2.1	0.5
Drink, tobacco, confectionery	74.3	9.7	6.4	6.4	0.8	0.2
Household goods	67.8	12.6	9.9	6.7	1.7	0.5
Mixed retail	68.2	13.0	8.6	5.5	1.5	0.3
Other	65.0	14.1	7.5	5.0	1.4	0.5
All	72.4	11.8	7.8	5.3	1.2	0.3

Source: based upon the Retail Cost Model of the Institute for Fiscal Studies (IFS), and adapted from Moir (1987, pp. 3–21).

Table 5.6   UK retail cost structure by sector

| Cost elements | Cost as % gross margin | | | | |
	Food	Clothing, footwear	Drink, tobacco, confectionery	Household goods	Mixed retail
Labour	47.7	45.7	39.9	39.2	41.0
Premises	28.6	35.4	25.0	29.8	27.1
Services, transport	20.3	20.4	22.8	19.6	16.3
Energy	4.3	5.1	3.0	4.9	4.3
Stockholding	0.7	1.3	0.8	1.4	0.9
Gross margin	20.72	39.76	25.66	32.23	31.82

Source: based upon the IFS Retail Cost Model, and adapted from Moir (1987, pp. 3–21).

multiples had paid around 10 per cent less for their supplies of biscuits than the other multiples. The organization of the retail buying function and the negotiation of buying terms are considered in some detail in Chapter 7.

Among the other cost elements, labour clearly dominates, especially in the highly labour-intensive sectors such as clothing and footwear. To illustrate contrasts at the individual company level, employee remuneration at Kwik Save discount food stores was reported to represent just 5.3 per cent of turnover, compared with 28.2 per cent of turnover at Horne Brothers menswear stores (Auld 1984). Kwik Save therefore is holding labour costs well below the norm for the food sector, whereas stores offering full-service delicatessens, bag packing at the checkouts, etc., are likely to have labour costs above the norm. In a phase when many companies are seeking a competitive edge through improved services (see Chapter 12), the importance of detailed cost analysis is clear. The attraction of measures that reduce labour while also providing a better service, such as PoS scanners, is also easy to understand.

A. ITEM PRICES
1. Can prices on certain lines be raised without significantly eroding competitive position?
2. Does an effective system exist for planning aggregate mark-up goals?
3. Is the present average level of mark-downs really necessary?
4. Can breadth or depth of assortment be modified to allocate more space to higher margin lines?

B. VOLUME
1. Can the market be expanded by innovating or modifying marketing strategy?
2. Are market share gains against competition possible?
3. How can marketing strategy, marketing mix and store image be improved?
4. Does a clear long-term marketing plan exist? Is it appropriate for today's trading conditions?

C. COST OF GOODS SOLD
1. Can buying discounts be improved?
2. Should purchasing be concentrated around fewer buyers?
3. Should more be bought direct or via wholesalers?
4. Are buying decisions effectively centralized?

D. OPERATING EXPENSES
1. Does a sound accounting and information system exist for controlling expenses and productivity by expense centres and selling units?
2. Is there an effective budgetary control system for planning expenses and relating them to financial goals?
3. Are periodic cost reduction and work simplification programmes undertaken by the company?
4. Are advertising and promotional budgets cost-effective and clearly related to store strategy?

E. ASSET TURNOVER
1. Are there advantages in leasing rather than owning stores, distribution centres and other fixed assets?
2. Do merchandise and display techniques make maximum use of store facilities?
3. Is the stock turnover rate acceptable? Is it consistent with the group's marketing and financial strategy?
4. Would reducing fringe sizes, duplicate brands and some price lines cut inventories sufficiently to offset any volume loss?
5. Does the information and control system effectively highlight slow-moving lines?
6. Could inventories be held down via increasing delivery frequency or persuading suppliers to hold them?
7. Are accounts receivable being systematically monitored?

F. LEVERAGE RATIO
1. What is the appropriate current ratio and long-term debt–equity ratio for this type of retailing?
2. What is the 'time-interest earned' figure? Is it sufficient for this type of retailing?
3. Can supplier finance be used more effectively to gear up return on net worth?
4. Should future expansion be financed via debt or equity?

Figure 5.4 Auditing financial structure
Source: Doyle and Cook (1985, p. 82).

The costs of premises, services and transport represented around 13 per cent of turnover on average, although there is again very considerable variation between companies and between individual outlets. A single-level store in an accessible area of low land value is likely to be operating at a far lower cost for these elements. In contrast, a multi-level store in an expensive city site is likely to incur high costs of rental, lift/escalator services and frequent, difficult deliveries. Energy costs, from the analyses of Tables 5.5 and 5.6, may appear to be of relatively slight significance. With net margins sometimes as low as 1 or 2 per cent, this would be an inaccurate interpretation. Furthermore, through the application of improved technology, energy costs can sometimes be reduced with no loss to services or to the shopping environment; this makes energy a highly suitable target for cost reductions.

There are clearly many possible areas for close cost scrutiny. In some cases retail planners must evaluate trade-offs between proposed enhancements to the retail offering and cost controls. In other cases costs can be reduced without a service trade-off, by revised working practices or through new technology. Doyle and Cook (1985) suggested a framework for auditing the financial structure of a retail company, illustrated in Figure 5.4. This takes the form of some 27 questions, to which companies may well add more to reflect their own specific circumstances. In the nature of any audit, this should be administered periodically to maintain pressure on costs and to avoid slippage towards higher costs that do not result in higher performance. The identification and analysis of key cost areas, including those within the general heading of 'overheads', leaves the retailer better able to determine expenditure priorities within the context of the strategic plan (Bendall 1985).

5.2.2 Productivity and profitability

A wide range of measures has evolved to measure different aspects of retail productivity and profitability, most of which provide useful indicators of retail performance. There has also been increased interest in retail productivity at sector and industry level, arising mainly from concern in the USA (e.g. Bucklin 1981) that retail productivity growth has appeared to lag behind that of manufacturing. It is not the purpose of this section to provide a full appraisal of theoretical and empirical developments in the study of retail productivity; an excellent collection of papers addresses this issue in the Fall 1984 edition of the *Journal of Retailing* (e.g. Achabal *et al.* 1984; Good 1984). The issue of labour productivity in retailing has received particular attention (e.g. Lusch and Moon 1984; Thurik and Van der Wijst 1984; Ingene 1984).

The meanings of the terms 'productivity', 'efficiency' and 'effectiveness' have frequently been blurred in discussions of retail performance. More distinct definitions were developed by Achabal *et al.* (1984) and were subsequently summarized by Goodman (1985):

a) productivity—relates a single input factor to an output measure, other inputs assumed constant;
b) efficiency—measures the effects of all inputs in combination and thus recognises that all inputs and the proportions in which they are employed may vary;
c) effectiveness—takes into account goal achievement as well.

These concepts are therefore quite distinct in their scope, but a hierarchical relationship may be seen to exist between them:

High productivity is a necessary but not sufficient condition for high efficiency, as individual productive factors may not be combined in an optimal manner. Similarly, high efficiency is a necessary but not sufficient condition for high effectiveness, as the efficient combination may be directed to less than optimal goals. (Goodman 1985)

Table 5.7 Productivity measures

Company	Sales per employee (£)	Company	Sales per square foot (£)
World of Leather	237,082	Colorvision	1,300
Bejam	146,300	Sainsbury	774
Shadow Photographic	135,354	Waitrose	748
Dixons	123,571	Dixons	700
Comet	123,450	Tie Rack	622
HMV	123,000	Savacentre	621
Wickes	119,763	Currys	600
Ultimate	115,978	Ratners	536
Majestic Wine	113,636	Wallis Frozen Foods	534
Kwik Save	110,693	Cecil Gee	518
Victoria Wine	110,351	Tesco	514
B & Q	105,245		

Source: Corporate Intelligence Group (1988).

Many different ratios can be calculated to measure aspects of retail productivity. Two of the most commonly quoted ratios are sales per employee (full-time equivalent) and sales per square foot of selling space. Table 5.7 shows these ratios for some of the 'best performers' in the UK, using these criteria. Clearly, the retailers of high-value products tend to perform well in terms of sales per employee; it is noticeable, however, that Kwik Save enters the list because of the unusually high degree of labour productivity in its discount food stores. In terms of sales per square foot, it is noticeable that the highest performances in the food sector are achieved by the more up-market Sainsbury and Waitrose. A measure of display productivity, sales per linear foot, is discussed further in Chapter 11.

There has been a tendency to 'borrow' concepts and measures of productivity from the manufacturing industry, although these may be less than appropriate as measures of retail performance. As Nooteboom (1986) observed:

[Manufacturing] industry provides a utility of form, while retailing provides a utility of time and place. In view of those differences, one should not too readily and uncritically employ concepts and tools from studies of productivity in industry.

The 'output' function in retailing is therefore especially difficult to establish. Good (1984) pointed out that a retailer's output is essentially a set of tangible services that make the goods sold more useful to consumers. It is because of these services that a margin can be earned between buying and selling prices. As noted within the introduction to this chapter, it is therefore essential to monitor consumers' perceptions of the retail 'package' as well as traditional performance measures.

An especially salient area of productivity analysis has been the attempts to measure economies of scale associated with larger stores. Dawson and Kirby (1977) found that labour productivity in the grocery trade increases with increased scale of operation; the Retail Outlets Research Unit (1974) also confirmed the existence of labour efficiencies in larger outlets. In a study with special reference to superstores, Thorpe and Shepherd (1977) found that scale economies tend to be clouded by certain aspects of a large store's cost profile, such as higher store advertising costs, a higher proportion of non-food selling and, in some cases, higher costs of occupancy (rent, rates, etc.). Personnel costs as a percentage of sales did however decline consistently with increasing store sizes, suggesting that superstores do enjoy distinct scale economies.

Interpretation of such analyses must be undertaken with considerable caution. Tucker (1975) identified many deficiencies in earlier studies of economies of scale. Variations in the 'output mix' had frequently been overlooked, as had differences in service and quality. Another problem identified was a failure to take into account differences in the way in which central/head office costs are allocated by multiple retailers. These and other difficulties led to the conclusion that far more rigorous methodologies were required to study economies of scale in retailing. The considerable differences between occupancy costs in different locations also present a problem. For example, a 100,000 sq. ft Tesco superstore in Hanley town centre costs £42 per sq. ft to develop, contrasting with a similarly sized store in Irlam which costs just £20 per sq. ft to develop (Evely 1978).

In appraising the financial performance of a retail company, the wide range of financial ratios common to most types of business can be applied. A full treatment of retail accounting would be beyond the scope of this text, but discussions of some of the major ratios as applied to retailing were provided by Chadwick (1984) and Norkett (1985). A summary of the more frequently used ratios is provided in Table 5.8; these are subdivided into profitability, liquidity, leverage and activity ratios.

The first of the profitability ratios, gross margin, indicates the total margin available to cover operating expenses and yield a profit. It is a ratio that is utilized at the company, category or individual item level, although some of its limitations are discussed in the next section. Table 5.9 summarizes gross margins by retail sectors; in 1984 these ranged from 40.8 per cent in the clothing and footwear sector to 15.2 per cent in confectioners, tobacconists, newsagents and off-licences. The operating profit margin indicates the retailers' profitability from current operations, before taking into account the interest charges accruing from the capital structure.

Net profit margins express profitability after all costs have been deducted. Table 5.10 shows the net margins and the turnover achieved by the eight largest retail companies in the UK; the strong performance of Marks & Spencer is clearly demonstrated. Return on total assets (ROA) is a measure of the return on total investment (ROI) in the company. Return on shareholders' equity, usually termed return on net worth (RONW), measures the rate of return on share-holders' investment in the company. Earnings per share (EPS) are the earnings available to ordinary shareholders. Liquidity ratios indicate the ability of the company to convert assets to cash. The current ratio indicates the extent to which the claims of creditors are covered by assets that are convertible on an appropriate time-scale. The quick or acid test ratio measures the ability to meet liabilities without selling inventories. Inventory to net working capital shows the extent to which working capital is tied up in inventories.

Leverage or gearing ratios provide an indication of the degree of risk that the company represents for lenders. The debt-to-assets ratio indicates the extent to which the firm's operations have been financed by borrowed funds. The debt-to-equity ratio relates funds provided by creditors to funds provided by shareholders. Times-interest-earned, or the coverage ratio, shows how far earnings can decline before the company would become unable to meet its interest commitments.

Among the activity ratios, inventory turnover is a key measure of how quickly the goods purchased are resold. Stock turn tends to vary greatly between sectors and between individual product lines, a factor that is further discussed in the next section. Fixed/total assets turnover indicates whether a sufficient volume of business is being generated, relative to the scale of the

Table 5.8   Summary of key financial ratios

Ratio	Method of calculation
Profitability ratios	
Gross profit margin	$\dfrac{\text{Sales} - \text{cost of goods sold}}{\text{Sales}}$
Operating profit margin	$\dfrac{\text{Profit before taxes and before interest}}{\text{Sales}}$
Net profit margin (or return on sales)	$\dfrac{\text{Profits after taxes}}{\text{Sales}}$
Return on total assets	$\dfrac{\text{Profits after taxes}}{\text{Total assets}}$
Return on shareholders' equity (or return on net work)	$\dfrac{\text{Profits after taxes}}{\text{Total shareholders' equity}}$
Earnings per share	$\dfrac{\text{Profit after taxes} - \text{performance dividends}}{\text{Number of ordinary shares outstanding}}$
Liquidity ratios	
Current ratio	$\dfrac{\text{Current assets}}{\text{Current liabilities}}$
Quick ratio (or acid test ratio)	$\dfrac{\text{Current assets} - \text{inventory}}{\text{Current liabilities}}$
Inventory to net working capital	$\dfrac{\text{Inventory}}{\text{Current assets} - \text{current liabilities}}$
Leverage ratios	
Debt to assets ratio	$\dfrac{\text{Total debt}}{\text{Total assets}}$
Debt to equity ratio	$\dfrac{\text{Total debt}}{\text{Total shareholders' equity}}$
Times-interest-earned (or coverage ratio)	$\dfrac{\text{Profits before interest and taxes}}{\text{Total interest charge}}$
Activity ratios	
Inventory turnover	$\dfrac{\text{Sales}}{\text{Inventory}}$
Fixed assets turnover	$\dfrac{\text{Sales}}{\text{Fixed assets}}$
Accounts receivable turnover	$\dfrac{\text{Annual credit sales}}{\text{Accounts receivable}}$
Average collection period	$\dfrac{\text{Accounts receivable}}{\text{Total sales} \div 365}$ or $\dfrac{\text{Accounts receivable}}{\text{Average daily sales}}$

Source: adapted from *Strategic Management: Concepts and Cases* by A. A. Thompson and A. J. Strickland. Copyright © 1987 Richard D. Irwin Inc.

Table 5.9   Gross margins by sector

Sector	Gross margin as % of turnover	
	1980	1984
Food retailers	20.4	21.3
CTNs/off-licences	14.8	15.2
Clothing, footwear	38.3	40.8
Household goods	31.1	33.0
Non-food	31.9	30.3
Mixed businesses	32.2	32.7
Total	26.9	27.6

Source: Euromonitor (1987, p. 43).

Table 5.10   Turnover and net margins, in UK retailing, 1986/7

Company	Turnover (£ 000)	Net margin (%)
J. Sainsbury	3,857,064	6.5
Marks & Spencer	3,809,100	10.8
Tesco	3,593,000	4.9
Asda–MFI	2,623,800	6.9
Dee Corporation	3,545,700	4.6
Argyll Group	1,855,180	4.0
Kingfisher	1,824,100	5.6
Boots	1,799,600	8.1

Source: Corporate Intelligence Group (1988 *The Retail Rankings*, Corporate Intelligence Research Publications, London).

company's assets. The measure of credit repayment periods are of increasing significance, especially to retailers financing their own credit schemes or store cards (see Chapter 12).

5.2.3   Measures of item profitability

The emphasis so far has been upon the evaluation of costs and profitability across the whole store or organization. In retailing, however, there are many decisions that require measures of profitability at the individual item, or product category, level. In the area loosely termed 'merchandise management', buyers must be able to appraise the profitability of their individual buying decisions; pricing decisions also require this type of input, as do decisions on own-brand products, promotions and shelf/display space allocation. Traditionally, mark-ups or gross margins have been at the core of the merchandise management function. These simple measures have acted as a rule of thumb (e.g. Preston 1963) in many pricing decisions; gross margins achieved have also served as one indicator of relative performance within the assortment.

Given that mark-ups and gross margins are such fundamental measures, it is unfortunate that confusion sometimes surrounds the use of the terms (Jolson 1973). Within this book, 'mark-up' is used to describe the difference between the buying and the selling price, expressed as a percentage of the former. The 'percentage gross margin' is the same quantity but expressed as a percentage of the selling price. To provide a simple example:

Cost of item to retailer	£40
Price at which item was sold	£50
Mark-up	25%
Gross margin	£10
Percentage gross margin	20%

In sectors such as clothing retailing, where it is quite common to reduce the price of items not sold by the end of a season, a distinction will usually be made between the 'initial' mark-up and the 'maintained' mark-up. The former is the percentage that would have been achieved at the price initially set, whereas the latter is the percentage realized after the price reduction. For example:

Cost of garment to retailer	£16
Price initially set	£40
Initial mark-up	150%
Price after reduction	£28
Maintained mark-up	75%

These interpretations of the terms are consistent with those used by Gabor (1977), but the reader will probably encounter other definitions. Sometimes the expressions 'percentage mark-up on retail price' and 'percentage mark-up on cost' are used to describe percentage gross margins and mark-ups, respectively. Sometimes the term 'mark-up' is reserved for the expression of profit on individual items, whereas the term 'margin' is used to describe profits on whole ranges of items. These inconsistencies arise partly from different sector or national conventions, but they can obviously cause difficulties when comparing sources. In some proprietary analyses, the definitions appear to be deliberately obscured. Profits expressed as mark-ups may be warmly received by senior management or shareholders; in dealing with manufacturers or consumer groups, it may be more tactful to express profits as percentage gross margins!

Quite apart from the problems of definitions, there has been a tendency to place too much emphasis upon mark-ups and gross margins in merchandise management. Sweeney (1973) noted that the rate of return on equity achieved by department stores had seriously declined, while over the same period percentage gross margins had increased. The particular limitations of percentage gross margins and mark-ups as 'major operating tools' were discussed over thirty years ago by McNair and May (1957). The adverse practices arising from over-dependence upon these ratios were summarized by Knee and Walters (1985):

1. a lack of attention to market-based pricing;
2. an assumption that all items had similar costs;
3. a disregard of possible elasticities of demand;
4. no distinctions being made between fixed and variable costs;
5. general acceptance of net sales as an appropriate basis of expense allocation;
6. over-confidence in final department net profit percentages after expense allocation;
7. frequent tie-in of the gross margin percentage with buyer's compensation;
8. the focus of attention on ratios of sales, rather than on 'dollars', and the use of convenient percentages as crutches.

Clearly, what is needed is a better measure of the contribution of an item to the firm's profits, although this is easier to say than to accomplish. A number of formulations have been suggested in recent years, although some were too cumbersome to gain widespread adoption. For example, the use of 'contribution margins' at the item or section level was criticized by Cross (1958) as being too cost-oriented, too difficult, too time-consuming and too expensive to install and maintain, as well as being of questionable differential value over simple gross margin measures. Naturally, many of the objections on time or difficulty grounds are now less valid because of the vast improvements in electronic information systems. Two measures of item profitability that have been highly influential in recent years are 'gross margin return on inventory investment' (GMROI) and 'direct product profitability' (DPP).

The importance of return on investment criteria in retail planning and control has been recognized for many years (e.g. Dalrymple and Thompson 1969). The approach was adapted to the product category level by Sweeney (1973), although he emphasized that it should be used exclusively for planning and controlling merchandising inventory investment. Gross margin return on inventory investment (GMROI) is defined as follows:

$$\text{GMROI} = \frac{\text{Gross margin dollars}}{\text{Average inventory investment}}.$$

Sweeney (1973) notes the following particular advantages of this measure as a criterion for merchandising decisions:

1. GMROI is a meaningful measure of the performance of buyers or other merchandising executives, measuring how well the major asset under his/her control, i.e. merchandising inventories, is being used to generate gross profit dollars.
2. At departmental level, GMROI goals can be set that have a clear and consistent relationship with the retailer's overall ROI goals.
3. The merchandising executive can define appropriate combinations of target gross margins and sales-to-inventory ratios to produce the target GMROI for the category or department.
4. GMROI offers a composite measure for comparing key performance characteristics between product categories.
5. GMROI is easily calculated from data that are routinely available within most retail companies.

Naturally, such a simple measure cannot accommodate the full complexity of retail cost structures. Serpkenci and Lusch (1983) particularly noted the limitation that GMROI does not take into account the costs of financing consumer credit or the benefits that a supplier may provide in the form of favourable credit terms. These particular costs and benefits can differ very considerably between different product lines. They observed that:

In a capital-scarce environment, GMROI has become misdirectional because it focuses the retail manager's attention only on a portion of the total operating cycle. Inventory turnover is considered but not the actual or real investment in merchandise.

Gilman (1988) argued that GMROI does not adequately consider the real profitability per square foot of selling space achieved by individual items. Some of the actions taken to improve margins have also tended to conflict with those taken to stimulate sales. He noted:

A question was raised as to whether or not gross margin return on investment really equates with profitability.

The key to retail profitability is to achieve the maximum profit contribution per square foot.

Sanghavi (1988) has also advocated a shift of emphasis from measures of sales per square foot towards measures of profit per square foot:

Until recently, sales per square foot was a widely accepted tool for judging the performance of various product categories. Today, retailers have realised that it is very easy to give stuff away. The name of the game now is not the big bucks but the bottom line. Profit per square foot has now become the tool to judge the performance of these product categories.

A measure that sets out to apportion all relevant costs, notably those of space and labour, is *direct product profitability*. This was explained in a detailed report by Pinnock (1986):

Direct product profitability (DPP) is a detailed measure of an individual item's actual profit contribution. In simple terms, the calculations involve adjusting the gross margin of a product to reflect allowances, payment discounts or any other form of 'income', and then subtracting any costs directly attributable to that product as it passes through the retail system.

The DPP of an item is therefore the gross margin, after adjustments, minus direct product costs (DPCs). These direct product costs arise at the warehouse, in transport, in the store and in head office functions. The largest single element of DPC is likely to be incurred in the store. Here a cost is allocated, possibly using work-study techniques, for the labour involved in receiving, sorting, moving, price-marking, shelf-loading and checking out the item. A space cost is allocated, being a function of the square or cubic footage occupied and the rate of stock turn of the item; in other words, within the cost accounting system, the item is in effect charged a rent for the space/time occupied. Table 5.11 shows the DPP and DPC calculations for typical items within the frozen, dry grocery and refrigerated food categories.

Although DPP has gained widespread adoption only recently, its origins can be traced back over thirty years. By the mid-1960s it had been utilized by some manufacturers and retailers in the USA, having been advocated by the McKinsey Company (Retail & Distribution Management 1987). The problem then was that it took too long to measure and calculate on a regular or detailed basis. Improvements in information systems, and the development of PC-based DPP models, have made the approach far more feasible. Harris (1987) summarized the advantages of DPP over gross profit as follows:

1. DPP attempts to consider all the revenue earned by the item.
2. It considers the cost of handling the item.
3. It can give some very different answers from those obtained using gross margin.

Table 5.11 provides examples of these very different results. The 'typical' frozen item has the most attractive gross margin but also rather high DPCs. This is not the case with the refrigerated item, however; being typically compact, this is relatively inexpensive to handle and to store.

Clearly, DPP is a measure that can usefully be applied by manufacturers and retailers alike. It can also promote better communication and co-operation between retailers and their suppliers (Walters 1986). There are of course still problems in terms of the costs of obtaining accurate data, and the number of companies that use the system extensively is still small (Retail Review 1989). Table 5.12, based upon a study by Touche Ross, indicated the proportions of retailers and manufacturers in the USA that have used DPP or are intending to do so within the next four years. The most common applications are in shelf space allocation, where the measure can provide an input to various space allocation models. It does however have the potential to assist in several other types of retailing marketing decisions, which are considered in Part Two of this book.

Table 5.11 DPP and DPC: typical items in categories[a]

	Frozen	Dry grocery	Refrigerated
Direct product profitability			
Adjusted gross margin (%)	30.0	20.6	26.4
Direct product costs (%)	17.8	10.6	8.9
Direct product profit (%)	12.2	10.0	17.5
DPP per item ($)	0.139	0.103	0.159
DPP per case ($)	2.104	1.795	3.118
Direct product costs			
(a) Warehouse			
Labour ($)	0.0136	0.0124	0.0077
Space ($)	0.0130	0.0068	0.0038
Total ($)	0.0266	0.0192	0.0115
(b) Transport ($)	0.0125	0.0092	0.0058
(c) Store			
Labour ($)	0.0602	0.0437	0.0405
Space ($)	0.0914	0.0281	0.0186
Total ($)	0.1516	0.0718	0.0591
(d) Headquarters			
Warehouse[b] ($)	0.0043	0.0040	0.0024
Store[b] ($)	0.0041	0.0039	0.0014
Invoicing ($)	0.0005	0.0004	0.0005
Total ($)	0.0089	0.0083	0.0043
Total DPC ($)	0.1996	0.1085	0.0807
DPC per case ($)	3.0442	1.8950	1.5795

[a] These data are illustrative and do not relate to specific items in these categories.
[b] Cost of capital tied up in stock.

Source: Pinnock (1986, p. 44).

SUMMARY

It is of vital importance for retailers to evaluate and frequently re-evaluate the performance of their retailing strategy. A number of standard accounting measures can be applied to assess the financial health of the company, but such measures should be supplemented with a detailed evaluation of retail marketing performance, from the viewpoint of the target customers. Such evaluations can provide early warnings of problems that, if not corrected, would exert a negative impact upon the balance sheet.

A serious gulf can exist between retailers' evaluations of their own stores and the images held by consumers. Most senior retail managers have very little direct contact with either existing or potential customers; even at store level, managers tend to be optimistic in their estimates of their own store image. Images are composed of consumers' feeling and beliefs; they are not an

Table 5.12   DPP: applications and attitudes in the USA

	Retailers	Manufacturers
DPP Review		
Familiar with DPP (%)	99	99
Using DPP now (%)	31	56
Will be using soon (%)	83	100
Perceive competitive advantage (%)	93	99
Conducted DPP studies (%)	41	59
Main applications		
Shelf space	X	X
Display types	X	
Retail pricing	X	
Promotion	X	X
Delivery methods	X	
New product selection		X
Product design		X
Packaging		X

Source: Robson (1987, p. 2) (based upon a study by Touche Ross).

amalgam of objective measures. They are also usually formed on the basis of relatively limited stimuli, not on a full appraisal of the store's attributes.

A major problem in image monitoring is to identify the image attributes that are most salient to consumers when selecting between stores. The most salient attributes are of course likely to vary between different market situations. An appropriate first stage in image research is to identify the detailed set of potentially salient attributes; some studies have identified between forty and fifty such attributes, often with further sub-categories. It is dangerous to over-generalize these attributes or to assume that images are composed of broad, functional dimensions, such as price, range or location.

The range of techniques available for the measurement of store images is very broad. Semantic differential scales have been widely used, although several other types of scale have evolved using more compact formats. Because of the rigidity of scales, and the problems of determining which attributes to measure, many researchers and consultants prefer to use open-ended techniques, at least at the outset of a study. Multivariate techniques, especially multi-dimensional scaling (MDS) and factor analysis, are being utilized increasingly to quantify images, without imposing a preconceived structure upon the data.

Image evaluation can achieve its full potential only if it compares store images, preferably also tracking these comparisons over time. The evaluation process need not be limited to the comparison of store images; for example, further insights can be achieved by comparing perceptions of stores' clienteles. Important diagnostic information can also be gained by comparing the images of individual stores within the chain, and the images of individual departments within a store. At a broader level, image evaluation may also be applied to competing shopping centres.

Few elements of retail marketing strategy can be pursued without costs, so it is important to monitor closely the cost-effectiveness of strategic actions. The objective of cost minimization must be carefully balanced with the requirements of the company's intended positioning. The major outgoings in most retail companies are the cost of goods sold, followed by labour costs, occupancy costs and the costs of transport and other services.

The evaluation of productivity in retailing is fraught with problems, particularly in defining the true 'output'. It is also necessary to distinguish clearly between measures of productivity, efficiency and effectiveness. An important area of productivity analysis has been the measurement of scale economies associated with larger retail outlets. Most of the standard accountancy measures can be applied to evaluate the financial health of a retail company, such as profitability, liquidity, leverage and activity ratios.

Many types of retail marketing decision require the evaluation of profitability at the department, product category or individual item level. The simple measures of gross margin and mark-up provide a starting point, but only a limited perspective on true profitability. The measure of gross margin return on inventory investment (GMROI) offers a composite ratio measure, but this too fails to take into account many aspects of cost. Direct product profitability (DPP) has emerged as a difficult but more thorough measure of the profitability of retailing specific items or categories.

REVIEW QUESTIONS

1. Illustrate how the use of financial analysis alone can fail to detect quickly problems in retail marketing strategy.
2. Why do retailers' images of their own stores tend to differ from those held by consumers? Show how this difference can hinder the retailer in formulating and evaluating retail strategy.
3. 'Store image is less like a photograph than a highly interpretative portrait.' Discuss.
4. With reference to a specific type of store, give an example of an image dimension and of the possible components and attributes within this. Why is it so essential to investigate beyond the level of broad dimensions when evaluating store images?
5. Compare the advantages and problems of using the following types of scale in the evaluation of store images:
   (a)   semantic differential scale;
   (b)   graphic positioning scale;
   (c)   numerical comparative scale;
   (d)   staple scale.
6. Outline the general principal of multi-dimensional scaling (MDS) in the evaluation of store images. What are the particular advantages of MDS in the monitoring of positioning?
7. Summarize the additional strategic benefits that can be achieved by extending image comparisons in each of the following ways:
   (a)   Images of different stores' clienteles
   (b)   Images of individual stores within the chain
   (c)   Images of different departments within a store
8. What are the main elements of cost within retail operations? With reference to a specific retailer, suggest the best options for cost reduction that may be available, without prejudicing the positioning of that company.
9. Distinguish between the terms 'productivity', 'efficiency' and 'effectiveness'. Give examples of measures of each that are relevant to the evaluation of retail performance.
10. Give two examples of each of the following, indicating how each ratio is calculated:
   (a)   Profitability ratio

    (b) Liquidity ratio
    (c) Leverage ratio
    (d) Activity ratio
What does each of these ratios tell retail management about the financial state of the company?
11. How does a retail company calculate gross margin return on inventory investment (GMROI)? Discuss the scope, strengths and limitations of this measure.
12. What is direct product profitability (DPP)? Show how this measure can be used to assist retail marketing decisions. Why has the adoption of DPP been relatively slow?

REFERENCES

Achabal, D. D., J. M. Heineke and S. H. McIntyre (1984), 'Issues and perspectives on retail productivity', *Journal of Retailing*, **60**(3), 107–27.

Arnold, S. J., T. H. Oum and D. J. Tigert (1983), 'Determinant attributes in retail patronage: seasonal, temporal, regional and international comparisons', *Journal of Marketing Research*, **20**(2), 149–57.

Arons, L. (1961), 'Does TV viewing influence store image and shopping frequency?' *Journal of Retailing*, **37**(3), 1–13.

Auld, R. (1984), *The Shops Acts: Late-Night and Sunday Opening*, HMSO, London.

Bellenger, D. N., W. W. Stanton and E. Steinberg (1976), 'The congruence of store image and self image as it relates to store loyalty', *Journal of Retailing*, **52**(1), 17–32.

Bendall, A. (1985), 'The battle for better margins', *Retail & Distribution Management*, **13**(5), 16–18.

Berelson, B. (1954), 'Content analysis', in G. Lindzey (ed.), *Handbook of Social Psychology: Theory and Method*, Vol. 1, Addison-Wesley, Reading, Mass., pp. 488–522.

Berry, L. L. (1969), 'The components of department store image: a theoretical and empirical analysis', *Journal of Retailing*, **45**(1), 3–20.

Boulding, K. E. (1956), *The Image*, University of Michigan Press, Ann Arbor.

Bucklin, L. P. (1981), 'Growth and productivity change in retailing', in R. W. Stampfl and E. C. Hirschman (eds.), *Theory in Retailing: Traditional and Nontraditional Sources*, AMA, Chicago.

Burstiner, I. (1974), 'A three-way mirror: comparative images of the clienteles of Macy's, Bloomingdale's, Korvettes', *Journal of Retailing*, **50**(1), 24–36, 90.

Cardozo, R. N. (1974), 'How images vary by product class', *Journal of Retailing*, **50**(4), 85–98.

Chadwick, L. (1984), 'Comparing financial performance: ratio analysis and retail management', *Retail & Distribution Management*, **12**(3), 35–7.

Corporate Intelligence Group (1988), *The Retail Rankings*, Corporate Intelligence Research Publications, London.

Cronin, J. J. and S. J. Skinner (1984), 'Marketing outcomes, financial conditions and retail profit performance', *Journal of Retailing*, **60**(4), 9–22.

Cross, G. B. (1958), 'A critical analysis of merchandise management accounting', *Journal of Retailing*, **34**(1), 21–9.

Dalrymple, D. J. and D. L. Thompson (1969), *Retailing: an Economic View*, Free Press, New York.

Davies, G. (1987), 'Monitoring retailing strategy by measuring customer perception', in G. Johnson (ed.), *Business Strategy and Retailing*, John Wiley, Chichester, pp. 133–52.

Dawson, J. A. and D. A. Kirby (1977), 'Shop size and productivity in British retailing in the 1960s', *European Journal of Marketing*, **11**(4), 262–71.

Doyle, P. (1975), 'Measuring store image', *ADMAP*, **11**(11), 391–3.

Doyle, P. and D. Cook (1985), 'Marketing strategies, financial structure and innovation in UK retailing', in J. Gattorna (ed.), *Insights into Strategic Retail Management*, MCB University Press, Bradford, pp. 75–88.

Doyle, P. and I. Fenwick (1974), 'How store image affects shopping habits in grocery chains', *Journal of Retailing*, **50**(4), 39–52.

Euromonitor (1987), *Retail Trade in the United Kingdom*, Euromonitor, London.

Evely, R. (1978), *Issues in Retailing*, Development Analysts, Croydon.

Gabor, A. (1977), *Pricing, Principles and Practices*, Heinemann, London.

Gilman, A. L. (1988), 'The benefits of looking below gross margin', *Retailing Issues Letter*, **1**(6), 1–4.

Golden, L. L., G. Albaum and M. Zimmer (1987), 'The numerical comparative scale: an economical format for retail image measurement', *Journal of Retailing*, **63**(4), 393–410.

Good, W. S. (1984), 'Productivity in the retail grocery trade', *Journal of Retailing*, **60**(3), 81–97.

Goodman, C. S. (1985), 'On output measures of retail performance', *Journal of Retailing*, **61**(3), 77–82.

Green, P. E., A. M. Krieger and J. D. Carroll (1987), 'Conjoint analysis and multidimensional scaling: a complementary approach', *Journal of Advertising Research*, **27**(5), 21–7.

Hansen, R. and T. Deutscher (1977), 'An empirical investigation of attribute importance in retail store selection', *Journal of Retailing*, **53**(4), 59–73.

Harris, D. (1987), 'DPP takes off with new technology', *Retail & Distribution Management*, **15**(2), 9–12.

Hawkins, D. I., R. Best and G. Albaum (1976), 'Reliability of retail store images as measured by the stapel scale', *Journal of Retailing*, **52**(4), 31–8, 92.

Hirschman, E. C., B. Greenberg and D. H. Robertson (1978), 'The intermarket reliability of retail image research: an empirical examination', *Journal of Retailing*, **54**(1), 3–12.

Ingene, C. A. (1984), 'Productivity and functional shifting in spatial retailing: private and social perspectives', *Journal of Retailing*, **60**(3), 15–36.

Jacoby, J. and D. Mazursky (1984), 'Linking brand and retailer images—do the potential risks outweigh the potential benefits?' *Journal of Retailing*, **60**(2), 105–22.

Jain, A. K. and M. Etgar (1976), 'Measuring store image through multidimensional scaling of free response data', *Journal of Retailing*, **52**(4), 61–70, 95.

James, D. L., R. M. Durand and R. A. Dreves (1976), 'The use of a multi-attribute attitude model in a store image study', *Journal of Retailing*, **52**(2), 23–32.

Jolson, M. A. (1973), 'Markup calculations—still a fuzzy area?' *Journal of Retailing*, **49**(3), 77–80.

Knee, D. and D. Walters (1985), *Strategy in Retailing: Theory and Application*, Philip Allan, Oxford.

Kunkel, J. H. and L. L. Berry (1968), 'A behavioral concept of retail images', *Journal of Marketing*, **32**(4), 21–7.

Likert, R. (1932), 'A technique for the measurement of attitudes', *Archives of Psychology*, no. 140.

Lindquist, J. D. (1974), 'Meaning of image: a survey of empirical and hypothetical evidence', *Journal of Retailing*, **50**(4), 29–38, 116.

Lusch, R. F. and S. Y. Moon (1984), 'An exploratory analysis of the correlates of labor productivity in retailing', *Journal of Retailing*, **60**(3), 37–61.

Marcus, B. H. (1972), 'Image variation and the multi-unit retail establishment', *Journal of Retailing*, **48**(2), 29–43.

Martineau, P. (1958), 'The personality of the retail store', *Harvard Business Review* **36**(1), 47–55.

May, E. G. (1971a), *Selection and Clustering of Image Dimensions*, Working Paper 71–137, Marketing Science Institute, Cambridge, Mass.

May, E. G. (1971b), *Simulated Shopping Trips in Retail Image Research*, Working Paper 71–138, Marketing Science Institute, Cambridge, Mass.

May, E. G. (1971c), *Image Evaluation of a Department Store*, Working Paper P–65, Marketing Science Institute, Cambridge, Mass.

May, E. G. (1973), *Management Applications of Retail Image Research*, Working Paper 73–109, Marketing Science Institute, Cambridge, Mass.

May, E. G. (1974), 'Practical applications of recent retail image research', *Journal of Retailing*, **50**(4), 15–20, 116.

Mazursky, D. and J. Jacoby (1986), 'Exploring the development of store images', *Journal of Retailing*, **62**(2), 145–65.

McClure, P. J. and J. K. Ryans (1968), 'Differences between retailers', *Journal of Marketing Research*, **5**(1), 35–40.

McDougall, G. H. G. and J. N. Fry (1974), 'Combining two methods of image measurement', *Journal of Retailing*, **50**(4), 53–61.

McGoldrick, P. J. (1979), 'Store image: how departmental images differ in a variety chain', *Retail & Distribution Management*, **7**(5), 21–4.

McNair, M. P. and E. G. May (1957), 'Pricing for profit—a revolutionary approach to retail accounting', *Harvard Business Review*, **35**(3), 105–22.

Moir, C. B. (1987), 'Research difficulties in the analysis of Sunday trading', *International Journal of Retailing*, **2**(1), 3–21.

Monopolies and Mergers Commission (1981), *Discounts to Retailers*, HMSO, London.

Myers, J. G. (1968), *Consumer Image and Attitudes*, Institute of Business and Economic Research, Berkeley, Cal.

Nevin, J. R. and M. J. Houston (1983), 'Image as a component of attraction to intraurban shopping areas', in W. R. Darden and R. F. Lusch (eds.), *Patronage Behavior and Retail Management*, Elsevier/North-Holland, New York, pp. 427–39.

Nooteboom, B. (1986), 'Costs, margins and competition: causes of structural change', in ESOMAR (eds.), *Retail Strategies for Profit and Growth*, ESOMAR, Amsterdam, pp. 186–98.

Norkett, P. (1985), 'A financial approach to supermarket success', *Retail & Distribution Management*, **13**(6), 53–8.

Oppenheim, A. N. (1976), *Questionnaire Design and Attitude Measurement*, Heinemann, London.

Osgood, C. E., G. J. Suci and P. H. Tannenbaum (1957), *The Measurement of Meaning*, University of Illinois Press, Urbana, Ill.

Oxenfeldt, A. R. (1974), 'Developing a favorable price–quality image', *Journal of Retailing*, **50**(4), 8–14, 115.

Pathak, D. S., W. J. Crissy and R. W. Sweitzer (1974), 'Customer image versus the retailer's anticipated image', *Journal of Retailing*, **50**(4), 21–8, 116.

Pessemier, E. A. (1980), 'Store image and positioning', *Journal of Retailing*, **56**(1), 94–106.

Peterson, R. A. and R. A. Kerin (1983), 'Store image measurement in patronage research: fact and artifact', in W. R. Darden and R. F. Lusch (eds.), *Patronage Behavior and Retail Management*, Elsevier North-Holland, New York, pp. 293–306.

Pinnock, A. K. (1986), *Direct Product Profitability: an Introduction for the Grocery Trade*, Institute of Grocery Distribution, Watford, Herts.

Preston, L. E. (1963), *Profits, Competition and Rules of Thumb in Retail Food Pricing*, Institute of Business and Economic Research, University of California, Berkeley.

Retail & Distribution Management (1987), 'Curtain up for DPP', *Retail & Distribution Management*, **15**(2), 6–7.

Retail Outlets Research Unit (1974), *The MBS/IGD Figures Exchange 1972/73*, RORU, Research Paper no. 8, Manchester Business School.

Retail Review (1989), 'But DPP not an easy option, say Americans', *Retail Review*, **149**, 3.

Robson, A. (1987), 'Professional trade management—the American perspective', *IGD News*, **52**, 1–2.

Rosenbloom, B. (1981), *Retail Marketing*, Random House, New York.

Sanghavi, N. (1988), 'Space management in shops: a new initiative', *Retail & Distribution Management*, **16**(1), 14–18.

Serpkenci, R. R. and R. F. Lusch (1983), 'New model offers retailers a realistic estimate of gross margin return from merchandise lines', *Marketing News*, 18 February, 6.

Sharma, S. and V. Mahajan (1980), 'Early warning indicators of business failure', *Journal of Marketing*, **44**(4), 80–9.

Singson, R. E. (1975), 'Multidimensional scaling analysis of store image and shopping behavior', *Journal of Retailing*, **51**(2), 38–52, 93.

Stewart, D. and N. Hood (1983), 'An empirical examination of customer store image components in three UK retail groups', *European Journal of Marketing*, **17**(4), 50–62.

Sweeney, D. J. (1973), 'Improving the profitability of retail merchandising decisions', *Journal of Marketing*, **37**(1), 60–8.

Thompson, A. A. and A. J. Strickland (1987), *Strategic Management: Concepts and Cases* (4th ed.), Richard D. Irwin Inc., Homewood, Ill.

Thorpe, D. and P. M. Shepherd (1977), *Some Aspects of Economies of Scale in Food Retailing*, Retail Outlets Research Unit, Manchester Business School.

Thurik, R. and N. Van der Wijst (1984), 'Part-time labor in retailing', *Journal of Retailing*, **60**(3), 62–80.

Tigert, D. J. (1982), 'Pushing the hot buttons for a successful retailing strategy', in ESOMAR (ed.), *Profitable Co-operation of Manufacturers and Retailers: The Contribution of Research*, ESOMAR, Amsterdam, pp. 119–62.

Tucker, K. A. (1975), *Economies of Scale in Retailing*, Saxon House, Farnborough, Hants.

Tull, D. S. and D. I. Hawkins (1987), *Marketing Research: Meaning, Measurement and Method*, Macmillan, New York.

Walters, D. (1986), 'Direct product profitability: cost-led or market-led retail management?' *Retail*, **4**(2), 44–8.

Weale, W. B. (1961), 'Measuring the customer's image of a department store', *Journal of Retailing*, **37**(2), 40–8.

Zimmer, M. R. and L. L. Golden (1988), 'Impressions of retail stores: a content analysis of consumer images', *Journal of Retailing*, **64**(3), 265–93.

TWO

—THE RETAIL MARKETING MIX

RETAIL LOCATION

INTRODUCTION

Store location decisions are frequently considered to be the single most important elements of retail marketing. Although a good location is unlikely in itself to compensate for mediocre overall strategy, a poor location can be a deficit that is very difficult to overcome. Even very small physical differences between locations can exert a major influence upon the stores' accessibility and attractiveness to customers.

The implementation time-scale also distinguishes location from other decision areas in retail marketing. Changes in merchandising or pricing, for example, can be administered almost immediately (although customer perceptions will of course change more slowly); the opening of a new store, on the other hand, is preceded by a planning and development process that can take years. The location decision represents a long-term investment and a very major investment, in the case of large, purpose-built outlets.

Rising property and land costs, coupled with competitive pressures to develop new store formats, have ensured that location decisions are also a major part of retailers' financial strategies. At a net book value of £532 million, the property assets of the Burton group were almost at the level of their annual turnover in 1985 (Mintel 1986). Marks & Spencer's UK property assets were valued at £1,244 million, 96 per cent of which was freehold property or on leases of over 50 years. Such organizations are therefore not just in the retailing business, but are deeply involved in the property business too. Each store location decision is therefore 'a long term financial commitment that will become either an asset or a liability' (Applebaum 1966).

In keeping with its importance within the strategic mix, the subject of store location has developed an extensive literature. The topic has been addressed from several perspectives, being of direct interest to researches in geography, marketing, town planning, operations research and economics. It will not be possible within this chapter to do justice to each of these perspectives, or to explore fully all the related theoretical approaches. A number of specialist texts (e.g. Davies and Rogers 1984; Wrigley 1988) are available to facilitate the exploration of specific topics in greater depth.

The first section of the chapter presents the techniques that may be used in identifying areas for geographical expansion and in evaluating specific sites. The section starts with a brief review of location practices, then presents a checklist of factors to be considered. The use of analogues in site assessment is discussed, followed by an account of trade area mapping techniques. A number of commercial agencies using very large computerized databases have now entered the field, and examples of their services are presented. Mathematical modelling techniques are then discussed, first multiple regression analysis, then spatial interaction or gravity models.

Up to this point, the influence of town planning is virtually ignored, although this represents a major constraint upon retail locations in most countries. The second section of the chapter therefore examines the planning framework in Britain and the procedures for obtaining planning permission. The key issues are discussed, notably those relating to land use, traffic and impact on other traders.

6.1 STORE LOCATION TECHNIQUES AND MODELS

This section will first examine the techniques most frequently used by retailers to help identify and evaluate potential new sites. Most of these techniques would serve equally well for the assessment of existing store performance, providing more objective performance yardsticks than those commonly used. Major distinctions are therefore not drawn here between techniques for store location and techniques for store assessment. Some of the more sophisticated modelling techniques are then discussed, representing the direction in which store location analysis is now moving.

6.1.1 Location techniques in practice

A number of researchers have suggested sequences that retail location decisions should follow, starting with the most general assessments of geographical areas, through to the detailed assessment of specific site characteristics. Davies (1976) points out, however, that the need for quick decisions often prevents such systematic ordering of the location decision process. In general, a retailer with a well defined, medium- to long-term location strategy is more likely to be in a position to follow a logical decision sequence than a retailer whose location decisions are mostly reactions to specific opportunities or threats.

Bowlby *et al.* (1984a) offer a sequence which could be considered part of an 'ideal' retail location strategy:

1. *Search*—the identification of geographical areas that may have potential for new outlet(s)
2. *Viability*—finding the best site(s) available within the given areas and forecasting the store turnover that may be derived from these
3. *Micro*—examination of all the detailed features of a specific site that are relevant to potential store performance

The characteristics of each level in this decision hierarchy clearly vary according to the nature of the retail company, in particular the level of product specialization and the importance of convenience in the strategic mix. It is therefore more difficult to classify rigidly the techniques that are appropriate to each stage of the decision. Many of the techniques outlined in the following sections may assist at more than one stage in this sequence.

There have been many case studies but few wider-scale surveys of retailer's location assessment practices. Table 6.1 summarizes evidence presented by Simkin *et al.* (1985), derived from 30 interviews and a postal questionnaire survey. These data illustrate the scale of the store location task within four of the retailer types studied. Not surprisingly, those operating discount warehouses and the grocery supermarket/superstore category were the most active in assessing potential sites. Although the sub-sample sizes in this study were not large, it was clear that most larger companies have specialist location assessment units within their property, estate or research departments.

Table 6.1 A survey of store location practices

Retailer type	Grocery s/market $ s/stores	Department stores	Variety stores	Discount warehouses
Stores opened per annum (mean)	6.2	1	3	9.5
Stores relocated per annum (mean)	1.4	—	4	4.5
Sites assessed fully per month	10	1	7	12
% companies with specialist research units	100	100	100	100
% companies conducting research continually	100	100	100	80
Main techniques used	Analogues Mathematical models	Checklists Financial appraisals	Checklists Analogues	Analogues Checklists
Main criteria				
Competition	X	X	X	X
Demographics	X	X	X	X
Local economy		X		
Site size, type		X	X	X
Accessibility	X			X
Turnover threshold			X	
Planning permission	X			X
Ratings (0–100 scale) of research				
Thoroughness	90	91	85	79
Quality	71	79	66	59

Source: derived from Simkin *et al.* (1985, pp. 21–6).

A major conclusion of this study was that many of the more sophisticated techniques to be found within the literature are not used by retailers in general. It was also noted that the more financially successful retailers, measured on a number of standard criteria, do not necessarily undertake location research more thoroughly or to a higher quality. 'Thoroughness' ratings were based upon a checklist of factors considered (or not), whereas 'Quality' ratings were based upon the use made by the retailers of supportive data and analysis. The larger-scale grocery retailers proved the most likely to have utilized mathematical modelling techniques, usually regression analysis. It is clear that checklists, comprising factors to be assessed, and analogues, based upon stores with comparable characteristics, are still the cornerstones of most retailers' location research. Indeed, even as more sophisticated techniques gain wider utilization, they are likely to complement rather than replace the use of checklists and analogues.

To a large extent, the choice of techniques must depend upon the needs and priorities for a particular situation. Choices are typically also subject to constraints of time, cost, data availability/quality, staff experience, software availability, etc. Beaumont (1987) suggested a list of questions which could assist a retailer in selecting the appropriate method(s) of store location analysis:

1. Decision-making process
   —What time period?
   —What type of results are required?
   —Is the method sophisticated?
   —Are structural changes likely?
2. Resources
   —Are the data available?
   —What are the software requirements?
   —What are the staffing implications?
   —What is the cost?

6.1.2 Location evaluation checklists

Most major retailers have developed detailed checklists of the factors to be considered when evaluating potential new trading areas and sites. Some elements of these checklists will be common to all retail types, but each retailer's list is likely to contain elements reflecting that company's particular trading style. It is obvious that a petrol retailer will have a very different checklist from that of a fashion retailer. It comes as more of a surprise to learn the extent of differences in the checklists of more comparable retailers, reflecting important differences in their positioning strategies and trading strengths.

The checklist technique was developed over thirty years ago. Nelson (1958) presented one of the most detailed checklist evaluation formats, comprising 8 major categories and 36 specific areas of evaluation. That checklist placed much emphasis upon changes in population and land use, reflecting a time of rapid building and growth. Rather more emphasis now tends to be placed upon the detailed characteristics of the population within the projected trading area.

A checklist primarily helps to avoid the danger of overlooking aspects of relevance to potential trading performance. You need only study a nearby shopping area to find many outcomes of location decisions that appear to have ignored important checklist factors. This may or may not in fact be true. Retailers and developers are limited in their choice of sites, and few locations are so good as to score highly on all elements of a checklist. If nothing else, at least a checklist may have served to highlight the deficits in order that these could be weighed in the decision, rather than ignored.

A checklist is only the starting point of an evaluation process; it essentially provides the questions, not the answers. Many of the techniques described in subsequent sections in fact build upon the checklist by providing detailed answers or estimates of specific elements. The checklist can also provide the framework of a strategic planning data base, developed on a long-term, rolling basis. Following extensive experience in shop development with the Boots company, Pope (1984) presented a database checklist, distinguishing between externally and internally derived data. Table 6.2 summarizes the main categories within that checklist.

In that a checklist forms the starting point of most store location evaluations, it may be helpful at this stage to note the factors that could be examined under each major heading. Table 6.3

Table 6.2 Checklist of data sources

External sources	Internal sources
Population totals	Retail sales
Population types	Sales areas
Income	Sales productivities
Unemployment	Stock and stock areas
Retail sales	Tenure type
Shopping centre composition	Other performance indicators
Competition	Sales forecasts
Branch position	
Inflation	

Source: 'Developing a strategic planning data base' by M. P. R. Pope in R. L. Davies and D. S. Rogers (eds.), *Store Location and Store Assessment Research*, Copyright © 1984 John Wiley & Sons Ltd. Reprinted by permission of John Wiley & Sons Ltd.

Table 6.3 Location checklist factors

Population	Accessibility	Competition	Costs
Population size	Pedestrian flow	Existing retail activity	Purchase price
Age profile	Pedestrian entry routes	Direct competitors	Leasing terms
Household size	Public transport	Indirect competitors	Site preparation
Income levels	Types	Anchor stores	Building restrictions
Disposable income per capita	Cost	Cumulative attraction	Building costs
Occupation classifications	Ease of use	Compatibility	Development concessions
Main employers	Potential	Existing retail specification	Rates payable
Economic stability	Car ownership levels	Selling areas	Refurbishment needs
Unemployment levels	Road network	Turnover estimates	Maintenance costs
Seasonal fluctuations	Conditions	Department/product	Security needs
Housing density	Driving speeds	analysis	Staff availability/rates
Housing age/type	Congestion	Trade areas	Delivery costs
Neighbourhood classification	Restrictions	Age of outlets	Promotional media/costs
Home ownership levels	Plans	Standard of design	Turnover loss—other
Building/demolition plans	Parking	Car parking	branches
Life-style measures	Capacity	Saturation index	
Cultural/ethnic groupings	Convenience	Competitive potential	
Current shopping patterns	Cost	Outlet expansion	
	Potential	Refurbishment	
	Visibility	Vacant sites	
	Access for staff	Interception	
	Access for transport and	Repositioning	
	deliveries	Competitor policy	

presents a very generalized checklist of the types of information that may be sought in order to estimate likely trading areas, forecast turnover and calculate the likely profitability of the proposed store. The issues relevant to obtaining planning permission, where this is required, are considered in Section 6.3.

Population Fundamental to any evaluation is a detailed review of the population character-istics within the relevant zones. Many of the key statistics relating to population size, age profiles, household composition and occupations can be obtained through the decennial cen-suses. However, this information eventually becomes outdated and the statistics for small areas may prove awkward to aggregate for the area under investigation. Local authorities may be able to provide more current information, and the commercial agencies, such as CACI and Pinpoint (see Section 6.1.5), are increasingly stepping in to supply these data. For a detailed review of the general data sources, see Jones (1984).

Several factors combine to indicate the present and potential spending power within an area. Income levels alone are a poor indication, unless linked to information about family and mortgage/housing commitments. Measures of disposable income and current spending propen-sities, if available, are therefore preferable. Local unemployment levels are now a key statistic, as broad regional data can disguise very major differences within smaller areas. The employment structure and stability of an area should be assessed. If for example a major steel production plant closes, the effect on the local economy would be drastic and previously viable retail sites may lose most of their value.

The location analyst should also seek information on the existing housing density, age and type. Levels of house ownership may also be important, for example in the evaluation of a DIY superstore site. Housing and neighbourhood types are increasingly being used as segmentation bases, but other bases may also be utilized, such as life-style measures and cultural, religious and ethnic groupings. If such information about the population can be obtained, a more thorough assessment of viability can be undertaken. If the site is selected, the information can then provide an input to the store and merchandise planning process.

Accessibility As car ownership continues to increase, accessibility is sometimes seen as synony-mous with driving times and parking provision. These are indeed key variables in most retail location decisions, but a detailed assessment requires consideration of many other factors that may facilitate, or deter, journeys to and from the store. Care must also be taken to give appropriate weightings to the factors most salient to the particular type of outlet proposed. A free-standing superstore may represent the primary purpose of most customers' journeys; many smaller stores, however, serve pedestrian or vehicle journeys. Very different criteria of accessibil-ity are therefore implied.

Within existing centres, the number of pedestrians moving past the proposed site is an essential measure. Even the most successful shopping centres have relative 'low spots', in spite of attempts by centre management to encourage circulation in all sections and levels. The entry routes to the site are also significant; subways are not popular with most shoppers, which was one of the factors inhibiting use of the Elephant and Castle centre in London.

Many traditional centres are still dependent upon public transport for a fairly high proportion of their customer traffic. Under such circumstances, the types currently and potentially avail-able, and their costs, should be part of the site evaluation. Centres such as Manchester are well served by rail services, but the long walk or short bus journey from the stations considerably increases the 'friction' of the journey. In this case, the local authority and British Rail are actively investigating new, lighter rail vehicles that can travel beyond the stations and into the shopping areas, using tram-type lines.

Although public transport continues to fulfil an important role in many shopping centres, most new retail developments must now pay utmost attention to their accessibility to car-borne shoppers. The overall level of car ownership continues to grow (see Chapter 2), but local measures of ownership help to judge the likely balance of car/public transport/pedestrian shoppers. No two retail locations are quite alike in terms of the surrounding road conditions, so the most detailed study of these is warranted.

The problems that can be caused by traffic congestion, difficult manoeuvres, traffic signals (or lack of them) and turning restrictions have long been recognized. Cohen and Applebaum (1960) presented a series of detailed maps which vividly illustrated the outcome of such problems for retail sites. The site assessor is well advised to calculate or obtain micro-isochrones, which represent the driving time/distance 'contours' around a site. These can provide graphic illustration of the areas within 5, 10, 15, (etc.) minutes' driving distances. For a large shopping development, effects of the new shopper traffic must also be estimated and the plans for road development should be consulted. I know of one very large store which lost 50 per cent of its existing customer traffic when a nearby motorway junction was closed during a three-year road improvement project.

The requirement for adequate car parking places a heavy additional demand upon space required for a new centre or free-standing store. Based upon the experience of Super Value Stores in the USA, Snow and Scott (1984) suggested an optimum ratio of 8 parking places per 1,000 sq. ft of building. Neafcy (1984) indicated that Asda consider 10 places per 1,000 sq. ft as ideal for their new superstores. The access routes to car parks require careful negotiation with local planners to avoid the creation of congestion points and, preferably, to enable necessary modifications to be made to relevant junctions and feeder roads. The site assessment must also weigh the potentials for ground-level and multi-level car parking. The former is usually preferred on cost and accessibility grounds, although an excessively large ground-level car park may be inconvenient to shoppers in bad weather and may also, at off-peak times, give the impression that the store is not popular.

The visibility of a store is an important facet of accessibility, plus a valuable measure of its ability to attract passing trade. In the case of new stores, the retailer's wish to maximize visibility is frequently at odds with the town planner's desire to blend or disguise new developments. An Asda superstore at Newport, for example, enjoyed convenient access to the M4 motorway but was rather less visible than the retailer would have preferred. Within the busy centre of Manchester's Piccadilly, a group of new shops failed, mainly because they were hardly visible from the outside and were accessible only by subways and escalators.

The checklist should also consider the accessibility of the store for staff; retail outlets situated on motorways or remote from public transport routes, for example, may incur the cost of transporting staff or be restricted in their recruitment scope. Within existing, congested centres, the access for delivery vehicles can be a major issue, particularly if loading times are restricted or if loading interferes with customer traffic.

Competition   If competition could be easily defined then it would be a simpler task to measure existing competition within an area. Very few retailers, however, trade within sectors that are not subject to a great deal of 'indirect' competition from other types of retailer. As competitors become less constrained and more aggressive in their diversification policies, this difficulty increases. A variety store or department store retailer may have to consider a very large number of indirect competitors in a new area; if only competitors of the same type were considered, serious deficiencies in the forecasts would result.

The evaluation must also weigh the positive effects of other retail activity in an area. The 'anchor stores' within a shopping centre may well offer competition to the proposed store, but they are crucial elements in maintaining the customer flow to and within the centre. Figure 6.1 shows the ground-floor layout of the Gateshead Metro centre, where the Carrefour, Marks & Spencer and House of Fraser stores provide the main anchors. Anderson (1985) demonstrated through regression analysis that anchor stores can be a powerful determinant of non-anchor stores' sales and profitability.

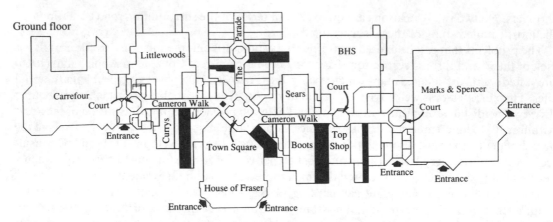

Figure 6.1 Metrocentre—ground floor plan
Source: CC Property Services.

A grouping of smaller, specialist outlets may also benefit from the concept of cumulative attraction, together providing a magnate that no one such store could have offered in isolation. The benefits of agglomerated centres are discussed in some detail by Ghosh (1986). Groupings may often be found of high-fashion stores, shoe shops or antique stalls, with the street or locality developing a favourable reputation for choice of products and stores. Larger-scale retailers may find that their trading style is compatible. For example, areas in which Marks & Spencer have a high share have been found particularly receptive to J. Sainsbury store developments. An empirical investigation of trading interdependency was undertaken by Brown (1987). Around 70 per cent of retailers surveyed felt that their trade was linked to that of businesses situated nearby; this linkage was especially strong in the case of clothing shops and department and variety stores, where comparison shopping is most likely to occur. This study helped to quantify the importance of 'magnate' stores and effects of cumulative attraction.

Having identified the relevant competition, an analysis of trading strengths and weaknesses should be conducted. Selling areas, if necessary broken down by product/department groupings, would be a basic element of this evaluation. Surveys may be undertaken to help estimate turnovers and calculate existing trade areas. The physical characteristics of the stores would also be assessed, including their age, standard of design and car parking provision.

When comparing alternative possible trading areas, it is tempting to reduce the assessment of competition and potential to an index of retail saturation (La Londe 1961). This can provide a useful comparative measure, provided that the relevant product/market competitive set(s) have been defined. This index may be calculated using the following formula:

$$IRS_{ji} = \frac{C_{ji} \times RE_{ji}}{RF_{ji}}$$

where IRS_{ji} = index of retail saturation for product j in area i
          C_{ji} = number of consumers in i who buy j
          RE_{ji} = retail expenditure per consumer in i on j
          RF_{ji} = total retail floorspace in i devoted to selling j.

It is clearly unrealistic to assume that competitors will not react to a new store opening or that they will not pursue their own development programmes. A study of the scope for outlet expansion or refurbishment may help to predict reactions. Other available sites should also be viewed as potential competition, presenting a particular concern if the site intercepts customers from the principle trading area. Most retailers try to maintain close contact with competitors' policies and plans so as to better predict changes in competition.

Costs The evaluation of population, accessibility and competition attributes are combined to produce a forecast of the likely turnover that could be derived from a site. The calculation of profit potential then requires a detailed study of all the likely development and running costs that will be incurred. As Bowlby *et al.* (1984a) concluded, the 'easy' sites, where a retailer could hardly fail to produce a profit, are mostly gone. Even a small outlet can cost over £200,000 to lease, equip and stock. As superstores are developed on more expensive land, especially in the South East of Britain, the development cost may be around £10 million for a superstore. Schiller (1987) has reported instances of £2 million per acre being paid for favourable superstore sites, indicating that the land alone could cost around £13 million.

Many of the cost data are obtained following negotiations with developers or lease owners and from detailed estimation of construction/refurbishment costs. In this respect, the figures are mostly derived from internal company sources, although many site-specific attributes must be taken into account. In comparing site cost/rental levels with national norms, Jones (1984) noted a paucity of data. A time-series analysis of shop rent levels is however provided by the Investors Chronicle in conjunction with Hillier-Parker (e.g. Hillier-Parker 1987).

When a new site is developed, the cost of site preparation may be greater than the purchase price, especially if extensive demolition is needed or unsuitable land has to be converted. The initial site of the Gateshead Metrocentre, for example, was bought for a relatively modest £1 million, but a far larger investment was then required to remove the waterlogged ashpits from the site. Building restrictions relating to height, architectural requirements or landscaping can also greatly influence building costs. The rates payable are frequently an area of contention between retailers and local authorities; they may present a major disincentive to develop inner-city sites, unless significant concessions are made.

The location, site and building design of a store greatly influence future running costs. A store requiring multi-level sales floors or car parking will have to cover the substantial maintenance costs of escalators or lifts. A location with a high crime rate is inevitably going to increase security costs and 'shrinkage' through theft. Retailers have been forced to close stores in some especially bad areas, when the theft of not only stock but also store equipment reached unacceptable levels. At the other end of the spectrum, an area with high employment and wage rates may bring problems of staff recruitment and retention.

Other cost factors include delivery costs; a site remote from the main distribution network may considerably increase such costs or require a major extension of the network. The costs of promoting the store locally could also be considered, although the proliferation of local media now provides suitable opportunities in most areas. Finally, and very importantly, the cost analysis must consider any possible impact of the new outlet on other branches. The higher the existing market share within an area, the greater the potential loss, although this has been accepted as a necessary trade-off by major grocery multiples expanding their superstore networks. In Section 6.1.7, some attempts to model the effects of multiple locations will be considered.

6.1.3 The analogue method

The study by Simkin *et al.* (1985), summarized in Table 6.1, illustrated the importance of analogues among the location techniques used by UK retailers. The analogue procedure is essentially as follows:

1. Identify other stores, preferably within the same chain, which have many essential features in common with the proposed store and location.
2. Quantify the key features of these stores and trading areas, then tabulate and summarize these data.
3. Extrapolate from these analogue stores to estimate the likely turnover and profitability of a store at the proposed location.

It may be noted from Table 6.1 that the department stores were least likely to have used the analogue method, mainly because they tend to have fewer and/or more varied stores. Although extrapolations are sometimes made based upon broadly analogous competitors' stores, this causes additional problems. Detailed turnover data are more difficult to obtain, and competitors' stores may be less truly analogous in terms of product ranges and overall images.

The analogue method therefore represents a systematic use of checklist data, which is designed to minimize the need for subjective judgement on the part of the analyst. Early examples of the method were presented by William Applebaum (1966), following its development as a forecasting technique with the Kroger Company. Retailers using the method now frequently update their analogue data, and, in common with most other forecasting techniques, it is also a valuable method for evaluating existing stores.

Table 6.4 presents a simple example of the analogue method, using the approach suggested by Applebaum but rebased on more recently derived UK superstore data. The first section of the table shows the proportion of trade derived by three analogue stores from each time/distance zone. The analyst will be able to establish the population living within each of these zones and thereby to calculate the per capita sales for each analogue/zone. The final section of the table shows the extrapolation for the proposed store. Note that the estimates are not based strictly upon the mean values for the analogue; the analyst is likely to exercise judgement as to likely deviations from the means. Typically, if the store is built, the realized sales/zone data will be collected in order that future forecasts can be further refined.

In that the analogue technique is based upon actual historical sales performances, it represents a considerable improvement upon generalizations such as the so-called 'share of space' method. This very crude rule of thumb was often used in the absence of systematic data. It worked on the assumption that the new store's share of sales within the likely trading area would be proportional to the store's share of selling space within that area. With the vast range of space productivities achieved, as an extreme comparison, by J. Sainsbury and the co-operatives, this is generally an unacceptable assumption.

Applebaum (1966) did not claim that the analogue method would replace subjective judgement; rather, he believed that it would both guide and limit it. As Drummey (1984) points out, subjective judgement inevitably has a role in evaluating new sites, as no two situations are ever exactly alike. The precision of the analogue can be further refined through the addition of survey data (Section 6.1.4) and information from computerized databases (Section 6.1.5). Rogers and Green (1979) do however identify problems in using the analogue approach alone: essentially, that the task of the analyst becomes extremely difficult as the database grows and more intricate causal relationships are identified. At that point it makes sense to start developing multivariate regression models, in order better to investigate the causal linkages (Section 6.1.6).

Table 6.4 Example of a superstore analogue

Driving time zones (min)	Proportion of analogue stores' sales from zones (%)			
	A	B	C	D
0–4	7	5	7	6
5–9	27	22	24	24
10–14	26	30	33	30
15–19	18	19	14	17
20 +	22	24	22	23

Zones (min)	Per capita sales of analogues (£)			
	A	B	C	D
0–4	3.70	3.09	4.42	3.74
5–9	0.52	0.39	0.44	0.45
10–14	0.24	0.26	0.32	0.27
15–19	0.10	0.11	0.08	0.10

	Application of analogues A–C to the new location			
Zones (min)	Population ('000)	Est. % sales from zone	Est. sales per capita (£)	Est. weekly sales (£000)
0–4	32.3	7	3.84	124.0
5–9	79.6	26	0.48	38.2
10–14	122.0	30	0.28	34.2
15–19	251.8	16	0.08	20.1
		79		216.5
20 +		21		57.6
		100		274.1

6.1.4 Trade area mapping

The methods utilized to survey and map stores' trading areas do not in themselves comprise forecasting techniques. They do however provide a valuable input to analogues or more sophisticated forecasting methods. Surveys at equivalent stores can provide estimates of trade area density and also show the effects of competition within that area. Such surveys can also provide inputs to promotional strategy and can assist in the evaluation of store performance.

Many detailed examples, showing the several applications of mapping techniques, were presented by Cohen and Applebaum (1960) and Applebaum (1968). At the simplest level, a map can depict with the use of dots the home addresses of each customer interviewed at the store. In the USA, maps of this type have sometimes been constructed based upon the licence plates of cars entering the car park, but in the UK a customer survey is usually necessary. Alternatively, if a retailer has comprehensive customer information derived from credit transactions, guarantee registrations, deliveries or service calls, this may provide the basis of a trade area map. Care must

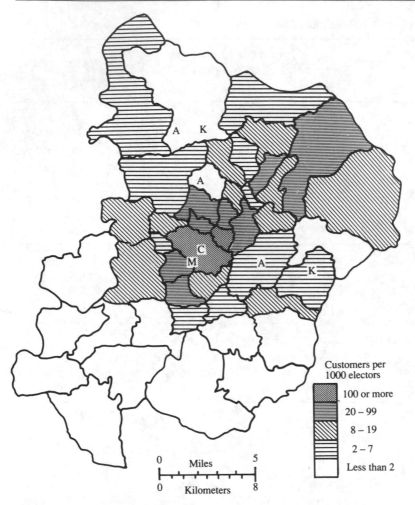

Figure 6.2   Mapping a superstore catchment area
Key: C, Co-op Superstore; M, Whelan (Morrisons) Store; A, Asda Superstores;
K, Kwik Save Stores
Source: Thomas *et al*. (1977).

be taken, however, to ensure that the information is truly representative of the overall customers, and not just of a specific subset.

When related to population data, a store survey can provide valuable estimates of market penetration within each part of the trading area. Figure 6.2 was based upon a survey (Thomas *et al*. 1977) at a Co-operative superstore to the north of Manchester. Data were obtained indicating the number of electors within 47 adjacent districts, which formed the basis of this map. The measure of catchment per 1,000 electors was calculated using the following formula:

$$S_j = [I_j \times \{(T/F)/N\}/E_j] \times 1,000$$

where S_j = shoppers per 1,000 electors in area j
I_j = interviewees from area j

T = mean transactions per week at store
F = mean weighted shopping frequency
N = survey sample size
E_j = electors in area j

A weighting system was applied to give less weight to the frequent users, who naturally tend to be over-represented in a store based sample. This and other sampling issues in drawing trade area maps were later discussed by Blair (1983). The figure illustrates that the trade area of this store could not have been estimated accurately using concentric circles or simple time/distance zones. Strong competition to the north creates a trough in the catchment area, whereas the primary area extends further to the north-east, assisted by good public and private transport accessibility, plus a relative lack of competition in that direction. In contrast, the trading area is truncated to the south by the city centre of Manchester.

Many of the cartographic tasks involved in mapping trade areas can be replaced by computer software systems, such as SYMAP. Epstein (1984) described this and other systems that exploit the capabilities of computer graphics in plotting black and white or colour maps. Rust and Brown (1986) reviewed some of the available procedures for continuous mapping and presented a refined system for estimating trade area densities. Such systems have now made mapping an easier and more flexible tool for reviewing detailed aspects of trade areas, such as the origins of customers at different times or the trade areas for specific products and departments. Similarly, the effects of changes in competition, promotional strategies or access routes can be depicted on a before and after basis.

6.1.5 Computerized databases

For many years the retail location analyst in the UK has suffered a paucity of basic marketing statistics (Jones 1984). There was a heavy dependence upon government department data, although these tended to be less well co-ordinated than, for example, the population and expenditure data of the Bureau of Censuses in the USA. The supply of UK information grew considerably worse following a series of government cuts, including the mid-term sample population census and the detailed Censuses of Distribution. It became clear that the UK government was no longer prepared to finance retail statistics; opportunities were therefore created for a new generation of 'data men', i.e. private companies specializing in database development, analysis and consultancy. In that these have now acquired an important role in retail location analysis, the services of two such companies will be briefly described here.

From 1983, Pinpoint Analysis Ltd has specialized in various forms of geographical analysis, many of which are relevant to retail location decisions. Specifically, this company manages and analyses large databases, including the Postcode Address File, containing some 23 million addresses. Each of the 1.3 million postcodes is linked to a grid reference. By 1988 the company had mapped the address code of every residential and commercial property in the UK to within 1 metre. Given this level of accuracy, customer or survey address lists can be used to computer-generate trade area and trade density maps. In order that these maps can relate to relevant boundaries, a variety of physical and administrative boundaries have been digitized as inputs to computer mapping procedures.

The company has also made available on a single disk pack the output of the 1981 census small area statistics, covering all 130,000 census enumeration districts in the UK. Variables within these census data include age, family, country of origin, employment type, qualifications, house specification, car ownership, and travel-to-work details. When linked to the postcode address file

Table 6.5 Extract from retail potential report (Pinpoint): CTNs within a two-mile radius of Sunderland

| | Aggregate spending | | |
Commodity	CTN (£000)	All businesses (£000)	Market index
Sweets and chocolates	1,374	2,512	92
Tobacco products	4,214	6,679	109
Cigarettes	3,881	6,151	109
Others	333	528	108
Newspapers, magazines and periodicals	1,533	1,823	83
Books, stationery and office supplies	194	1,670	80
Groceries and provisions	415	18,059	91
Toys, sports goods	87	1,497	77
Other goods	517		
Total	8,334		100

Estimates supportable stores = 62

Source: based upon information supplied by DSR Marketing and PINPOINT Analysis Ltd.

and other household-specific data sources, this provides a means of identifying areas or addresses meeting specified criteria. A further database, 'Lupin', is being developed from over 60,000 telephone interviews, which eventually aims to cover one in 200 telephone-owning homes. Details of shopping behaviour are obtained, which can provide estimates of existing patronage patterns within an area and also help in the calibration of gravity models (see Section 6.1.7).

In conjunction with DSR Marketing Systems, Pinpoint provide retail potential reports for specified areas, drawing also upon data from the Department of Employment's Family Expenditure surveys. Table 6.5 shows an extract from such a report, indicating the estimated expenditure on confectioners', tobacconists' and newsagents' product groups around Sunderland. These data are derived from 'per household' expenditures, scaled up to the known number of households within the area. The proportion of expenditure in each product class that would be expected to be made through CTNs is identified and, from this, an estimate of 'supportable stores', based upon national norms, is produced. When linked to information on existing stores within the defined area, this technique is similar in approach to the 'vacuum method' described by Davies (1976, pp. 270–2). The 'market index' shown in the final column of Table 6.5 indicates whether the expenditure in that area is above or below the national average.

The first company in the UK to develop a computerized database from the census was CACI, well known for its classification of residential neighbourhoods (ACORN), described in Chapter 3. Since 1977 this company has developed a range of data services, some of which compete directly with those described above. It claims to have provided these to 75 per cent of major retailers and is generally regarded as the market leader in this field.

A number of case studies of retailers using CACI services have been reported (e.g. Retail & Distribution Management 1983). Dingles, part of the House of Fraser group, used CACI to analyse store catchment areas and to better define their key target groups. Because of their relatively up-market profile, they found that market penetration was sometimes highest in areas some distance away from their stores, rather than in the immediate vicinity. This spelt a clear

Table 6.6   Extract from Shop Count Report (CACI) Centre: Basildon, Essex

Distribution of outlets by activity type	Outlets		Base	
	N	%	%	Index
Convenience outlets				
1. Bakers	5	1.9	2.3	86
2. Butchers	6	2.3	2.4	96
3. Greengrocers & fishmongers	0	0.0	2.1	0
4. Grocers & provision dealers	4	1.5	3.3	47
5. Off-licences	1	0.4	1.2	33
6. Confectioners, tobacconists, newsagents	7	2.7	3.7	73
Total convenience outlets	23	8.9	14.9	60
Comparison outlets				
7. Footwear shops & repairs	21	8.1	4.0	201
8. Mens & boyswear	12	4.6	3.0	155
9. Ladies & girlswear/drapers/woolshops	33	12.7	9.0	142
10. Furniture, furnishings, carpets	10	3.9	5.2	75
11. Books, art, stationery, cards, printing	8	3.1	3.3	94
12. Gas, electrical, hi-fi, optical goods	22	8.5	7.4	115
13. Building, decorating, ironmongery	6	2.3	3.0	78
14. China, glassware, leather, fancy goods	2	0.8	2.1	37
15. Cycle, pram, motor accessory	2	0.8	1.3	59
16. Chemists, opticians & surgical suppliers	10	3.9	3.5	110
17. Variety, department & general household	11	4.2	2.1	201
18. Florists & horticultural	1	0.4	1.1	36
19. Hobby, craft, toys, sports shops	6	2.3	2.3	101
20. Jewellers, watchmakers, engravers	10	3.9	2.8	136
21. Petshops & petfood	1	0.4	0.6	67
22. Camping, gov't surplus, secondhand	1	0.4	0.7	54
Total comparison outlets	156	60.2	51.3	117
Services outlets (categories 23–29)				
30. Unclassified & Misc.	6	2.3	2.6	88
31. Vacant & Under Construction	31	12.0	8.2	145

Car park spaces per outlet = 12.2   Base = 3.9   Index = 312

Source: based upon information supplied by CACI Market Analysis Division.

warning about the dangers of oversimplified trade area assumptions. Comet has also made extensive use of CACI services. From 150,000 customer addresses derived from product guarantee registrations, it was possible to develop a detailed profile of customer types and to model the effects of opening stores in new areas.

Among the new services developed primarily for retail location analysis, CACI has assembled a data file of road types and congestion levels. From this, a computerized isochrone system has been developed which indicates drive-time-bands for any site in the UK. Another recent enhancement is a system called 'Shopping Centre Planner', which identifies competition in an area. Table 6.6 shows an excerpt from these data, relating to Basildon. The index in the final column compares the proportion of outlets of each type with a national base of 1,016 centres and 197,632 outlets. In this specific example, footwear shops are heavily represented, whereas florists have a low representation. A similar analysis can also be provided indicating relative proportions of floorspace. Clearly, more needs to be known about the nature of outlets within an area, although this type of analysis provides a useful starting point in the identification of suitable areas for store development.

A number of criticisms have been levelled against this new generation of commercial data. For example, Bowlby *et al.* (1984b) pointed out that typologies such as ACORN are very general and may not be best fitted to a specific type of store. Assumptions about the shopping behaviour of a specific ACORN or census-based segment may also be based on a survey including a rather modest number of shoppers within that segment. Such criticisms can of course be made of many forms of segmentation-based analysis, and the 'datamen' have responded to such criticisms by diversifying their databases and introducing more flexibility into their approaches to clients' problems. A major concern to the retail location analyst is that, given the assertive marketing of such companies, it is more difficult critically to evaluate the bases and the appropriateness of the packages offered. Some caution is therefore required, although there seems little doubt that commercial, computerized databases will continue to develop and help to fill the many information gaps that still remain in retail location decision-making.

6.1.6 Multiple-regression analysis

Given the increasingly complex array of data potentially available to the location analyst, there is a need to utilize more sophisticated procedures to identify the relationships between store sales and the various predictor variables. For example, measures of population, per capita income, competition and store size may each be known to relate to potential sales. Using multiple-regression analysis, a model can be constructed which harnesses the predictive power of all, or the most appropriate subset, of the available predictor variables. Few applications of this technique have been published in detail, although Simkin *et al.* (1985) note that regression models are now being used in the UK, particularly by major grocery retailers (see Table 6.1). Davies (1973) presents an example, based on tailoring stores, in which multiple regression was used to explain, and possibly predict, sales of the major product. Table 6.7 summarizes the results of these analyses. It can be seen that five variables account for over 71 per cent of variance in sales for the stores as a whole ($R_2 = 0.712$). Higher levels of explanation were achieved when two sub-groups of the stores were analysed independently, 80 per cent in the case of corner-site stores. Different combinations of predictor variables proved to be most appropriate in the three models.

As in this example, multiple regression is usually conducted in the 'step-wise' mode; i.e., the predictor variables are entered into the equation one at a time, starting with the one accounting for the highest proportion of variance. The next best 'predictor' is then added, and at any stage variables may be dropped from the equation if they no longer contribute significantly. The process continues until no significant benefit could be derived by entering further variables, using significance criteria pre-set by the analyst, or until all the variables have entered. Having identified the most appropriate set of independent (predictor) variables, the multiple-regression procedure provides the equation that could help to forecast values of the dependent variable, in this case sales.

A regression analysis of the type shown in Table 6.7 requires a reasonable number of analogous stores. Bowlby *et al.* (1985) illustrate alternative regression strategies which can be

Table 6.7   Examples of multiple-regression analysis

Variables entered	Step	R^2	R^2 change
Total stores			
Gross selling area	1	0.544	0.544
Rent and rates	2	0.635	0.091
Distance to car park	3	0.657	0.021
No. of branches	4	0.680	0.024
Store accessibility	5	0.712	0.031
Corner-site stores			
Gross floor area	1	0.650	0.650
Store accessibility	2	0.692	0.042
No. of branches	3	0.723	0.030
Urban growth rate	4	0.762	0.039
Distance to car park	5	0.800	0.038
Intermediate sites			
Total urban retail expenditure	1	0.473	0.473
Store accessibility	2	0.649	0.176
Gross selling area	3	0.712	0.063
Gross floor area	4	0.738	0.026
No. of multiples	5	0.761	0.023

Source: Davies (1973).

used when few equivalent stores are available. Instead of making each store a unit of analysis, the trade areas of a few stores may be divided into grid squares, which become the units of analysis. The regression equation then estimates potential sales derived from each grid square within a new trade area. Clearly, this regression approach requires far more detailed surveys of the catchment and trade area characteristics of the analogous stores. If a sufficient database is available, different regression equations can be derived for different types of grid square, for example those representing high-, medium- and low-status areas.

Regression analysis can also be applied to the estimation of market potential, as part of the initial process of selecting geographical areas for expansion. Ingene (1984) illustrates how the available expenditure per household for a number of store types can be predicted on the basis of several demographic and marketing variables. If sufficient data were available relating to the population and competition within an area, this approach could offer an improvement upon the rather basic index of retail saturation, described in Section 6.1.2.

Rogers and Green (1979) summarize the main advantages of multiple-regression analysis, relative to other sales forecasting techniques:

1. The structure of the model is not limited to a set number of variables.
2. By determining which variables are important in forecasting sales, the model imposes an objective discipline upon the analyst.
3. The range of potential error in the sales estimates can be determined statistically.
4. The model may require expensive data and some computer time to develop but it can be applied easily and cheaply.

Regression also provides a useful technique for the evaluation of existing stores. The 'residuals' enable the performance predictions of the model to be compared with actual performance levels.

Inevitably, multiple-regression analysis has its dangers and drawbacks. It does require a large database; if each store is treated as a unit of analysis, Rogers suggests that each variable must equate to approximately six stores (Poyner 1984). A company with less than 15–20 analogous stores would therefore not be able fully to utilize this regression approach. Davies (1976) also points to the need to distinguish cause and effect clearly when selecting 'predictor' variables. For example, store size may, in some cases, be more a long-term effect than a cause of sales levels. Wilson (1984) also warns that the accuracy of the forecast deteriorates as the sites being evaluated become increasingly different from the types of store upon which the model was initially calibrated.

Where a number of interrelated variables are considered as possible predictors, the analyst must also avoid the dangers of multicollinearity. If two or more independent variables are strongly associated, the model will become less stable. One solution to this problem, especially where the number of variables is large, is to apply factor analysis in order to identify the common dimensions within the variables. In the study of 72 tailoring stores by Davies (1973), 6 factors emerged from a factor analysis of 43 variables. Ingene (1984) also utilized factor analysis, which provided the inputs to his regression model and avoided a severe multicollinearity problem. Before using multiple regression analysis, readers are urged to consult a statistical text for a more detailed discussion of the procedures and constraints.

A number of alternative statistical approaches have been suggested to help understand the relationship between measures of performance and the predictor variables. The Automatic Interaction Detector (AID) programme, developed by Sonquist et al. (1971), provides an appealingly clear way of searching for structure among the variables. Unfortunately, at least 1,000 cases are required for the reliable use of the technique, and few retailers have that many stores. If the individual customer, or some other more numerous unit of analysis, is used, the technique is more likely to be feasible. Simmons (1984) presents an example in which AID was used to show the variables that best explain why 1,023 consumers spent a high or low proportion at a store. If AID is feasible, it may be used to examine the structure of the relationships prior to using multiple regression.

The use of discriminant analysis has also been suggested as a technique to assist site selection. Like multiple regression, it constructs a model based upon a number of predictor variables. Unlike regression, it predicts category membership, rather than the actual expected sales or profits. Sands and Moore (1981) illustrate how discriminant analysis, using four demographic variables, predicted whether stores would fall into the break-even or non-break-even categories, achieving 72 per cent accuracy. This was advocated as an initial screening technique, although in this particular case multiple regression could have been used instead to forecast profit (or loss) on the basis of the same set of variables. Again, readers are referred to an appropriate statistical text for a fuller exposition of the technique (e.g. Hair et al. 1979).

The multivariate techniques described in this section clearly demand a higher level of statistical sophistication than the more straightforward techniques discussed earlier. However, they should not be seen as a 'packaged' solution to retail location problems or as likely to replace the judgement of the analyst. They are merely analytical tools, which help to understand and measure the influence of the predictor variables. As Jones and Mock (1984) point out, their success is dependent largely upon the quality of the initial data, the proper application of statistical procedures, and the analysts' intuitive understanding of the problem.

6.1.7 Spatial interaction models

This 'family' of models, also referred to as gravity models, has evolved as part of a major stream of development in retail location theory. A comprehensive discussion of the earlier model developments was provided by the National Economic Development Office (1970), and a review of more recent developments by Craig *et al.* (1984).

The basic principle of spatial interaction models is that the aggregate movements of shoppers are positively related to the attractiveness of a shop/centre and inversely related to the distances, or some other 'deterrence' measure. The basic principle of spatial interaction has been widely accepted, and various forms of gravity model have been applied by more sophisticated retailers and database agencies (see Section 6.1.5). There is however considerable debate as to the most appropriate attraction and deterrence measures and as to the nature of the relationship between them.

One of the earliest models of this type was that of Reilly (1931). 'Reilly's Law' states that the frequency with which the residents of an intermediate settlement trade with two towns is directly proportional to the populations of the two towns and inversely proportional to the square of the distances from the two towns to the intermediate settlement. From this 'law' was derived a formula to describe the 'breaking-point' between two towns, defined as the point up to which one town dominates and beyond which the other is dominant. This is of the following form:

$$d_{01} = \frac{d_{12}}{1 + \sqrt{(A_2/A_1)}}$$

where d_{01} = is the distance, or journey time, of the breaking point 0 from town 1
d_{12} = is the distance, or journey time, between towns 1 and 2
A_1, A_2 = are measures of the 'attractiveness' of towns 1 and 2.

This crude formulation, based upon an analogy with the physical laws of gravity, formed the basis of many subsequent models. The early gravity models suffered many serious limitations, as noted by Huff (1964):

1. The breaking-point formula provided no graduated estimates above or below the break-even position between two centres.
2. The model was ill-equipped to predict trade areas of more than two centres.
3. The form of the function will vary between types of shopping trip, and will not be a constant across all types.

In order to overcome these specific problems, Huff developed a model founded upon the 'utility' that a customer derives from shopping at a store or centre for a particular type of product. From this, the probabilities of patronizing each of a series of shops or centres could be calculated:

$$P_{ij} = \frac{F_j/t_{ij}b}{\Sigma F_j/t_{ij}b}$$

where P_{ij} = is the probability of a consumer resident at i visiting centre j
F_j = is the floor space of centre j
t_{ij} = is the travel time from the consumer's residence i to centre j
b = is a parameter taking different values for different classes of goods.

Having tested the Huff model in relation to food shopping by various urban shopper types, Haines *et al.* (1972) found a reasonably high degree of conformity between the groups to the model's predictions; it was noted, however, that very different trading areas existed for major food shopping trips and for intermediary, 'fill-in', trips.

Refinements upon the early gravity models include the work of Lakshmanan and Hansen (1965), who evolved a model to predict the effects of several existent and proposed centres in the Baltimore area. Their approach provided a basis for a model produced by Manchester University (1966), relating to the impact of a possible centre at Haydock. Partly because of a lack of floorspace data, the 'attractiveness' function within the Haydock shopping model was constructed as an empirically derived index of the number of certain store types in any given centre. The Lakshmanan–Hansen model was also shown by Gilligan *et al.* (1974) to be reasonably effective in forecasting the impact of a large, individual retail outlet.

Although the concept of spatial interaction has retained its appeal, the extreme parsimony of some of the models has been criticized. Mason and Moore (1970) question the concepts of mass and distance as suitable delineators of trade areas in basic gravity models. It was pointed out that this assumes similar patronage decisions from various income, educational and occupational categories.

The calculation of 'deterrence' as a direct function of distance or journey time can also lead to serious oversimplifications. Whereas driving time has been found to be highly influential in patronage decisions in relatively simple retail networks, the relationship is less consistent in more complex, urban areas (Cox and Cooke 1970). Bucklin (1971) notes that the propensity to search differs greatly between customers; 'travel sensitivity' is affected by perceptions of direct cost and opportunity time/cost. Another problem with most spatial interaction models is that the distance is assumed to relate to a single-stop shopping journey, whereas consumers often incorporate multiple stops on one journey. It has also been found that shoppers' perceptions of store locations can differ considerably from their actual locations (Olshavsky *et al.* 1975). Naturally, the perceptions of location are more likely to be important determinants of patronage than the actual distances, although this is more difficult to research. The procedure of cognitive mapping could be used to measure these distance perceptions (MacKay and Olshavsky 1975; Mazze 1974). Differences between perceived and actual distances appear to relate to 'frictional' factors, such as volume of traffic or ease of parking, and aspects of the store's or centre's attractiveness.

A more refined but data-demanding specification of deterrence has been suggested by Gautshi (1981). He included factors relating to transport cost, parking, travel atmosphere (clean, attractive environs), convenience, reliability, flexibility and safety (from accidents and vandalism). The model therefore sought to quantify and include many more of the 'accessibility' factors discussed in Section 6.1.2. Not all these factors contributed significantly to the explanation of retail patronage, although they demonstrate the diversity of factors associated with evaluations of 'distance' and 'convenience'.

Concern has also been expressed as to the adequacy of population, floorspace or other crude measures of attractiveness in spatial interaction models. Cox and Cooke (1970) used measures of the size of department stores, supermarkets and car parks, in addition to total store space. In fact, presumably because of a high degree of correlation between these variables, they did not add significantly to the explanatory power of the model. As noted above, the Haydock shopping model contained a composite index of facilities. All such measures of attractiveness, however intricately constructed, are limited in that they relate to the physical properties of the shop or centre, ignoring the great diversity of image characteristics.

The realization that image factors represent significant determinants of attractiveness grew with the development of image research through the 1970s. Mason and Moore (1970) concluded that images of shopping centres significantly influence the shape of their trading area. Stanley and Sewall (1976, 1978) set out to integrate image components into spatial interaction models. From a study of 372 shoppers and 21 supermarkets, they constructed image indices using three alternative measurement techniques, namely, individual difference scaling, multi-dimensional preference analysis, and a semantic differential scale (see Chapter 5). In each case, the image measurements were reduced to a single-image index and added to an extension of Huff's model.

Each of the three image measures made a significant improvement to the explanatory power of the model, and there was no significant difference between the effectiveness of the three measures. Driving time, however, still accounted for more variation than did image. Nevin and Houston (1980) found that the inclusion of three image variables did not significantly improve the predictive power of the model although it was a major determinant of shopping centre preference. In both these studies, the reduction of image to indices may have lost them some of their explanatory power.

Important extensions upon the basic forms of spatial interaction models include the multiplicative competitive interaction model (MCI). This was considerably developed by Nakanishi and Cooper (1974), building upon the Huff model to include more explicitly the specific competitive situation. They also demonstrated that the parameters of the model could be effectively estimated using the least squares approach, as in multiple regression analysis. This development considerably increased the usefulness of the model as a practical tool. Nakanishi and Cooper did not relate the MCI model specifically to retail patronage forecasting, although Achabal *et al.* (1982) subsequently reported that several retailers in the USA have used such formulations in this context. The MCI models are of the following form:

$$P_{ij} = \frac{\prod_{h=1}^{m} X_{hij}^{Bh}}{\sum_{k=1}^{n} \prod_{h=1}^{m} X_{hij}^{Bh}}$$

where P_{ij} = the probability that consumer i chooses shopping alternative j, $j = 1, \ldots, n$
X_{hij}, X_{hik} = any of $h = 1, \ldots, m$ attributes of alternatives j and k for consumer i
B = parameters that determine the effect of each attribute on the choice probability.

It will be noted that this model is of considerably more flexible form than the gravity models, specified earlier. The models can be expanded to include a wide range of attributes (e.g. Jain and Mahajan 1979) and can cope with a number of shopping alternatives. These characteristics reflect in part the increases that have occurred in available computing power, the more extensive data sets now available, and a recognition that the consumers' shopping choice is usually a more complex interaction between available alternatives.

Progress has also been made in the development of multinomial logit (MNL) models as an alternative to MCI. Again, this approach operates initially at the disaggregate level, i.e. predicting individual shopper choice behaviour. Such predictions can of course be combined to produce estimates of aggregate consumer behaviour. MNL models are currently being developed and tested in the retail location context, so a full exposition is not appropriate at this stage. Weisbrod *et al.* (1984) provide an example of an MNL model, used to forecast aggregate travel patterns among major shopping centres. They illustrated that the approach could be useful in forecasting response to possible changes in population distribution, road and transport characteristics or changes in the competitive mix.

There has been increased interest also in modelling the optimal location of multiple branches. Retailers moving into new areas often set out to establish a network of outlets in each area, thereby increasing the effectiveness of their advertising, management and distribution systems. Most models have addressed themselves to improving decisions on individual locations, which may not result in the best network overall. An exception is the MULTILOC model, presented by Achabal *et al.* (1982). This extends the MCI model to take into account effects upon other units within the same chain. Alternative approaches to assist in the development of branch networks have also been suggested by Mahajan *et al.* (1985) and by Ghosh and Graig (1986).

6.2 TOWN PLANNING AND RETAILING

So far, the emphasis has been upon the approaches, techniques and models that can assist the retailer in the tasks of site finding and site assessment. There are however many ways in which retail locations are influenced and constrained by local and central government planning policies. Even the change of use of an existing building may require planning permission, depending upon the building's previous purpose. As discussed in Chapter 2, the major thrust of retail development is now of a far more radical nature, involving large new stores and centres, often in locations not previously used for retail purposes.

The task of obtaining planning permission can easily consume more time and management resources than all the location evaluation procedures. Neafcy (1984) quotes the extreme example of the Brent Cross Centre in north London, which required 14 years of negotiation with local government and several revisions of the design along the way. This is of course not typical, although the total process of site negotiation, planning applications, appeal against refusal, and planning inquiry is still very protracted. When a proposal becomes the subject of a planning inquiry, this alone tends to add 8–10 months from initiation to final decision. Success in obtaining planning permission is influenced by the judicious choice of the site, with regard to planning issues, and by the skilful preparation and pursuit of the application. The interface between town planning and retailing is therefore an integral element in the development of new retail locations.

6.2.1 The framework

Dawson (1980) points out that all governments in the Western industrial nations intervene in the retail sector. The extent of this intervention does however differ considerably, as do the structures and processes of planning. In the UK and many European countries, retailers and developers have been more constrained than their counterparts in the USA. The modest number of out-of-town shopping centres in the UK and the uneven distribution of large stores are indicative of these constraints. Central and local government in this country have also tended to be more proactive themselves in the development process, for example concerning the New Towns and some central area developments. In the majority of cases, the retail elements of these schemes involve private developers, although their flexibility is obviously restricted.

An understanding of the relevant planning framework requires a brief description of the respective roles of central and local government. Through the Town and Country Planning Act of 1971, local authorities were required to prepare structure plans, which would include provision for retail uses. These plans usually took some time to research, draft and debate, before being submitted to central government for approval. The administration and consideration of individual planning applications is part of the local government role, but operating within central government guidelines. If an application is turned down at local level, the retailer or developer has the right to appeal to central government. For major appeals, the Department of the Environment would normally appoint an inspector to conduct a public inquiry into the case. For a comprehensive discussion of the planning process, see for example Guy (1980) or Davies (1984).

The relationship between central and local government in this context has been compared with that between an over-anxious parent and an adolescent child (Schiller 1985). Local authorities are allowed to form their own policies, within general guidelines, but the Department of the Environment reserves the right to intervene. Central government has been criticized (e.g. Gayler 1984) for limited and diffused involvement and for guidelines that are often ambiguous. Local governments, for their part, are often accused of defending too rigidly the status quo and therefore turning down the majority of retail planning applications that would involve a major change in land use. Not that local authorities are uniform in their attitudes towards retail issues, as Summer and Davies (1978) illustrated with respect to superstores and hypermarkets.

In addition to its roles in plan formation and planning administration, local government has other important powers. Compulsory purchase powers in particular enable a local authority to assemble a land package that would have been very difficult or protracted by private negotiation. For example, without the aid of compulsory purchase, over 30 interests had to be acquired to assemble the 8 acre site for the first Arndale Centre at Crossgates, Leeds (Neafcy 1984). Local authorities also have powers in relation to traffic management, car parking and general improvements, powers that may or may not be used to facilitate a specific retail development. In granting planning permission, conditions may be imposed upon the forms of retailing, for example DIY but not groceries. The permission may be granted only if the retailer or developer pays for new access roads, drainage or other improvements associated with the scheme.

Central government does not intervene directly in these processes, unless the local authority decision is taken to appeal. However, the Department of the Environment (1972, 1977) has issued Development Control Policy Notes which briefly express the advantages and disadvantages of developments outside existing centres. For example, the form of these Policy Notes indicated that such developments:

may, by efficient retailing help to keep prices down, be convenient to shoppers by car and relieve traffic congestion in the towns. They may too disfigure the countryside, detract custom from and cause deterioration of existing centres and produce traffic problems on inter-urban and country roads.

The note also asked local authorities to inform the Department of the Environment, or the Welsh office, of any applications for a store or shopping centre of 50,000 sq. ft or more of gross floor area outside existing city, town or district centres. The 1977 note raised this notification level to 100,000 sq. ft, indicative of some relaxation of central government attitude.

In that many major planning applications go to appeal and public inquiry, the Department of the Environment is clearly able to exert a major influence at this stage. The final decision in such cases rests with the Secretary of State for the Environment, who usually follows the recommendation of the inspector appointed. The public inquiry can last several days, sometimes weeks. The retailer or developer's case is usually presented by a specialist barrister or QC, normally assisted by other lawyers or company personnel. The inquiry typically hears cases presented by various expert witnesses, trade representatives, vested interest groups and local authority officers. Naturally, the legal and other costs incurred by the retailer up to and including this stage are very considerable indeed, providing a major disincentive against making proposals with low probabilities of success.

It is obviously in the interests of a retailer to try to enhance its chances of success by favourably influencing the opinions of planners and the local community. This may be regarded as a special area of retail marketing, communicating the benefits of a proposed store to the relevant public. Asda has shown considerable flair in this area; Neafcy (1984) describes the inquiry at Rawtenstall, where the local community turned out in force, mostly to support the proposal. The inquiry was delayed while a larger hall was found to accommodate the crowds! Asda have used large advertisements in newspapers to convey specific messages. In one series, the benefits of superstores in transforming derelict land were illustrated by before and after pictures. In another, the focus was upon the benefits of increasing competition in the London area, when that region had seen little superstore competition (Whysall 1985).

From central government, there has been evidence of a desire to loosen planning controls. In 1985 the Secretary of State stated that:

it is not the function of the planning system to inhibit competition among retailers or among methods of retailing, nor to preserve existing commercial interests as such; it must take into account the benefits to the public which flow from new developments in the distributive and retailing fields.

Although this view has been welcomed by many prospective developers and retailers, the lack of clarity in government policy has been criticized. Specifically, a long awaited revision to the Development Control Policy Note of 1977 did not materialize. Ross Davies had referred to retail planning 'in disarray', concluding that there appears to be no co-ordinated body of controls dealing consistently and rationally with the retail trades. From the John Lewis Partnership, Stuart Hampson accused the Department of the Environment of pursuing conflicting goals in relation to inner cities and also cited other policy inconsistencies (Retail & Distribution Management 1987). Against this somewhat complex and ill defined policy framework, it will be apparent that planning matters will continue to be a major preoccupation within UK retailers' location decisions.

6.2.2 The issues

In Section 6.1.2 checklists were presented which could help in evaluating the economic viability of potential sites. Equivalent checklists could well be constructed to help appraise the planning viability of a location. In view of the importance of obtaining planning permissions, the identification and understanding of the key issues is vital to success. Sites that are most unlikely to be acceptable in planning terms can be eliminated at an early stage in the screening process. In other cases, the most detailed attention can be directed to those issues that are likely to be foremost at the planning inquiry.

A great deal of evidence has accumulated from planning inquiries over the last twenty years, which is of considerable interest to students of town planning and retailing. Within this chapter it is possible only to summarize the main issues, noting particularly the most frequent causes of planning refusals. Extensive reviews of planning appeals in respect of superstores and shopping centres are presented by Lee Donaldson Associates (1986a, 1986b).

Table 6.8 summarizes the major advantages and problems that tend to be cited in relation to large new stores. These are often broadly classified as economic, environmental or social issues, although overlap obviously occurs. In the case of superstores, lower prices are usually cited as the major economic advantage from the consumer viewpoint. Taking the wider perspective, they also create new employment, generate rates, and may be used to enhance the appeal of an existing centre. On the environmental side, large new stores usually offer the advantage of a safer and more comfortable shopping environment, free of traffic and not subject to the vagaries of the weather. In certain circumstances, the environmental case may focus upon the improvement of a derelict/run-down area or on the reduction of congestion in existing centres. It tends to be

Table 6.8 Large new stores: planning issues

Possible advantages	Possible problems
Economic	
Lower prices	Affects other traders
Enhancement of centre (if integrated)	Depletion of other centres
New employment	Changes employment structure
Generates rates and revenue	Extra infrastructure costs, e.g. roads
Meets demand in growth area	
Environment	
Improvement of run-down areas	Visual intrusion
Reduction of congestion in existing centres	New congestion points
Safe, comfortable environment	Less character than old centres
	Inhibition of other development
Social	
Convenient shopping	Favour car-borne shoppers
Efficient shopping	Lack social role of small shops
Increases choice	May isolate elderly and immobile
Popular with majority	Local monopolies

Source: Davies and Reynolds (1986).

assumed that other advantages will accrue to the shopper, notably more convenient and efficient shopping, assuming that access and car parking are satisfactory. Greater choice of merchandise is also normally claimed, although one counter-argument is that large stores may lead to local monopolies and ultimately may reduce the real choice available.

Indeed, there are counter-arguments to most of the cited advantages, so most attention tends to be focused upon the reasons why planning permission is refused. Neafcy (1984) notes that up to a dozen reasons may be given for refusal in any one case, although these are mostly centred around three themes: land use, traffic, and impact.

Land use issues may be further classified into those relating to designation, intrusion or nuisance (Lee and Kent 1978). When a site is within a designated Green Belt, in particular, the chances of success have tended to be low. There were however inconsistencies in the treatment of the Green Belt issue, and the Department of Environment was called upon to clarify its view. In 1987 a draft DoE circular ruled out further Green Belt developments and also indicated that other open countryside developments would generally be opposed. A more flexible attitude tends to be shown with regard to land designated for industrial use, provided that alternative industrial land is available. Objections to new stores simply on the grounds that land is not designated for retail use are rarely accepted, in that many designations were drawn up before the demand for such retail forms was fully recognized.

In cases where Green Belt designation does not apply, the objection of intrusion can still be a major reason for refusals. Numerous commercially attractive sites have been identified on the outskirts of towns and cities; many have been refused planning permission on the grounds of physical and visual intrusion. Retailers have submitted elaborate proposals for landscaping such sites in order to blend into the rural area, although such measures are usually considered unlikely to be effective. In Britain there is a general planning preference for urban containment and the prevention of scattered development. In contrast, the likelihood of nuisance to adjoining residents or other land users tends to be regarded as a lesser issue, unlikely to be the primary cause of refusal.

Traffic issues generally relate to the immediate access to the proposed store or the increased load on surrounding roads. In that large new stores and centres are especially attractive to car-borne shoppers, these issues are raised at most inquiries but are usually not a primary reason for refusal. In some cases the retailer or developer offers to bear the cost of junction modifications or even new road construction. For example, Marks & Spencer and Tesco offered to contribute £19 million for the cost of a bypass around Handforth in Cheshire, if they received permission to build two large superstores there.

In that traffic flows and road capacities can be estimated by established procedures, it is usually possible for retailers to anticipate objections on traffic grounds. For example, it was estimated that one development by J. Sainsbury would generate around 4,320 vehicle trips per shopping day. The results of failing to anticipate traffic increases correctly were seen in some early cases. I can recall the opening of (arguably) Britain's first hypermarket at Caerphilly (Thorpe and McGoldrick 1974); the existing road network was quite inadequate to carry the extra load, and major traffic jams resulted. The store manager actually appeared on television asking people to stay away, with the inevitable effect that yet more came! Subsequently it was necessary for road schemes to be initiated or given higher priority to cope with the increased traffic.

Impact issues have been argued in terms of the likely adverse effects upon individual retailers or existing shopping centres. The former now carries little weight *per se* at inquiries, unless the cumulative effect of such impacts would markedly jeopardize the viability of important existing shopping areas. The Secretary of State for the Environment has stated that the planning system is not designed to inhibit competition between retailers or between retail types. The major impact issues therefore revolve around effects upon the shopping hierarchy, the consequences for inner cities, and the social effects of more car-oriented shopping provision.

The concept of a retail hierarchy has been developed from the 1930s with the emergence of central place theory. An extensive body of literature has accumulated and the limitations of the theory are well documented (e.g. Huff 1981; Craig *et al.* 1984). The essential postulates of the theory were summarized by the National Economic Development Office (1970):

for any given commodity there is a level of demand below which it will not be offered for sale. Dealers in commodities with a high (threshold) level of demand will be located in relatively few centres with large trade areas; businesses offering commodities with a low threshold demand level will be located in many more centres having small trade areas. Businesses with intermediate threshold demand level will be found in centres which lie between these extremes both in number and in the size of their trade areas. On this basis a stepped hierarchy of trading centres may be constructed.

It is widely accepted that central place theory has provided a normative rather than a prescriptive model of the retail hierarchy. None the less, there has been a tendency within town planning to defend the established hierarchy, whereby comparison shopping is grouped within larger centres and convenience shopping is more widely dispersed.

In the 1960s, a major challenge to this hierarchy would not be accepted; the proposal for a major centre at Haydock Park was turned down when the likely impact upon existing centres was demonstrated (Gayler 1984). In the 1970s, the rapid development of superstores challenged the hierarchy but their emphasis was upon convenience goods; comparison shopping remained essentially a town centre activity. Then specialist durable goods stores developed outside existing centres, notably electrical, carpet and furniture stores. Now, centres of regional proportions are developing in fringe and out-of-town areas.

It has therefore been accepted by successive stages that impact upon the established hierarchy cannot be avoided, while catering for the demand for new retail formats. The fact that more shop vacancies will occur in an existing centre as a consequence of a new proposal is not usually adequate justification for refusal. This may be of more concern if the centre is of particular historical importance and the loss of trade would significantly affect its character. Alternatively, if the anchor tenant(s) of a local or district centre would be forced to close, thereby making the whole centre non-viable, then the impact argument might carry more weight.

The rush of planning applications to build out-of-town centres has caused renewed alarm at the likely impact upon city centres. Ross Davies points to the threat of the 'death of downtown' scenario, which occurred in many US cities. Stuart Hampson notes the illogical position of the Department of the Environment, on the one hand bemoaning the lack of investment in the inner cities, on the other seemingly encouraging development which will increase the problems of the traditional centres (Retail & Distribution Management 1987). For some time now, government has been urged to more positively encourage superstore and other retail developments in the inner cities (Eliot 1982; Sparks 1983). Clearly, such development could help to alleviate some inner-city problems, although financial and planning concessions would be required to help offset the disadvantages of such locations.

Concern has also been expressed about the impact of large new developments upon consumer welfare (Cassells 1980; Davies and Reynolds 1986). If such developments cause local shops and centres to close, then older, poorer and less mobile shoppers are placed at an increased disadvantage. The effect may also be to create undesirable monopolies, at least for those shoppers without the mobility to get to competing stores some distance away.

A major problem in assessing impact is that of accurate quantification. Many of the modelling approaches discussed in Sections 6.1.6 and 6.1.7 have been applied to impact estimation, although the task is more complex than that of potential turnover assessment. The 1977 Development Control Policy Note expressed considerable reservations about the use of mathematical models:

These models may be complicated and based on a number of arguable assumptions; they have not, so far, been of great help to Inspectors at Inquiries. They are most likely to be of value where there is agreement on the basic assumptions underlying their use and where, if different models are used, any difference in results can be identified and explained.

One problem, of course, is that selectivity in the choice of procedures and inputs to such models can greatly influence the outcome. Whysall (1981) cites an inquiry in Nottingham, at which the opposing parties had each produced quantitative impact assessments. Not only did these assessments not agree; they were in fact inversely correlated! Rather more basic forms of quantification, within which the assumptions and procedure are more readily explained, therefore tend to be preferred. A comprehensive review of impact assessment procedures was presented by Wade (1983).

SUMMARY

Location decisions are among the most crucial and long-term elements of retail marketing strategy. Large new stores can now cost many millions of pounds to develop, so the consequences of poor location decisions are extremely serious in both marketing and financial terms. Major retailers are now using a range of techniques and expert assistance in order to reduce the risks. The relatively straightforward checklist and analogue approaches are still most widely used, although computerized databases and mathematical modelling techniques are gaining an important role in location decision-making.

A comprehensive checklist of factors is the starting point of most location evaluations. These may be considered under the general headings of population, accessibility, competition and costs. Population factors relate to the demographic, economic, life-style and behavioural characteristics of those resident within the catchment area. Accessibility measures require the detailed study of pedestrian flows, public transport, road access and car parking. The competition analysis should examine existing retail activity and specification, plus likely competitive reactions. The cost estimates will include all the store development costs and the running costs at a specific location.

The analogue method can be used if a number of existing stores and locations are analogous to the one proposed. Key features of their performance and trading areas can be tabulated; an extrapolation for the proposed store can then be made, based upon equivalent trading area data. Detailed trade area maps based upon existing stores can be a valuable input to analogue studies. These maps may be based upon customer address information held for credit or guarantee purposes, or a survey may be required.

The demand for comprehensive, local-area statistics to assist location decision-making is increasingly being met by commercial, non-government organizations. Companies such as CACI and Pinpoint have now accumulated very large, computerized databases, including detailed local information on population characteristics, existing retail activities and driving times. These databases continue to grow, and the agencies have become increasingly flexible in their range of services.

More complex mathematical models have been extensively developed and reported within the academic literature but have been used in practice only by some of the more sophisticated retail companies. Approaches involving multiple-regression analysis and forms of spatial interaction modelling are now gaining wider acceptance. As the volume of data available to the decision-makers continues to grow, it is likely that such models will increasingly be required to cope systematically with the information. They are likely to complement, not replace, the checklists and the judgement of the analyst.

In most countries, retail locations are constrained to a greater or lesser degree by government regulations and planning restrictions. In Britain, the local authority is responsible initially for granting or refusing planning permissions, although appeal inquiries are administered through central government. A wide range of issues is considered at these inquiries, and the reasons for refusals relate mostly to land use, traffic, and impact on existing centres. Even the most sophisticated location procedures serve little purpose if planning permission cannot be obtained. An understanding of the relevant planning framework and issues is therefore a crucial part of the retail location process.

REVIEW QUESTIONS

1. What are the logical stages of the store location process? What circumstances may prevent a retailer from going through these stages in an ideal sequence?
2. Why do different types of retailer tend to utilize different combinations of store location techniques?
3. Illustrate how some store location techniques can also be used for the assessment of existing stores.
4. Select a specific retail type and strategic positioning: what would be the main considerations in locating additional branches for company of that type?
5. Using the example selected above, develop a checklist of factors to be evaluated and data to be collected in the location process.

6. What is the analogue method? Discuss the limitations of the method and the problems that may be encountered in using it.
7. How would you set about identifying and mapping the trading areas of existing
   (a) superstores?
   (b) High Street fashion stores?
8. In locating the store type of your choice, what assistance would be available from the commercial database agencies? What stages would you go through in utilizing such an agency?
9. Illustrate how multiple-regression analysis can be used to assist location decisions. What are the main pitfalls to be avoided in using this analytical procedure?
10. What is the basic principle of spatial interaction or gravity models? Outline the progress that has been made in defining the main functions within such models.
11. To what extent is the location decision constrained and influenced by
    (a) local authorities?
    (b) central government?
12. Your bid to build a superstore on the fringe of a town has become the subject of a public inquiry. What would you expect to be the key issues at the inquiry, and what would be your strategy to maximize chances of success?

REFERENCES

Achabal, D. D., W. L. Gorr and V. Mahajan (1982), 'MULTILOC: a multiple store location decision model', *Journal of Retailing*, **58**(2), 5–25.

Anderson, P. M. (1985), 'Association of shopping centre anchors with performance of a nonanchor speciality chain's stores', *Journal of Retailing*, **61**(2), 61–74.

Applebaum, W. (1966), 'Methods for determining store trade areas, market penetration, and potential sales', *Journal of Marketing Research*, **3**(2), 127–41.

Applebaum, W. (1968), *Store Location Strategy Cases*, Addison-Wesley, Reading, Mass.

Beaumont, J. R. (1987), 'Retail location analysis: some management perspectives', *International Journal of Retailing*, **23**, 22–35.

Blair, E. (1983), 'Sampling issues in trade area maps drawn from shopper surveys', *Journal of Marketing*, **47**(1), 98–106.

Bowlby, S., M. Breheny and D. Foot (1984a), 'Store location: problems and methods 1', *Retail & Distribution Management*, **12**(5), 31–3.

Bowlby, S., M. Breheny and D. Foot (1984b), 'Store location: problems and methods 2', *Retail & Distribution Management*, **12**(6), 41–6.

Bowlby, S., M. Breheny and D. Foot (1985), 'Store location: problems and methods 3', *Retail & Distribution Management*, **13**(1), 44–8.

Brown, S. (1987), 'Retailers and micro-retail location: a perceptual perspective', *International Journal of Retailing*, **2**(3), 3–21.

Bucklin, L. P. (1971), 'Trade area boundaries: some issues in theory and methodology', *Journal of Marketing Research*, **8**(1), 30–7.

Cassells, S. C. (1980), 'Retail competition and planning', *Retail & Distribution Management*, **8**(6), 32–7.

Cohen, S. B. and W. Applebaum (1960), 'Evaluating store sites and determining store rents', *Economic Geography*, **36**, 1–35.

Cox, W. E. and E. F. Cooke (1970), 'Other dimensions involved in shopping centre preference', *Journal of Marketing*, **34**(4), 12–17.

Craig, C. S., A. Ghosh and S. McLafferty (1984), 'Models of the retail location process: a review', *Journal of Retailing*, **60**(1), 5–35.

Davies, R. L. (1973), 'Evaluation of retail store attributes and sales performance', *European Journal of Marketing*, **7**(2), 89–102.

Davies, R. L. (1976), *Marketing Geography, with Special Reference to Retailing*, Retailing and Planning Associates, Corbridge.

Davies, R. L. (1984), *Retail and Commercial Planning*, Croom Helm, London.

Davies, R. L. and J. Reynolds (1986), 'Retail development pressures on Greater London', *Retail*, **3**(4), 42–4.

Davies, R. L. and D. S. Rogers (1984), *Store Location and Store Assessment Research*, John Wiley, Chichester.

Dawson, J. A. (1980), *Retail Geography*, Croom Helm, London.

Department of the Environment (1972), *Out of Town Shops and Shopping Centres*, Development Control Policy Note 13, HMSO, London.

Department of the Environment (1977), *Large New Stores*, Revisions to Development Control Policy Note 13, HMSO, London.

Drummey, G. L. (1984), 'Traditional methods of sales forecasting', in *Store Location and Store Assessment Research*, John Wiley, Chichester, pp. 279–99.

Eliot, S. J. (1982), 'Superstore boost for inner city areas', *Retail & Distribution Management*, **10**(3), 16–20.

Epstein, B. J. (1984), 'Market appraisals' in R. L. Davies and D. S. Rogers (eds.), *Store Location and Store Assessment Research*, John Wiley, Chichester, pp. 195–214.

Gautschi, D. A. (1981), 'Specification of patronage models for retail center choice', *Journal of Marketing Research*, **18**(2), 162–74.

Gayler, H. J. (1984), *Retail Innovation in Britain: The Problems of Out-of-Town Shopping Centre Development*, Geo Books, Norwich.

Ghosh, A. (1986), 'The value of a mall and other insights from a revised central place model', *Journal of Retailing*, **61**(1), 79–97.

Ghosh, A., and C. S. Craig (1986), 'An approach to determining optimal locations for new services', *Journal of Marketing Research*, **23**(4), 354–62.

Gilligan, C. T., P. M. Rainford and A. R. Thorne (1974), 'The impact of out-of-town shopping, a test of the Lakshmanan–Hansen model', *European Journal of Marketing*, **8**(1), 42–56.

Guy, C. (1980), *Retail Location and Retail Planning in Britain*, Gower Press, Farnborough, Hants.

Haines, G. H., L. S. Simon and M. Alexis (1972), 'Maximum likelihood estimation of central-city food trading areas', *Journal of Marketing Research*, **9**(2), 154–9.

Hair, J. F., R. E. Anderson, R. L. Tatham and B. J. Grablowsky (1979), *Multivariate Data Analysis*, Petroleum Publishing Company, Tulsa, Oklahoma.

Hillier Parker (1987), *ICHP Rent Index*, Hillier Parker, London.

Huff, D. L. (1964), 'Defining and estimating a trading area', *Journal of Marketing*, **28**(3), 34–8.

Huff, D. L. (1981), 'Retail location theory' in R. W. Stampfl and E. C. Hirschman (eds.), *Theory in Retailing: Traditional and Nontraditional Sources*, American Marketing Association, Chicago, pp. 108–21.

Ingene, C. A. (1984), 'Structural determinants of market potential', *Journal of Retailing*, **60**(1), 37–64.

Jain, A. K., and V. Mahajan (1979), 'Evaluating the competitive environment in retailing using multiplicative competitive interactive model', in J. Sheth (ed.), *Research in Marketing*, JAI Press, Greenwich, Conn., pp. 217–35.

Jones, K. G. and D. R. Mock (1984), 'Evaluating retail trading performances', in R. L. Davies and D. S. Rogers (eds.), *Store Location and Store Assessment Research*, John Wiley, Chichester, pp. 333–60.

Jones, P. M. (1984), 'General sources of information', in R. L. Davies and D. S. Rogers (eds.), *Store Location and Store Assessment Research*, John Wiley, Chichester, pp. 139–62.

Lakshmanan, T. R. and W. G. Hansen (1965), 'A retail market prediction model', *Journal of American Institute of Planners*, **31**, 134–43.

La Londe, B. J. (1961), 'The logistics of retail location', in W. D. Stevens (ed.), *The Social Responsibilities of Marketing*, American Marketing Association, Chicago, pp. 567–73.

Lee, M. and E. Kent (1978), *Planning Inquiry: Study Two*, Donaldsons Research Report 5, London.

Lee Donaldson Associates (1986a), *Superstore Appeals Review 1986*, Lee Donaldson Associates, London.

Lee Donaldson Associates (1986b), *Shopping Centre Appeals Review*, Lee Donaldson Associates, London.

Mackay, D. B. and R. W. Olshavsky (1975), 'Cognitive maps of retail locations: an investigation of some basic issues', *Journal of Consumer Research*, **2**(3), 197–205.

Mahajan, V., S. Sharma and D. Srinivas (1985), 'An application of portfolio analysis for identifying attractive retail locations', *Journal of Retailing*, **61**(4), 19–34.

Manchester University (1966), *Regional Shopping Centres in North-West England Part II: A Retail Shopping Model*, Department of Town Planning, University of Manchester.

Mason, J. B. and C. T. Moore (1970), 'An empirical reappraisal of behaviouristic assumptions in trading area studies', *Journal of Retailing*, **46**(4), 31–7.

Mazze, E. M. (1974), 'Determining shopper movement problems by cognitive maps', *Journal of Retailing*, **50**(3), 43–48.

Mintel (1986), 'Store Location', *Mintel Retail Intelligence*, Autumn, 102–31.

Nakanishi, M. and L. G. Cooper (1974), 'Parameter estimation for a multiplicative interaction model—least squares approach', *Journal of Marketing Research*, **11**(3), 303–11.

National Economic Development Office (1970), *Urban Models in Shopping Studies*, HMSO, London.

Neafcy, E. (1984), 'The impact of the development process' in R. L. Davies and D. S. Rogers (eds.), *Store Location and Store Assessment Research*, John Wiley, Chichester, pp. 99–115.

Nelson, R. L. (1958), *The Selection of Retail Locations*, Dodge (McGraw-Hill), New York.

Nevin, J. R. and M. J. Houston (1980), 'Image as a component of attraction to intra urban shopping areas', *Journal of Retailing*, 56(1), 77–93.

Olshavsky, R. W., D. B. MacKay and G. Sentell (1975), 'Perceptual maps of supermarket locations, *Journal of Applied Psychology*, 60(1), 80–6.

Pope, M. P. R. (1984), 'Developing a strategic planning data base', in R. L. Davies and D. S. Rogers (eds.), *Store Location and Store Assessment Research*, John Wiley, Chichester, pp. 181–94.

Poyner, M. W. (1984), 'Getting the shop in the right place', *Retail & Distribution Management*, 12(4), 20–4.

Reilly, W. J. (1931), *The Law of Retail Gravitation*, Knickerbocker Press, New York.

Retail & Distribution Management (1983), 'Approach to store location analysis', *Retail & Distribution Management*, 11(2), 25–30.

Retail & Distribution Management (1987), 'An unstable environment', *Retail & Distribution Management*, 15(3), 6–7.

Rogers, D. S. and H. L. Green (1979), 'A new perspective on forecasting store sales: applying statistical models and techniques in the analog approach', *Geographical Review*, 69(4), 449–58.

Rust, R. T. and J. A. N. Brown (1986), 'Estimation and comparison of market area densities', *Journal of Retailing*, 62(4), 410–430.

Sands, S. and P. Moore (1981), 'Store site selection by discriminant analysis', *Journal of the Market Research Society*, 23(1), 40–51.

Schiller, R. (1985), 'Land use controls on UK shopping centres', in *Shopping Centre Development: Policies and Prospects*, Croom Helm, London.

Schiller, R. (1987), 'Out-of-town exodus', in E. McFadyen (ed.), *The Changing Face of British Retailing*, Newman, London, pp. 64–73.

Simkin, L. P., P. Doyle and J. Saunders (1985), 'How retailers put site location techniques into operation', *Retail & Distribution Management*, 13(3), 21–6.

Simmons, M. (1984), 'Store assessment procedures', in R. L. Davies and D. S. Rogers (eds.), *Store Location and Store Assessment Research*, John Wiley, Chichester, pp. 263–78.

Snow, W. and K. Scott (1984), 'Site appraisals', in R. L. Davies and D. S. Rogers (eds.), *Store Location and Store Assessment Research*, John Wiley, Chichester, pp. 215–31.

Sonquist, J. A., E. L. Baker and J. N. Morgan (1971), *Searching for Structure: Alias AID III*, University of Michigan.

Sparks, L. (1983), 'Superstores and the inner city', *Retail & Distribution Management*, 11(1), 21–5.

Stanley, T. J. and M. A. Sewall (1976), 'Image inputs to a probabilistic model: predicting retail potential', *Journal of Marketing*, 40(3), 48–53.

Stanley, T. J. and M. A. Sewall (1978), 'Predicting supermarket trade: implications for marketing management', *Journal of Retailing*, 54(2), 13–22, 91, 92.

Sumner, J. and K. Davies (1978), 'Hypermarkets and superstores: what do the planners really think?', *Retail & Distribution Management*, 6(4), 8–15.

Thomas, C. J., D. Thorpe and P. J. McGoldrick (1977), *Co-operative Society Superstores*, RORU, Manchester Business School.

Thorpe, D. and P. J. McGoldrick (1974), *Carrefour, Caerphilly: Consumer Reaction*, Retail Outlets Research Unit, Manchester Business School.

Wade, B. (1983), *Superstore Appeals—Alternative Impact Assessment Methods*, Unit for Retail Planning Information, Reading.

Weisbrod, G. E., R. J. Parcells and C. Kern (1984), 'A disaggregate model for predicting shopping area market attraction', *Journal of Retailing*, 60(1), 65–83.

Whysall, P. (1981), 'Retail competition and the planner', *Retail & Distribution Management*, 9(3), 44–7.

Whysall, P. (1985), 'Changing planning policies for large stores', *Retail & Distribution Management*, 13(1), 8–12.

Wilson, B. L. (1984), 'Modern methods of sales forecasting: regression models', in R. L. Davies and D. S. Rogers (eds.), *Store Location and Store Assessment Research*, John Wiley, Chichester, pp. 301–18.

Wrigley, N. (1988), *Store Choice, Store Location and Market Analysis*, Routledge, New York.

SEVEN
PRODUCT SELECTION AND BUYING

INTRODUCTION

Buying represents the translation of a retailer's strategic positioning statement into the overall assortment and the specific products to support that statement. The retail buyer therefore holds a pivotal role in the implementation of retail strategy and, especially within smaller organizations, may be a principle architect of that strategy. It would therefore be an understatement to say that buying is an important element within the retail mix; the work of the buyer largely underpins many of the pricing, merchandising and communications decisions that will be examined in later chapters.

This chapter first considers the nature of the buying function within retail organizations, the role of the buyer, some organizational structures for buying, and the use of buying committees. The tasks of determining appropriate order sizes are then examined. Attention next turns to the product and supplier selection decisions, the criteria used to evaluate new products, supplier selection criteria, and attempts to model the retail buying decision. The final section looks at the negotiation of the exact terms of trade and at evidence relating to discounts and other incentives. Ettenson and Wagner (1986) have noted the lack of both conceptual and empirical information within the literature which directly relates to retail buyer's decisions. The topic has however also been researched from the viewpoint of the manufacturer selling into retail; evidence derived from this perspective will be utilized when appropriate.

7.1 THE BUYING FUNCTION

This section focuses upon buying *within* retail organizations, rather than the external purchasing channels that may be utilized. It should be recognized, however, that some retailers prefer to delegate part of their buying functions to brokers or to resident buying offices, possibly situated in major centres of supply in other countries (Diamond and Pintel 1985). As noted in Chapter 2, retailers within voluntary groups also delegate most of the purchasing role to the group wholesalers or head office. There is in fact an enormous diversity of purchasing structures, and the same holds true of the internal organization of retailers' buying functions.

7.1.1 The role of the retail buyer

Within small retail companies, buying may be one of the numerous management roles undertaken by the individual owner or store manager. If a buyer is employed, he or she is likely to have a very extended role, which may include most of the pricing, merchandising and promotional functions. Within larger retail companies, a two-fold change is occurring in the role of buyers. On the one hand, the importance and complexity of the buying task is becoming greater as organizations grow larger, product assortments expand and competition intensifies. It is now the responsibility of the buyers to utilize this purchasing power to the best possible advantage, and mistakes become increasingly costly. On the other hand, as companies become sufficiently large to justify, or realize the need for, specialist marketing management, some of the functions traditionally undertaken by buyers are being taken over by other management.

There are arguments for and against the separation of buying and the other marketing functions. Possibly the most persuasive argument is that they are different jobs, requiring different types of ability, personality and training. Rosenbloom (1981) also noted the lack of effective integration within some retail organizations when marketing decisions are scattered between buying and other functional divisions. On the other hand, it is obviously essential for the buyer to be involved in, or closely aware of, the relevant pricing and other merchandising decision. Rapid feedback on customer reactions at store level is also essential.

Some problems of co-ordination can now be overcome through the use of improved information systems. For example, a retailer with a full point-of-sale data capture system can process all this information overnight to provide buyers in the morning with a completely up-to-date picture of sales trends by item and by store. Not only does this enable immediate adjustments to be made to reorder levels, it also provides a formidable weapon in negotiating with suppliers. It would be quite wrong, however, to assume that this type of information, however comprehensive and rapidly available, is a complete substitute for liaison between buyers and store personnel. The buyer also needs to know about customer needs *not* satisfied by the product range. A detailed system of recording reasons for product returns is one approach, although this relates only to the existing range.

I have been closely involved with one company with an unusually high level of PoS computing, which had developed a strongly centralized buying function. Because the electronic links between the stores and the head office had become so extensive, the informal links had largely broken down and the buyers had become too isolated from the interface with the final consumers. This problem has now been recognized and a programme initiated to develop both formal reporting procedures of customer reactions and increased informal contact between store management and the buyers.

The tendency within large organizations for buying to become a more specialist role has brought a realization of the need for more specific training. In the 1970s it was observed that both the qualifications and the training of buyers had improved considerably in the USA (Wingate and Friedlander 1978). In the UK, Forrester (1981, 1987) has helped to dispel the myth that 'flair' alone is sufficient to make an effective buyer. There are many other skills involved which can generally be enhanced by an effective training programme. It has been pointed out that the sales representatives of major companies undergo regular training programmes, whereas the retail buyers dealing with these salesmen have sometimes received minimal training.

Diamond and Pintel (1985) have identified ten main personal qualifications for an effective retail buyer:

- Education
- Enthusiasm
- Analytical Excellence
- Ability to Articulate
- Product Knowledge

- Objective Reasoning
- Dedication
- Leadership
- Appearance
- Flexibility

The complexity of retail buying decisions, examined in the following section, now place considerable demands upon buyers. They need effectively to assimilate large volumes of information, be highly competent in the mathematical appraisal of suppliers' terms and also be effective communicators and negotiators. Buying is now offering a challenging and rewarding career for many graduates, as some large organizations are developing a specialist career track within the buying function.

The effectiveness of buyers has long been recognized as an important component in the performance of retail companies. In one of the most systematic studies of this relationship, Martin (1973) compared the buyers of two stores, one highly successful and one with declining sales. From detailed interviews and evaluations of the buyers, it was found that those of the successful store were more self-confident, more aggressive, and more likely to show leadership in new product trends. It was held that these traits contributed to the successful pattern of sales growth for that store, whereas the lack of these traits contributed to the other store's decline.

7.1.2 Organization of retail buying

The organization of the buying function must be developed to suit the size and structure of the retail operation, the types and assortments of products sold and the strategic focus of the company. A chain of largely homogeneous DIY stores may be best served by strongly centralized buying, whereas a diverse grouping of department stores may need to allow limited buying at branch level. Some retailers allow their specialist product buyers considerable individual autonomy, whereas others utilize formal or informal buying committees to oversee a wide range of buying decisions. Companies heavily involved in own labels and product innovation, like Marks & Spencer, require a major technical input in the buying process, whereas others see this as purely the domain of the manufacturer.

Retailers specializing in staple goods in steady demand, such as branded groceries, will focus the buying operation upon the negotiation of the best possible terms; those specializing in high-fashion goods will be no less interested in terms but will also have to take on board the task of forecasting demand in areas where sales can fluctuate violently. Buying within the larger retail operations has tended to be organized according to traditional product categorizations, such as mens' outerwear. With increased attention to target marketing, this structure is starting to give way to specialist buying for specific target groups, such as teenage fashion wear. A retailer must also decide how much of the buying function to undertake internally and how much to rely upon outside agencies. In other words, there are numerous possible configurations of the buying function; a structure that is optimal for one retail company may be quite unsuitable for another.

One characteristic that has been common across most large retail organizations has been the increased centralization of the buying function. Wingate and Friedlander (1978) examined in some detail the advantages and disadvantages of this trend. In summary, the major advantages of centralized buying are now as follows:

1. More effective use of buying power in negotiation of supply prices and other terms.
2. Specialist buyers can devote more time to the analysis of market trends and the identification of new product opportunities.

3. With access to more and aggregated sales data, forecasts are likely to be more accurate than those based upon limited, localized observations.
4. The cost of the buying function is lower as economies of scale are obtained.
5. Better and more rapid quality control procedures can be implemented, either at the manufacturer/importer's distribution point or within the retailer's own warehouse; time consuming returns and customer complaints are therefore minimized.
6. A more consistent assortment can be presented across all the stores to back up national promotions and image building.
7. The quality of buying and stock control decisions is equalized across stores.
8. Store personnel need not be selectors and negotiators; their time is freed to concentrate upon store organization and selling activities.

The trend towards fewer, larger retail companies has increased the benefits to be derived from central buying but has also highlighted some of the problems. Accordingly, various attempts have been made to increase sensitivity to local needs while retaining the advantages of central buying. With improved information systems, more analyses can be undertaken at store level to identify different demand patterns and/or performance levels. In companies with very large numbers of outlets, classification systems have been introduced to better fit assortments and prices to local conditions (see Chapter 8). Increased dialogue between store personnel and buyers has also been encouraged, both to keep the buyers appraised of local considerations and to better motivate those responsible for selling the products. Unfortunately, central buying usually results in sellers blaming buyers for poor sales performances, and vice versa; improved communications can reduce this tendency.

Given the diversity of buying organizations within retail companies, it is not considered meaningful to represent a 'typical' buying structure. It is of interest, however, to look at a buying function that is far from typical but is highly successful, namely, that of Marks & Spencer. Tse (1985) undertook a detailed examination of this company, and Figure 7.1 depicts the personnel and activities normally involved in the procurement process. Of particular interest in this case is the breakdown of the buying function into four major elements, those undertaken by selectors, merchandisers, technologists and quality controllers. The prominent role of the technologist in the buying function, not just as a 'back room' expert, was unusual in retailing. The concept of specification buying, with a very close involvement with the manufacturer, was more a characteristic of industrial than retail buying. As retailers become more proactive in product development, this type of involvement will become more common.

Although the buying structure depicted in the figure is unusual, most larger retail companies use some form of buying committee, thereby reducing the autonomy of individual buyers. In an early study of chain stores in the USA, Gordon (1961) noted that 86 per cent of those with 30 or more branches used a buying committee. The benefits of committee buying may be summarized as follows:

1. A wider range of experience is applied to the decision-making process.
2. Decisions are made in a more scientific atmosphere.
3. The level of pressure in the buyer–salesperson relationship is lowered.

An element of the buyer–seller relationship that receives little attention in the literature is that of bribes and personal incentives to the buyers. In the study reported by McGoldrick and Douglas (1983), inducements were found to range from car stereos for junior buyers to tickets for Ascot or weekends in Paris for senior buyers. Retail companies naturally take a dim view of such practices, and most have instituted rigorous regulations to inhibit the acceptance of such favours. One multiple retailer was obliged to dismiss many of its buyers, some at very senior

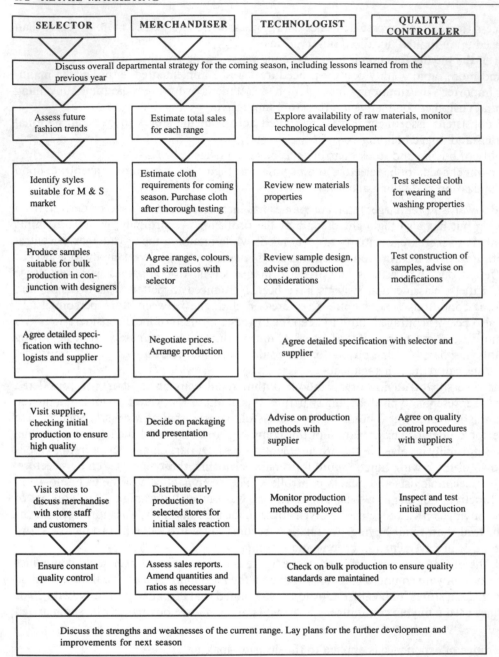

Figure 7.1 Marks & Spencer buying team composition
Source: Reprinted with permission from K. K. Tse, *Marks & Spencer: Anatomy of Britain's Most Efficiently Managed Company.* Copyright © 1985, Pergamon Books Ltd.

BUYERS	BUYING COMMITTEE MEMBERS
Special knowledge about	Special knowledge about
– suppliers	– stores
– tactics	– physical distribution
– production	– warehousing
– products	– regional demand
Special interests	Special interests
– uniform, nationwide assortment	– regionally adapted assortment
– prevent back entrance purchases	– total sales
– sales of private brands	– low retail prices
– moderate retail prices	– local suppliers are supported
– location of the supplier of no interest	
Assortment building is the main issue	Assortment building is a task among many others

Figure 7.2   Buyers and buying committees
Source: Nilsson (1980, p. 270).

level, when the taking of inducements had reached serious proportions. Such experiences are one factor that has encouraged retailers to institute more structured buying committees and procedures.

From a study of buying within one of Sweden's largest supermarket chains, Host and Nilsson (1983) identified the respective roles and orientations of individual buyers and the buying committee. The buyers receive tenders, gather information, negotiate, and analyse the offers. Then they combine a number of facts on individual 'item sheets', which are then presented to a formal committee which meets once a month. The overall goals of the buyers and the committee members have much in common, although the different responsibilities and perspectives create the possibility of conflicts. Figure 7.2, derived from Nilsson (1980), summarizes the major differences between the individual buyers and the committee members.

An early study of buying committees by Hileman and Rosenstein (1961) found that little time was spent on studying proposals before the meetings by most members of the committee. The buyer who made the presentation was expected to be well informed about all facets of the case. Sessions were considered to be democratic, but the greatest weight was given to the comments of store managers, the merchandise manager and the buyer. More recently, Hutt (1979) observed that effective leadership patterns are likely to exist within a committee which may or may not relate to the hierarchy. Having attended meetings of buying committees, the author can confirm that an especially vociferous group member can influence or even dominate the deliberations, sometimes to the detriment of the decision process.

A number of factors have been found to relate to the composition of a buying group or, indeed, to whether one existed at all. Wallace (1976) concluded that 'buying centre' composition was usually linked to the following factors:

1. The technical complexity of the product
2. The value of the item

3. The frequency of purchase
4. The product's essentiality to an organization
5. The consequences of making a wrong decision

In a UK study, McGoldrick and Douglas (1983) found that 25 per cent of the smaller multiples used committee buying, compared with 43 per cent of the larger multiples. The study was however restricted to the buying of snack food products, and it was apparent that committee buying was more prevalent for more complex products. In a study of 30 grocery retailers by Mintel (1987), 9 indicated that buyers deal with negotiations but that final authority rests with a committee or a senior buyer. There clearly remains a great diversity of retail buying practices, although the evidence would suggest that formal committee participation is more likely to occur in the larger retail organizations. In spite of this trend, it is recognized that the style of individual buyers should not be completely stifled. In the words of Leigh (1974):

Even in the modern environment, with all the inhibitions imposed by systems in a large company, creative effort from each person must be allowed to contribute effectively to the cumulative effort which the modern company represents.

7.1.3 Determining order quantities

At least part of the responsibility for sales forecasting and stock decisions usually rests with the retail buyer. In a small retail organization, the buyer might in fact have complete responsibility for these functions. In a large organization, merchandise managers and those responsible for physical distribution are also likely to be closely involved. For example, the merchandise manager may be responsible for estimating/forecasting sales and required stock levels within defined commodity groups, for example men's raincoats. The buyer then translates these projections into actual purchases, and may hold the responsibility for allocations between specific colours, styles and sizes. Until the item is delisted by the buyer or merchandise manager, the day-to-day control of stock levels and reorders may be delegated to store personnel or even to an external distribution agency, if one is used. Again, many different organizational structures will be encountered in different retail companies.

There is a considerable contrast between the tasks of estimating demand for staples and fashion goods (Cravens and Finn 1983). In the grocery sector, for example, most commodity group sales can be forecast reasonably accurately on the basis of former sales. The forecast can be refined by allowing for long-term upward or downward trends and for fairly predictable seasonal influences. In the fashion sector, however, forecasting is far more difficult. Not only are fashions subject to rapid change, but it is also difficult to judge how successfully the fashion(s) have been interpreted in the style of a specific garment. Although uncertainty can be reduced through in-house market test procedures, it still remains difficult to forecast demand for a season that has not yet commenced. Risk can be reduced by minimizing initial orders and negotiating rapid replenishment cycles with manufacturers, although this will increase the risk of running out of stock at the peak of the season.

In the fashion sector, the forecast must be broken down into a very detailed specification of quantities required. Diamond and Pintel (1985) suggest the following breakdown:

1. *Classification*—the specific types of goods within a department, such as trousers, suits, shirts, ties, etc. Various information sources indicating trends and competition may be used to adjust quantity estimates between classifications.
2. *Style*—relating to skirt lengths, trouser widths, etc. Past sales may be a poor indicator of

future needs, although buyers in many contexts will phase out old styles gradually to cater for their more conservative customers.

3. *Price lines*—the price zones within which the items must be positioned. Few stores wish to offer an item and style within just one price zone. (For further discussion of price lining, please see following chapter.)

4. *Sizes*—generally these can be determined from past records, although particular styles may be manifestly unsuitable for larger customers!

5. *Colour*—again, a decision requiring sensitivity to what is expected to be sought in the forthcoming season. There is also a need for co-ordination between classifications to encourage combined purchases.

The more accurately these elements can be estimated, the less chance there is of losing potential sales on the one hand, or having to mark down the prices of surplus stock on the other. It should be noted, however, that many buyers and merchandisers incorporate 'planned mark-downs' within their purchasing plans, given the high volume of business conducted within 'sales' periods. Usually a number of items are bought primarily for selling within such periods.

Given these many dimensions of quantity decisions and the fluctuations of fashion, many retailers do not make use of statistical forecasting techniques. Rosenbloom (1981) also attributed this to the problems of gathering adequate data, time and cost considerations, and a general unfamiliarity with such techniques. Olson and Olson (1970) referred to 'non-quantitative approaches' to sales forecasting by retailers, often used because of a lack of knowledge of statistical procedures. They point out that a lack of such knowledge can lead to a tendency not to plan at all, unless the retail manager has high confidence in subjective estimates. Non-quantitative approaches can also waste management time that could be better applied elsewhere. There is however an emerging interest in more rigorous forecasting methods as retailers acquire extensive computer facilities and the personnel become familiar with their use.

Bowersox (1978) describes several of the statistically based forecasting techniques, based either upon time-series projections from past sales trends or upon known correlations between sales and various independent variables. These techniques include:

1. *Moving averages*   Item sales are recorded, for example weekly, and the forecast is based upon the average over the last four weeks. As each new weekly sales figure becomes available, it replaces the oldest sales figure in the calculation. This approach has the advantage of being easy to calculate, but forecasts are unresponsive to rapid change.

2. *Exponential smoothing*   Each new forecast is a function of the last forecast, adjusted according to the accuracy of that forecast. The extent to which the forecast is adjusted is determined by setting the alpha factor in this equation:

$$F(t) = F(t-1) + \propto \{S(t-1) - F(t-1)\}$$

where
F = forecasted sales for time period
t = time period of constant duration
S = most recent actual sales
$\propto$ = alpha factor

If an alpha factor of 1 is set, the effect is to set the forecast equal to the most recent sales figure. A low alpha factor, such as 0.2, makes the forecast less responsive to short-term changes; judgement is therefore required to establish the most appropriate alpha.

3. *Extended smoothing*   This entails a refinement of exponential smoothing to incorporate the overall sales trend and/or seasonality in deriving the forecast. The technique may be referred to as double or triple exponential smoothing if one or both of these factors is included.
4. *Regression*   Instead of basing forecasts upon past sales trends, relationships between sales and other factors are determined by correlation analysis. For example, the sales of fur coats may be found to be sensitive to fashion trends, levels of disposable income and expectations of cold weather. A regression equation could then be constructed which produced a forecast based upon estimates of these three factors, plus any others that were found significantly to improve the forecast. A suitable statistical text should be consulted for a detailed treatment of regression procedures.

Having estimated or forecasted sales levels, the economic order quantity (EOQ) must then be determined. This concept seeks to minimize total costs by establishing the optimum balance between ordering costs and stock-holding costs. In many retail contexts, however, the order quantity is very tightly constrained by available shelf space, sometimes effectively the only storage space available to the retailer. Suppliers' or distributors' delivery cycles may also largely determine order quantities.

A fine balance must also be achieved between the costs of holding stock and the costs of running out of stock. Chadwick (1982) pointed out that the value of stocks held by UK retailers amounted to £7,262 million. Naturally, there is a strong motivation to reduce stock-holding as far as possible. Stock-holding costs can be estimated with reasonable accuracy and include the costs of rent, rates, energy, handling, administration, depreciation, insurance and interest charges. Costs of running out of stock, on the other hand, are rather more difficult to determine. Nielsen (1975) provided indications of customer reactions to out-of-stock situations in supermarkets, as shown in Table 7.1. In immediate terms, the most serious category from the retailer's viewpoint was the 39 per cent of items subsequently bought elsewhere. It must be recognized, however, that out-of-stock situations are also likely to have adverse effects upon images and longer-term patronage decisions. Zinszer and Lesser (1980) found that shoppers who had experienced stock-outs left the store with a lower store image and less satisfaction, measured on several scales.

Given the wide range of factors relevant to the forecasting of sales and stock levels, a large retail organization requires a control system within which buyers determine their order quantities. The open-to-buy (OTB) system is a commonly used approach, wherein buyers are allocated a 'budget' for a given time period. From sales forecasts and the overall merchandise plan, the planned purchases within a commodity group are determined. The OTB amount equals these planned purchases, less the goods already bought.

The OTB system provides a useful discipline for buyers and, if based upon sound merchandise plans and forecasts, can prevent over- or under-buying. It can also provide a useful diagnostic tool if the OTB appears to indicate either more or fewer purchases than the buyer seems to require. The system is particularly useful in situations where some or all of the buying role is geographically dispersed, limiting the scope for joint planning by merchandise managers and buyers. As Wingate and Friedlander (1978) point out, however, it should not be used as a rigid constraint upon buying, any more than it should be totally ignored by the 'prodigal buyer'.

7.2   PRODUCT AND SUPPLIER SELECTION DECISIONS

Whether retail buying decisions are made by individuals or by groups, the complexity of the decisions is enormous. In the first place, the number of decisions in most retail contexts is very high, as buyers must frequently evaluate new product ideas and also constantly re-evaluate the

Table 7.1 Customer reactions to out-of-stock situations

Reaction	Extended-use food (%)	Immediate-use food (%)	Non-food (%)	All (%)
Bought substitute	32	48	26	35
Different size/same brand	5	7	2	5
Different brand/same category	22	35	22	25
Other product	5	6	2	5
Did not buy	68	52	74	65
Buy here later	23	21	33	26
Buy elsewhere	45	31	41	39

Source: Nielsen (1975, p. 5).

existing product assortment. The complexity is compounded by the numerous product-, market- and supplier-related factors that are relevant to each decision. A closer understanding of the decision process is a worth-while objective, either for retailers seeking to improve the effectiveness of the buying function or for suppliers wishing to fine-tune their selling efforts.

This section first considers the types of retail buying decisions and the information sources used to assist them. Attention then turns to the criteria involved in evaluating products and suppliers; a limited but very relevant body of research has now accumulated, investigating the relative importance of these criteria. Finally, consideration is given to the actual process of the buying decision, including attempts to model this process.

7.2.1 Decision types and information sources

A number of circumstances may precipitate a retail buying decision, including the following:

1. New or different products/brands are offered to the buying unit.
2. A need is perceived to introduce new product lines.
3. A need is perceived to widen the choice of brands available.
4. A lack of satisfaction is noted with existing products/brands.
5. A routine review is undertaken of all or part of the existing assortment.

In practice, circumstances 1–3 can be classified simply as new product decisions, 4 and 5 as old product or rebuy decisions. Nilsson and Host (1987) have underlined the importance of this distinction between new and old product decisions, in terms of both the information used and the consequences of the decision. Figure 7.3 develops this distinction into eight outcome categories, four representing correct decisions, the other four representing mistakes. This latter group provides particular insights into the way that buyers tend to treat old and new product decisions rather differently.

The figure illustrates that the consequences of mistakenly accepting a new product are rather high, in terms of the costs of introduction, the costs of slow-moving stock, and the mark-downs probably required to clear this stock. The mistaken rejection of a new product, on the other hand, is likely to cause only minor losses, as an error can soon be corrected before many sales are lost. In general, the reverse is true of decisions relating to existing products, in that mistaken

Decision outcome	Decision consequences The product's performance is/will be/would be... ... satisfactory	... unsatisfactory
I *Retention* **Old products**	Ideal situation	Mistake! The product can, however, be deleted later with only minor losses arising from the delay. The mistake is easily discovered: good *a posteriori* knowledge
II *Deletion*	Mistake! Large losses occur in lost sales, in selling out old stock, and possibly also in reintroducing the product. The mistake is difficult to discover: poor *a posteriori* knowledge	Ideal Situation
III *Acceptance* **New Products**	Ideal situation	Mistake! Large losses occur in market introduction and then in selling out the stock. The mistake is easily discovered: good *a posteriori* knowledge
IV *Rejection*	Mistake! The product can, however, be accepted later with only minor losses (lost sales) owing to the delay. The mistake is difficult to discover: poor *a posteriori* knowledge	Ideal situation

Figure 7.3   Different decision outcomes
Source: Nilsson and Host (1987, p. 24).

retention can soon be reversed with little loss. A mistaken deletion, on the other hand, may cause large sales losses, loss of customer goodwill, inappropriate mark-downs and possibly the additional costs of reintroduction. Doyle and Weinberg (1973) suggested an approach by which supermarket buyers could quantify some of the opportunity costs of mistakes, specifically as an aid to their *new* product decisions.

Nilsson and Host (1987) point out that the contrasting consequences of old and new product decisions tend to lead to conservative decisions. In conditions of uncertainty, it is generally safer to retain the status quo. The situation is compounded by the fact that wrong decisions to reject new products, unlike other mistakes, may never be discovered by those responsible for evaluating the buyers' performance. Furthermore, buyers usually have extensive information about existing products, much of which is internally generated and therefore more likely to be trusted than information supplied in relation to new products.

As noted earlier, the flow of information on existing product performance is improving rapidly in line with point-of-sale computer developments. In the early 1970s, Doyle and Weinberg (1973) and Grashof (1970) criticized the use made of computer printouts by the retail buyers studied. Such information is now being presented to buyers in a far more immediate and 'user-friendly' format, usually with on-line access from the buyer's own terminal to the sales data files. In contrast, information to support new product decisions is developing more slowly.

Nilsson (1977) identified three main types of new product information source. First, direct contact with supplier representatives provides a great deal of information, although the attention that the buyers give to this is not usually especially high. Second, written information, in the form of letters, pamphlets, trade advertisement, etc., is fairly copious, although the standard of this had been criticized (e.g. Johnson 1976) and the credibility is low. In view of the high cost of personal communications, suppliers have sought to improve such non-personal communication channels, although the credibility problem remains. Third, the buyer can generate more objective information to assist new product decisions through product testing. Nilsson (1977) reports a range of practices in different countries, ranging from carefully controlled laboratory analysis to far less rigorous trials by the buyers or their families. In-house testing of new products can clearly help improve buying decisions, and many major retailers with the resources to undertake such tests are developing these procedures.

From the study of snack food buyers, Douglas and McGoldrick (1981) observed a strong recognition of the need to remain aware of what was happening in the commodity group as a whole. Among the buyers in multiple retail firms, 71 per cent claimed to maintain regular contact with the national accounts personnel of manufacturers with whom they did not currently trade. Others maintained contact with their sales personnel, very few depending upon direct mail or trade publications. Benn (1979) presented the results of a survey of nearly 500 retailers/buyers in three sectors, the majority of whom were independents. The main sources of information about new products were representatives (76 per cent) and the trade press (51 per cent).

From a study of department store buyers in the USA, Mazursky and Hirschman (1987) found a greater reliance upon external, non-personal information sources, such as the trade press. This contrast with some European studies may reflect the geographical area of the USA, and the fact that many respondents were not the central office buyers. As a framework for this study, Mazursky and Hirschman suggested a two-dimensional typology of retail buyers' information sources, based upon the personal/non-personal and the external/internal distinctions.

Although evidence varies between studies, it is clear that buying decisions can be only as good as the information upon which they are based, a particular issue in the case of new product decisions.

7.2.2 Selection criteria

In any selection decision, it is likely that a number of different criteria will be considered, some relating to the product itself, others to characteristics of the supplier. It is of benefit to the consistency and objectivity of buying decisions if these can be identified and evaluated using a more scientific framework. There are however a number of problems involved in researching these criteria, not least of which may be the difficulty/reluctance of buyers in articulating all the factors involved in their decisions. It is also dangerous to generalize too widely from the factors identified in one particular country, store type or product area. In spite of these reservations, it is useful to briefly examine some of the evidence that has now emerged indicating the wide diversity of criteria potentially relevant to retail buying decisions.

In their study of new product stocking decisions by supermarket buyers, Doyle and Weinberg (1973) found them to be based generally upon ratings of some or all of these eight criteria:

1. Potential opportunities in relevant product class
2. Marketing reputation of the manufacturer
3. Price of the brand compared with competitors

4. Quality of the brand compared with competitors
5. Contribution margin
6. Rating of proposed product launch
7. Expected volume compared with others in product class
8. Potential profitability to the supermarket if launch successful

Doyle and Weinberg recognized that many more factors had been identified in previous studies, sometimes as many as 45. However, they held that a more parsimonious rating system was justified in this case in order to provide the basis for an efficient screening process. Also from a study of supermarket's new product decisions, Montgomery (1975) isolated 18 criteria and utilized discriminant analysis to examine their relationships with decisions to reject or accept.

Following a review of previous work and an empirical study of supplier selection within the two largest Swedish grocery distributors, Nilsson (1977) identified eight types of criteria as being especially important in buying decisions:

1. Profitability and sales—regarded by many to be the ultimate criteria within buying decisions, all other factors acting only as indicators of how well these criteria are likely to be met.
2. Assortment—increasing the number of brands stocked within a product group will not normally increase total sales volume. It may reduce individual sales volumes, increase pressures upon distribution and shelf space and result in poorer buying terms. An addition is therefore usually accompanied by a deletion, so a potential supplier will have to show that his product offers advantages, in terms of profitability and sales, over one which is currently stocked.
3. Consumer Value—the critical determinant of a product's sales potential within an outlet is the value of the product to the consumer, which buyers attempt to evaluate by examining such attributes as price, taste, quality and packaging.
4. Introductory Marketing—in relation to new products and attempting to stimulate customer trial. It is of interest to assess the relative importance which buyers attribute to above and below the line marketing strategies.
5. Supplier Characteristics—a number of concepts of supplier reliability, including delivery timing and business consistency.
6. Tactical Considerations—for example, always retaining at least two suppliers of major products, in order that they can be played off against each other.
7. Prices and Economic Conditions—the importance of a competitive pricing strategy by suppliers to ensure adequate market share in distribution channels dominated by discount pricing strategies.
8. Distribution Channel Requirements—factors within the physical distribution system which buyers must consider when arriving at a stocking decision.

Several studies have subsequently drawn contrasts between the most important criteria in different buying situations, Brown and Purwar (1980) compared the importance of supplier selection factors in three different types of marketing channel. Hirschman (1983) compared the criteria cited by buyers for chain stores and department stores. McGoldrick and Douglas (1983) compared the importance ratings of factors considered by multiple and cash-and-carry buyers. From a major survey of buyers, Shipley (1985) drew comparisons between several product fields and between samples in the USA and the UK. The differences between the two countries were not in fact great, although prices and delivery were more important criteria in the UK. A rather different perspective was adopted by Wright (1985), who compared the importance ratings of retailers and suppliers, based upon an Australian survey. This illustrated that suppliers frequently do not accurately interpret the priorities of the retail buyers.

Table 7.2 Classification of decision criteria

Category of criteria	Criteria previously mentioned in studies	
	N	%
A. Profitability and sales	50	13
Overall profitability	12	3
Rate of turnover	7	2
Sales potential	31	8
B. Financial terms	75	19
Suppliers' price	6	2
Gross margin	14	4
Allowances and rebates	17	4
Support to co-operative advertising	13	3
Credit terms	7	2
Other economic conditions	18	5
C. Assortment considerations	21	5
Existence of private brands	3	1
Relations with other products	18	5
D. Consumer evaluation	75	19
Overall consumer value	20	5
Retail price	11	3
Product's physical characteristics	18	5
Product's psychological characteristics	13	3
Packaging	13	3
E. Supplier marketing	51	13
Introductory campaign	34	9
Continual marketing	17	4
F. Supplier characteristics	79	20
Supplier representative	5	1
Reputation and reliability	30	8
Sales force organization	5	1
Services and functions	33	8
Other characteristics	6	2
G. Competitive considerations	13	3
H. Distributive factors	15	4
Transportation adaptations	4	1
Adaptation to store needs	11	3
I. Tactical considerations	3	1
J. Salesman presentation	7	2
Total	389	100

Source: Nilsson and Host (1987, p. 50).

A review of organizational buying criteria was presented by Cravens and Finn (1983), including studies of both industrial and retail buying. An excellent review and analysis of studies in this specific field was provided by Nilsson and Host (1987). In all, nearly 400 criteria were mentioned in the studies reviewed, although many of these are of course closely related. A classification of the criteria was therefore undertaken, a summary of which is presented in Table 7.2. The numbers and percentages indicate the number of criteria within each heading that were mentioned in previous studies. These suggest the relative importance of the factors but were not intended to suggest the weightings that should be attached to each criterion. In fact, Nilsson and Host pointed out that it would be impossible to determine such weightings in a general way from previous research. Given the wide diversity of retail buying situations, weightings will inevitably differ considerably. However, the framework has been established for a more rigorous approach to product and supplier appraisal.

7.2.3 The decision process

Having identified the types of retail buying decision, the information sources used and the criteria typically utilized, the next stage is to try to develop an understanding of the actual decision process. A number of attempts to model this process have been reported, using flow diagrams or a range of mathematical techniques. It has also been pointed out (e.g. Ettenson and Wagner 1986) that retail buying has many characteristics in common with the more extensively researched area of industrial buying. Models developed in that context, for example those of Webster (1965) and Sheth (1973), have therefore influenced the development of retail buying models.

An early attempt to depict the decision process of retail buyers was the 'logical flow model' of Massy and Savvas (1964). This was based upon decisions regarding the purchasing of consumer durables, and through a detailed flow diagram depicted each stage of the buyer's decision and the alternative outcomes. The model highlighted the need for a buyer to maximize the profitability of the total range stocked but did not incorporate the full range of factors likely to influence the selection of a supplier. A model with an emphasis upon inputs of information from both distributor and manufacturer was developed by Grashof (1970), following his study of new product stocking decisions by supermarkets. From a set of product-related data, an assessment of likely sales and profitability is derived and compared with a specified target. Although somewhat oversimplified, this model has the benefit of being a concise, functional representation that can also be applied to product reappraisals.

McGoldrick and Douglas (1983) set out to develop this approach by suggesting the type of information sources that should be utilized, the criteria typically adopted, and the process of product evaluation and re-evaluation to buyers. Figure 7.4 depicts the decision process adopted, specifically in relation to the selection of a supplier of potato crisps. In this particular case, factors such as the choice of sizes and flavours were important criteria, whereas prices to the end consumer were scarcely differentiated. As illustrated in the previous section, the criteria utilized should not be generalized across products and retail sectors. Attention is drawn to the 'non-task' factors that influence the decision process, including individual buyers' psychological traits and the interpersonal influences within a buying centre (i.e. the group of people and/or committee involved in the buying process).

At the very core of any buying model is the process by which the many different attributes are combined and evaluated in order to arrive at the final decision. If a systematic product-screening process is to be devised, it is essential to understand the decision rules that are being used. Furthermore, the examination of these rules may lead to an improvement, or at least to a greater

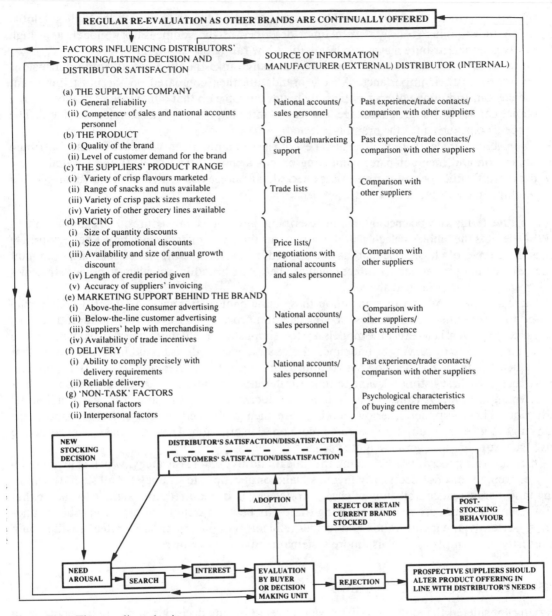

Figure 7.4   The supplier selection process
  Source: McGoldrick and Douglas (1983, p. 25).

consistency, in the buying process. Heeler *et al.* (1973) discussed three alternative choice strategies and their respective mathematical formulae. A comprehensive listing of choice strategies is reproduced by Stern and El-Ansary (1987). Three of the more frequently encountered ones are described as follows:

1. *Linear additive choice strategy*   By this method, a buyer assigns evaluative weights to each attribute of a brand, according to its perceived importance. Each brand under consideration then receives a rating on each attribute dimension. These are combined linearly to form an

overall judgement for each brand. The one selected would be the one with the highest 'global utility index'. This strategy is sometimes described as the compensatory model, as a high rating on one attribute may compensate for a low rating on another.

2. *Lexicographic choice strategy* The buyer initially ranks the different attribute dimensions according to their importance. All the brands are then compared on the most important dimension, and, if one offers a noticeably better outcome on that dimension, it is selected. If a choice cannot be made at this stage, the second most important dimension is considered. The process continues until the brand is selected.

3. *Conjunctive choice strategy* The buyer establishes minimum cut-off values for each attribute dimension and then compares competing brands against these values. If any is rated below the cut-off values of any attribute, it is rejected as a choice possibility. This is an example of a 'multiple cut-off' model.

Alternative terms may be encountered in describing these choice procedures. For example, Sheth (1981) depicts the 'choice calculus' at the core of his theory of merchandise buyer behaviour. He cites three types of choice rule that may be applied, namely, trade-off choice calculus, dominant choice calculus, and sequential choice calculus. These are broadly equivalent to choice strategies 1–3 respectively, as outlined above.

There are many other variations upon these basic choice strategies. As described they may sound too mechanistic really to describe the decision process of a buyer. The question that must be asked, however, is whether the models are too simplistic, or whether buyers are sometimes too erratic in their use of varying or undefined choice strategies. A decision aid for retail buyers that is frequently cited is the 'decision matrix approach', suggested by Berens (1971–2). The matrix is constructed by first listing relevant selection criteria; then these are ranked according to their relative importance. All the suppliers under consideration are then ranked on each individual criterion. These supplier/criterion rankings are then multiplied by the criterion importance rankings to give each supplier a weighted score on each criterion. These scores are then added to give each supplier an overall weighted score.

In effect, this procedure is assuming the 'linear additive' choice strategy, which is arithmetically convenient but not necessarily the most valid or appropriate strategy for all such decisions. In many instances a combination of choice strategies will be required, for example to ensure that minimum standards are met but allowing trade-offs between criteria within acceptable boundaries. Certainly, the identification and further refinement of buyers' choice strategies will remain a priority in attempts to establish more systematic buying procedures.

7.3 NEGOTIATION OF TERMS

Having considered the many criteria relevant to retail buying decisions, it would be incorrect to assume that terms of trade are mostly fixed. There are in fact very few elements that cannot be the subject of negotiation. As Marks & Spencer in particular have so powerfully illustrated, even the most detailed characteristics of the product itself can be negotiated. In the UK and many other countries, all elements of the supply price and discounts are typically the subject of negotiation, as are delivery conditions, advertising allowances and many other elements of 'the deal'.

The value to retailers of effective negotiation can be very large indeed. As Forrester (1983) illustrated, a negotiated reduction in the supply price of just 1.5 per cent could well contribute an increase of 20 per cent or more in net profits. He also noted a surprising reluctance on the part of some buyers to explore new opportunities for negotiation. In the retailing of fast moving/mostly low-value items such as groceries, a difference of a fraction of a penny per unit could contribute thousands of pounds to final profits. Similarly, improvements that can be negotiated in the other terms of trade can yield substantial benefits. A full discussion of bargaining techniques would be beyond the scope of this text, but a lively introduction to this topic is provided by Winkler (1981).

As noted in Chapter 1, the scope for effective negotiation is rather greater in the UK than in some other countries. In the USA, for example, the Robinson–Patman Act limits the scope of major retail buyers to obtain better terms purely on account of their buying power. A summary of this and other relevant legislation can be found in Chapter 6 of Office of Fair Trading (1985). Legislation of this sort has frequently been advocated in the UK, but the investigations of the Monopolies and Mergers Commission (1981) and the Office of Fair Trading (1985) both concluded with recommendations against this. The exact term of trade negotiated by major retailers are under-researched and highly confidential, as neither buyers nor sellers wish to reveal to others the terms established with specific suppliers/retailers.

7.3.1 Terms of trade

The study by the Monopolies and Mergers Commission (1981) helped to clarify the range of discount types and other inducements offered to retailers, although there was clearly reluctance on the part of retailers and manufacturers to quantify these terms. The published terms of trade, in addition to the basic supply price, sometimes included formalized scales of discounts. These tended to relate to one or more of the following:

1. Size of the order overall
2. Size of orders at each delivery point
3. Total purchases of the whole product range over a given period of time
4. Period of credit given or taken
5. Extent of promotional support by the retailer or compliance with specified stocking arrangements

The unpublished terms are inevitably a good deal more complex and difficult to evaluate, but they are a major element of buying. Phillips (1980) refers to one manufacturer that had to offer 'best' or 'next to best' terms on 98 per cent of its business. These terms may include the following types of special concessions, negotiated with specific retailers (Monopolies and Mergers Commission 1981):

1. Favourable terms for smaller delivery drops, typically favouring large retailers requiring branch delivery to many small or medium sized outlets.
2. Special discounts or prices, negotiated by large retailers, irrespective of published lists. The special prices in one case were 15% lower than list prices and 8% lower than average prices.
3. Retrospective discounts or rebates, frequently described as 'overriders' and sometimes more than one is awarded to a specific retailer. These usually represent a form of reward for reaching some specified sales target and sometimes ascending targets are rewarded by ascending rates of discount.
4. Favourable credit terms, rarely awarded formally but frequently taken by powerful retailers; manufacturers are simply obliged to refrain from strictly applying their credit terms.
5. Special promotions, usually linked to an agreed special price in the retailer's stores; these may or may not involve a reduction in the gross margin normally enjoyed by the retailer.
6. Disposal of seasonal lines or other surpluses, which may not be offered on equal terms to all retail customers.
7. Supply of goods in special containers to customers' requirements.

Table 7.3   Cost to manufacturers of special buying terms

	1981 (£m)	1981 (%)	1985 (%)
(a) Total sales by manufacturers	963		
(b) Cost of special terms as % of (a)		6.6	8.6
(c) Total sales to top 10 retail customers	311		
(d) Cost of special terms as % of (c)		8.7	10.0
(e) Total sales to top 4 retail customers	206		
(f) Cost of special terms as % of (e)		9.2	10.5

Sources: Monopolies and Mergers Commission (1981); Office of Fair Trading (1985).

Table 7.3 summarizes two major attempts to quantify the special terms offered by samples of manufacturers to their top ten retail customers. Although the two surveys differed in many ways, it would appear that the value of the special terms had increased. Among the problems encountered in compiling the data for the table was the genuine difficulty of manufacturers in allocating marketing expenditures to specific accounts. For example, a special delivery service can involve a considerable cost but one that is difficult to isolate from total physical distribution costs. There must also be some doubt as to whether the quasi-legal forms of incentive will have been included. In spite of such inevitable reservations, these data represent some of the most substantive published evidence available in this highly secretive area of company operation.

There are also several types of benefit that may be offered to the retailer which do not involve reduced prices as such:

1. Advertising support, by way of a contribution to the retailer's advertising which (hopefully) benefits the supplier's products
2. Promotional fees, to cover part or all of a retailer's cost in entering a joint promotion with a supplier
3. Coupons, representing a promotional payment or discount for involvement in a coupon scheme
4. Payments in return for a guarantee of immediate distribution in all the retailer's outlets
5. Payments for special displays in addition to normal displays
6. New distribution payments, to persuade the retailer to take the risk of stocking an unproven product

There are other types of benefit negotiated by some retailers which do not represent direct payments as such, for example:

1. Shelf filling, labelling and/or price-marking services
2. Provision of training for sales staff
3. Special delivery services, such as extra, smaller deliveries
4. Provision of shop equipment, such as refrigerated cabinets
5. Special credit facilities or loans

Using a sample base of 15 manufacturers supplying the three largest grocery multiples, the Monopolies and Mergers Commission (1981) estimated the following relationship between their total sales to each retailer and the percentage cost of special terms to each:

	Total sales of the 15 manufacturers' brands (£m)	Cost of special terms (%)
Tesco	87.0	8.35
Sainsbury	21.4	7.77
Asda	49.8	7.06

As may be anticipated, the value of these special terms reflected the relative size of these retailers, Tesco having the largest market share of branded goods at the time of the investigation. It is noticeable, however, that the total sales of branded goods from these 15 manufacturers to Sainsbury were relatively low, because of the large proportion of own-labels sold by this retailer (see Chapter 9). In spite of this, Sainsbury appeared to be enjoying better special terms than Asda.

From enquiries that I conducted, it is clear that the Commission was not comparing similar special terms in the cases of these three retailers. The most significant areas of difference are in the delivery and in-store assistance requirements of each retailer. At the time of the Commission's enquiry, Tesco demanded an extensive branch delivery service from most suppliers, although subsequently it started to develop links with 'third-party' distribution agencies. Equally or possibly more difficult to quantify would have been the extensive price-marking, shelf-filling and merchandising services demanded by Asda. By contrast, Sainsbury prefer, in general, to keep manufacturer agents or representatives away from their stores, believing that they can lead to less efficient delivery systems and less integrated in-store merchandising arrangements.

As part of its investigations, the Commission undertook a survey of both the buying prices and the retail prices in a sample of 170 retail outlets in three selected areas. It is of interest to compare the buying terms enjoyed by the different types of retailer. Table 7.4 summarizes these different buying prices for eight product categories, with prices expressed as indices, the lowest retail price being equated to 100. The four major multiples were Sainsbury, Tesco, Asda and Fine Fare, and with each product group between two and five brands or sizes were observed.

For all the products surveyed, the average buying prices of the independents were higher than those of the multiples or the co-operatives. The four major multiples clearly enjoy a significant buying advantage over the other multiples in the major grocery product fields, although this is not true of all the products that are the speciality of non-grocery outlets. Although a useful contribution to the available evidence on retail buying terms, this survey was relatively small and actually included only eight co-operative outlets. Furthermore, in order to make the buying prices comparable, estimates were made of the cost of deliveries, when undertaken by the retailer, and the benefits of possible retrospective discounts.

SUMMARY

The retail buying function represents a vital linkage between overall merchandise strategy and the elements of the retail marketing mix. Consequently, the effectiveness of buyers exerts a major influence upon the level of success enjoyed by the company. As firms have grown larger and more sophisticated, retail buying has become a more specialized function, while still retaining close linkages with pricing, product development, advertising and in-store merchandising.

A wide range of alternative structures exist to manage the buying function, depending upon the size, sector and objectives of the company. There has been a fairly consistent trend towards

Table 7.4   Buying prices paid by different types of retailer

Product group	4 major multiples	Index (lowest retail price = 100) Other multiples	Co-ops	Independents
Baked beans	95	112	98	120
Biscuits	100	111	105	114
Bread	101	102	102	113
Confectionery	98	101	98	107
Paper handkerchiefs	103	100	92	105
Toothpaste	92	93	94	114
Canned beer	105	103	96	106
Cigarettes	98	99	93	103

Source: Monopolies and Mergers Commission (1981).

more centralized buying in large firms, in order to better exploit specialization and economies of scale. The buying committee (or centre) has also increased in importance, which widens involvement in buying decisions and also shifts some responsibility from individual buyers.

The determination of order quantities is a major part of the buying process, a particularly difficult task in areas subject to current fashion and sudden change. Various statistical procedures exist to assist forecasting, although many retailers have been reluctant to utilize them. Reductions in stocks held and improvements in stock turnover are constantly being sought, but the costs of out-of-stock situations must be carefully evaluated. Many retail organizations use the open-to-buy (OTB) system to control the quantities purchased within given time periods and commodity groups.

The volume of selection decisions confronting retail buyers from day to day is very large. A stream of new products must be screened and the existing range should be constantly re-evaluated. Existing product decisions tend to be well supported with internally generated information, sometimes from point-of-sale computers. Information about new products tends to be less copious and reliable, so more sophisticated retailers are developing their own product analysis and testing facilities.

The criteria used by retail buyers in making their decisions vary considerably between sectors and product types. A major review of product/supplier selection criteria by Nilsson and Host (1987) identified nearly 400 possible criteria, classified as relating to profitability and sales, financial terms, assortment considerations, consumer evaluation, supplier's marketing, supplier characteristics, competitive considerations, distributive factors, tactical considerations and salesman presentation.

Given the wide range of financial, marketing and logistical inputs to the decision, a buyer needs to develop a process for evaluating the combinations of attributes. In essence, attributes may be allowed to compensate for one another, choices may be made on the most important attribute, or products may be judged against minimum cut-off points on each attribute. When the most appropriate choice strategy has been identified, a systematic screening process for products and suppliers can be evolved.

In large retail companies particularly, few elements of the terms of trade are regarded as fixed; the ability to negotiate effectively is an essential skill for a retail buyer. In the UK, the value of the special, unpublished buying terms secured by major retailers can greatly exceed the value of standard, quantity discounts. These special terms can include additional forms of discount, support for the retailer's marketing effort, or services that reduce the retailer's costs in other ways.

REVIEW QUESTIONS

1. Contrast the likely roles of the buyers in these three organizations:
   (a) An independent chain of six fashion stores
   (b) A chain of 20 department stores
   (c) A major grocery multiple
2. Discuss the benefits and the drawbacks of centralized buying within large retail companies. What measures would you recommend to overcome the drawbacks?
3. Do you consider that committee buying represents an improvement upon individual buying? Justify your answer.
4. Select a category of fashion merchandise of your choice. How would you set about improving forecasts of merchandise requirements through the application of statistical techniques?
5. What do you consider to be the main benefits and drawbacks of open-to-buy (OTB) controls?
6. Wrong decisions regarding new products may bring very different consequences to the buyer, compared with wrong decisions regarding existing products. Explain.
7. How can a retail organization improve the information available to assist buyers in their choices between products and suppliers?
8. In selecting specific products and suppliers, what would you estimate to be the principal criteria in the decision of:
   (a) a department store fashion buyer?
   (b) a buyer of packaged groceries?
9. Explain the distinctions between the 'linear additive', 'lexicographic', and 'conjunctive' choice strategies.
10. Construct a flow diagram to depict the normal decision processes of a retail buyer within a chain of shoe shops.
11. Why, and in what respects, is the scope for negotiation by UK retail buyers greater than that of their counterparts in the USA?
12. In addition to normal quantity discounts, what other terms would you seek to negotiate if you were responsible for buying:
    (a) paper goods for a large supermarket chain?
    (b) cosmetics for a voluntary grouping of small pharmacies?

REFERENCES

Benn, J. (1979), *How Retailers Buy*, Benn Publications, Tunbridge Wells.

Berens, J. S. (1971–2), 'A decision matrix approach to supplier selection', *Journal of Retailing*, **47**(4), 47–53.

Bowersox, D. J. (1978), *Logistical Management*, Macmillan, New York.

Brown, J. R. and P. C. Purwar (1980), 'A cross-channel comparison of retail supplier selection factors', in R. P. Bagozzi *et al.* (eds.), *Marketing in the 80's*, American Marketing Association, Chicago, pp. 217–20.

Chadwick, L. (1982), 'Inventory control: how to reduce stockholding costs', *Retail & Distribution Management*, **10**(3), 61–2.

Cravens, D. W. and D. W. Finn (1983), 'Supplier selection by retailers: research progress and needs', in W. R. Darden and R. F. Lusch (eds.), *Patronage Behavior and Retail Management*, Elsevier/North-Holland, New York, pp. 225–44.

Diamond, J. and G. Pintel (1985), *Retail Buying*, Prentice-Hall, Englewood Cliffs, NJ.

Douglas, R. A. and P. J. McGoldrick (1981), 'A study of supplier selection by multiple retailers and cash and carries', *Occasional Papers in Management Sciences*, 8109, UMIST, Manchester.

Doyle, P. and C. B. Weinberg (1973), 'Effective new product decisions for supermarkets', *Operational Research Quarterly*, 24(1), 45–54.

Ettenson, R. and J. Wagner (1986), 'Retail buyers' saleability judgements: a comparison of information use across three levels of experience', *Journal of Retailing*, **62**(1), 41–63.

Forrester, R. A. (1981), 'The perspiration zone', *Retail & Distribution Management*, **9**(4), 31–3.

Forrester, R. A. (1983), 'Buying for profit,' *Retail & Distribution Management*, **11**(2), 14–16.

Forrester, R. A. (1987), 'Buying for profitability', *Retail & Distribution Management*, **15**(3), 25–6.

Gordon, H. L. (1961), 'How important is the chain store buying committee', *Journal of Marketing*, **25**(3), 56–60.

Grashof, J. F. (1970), 'Supermarket chain product mix decision criteria: a simulation experiment', *Journal of Marketing Research*, **7**(2), 235–42.

Heeler, R. M., M. J. Kearney and B. J. Mehaffey (1973), 'Modeling supermarket product selection', *Journal of Marketing Research*, **10**(1), 34–7.

Hileman, D. G. and L. A. Rosenstein (1961), 'Deliberations of a chain grocery buying committee', *Journal of Marketing*, **25**(3), 52–4.

Hirschman, E. (1983), 'An exploratory comparison of decision criteria used by retail buyers', in W. R. Darden and R. F. Lusch (eds.), *Retail Patronage Theory*, Elsevier-North Holland, New York, p. 5.

Host, V. and J. Nilsson (1983), 'Choice criteria for the assortment decisions in a supermarket chain', paper presented at the Annual Conference of the European Marketing Academy, April, Grenoble.

Hutt, M. D. (1979), 'The retail buying committee: a look at cohesiveness and leadership', *Journal of Retailing*, **55**(4), 87–97.

Johnson, M. (1976), *New Product Marketing and the Major Multiples*, Market Research Ltd., London.

Leigh, L. (1974), 'Buying—its function in the marketing concept', *Retail & Distribution Management*, **2**(4), 21–3.

Martin, C. R. (1973), 'The contribution of the professional buyer to a store's success or failure', *Journal of Retailing*, **49**(2), 69–80.

Massy, W. F. and J. D. Savvas (1964), 'Logical flow models for marketing analysis', *Journal of Marketing*, **28**(1), 30–7.

Mazursky, D. and E. Hirschman (1987), 'A cross-organisational comparison of retail buyers' information source utilisation', *International Journal of Retailing*, **2**(1), 44–61.

McGoldrick, P. J. and R. A. Douglas (1983), 'Factors influencing the choice of a supplier by grocery distributors', *European Journal of Marketing*, **17**(5), 13–27.

Mintel (1987), 'Retail practices', *Mintel Retail Intelligence*, **5**, 3.25–3.28.

Monopolies and Mergers Commission (1981), *Discounts to Retailers*, HMSO, London.

Montgomery, D. B. (1975), 'New product distribution: an analysis of supermarket buyer decisions', *Journal of Marketing Research*, **12**(3), 255–64.

Nielsen (1975), 'Distribution—a perennial problem', *Nielsen Researcher*, **3**, 1–6.

Nilsson, J. (1977), 'Purchasing by Swedish grocery chains', *Industrial Marketing Management*, **6**, 317–28.

Nilsson, J. (1980), *Sortiments-Byggande* (summary in English), EFL, Lund, Sweden.

Nilsson, J. and V. Host (1987), *Reseller Assortment Decision Criteria*, Aarhus University Press, Aarhus.

Office of Fair Trading (1985), *Competition and Retailing*, OFT, London.

Olson, L. G. and R. H. Olson (1970), 'A computerized merchandise budget for use in retailing', *Journal of Retailing*, **46**(2), 3–17, 88.

Phillips, J. (1980), 'Terms of trade-changing practice', *Market Place*, April/May, 3–9, 14.

Rosenbloom, B. (1981), *Retail Marketing*, Random House, New York.

Sheth, J. N. (1973), 'A model of industrial buyer behavior', *Journal of Marketing*, **37**(4), 50–6.

Sheth, J. N. (1981), 'A theory of merchandise buying behavior', in R. W. Stampfl and E. C. Hirshman (eds.), *Theory in Retailing: Traditional and Nontraditional Sources*, American Marketing Association, Chicago.

Shipley, D. D. (1985), 'Resellers' supplier selection criteria for different consumer products', *European Journal of Marketing*, **19**(7), 26–36.

Stern, L. W. and A. I. El-Ansary (1987), *Marketing Channels*, Prentice-Hall, Englewood Cliffs, NJ.

Tse, K. K. (1985), *Marks & Spencer: Anatomy of Britain's Most Efficiently Managed Company*, Pergamon Press, Oxford.

Wallace, A. (1976), *A Study of the Buying Process for New Products by Intermediate Marketing Organisations in the Channels of Distribution for Grocery Products*, unpublished PhD thesis, UMIST, Manchester.

Webster, F. W. (1965), 'Modelling the industrial buying process', *Journal of Marketing Research*, **2**(4), 370–6.

Wingate, J. W. and J. S. Friedlander (1978), *The Management of Retail Buying*, Prentice-Hall, Englewood Cliffs, NJ.

Winkler, J. (1981), *Bargaining for Results*, Heinemann, London.

Wright, J. (1985), 'Trade marketing: an Australian survey', in J. Gattorna (ed.), *Insights in Strategic Retail Management*, MCB, Bradford.

Zinszer, P. H. and J. A. Lesser (1980), 'An empirical evaluation of the role of stock-out on shopper patronage processes', in R. P. Bagozzi *et al.* (eds.), *Marketing in the 80's*, American Marketing Association, Chicago, pp. 221–4.

EIGHT
RETAIL PRICING

INTRODUCTION

The role, complexity and importance of the retail pricing function varies enormously between different sectors and types of retailing institution. In the few areas where resale price maintenance is still permitted, the setting of retail prices is primarily the responsibility of the manufacturer; the retailer's pricing role is therefore rather limited. In the retailing of cars or other major consumer durables, the task of retail pricing has much in common with that of manufacturer pricing, in that the transaction is typically the purchase of a specific product and the buyer is likely to be relatively well informed. These instances do not however represent the broad base of retailing, and accordingly will not be the main focus of this chapter. In department stores, grocery stores and other types of retailing characterized by large product assortments, pricing requires a very different approach from that implied within the conventional manufacturer-oriented view.

In most sectors of retailing, pricing decisons are regarded as being among the most crucial and difficult aspects of retail marketing. Whereas a range of 100 products may represent a fairly wide assortment for a manufacturer, it is not uncommon for a retailer to be responsible for the pricing of 10,000 or more items. Compounding upon this complexity is the fact that many multiple retailers differentiate at least some of their prices in response to different local markets. The assumption of well informed customers, inherent in traditional pricing theory, clearly cannot be considered valid in relation to most retail markets. Neither can it be assumed that those responsible for the setting of the prices, or their competitors, are aware of all the relevant prevailing price levels.

Since the abolition of resale price maintenance in many areas, retailers have found that price competition can exert a very powerful influence upon consumer purchase decisions. Ironically, the price function has tended to be somewhat fragmented within retail organizations. It is not unusual for most day-to-day pricing decisions to be made by different groups of buyers, working within broad policy directives evolved by senior marketing and/or financial management. From elsewhere in the organization may be added various strategic or tactical overlays, such as the pricing decisions related to special offers, own brand items or a newly opened store. However, the need to achieve greater co-ordination both within the pricing function and between different elements of the mix has been recognized by major retailers.

This evolving retail pricing function has not been especially well served by the existing literature. Having undertaken an extensive review of the models and approaches that exist to help or depict various types of pricing decision, Monroe and Della Bitta (1978) concluded that no greater deficiency existed in any other major decision area of marketing. This problem is even more acute in relation to retail pricing, where the evidence is extremely fragmented and the multi-dimensional nature of the function has not been fully explored. Various attempts have been made to extend the economist's theory of the firm to the retail case, including the early work of Holton (1957) and Holdren (1960); the rigidity of traditional microeconomic frameworks did however present problems in extending to the wide assortments typical in retailing.

This chapter will therefore present the many facets of retail pricing within a less conventional framework, which is considered better fitted to most retail applications. The relevance of traditional economic models to certain retail pricing decision is acknowledged, but the format adopted here underlines the multi-dimensional character of retail pricing. Having considered some of the basic terms and concepts of retail pricing, a framework is introduced which focuses upon the assortment, time, geographical and comparative dimensions. Relevant pricing strategies and research contributions are considered in relation to these major dimensions of retail pricing.

Having discussed the formulation of retail strategy within Part One of this volume, most of the pricing policies, strategies and tactics discussed in this chapter can be set within that overall context. It may be helpful, however, to summarize at this stage the objectives that tend to underlie most retail pricing decisions:

1. *Long-term profit maximization*   This is assumed to be the general goal of all retail companies, although shorter-term objectives frequently take precedence. Exceptions may include the co-operatives, which in their initial concept also pursued social policy goals, and some independent retailers, who may pursue a blend of personal, social and financial goals.
2. *Short-term profit maximization*   This may be pursued if maximum funds are required for new stores, major refurbishments, new EPoS systems, etc. Improved short-term profits may also be required for tactical reasons, to attract investment or to help ward off an unwelcome takeover bid.
3. *Market penetration*   The need to establish a place in a market or to capture a better share may indicate pricing policies that are unlikely to yield the best short-term profits. This may be the objective of an entirely new retail organization, such as the discounters that have emerged in many sectors, or of specific stores, sections or departments within an existing organization. From time to time, existing companies recognize the need for a major programme of market penetration, such as Tesco's 'Operation Checkout'. This campaign increased sales by 43 per cent in one year but made considerable inroads into profitability (Retail & Distribution Management 1978). The problems of trading up from an initial low-price position were noted by Marbeau (1987).
4. *Market defence*   This may follow the specific penetration activities of a competitor. For example, J. Sainsbury's 'Discount 78' was largely a response to Tesco's 'Operation Checkout'. Defensive pricing may be localized or confined to a few commodity groups.
5. *Market stabilization*   This entails avoiding the use or provocation of aggressive price competition. It can also help to shift consumer attention away from prices and usually leads to more profitable operations, if also pursued by major competitors.
6. *Quality image*   An extensive literature has developed indicating a positive relationship between prices and perceptions of quality (e.g. Riesz 1978). This serves as a warning against the use of certain pricing tactics, especially in exclusive markets and where quality and style are of paramount importance to shoppers.
7. *Pricing integrity*   This means being seen as fair by consumers. Excessive price fluctuations because of special offers, for example, may suggest that the usual prices are not fair (Miller 1987). Similarly, bargain offer claims that do not meet legal requirements (Office of Fair Trading 1981) can bring adverse publicity.

8. *Rundown Pricing* If a particular item or department is being phased out, the primary objective may be to clear stocks to make space for more profitable merchandise. If a store is to be closed or sold, the retailer may use low prices and 'spoil the market' to maximize turnover and get the best sale price/compulsory purchase compensation.

These objectives are of course not mutually exclusive. Furthermore, a retailer may well pursue somewhat different pricing objectives at different points in time, in different outlets, or within different departments of the same store.

8.1 PRICE–DEMAND RELATIONSHIPS

In most retail settings, the objective of pricing is to maximize the overall profitability and/or sales within the total assortment. Models depicting the price–demand relationship for a single or just a few products are therefore of limited use to most retail price-makers. An understanding of the effects of price upon demand is however essential, in terms of both profit maximization and forecasting inventory requirements. A great deal of economic theory is centred upon the price–demand relationship, although traditional models fail adequately to depict the retail pricing function. More recently there has been a growing interest in the psychological components of prices, which exert strong influences upon the price–demand relationship. The purpose of this section is to briefly introduce some of the basic concepts and terminology relevant to this relationship, including price elasticity, price sensitivity and price thresholds. Finally, consideration is given to the complex network of price–demand relationships within the multi-product, retail pricing situation.

8.1.1 Price elasticity

The elasticity of demand to changes in price is an expression of the extent to which the quantity sold changes as prices are increased or decreased. The measure represents the division of the percentage change in demand by the percentage change in price. Demand is said to be elastic if the percentage change in demand is greater than the percentage change in price; if the reverse is true, the demand is said to be inelastic. For example:

	Week 1	Week 2	% change
Price (£)	50	44	12
Demand (units)	450	531	18

Elasticity = 18/12 = 1.5 (elastic)

The general concept of elasticity is of interest to the retailer in helping to assess likely responses to prices marked down for a seasonal sale, items used as special offers, or when a price is increased. In their most simple form, however, elasticity data may wrongly imply that the changes in demand will occur at an even rate across a wide range of price adjustments. One interesting elaboration upon the basic elasticity concept was termed the 'kinked demand curve' (Hall and Hitch 1939). This suggests that increases in price may generate a more elastic response than decreases, thus the kink in the demand curve. The theory suggests that increases will cause a rapid loss of market share to competitors, whereas competitors will tend to follow decreases, thereby suppressing much of the additional demand that may otherwise have accrued to the individual company.

It could be somewhat misleading to construct a series of profit maximization models based upon generalized elasticity data and known cost functions. Essentially, retailers are unlikely to have sufficiently detailed or timely data available, unless perhaps they are selling a very small range of high-value items. It has been suggested that product elasticity data issued at the national level could be utilized to assist retail pricing decisions (e.g. Bowbrick 1973), although this approach contains many weaknesses.

Aggregated data give little indication of the likely reactions of various types of competitor. Neither do they distinguish between the reactions of different shopper types. For example, a more affluent or brand-loyal shopper may be less prone to vary purchase levels in response to modest price changes. Furthermore, general product elasticity data do not necessarily reflect the demand functions of individual brands, sizes, flavour, styles or colours. Because of a lack of precise and relevant elasticity data, Pfouts (1978) found that retailers tend to have in mind a range of possible sales responses, in other words an 'interval' rather than a 'point' anticipation. One effect of this is that they tend to be less responsive to changes in demand, in that they have no precise yardstick against which to measure sales response.

8.1.2 Price sensitivity and thresholds

Although at first sight the concept of price sensitivity may appear directly analogous to that of price elasticity, there are important differences. Gabor and Granger (1964) and Sampson (1964) were among the earlier writers to develop the concept of price sensitivity as distinct from traditional measurements of elasticity. In Sampson's view, the latter tend to oversimplify the price–demand relationship, to be too generalized, and also to lead managers to anticipate more sensitivity to price than usually exists. Among the many factors that may desensitize customers, at least to more modest price changes, are the following:

1. The effects of product differentiation
2. Multiple dimensions of quality and preferences
3. Consumer loyalty to products or stores
4. Local competitive conditions
5. A reduction in levels of price awareness

In these respects, studies indicating sensitivity levels represent an improvement upon elasticity measures but generally share the weakness of relating only to specific product demand functions, measured in isolation. Several methods have been used to obtain sensitivity estimates, including the use of somewhat subjective trade or consumer surveys. In-store experiments potentially provide more objective results, and the spread of PoS computing will facilitate the measurement of sales on an hour-by-hour basis. Such experiments are not however free of potentially serious pitfalls, especially when conducted without adequate controls for the impact of the numerous extraneous variables, such as competitors' strategies. Critical discussion of the various designs and weaknesses of in-store experiments have been presented by Doyle and Gidengil (1977) and Lipstein (1981). It may also be considered unrealistic to measure reactions to price in isolation from other marketing variables, as interactions between price, display and advertising have been illustrated in multi-factor studies (e.g. Chevalier 1975; Wilkinson *et al.* 1982).

Some of the practical problems of in-store pricing experiments can be avoided by the use of approaches generally classified as 'hypothetical shopping situations'. These include simulations of the shopper's buying situation conducted in hall tests, at respondents' homes, or at clubs, meeting places, etc. (e.g. Tinn 1982; French and Lynn 1971). 'Laboratory' studies are also sometimes reported, although this can sometimes be a euphemism for studies conducted within the classroom! Even the better laboratory studies are subject to many limitations, including the possibility that subjects in this setting are likely to exhibit greater 'rationality' than they would within an actual store (Huber *et al.* 1986). Gabor *et al.* (1970) presented a major comparison of real and hypothetical shop situations, concluding that perfect correspondence of the results with behaviour under actual shop conditions could not be expected.

Within the general framework of price sensitivity, a number of researchers have suggested that there are certain ranges of prices that are 'acceptable' to consumers (e.g. Stoetzel 1954). It is held that the consumer has two price limits in mind: an upper limit, beyond which the product is considered too expensive, and a lower limit, below which the quality would be suspect. This introduces two further departures from the basic elasticity concept: first, that demand responds more to price changes beyond a certain threshold, and second, that too low a price may cause doubts about quality and therefore may deter, rather than attract, purchases. There have been many studies demonstrating a price–perceived-quality relationship, although many of the study methods used are open to serious criticism. Reviews of this literature have been provided by Monroe (1973) and Riesz (1978).

Whereas some of the early investigators of price thresholds used direct questions to establish upper and lower limits, Gabor and Granger (1966) pointed out that this was an unrealistic task to request of consumers. In their research, they called out six different product prices to a large sample of respondents, who are simply asked to respond 'buy', 'no, too expensive' or 'no, too cheap'. By varying the prices called across the whole range of interest to management, they were able to plot 'buy response curves' for each product. These showed the percentage of respondents willing to buy at each price level. Buy response curves derived in this way can reveal the thresholds that appear to trigger greater changes in demand and can also illustrate when the price currently set is too high or too low.

More practical concepts and methodologies have therefore been developed which are of considerable potential use to retail price-makers. The necessity remains, however, to test for price sensitivity and price thresholds in relation to the products, market conditions and customer types of interest to the specific retailer.

8.1.3 Multi-product pricing

Price sensitivity can now be estimated with reasonable accuracy at the individual product level, but the existence of interrelated demand remains a complex issue in most sectors of retailing. For example, a price reduction on a suit may generate additional sales of that item, but can either positively or negatively influence the sales of other items in the store. Additional sales of shirts and ties may be generated, but the extra suits sold may cannibalize the demand for other suits. Conversely, the total store sales may be sufficiently boosted to increase the sales of all suits, whether or not their prices are reduced. These demand interrelationships, usually described as 'cross-elasticities' (e.g. Cassady 1962; Reibstein and Gatignon 1984), are even more complex in a supermarket, within which a very large number of demand linkages exist.

The problems of interrelated demand, in terms of measurement, model-building and conceptual development, have seriously hindered developments in the theory of retail pricing. Much of the work in this area has been found within the microeconomic traditions; Moyer (1972), among others, was critical of the scope of traditional economic theory, which has tended to envisage a world in which middlemen do not exist and which is not readily adapted to the pricing of large product assortments. In conclusion to this section, a few notable studies will be mentioned which present a progression towards a more realistic and workable theory of retail pricing.

Holton (1957) suggested a model to explain multi-product profit maximization by retailers, explicitly considering cross-elasticities of demand between products. He developed the concept that retailers must pursue a form of price discrimination between products within their assort-ment in order to maximize profits. However, the model was constrained by assumption of rational economic behaviour among both retailers and consumers. Holdren (1960) subsequently presented a major attempt to describe and model the multi-product retail pricing function; the study provided valuable insights into alternative pricing structures, but the models suggested were probably too complex and demanding of inaccessible/expensive data to be entirely helpful to retailers.

A later contribution by Padberg (1968) was based upon a very large volume of data collected at the national level in the USA. Rather than attempt to construct formal pricing models, it drew attention to the various ways of differentiating product gross margins and also noted the importance of local pricing by chain stores. A further departure from traditional pricing models was made by Nystrom (1970), who set out to integrate concepts of economics and psychology relevant to the study of retail pricing. He particularly explored the assortment and time dimensions, noting that consumers tend to form longer-term price images of stores, usually based upon a relatively small number of item price discriminations. At least implicitly, this study formed a valuable linkage with the emerging stream of research on the formation of retail images, discussed in Chapter 5.

More recently, Little and Shapiro (1980) noted that PoS scanners could increasingly facilitate the calculation of timely and more specific elasticity and cross-elasticity data. They also drew attention to the important distinctions between short-term product purchase decisions and longer-term store patronage decisions. An appreciation has therefore emerged that retail pricing cannot readily or adequately be encompassed within the traditional, economic framework.

8.2 THE DIMENSIONS OF RETAIL PRICING

It is hoped that the previous section will have illustrated that most studies of retail pricing have taken only a partial view of this complex function. The microeconomic tradition has tended to focus largely upon the cost and competition elements and has found difficulty in accommodating the wide assortments characteristic of most forms of retailing. Noteworthy attempts to overcome this particular problem have been made, and Nystrom (1970) made a significant conceptual contribution in exploring the assortment and time dimensions of retail pricing. Practising retail managers do however need to recognize and effectively control all the relevant dimensions of retail pricing; the further development of retail pricing theory also requires a more comprehen-sive and realistic framework.

A potentially helpful contribution, developed in relation to manufacturer pricing, was the 'differential pricing approach', expounded by Oxenfeldt (1979). Although concepts of price discrimination are not new, this approach provides a view of pricing in terms of an interrelated network of differentials, applied to certain cost and competition bases. In particular, the potential use of geographical price differentials, ignored in many previous studies, is given explicit consideration. It is felt that this approach can be usefully adapted and extended to the retail case. The purpose of this section is to develop this framework, which will focus the attention of both researchers and decision-makers upon the several important dimensions of retail pricing. Some changes of terminology have been considered desirable, both to clarify meanings and to provide greater consistency with previous studies that have considered specific elements of retail pricing.

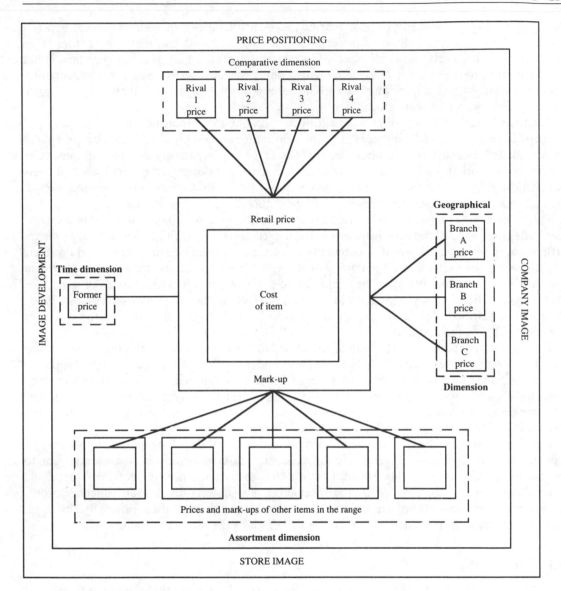

Figure 8.1 The dimensions of retail pricing
Source: McGoldrick (1987).

8.2.1 A multi-dimensional framework

Figure 8.1 illustrates, in necessarily simplified form, the major dimensions of the retail price decision. The following sections examine each of these in relation to the pricing strategies employed and the conceptual insights available. The core of the retail pricing function is seen as the establishment of different mark-up levels; each of these decisions, however, must have regard for the comparative prices in rival stores, previous prices, prevailing price levels in local areas, and the numerous other prices within the product assortment. The outer frame comprises the related facets of overall price image, which both constrain and are influenced by these pricing decisions.

The comparative dimension of retail pricing represents the many differences in price between those of the retailer and those of direct and indirect, local and national competitors. This dimension has been relatively well explored in early studies, although adequate recognition has not been given to the problems associated with gaining the necessary comparative information. The discussion of this dimension therefore includes a consideration of systems of retail price auditing and sources of such information.

The time dimension is also of great significance in retailing; in department stores, grocery and other wide-range retailing companies, it is not unusual for several hundred price adjustments to be administered each week. In addition, short-term pricing represents a major, if sometimes overworked, promotional tool, either in the form of general 'sales' or temporary offers on a few items in the range. In terms of consumer perceptions of store price levels, the time dimension is also relevant to the longer-term processes of favourably developing price images.

The assortment dimension has in recent years been the focus of considerable retail management attention. It has long been recognized that a fixed mark-up on all items in the range makes little sense either in terms of cost or competition factors, so varying mark-ups between products tend to be the norm. It has also been increasingly recognized that certain items in the assortment are more powerful than others in the formation of price images; differential levels of item price awareness are therefore highly relevant in this context. As a further overlay to assortment pricing decisions, a number of concepts and strategies have been evolved with regard to the choice of specific price levels and endings.

The geographical dimension has rapidly increased in relevance as more retailing is undertaken by chain stores, rather than single-location independents. Even if a chain retailer decides to charge the same prices in all outlets, this dimension cannot be ignored, as this set of prices will be differently positioned in different locations. The practice of geographical differentiation is becoming an increasingly important element of major retailers' pricing strategies, albeit within the limits constrained by the price image of the company as a whole.

This framework, at least in this simplified form, is clearly not designed to supply precise answers to the many individual retail pricing decisions. It does however seek to draw attention to the essential complexity of this pricing function and to help the price-maker focus upon the dimensions that may be affected by the specific set of decisions. In the subsequent sections, pricing strategies and tactics are discussed in relation to the dimension primarily involved, although virtually all price actions influence some or all of the other dimensions.

8.3 THE TIME DIMENSION

This dimension is considered first to underline the essential principal that pricing in retailing is not usually concerned simply with the maximization of individual product, short-term sales. A longer-term objective normally exists in attempting progressively to create the most favourable price image for the store or company. One type of approach to this, which will be considered within this section, is the use of temporary special offers or more widespread seasonal 'sales'. These are clearly not the only routes towards the longer-term development of a lower-priced image, although they are ones that are widely used in most retail sectors. In that temporary offers are usually administered very selectively within the product range, it will be seen that they also comprise an important component of the assortment dimension.

8.3.1 Formation of price images

The wider question of store images has already been considered in detail in Chapter 5. However, the specific issue of price images is highly relevant in this context, as retailer strategies and tactics are increasingly focused upon image formation. This facet of retail pricing was largely ignored within many early studies, but Nystrom (1970) effectively harnessed the concept within a simple model. The core of this was a recognition that consumers, even if they wish to be economically rational in their purchasing decisions, are prevented by lack of information and/or cognitive limitations. Accordingly, they are prone to generalize an image of the retailer's overall price level which is based upon a relatively small number of (or maybe just one) individual price discrimination(s).

This concept of generalization on the basis of very limited discriminations is clearly valid in relation to the longer-term price images of retailers with large product assortments, such as variety stores or grocery stores. Nystrom also depicted the situation within which the existing image held of the store prices influences the customer's evaluation of an individual price offering. This effect was later demonstrated by Fry and McDougall (1974); they illustrated that the more traditional retailer may find it harder to convince customers that a cut price is really the lowest in the area than a retailer with a discounter image.

When a prior generalization leads to a favourable evaluation, it is quite likely that the consumer will undertake specific comparison, the process of discrimination, at a later stage. For example, a consumer patronizing a discount store may be easily convinced, because of store images held, that a sofa priced at £399 represents a good deal. If it is later observed that the sofa is being sold for £450 elsewhere, that price image will be reinforced. If on the other hand the sofa is observed for sale at £349 elsewhere, this one discrimination may be generalized to modify considerably the image held, especially if the item was actually purchased at £399! Figure 8.2 illustrates the alternative processes of generalization and discrimination.

8.3.2 Temporary price offers

As a device for conveying an image of competitive prices to the consumer, short-term price reductions have had a long history in most forms of retailing. Briggs and Smyth (1967) noted that they convey an 'image of cheapness' and also that more expensive firms often used the deepest cuts. Alderson (1963) summarized the process of heavily promoting a selection of special prices as the desire to 'minimize the cost of appearing competitive'. Cassady (1962) considered that it would be 'foolish as well as futile' to try to undercut rivals on all items. The advantages of temporary offers were summarized: being short-term, they are less likely to provoke direct retaliation; concentration upon a few lines gives a flexibility in accordance with market conditions; and special offers may be used to attract certain types of customers.

The choice of products for temporary price offers represents a difficult task for retail price-makers. Willsmer (1970) reported that one retailer was offered over 600 promotions each month, yet wished to feature only 20 items every two weeks. Various recommendations have emerged as to how a retailer should select special-offer items. Preston (1963) suggested that more expensive and/or bulky items should be used in order to inhibit stocking up by consumers; in contrast, Cassady (1962) considered that lower-priced items would deter 'cherry picking' of the offers. Litvack et al. (1985) explained widely varying levels of response to short-term price offers in terms of the 'stockability' of different products by consumers. In the context of special-offer item choice, Livesey (1976) noted the dangers of price cuts on the type of items for which lower quality may therefore be assumed. Holdren (1960) made a systematic attempt to identify the

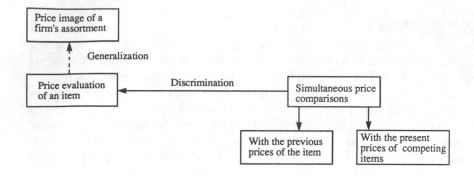

Case 1: Item specific price information dominates

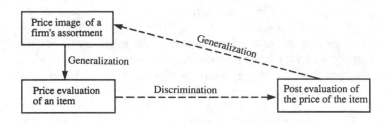

Case 2: Price image dominates

Figure 8.2   Generalization and discrimination in retail price evaluations
Source: adapted from Nystrom (1970).

types of item with a strong 'transfer effect'; this denotes changes in the sales of a store resulting from the transfer of custom from one store to another, rather than from one product to another.

Although retailers are becoming more discriminating in their choice of offers, in the UK grocery industry, for example, most cuts are 'subsidized' by at least 40 per cent by manufacturers; in some cases the manufacturer meets 100 per cent of the price cut, plus a contribution towards advertising and display costs. The former chairman of one major grocery chain defined sales promotion as 'manufacturers' contribution to my profits'. Manufacturers generally agree that they require retailer assistance with promotions (e.g. Thijm 1976), although retailer's views are more varied. Chevalier and Curhan (1976) observed frequent retailer–manufacturer conflicts, with retailers feeling that manufacturer-initiated promotions simply encouraged 'profitless brand-switching'. In a study of loss-leader promotions in Finland, Rinne *et al.* (1986) found that about half of them had a negative effect on store profits. An aspect of product choice for which some evidence is available is the extent to which retailers follow or avoid their competitors' offers. Alderson and Shapiro (1964), Nelson and Preston (1966) and Swan (1971) all tended to find overlap of 10 per cent or less. It appeared that retailers were able to make reasonable estimates of rivals' offers and generally sought to avoid direct competition on the same items.

The appropriate depth of price cut has received relatively little attention. Padberg (1968) observed temporary reductions of 6–24 per cent, but some items listed among 'specials' may include no reduction at all (e.g. Gray and Anderson 1962). Chevalier (1974) concluded that, if direct sales response were the only criterion, there would be 'little rationale for deep price cuts'. Walters and Rinne (1986) found no significant increases in the sales of non-promoted products resulting from loss-leader special-offer promotions. Several studies have reported the short-term effects of price cuts coupled with increases in advertising and/or display (e.g. Chevalier 1975; Wilkinson et al. 1982). In the early 'Dillon Study' in the USA, sales of price-cut items increased by an average of 808 per cent (Progressive Grocer 1960). Rather more extravagant claims are made by those with an interest in stimulating promotional activities; such claims may however make no reference to the demonstrated propensity of sales to fall away again to about the previous level after the temporary offer period (e.g. Ehrenberg 1976; Shoemaker and Shoaf 1977; Cotton and Babb 1978). In spite of these important qualifications, plus the somewhat uncertain impact of the offers upon the retailer's longer-term image, the lure of temporary price cuts remains strong.

8.4 THE ASSORTMENT DIMENSION

With the exception of petrol stations, car dealers and other narrow-range retailers, most retail companies are concerned with the pricing of very large product assortments. A major problem arises therefore in setting mark-ups for each item in the range that will maximize the overall company profitability. The practice of applying the same mark-up to every item in the range has long since been discredited (e.g. Holton 1957; Holdren 1960), being justified neither in cost nor in competition terms. Many systems of allocating item costs as an aid to such decisions have been offered to retailers. In recent years the concept of direct product profitability (see Section 5.2.3) has been advocated, and such approaches can provide useful inputs to many assortment decisions including pricing decisions, provided of course that the cost of the information does not outweigh the benefit derived.

While not ignoring these approaches to the analysis of item profitability, the discussion in this section will focus upon the strategies and concepts most relevant to the maximization of total assortment profitability. In the final analysis, the mark-up that can actually be achieved on each item is more a function of competitive prices, consumer awareness of specific item prices, their sensitivity to changes in those prices, and the effect that an item price exerts upon the overall assortment price image. The 'leader line pricing' technique is described as a longer-term approach to selective discounting and favourable image formation. The concept of item price awareness is explored as a major component of such strategies. Unit prices are then considered, in that many assortment pricing decisions relate to the different sizes of the same product. Finally, the tasks of setting the specific price points are examined, including the use of price lining and certain price endings. Price differentials between own brands and equivalent manufacturer brands are also highly relevant to the assortment dimensions; this topic is considered in detail in the following chapter.

8.4.1   Leader line pricing

The types of strategy that have generally come to be known as 'leader line pricing' represent an evolution of the temporary price-cutting strategies discussed in Section 8.3.2. The core concept is very similar, in that certain items within the assortment are made the subject of more competitive pricing, in order to convey a better price image which hopefully is generalized to the whole company or store. The difference is that these prices are usually not cut as deeply as in the case of short-term offers; there tend to be more items involved, and the selectively discounted prices are held long-term, apart from occasional fine-tuning of the leader line items. The logic of the approach is well established. In an early study by Nelson (1962), an example is cited of a reasonably inexpensive chain that had developed a high-priced image by failing to identify the product prices that were most instrumental in forming images of the company's overall prices. Conversely, Parsons and Price (1972) noted that even stores carrying the 'discount' title do not need to place low prices on every product in order to sustain that image. In other words, because of the processes by which consumer's form their overall price images, there is much to be gained by identifying the 'key indicators' within the assortment.

Pressures towards leader line pricing came from emerging evidence that many consumers were increasingly disenchanted with short-term offers. McClelland (1963) declared himself to be in favour of a wider range of lesser price cuts but concluded at that time that the preference of the public, and the American experience, seemed to drive the retailer towards fewer, deeper cuts. Lynn (1967) noted the dangers of arousing distrust and resentment through this strategy. By the mid-1970s, a view had been widely circulated by the Harris International organization that shoppers were becoming decreasingly prone to shop around for special offers (Louis Harris International 1974). While this is to be expected as more shoppers switch to using fewer but larger stores, it does not necessarily mean that special offers do not still have a role in favourably influencing price images.

Several interesting case studies of leader line pricing were provided by the UK grocery retailers in the late 1970s. By 1977, the management of the large Tesco chain had decided that their long used mix of temporary price offers, trading stamps and only moderately competitive prices was not destined to keep them among the market leaders for many more years. They were being threatened on the one side by the slightly more up-market operations of their major rival J. Sainsbury, and on the other side by the new and vigorous growth of grocery discounters. The use of more special offers was not an adequate answer; surveys undertaken by myself early in 1977 with the collaboration of Tesco confirmed their belief that few of their 60–70 offers at any one time were making any significant impact or were even being noticed.

Tesco's answer was a drastic and somewhat courageous alteration of their pricing and overall marketing policy, which was labelled 'Operation Checkout'. The most obvious manifestations were the dropping of trading stamps and a great deal of advertising. Less obvious but highly effective was a switch to a leader line pricing system, involving long-term reductions on approximately 150 lines. In order to avoid the impression that they had completely abandoned special offers, Tesco retained 6–10 short-term, very deep cut offers—as many, in fact, as tended to be noticed when they previously used far more. For this company, the leader line approach possibly offered the only medium-term solution to gaining a price image comparable with the new discounters. Although rapidly rationalizing its outlets, Tesco could not instantly transform its cost structure to allow truly 'across-the-board' discounting. The process was however highly successful in increasing turnover by 43 per cent in the first year alone. The approach was soon followed by several of the rival retailers, including at least one of the newer discounters.

8.4.2 Consumer awareness of item prices

Both long- and short-term promotional pricing strategies are generally pursued in the recognition that consumer awareness of specific item prices is now relatively low. Assumptions of high price awareness, implicit in early economic theory, have long since been discredited. Padberg (1968) noted that consumers may be aware of possibly 20, 50 or, at the most, 200 prices among the several thousand in a supermarket range. Subsequently it was reported that only 15 per cent of housewives could correctly state the cost of a branded drink that they had just bought (Thorncroft 1973). There are sound reasons to anticipate that awareness should have declined still further, including inflation, the metrication of some package sizes (in the UK), product range diversification, and the greater spatial separation of new, larger stores. To these factors can be added the far greater degree of variability both between and within retailers' prices since the abolition of resale price maintenance in most areas.

With regard to assortment pricing decisions, studies that have examined awareness of specific *item* prices, as opposed to overall store price *levels*, are especially relevant. From a study in the late 1950s, Gabor and Granger (1961) found considerable differences between the accuracy of recall of different product prices; 79 per cent correctly recalled tea prices, whereas only 35 per cent correctly recalled breakfast cereal prices. A Progressive Grocer (1964) study used a very different methodology but found an even wider range of awareness levels; using the measure of recall of within 5 per cent of the correct price, awareness levels varied between 12 and 91 per cent among the 59 products investigated. A follow-up study demonstrated considerably reduced awareness levels (Heller 1974). Other studies have confirmed falling levels of price awareness, and some have investigated relationships with customer characteristics. Goldman (1977) produced evidence that lower-income shoppers tend to be more price-aware, although the study focused upon items of higher budgetary importance.

A recent study by McGoldrick and Marks (1987) produced indications of awareness levels in ten grocery product categories. These results are summarized within Table 8.1. Various measures of awareness were utilized, of which three are shown in the table. The level of exact recall is especially relevant when deciding upon the exact price point, whereas the measures of approximate recall are more appropriate to wider decisions on relative price positioning within the assortment. Using the mean percentage recall error measure, the products can be grouped into three significantly different groups, as shown in the table. Extensive proprietary research has been undertaken on behalf of specific retailers to measure item price awareness levels, from which leader line and other pricing strategies have been evolved. Clearly, far more detail is required than the general category means represented in Table 8.1. Assortment pricing decisions must not only determine the marks-ups on broad product categories but also establish prices for individual brands, varieties and sizes within each category.

8.4.3 Unit prices

In many sectors of retailing, the price-makers must decide upon the relative prices of the different sizes or quantities of the same items. The term 'unit price' is used to denote the price expressed in relation to an appropriate standard unit of measure, such as price per kilogram or price per litre. It would normally be assumed by consumers that larger sizes, or multipacks, cost less per unit than smaller sizes, although several studies have illustrated departures from this assumption.

A 'quantity surcharge' is said to exist when the larger size actually costs more per unit than the smaller size(s). Examples of quantity surcharges were identified in studies by Lamont *et al.* (1972)

Table 8.1 Levels of item price awareness (%)

Product	Exact recall	Recall ± 5%	Recall error mean
Coffee	22	65	6.7
Beans	39	59	6.9
Fish fingers	25	69	6.9
Muesli	23	46	7.0
Canned soup	39	51	8.9
Flour	29	60	9.0
Sauces	20	52	9.5
Extracts	20	20	10.3
Vegetable oil	18	43	11.9
Digestives	23	46	12.0
All items	29	55	8.7

Source: McGoldrick and Marks (1987).

and Widrick (1974). More recently, Nason and Della Bitta (1983) found that 25 and 29 per cent of items in two price audits included at least one quantity surcharge in the various size comparisons. Managers interviewed in the UK indicated that quantity surcharges are usually the result of errors or special offers on smaller sizes; they were less prepared to acknowledge that some may be the outcome of deliberate strategies, for example leader line pricing featuring the smaller sizes (McGoldrick and Marks 1985). Whatever the reason, quantity surcharges, if noticed, clearly may alienate shoppers.

The ability of consumers to compare unit prices both within and between brands is considerably hampered by the chaotic state of package sizes in the UK. Although some products are sold in an orderly size progression, in others it is impossible to compare unit prices without an electronic calculator and conversion chart. In the USA it is common to find unit price information displayed either alongside the item price or on a composite list nearby. This practice has been vigorously resisted by most UK retailers, so unit prices tend to be displayed only where required by law, e.g. on pre-packaged meats and cheeses. An extensive literature has developed on consumer usage of unit pricing information in the USA, a review of which was provided by Aaker and Ford (1983).

Most of the studies have been concerned with consumers' awareness of the information, its usage, and the reactions to different modes of information display. There is little direct evidence as to the effects of unit pricing upon price awareness in general. It could well be that unit pricing may reduce awareness of actual shelf prices, having given consumers an alternative yardstick by which to compare value. At the point of purchase, however, awareness of interproduct and intersize differentials is likely to be increased, potentially increasing sensitivity to differentials within the retailer's assortment. The spread of PoS computer systems will considerably facilitate the automatic printing of unit pricing information; it is yet to be seen how many retailers will avail themselves of the facility.

8.4.4 Selecting specific price points

Various concepts and strategies have so far been examined which are relevant to the task of setting differential mark-ups for items within the assortment. It would however be incorrect to assume that the specific price point chosen is an unimportant issue; there are firmly held beliefs that certain price endings are more effective than others, such as £9.95 or £9.99 rather than £10.00. Twedt (1965) suggested that this practice was originated by department stores to force cashiers to ring up sales and open the till to give change, thereby reducing cashier fraud. Whatever the origins, it has created customary prices in some product fields. When researching the buy-response curve (see Section 8.1.2), Gabor and Granger (1966) noticed sharp kinks in demand just below whole-number prices. Certain unaccustomed prices were simply not seen as 'real prices' by their respondents.

Customary endings are by no means restricted to department stores and clothing outlets. Twedt (1965) found that 64 per cent of prices in grocery advertisements ended in 9s. He urged further research into the '9 fixation' to establish whether such prices really promote sales or are simply 'sticky prices' which obstruct more scientific pricing decisions. Friedman (1967) found that 80 per cent of prices observed ended in a 9 or a 5; odd prices also tend to be common in the pricing of multiple units (Progressive Grocer 1971). Following an elaborate study of odd price endings, Georgoff (1972) concluded that endings do appear to affect price illusions; direct effects upon sales could not however be detected. The possible effects upon price illusions are none the less important, as the image of assortment prices is more important in most contexts than the sales of specific items.

A major problem in research terms is that certain types of price have developed symbolic meanings in some product areas but not in others. Gabor (1974) noted the powerful effects of 'odd-ball' prices under certain circumstances, and Gardner (1970) pointed out that many retailers set prices as though they conveyed special meanings. Even-number prices may be used to signify prestige or quality, whereas prices such as 88¢ may be used to indicate a bargain. A few retailers in recent years have conducted limited studies to assess whether the use of such endings is a valid assortment pricing strategy, although a wide range of practices remains.

Another common approach in the setting of specific price points is the use of price lining, although there is little published evidence as to its effectiveness. Price lining implies the use of very few different price points for a range of items, rather than a wide variety of prices. Table 8.2 provides examples of different types of price lining, illustrating also the common use of odd endings at the cheaper end of the scale.

One justification of price lining is that it simplifies the assortment pricing and, to an extent, the buying process. Having established price lines that appear appropriate to specific consumer segments and needs, the retailer can buy, or have produced, items that yield acceptable margins when sold at those price points. Gabor (1977) pointed to certain problems in using price lines, notably a reluctance to sell items that do not fit into the structure, even if they would be attractive to the consumer. Rigid price lines can also prove difficult to adjust in times of rapid inflation. However, price lines are thought to have advantages in simplifying the consumer's choice process in the store. Particularly when purchasing clothing items, a consumer is typically faced with a wide choice of styles, colours, etc., in several different stores. If many different price levels within one store must also be evaluated within the complex choice process, the effect can be severe dissonance and an instinct to retreat from the store. When price lines are encountered, the consumer is likely to select from among the items at one or possibly two points, thereby considerably reducing the task of deciding upon the purchase.

Various alternative strategies may be employed in setting the differentials between price lines.

Table 8.2 Examples of price lining

Ties		Suits		Watches	
Prices (£)	Diff. (%)	Prices (£)	Diff. (%)	Prices (£)	Diff. (%)
2.99		79.95		14.95	
	50.2		25.0		33.4
4.49		99.95		19.95	
	50.3		20.0		102.2
6.75		120.00		39.95	
	48.1		16.7		275.5
10.00		140.00		150.00	

In the first example in Table 8.2, the constant percentage differential is attempting to create an even spread across the mass market for ties. The second example, the diminishing percentage differential may be used to encourage consumers to move up to the next price point above their intended purchase price for a suit. In the final example, a jeweller may be attempting to cater for a very diverse range of needs, from the basic utility watches to the more expensive fashion watches. Where very diverse segments are being catered for within one store, 'price clustering' may be used as a variant upon price lining. In such cases, prices are clustered around certain levels, rather than strictly adhering to specific price points. Of all the elements of assortment pricing, the practice of price lining is the least well analysed within the published research literature.

8.5 THE GEOGRAPHICAL DIMENSION

Every retail store of a multiple chain operates within a local market that is at least slightly different from that experienced by other stores in the group. In spite of the rapid growth of the multiple chains in most sectors, this quite fundamental property of retail marketing has received very little detailed attention in the literature. Within this section, a distinction is drawn between studies of price differences between areas, including whichever retailers are trading in those areas, and studies of geographical differentiation within the pricing strategies of individual companies. The former have received rather more attention, including comparisons of prices in urban and rural areas, the particular issues of prices in minority/poverty areas, and studies of local prices in relation to levels of local concentration. This body of evidence will be very briefly summarized, then attention turns to the strategy of geographical differentiation from the viewpoint of the specific chain retailer.

8.5.1 Area price differences

The existence of area price differences has been firmly established from work undertaken in the USA, Europe and Australia. Naturally, such differences can emerge only when the geographical dimension is included within the study methodology; it represents a major weakness of many otherwise excellent studies of retail pricing that the spatial aspects were virtually ignored.

It is possibly not surprising that Jamison (1968) found considerable price differences between Honolulu and San Francisco, given regional taste differences and very unequal transport cost factors. In a study of prices in several Australian cities, Briggs and Smyth (1967) noted that an equivalent group of items in Hobart was 15.5 per cent more expensive than in Adelaide. More surprising was the finding that prices were lower in Perth than in Melbourne, in spite of the higher transport costs of most items to Perth. Clearly, the importance of competitive structure and style of retailing in each area outweighed transport cost considerations. Similarly, Murray (1977) noted major differences between grocery prices within England, with shoppers in Yorkshire being able to buy groceries for about 11 per cent less than their counterparts in less competitive Surrey.

Other studies have compared urban, suburban and rural price levels and illustrated differences within rather smaller geographical areas. Campbell and Chisholm (1970) found that prices generally increased as one moved away from the centre of Swansea, mainly because of the mix of retailers operating in the different areas. Parker (1979), on the other hand, found no strong relationship between prices and proximity to the centre of Dublin, although that study was confined to the city and suburbs. It is to be expected that prices may be higher in more isolated areas; Briggs and Smyth (1967) reported growing price differences with increasing distances from Perth, and in the UK the Price Commission (1975) produced some evidence of higher prices in outlying areas.

Prices in poverty and/or racial minority areas have been the subject of more extensive, if not entirely conclusive, studies. Parker (1979) reviewed several of the early studies of price variation within North American cities and found some evidence of 'price-gouging' of lower-income consumers. Alexis and Simon (1967) concluded that a nonlinear relationship appeared to exist, with the middle classes paying the least, the upper and lower classes the most. Samli and French (1971) noted that area differences do not always discriminate against the poor but observed that the rural poor rather than the urban poor tended to pay more. Wilkinson et al. (1973) also found that the non-urban poor tended to be offered fewer special offers, thereby demonstrating that geographical price differentiation may be concentrated on temporary offers. A critical review of the early studies in this area was provided by Sexton (1974), who identified many methodological weaknesses.

Relationships between local concentration and area prices have not been as widely researched. From an early review of the somewhat fragmentary evidence, Bucklin (1972) concluded that some association appeared to exist. Extensive evidence was subsequently presented by Marion et al. (1979), illustrating relationships between local concentration and food prices. A measure of the proportion of local trade in the hands of the four largest firms proved to be far more strongly related to retail prices than did several measures of retail costs. The relationship derived suggested that a group of items costing $93 in areas where the four largest firms held 45 per cent of the market would typically cost $98 where the equivalent concentration measure was 75 per cent. In that local markets are becoming more highly concentrated with the growth of the multiple chains, this relationship will be of increasing interest both to policy-makers and to retail management.

8.5.2 Strategies of geographical differentiation

In that every local market is unique in terms of its level and type of competition, to exploit the potential fully a multiple retailer would need to charge different prices in each individual outlet. In most cases, the benefits to be gained from such a policy would be more than outweighed by the costs involved in collecting the necessary comparative information and in the administration of the system. Among the major retailers in the UK, it would appear that the Carrefour company operated with a considerable degree of branch autonomy to adapt to local conditions. At the other extreme, some of the discounters operate a rigid pricing policy across all their stores, taking the view that their prices are competitive in any location. Although this leads to more simple administration and control procedures, the weakness of the policy is clearly that the prices are only just competitive in some areas but almost too competitive in others.

The Asda superstore group in the UK used frequently to boast a policy of identical prices in all their stores. When they opened a large store in the (then) high-priced Edinburgh area, consumers travelled to it from unusually great distances, reflecting in part the fact that the prices were very much lower than the local norm. Most multiple retailers operate a compromise between these two solutions, using a classification system which allows a manageable approximation to be made to local competitive conditions. It has for example been reported that the Tesco company operates seven or more pricing strata, and other, smaller multiples have been found to operate two or three.

The McKinsey company has declared that, in pricing terms, the UK may be divided into 'hard', 'medium' and 'soft' areas. The Consumers' Association (1978) offered comparisons indicating that a 'basket' of goods costing £9.22 at Fine Fare stores in Yorkshire and Humberside would cost £8.93 at Fine Fare stores in the West Midlands. As many multiples found themselves with a diversity of store sizes and types, geographical differentiation was often justified in terms of differing store cost structures. This can be only a short-term consideration, however, as conditions of local competition constrain the prices that can be charged and ultimately the cost structure that is viable within the area.

As part of a study of geographical price differentiation, McGoldrick (1985) obtained 19,600 almost simultaneous price observations, comprising 98 item prices in each of 200 stores. A price index was constructed for each individual store, using an appropriate weighting system, as discussed in Section 8.6.1. Table 8.3 shows the dispersion of store price levels between the stores of the eight retailers involved, the levels being expressed relative to an overall mean index of 100. Very different policies towards geographical differentiation may be implied from these analyses. The difference between the cheapest and most expensive stores in Company E was less than half of a percentage point; given that small time-lags can occur in the administration of price changes, this is indicative of no geographical differentiation by that company. The contrast, the most expensive store of Company B had a price level some 13 per cent higher than that of its cheapest store. These data illustrate both the extent of geographical differentiation by some companies and also the fact that some hardly use the strategy at all.

Evidence to emerge from the literature is somewhat fragmentary. Padberg (1968) referred to an early anti-trust case against Safeway, which was deemed to have pursued market share goals in Dallas and El Paso through intensive local price reductions. Preston (1963) studied price advertisements of the same retailers in different areas and found many differences in the products and prices offered. During a period of intensive price competition in Northern Ireland, Bell and Brown (1986) noted evidence of 'dual pricing' by an established chain which had decreased prices in some branches to meet local competition. From a study of chain drug stores, Parsons and Price (1972) noted a form of 'restricted autonomy', whereby store managers could alter certain key product prices without first consulting the head office. Other researchers have also pointed to the gross margin differences caused by local price adaptations (e.g. Cottrell 1973; Will 1970).

More obvious examples of geographical price differentiation can be seen when a retailer positions certain outlets as discount stores or convenience stores. In these instances, all elements of the retailing mix, including prices, are likely to be focused upon the competitive objectives of the specific outlet and the local market conditions. This strategy, which may extend to using a different name on certain stores, can help to overcome the constraints imposed by the overall

Table 8.3 Within-company price level differences

Company	No. of stores sampled	Mean index level	St. dev.	Index range Lowest	Highest
A	40	104.10	159.7	98.41	106.51
B	40	103.20	316.2	94.91	107.27
C	40	100.51	92.5	97.25	102.52
D	40	93.42	75.9	91.60	95.63
E	10	92.28	15.3	92.09	92.51
F	10	95.52	29.9	94.84	95.83
G	10	102.00	59.2	100.75	103.10
H	10	105.32	119.5	102.90	106.98

Source: McGoldrick (1985).

price image of the company. Instances of short-term geographical differentiation may also be observed when a new store is opened or as a reaction to an opening by a competitor. Such pricing tactics illustrate all the dimensions so far discussed, being localized, temporary and typically involving selected items within the total assortment.

8.6 THE COMPARATIVE DIMENSION

This important dimension has been left until now as it clearly represents an overlay to the other dimensions and specific issues already discussed. All other pricing decisions, whether long-term or short-term, item-level or assortment-level, local or national, must be taken with a view to the resulting comparative price position *vis à vis* competitors. The title 'competitive dimension' was considered for this element of the framework but was rejected on the grounds that it blurred the scope of this dimension. All the dimensions reflect part of the competitive pricing function; this one relates more specifically to the tasks of price comparison and positioning.

In numerous marketing and retailing texts, we are told that the price-maker faces the options of positioning prices below, at, or above the market. Although this basic logic is difficult to refute, broad classifications of strategic options along these lines suggest a certain simplicity in retail marketing which is rarely encountered. In the first place, it is rather more difficult in retailing than in most forms of manufacturing to actually know what 'the market' is, in pricing terms. Large assortments of prices are typically competing with other large, but usually different, assortments; the bases of comparisons are therefore somewhat more complex.

As noted in Section 8.3.1, it is essential to be aware not only of comparative price positions but also of the resulting comparative price images. Rather than dwell upon the general issue of price positioning, which has already been discussed in Chapter 4, this section will focus upon the specific issues of obtaining retail price comparisons. First, the techniques and problems of retail price auditing are discussed, then examples are presented to illustrate essential differences between objective and subjective comparison systems.

8.6.1   Price auditing

It has already been noted that shoppers tend to be aware of only a small proportion of retail prices; the implication may have arisen that retail managers are, on the other hand, in possession of comprehensive, reliable and objective information about comparative price levels in each others' stores. Although audits, or surveys of prices, are undertaken to report prices of particular products, in certain stores at particular points in time, these typically represent only a very small sample of the total. As in any sampling exercise, there is inevitably a trade-off between the sample size, therefore the cost, and the reliability of the information produced. Most *ad hoc* audits of prices in grocery or other wide-range stores collect between 50 and 125 item prices, depending upon the resources available and the other sample dimensions, notably the number of stores audited. Wood (1976) collected 105 item prices and Thorpe (1972) 123 in studies of prices at or near major superstores. As an indication of the time/cost involved, Holdren (1960) reflected that it took him about 300 man-hours to collect and compute indices from 74 prices in eight stores. Clearly, as the sample of products becomes large, it is increasingly difficult to undertake the audit without the knowledge of the store management.

Price audits exert an important influence upon retail pricing in a number of different ways. First, published audits that are available to consumers, such as those sometimes included in the *Which?* reports published by the Consumers' Association in the UK, may be very instrumental in the formation of price images by consumers who notice or seek this information. Accordingly, some retailers take a special interest in the sample of products audited to ensure that their price ratings emerge as favourably as possible. Second, major 'trade-oriented' audits exist, such as those conducted on a continuous basis by Audits of Great Britain and A. C. Nielsen. These tend to identify a wider range of product prices at individual store level, therefore providing retailers and manufacturers with a more comprehensive check upon the prices charged for those items by most major retailers. Third, *ad hoc* price audits are regularly conducted by retailers to monitor competitor activities and, in some cases, to ensure that their own stores are complying with head office policy.

The validity of price comparisons derived through price auditing is highly dependent upon the sampling and analytical methods employed. If a product sample is to be absolutely comparable between retailers, only those items could be included that are widely available brands and sizes. This would however limit the scope of the audit and would concentrate too heavily upon more strongly promoted items. Many researchers have therefore accepted some variability in the product specification in order to include private labels, less popular sizes and/or fresh foods (e.g. Padberg 1968; Wood 1976). Another decision is the extent to which observations are repeated over time. In comparing prices of women's clothing in discount and department stores, Hutchinson-Kirby and Dardis (1986) noted the prices every week for 13 weeks.

Having audited a selection of items, the construction of an index to represent comparative price levels requires a method of combining the item price observations. A commonly used approach is simply to add up the item prices, but this can overweight the importance of expensive items and/or items less frequently purchased. A somewhat better approach is to weight each item price statistically before combining them to form the price level index. Usually a weighting system is used that reflects 'average' allocations of expenditure to the various commodities, although it is recognized that difference weightings will be appropriate for different consumer groups. A detailed description of one relatively elaborate price auditing and weighting system was provided by Wood (1976).

8.6.2 Objective and subjective comparisons

The problems outlined in attempting to gain measures of relative price levels clearly leaves some doubt as to whether such comparisons can be entirely objective. In evaluating the longer-term effects of pricing activities, the retailer is even more concerned to assess the entirely subjective evaluations of relative price levels formed by consumers. Relatively few studies have investigated consumer awareness of relative price levels, as opposed to awareness of individual item prices. A major study by Brown (1969) involved over 1,000 shoppers in five different areas using 27 different stores. The prices of 80 items were audited twice in each store and then combined, using statistical weightings, to produce an index of price level for each store. Respondents were invited to rank up to four stores from the most to the least expensive; these rankings were then contrasted with the audit indices to produce 'perceptual validity' sources. Certain cues were important in the formation of price images, given that consumers could not really objectively compare price levels. A large shopping centre, heavy advertising or a wide assortment were signs of low prices, whereas extra services, late hours, expensive interiors and trading stamps conveyed the image of high prices. Major changes in retailing, notably the emergence of the narrow-range discounter, will probably have changed the effects of these cues, although the concept is still valid. A more limited survey of this type was later undertaken by Thompson (1975), although both studies unfortunately audited the most popular items and brands, i.e. the ones most carefully priced by the retailers.

An opportunity arose to monitor consumers' subjective assessments of prices in a Tesco store before and after their 'Operation Checkout' campaign, discussed in Section 8.4.1. A survey of shoppers was conducted a few months before the change in strategy and a follow-up study was undertaken one year later. Table 8.4 summarizes some of the results of these two surveys. Clearly, the perceived price position of Tesco in this particular case had improved very considerably, although the table showed that 28 per cent of respondents were still unconvinced, even after a campaign of the vigour of 'Operation Checkout'. Relatively objective information indicating the likely 'real' differences between the store and its adjacent rivals would suggest that the perceived saving of 9.1p/£ was fairly valid. Of considerable interest were the perceptions of special offer availability before and after. Temporary offers had been reduced in number but promoted more vigorously, the outcome of which was an improved image in this respect, since most of the early offers had not been widely noted.

Table 8.4 Shoppers' evaluations before and after 'Operation Checkout'

	Before	After
% of shoppers believing Tesco to be the cheapest store	40.9	72.0
Perceived saving by shopping at Tesco (mean pence/£)	2.2	9.1
% of shoppers believing Tesco to have the most special offers	60.0	75.1
No. of offers perceived to be available in Tesco (mean)	9.8	19.2

SUMMARY

Pricing is one of the most important decision areas of retail marketing, yet traditionally it has not received the attention merited from either researchers or retail management. Specific decisions are frequently made in isolation, and in many companies the pricing activities are dispersed between different parts of the organization. A clear and co-ordinated pricing function is required which recognized the vital role of pricing within the marketing process and the important interrelationships between the various elements. The objectives of retail pricing must be set within the overall strategic plan but equally must be clearly defined to guide the choice of appropriate strategies and tactics.

Some of the basic concepts of pricing can be of assistance to the retailer, provided that their constraints are recognized. For example, elasticity of demand to price is a useful concept in making price adjustments, but the traditional assumptions are very rigid. A more flexible approach is to consider the sensitivity of customers to price, which may include reactions against prices that are too low or too high, and some degree of indifference to prices between certain thresholds. Such considerations can provide a valuable input to pricing decisions, particularly those of narrow-range retailers whose pricing decisions are focused upon one or just a few products. In the retailing of large product assortments in many different stores, as in the case of variety stores or grocery chains, rather more pricing dimensions need to be considered. Most of the strategies and concepts considered within this chapter are presented within a framework that draws attention to the multi-dimensional character of retail pricing, focusing upon the time, assortment, geographical and comparative dimensions.

One essential property of retail pricing is that the effects are not only the immediate item sales. A longer-term process of price image formation is constantly in progress; as consumers are unable really to compare more than a handful of item prices, they naturally tend to generalize longer-term images from those few comparisons. A traditional approach in attracting customers to the stores is to offer short-term, price cuts on a few items. Several suggestions have been evolved as to how items should be selected to maximize overall sales improvement, rather than simply sell more of the offered items.

Some major retailers are trying now to take a more co-ordinated view of the task of pricing a large assortment of products. Short-term offers have partly given way to longer-term 'leader line' pricing systems, whereby key items are selected for discounting to enhance the overall image. Studies of consumers' price awareness have provided guidelines as to the products upon which such pricing tactics may be most effectively concentrated. The pricing of a large assortment involves other major decisions, such as the price differentials between different package sizes or between private and manufacturer brands. It is also necessary to consider the exact price points then to be used, and some sectors make extensive use of 'odd ending' prices and 'price lining'.

The geographical dimension of pricing is salient to all multiple chains, in that each store trades under different market conditions. Some evidence has emerged that prices tend to be higher in more outlying areas, more down-market areas, and when a few major retailers hold a large local market share. Various strategies have been evolved to differentiate prices between stores to better exploit local conditions. A form of local and temporary price differentiation is also often utilized when a new store is opened.

All retail pricing decisions, whether long- or short-term, item-specific or general to the range, local or company-wide, must be taken with regard to the resulting price positions *vis à vis* competitors. This is not in itself a simple task, as the information required is not usually readily available; techniques of price auditing are evolving, although serious errors of methods and/or interpretation are frequently encountered. Although the surveys of comparative prices are important, it must be recognized that the consumers' subjective impressions of comparative prices are the essential indicator of the outcome of retail pricing activities.

REVIEW QUESTIONS

1. What considerations should be taken into account when allocating responsibility for the tasks of retail pricing within a large retail organization?
2. Under what circumstances would a retailer's pricing strategies be primarily oriented towards
   (a) market penetration?
   (b) market stabilization?
3. Compare and contrast the concepts of price elasticity and price sensitivity. Discuss the problems involved in deriving and using measures of each.
4. What particular facets of retail pricing make the function quite different to that of pricing by a manufacturer?
5. Discuss the processes of discrimination and generalization in the formation of retail price images by consumers.
6. Under what circumstances is the use of temporary price reductions an appropriate retail pricing strategy in the context of
   (a) grocery retailing?
   (b) department store retailing?
7. Why has the 'leader line' pricing strategy been adopted increasingly in recent years? How should a retailer select the products to be price-discounted within such a strategy?
8. Define 'unit prices' and 'quantity surcharges'. What could a retailer gain by providing unit price information beyond that required by law?
9. Discuss the advantages and dangers of using
   (a) odd-ending prices;
   (b) price lining.
10. What factors tend to influence the prevailing retail price levels within different geographical areas?
11. Why would a multiple retailer consider charging different sets of prices in different stores within the chain? How could such a policy of geographical differentiation be best administered?
12. What problems may be encountered by a wide-range retailer in attempting objectively to compare store price levels with those of competitors?

REFERENCES

Aaker, D. A. and G. T. Ford (1983), 'Unit pricing ten years later: a replication', *Journal of Marketing*, **47**(1), 118–22.

Alderson, W. (1963), 'Administered prices and retail grocery advertising', *Journal of Advertising Research*, **3**(1), 2–6.

Alderson, W. and S. J. Shapiro (1964), 'Towards a theory of retail competition', in R. Cox, W. Alderson and S. J. Shapiro (eds.), *Theory in Marketing*, Richard D. Irwin, Homewood, Ill.

Alexis, M. and L. S. Simon (1967), 'The Food Marketing Commission and food prices by income groups', *Journal of Farm Economics*, **48**(2), 436–46.

Bell, J. and S. Brown (1986), 'Anatomy of a supermarket price war', *Irish Marketing Review*, **1**, 109–17.

Bowbrick, P. (1973), 'Consumers and price changes', *Super Marketing*, 6 April, 16–17.

Briggs, D. H. and R. L. Smyth (1967), *Distribution of Groceries: Economic Aspects of the Distribution of Groceries with Special Reference to Western Australia*, University of Western Australia Press, Nedlands.

Brown, F. E. (1969), 'Price image versus price reality', *Journal of Marketing Research*, **6**(2), 185–91.

Bucklin, L. P. (1972), *Competition and Evolution in the Distributive Trades*, Prentice-Hall, Englewood Cliffs, NJ.

Campbell, W. J. and M. Chisholm (1970), 'Local variations in retail grocery prices', *Urban Studies*, **7**, 76–81.

Cassady, R. (1962), *Competition and Price Making in Food Retailing*, Ronald Press, New York.

Chevalier, M. (1974), *The Impact of Display with Price Reduction on Sales Volume and Profitability of Supermarket Products*, DBA, dissertation, Harvard University.

Chevalier, M. (1975), 'Increase in sales due to in-store display', *Journal of Marketing Research*, 12(4), 426–31.

Chevalier, M. and R. C. Curhan (1976), 'Retail promotions as a function of trade promotions: a descriptive analysis', *Sloan Management Review*, 18(1), 19–32.

Consumers' Association (1978), 'Grocery prices', *Which?* October, 543–5.

Cotton, B. C. and E. M. Babb (1978), 'Consumer response to promotional deals', *Journal of Marketing*, 42(3), 109–13.

Cottrell, J. L. (1973), 'An environmental model for performance measurement in a chain of supermarkets', *Journal of Retailing*, 49(3), 51–63.

Doyle, P. and B. Z. Gidengil (1977), 'A review of in-store experiments', *Journal of Retailing*, 53(2), 47–62.

Ehrenberg, A. S. C. (1976), 'Learning about promotions', in *The Contribution of Research to Decision Making on Promotions*, ESOMAR, Amsterdam, pp. 23–9.

French, N. D. and R. A. Lynn (1971), 'Consumer income and response to price changes: a shopping simulation', *Journal of Retailing*, 47(4), 21–31, 95.

Friedman, L. (1967), 'Psychological pricing in the food industry', in A. Phillips and O. Williamson (eds.), *Prices: Issues in Theory, Practice and Public Policy*, University of Pennsylvania Press, Philadelphia.

Fry, J. N. and G. H. McDougall (1974), 'Consumer appraisal of retail price advertisements', *Journal of Marketing*, 38(3), 64–7.

Gabor, A. (1974), 'Customer oriented pricing', in D. Thorpe (ed.), *Research into Retailing and Distribution*, Saxon House, Farnborough, Hants.

Gabor, A. (1977), *Pricing, Principles and Practices*, Heinemann, London.

Gabor, A. and C. W. J. Granger (1961), 'On the price consciousness of consumers', *Applied Statistics*, 10(1), 170–88.

Gabor, A. and C. W. J. Granger (1964), 'Price sensitivity of the consumer', *Journal of Advertising Research*, 4(4), 40–4.

Gabor, A. and C. W. J. Granger (1966), 'Price as an indicator of quality: report on an enquiry', *Economica*, 33, 43–70.

Gabor, A., C. W. J. Granger and A. P. Sowter (1970), 'Real and hypothetical shop situations in market research', *Journal of Marketing Research*, 7(3), 355–9.

Gardner, D. M. (1970), 'An experimental investigation of the price/quality relationship', *Journal of Retailing*, 46(3), 25–41.

Georgoff, D. M. (1972), *Odd–Even Retail Price Endings*, MSU Business Studies, Michigan.

Goldman, A. (1977), 'Consumer knowledge of food prices as an indicator of shopping effectiveness', *Journal of Marketing*, 41(4), 67–75.

Gray, R. W. and R. Anderson (1962), 'Advertised specials and local competition among supermarkets', *Food Research Institute Studies*, 3(2), 128.

Hall, R. L. and C. J. Hitch (1939), 'Price theory and business behaviour', *Oxford Economic Papers*, 2, 12–45.

Heller, W. H. (1974), 'What shoppers know and don't know about prices', *Progressive Grocer*, 53(11), 39–41.

Holdren, B. R. (1960), *The Structure of a Retail Market and the Market Behaviour of Retail Units*, Prentice-Hall, Englewood Cliffs, NJ.

Holton, R. H. (1957), 'Price discrimination at retail: the supermarket case', *Journal of Industrial Economics*, 6(1), 13–32.

Huber, J., M. B. Holbrook and B. Kahn (1986), 'Effects of competitive context and of additional information on price sensitivity', *Journal of Marketing Research*, 23(3), 250–60.

Hutchinson-Kirby, G. and R. Dardis (1986), 'Research note: a pricing study of women's apparel in off-price and department stores', *Journal of Retailing*, 62(3), 321–30.

Jamison, J. A. (1968), 'Inter-market food cost differentials: a case study of Honolulu and the San Francisco Bay area', *Food Research Institute Studies*, 8(2), 155–89.

Lamont, L., J. Rother and C. Slater (1972), 'Unit pricing: a positive response to consumerism', *European Journal of Marketing*, 6(4), 223–33.

Lipstein, B. (1981), 'A review of retail store experiments', in R. W. Stampfl and E. C. Hirschman (eds.), *Theory in Retailing: Traditional and Nontraditional Sources*, American Marketing Association, Chicago, pp. 95–107.

Little, J. D. C. and J. F. Shapiro (1980), 'A theory of pricing nonfeatured products in supermarkets', *Journal of Business*, 53(3) (pt. 2), S199–S209.

Litvack, D. S., R. J. Calatone and P. R. Warshaw (1985), 'An examination of short-term retail grocery price effects', *Journal of Retailing*, 61(3), 9–25.

Livesey, F. (1976), *Pricing*, Macmillan, London.

Louis Harris International (1974), *Qualitative Research into Shopping Motivations*, Louis Harris International, London.

Lynn, R. A. (1967), *Price Policies and Marketing Management*, Richard D. Irwin, Homewood, Ill.

Marbeau, Y. (1987), 'What value pricing research today?' *Journal of the Market Research Society*, 29(2), 153–82.

Marion, B. W., W. F. Mueller, R. W. Colterill, F. E. Geithman and J. R. Smelzer (1979), *The Food Retailing Industry: Market Structure, Profits and Prices*, Praeger, New York.

McClelland, W. G. (1963), *Studies in Retailing*, Basil Blackwell, Oxford.

McGoldrick, P. J. (1985), 'The geographical dimension of grocery pricing', in *Proceedings of the Second World Marketing Congress*, University of Stirling, pp. 820–30.

McGoldrick, P. J. (1987), 'A multi-dimensional framework for retail pricing', *International Journal of Retailing*, **2**(2), 3–26.

McGoldrick, P. J. and H. J. Marks (1985), 'Price–size relationships and customer reactions to a limited unit pricing programme', *European Journal of Marketing*, **19**(1), 47–64.

McGoldrick, P. J. and H. J. Marks (1987), 'Shoppers' awareness of retail grocery prices', *European Journal of Marketing*, **21**(3), 63–76.

Miller, B. (1981), 'Do price cuts really work?' *Marketing*, **4**(2), 28–9.

Monroe, K. B. (1973), 'Buyers' subjective perceptions of price', *Journal of Marketing Research*, **10**(1), 70–80.

Monroe, K. B. and A. J. Della Bitta (1978), 'Models for pricing decisions', *Journal of Marketing Research*, **15**(3), 413–28.

Moyer, M. S. (1972), 'Management science in retailing', *Journal of Marketing*, **36**(1), 3–9.

Murray, I. (1977), 'Blazing the discount trail', *Campaign*, 18 November, 47.

Nason, R. W. and A. J. Della Bitta (1983), 'The incidence and consumer perceptions of quantity surcharges', *Journal of Retailing*, **59**(2), 40–54.

Nelson, D. H. (1962), 'Seven principles in image formation', *Journal of Marketing*, **26**(1), 67–71.

Nelson, P. E. and L. E. Preston (1966), *Price Merchandising in Food Retailing: a Case Study*, Institute of Business and Economic Research, University of California, Berkeley.

Nystrom, H. (1970), *Retail Pricing: an Integrated Economic and Psychological Approach*, Economic Research Unit, Stockholm School of Economics.

Office of Fair Trading (1981), *Review of the Price Marking (Bargain Offers) Orders 1979*, OFT, London.

Oxenfeldt, A. R. (1979), 'The differential method of pricing', *European Journal of Marketing*, **13**(4), 199–212.

Padberg, D. I. (1968), *Economics of Food Retailing*, Cornell University, Ithaca, NY.

Parker, A. J. (1979), 'A review and comparative analysis of retail grocery price variations', *Environment and Planning*, **11**, 1267–88.

Parsons, L. J. and W. B. Price (1972), 'Adaptive pricing by a retailer', *Journal of Marketing Research*, **4**(2), 127–33.

Pfouts, R. W. (1978), 'Profit maximisation in chain retail stores', *Journal of Industrial Economics*, **27**(1), 69–83.

Preston, L. E. (1963), *Profits, Competition and Rules of Thumb in Retail Food Pricing*, Institute of Business and Economic Research, University of California, Berkeley.

Price Commission (1975), *Food Prices in Outlying Areas*, Report no. 10, HMSO, London.

Progressive Grocer (1960), 'Dillon study: how to build more profits into your special display program', *Progressive Grocer*, **39**(1), 49–72.

Progressive Grocer (1964), 'How much do customers know about retail prices?' *Progressive Grocer*, **43**(2), 104–6.

Progressive Grocer (1971), 'How multiple-unit pricing helps—and hurts', *Progressive Grocer*, **50**(6), 52–8.

Reibstein, D. J. and H. Gatignon (1984), 'Optimal product line pricing: the influence of elasticities and cross-elasticities', *Journal of Marketing Research*, **21**(3), 259–67.

Retail & Distribution Management (1978), 'Tesco: how profitable is the pursuit of volume?' *Retail & Distribution Management*, **6**(4), 65–7.

Riesz, P. C. (1978), 'Price versus quality in the market place, 1961–1975', *Journal of Retailing*, **54**(4), 15–28.

Rinne, H. J., S. W. Bither and M. D. Henry (1986), 'The effect of price deals on retail store performance: an empirical investigation', *International Journal of Retailing*, **1**(3), 3–16.

Samli, A. C. and L. J. French (1971), 'De facto price discrimination in the food purchases of the rural poor', *Journal of Retailing*, **47**(3), 48–60.

Sampson, R. T. (1964), 'Sense and sensitivity in pricing', *Harvard Business Review*, **42**(6), 99–105.

Sexton, D. E. (1974), 'Differences in food shopping habits by area of residence, race and income', *Journal of Retailing*, **50**(1), 37–48, 91.

Shoemaker, R. W. and F. R. Shoaf (1977), 'Repeat rates of deal purchases', *Journal of Advertising Research*, **17**(2), 47–53.

Stoetzel, J. (1954), 'Le prix comme limite', in P. L. Reynaud (ed.), *La Psychologie Economique*, Librarie Marcel Riviere et Cie, Paris, pp. 184–8.

Swan, J. E. (1971), 'Patterns of competition for differential advantage in two types of retail institutions', *Journal of Retailing*, **47**(1), 25–35, 96.

Thijm, K. J. L. A. (1976), 'Promotion and the retailer', in *The Contribution of Research to Decision Making in Promotions*, ESOMAR, Amsterdam, pp. 213–20.

Thompson, W. W. (1975), *An Inquiry into the Determinants of Price Awareness of Supermarket Shoppers*, PhD dissertation, University of Arkansas.

Thorncroft, A. (1973), 'Do housewives count the cost?' *Financial Times*, 20 September, 15.

Thorpe, D. (1972), *Food Prices: a Study of Some Northern Discount and Superstores*, RORU, Manchester Business School.

Tinn, I. (1982), 'Some problems with pricing research', *Journal of the Market Research Society*, 24(4), 317–34.

Twedt, D. W. (1965), 'Does the "9 fixation" in retail pricing really promote sales?', *Journal of Marketing*, 29(4), 54–5.

Walters, R. G. and H. J. Rinne (1986), 'An empirical investigation into the impact of price promotions on retail store performance', *Journal of Retailing*, 62(3), 237–66.

Widrick, S. M. (1979), 'Quantity surcharge: a pricing practice among grocery store items—validation and extension', *Journal of Retailing*, 55(2), 47–58.

Wilkinson, J. B., J. B. Mason and C. H. Paksoy (1982), 'Assessing the impact of short-term supermarket strategy variables', *Journal of Marketing Research*, 19(1), 72–86.

Wilkinson, J. B., E. M. Smith and J. B. Mason (1973), 'Number and value of food specials in different socioeconomic areas', *Journal of Retailing*, 49(3), 34–41.

Will, R. T. (1970), 'Causation of gross margin percentage differences between intra-firm discount stores', *Journal of Retailing*, 46(1), 61–71.

Willsmer, R. (1970), 'Promotion in retailing', in G. Wills (ed.), *New Ideas in Retail Management*, Staples, London.

Wood, D. (1976), *Food Prices Near Three Superstores*, Social and Community Planning Research, London.

NINE

RETAILERS' OWN BRANDS

INTRODUCTION

A major cornerstone of retail marketing in recent years has been the development of the retailer's name as a brand, rather than simply a name over the shop. We have now arrived at a situation where the names of major retailers are better known to consumers than any but the biggest of the manufacturer brand names. An important part of this change has been the development of retailer's own-brand products, to the point that they now represent over 22 per cent of retail turnover in the UK. It is also noticeable that some of the most successful retail companies have a very strong commitment to own brands; in the case of Marks & Spencer, the commitment is 100 per cent. The value of own-brand sales in Marks & Spencer, Tesco and Sainsbury alone has been estimated at around £6,000 million per year (Euromonitor 1986).

This represents just one reason why the topic of own brands merits individual consideration, rather than simply being treated as a special issue within retail pricing and merchandising. Own brands also tend to receive a higher proportion of management attention within retail companies than their turnover alone would indicate. Not only is the retailer typically more involved in product development or specification, the own brand also tends to receive special emphasis in space allocations and retailer advertising. A body of relevant literature has therefore developed, as the subject has attracted increased attention from practitioners and researchers.

In line with Euromonitor (1984, 1986), the term 'own *brand*' is used in preference to 'own *label*', in spite of the fact that the latter term is commonly used in the UK. It is felt that 'own *label*' implies that the concept is mostly about groceries, which is quite inappropriate. Also, the term 'own *brand*' better depicts the actual, or potential, role of such product ranges in building consumer confidence and loyalty. There has in fact been a serious problem of terminology in the development of this subject. Martell (1986) referred to language that is 'vague, if not misleading' being used to describe own brands. In an early discussion of this problem, Schutte (1969) listed no less than 17 alternative terms that have been used to describe distributor-oriented brands; ironically, neither 'own label' nor 'own brand' was among them!

A frequently cited definition was published by J. Walter Thompson (Rousell and White 1970):

Products sold under a retail organisation's house brand name, which are sold exclusively through that retail organisation's outlets.

In fact, there are many different approaches to own-branding, some of which now stretch the boundaries of this definition. Euromonitor (1986) identified six main 'species' of private branding:

1. The own brand using the retailer's own name, such as BHS and Sainsbury
2. The own brand using a different name, which may become as well known as that of the retailer itself, such as St Michael products at Marks & Spencer
3. 'Super' own brands, such as the Sainsbury Supreme range
4. Generics, a plain-label variant upon the own brand concept, such as the Tesco Economy brand
5. The 'exclusive', introduced usually as a temporary promotion but not using the retailer's usual own brand name. For example, 'House of Fraser Exclusives', not using the company's usual Allander own-brand name
6. Surrogate brands—not truly a retailer brand but a manufacturer brand that is exclusive to a chain of stores; for example, Cover Plus is manufactured by MacPhersons for the Woolworth group

This chapter will first examine the development of own brands within different retail sectors and specific companies. Attention then turns to strategies of own-branding, the opportunities and threats to the retailer, approaches and problems in recruiting suppliers, and the task of positioning the range(s). The final section considers consumer responses to own brands, their purchase patterns, and their perceptions of price and quality.

9.1   DEVELOPMENTS IN OWN BRANDS

This section first presents a brief statistical summary to illustrate the growth in own-brand market share in recent years. Specific sectors in the UK are identified, and some comparisons are drawn with the experiences of other European countries. The own-brand developments of specific companies are then considered, including wholesale and symbol groups. Finally, the progress of 'generics' is considered, these having been a notable feature of grocery markets in particular since their initial launch in France in 1976.

9.1.1   The growth in market shares

In one sense, the history of own brands is as long as that of retailing itself, with tailors, shoemakers, bakers, etc., making and selling their own products. In another sense, own brands as we know them today are a relatively recent phenomenon, representing an integral component of retailers' increasing power and marketing sophistication. The late 1960s was the time when own brands started to be widely noted as a threat to manufacturers' brands, especially in packaged grocery markets. Surprisingly little attention was given to their growth in other markets; it tended to be taken for granted that many clothes were sold as own brands and that all of Marks & Spencer's sales were in own brands. This situation changed rapidly in the late 1970s, when it was acknowledged that few product markets had escaped significant inroads from retailers' own brands.

Table 9.1 represents a summary of own-brand growth across all retail product categories in the UK. Because the data are based upon sales turnover, these may understate the volume growth of own brands, with many own brands selling at lower retail prices. Progress in the 1980s has therefore been very significant, with annual growth rates since 1981 averaging 7.6 per cent. The slight loss of share between 1980 and 1981 represented the end of a short period when own brands appeared to have entered the doldrums. This is reflected in Table 9.2, which relates specifically to the packaged grocery market.

There are various explanations for the apparent stagnation of own brands in the late 1970s. Goodwin (1982) pointed to the anxiety among some multiples that consumer choice was being limited, especially by 'me too' own brands offering few innovatory features. McLaren (1977) suggested four factors that had retarded growth in the grocery sector in the 1970s:

Table 9.1 Growth in UK own-brand market shares, 1980–86 (%)

	Own-brand share	Annual real growth
1980	17.1	—
1981	17.5	− 1.2
1982	18.4	+ 4.9
1983	19.4	+ 9.6
1984	20.6	+ 8.8
1985	21.1	+ 6.0
1986	22.3	+ 8.8

Source: Euromonitor (1986).

Table 9.2 Own-brand share of packaged grocery turnover, 1977–85 (%)

	1977	1980	1983	1985
All multiples	22.9	21.9	26.9	32.0
Co-op	33.0	29.7	33.4	33.0
All major symbols	17.3	15.3	14.9	15.0
Total (packaged groceries)	—	22.5	24.9	28.0

Sources: Euromonitor (1986); Mintel (1985/86).

1. The retail/manufacturer brand price differentials had declined rapidly, in some cases halved in two years.
2. Successful discounters, such as Kwik Save and Asda, had concentrated mainly or entirely upon manufacturer brands.
3. Some retailers, such as Sainsbury, had started to use 'fighting brands' as their lowest price offering, to avoid devaluing the image of their own brand.
4. Temporary shortages in the early 1970s had adversely affected some own brand supplies.

These provide examples of the hazards in own-brand development, some of which could affect other sectors in the future. The 1980s, however, saw renewed confidence in own brands and a recognition by retailers that the most successful own brands tended to offer more than just a price reduction. The renewed vigour also reflects the growth of major multiples with a strong commitment to own brands.

A strong linkage inevitably exists between retail concentration (see Chapter 2) and the share of trade taken by retail brands. This point was demonstrated in an international comparison by Clark (1981), who illustrated high levels of retailer concentration and branding in the UK and USA, low levels of both in Italy and Belgium. European comparisons of retailer branding within grocery product classes have been presented by the A. C. Nielsen company (e.g. Nielsen 1980). Table 9.3 shows that grocery own brands have recently increased their share in most European countries, especially in Austria, the Netherlands and Germany. However, these data are based on *volume* trends and on selected product classes; they are not therefore directly comparable with those of Table 9.2.

Table 9.3 Own-brand grocery volume shares—European comparisons

Country	No. of product classes measured	1978/9 (%)	1984/5 (%)
Great Britain	12	17.5	22.1
Sweden	22	20.0	18.4
France	9	17.8	18.4
Austria	6	12.5	18.1
Netherlands	12	13.7	18.0
Belgium	14	15.5	16.6
Norway	19	n/a	10.7
Switzerland	9	10.7	10.1
Germany	15	3.8	9.7
Italy	11	4.3	5.3
Mean (excl. Norway)	12	12.9	15.3

Source: based on Nielsen data presented by Salimans (1986).

Turning now to comparisons between product sectors, Table 9.4 shows the estimated share of own-brand sales through each category of outlet. Again, these data are not directly comparable with those in Tables 9.1 and 9.2, being based upon slightly different classifications. A consistent pattern emerges, however, in that own-brand share increased in every major category between 1980 and 1985. In the clothing sector, own brands have traditionally been stronger in menswear than in womenswear, although the growth of the multiples is helping to increase their penetration in both these categories (Hollis 1986). In footwear, the high level of vertical integration, including the extensive retail interests of the British Shoe Corporation, has ensured a strong presence of own brands. Growth has been slower in the durable goods categories, where the perceived risks of purchases may be higher. Progress has however been made in DIY, with the rapid spread of multiples such as B&Q, and in some furniture categories, such as the MFI self-assembly products.

In that own-brand growth is strongly related to the growth of the multiples, the process is likely to continue, but probably at a slower rate of increase. Marketpower (1988) forecast that the pace would slacken, partly because multiples will be cautious of complaints that they are reducing consumers' real choice. In some sectors, concentration has also come close to the level at which government intervention could occur. There is however a growing tendency towards more innovatory retailer brands, which should ensure continued growth. Euromonitor (1986) estimated that the own-brand share of total retail sales would reach 27 per cent by 1990.

9.1.2 Retailers' brand developments

A summary of own-brand activity by individual retailers is provided in Table 9.5. The biggest own brand in the UK is Marks & Spencer's 'St Michael', which achieved a turnover of £3,000 million in 1985. Although sold only through the company's outlets, this represents a major brand in its own right. For example, 'St Michael' holds 15 per cent of the clothing market, with far

Table 9.4 Own-brand shares by types of retailer, 1980 and 1985

Retailer type	Own-brand share (%) 1980	1985
Food retailers	16	22
Large grocers	18	25
Other grocers	9	12
Specialists (e.g. butchers)	15	16
Drinks confectionery, tobacco	8	10
CTNs	7	9
Off-licences	10	14
Clothing, footwear, leather goods	22	24
Footwear	44	49
Menswear	38	45
Women's & infants' clothing	7	
General clothing	5	9
Leather & travel goods	6	
Household goods	9	12
Gas & electricity showrooms	10	10
Furniture & furnishings	11	13
TV & other hire/repair	12	12
Electrical & musical	8	10
Hardware & china	2	2
DIY	11	15
Other non-food retailers	11	12
Chemists (excl. prescriptions)	30	32
Booksellers, stationers	4	5
Jewellers	10	10
Toys, sports & cycles	2	3
Other (incl. photographic)	10	10
Mixed retail businesses	32	35
Large mixed	39	41
Other mixed	5	5
General mail order	18	19
Total	17	19

Source: Euromonitor (1986).

higher levels in some commodity groups, such as lingerie (34 per cent) and men's underwear (33 per cent). Marks & Spencer's food retailing is a highly selective operation, yet still commands 4 per cent of the food market, with especially high levels in meat pies (18 per cent) and poultry (15 per cent).

The own-brand percentage share at J. Sainsbury has varied somewhat over recent years, dropping from 63 per cent in 1977 to 53 per cent in 1983, then being partly restored by 1985. To

Table 9.5 Own-brand turnover of selected retailers, 1985

Retailer	£m	% of sales
Marks & Spencer	3,000	100
Sainsbury	1,800	60
Co-op	1,500	33
Tesco	1,200	40
BHS	500	91
Boots	475	32
C & A	350	75
Littlewoods	300	60
Waitrose	300	55
MFI	300	90
Argyll Foods	270	20
Dee Corporation	250	10
British Shoe Corporation	250	60
Safeway	200	24
Mothercare/Habitat	200	65
House of Fraser	150	15
John Lewis	150	27
Lewis's/Selfridge's	100	29
Spar	100	25
Burton Group	100	18
Electricity Boards	95	10
W. H. Smith	80	7
Mace	50	20
Currys	35	18
Comet	30	9
Superdrug	30	15
Dixons	30	11

Source: Euromonitor (1986).

an extent, this fluctuation reflected the opening of many larger stores by that company, bringing the need and opportunity to diversify into new products more quickly. The company also cultivated manufacturer-named 'fighting brands' in the late 1970s, largely in response to the competition from other retailers' generic ranges. In spite of the high turnover share of the Sainsbury brand, however, it comprises only about a third of the product range sold by the company (Key Note 1986). This is indicative of a concentration on the higher-volume items, plus a strong marketing effort behind the own brand; the own-brand range does however extend into some speciality areas.

The Co-op represents a major own-brand retailer across a wide spectrum of commodity groups. Traditionally, this reflected the large manufacturing and farming capacity of the Co-operative movement, although these now supply only about 13 per cent of goods sold in Co-op stores. The manufacturing and wholesaling division has increasingly been obliged to compete with outside suppliers and to become suppliers to other organizations. For example, the

Table 9.6 Own brands of cash-and-carry groups

Group	Own brand	Approx. no. of lines
Batleys	Batleys	60
	Best Buy (generics)	32
Booker	Family Choice	122
	Summergold (catering)	
	First Cigarettes	
ICCG	Stirling	320
Landmark	Landmark	170
	Own Brand (generics)	59
Linfood	My Mums	
	Hallmark	350
Makro	Aro	300
	Charles House	
Nurdin & Peacock	Peacock	450
	Happy Shopper (generics)	26
	Red Band Cigarettes	
	Jacobite Whisky	
	Best Buy (generics)	

Source: Key Note (1986).

Co-op biscuit factories have produced own-brand products for other retailers. Possibly the best known of the Co-op branded items is their '99 tea', which holds 14 per cent of the packet tea market (Euromonitor 1984).

In the chemists' sector the dominant company is Boots, with 40 per cent of the retail market. Their high level of own-brand participation too had its roots in a large manufacturing division, which is also a major supplier to the chemists' trade in general. Boots manufactures many products that do not carry the company brand name as such, for example Optrex eye care products, Virol baby foods and Strepsils throat lozenges. As the Boots stores diversify into many new fields, such as photographic goods and speciality foods, the powerful Boots brand name is increasingly utilized on products brought from outside suppliers. W. H. Smith is another company that has utilized own labels as part of a strategy of diversification from its original product base. That company too introduced special own-brand names with just a low-key mention of the W. H. Smith name, such as 'Messenger' prestige products and 'Expressions' gift stationery (Hill 1985).

It would be incorrect to assume that own brands are restricted to large stores operated by the multiples. The symbol groups, such as Spar in the grocery sector and Numark in the chemists' sector, have also been active in own-brand development. The UK's biggest group of convenience stores, Circle K, also developed an own-brand range (Hoggan 1987). There may seem little scope for own brands to be sold in completely independent outlets, although those of cash-and-carry groups may be sold. As Simmons and Meredith (1984) pointed out, the wholesaler's name probably means little to the independent store's customers, although some advantages of own brands can still be achieved through this channel. Table 9.6 shows some of the own-brand names available within cash-and-carry outlets. In the case of symbol groups, own brands offer an additional method of cohesion for stores that are typically more diverse than is ideal. For cash-and-carry wholesalers, own brands attempt also to increase the loyalty of independent retailers, as the own brands become established within their stores.

9.1.3 Retailers' generic ranges

Own brands demonstrate a very wide range of product positioning strategies, but the most extreme examples are the ranges of generics. These have also been described as 'brand-free', 'no-name' and 'unbranded' products, although some would argue that they simply represent a different form of retailer branding. Generics have in common a deliberate austerity in packaging, most being packed in plain white or with a single-colour background. The product description is normally in black, stencil-like lettering, and the pack carries little more than the required label information. Prices are normally significantly below those of comparable brands (McGoldrick 1984).

The initiation of generics is usually attributed to Carrefour, who launched their 'Produits Libres' in France in 1976 (Management Horizons 1979). This introduction was accompanied by a blaze of publicity, not all of which was favourable but most of which was effective in achieving high rates of awareness and adoption (Hawes 1982). Within a year, the concept had been taken up by retailers in the USA and by International in the UK (Sheath and McGoldrick 1981); it then spread quickly to other countries, including Belgium (Goormans 1981), Holland, West Germany, Sweden, Canada, Australia and Japan.

Generics offer retailers a chance to build market share, but the strategy is not without risks, notably:

1. Overall margins can suffer significantly unless buying terms are very favourable and unless sales of other items are also stimulated.
2. If the generic range is perceived to be of primarily down-market appeal, the retailer's image could be adversely affected.
3. An existing own-brand range could be weakened if the generic range is not appropriately positioned.

These and other factors have limited the impact achieved by generics in the UK. Table 9.7 summarizes the main ranges within the grocery sector; the generic concept has also been explored in other sectors, including certain chemists and DIY products. The most successful generic ranges in the UK, at least in turnover terms, were Fine Fare's 'Yellow Packs' and Carrefour's 'Brand Free'. Yellow Packs were strongly promoted and positioned alongside an existing own-brand range. Brand Free was introduced as Carrefour's only private brand range and positioned as a quality/high-value generic. Tesco has entered a second phase of generic development, initially launching a 'Value Lines' range in 1981, then repositioning and extending the concept under the 'Economy Lines' banner in 1986.

The price differentials between generics and manufacturer brands are usually considerable. In the USA, Nielsen (1981) found generics to be around 30 per cent cheaper than overall product category prices, around 15 per cent cheaper than own-brand prices. In a study of five generic ranges in the UK, they were found to be on average between 25–46 per cent cheaper than leading brands and 17–29 per cent cheaper than own brands, where these were also available (Nielsen 1982). It is therefore of some interest to consider just how these lower prices are achieved.

There are real few economies made in the packaging. One manufacturer complained, for example, that it cost him more to pack in generic plastic bags than in his standard cardboard boxes; packaging 'economies' are used mainly to create the generic impression. Some differences

Table 9.7 Generics in grocery multiples

Company	Name of range	No. of items	Est. share of turnover (%)
Fine Fare	Yellow Packs	250	8
Tesco	Economy Lines	30–40	1
Presto	Basics	20	1
Carrefour	Brand Free	100	4
Mace	Basic Buys	25	n.a.
Spar	Economy Brand	—	n.a.

Source: Euromonitor (1986).

in the costs of ingredients are apparent, but this is not the major saving. The ability to buy very aggressively is the main area of cost reduction. With considerable over-capacity in manufacturing, orders can be switched between suppliers and different suppliers can be used in different regions, provided that slight variability of product characteristics is acceptable. Accordingly, smaller manufacturers, who would not necessarily be able to supply a major own-brand range, can be used to supply some generic lines.

Ironically, some of the main developers of generics in the UK, including Fine Fare and Carrefour, have since been subsumed within the Dee Corporation, thereby losing their individual, own-brand identities. This is one reason why generics have achieved only a 2 per cent share of grocery sales in the UK. The prior existence of many budget-price, own-brand ranges in the UK also limited scope for growth. Elsewhere they have made more progress; estimates of their share in France are between 5 and 10 per cent, and in West Germany between 10 and 12 per cent (Key Note 1986). In the USA, Harris and Strang (1985) concluded that generics had demonstrated their long-term viability, with share estimates in the 5–10 per cent range. They have tended to evolve away from their very basic origins, towards being more like mainstream but low-priced own brands (Bauschard 1982). Another development on the generics theme has been the concept of 'pack-your-own', traditional in fresh fruit and vegetables but now extended to such items as sugar, flour and sweets (Key Note 1986).

9.2 STRATEGIES OF OWN-BRANDING

From this brief account of own-brand developments, it will be apparent that very different levels of success have been achieved by different retailers. In some cases, such as Marks & Spencer and J. Sainsbury, the own brand has been a major and integral part of the company's growth. In other cases, the own brands have never risen beyond mediocrity, typically when they are introduced as a defensive rather than a positive strategy. The route to a successful own-branding strategy is first to determine the precise objectives to be fulfilled by the introduction/extension of the range(s). Then, appropriate sources of supply must be found that can deliver the required price–quality mix. Through their launch and development, the own brand(s) must be clearly differentiated both within the store's own assortment and within the retail sector as a whole.

Table 9.8 Advantages of own brands for retailers

Store image/customer loyalty
1. Good value enhances store image.
2. Good value builds loyalty to the store and own brand.
3. Own brand may be perceived as equal to or better than manufacturers' brand.
4. It is widely assumed that own brands are made by leading manufacturers.
5. Own brands can give a distinctive corporate image.
6. Own brands carry the retailer's name into the consumer's home.
7. Retailer advertising can benefit both the stores and the own brand.
8. Better design co-ordination can be achieved between the stores and the products.

Competitive edge/extra turnover
1. Advantage over competitors with no own brand.
2. Offer benefits distinct from competitors.
3. More control of product specification and quality.
4. Allows more retailer-led product innovation.
5. More control over composition of product range.
6. Own brand products cannot be obtained elsewhere.
7. Can be sold at lower prices.
8. Offer more price variety to the consumer.
9. Inducement to use the store, leading to other purchases.

Higher profits/better margins
1. Margins tend to be 5–10 per cent better.
2. Manufacturers' promotional expenses are avoided.
3. Display space can be manipulated for better returns.
4. Sales can be promoted by placing own brands next to major brands.
5. Tighter stock control is usually possible.
6. There is more control over pricing.
7. Favourable buying terms occur where excess supply capacity exists.
8. Bargaining power increases as it becomes easier to switch suppliers.
9. They can help to break down manufacturers' hold of certain markets.

Source: adapted from Euromonitor (1986).

9.2.1 Retailers' objectives

The overall objective of own-branding must clearly be to achieve competitive advantage, although there are many forms that this may take. The potential advantages to the retailer can be broadly classified as relating to:

- Store image/customer loyalty
- Competitive edge/extra turnover
- Higher profits/better margins

Using this framework, Table 9.8 summarizes the main possible advantages to retailers of own-branding. A successful own-brand range is likely to yield benefits under each of these three headings, although it is most unlikely that all the cited advantages will apply.

The objective of building customer loyalty and store image must be a major long-term consideration. Some of the most respected and sought after own brands are also those that have been longest established, such as the Sainsbury and St Michael brands. The considerable loyalty to the Sainsbury brand was most ironically demonstrated when the company suffered own-brand supply shortages during a transport drivers' strike; it was found that many Sainsbury brand-loyal customers became most irate and refused to switch to leading manufacturer brands during that short phase. It would be incorrect, however, to assume that own-brand longevity guarantees success, as the Co-op must be all too well aware. Neither is it impossible to develop own-brand strength more quickly. Asda has recently engaged in an extensive and aggressive development programme, although the cost of the necessary marketing support has been considerable.

In the early stages of own-brand development, it was frequently claimed that they offered a means of avoiding the cost of advertising and promotion. This claim is now more difficult to sustain, in that much of that cost is now simply being borne by the retailers. However, a large retail organization can achieve considerable advertising 'efficiency', in that the company and own-brand name can be jointly promoted and the benefits spread over the whole product range. De Chernatony (1986) commented upon the shift in emphasis within much retail advertising, from a cut-price to an own-brand orientation. Mintel (1985/6) estimated that £7.5 million had been spent in 1985 on own-brand advertising; Key Note (1986) claimed that J. Sainsbury alone has spent £2.7 million in this way in 1985. Not surprisingly, the personality of own brands has developed, while the personality of some manufacturer brands has weakened (King 1985).

The objective of achieving a competitive edge through own-branding can be pursued in various ways. The most common approach has tended to be to present the own brands as a lower-price alternative. Unfortunately, this ceases to provide a competitive edge if most competitors are doing the same, and if leading brands are also being heavily discounted. Therefore more retailers have sought to follow the alternative methods of differentiation through quality, innovation and/or design. Tse (1985) describes in detail the product innovation role within Marks & Spencer; over fifty years ago, this company found that it could hardly obtain the products that it knew it could sell, often because they did not yet exist! A major product development function therefore developed within the company. J. Sainsbury also has a long history of close participation in product development, having established a food technology department in the 1920s. Senker (1986) observed rapid growth in food retailers' technological capabilities, with three firms employing 70 or more food technology staff.

Production innovation is certainly not limited to the food retailers. Body Shop, for example, has developed a strongly innovatory own-brand concept, based upon the 'healthy' and 'natural' properties of their hair and skin care preparations (Sharples 1985). In the fashion sector, Benetton and Laura Ashley have successfully developed a synergy between their store and product developments. Salmon and Cmar (1987) note the competitive edge that can be achieved through greater cohesiveness between the merchandise and the retail presentation.

Any retailer involved in own-branding is likely to see profit improvement as a major objective, although there are different routes to achieving this. In some cases an objective is to break down a monopoly/oligopoly position when strong manufacturers dominate specific markets (Simmons and Meredith 1984). At the very least, the existence of the private brand is likely to increase bargaining power, both with suppliers of the own brand and with those competing for the remaining shelf space. Stern and El-Ansary (1987) identified own-brand programmes as one means by which retailers secure greater control within the marketing channel.

Unlike the manufacturer, a retailer is able directly to control the selling environment of its brands so as to enhance their turnover and, hopefully, profitability. It is quite usual for leading brands to be displayed alongside the own-brand alternatives, to provide an attraction to the section and to emphasize own-brand advantages. Manufacturers often claim that retailers give a disproportionate amount of display space to their own brands. A study for *Marketing* magazine substantiated this claim in many cases (Bond 1984), at least in the packaged grocery sector. Some retailers can defend this in terms of the superior sales volume of their own brands, although excessive bias in space allocations can damage the retailer's image for product choice. Clearly, retailers must carefully balance the objectives to be achieved through own-branding.

9.2.2 The supply of own brands

With excess capacity in most areas of domestic manufacturing, plus strong competition from overseas manufacturers, it may be assumed that the supply of own brands presents few problems for retailers. In fact, this is not entirely true, in that there are still sectors within which manufacturers can inhibit the supply of own brands. Even within the grocery sector, problems were encountered in developing own-brand cornflakes; Kelloggs previously held a monopoly supply position, and the product was not easy to import (Clark 1981). Problems can also be encountered in obtaining reliable supplies to an acceptable standard.

As retailers became more demanding in their product specifications and the sheer volume of own brands increases, the choice of suppliers with the required capability becomes more limited. Also, the identification of suitable sources for new own-brand products can require extensive information and more time than some retailers are able to devote to the task. Loblaws, a Canadian supermarket chain, uses a subsidiary called Intersave to source and thoroughly test their own brand/generic lines, both for performance and for value (Fitzell 1982). Intermediaries, such as food brokers, are sometimes used in this capacity. In the USA, manufacturing consultants have developed to co-ordinate the specification, design and production of own-brand products, usually those supplied by smaller manufacturers. One example is Mitchell Paige, which now has a network of 30 contractors producing fashion wear (Diamond and Pintel 1985).

It could be argued that organizations with their own manufacturing capacity, such as the Co-op, Boots and the British Shoe Corporation, encounter fewer supply problems. In none of these cases, however, is the manufacturing division the sole source of supply; vertical integration may also be regarded, at least by the retail divisions, as an obstacle to aggressive buying. Britain's largest own brand retailer, Marks & Spencer, has no manufacturing capacity under its direct control. Because of its close involvement in the design and production of own brands, Marks & Spencer has been described as a 'manufacturer without factories' (Tse 1985). The company has set new standards in specification buying, which attempts to leave no aspect of the product to chance or to arbitrary decisions by suppliers. Expressed very simply, if you cannot specify what you want, it is most unlikely that you will get it. Obvious though this may seem, many other retailers still purchase own-brand products using weak or partial specifications.

Euromonitor (1984) reported that there are about 700 suppliers producing St Michael goods, including major brand manufacturers such as United Biscuits and Lotus Shoes. The major supplier of St Michael foods is Northern Foods; this company operates what is sometimes termed a 'mixed brand' policy, producing own labels and a number of well-known brands, such as Fox's Biscuits and Bowyers. A very close involvement is maintained between Northern Foods and Marks & Spencer from senior management to shop-floor levels (Retail 1988a). A survey of 100 grocery suppliers by Euromonitor (1986) showed a surprisingly high level of involvement with own brands. Only 24 did not supply own brands, and only 16 of these were convinced that they would not supply them in the future. Among those that did supply them, 76 per cent indicated that at least some of the own brands are specially formulated for the specific retailer(s). More than half reported an increase in own-brand production, only 12 per cent a decrease.

Table 9.9 Advantages and problems of supplying own brands for retailers

Advantages
1. Excess production capacity can be utilized.
2. There is a more efficient utilization of manufacturing and distribution facilities, exploiting economies of scale.
3. Own brands help absorb fixed costs.
4. Refusal to supply own brands may simply transfer more volume to competitors who will supply them.
5. Own brands may provide a base for expansion.
6. Small manufacturers can enter/stay in the market without incurring costs of branding.
7. Some warranty liabilities may transfer to the retailers.
8. Large manufacturers using a mixed-brand policy may retain more control and discriminate between product images, specifications and prices.
9. Brand leaders may benefit as own brands have tended to compete more with minor brands.
10. Retailers may refuse to stock manufacturer's brand unless it agrees to also produce own brands.
11. Own-brand supply fosters a closer relationship with the retailers.
12. The retailer has an equal interest in selling the goods.

Problems
1. Advantages may be short-lived.
2. It may be difficult to re-establish a manufacturer-brand position once promotion and advertising have been phased down.
3. Own brands may undermine sales of manufacturer's brands in the same store.
4. Retailers may restrict display and promotion of manufacturer brands to emphasize own brands.
5. Own brands can lead to excessive reliance on a few customers (at worst, just one customer).
6. Bargaining power is lost as the retailer can usually switch to alternative channels of supply.
7. Using own brands to recover overheads may simply postpone solving a problem of excessive overheads.
8. Investment in technical development and competitive advantage is given away 'free' to own brands.
9. Expensively developed expertise may in effect be handed over to rival domestic or foreign manufacturers if retailer decides to switch suppliers.
10. Margins can be 20 per cent less, and own-brand supply tends to achieve lower profitability.

Source: adapted from Euromonitor (1986).

A variety of reasons have been cited by manufacturers for becoming involved in, or staying out of, own brands. Table 9.9 summarizes the main advantages and problems of supplying own brands, from the viewpoint of the manufacturers. The arguments most frequently given in favour of supplying own brands relate to the economic factors (e.g. Morris 1979). When excess capacity exists, the production of own labels at least helps to absorb fixed costs. Greater economies of scale can also be achieved, an argument that may also be applied to distribution facilities. In this case, however, the strategy may backfire; for example, a frozen food manufacturer with a mixed-brand policy found that its expensive warehousing and transport system was increasingly difficult to sustain, as their own brands were increasingly distributed by the retailers or their agency distributors.

Other cost savings may also be achieved by the own-brand supplier. In the electrical goods sector, some of the warranty liability normally accepted by the manufacturer may be transferred to the retailer (Monopolies and Mergers Commission 1981). Unfortunately, this again may fail to yield real savings if an existing repair network is then used less intensively. Where a manufacturer does not promote brands of its own, considerable savings in advertising costs will occur. McKinsey recently analysed the costs of a large branded foods manufacturer and found that no less than 23 per cent of total costs were related, directly or indirectly, to the branding exercise (Caulkin 1987).

There could also be strategic considerations in the supply of own brands. Foremost among these may be the simple fact that a competitor will almost certainly supply them if you refuse. This not only leads to reduced economies of scale, it also further reduces control over the product market. Although retailers are becoming increasingly demanding in their product specifications, the own-brand supplier can at least retain some influence, if not control, over product images and prices. For example, in the 1970s the Wickes DIY chain was actually encouraged by ICI to develop own-brand paints. The motive was to persuade Wickes to drop the Crown range of paints, the main rival of ICI's Dulux range. In this way, the manufacturer sought to increase control over this sector of the market by supplying both the brand leader and the own brand (Ody 1987). The development of surrogate brands, sometimes using old but respected brand names phased out after mergers, is another approach to retaining some control. Although these may be supplied exclusively to one retail group, the source of supply is far more difficult to switch.

There are of course major problems involved in supplying own brands, which have motivated some manufacturers to avoid them. At the most general level, own brands are likely to receive more emphasis in store and to take sales from the manufacturer's brands. This is of course no argument for staying out of own-brand supply, if rival companies could supply them equally well. Some leading brand manufacturers consider that own-brand production would be a 'downhill slope', with short-lived gains and very little chance of reverting to becoming a strong brand if promotional expenditure is allowed to decline. There are also strong fears expressed that technical expertise, even 'trade secrets', may be transferred to another manufacturer if the retailer changes its source of supply. Probably the most fundamental problem is the weak bargaining position of the manufacturer, most particularly if one retailer takes a high proportion of output. For example, Marks & Spencer takes over 95 per cent of Gent's and 90 per cent of Dewhirst's output, although on average it takes about 30 per cent of its suppliers' output (Tse 1985). In view of these factors, it is not surprising that the supply of own labels has usually been found to be less profitable to the manufacturers (e.g. Cook and Schutte 1967).

There are many instances of both conflict and co-operation in the supply of own brands for retailers. McMaster (1987) cites examples of arbitrary threats and suppliers being played off against each other. Tesco was quoted in the early 1980s as saying that 'there is always someone willing to sell for less'. As one manufacturer expressed the situation, 'when a supplier is asked to jump, his only response these days is how high?' (Caulkin 1987). On the other hand, there are also many examples of long-term supplier–retailer relationships and successful joint development activities. For example, high-juice squash and vitamin-fortified milk are among the items first launched in the UK as Sainsbury own brands. Marks & Spencer also has a strong record of product innovation and has maintained long-term relationships with many suppliers; more than 100 have supplied the company for over thirty years (Tse 1985). As retailers seek to achieve higher quality and distinctiveness in their own-brand ranges, it is likely that a balance will increasingly be struck between hard bargaining and the need to co-operate closely with suppliers.

Table 9.10   Own-brand differentials: UK grocery products

Product category	% price difference on standard sizes			
	Waitrose	Sainsbury	Tesco	Co-op
Cooking oil	12.6	12.6	8.5	9.4
Flour	15.0	10.2	7.7	—
Baked beans	7.7	10.2	10.2	10.8
Fruit squash	5.7	—	13.5	13.5
Instant coffee	12.8	23.0	13.3	38.3
Washing-up liquid	6.3	25.4	32.2	25.6
Margarine	18.4	17.0	23.5	—
Dog food	12.9	4.8	11.8	21.9
Average	11.4	14.7	15.0	19.8

Source: Themistocli & Associates (1984).

9.2.3   Differentiating own brands

The majority of retailers have used prices as a major method of achieving competitive advantage for their own brands. As manufacturers have responded to the challenge, by paring down their own costs and margins, it has become increasingly difficult to achieve successful differentiation through price alone. Where own and manufacturer brands compete directly, however, there are still few examples of own brands being sold at the same or higher prices. It is normally assumed that the equivalent own brand will be noticeably cheaper; Dore (1976) suggested that an own brand should be at least 15 per cent cheaper.

Evidence relating to the packaged grocery market would suggest that this generalization still holds largely true. Table 9.10 contains examples of price differentials within eight product categories in four supermarket chains. Noticeably, the differentials in the up-market Waitrose chain averaged only 11.4 per cent, yet it will be recalled that own brands account for 55 per cent of that company's turnover (see Table 9.5). At the other extreme, the Co-op own brand offers nearly a 20 per cent price saving, yet accounts for only 33 per cent of Co-op turnover. Clearly, the Waitrose own brand is perceived as a strong brand in itself, which can succeed without major price differentials. It is also noticeable that differentials vary somewhat between product categories, tending to be high in the case of coffee and washing-up liquid. In these categories there is considerable scope for reducing product quality, although this can be a most dangerous strategy and is not the only method of achieving lower prices.

Internationally, there is considerable variation in the extent to which own brands offer lower prices. Salimans (1986) showed the observed price differentials within the Nielsen product classes tracked in ten different countries. These varied greatly, being around 39 per cent in West Germany, 29 per cent in the USA, 19 per cent in France and 11 per cent in Sweden. There are many factors relevant to these international differences. In Germany, for example, the own-brand share is still relatively low but increasing (Table 9.3), so the development may be regarded as still within its main growth phase; generics have also made a significant impact in that country. As own-brand developments mature and shift towards the less price-sensitive product areas, it is inevitable that average price differentials tend to fall.

A variety of positioning strategies may be employed in developing own brands. Euromonitor

(1986) defined three types of role that could be fulfilled by own brands, in terms of consumers' motivations:

1. 'Cheapest will do'—motivated by economy or lack of pressure to select anything else. Shopping in this mood clearly favours own brands, including generics.
2. 'Rational choice'—a conscious quality/value judgement strongly associated with the store itself. This could favour own brands or premium brands, depending on the shopper's feelings about the store.
3. 'Worth paying for quality'—when there is some rejection of economy or even rationality, or when the shopper is under pressure to make an impression on others. This kind of motivation favours premium brands or the own brands of up-market stores, e.g. Harrods.

It is clearly important for the retailer to identify the particular position within the relevant market(s) to be filled by the own brands. The tendency to introduce 'me too' own brand ranges, mainly because everyone else seemed to have them, did not lead to clear positioning. Even the first generic range in the UK ran into serious positioning problems. International's 'Plain and Simple' range was introduced with fairly standard quality and packaging, but at lower prices. When low profitability provoked the redevelopment of the mainstream own-brand range, this proved difficult to position alongside the generics; 'Plain and Simple' was subsequently phased out. The most successful generic range in the UK was Fine Fare's 'Yellow Pack', the packaging and pricing of which made a very clear, generic statement.

Indeterminacy in positioning is therefore unlikely to result in success, in relation to either stores or own brands. Furthermore, the positioning does not have to be mainly price-based. As Clark (1981) observed, the most successful own brands have been those with clearly differentiatied 'product pluses' compared with existing branded products. These 'pluses' may relate to several factors, including quality, convenience, innovation, assortment and price. As noted earlier, two of the most successful own-brand retailers, J. Sainsbury and Marks & Spencer, have made massive investments in the specification of quality products and the development of unusual additions to their assortments. Innovatory forms of convenience packaging have also contributed to the success of St Michael foods (Retail 1988b). Ikea and MFI have achieved considerable success with their self-assembly furniture, which can usually be collected and transported immediately by the customers. This innovation incorporated the major 'pluses' of convenience and price, relative to standard furniture. There are also many other examples of differentiation through product design, such as new safety features on Mothercare's products and the natural preparations developed by the Body Shop.

In view of the success of these approaches, it seems inevitable that retailers will take an increasingly strong role in product development and innovation. Without this, they would have to be content with competing from a primarily price-based platform, which is a difficult position from which to maintain competitive advantage in the long term. It is often pointed out that the retailer is far closer to the customer than the manufacturer, although the identification of needs and the interpretation of these into successful product concepts is unlikely to happen through proximity alone. In the future, it is likely that more retailers will adopt a role ascribed to Marks & Spencer, that of a 'manufacturer without factories'.

9.3   CONSUMER RESPONSE TO OWN BRANDS

In common with any marketing strategy, own-branding requires the close monitoring of consumers' reactions, in terms of both perceptions and actual purchase patterns. It tends to be assumed, for example, that own brands increase loyalty, which may or may not be true in relation to a particular retailer's brand. It may also be assumed that consumers perceive a particular range to represent high value, but these perceptions should be regularly checked. This section looks briefly at some of the studies undertaken to assess consumer reactions to own-brand ranges. From the earlier discussion, however, it will be recognized, that own brands come in many different forms; the results of any one specific study, therefore, should not be assumed to apply to own brands in general.

9.3.1   Own-brand purchasers

There has been considerable research interest in identifying the types of consumer who are most prone to purchase own brands. Early studies in the UK generally confirmed a slightly higher propensity to purchase own brands among up-market and young consumers (e.g. Economist Intelligence Unit 1971; Mintel 1976). This has been attributed to the higher perceived risk in buying own brands, and the greater security of these up-market consumers. This obviously cannot be generalized across all own brands; St Michael and Sainsbury brand products, for example, are regarded as extremely 'safe' purchases. Clearly, the extent of the perceived risk now depends upon the length of time that the own brand has been established, the marketing support invested by the retailer, and consumers' perceptions of the retailer's overall reputation.

Among researchers in the USA, there has been some disagreement as to the importance of socioeconomic variables. Coe (1971) and Murphy (1978) found clear evidence that lower-income shoppers were less likely to purchase own brands, whereas no distinct association was found by Myers (1967), or Frank and Boyd (1965). Some of these differences could be explained by the differences between the ranges studied and/or the shifting over time of the position of many own-brand ranges.

Some insights into purchasing patterns of own brands in the UK were provided by Mintel (1985/6). Table 9.11 summarizes the proportions among a sample of 1,005 adults who purchased own brands within four product categories. The overall proportions reflect to an extent the different levels of own-brand availability within the four categories, in particular the small minority purchasing own-brand electrical goods. Even in the food sector, some 28 per cent of the 'housewives' interviewed claimed that they had not purchased own brands. In part, this will reflect low or non-availability in some stores, but it also signals the need for caution among retailers contemplating phasing out more of the leading grocery brands.

Only tentative conclusions can be drawn from the breakdowns in the table of social class and age, as these do not control for differences in availability or overall category purchasing habits (e.g. the greater expenditure on alcoholic drinks for home consumption by the higher social groups). The analyses seem to point to an up-market bias in own-brand purchasing. Inevitably, there is a problem in identifying the direction of causation. Many of the up-market shoppers patronize Sainsbury and Waitrose, therefore are offered extensive opportunities to buy own labels. Loyal Kwik Save shoppers, many of whom are more down-market, are offered no own labels in these stores. Therefore care must be taken in the interpretation of such analyses. They do however at least confirm a more widespread familiarity with, and acceptance of, own brands among the more affluent respondents. The results of the age breakdown are more difficult to interpret, although they would seem to suggest a low propensity to purchase own brands among the oldest group.

It is also important to try to measure the degree of loyalty to the own-brand range. If this is low, then the range may be doing little more than encouraging consumers to shop around for the best prices of the day. On the basis of detailed records of past purchases, Rao (1969) found that repurchase rates varied considerably between different retailers' own brands. It was also found

Table 9.11   Consumers of selected own-brand products (%)

N = 1,005 adults	Food	Clothes	Proportion purchasing own brand versions of: Alcoholic drinks	Electrical goods
All	62	49	27	8
Housewives	72	54	27	6
Class:				
AB	69	64	39	6
C1	71	55	33	11
C2	60	48	22	8
D	53	39	25	7
E	56	41	18	5
Age:				
15–24	55	48	26	8
25–34	69	48	37	7
35–44	72	52	30	14
45–54	62	51	32	9
55–64	62	53	27	4
65 +	55	47	12	6

Source: Mintel (1985/6).

that many of the consumers who preferred own brands tended to transfer that preference, even when they switched to another store. Uncles and Ellis (1987) also examined levels of loyalty, in the purchasing of coffee at Safeway in the USA. In this case, the own brand had gained a higher level of loyalty than the other two main brands, with some 48 per cent of all the coffee buyers at Safeway purchasing only the own brand.

The purchasers of generic products have also been the subject of several studies. For example, Murphy and Laczniak (1979) found that 73 per cent of Jewel shoppers had tried generics within six months of their introduction. They found no significant differences between the ages, occupations or incomes of the buyers and non-buyers, although the more highly educated were significantly more likely to be buyers. These were assumed to have 'more confidence in their evaluative abilities', and therefore to be less likely to rely upon 'the brand name as an indicator of product performance'. The concept of own brands appealing to the more discerning consumers have been effectively harnessed by a number of retailers. Tesco, for example, pursued a strong programme of nutritional labelling in product categories where this had not usually been provided.

One of the most extensive academic studies of generic purchasers was published by McEnally and Hawes (1984), based upon panel data covering 18 months and 1,442 households. Using discriminant analysis, they eveluted the ability of several demographic and psychographic variables to differentiate between generic users and non-users. Generally, the users were concentrated in the middle-income, larger households; they also tended to be less brand-loyal and prone to select cheaper alternatives. Price-based own brands, such as generics, clearly do have the ability to capture share by encouraging brand-switching. There must however be some doubt as to whether they have the power to retain consumer loyalty if the price advantage is significantly reduced.

Given the proliferation of studies on the characteristics of generics users, Szymanski and Busch (1987) were able to apply the technique of meta-analysis. Meta-analysis uses statistical measures to summarize findings across a number of studies; in this case, 24 could be used. They observed that it will become increasingly difficult to find meaningful differences between generics users and non-users as the purchase of generics becomes more diffused throughout the population. They concluded that 'marketing scholars have overemphasized the analysis of consumer descriptors while neglecting the study of the determinants of quality perceptions and their role in the consumer decision-making process for generics'.

9.3.2   Perceptions of price and quality

Objective quality data, such as Consumers' Association test reports, are available on a limited scale but are not utilized by the majority of consumers. Perceptions of quality are therefore a key determinant of the positioning achieved by an own-brand range. Over a period of many years, the 'St Michael' own brand has achieved an enviable reputation for quality and value. From its survey of over 1,000 adults in the UK, Mintel (1985/6) found that the largest single proportion, 57 per cent, named Marks & Spencer as a shop with particularly good-value own-brand products. This type of reputation cannot however be achieved overnight; the process of establishing a new own-brand range inevitably takes time and/or a good deal of marketing support.

In the vigorous early growth period for many own brands in the 1970s, there was some concern about quality perceptions. The available evidence, however, suggested that the standing of own brands started to converge with that of manufacturers' brands. For example, Mintel (1973) reported that 35 per cent of respondents considered own brands to be the same as well-known brands, whereas this figure had risen to 50 per cent by the time of the Mintel (1976) study. This result was broadly confirmed by a survey conducted in 1974, in which 48 per cent considered the quality to be the same (Livesey and Lennon 1978).

There is inevitably a dilemma facing a retailer launching an own brand based primarily upon a low-price proposition. As noted in the previous chapter, consumers have a propensity to impute quality on the basis of price, particularly when there are not other strong quality cues available (see for example Riesz 1978). One such cue, of course, is the reputation of the retailer itself. It is significant that Asda postponed the main development of its own brands until the mid-1980s. In the early 1970s, the company was still trading largely from converted old mills and was unknown in most parts of the country. After years of new store development, geographical expansion and heavy media advertising, Asda achieved a solid, national reputation. The time was therefore more appropriate to start expanding the own-brand range.

Generics represent an interesting attempt to overcome the problem that low price will tend to signal low quality. The essence of the generic concept is the communication to the consumer of a simple no-frills approach; the message implied is that they offer an escape route from the perceived 'marketing surcharge' commonly associated with leading brands. Early studies in the USA suggested that the approach was at least in part successful. Zybthiewski and Heller (1979) reported that most generics buyers attributed the lower prices to savings in advertising or packaging. Only 15 per cent of the buyers felt that lower quality was the reason, although this view was held by 38 per cent of the non-buyers.

A useful framework for examining the interplay between perceptions and purchases is that of perceived risk. This may be defined as the expected negative utility associated with the purchase

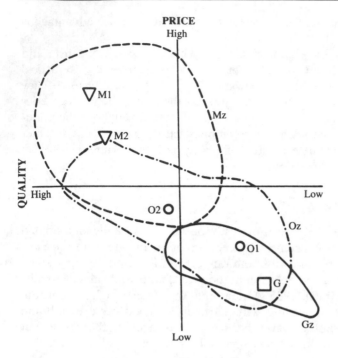

Figure 9.1 Perceived positioning of own labels
Source: McGoldrick (1984).

of a particular product or brand. Dunn *et al.* (1986) looked at the types of perceived risk associated with buying national brands, own brands and generic brands. Not surprisingly, the greatest *performance* risk tended to be associated with generics, the greatest *financial* risk with national brands. In this particular study, *social* risk was not found to be a major issue, although this could be because the products studied were all fairly basic.

It is felt that social risk should not be eliminated as an issue in own-brand purchasing behaviour. In the study of generics buyers in the UK, Sheath and McGoldrick (1981) found instances of leading brands being bought to offer to friends, whereas generics were bought for own use. There was also some resistance to the purchase of own-brand wines for gifts or for serving to others, even wines that carried some of the most reputable retailer names. A combination of social and performance risk could also slow the growth of own brands in some of the high-cost, high-prestige consumer durables sectors. However, the extent of perceived risk will vary enormously between retailers and is also likely to change over time.

The relative positioning of most grocery own-brand ranges shifted considerably through the 1970s and 1980s. Retailers' names, and their own brands, gained much of the marketing support formerly given to manufacturer brands; by the same process, however, they lost much of the 'brand-free' appeal of their early phase. To a large extent, retailers' conventional own brands therefore vacated the position now adopted by generic ranges in the UK and elsewhere.

Figure 9.1 attempts to depict this process, using a perceptual map with axes based upon price and quality perceptions. On this largely hypothetical chart, M1 and O1 represent the average perceived positions of manufacturer brands and own brands, respectively, in the early 1970s. M2 and O2 represent the perceived positions currently, and G shows the position typically held by generics. The gap between manufacturer and own brands has certainly diminished; both have shifted their position. Manufacturers have engaged in frequent promotions, discounting and cost reduction programmes; own brands, on the other hand, have tended to trade up from their initial position.

There is of course a great deal of variation between the positions of different brands and products. On the perceptual map, Mz, Oz and Gz indicate the 'zones' typically occupied by the three brand types. Some manufacturer 'fighting brands' have taken their place in the low perceived quality/price sector, whereas the strongest own brands are well established in the high perceived quality, reasonable (but not low) price area. Empirical work by De Chernatony (1985) illustrated some of the contrasts in the perceived quality positions of own brands, with Sainsbury tea being close to the branded segment and International and Fine Fare teas close to the generic sector. De Chernatony (1988) subsequently confirmed that some retailers' own brands and generics were not sufficiently differentiated in consumers' perceptions; under these circumstances sales of generics are more likely to detract from sales of the more profitable own brands.

Depicting own brands in terms of price and quality perceptions illustrates that there is a limited amount of space within which successfully to position an own-brand range. Considerable buying power and operating efficiency is required to achieve the reasonable price/good quality position of Marks & Spencer and J. Sainsbury. Some of the lower perceived quality positions, while possibly commanding a viable share of turnover, may be in conflict with the retailer's overall need to develop a quality image. As discussed in the previous section, it is therefore increasingly necessary to look at dimensions other than just price and quality to achieve successful own-brand differentiation.

SUMMARY

Many alternative terms are used to describe own brands, including 'private labels', 'own labels', 'house brands' and 'retailer brands'. These are all descriptions of product ranges that are sold only within the stores of a particular retail organization. The range may carry the name of the retailer or a brand name specific to that retailer. There are also variants upon the own-brand concept, including generics, retailer 'exclusives' and surrogate brands.

The market share held by own brands grew steadily from the late 1960s but faltered in the late 1970s, following heavy price discounting of manufacturer brands. The 1980s have seen renewed growth, from 17.1 per cent of retail sales in 1980 to 22.3 per cent in 1986, with 27 per cent forecast by 1990. Own-branding is particularly strong in footwear, menswear, chemists, grocery and large 'mixed' retail businesses. The proportion of own-branding in the UK is higher than in other European countries, reflecting the particular strength of the UK multiples, although most countries have seen increases in recent years.

Many own-brand ranges rank alongside major manufacturer brands in scale; those of Marks & Spencer, Sainsbury, the Co-op and Tesco now each have a turnover in excess of £1,000 million per annum. Own brands have grown with the major multiples, although not all multiples have been committed to their development. Neither are own brands to be found solely in the multiples and co-operatives. In the symbol sector own brands have been developed partly to maintain group cohesion, and in the cash-and-carry sector they have helped to increase the loyalty of independent retailers.

Generic ranges, otherwise known as 'brand-free' and 'no-names', have been introduced by some retailers, especially in the grocery sector. These products use very basic labelling and sell at prices well below those of leading brands. Their growth has been limited in the UK, partly because of difficulties in positioning them alongside existing own brands. Generics have achieved rather more impact elsewhere, including France, Germany and the United States.

Some own brands have been introduced as defensive, 'me-too' ranges; others have demonstrated more positive approaches to gaining competitive advantage. This may be achieved through enhancement or reinforcement of the store image, hopefully leading to increased store loyalty. The ability to innovate and better control the product range can also help to create a competitive edge, while at the same time improving turnover. On the cost side, the stronger bargaining position with suppliers can lead to both better shelf prices and considerably enhanced margins.

With excess capacity in most areas of manufacturing, it is usually not difficult to find one or more potential suppliers of own brands. Many retailers have exploited this opportunity to the full in order to gain maximum price advantage. As retailers increasingly recognize the need to innovate and maintain high quality in own brands, more care has to be given to establishing appropriate and reliable channels of supply. Buying specifications have tended to become more exacting, and some retailers have established long-term working relationships with their best suppliers.

Where own brands are directly comparable with manufacturer brands, they tend on average to be 10–20 per cent cheaper. It has become obvious, however, that a range with little more than just a price advantage is unlikely to retain that for very long. The renewed vigour of own brands owes much to a phase of more effective product differentiation, rather than simply imitation. Some of the most successful own-brand ranges are those that offer innovatory items or features not currently available elsewhere.

Considerable research attention has focused upon trying to identify the types of shopper most prone to buy own brands. There is tentative evidence that older and more down-market shoppers are the least likely to buy them, but this may largely reflect different levels of availability. The degree of consumer loyalty achieved by the own brand is an important measure of its success; again, the most effectively differentiated own brands inevitably achieve the highest loyalty.

In the early development phase of most grocery own-brand ranges, there is evidence that they were often perceived as low-price, low-quality alternatives. As own brands became better developed and more vigorously advertised, the perceived quality distinctions between them and the manufacturers' brands became more blurred. In some cases, there is now less perceived risk in buying the retailer's brand. As own-brand development increases in other product areas, there will however be a need to identify and overcome the potential sources of perceived risk.

REVIEW QUESTIONS

1. What factors have influenced the pattern of growth in own-brand market share? Do you expect this growth to continue?
2. Explain why own brands have achieved far more impact in some product sectors than in others.
3. To what extent has vertical integration influenced the development of own brands within certain retail organizations?
4. How would you define the role of own brands in
    (a) a symbol group?
    (b) a cash-and-carry group?
5. From the viewpoint of a major grocery retailer, how would you appraise the opportunities and the threats of introducing a range of generics?
6. What would be the principal objectives in developing an own-brand range for
    (a) an established chain of department stores?
    (b) an expanding chain of DIY superstores?

7. Identify the ways in which a grocery retailer may reduce costs and improve margins through own-brand development.

8. What factors could motivate a manufacturer of branded goods to also supply own brands? What risks are involved in this strategy?

9. Discuss the role of specification buying within retailers' own-brand programmes.

10. 'The most successful own brands have been those with clearly differentiated "product pluses" compared with existing branded products.' Discuss.

11. Why do some own-brand positioning strategies fail to achieve high consumer loyalty to the range?

12. What types of perceived risk should be taken into account in developing own brand ranges of
    (a) women's blouses?
    (b) washing machines?
    How would you overcome the problem of perceived risks in each case?

REFERENCES

Bauschard, S. F. (1982), 'The generic metamorphosis: now they're third-tier brands with names, colorful labels', *Marketing News*, 15(22), 1, 7.

Bond, C. (1984), 'Own-labels vs the brands', *Marketing*, 6(10), 24–7.

Caulkin, S. (1987), 'The fall & rise of brands', *Management Today*, July, 45–9, 104.

Clark, I. M. (1981), *Retailer Branding: Profit Improvement Opportunities*, Management Horizons, Richmond.

Coe, B. D. (1971), 'Private versus national preference among lower- and middle-income shoppers', *Journal of Retailing*, 47(3), 61–72.

Cook, V. J. and T. J. Schutte (1976), *Brand Policy Determination*, Allyn and Bacon, Boston.

De Chernatony, L. (1985), 'How consumers see the packaged grocery markets', *Retail & Distribution Management*, 13(4), 45–7.

De Chernatony, L. (1986), 'The impact of the changed balance of power from manufacturer to retailer in the UK packaged groceries market', *Fourth International Conference on Distribution*, CESCOM, Milan.

De Chernatony, L. (1988), 'Own labels: an adjunct to brands?' *Retail & Distribution Management*, 6(4), 18–20.

Diamond, J. and G. Pintel (1985), *Retail Buying*, Prentice-Hall, Englewood Cliffs, NJ.

Dore, B. (1976), 'Own labels—are they still worth the trouble to grocers?' *Advertising and Marketing*, 13(2), 58–63.

Dunn, M. G., P. E. Murphy and G. U. Skelly (1986), 'The influence of perceived risk on brand preference for supermarket products', *Journal of Retailing*, 62(2), 204–16.

Economist Intelligence Unit (1971), 'The development of own brands in the grocery market', *Retail Business*, no. 166, 27–34.

Euromonitor (1984), *The Own Brands Report*, Euromonitor, London.

Euromonitor (1986), *The Own Brands Report*, Euromonitor, London.

Fitzell, P. B. (1982), *Private Labels: Store Brands & Generic Products*, AVI, Westport, Conn.

Frank, R. E. and H. W. Boyd (1965), 'Are private-brand-prone grocery customers really different?' *Journal of Advertising Research*, 5(4), 27–35.

Goodwin (1982), 'Private label's erratic ascent', *Marketing*, 10(11), 25–32.

Goormans, M. (1981), 'Generic products in Belgium: introduction and conditions', *European Journal of Marketing*, 15(1), 78–87.

Harris, B. F. and R. A. Strang (1985), 'Marketing strategies in the age of generics', *Journal of Marketing*, 49(4), 70–81.

Hawes, J. M. (1982), *Retailing Strategies for Generic Grocery Products*, UMI, Ann Arbor, Mich.

Hill, M. (1985), 'W. H. Smith: endorsing quality in own label', *Marketing Week*, 8(35), 47–8.

Hoggan, K. (1987), 'Label laws', *Convenience Store*, 21 August, 35–8.

Holliss, R. (1986), 'The changing marketplace in fashion', *Retail & Distribution Management*, 14(1), 9–12.

Key Note (1986), *Own Brands*, Key Note Publications, London.

King, S. (1985), 'Another turning point for brands?' *ADMAP*, 21, 480–4, 519.

Livesey, F. and P. Lennon (1978), 'Factors affecting consumers' choice between manufacturer brands and retailer own labels', *European Journal of Marketing*, 12(2), 158–70.

Management Horizons (1979), *Generic Merchandising in Europe and the Impact on North America*, Management Horizons, Richmond.

Marketpower (1988), *Own Label Statistical Review 1986–1990*, Marketpower, London.

Martell, D. (1986), 'Own labels: problem child or infant prodigy', *Quarterly Review of Marketing*, 11(4), 7–12.

McEnally, M. R. and J. M. Hawes (1984), 'The market for generic brand grocery products: a review and extension', *Journal of Marketing*, 48(1), 75–83.

McGoldrick, P. J. (1984), 'Grocery generics—an extension of the private label concept', *European Journal of Marketing*, 18(1), 5–24.

McLaren, D. (1977), 'Where does own-label go from here?', *Campaign*, 18 November, 45.

McMaster, D. (1987), 'Own brands and the cookware market', *European Journal of Marketing*, 21(1), 83–94.

Mintel (1973), 'Own labels', *Market Intelligence Reports*, 1(12), 4–15.

Mintel (1976), 'Own labels', *Market Intelligence Reports*, 4(10), 44–53.

Mintel (1985/6), 'Own brands', *Mintel Retail Intelligence*, Winter, 109–43.

Monopolies and Mergers Commission (1981), *Discounts to Retailers*, HMSO, London.

Morris, D. (1979), 'The strategy of own brands', *European Journal of Marketing*, 13(2), 59–78.

Murphy, P. E. (1978), 'The effect of social class on brand and price consciousness for supermarket products', *Journal of Retailing*, 54(2), 33–42, 89, 90.

Murphy, P. E. and G. R. Laczniak (1979), 'Generic supermarket items: a product and consumer analysis', *Journal of Retailing*, 55(2), 3–14.

Myers, J. G. (1967), 'Determinants of private brand attitude', *Journal of Marketing Research*, 4(1), 73–81.

Nielsen (1980), *Nielsen Study of Private Labels in the Grocery Retail Trade of Europe*, A. C. Nielsen, Oxford.

Nielsen (1981), *Generics in Supermarkets: Myth or Magic?* A. C. Nielsen, Northbrook, Ill.

Nielsen (1982), 'Generics, a first look', *Nielsen Researcher*, 1, 3–7.

Nielsen, A. C. (1984), 'The development of industry brands and distributor brands in Europe and the United States', *Marketing Trends*, 2, 1–4.

Ody, P. (1987), 'The growth in private brands', *Retail & Distribution Management*, 15(3), 9–11.

Rao, T. R. (1969), 'Are some consumers more prone to purchase private brands?' *Journal of Marketing Research*, 6(4), 447–50.

Retail (1988a), 'Own label development', *Retail*, 6(2), 41–2.

Retail (1988b), 'Package designing', *Retail*, 6(2), 15.

Riesz, P. C. (1978), 'Price versus quality in the marketplace 1961–75', *Journal of Retailing*, 54(4), 15–28.

Rousell, D. and R. White (1970), *Private Label Reviewed*, J. Walter Thompson, London.

Salimans, R. W. J. (1986), 'Brands and own brands in Europe' in *Strategies for Retailer Growth*, ESOMAR, Amsterdam, 125–51. *Note:* ESOMAR seminar papers available from the ESOMAR Secretariat, J. J. Viottastraat 29, 1071 JP AMSTERDAM, The Netherlands.

Salmon, W. J. and K. A. Cmar (1987), 'Private labels are back in fashion', *Harvard Business Review*, 87(3), 99–106.

Schutte, J. F. (1969), 'The semantics of branding', *Journal of Marketing*, 33(2), 5–11.

Senker, J. M. (1986), 'Technological co-operation between manufacturers and retailers to meet market demand', *Food Marketing*, 2(3), 88–100.

Sharples, S. (1985), 'Differentiation by product design', *Retail & Distribution Management*, 13(3), 28–31.

Sheath, K. J. and P. J. McGoldrick (1981), *Generics: their Development in Grocery Retailing and the Reactions of Consumers*, UMIST, Manchester.

Simmons, M. and B. Meredith (1984), 'Own label profile and purpose', *Journal of the Market Research Society*, 26(1), 3–27.

Stern, L. W. and A. I. El-Ansary (1987), *Marketing Channels*, Prentice-Hall, Englewood Cliffs, NJ.

Szymanski, D. M. and P. S. Busch (1987), 'Identifying the generics-prone consumer: a meta-analysis', *Journal of Marketing Research*, 24(4), 425–31.

Themistocli & Associates (1984), *The Secret of the Own-Brand*, Institute of Marketing, London.

Tse, K. K. (1985), *Marks & Spencer: Anatomy of Britain's Most Efficiently Managed Company*, Pergamon, Oxford.

Uncles, M. D. and K. Ellis (1987), 'Own labels: beliefs and reality', *Fourth International Conference on Distribution*, CESCOM, Milan.

Zbythiewski, J. A. and W. H. Heller (1979), 'Generics—who buys? Rich shopper, poor shopper, they're all trying generics', *Progressive Grocer*, March, 92–106.

ADVERTISING AND PROMOTION

INTRODUCTION

Advertising has become a major area of marketing expenditure and a key element of the marketing mix for most large-scale retailers. Several companies now spend over £10 million annually on media advertising, in addition to their expenditures on other forms of promotional activity. Advertising is usually defined as non-personal or one-way forms of communication conducted through paid media under clear sponsorship (e.g. Kotler 1988). In most retail marketing contexts, the store itself also provides many forms of non-personal communications, such as displays, design and the overall ambiance; these store-based influences are the subject of the next chapter. The main focus of this chapter is on the out-of-store communication channels. Although the main emphasis is on media advertising decisions, consideration is also given to sponsorship and other forms of public relations activity.

It would appear obvious that retail advertising must be an integral component of overall marketing strategy. There have however been many instances of advertising being pursued almost independently of, or as a substitute for, an adequate retail strategy; under such circumstances, any benefits gained through the expenditure on advertising are likely to be very short-lived. There is little point in making specific claims or attempting to build images that are not reinforced by the product–service mix of the stores themselves. It is important therefore that the communication objectives be clearly defined, whether these be strategic or short-term tactical; for example:

1. *To develop new customers*   The emphasis may be upon customers entering the geographical area or the relevant age category for the first time; in most cases, however, new customers must be won from competitors by communicating the differential advantages of the store. When a new store is opened, an intensive local campaign is usually launched to create an awareness among target groups. In forms of non-store retailing, the advertising objective may be to attract initial enquiries from potential new customers.
2. *To increase expenditure by existing customers*   By increasing awareness of new departments or products, the variety and volume of sales to existing customers may increase. Some campaigns have as a primary objective the promotion of store credit card usage, to increase loyalty and provide better communications with customers. With more customer-specific information, subsequent campaigns can be targeted at specific market segments or may seek to increase the visit frequency of irregular shoppers.
3. *To increase store traffic*   Special sales are frequently promoted to increase traffic during the dull periods. Alternatively, the promotion may seek to capture the maximum share of

peak-season traffic by emphasizing particular advantages. In that many stores operate within shopping centres, such traffic-building promotions are sometimes conducted in co-operation with other retailers or shopping centre management.

4. *To increase product sales* The emphasis may be upon specific products, to clear particular lines of merchandise or to utilize opportunities for co-operative advertising with manufacturers. A campaign may seek to establish association with well-known branded products or be used to announce the arrival of new lines. Alternatively, the focus may be upon promoting the quality, value and/or uniqueness of the retailer's own-brand products.

5. *To develop the store image* All advertising is likely to influence image, but some campaigns are primarily image-oriented. These usually seek to build the longer-term reputation and increase consumer confidence in the retailer's product and service expertise. Advertising may be used to increase awareness of the retailer's positive attributes and to communicate store policies; a secondary objective may also be to build the loyalty and confidence of staff. A campaign may be linked to specific public relations efforts to create goodwill for the retailer.

Retail advertising may therefore have many different primary and secondary goals, which require the use of different creative and media treatments. Some retailers, including J. Sainsbury, have used more than one agency to deal with their different advertising requirements. Sometimes different promotional objectives are pursued in different areas, according to local competitive and market conditions. While some of the objectives summarized above are quite compatible, others clearly are not. In defining the communication objectives, the retail advertiser must therefore ensure that local or short-term expedients are not in conflict with overall image requirements.

10.1 TRENDS IN RETAIL ADVERTISING

This section looks at four main elements of retail advertising trends. First, the growth in expenditure on media advertising and the major differences that exist between companies are summarized. Second, the importance of co-operative advertising is considered, i.e. advertising that is financed at least partially by the manufacturers. Third, the major shift in advertising content and style is reviewed, from an emphasis on individual products and prices to a greater proportion of theme or store-image-oriented advertising. Finally, the growth of sponsorship and other forms of publicity is discussed.

10.1.1 Advertising expenditure

Summaries of retail advertising expenditures say little about the effectiveness of this advertising, but they do indicate the strong commitment to media advertising of many major retailers. The most rapid growth in retail advertising, in real terms, occurred in the early 1970s. Between 1972 and 1977 there was an almost three-fold real growth in retail advertising, having allowed for a high rate of media cost inflation (Challiner 1982). Since that time there has been some levelling off in real growth, but retailers have continued to be among the major spenders. In 1987 retailers were listed as seven of the top ten spending 'brands' (Marketing 1988).

Table 10.1 shows the levels of expenditure, broken down by retail sector. Based upon MEAL (Media Expenditure Analysis Limited) and Advertising Association data, Mintel (1988) estimated an overall level of retail advertising expenditure of £440.6 million. This represents an increase of almost 50 per cent over a five-year period, although very little of this represents real growth; over that same period, media costs inflated by approximately 48 per cent. Many sectors therefore decreased their levels of advertising expenditure in real terms. For example, the grocery

Table 10.1   Advertising expenditures by retail sector, 1982–1987

Sector	1982 (£m)	1987 (£m)	Index (1982 = 100)
Chain grocery and co-ops	63.8	65.6	102.7
Department and retail stores	157.7	284.1	180.2
Direct response catalogues	5.7	12.7	221.5
Direct response mail order	43.5	53.3	122.6
Other mail order	11.5	11.8	102.6
Other retail	11.8	13.1	111.6
Total	294.0	440.6	149.9

Source: Mintel (1988).

chains and co-operatives overall held their expenditure at a fairly constant level, representing a decrease in real terms of around 30 per cent. Some of this decrease has been attributed to merger activity in this sector (see Chapter 4), notably that of Argyll and the Dee Corporation, which has reduced the number of separate retail accounts. However, there has also been some reaction against the escalation of media costs. Some retailers have reduced the emphasis upon media advertising within their marketing mix, and expenditure has also been diverted to other forms of advertising and promotion. It will be apparent from Table 10.1, however, that many companies within the large and diverse 'department and retail stores' category have continued to increase their levels of media advertising in real terms.

A more detailed breakdown of the top 16 retail advertisers, in terms of their media expenditures, is provided by Table 10.2. In 1987 there were eight retailers with media expenditures in excess of £10 million. It is noticeable that ranks 4–6 are held by Woolworths, B & Q and Comet, spending a total of £37.8 million. There are many good reasons why these three sections of Kingfisher continue to trade under their own names, but the group as a whole obviously incurs a heavy media cost in so doing. Similarly, Dixons and Currys, though parts of the same group, spend £29.2 million in promoting their individual identities. MFI has maintained the position of top retail advertising spender since 1983 and peaked at £21.4 million in 1986. This represents an unusually high 6.4 per cent of sales, exceeded only by former trading partner Allied Carpets at 9.3 per cent. These represent exceptional advertising-to-sales ratios for the mainstream retailing industry, indicative of a very strong emphasis on media advertising within the marketing mix of these companies.

In the majority of cases, advertising accounts for around 2 per cent or less of sales. In the grocery sector, where more slender gross margins are the norm, the proportions tend to be far smaller, Asda being a high spender at 0.5 per cent of sales. Asda has felt the need to increase media spending in order to support continued geographical expansion, the development of its own brands and a general upgrading of the company image. Tesco on the other hand has reduced media spending considerably, from being the top spender in 1982. Taking into account media inflation, Tesco's media advertising decreased in real terms by around 54 per cent over the five-year period. This partly reflects a far lower proportion of expenditure on television—2 per cent in 1987 compared with 55 per cent in 1982; there has also been a strategic decision to divert more funds to store developments and other improvements in customer services.

Table 10.2   Major retail advertisers, 1982–1987

Retailer	Advertising expenditure 1982 (£m)	1987 (£m)	Index (1982 = 100)	Advertising as % of sales 1986
MFI	10.0	19.8	198	6.41
Dixons	4.0	14.9	372	2.31
Currys	6.0	14.3	357	2.01
Woolworths	8.5	13.1	154	0.43
B & Q	1.3	12.4	954	2.16
Comet	6.4	12.3	192	2.14
Asda	7.0	12.1	173	0.51
W. H. Smith	5.2	10.5	202	0.66
Rumbelows	4.3	9.7	226	2.29
Texas Homecare	4.1	9.4	229	5.00
Boots	9.7	8.2	85	0.50
Tesco	11.8	8.1	68	0.29
Allied Carpets	6.1	7.9	130	9.29
Queensway	4.3	6.1	142	1.39
Sainsbury	3.6	5.5	153	0.20
Co-op (local)	5.0	5.2	140	n.a.

Source: Mintel (1988).

10.1.2   Co-operative advertising

Co-operative advertising occurs when two or more organizations sponsor an advertisement to promote their goods/services jointly. It is necessary to distinguish between horizontal and vertical co-operative advertising. In the former case, two or more retailers may get together to promote their advantages in common or to build traffic in their shopping centre (e.g. Kleimenhagen *et al*. 1972). Vertical co-operative advertising, on the other hand, signifies agreements between suppliers and retailers to promote the product(s) and the stores jointly. Horizontal and vertical arrangements sometimes operate together, for example when a specific product or range is advertised and a number of retailers are listed or mentioned within the advertisement.

Vertical co-operative advertising can result in many different formats. Where the manufacturer is the dominant partner and the retailer or dealer is a small independent, the format may essentially be a product advertisement with the retailer's name inserted within the copy or at the end of the sound track. Where the retailer holds the balance of power and is in control of the advertising programme, the manufacturer's product may simply be one of many that are listed, pictured or mentioned within the advertisement. In that neither of these extremes provides a 'fair' balance of exposure, formats have been developed which give more equal emphasis to both parties. For example, some Kwik Save television commercials feature a specific well-known product for the first half, then switch to promoting the attributes of the store. Given the bargaining power of Kwik Save, however, one can be sure that the manufacturer and retailer contributions to the cost would be far from equal!

In the UK, advertising allowances have tended to become just another element within the negotiations between major retail buyers and their suppliers. Manufacturers often complain that such allowances are simply treated as a further price reduction or contribution to the retailer's gross margin. One industry commentator described major retailers' co-operative advertising policies as 'sheer blackmail' (Jones 1977). Many manufacturers feel that the advertising appropriation is simply being used to develop retailers' images (Mintel 1988). Even when the product is given reasonable exposure within the advertisement, manufacturers often feel that they have lost full control of the copy, placement, timing and media, possibly to the detriment of their promotional objectives.

In spite of these major reservations, there are reasons why manufacturers continue to offer co-operative advertising allowances. Curhan and Kopp (1987/8) noted that packaged goods manufacturers in the USA offer around twenty times more promotions than can be adequately supported by the retail trade; a similar 'promotional overload' exists in many other countries. Advertising allowances may be a requirement for obtaining retailer support, or even retail listing. There are however some positive benefits for the manufacturer. Linkages with retail advertising can achieve greater local penetration of message and can stress local availability. The advertisements may also spur other retailers to promote or at least stock the product. In some cases, the image of the product may also be enhanced if linked to the name of a prestigious store.

Given the widespread availability of co-operative advertising allowances, the benefits and drawbacks of such advertising must be carefully evaluated by the retailer. Advantages may be summarized in the following terms, although some of these factors are clearly more applicable to smaller retail firms:

1. Advertising funds are increased, which in turn may lead to better discounts on media costs or agency commissions.
2. The increased funds may provide access to more diverse and/or powerful media than the retailer alone would have wished to finance.
3. A judicious selection of co-operative advertising partnerships can bring additional profits and prestige to the retailer.
4. A tie-up to a manufacturer's major advertising campaign can bring benefits beyond those yielded directly by the co-operative advertisements themselves.
5. Smaller retailers, without their own advertising staff or agency resources, can benefit from the quality of more professionally prepared copy.
6. Similarly, the retailer can benefit from the manufacturer's research into the best focus, timing, etc., for the advertisements.
7. If a retailer is not in a powerful bargaining position, the costs of such allowances may in any event be 'built into' the supply prices offered by the manufacturer.

There are however major drawbacks associated with co-operative advertising, which have caused some major retailers to limit such activities. The main drawbacks can be summarized as follows:

1. The products with the best advertising allowance may not offer the best short- or long-term profitability to the store; buyers should therefore take care to buy the products, not the allowances.
2. Excessive promotion of specific items may reduce the stores' perceived integrity as the provider of product choice and impartial advice; largely for this reason, the Neiman-Marcus chain specified that no more than 20 per cent of advertising could be run with co-operative funds (Spitzer and Schwartz 1982).
3. Too great a proportion of co-operative advertising may limit the scope for the retailer's own local or seasonal promotions.

4. The image of the products may not be consistent with the retailer's image building requirements; for example, the co-operative allowances offered to promote a packaged 'junk-food' may be excellent, but this could be in total conflict with a strategy of promoting the retailer as a supplier of fresh and healthy foods.
5. Co-operative advertising may lead to a 'sameness' if the emphasis is upon products and prices; this is in conflict with most retailers' need to differentiate themselves using more theme or institutional advertising.
6. Unless handled professionally, some forms of co-operative advertising for small stores can create ambiguity; for example, a glossy product advertisement shown in a cinema with a badly recorded retail announcement at the end can provoke entirely the wrong reaction from the audience!
7. The task of obtaining or supplying evidence of advertising exposure may prove a burden to the smaller retailer and may also lead to disputes with suppliers.

In spite of these major reservations, co-operative advertising is estimated to be worth around £50 million in the UK (Mintel 1988). As discussed in Chapter 7, much secrecy surrounds terms of trade, so it is not possible to quantify co-operative advertising deals precisely. From a study of 381 contracts in the USA, Haight (1976) found the following breakdown of manufacturer contributions:

Proportion of advertising cost paid by manufacturer	*Proportion of contracts in survey*
Below 50%	1.3%
50%	61.9%
60–80%	15.7%
100%	21.0%

One of the most systematic studies of co-operative advertising was undertaken, also in the USA, by Young and Greyser (1983). They considered the 'dual-signature' problem, the question of just whose name is primarily associated with the advertisement by consumers. One manufacturer was quoted as saying:

Co-op is by definition a program of conflict. Two organisations, which by their very nature have different objectives, are sharing the costs of a common effort.

It should be borne in mind, however, that advertising and promotional allowances are subject to many federal and local regulations in the USA, including the Robinson–Patman Act. A summary of these compulsory and voluntary regulations is provided by Edwards and Lebowitz (1981). In the UK, there are few external regulations upon the retail buyers' ability to demand advertising allowances, or upon the use that is made of these. Extensive allowances therefore continue to be paid to the more powerful retailers, even though there has been a marked decline in the product and specific price emphasis within their retail advertisements.

10.1.3 Building the retail brands

Increased awareness of the need for strategic thinking in retail marketing has contributed to a major change in the emphasis and style of retail advertising. Until relatively recently, retail advertising was dominated by specific product price announcements, with rather less attention given to the promotion of other store attributes. The lure of co-operative advertising undoubtedly contributed to this tendency, as did the 'security' of the fast sales response that this type of advertising can achieve. The typical characteristics of retail advertising were summed up by Berman and Evans (1979):

retail advertising emphasizes immediacy. Individual items are placed on sale and advertised during specific, short time periods. Immediate purchases are sought.

This style of advertising does little to enhance customer loyalty; in fact, it could diminish loyalty by encouraging shopping around. Nielsen (1974) described the attraction of price cuts as the 'most promiscuous of consumer motivation'. Neither could distinctive identities be created by using similar combinations of products and prices within similar formats. Kapferer (1986) expressed the problem:

Each store sings the same song: 'here tomatoes are cheaper'. The result is a poor attribution of advertising claims and some lack of credibility.

Many retailers were reluctant to be seen as shifting away from price appeal but recognized the need for a more individual identity in their advertising. A number of devices were therefore introduced to convey a more general image of good prices, rather than presenting a rather dull list of claimed reductions. For example, 'Asda Price' and Sainsbury's series of 'Discount' campaigns sought to establish a longer-term belief in the stores' value for money. Various discounters and department stores have used themes such as 'never knowingly undersold' or 'we will match any competitor's price'. Some customers take advantage of these claims and obtain a discount from the stated price. In most cases, however, the message simply serves as a price reassurance, allowing attention to be shifted to other store attributes.

Although prices play a major role in retail advertising, in very few cases can they provide the basis of a viable major strategy. Few retailers can enjoy the best available buying terms and retail cost structures. Those that do enjoy this happy position may well benefit more from placing emphasis upon factors other than prices. Those that do not are unlikely to be able to maintain a credible lowest-price position. This led Neill (1980) to conclude that 'price as a platform can only ever be your tactical weapon—it can never be your strategy'.

One can find exceptions to most generalizations, but it is true that price advertising now tends to be regarded as tactical and short-term, usually with the aim of building traffic or persuading shoppers to try out a new store or product area. As discussed in Chapter 4, effective differentiation cannot be achieved by adopting similar positioning statements. Retailers have therefore started to promote themselves as retail environments with wider packages of features (Davies *et al.* 1985). Emphasis has shifted to factors such as quality and service, with price benefits portrayed more in terms of value. The widespread development and promotion of retailers' own-brand products, discussed in the previous chapter, has also served to reinforce the brand value of many retailers' names.

The sheer scale of the major retail multiples has made possible the type of branding exercises that were previously the exclusive domain of major manufacturers such as Heinz and Ford. Where retail groups expand through acquisition, many seek a uniformity of name in order to achieve economies of scale in this 'branding' operation. In some cases this involves painful decisions to abandon existing names that had developed customer loyalty. For example, the incorporation of the Carrefour and Fine Fare stores under the Gateway name will require a considerable investment of marketing support to achieve greater levels of recognition. The costs of supporting parallel names, however, were illustrated in Table 10.2.

The decision to merge names or to continue separate identities depends upon a number of factors, including the following:

1. The compatibility of the store groups' positioning and product ranges
2. The strength of consumer loyalty to specific store names in local areas
3. The segmentation benefits that may be derived from retaining or creating different names
4. The extent to which promotion by national media is appropriate and viable using different names

Accordingly, House of Fraser has continued to operate stores under a large number of famous names, including Harrods, Dingles, Binns and Rackhams. The Burton group has retained and developed names to position and promote specific outlets for specific market segments. Grocery retailers, on the other hand, have been reluctant to focus their overall store offerings on such tightly defined segments. However, retail advertising does play an increasing role in promoting specific attributes of their stores to certain target groups. For example, while wishing to retain its traditional base of price–value-oriented shoppers, Tesco has promoted strongly the more up-market appeals of its health foods and delicatessens.

A major problem remains, however, in establishing unique brand identities for retail groups, many of which share essentially the same strategy. Much is said of repositioning today but this does not necessarily lead to effective differentiation; in fact, it may well achieve the opposite effect. Kapferer (1986) also noted:

The positioning concept has another limitation: it leaves totally free advertising creativity. Focusing on such attributes as products, price, location, service etc.—it is not really concerned with the language, the signs that will be used in the communication, as long as they are understandable. This position is no longer tenable: today everything communicates. In an age where the basic messages are more and more alike, we have to rely on signs and symbols to create and maintain an identity.

More detailed attention is given to decisions on advertising content and message in Section 10.2.3.

10.1.4 Publicity and sponsorships

With the rising cost of media advertising, increased attention is now being paid to other forms of publicity. This has also been stimulated by the advertising 'clutter' that exists in many traditional media and the problems therefore of conveying a clear and distinctive message within those media. The trend towards more powerful 'retailer branding' has also favoured the use of longer-term publicity devices, such as sponsorships. Used judiciously, publicity may also achieve higher credibility than conventional advertising, in that the communication usually reaches the consumer through an impartial intermediary such as a journalist or a television commentator. Publicity has been defined as:

non-personal stimulation of demand for a product, service or business unit by planting commercially significant news about it in a published medium or obtaining favourable presentation of it on radio, television or stage that is not paid for by the sponsor. (Alexander 1960).

Retailing has always had its share of entrepreneurs with a flair for publicity, but few retail organizations now leave this to chance. Even modest-sized companies tend to have a press officer or a member of the sales promotion staff nominated for press liaison. Most larger companies now have public relations sections and/or utilize the services of specialist PR agencies. It is not sufficient just to do things that are 'newsworthy'; a professional approach is required to ensure that press notices reach the right people in the right format and at the right time. Given the appropriate written and pictorial material, journalists and editors may be highly receptive, as it is 'easy' news and it satisfies a demand for local, consumer-oriented information. They are naturally less receptive to press releases that are low on news and high on advertising content, these being regarded simply as an attempt to avoid paying for advertising.

New store openings provide some of the best opportunities for publicity, a one-off opportunity which obviously should be exploited to the full. Sometimes the publicity is not quite of the nature intended; for example, the new Carrefour hypermarket at Caerphilly caused such traffic jams that these received considerable publicity. However, this television exposure persuaded even more people to come and visit the new attraction. Sometimes the opening of a new sales floor or department may be also able to attract press publicity. Marks & Spencer have been particularly successful in the use of publicity; this probably results from a high level of consumer interest in the company, a very well organized PR function, and a reluctance to use conventional advertising formats.

Sometimes particularly notable strategic moves are able to attract widespread publicity, such as Tesco's 'Operation Checkout' (see Section 8.4.1), or the same company's decision to delist major brands of coffee, accusing manufacturers of conspiring to inflate the prices. The various diversifications and extensions of the 'Next' concept have also been widely reported. The spate of retail takeover bids has attracted publicity, although much of this has been unfavourable. Sometimes, therefore, the role of publicity management is to try to attenuate the effects of potentially bad publicity.

Sales promotion activities and special events form the more regular basis of retail publicity. Fashion shows are held in many department stores, and Marks & Spencer has used them to good effect, including a major televised fashion show. Visits by television personalities to stores can also be used to attract crowds and newspaper publicity after the event. Forms of entertainment, such as fireworks displays sponsored by Arndale shopping centres, can also be used to create goodwill and name awareness. Coloroll, the home furnishings company, has been backing the Red Devils free-fall parachute team, which has held a series of displays, for example, to mark store openings (McEwan 1987).

Sponsorship has now become a major route to publicity, although it may also be motivated by personnel policies, a degree of altruism and/or the particular interests of senior directors. Mintel (1987) estimated all forms of sponsorship to be worth about £200 million annually; Otker (1988) predicted a ten-fold increase in sponsorship funding between 1980 and 1991. Retailers are among the major sponsors; they are involved in the full spectrum of activities, including sports, the arts, education, the environment and charities. For example, Marks & Spencer gives £0.5 million each year to the arts, mainly concentrated on youth ventures in deprived parts of the country (Thorncroft 1987). The biggest area of sponsorship overall, however, is sport, which attracts approximately 70 per cent of sponsorship funds (Mintel 1987). Some of the anticipated advantages from effective sponsorships are described by Turner (1987); these include:

1. Valuable media exposure
2. Employee involvement/interest
3. Name exposure at events
4. Company names on participants' and supporters' clothing
5. Company names on the ticket of the event
6. Special ticket allocations or entertainment opportunities for the company and its guests

The number of hours of media exposure varies considerably between sports. Based upon the evaluation of Sportscan of commercial television exposure, Miles (1987) reported that snooker received a massive 394 hours in 1986, with soccer receiving 261, tennis 188, athletics 131 and bowls 112 hours. The selection of a suitable sponsorship must consider several factors in addition to the hours of exposure, including how 'congested' the sport is with sponsors. For example, motor racing needs much sponsorship; when spectators at race meetings were asked to name up to three sponsors, five other sponsors were mentioned more frequently than B & Q (Sponsorship News 1986).

The compatibility of the sport or activity with the store image is also an important criterion. For example, in sponsoring darts competitions, MFI is reinforcing a mass market appeal, but the sport does have several negative connotations for many up-market consumers. Littlewoods has invested £2 million in sponsoring the soccer cup competition which carries its name. Guha (1987) has expressed satisfaction with the outcome, the draws and games having received over 300 minutes of BBC or IBA transmission time during the first year of the sponsorship. He points out that soccer is still the biggest participation sport in the UK and that television coverage attracts a relatively high proportion (45 per cent) of women and children viewers. Interest in football also spreads across most age and social class segments (Wright 1988).

The investment in a sponsorship does not always achieve the required level of publicity, especially if it is not supported by sufficient and related promotional expenditure. Miles (1987) suggests that this related expenditure should usually equal or exceed the actual cost of the sponsorship. Having reviewed the problems and benefits of sponsorship arrangements, Otker (1988) observed:

many sponsorships are still entered into without proper and detailed objective in mind.

sponsorship should be judged (and researched) as a reinforcing and catalytic factor, rather than an initiating or 'locomotive' factor.

Unlike the direct effects of special event publicity, which are relatively easy to calculate, the effectiveness of long-term publicity formats is difficult to quantify. Current indications, however, are that forms of publicity and sponsorship will become increasingly important means by which retailers can attract interest and further establish their brand identities.

10.2 ADVERTISING DECISIONS

This section considers five of the major decision areas facing the retail advertiser. First, alternative approaches to establishing the level of advertising expenditure are compared. The choice of an advertising agency is next considered, in that most major retailers use the service of at least one agency. Attention then turns to the creation of advertisements, specifically, ways of establishing the most appropriate advertising content and message. The relative merits of television, press and other available advertising media are then compared. The final part of this section examines approaches to the timing of advertisements, including considerations of seasonality.

10.2.1 Determining expenditure levels

The opportunities to advertise are almost without limit, and retailers are constantly under pressure to increase their advertising expenditures. Media owners naturally have a vested interest in advocating increased advertising, and agencies too are likely to benefit from larger expenditures. Pressure from the retailers' own branch and merchandise management, plus manufacturers' co-operative deals, may also contribute to an upwards drift in advertising expenditures. An objective approach to the task of establishing budgets is therefore required, in order to resist these pressures and to impose a financial discipline upon advertising managers and the agency. The budgets also form the framework within which the details of creative treatment and media schedules can be planned. Most companies do however allow a modest contingency fund, in order to allow reaction to unexpected opportunities or threats.

There are several different approaches that may be taken to establishing budgets, with varying degrees of merit. Among the least meritorious are the 'historical' methods, whereby budgets are simply an adjustment of previous years' budgets; obviously, the approach has little logic, in terms of either financial or marketing objectives. The 'arbitrary' or 'affordable' method bases allocations upon the level that controllers feel could be met that year, based upon financial estimates. This ignores the effects of advertising upon sales, introduces instability in the advertising programme from year to year and also tends to reduce advertising when it may be most needed. Elements of these approaches are still found within the budget planning of some retailers, although most now use one or a combination of the following methods:

1. *Percentage-of-sales method*   Using this method, the advertising budget is set as a percentage of recent or expected sales. The advertising expenditure of 16 of the UK's major retailer advertisers are expressed in Table 10.2 as a percentage of their sales. One merit of the approach is that advertising tends to remain within the affordable range; it may also encourage competitive stability within a sector if most other retailers use the same method. The approach may be useful for a wide-assortment retailer in allocation advertising funds between departments, in that the industry norms in each product sector can be used as a guide (Kaufman 1980). The drawbacks are that sales are allowed to determine advertising levels, whereas advertising should be regarded as a determinant of sales. The approach also tends to inhibit flexibility and experimentation with different inputs of advertising. It is not based upon a systematic analysis of the cost-effectiveness of advertising in achieving the various national and local, long-term and short-term goals of the company.

2. *Competitive parity method*   The retailer establishes a budget equal to or above that of competitors. Typically, this would be based upon competitors' recent expenditures, as published by Media Expenditure Analysis Ltd or the Media Register. It should be noted, however, that the calculation procedures of these two sources are very different, leading to a difference of almost £2 million between their estimates of MFI expenditures in 1986 (Bowen-Jones 1987). It is claimed that the competitive parity approach draws upon the collective wisdom of the sector and also tends to inhibit promotion wars, although neither claim is entirely valid. In that each company has different strategic objectives and is faced with different problems and opportunities, there is no reason why advertising expenditures should equate with those of competitors.

3. *Objective and task method*   Using this approach, the retail marketer is required to define detailed objectives, establish the tasks required to achieve these, and then estimate the costs of undertaking the tasks. The total of these costs forms the basis of the advertising budget. The method imposes a useful discipline in that managers must more precisely define objectives and assumptions about relationships between advertising and sales, new customers, store image and/or customer loyalty. It also permits more systematic evaluations of the effects of the advertising in relation to each objective.

Of these three methods, the objective and task method clearly offers the most rigorous but difficult approach to determining advertising expenditure levels. Whitaker (1983) analysed how both Sainsbury and Tesco increased their expenditures in pursuit of market share objectives. Their advertising-to-sales ratios increased considerably between 1976 and 1981, but at no stage was there competitive parity between the budgets of the two companies. Fulop (1987) further described the specific objectives of Sainsbury in increasing its expenditure. Research had indicated a need to improve price perceptions; awareness of the company had to be built in new geographical areas; and awareness needed to be developed of the wider product ranges in their newer, larger stores.

It is also necessary to view the advertising budget as a part, albeit perhaps a major part, of the sales promotion budget. Intended allocations should also therefore be evaluated in terms of alternative uses for those funds, such as special events, publicity, displays or simply price cuts. In many companies this concept is taken a logical stage further, advertising expenditures being seen as an element of an overall 'strategic mix budget' or the 'customer motivation budget'. This philosophy encourages a more demanding and critical approach to advertising budgets, evaluating them against the effectiveness of other expenditures, such as store developments, refurbishments, product developments or additional customer services.

10.2.2   Selecting an agency

The choice of an advertising agency can exert a major influence upon the results achieved from a given level of advertising expenditure. Retailers are faced with a wide choice of agencies, from the large, international organizations to the very small, often regionally based agencies. Some provide a full range of advertising and marketing services; others are specialists in specific functions, such as a creative work or media buying. A retailer may decide to use different agencies to service its different advertising needs. For example, Sainsbury previously used Saatchi & Saatchi for television and national press, Abbott Mead Vickers/SMS for colour magazine work and Broadbent for local press advertising (Marketing Week 1985).

Some retailers prefer to undertake all or part of their advertising work 'in-house'; for example, Next refused to use an agency for the launch of the 'Next Directory' home shopping catalogue, declaring that agencies were too expensive (Britton 1988). Most major retailers could develop the resources and media buying power to advertise without the help of agencies, but few elect to take this approach. Although a retailer would be unwise to delegate its strategic thinking to an agency, the input and stimulus provided by the agency can be a valuable contribution to its strategic planning. The creative and media buying services of an agency involve a range of specialist skills; to develop these in-house could reduce their flexibility in advertising approach. At the end of the day, the ability of clients to switch agencies relatively easily imposes a continuous pressure to produce results.

The precise range and balance of services provided to retailers by their agencies differs in every case, depending upon the resources of each party and the specific needs of the retailer. The services are likely to include some or all of the following activities:

1. To assess the strengths and weaknesses of the client's stores, merchandise and image, *vis-à-vis* those of competitors
2. To analyse the characteristics of the present and potential market, and of the client's competitive position
3. In collaboration with the client, to determine the strategic plan, including relationships between advertising and other elements of the mix
4. To define the specific objectives to be achieved by advertising
5. To evolve a creative and media plan for presentation to the client
6. To create and produce advertising copy, illustrations, sound track and television/film material for commercials
7. To buy media space and time that will reach the maximum number of target customers at the lowest costs

Table 10.3   Reasons for switching agency[a]

Why clients sack their agencies	
8 main reasons	*% of respondents quoting reason*
Results fell short of expectations	40
In a rut—needed new ideas	36
Poor client service	20
Needed to rationalize agencies used	18
Not getting value for money	14
Agency clearly in decline	12
Outgrown the agency	12
Agency didn't understand our problems	12

Factors in selecting a new agency	
8 main factors	*% of respondents quoting factor*
Evidence that agency understands our problems	50
Agency made the best pitch	44
Creative record	38
Good personal chemistry with staff	24
Strong planning function	22
Appropriate size	12
Good media buying record	10
Specialist knowledge of our industry	10

[a] *Base*: 120 companies from all sectors that switched agencies in 1987; each was asked to cite up to three main reasons for sacking the agency and up to three main factors in selecting a new one.
Source: Gofton (1988).

8. To evaluate the effectiveness of the advertising through both pre- and post-testing procedures

Compared with most other types of clients, retailers tend to be very demanding of their agencies. Having handled Tesco's press business for 11 years, Carter (1977) described some of the problems in dealing with a large volume of local press advertising:

an advertising agency handling a lot of retail advertising has to be able to produce a large volume of advertising per £ spent, and be able to do so quickly. We might produce 10,000 ads. in a year . . . From copy brief to finished art, the studio produces a retail ad. in an average of five hours.

Although there has been a shift towards more theme advertising and less emphasis on short-term price offers, there is still a strong bias towards press advertising among retailers. They are also not averse to wielding their buying power, and most demand a volume discount on commission from their agencies (Ward 1985).

Long-term loyalty to a particular agency is relatively uncommon. Mintel (1988) reported that only 29 per cent of retail accounts were retained over a five-year period, 11.2 per cent over a ten-year period. Some of the results of a survey of companies that switched agency recently are shown in Table 10.3. The main reasons for leaving an agency are dissatisfaction with results achieved, the creative ideas being produced or the service offered. In selecting a new agency, the quality of the 'pitch' was important, but not as important as evidence that the client's needs were understood by the agency. The creative record, strength of the planning function, media buying record, industry knowledge and appropriateness of size were also important factors. It is also noticeable that 24 per cent of respondents mentioned good 'personal chemistry' with staff; the need for a close and interactive relationship with the agency is increasingly recognized:

clients are more interested in appointing a business partner, as opposed to someone who is just going to solve their creative problem. They are seeking someone who can be involved in their strategic planning and thinking, all the way through. (Gofton 1988)

10.2.3   Content and message

In that many retailers have shifted away from price as the major theme within their advertising, the selection of appropriate content and message formats has become major decision area for retailers and their agencies. Although creativity has a major role to play in the production of advertisements, decisions on advertising content should be based upon sound research into consumers' motivations and the images held of the relevant stores. For example, although Sainsbury's is regarded as a high-quality and reliable supermarket, research indicated that it had also acquired an austere and authoritarian image. The new advertising has therefore sought to portray a friendlier face and to create more of a relationship with the store's customers (Warner 1988). Similarly, the image of Halfords was found to be solid, dependable and reliable; it was however perceived as a little boring, an impression that the company has set out to overcome.

Based upon a technique developed by QED Research Ltd, Walters and White (1987) suggested a stage-by-stage route to the appropriate creative solution, which is summarized as follows:

1. Identify the store attributes and requirements that consumers consider to be most important when shopping in the particular retail sector.
2. Promotional emphasis should be reduced on attributes and requirements of low importance, as these are likely to be least effective in improving overall image.
3. Based upon the important factors, the store should be evaluated against competition to establish relevant strengths and weaknesses.
4. By reference to those with experience and greatest familiarity with the store, these strengths and weaknesses should be subdivided into those that are real and those that are 'illusory'.
5. Serious consideration should be given to changing the store's actual attributes to correct real weaknesses and give substance to perceived strengths which are currently merely illusory.
6. The advertising strategy and creative solution is then formulated on the bases of (a) maintaining perceptions of real strengths, (b) correcting perceptions of illusory weaknesses, and (c) promoting any real improvements made to the store package.
7. The process of assessment and monitoring should continue, so as to provide inputs to retail strategy and advertising decisions.

There are of course significant methodological difficulties in ranking the importance of store attributes and in rating store images, as is discussed in Chapters 3 and 5. This approach does however offer a systematic route between the consumer research and the creative solution. It can provide guidance on the general content of the advertisements, although decisions on how best to convey that content remain. Kapferer (1986) pointed out:

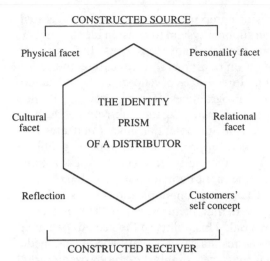

CONSTRUCTED SOURCE

Physical facet

Personality facet

THE IDENTITY

Cultural facet

PRISM

Relational facet

OF A DISTRIBUTOR

Reflection

Customers' self concept

CONSTRUCTED RECEIVER

Figure 10.1 The identity prism: facets of identity
Source: Kapferer (1986, p. 171).

Traditionally, strategic communication platforms were only concerned by 'what to say'. Nowadays 'how to say it' is as important. It just cannot be abandoned to the hazards of mere creativity.

In order to provide a framework for the creation of retail advertising, Kapferer presented the concept of an 'identity prism', illustrated in Figure 10.1. The 'constructed sender' represents the physical and personality facets of the retail communicator; the 'constructed receiver' is the person to whom the advertising message is addressed. The six interrelated facets of the identity prism are as follows:

1. *The physical facet*—the basic characteristics of the store, including prices, assortment, services, etc.: these are the traditional content of retail communications.
2. *The personality facet*—the intangible personality characteristics ascribed to the store, such as the elitist store or the pioneering store: various projective techniques have been used to identify consumers' symbolic images of stores.
3. *The relational facet*—all retail activities involve a relationship between company and customers: this can be projected, for example, as a protection relationship, fighting against high prices, or as a guidance relationship, helping the customer through complex choices.
4. *The cultural facet*—particularly in the more specialized trades, stores may have cultural roots which can be utilized; for example, IKEA projects its Scandinavian origins, and their associations with good living, affluence and style; associations with various forms of popular culture may be projected by record and teenage fashion stores.
5. *The reflection facet*—the image of the customers that the store wishes to convey, which may not be a description of the target customers: this can be particularly important if research indicates that a low opinion is held of a store's customers. The choice of actors and models in advertisements makes a strong statement about this facet.
6. *The self-concept fact*—the instrumental role of the store for customers' self-images; for example, in using a particular store a customer may feel him- or herself to be an astute shopper, a person 'in' fashion or a member of a restricted circle.

These six facets of the store identity provide useful directions for advertising research and creative solutions. They also draw attention to the dangers of creating a confused identity or ambiguity in advertisements if the facets are dissonant.

Quantitative approaches to the selection of advertising components have also been suggested. Green *et al.* (1984) presented the BENEMAX decision support system to assist in identifying sets of product features, benefits and image components for retail advertisements. Inputs to the system would comprise routinely collected survey data on consumers' store-feature and retail-feature preferences; background variables regarding store usage, psychographics and demographics would also be input. The initial BENEMAX programmes develop a set of optimum advertising claims, i.e. the features, benefits and image components; further sub-routines develop perceptual/preference maps and identify the characteristics of potential buyers that are most highly associated with the 'feature package'. This type of approach would appear to offer a useful means to derive suitable advertising content from potentially large volumes of consumer survey data, provided that the limitations of the available input data are not forgotten.

The appropriate balance between pictures and words in retail communications was studied by Gardner and Houston (1986). Their evidence suggested that pictures retain their effects on memory and evaluations rather more than verbal material. This points to the need to pay great attention to the pictorial aspects of the store itself. The results suggest that, when using media with less exposure time such as television, pictorial messages should be emphasized; verbal portrayal of store features should be given more emphasis when the consumer has adequate time to examine the advertisement, for example in a newspaper.

10.2.4 Evaluating media alternatives

The retail advertiser is faced with a wide choice of media, including television, radio, newspapers, magazines, direct mail, posters and many more. The choice of specific media vehicles is quite vast, especially in the printed media, where new magazine titles continue to proliferate. Each has its particular advantages and its limitations, which should be evaluated in relation to the retailer's communication requirements. Table 10.4 shows the allocation of expenditures of 15 major retail advertisers between press and broadcast media. This illustrates the importance of newspapers, taking over 50 per cent of expenditure in all but two cases. In 1987, all of the 'top 10' newspaper advertisers were retailers (Douglas 1988).

Television advertising takes the second largest share of expenditure in most cases. It should be noted, however, that Tesco and Queensway, the two companies with the highest weighting towards television in 1986, both reduced this the following year; in Tesco's case, television advertising was cut from £2.9 million to just £0.25 million. Magazines have become the major media type used by W. H. Smith, and they also play a very significant role for Sainsbury, Woolworths, Boots and MFI. Radio advertising proved useful for local advertising in some cases, especially the co-ops. Not included within this analysis are retailers' expenditures on direct mail, outdoor posters, in-store advertising and other media. A detailed evaluation of the media alternatives is beyond the scope of this text; for this purpose readers may wish to consult a specialist retail advertising text (e.g. Haight 1976; Edwards and Lebowitz 1981; Spitzer and Schwartz 1982). It may be useful at this stage, however, briefly to review the advantages and problems of the major media.

Newspapers A major advantage of newspapers is their selectivity; local newspapers have a clearly defined geographical circulation, allowing retailers to advertise with minimum waste circulation. Nationals usually do not share this advantage, but detailed data are available relating to reader characteristics, allowing some selectivity by market segments. Although advertising rates vary enormously between papers, the 'cost per thousand' tends to be lower than television and the costs of producing the adverts is usually considerably lower. The advertiser

Table 10.4 Use of press and broadcast media, 1986

Major retail advertisers	% press/broadcast media expenditure on:			
	Newspapers	TV	Magazines	Radio
MFI	74.3	12.9	12.4	0.4
Dixons	80.8	16.1	1.0	2.2
Currys	84.6	14.5	0.5	0.5
Comet	86.4	10.1	3.3	0.2
Asda	67.5	24.0	7.5	1.1
Rumbelows	77.5	19.5	1.5	1.5
Texas Homecare	71.3	25.9	0.3	2.5
Woolworths	47.9	24.6	23.9	3.6
Tesco	60.7	34.9	2.5	1.9
Boots	63.0	18.6	18.4	—
Co-ops	68.6	21.3	3.6	6.5
B & Q	67.1	24.7	5.6	2.5
Queensway	57.3	32.6	5.5	4.6
Sainsbury	54.1	17.4	28.3	0.2
W. H. Smith	40.5	6.3	51.3	1.9

Source: derived from Sharman (1987).

also enjoys much flexibility of format in newspapers, and the lead time for preparing and inserting advertisements is very short. It is claimed that newspapers enjoy high credibility; Lynn (1981) found that 74 per cent of respondents preferred them as a source of information on where to shop.

The limitations of newspapers include the poor print and paper quality, plus the difficulties of using colour in advertisements. In that papers carry a large volume of advertisements, there is also a problem of 'clutter', which may limit impact unless the creative treatment is particularly effective. Daily papers have a very short life and little additional 'pass-on' exposure. By no means all newspaper buyers actually read the advertisements, although the proportion can be increased by careful positioning within the paper (Soley and James 1982).

Television In combining sight, sound and movement, television may achieve greater impact than most other media; it also allows a very wide range of creative treatments. Cohen and Jones (1978) described television as the 'ideal medium' for promoting brand images. Television advertising therefore should make the most effective use of its special advantages, and not convey dull or detailed information that would be better and more economically communicated in print form. Also, the use of television may in itself bring some prestige to the advertiser.

The main problems of television advertising relate to the very high and rising costs, which inflated by 25 per cent during 1987 alone (Snoddy 1988). Furthermore, the system for selling television time is such that a media buyer must offer a price at or close to the station's rate card level in order to be fairly sure of getting a specific time slot; otherwise, the booking can be pre-empted by a higher bid from another advertiser, possibly with serious consequences for the timing of a promotional campaign. The differences between rate card levels and prices actually paid are therefore highly sensitive to the demand for air time. This difference has averaged between 45 and 16 per cent since 1980 but has been at its lowest level in recent years (Admap 1987).

There are other problems too. Television lacks geographical selectivity, which means much wasted advertising unless a retailer has a high density of stores in a television area. Although special rates may be available to reflect limited trading areas, these are unlikely to be available for more desirable time slots. Furthermore, the message time for television adverts is fleeting; the more widespread use of television and video remote controls is also leading to more people switching off the sound, switching channels or fast winding tapes during commercial breaks (Yorke and Kitchen 1985). Another drawback is that the production of high-quality television advertising is very expensive and relatively slow; therefore promotional lead times are much longer.

Magazines   These are now a very important medium for some retail advertisers (Table 10.4). Given the very wide range of titles, advertising can be closely targeted on specific demographic or life-style segments, for example *Amateur Photographer*, *Mother & Baby*, *Practical Householder* and *Fitness* (Henry 1988). Although some 'magazines' are closer to newspapers in their print and paper quality, the majority offer excellent reproduction quality; this allows the use of highly colourful and glossy creative treatment. Magazines tend to be kept around longer for reading at leisure and also are more likely to be passed on to others. Sainsbury has used advertisements containing recipe suggestions, printed on very stiff paper; these are designed to be pulled out of the magazine and retained longer.

Inevitably, it costs more to produce an effective advertisement for a magazine than for a newspaper. This is a particular problem if different ones are designed with highly selective appeals for each magazine audience. Most magazines have a relatively small circulation, although this is less of a problem if it closely matches the target group. Production lead times tend to be considerably longer than those of newspapers.

Direct mail   These communications range from basic leaflets to full-colour catalogues; some companies mail promotional information or store magazines directly to their customers on a regular basis. Direct mail as a whole grew by 37 per cent between 1984 and 1985 (Coles 1987). Since 1983 it was estimated that over 100 million direct mail items per year were sent out by store-based retailers, many more by mail order companies (Rowney 1986). The use of direct mail by retailers is now growing faster than among any other category (Mintel 1988). A Management Horizons survey (Ody 1987) found that direct mail, including catalogues, account for the following proportions of promotional spending:

Supermarkets	9%
Retail warehouses	6%
Department stores	5%
Variety/chainstores	8%
Mail order	74%

The main advantage of direct mail is the minimal wastage of circulation; every recipient can be selected to be an actual or potential customer. Lists of store credit card users (see Chapter 12) or name/address files held by specialist agencies enable direct mail to be accurately targeted at specific segments. Letters can be personalized by name and the message or contents adjusted to the known characteristics or spending habits of the recipient. The opportunities to experiment are also numerous, especially if store credit card usage allows a precise monitoring of specific customers' reactions.

Inevitably, direct mail involves a higher cost per recipient than any other medium. In those terms, the costs of production can also be relatively high, especially some of the more elaborate catalogues. Given the rapid proliferation of direct mail, it may also be treated as junk mail and quickly discarded, possibly not even opened. This problem may be partially overcome by enclosing direct mail advertising with credit statements or by incorporating a consumer competition to stimulate interest and retention of the material.

Outdoor It was estimated that retailers accounted for only 2.5 per cent of expenditure on outdoor posters in 1986 (Poster Scene 1987), although the proportion increased in 1987. The poster industry claims to offer a far lower 'cost per thousand' than the other main media and also claims the highest coverage of the adult population. Posters have been used to particularly good effect by retailers to announce new store openings and to provide direction signs to the store. Posters also offer scope for dramatic creative effects, and impact can be further increased with lighting, mobile effects or three-dimensional displays. On the negative side, the audience selectivity of posters is low and the clutter of outdoor advertising is high in some areas. The message content of the poster must also be brief; it should be designed to be completely understood within five seconds, if observed mainly from passing vehicles (Bolen 1988).

Internal Retailers have numerous potential advertising opportunities within their own stores. These include posters, carrier bags, packages, leaflets or catalogues given away at the checkout, messages on sales receipts, etc. In-store advertising may also include audio announcements, videos or slide presentations promoting specific products or store benefits. Littlewoods has developed electronic information points, based upon interactive video disks, which provide both a screen display and printed information, if requested by the customer. A store can therefore provide many opportunities to reinforce the retailer's 'brand image' and stimulate further purchases (see Chapter 11); the limit is imposed by the need to avoid excessive clutter and confusion. Although packages and carrier bags carry the name of the retailer beyond the store, the limitation of most in-store advertising is that it only reaches existing customers.

Other media There are many other communication methods that may form part of the retailer's media mix. Local commercial radio channels provide reasonable selectivity and flexibility, at relatively low cost. 'Transit' advertising, on buses or underground trains, can deliver a timely message, just before a potential customer reaches a store. Cinema screen or theatre programme adverts tend to reach relatively small audiences, but this may not be a problem if the audience is particularly appropriate. Local 'Shopper guides' or 'free sheets' have also developed, in some areas presenting a real challenge to the local newspapers (White *et al.* 1980). The telephone yellow pages can provide a valuable source of new customers, especially for goods and services required less frequently. Some retailers have employed leaflet distributors to target specific customer types within shopping centres or car parks. The exterior of the store itself also provides many opportunities to communicate with passers-by.

10.2.5 Media planning

The choice between the alternative media must depend upon several factors, including the detailed objectives of the campaign(s), the type of message to be conveyed, the products (if any) to be featured, the media habits of target customers, and the costs of specific media in relation to the total budget. The previous section will have illustrated that each media type has its particular strengths and its problems; there is no simple formula for determining the appropriate media mix. The first stage in the process is obviously to eliminate alternatives that are unavailable in the relevant areas or that are completely beyond the budget constraints. This is still likely to leave a wide choice of media and media vehicles, so a number of criteria may be used to assist in the choice.

Cost-per-thousand Sometimes abbreviated CPT or CPM, this is simply an expression of the cost of reaching each 1,000 households or people, using a specific media vehicle. For example, a half-page display in a major regional newspaper may cost £2,300 and reach a circulation of 350,000; the cost-per-thousand would therefore be 657p. The calculation can be modified to reflect 'audience' rather than circulation, if audience is larger because of pass-on readership. Alternatively, the 'effective audience' may be the criterion, this being the people within the retailers' target groups who are exposed to the media vehicle. Further refinements to the calculation can be made to reflect the fact that some of the effective audience would not actually see the advertisement. Jolson (1979) discussed the different criteria that a retailer could apply in evaluating possible print media vehicles.

Cost-per-thousand measures can be a useful starting point in choosing between media of similar type. Comparisons between different media are fraught with difficulties but are sometimes encountered. For example, Poster Scene (1987) cited a comparison of major media on the basis of costs-per-thousand, compiled by Saatchi & Saatchi Compton:

Cinema	1830p
Television	322p
National newspaper	295p
Colour supplements	137p
Radio	81p
Outdoor	31p

This was based upon a 30-second cinema, television or radio commercial, a full-page monochrome newspaper advertisement, a colour page in supplements, and a weighted average of large and small outdoor posters. In attempting such inter-media comparisons, it is essential to recognize the very different levels of audience attention and impact achieved by these different media.

Impact Certain media have inherent advantages in achieving impact, notably cinema and television, although impact also depends upon characteristics of the message and the target audience. A relatively complex series of price comparisons or technical specifications of particular products would clearly require the opportunity to be read carefully; newspapers or magazines would therefore achieve the highest impact. For other creative treatments, the availability of colour is essential, in which case television or magazines are likely to be preferred. Analysis of the media habits of the target consumers also provides guidelines in choosing between media vehicles. Many magazines are very closely targeted upon specific groups, whereas television and national newspapers have somewhat wider appeal. The choice of specific TV programme slots or locations within newspapers can however improve the impact. Higie *et al.* (1987) suggested that particular attention should be paid to the media habits of 'market mavens', defined as:

individuals who have information about many kinds of products, places to shop, and other facets of markets, and initiate discussions with consumers and respond to requests from consumers for market information. (Feick and Price 1987)

They suggest that direct mail and women's homemaking magazines are useful vehicles for targeting this group. In so doing, the retail advertiser may most favourably influence the frequent word-of-mouth communications in which this type of consumer is likely to be involved.

Exposure Exposures, sometimes referred to as 'impressions', are the number of times that an advert is seen by the media audience. Inevitably, exposure (E) is a function of reach (R) and frequency (F):

$$E = R \times F.$$

For example, 12 million exposures could be achieved by reaching 4 million people an average of three times during the campaign period, or 2 million people an average of six times. If a well-known retailer is concerned primarily with expanding territory or announcing the arrival of a new product range, the emphasis could be on achieving a wide reach. A retailer as yet unknown in the area, on the other hand, might wish to achieve a higher frequency of exposure. Gross rating points (GRPs) are a measure of frequency times the percentage of the audience reached ($R\%$):

$$GRP = R\% \times F.$$

A schedule that reached 80 per cent of the audience an average of four times each would therefore have a GRP of 320.

The appropriate number of exposures varies according to the communication objectives of the retailer. From a review of previous research, Teel and Bearden (1980) noted:

Although there is disagreement on the precise values of the upper and lower limits of the 'optimal effect' range, fewer than three message exposures are likely to fail to register, and more than ten exposures are probably unnecessary, for products advertised on broadcast media.

It should be noted that an exposure does not necessarily occur every time a person reads a newspaper or watches television at a specific time. Less than half the people who had 'vehicle exposure' may have had 'actual exposure' to the advertisement, particularly with the relatively low-involvement media, such as television and radio (Krugman 1975). To achieve high 'cumulative reach' (cume) over a series of advertisements in order to reach a high proportion of the target audience, the media planner may have to accept that many customers will have an excessive exposure frequency. This may be partially overcome by selecting different media vehicles with low audience duplication, for example two daily papers with very little reader overlap.

Media selection is therefore 'the problem of finding the most cost effective media to deliver the desired number of exposures to the target audience' (Kotler 1988). However, the media planner is also concerned with the timing of the advertisements, in terms of both the overall seasonality (if any) in the advertising and the precise timing within the campaign. These two aspects of media planning are 'macro-scheduling' and 'micro-scheduling' problems.

Macro scheduling At this level, the planner may decide to maintain a fairly constant level of advertising over the whole year, to concentrate advertising in seasons with high expected sales levels, or to use advertising to stimulate sales during the normally quiet seasons. Table 10.5 shows the seasonal trends in advertising by broad groupings of retailers. In the grocery, department store and mail order retail categories, there is a strong bias towards the final quarter; even much of the post-Christmas sales advertising falls within the last part of this quarter. In some specific sectors the bias may be even more pronounced. Ward (1985) reported that 54 per cent of advertising by the jewellery sector occurs in that final quarter. Not surprisingly, film process advertising is heavily concentrated around the main holiday months.

In contrast, the direct response mail order companies adopted an even pattern of expenditure over the year; in their case, the advertising is in a sense the store. The product emphasis within

Table 10.5   Retail advertising by season, 1987

Retail category	% of advertising expenditure in each quarter			
	1st	2nd	3rd	4th
Grocery multiples and co-ops	17.8	20.3	23.7	37.7
Department and retail stores	18.0	23.7	22.5	35.4
Film process-retail and mail order	5.8	38.6	42.2	13.4
Direct response mail order	25.6	23.4	23.1	27.9
Mail order retailers	13.4	15.3	22.7	48.6
All retailers	20.4	23.0	26.4	30.1

Source: based upon MEAL data compiled in Mintel (1988).

this advertising, however, is highly seasonal. Haight (1976) depicted the trends of nine product categories; sales of lawn and garden items peak in the spring, paint and paint sundries in the summer, and gift items in December. The timing of advertising to gain maximum awareness at peak seasons depends upon the degree of advertising carry-over, i.e. the extent to which the effect of the advertising continues or wears out over time. If carry-over is high, the campaign may be initiated some time before the peak demand period. There are of course arguments against concentrating advertising at peak seasons. At such times, advertising clutter in the media can be high and the discounts obtainable by media buyers are likely to be low.

The cheapest months in which to advertise tend to be January, February, July and August (Roberts and Prentice 1978). In that many retailing costs are fixed, it also makes sense to attract customers at times that some types of stores would be under-utilized. The emphasis on long-term image building, as opposed to short-term sales promotion, also suggests a more even pattern of advertising. Few retailers, however, can afford to ignore the sales opportunities provided by peak demand seasons, not least because competitors are likely to be promoting hard to gain maximum share of the temporarily increased market.

Micro scheduling   At this level, the objective is to allocate the exposure within short time periods in order to achieve the highest impact. Advertising may be concentrated in a 'burst' pattern over a period of a few days, for example, in order to announce the start of a major sale. Other objectives may call for a more continuous 'drip' pattern. For example, prior to major hypermarket openings, Carrefour used a series of teaser advertisements in local newspapers. By providing a little more information each day, these built up interest and awareness of the company logo. The advertising then rose to a peak immediately prior to the store opening.

Some schedules use an intermittent pattern, possibly concentrating the advertising around the most popular shopping days. From a study of grocery store advertising in a regional newspaper, the author found that 64 per cent of advertisements appeared on a Wednesday or Thursday evening, and only 9 per cent on a Saturday or Monday. Many media planners target common pay days, although the shift away from weekly, cash payment of wages means that payment dates are more highly concentrated in the middle or the ends of months.

A number of computer-based decision support models have now been developed to assist in the selection and scheduling of the promotion mix. Based upon three years of sales and promotion expenditure data for a large speciality store, Allaway *et al.* (1987) developed a series of equations relating overall and department sales to promotional variables. These included the number of newspaper column inches, the contents of the adverts, the rates paid, whether a coupon was used, the price discount (if any), the timing and content of radio and television adverts, the size and content of billboards, and other variables. Optimal control modelling was used to derive the most cost-effective mix of media and the size, timing and promotional content of the adverts.

The model suggested a number of major changes from the store's usual promotional plan. These included a large increase in the use of billboards during certain weeks and a drastic decrease in the column inches featuring a leading brand of jeans; the results of the model suggested that the brand had been overpromoted from the store's viewpoint, largely because of the desire to use co-operative advertising funds. Models of this type are obviously not designed to replace management judgement in making advertising decisions; however, they can encourage more objective analysis of major alternatives and help to answer many 'what-if' questions. Given the more widespread availability of detailed and timely point-of-sale data, the scope for developing and using such models is now extensive.

10.3 MONITORING ADVERTISING EFFECTS

Having considered some of the major decision areas facing the retail advertiser, it is appropriate to conclude with a brief look at the ways in which advertising effects can be monitored. In that several retailers now spend over £10 million annually on media advertising, the need to assess performance is very strong. A survey by Management Horizons indicated that, for some major retailers, their only test of advertising effectiveness was 'gut feel' (Ody 1987). Less than half the retailers in the sample attempted to relate advertising to improvements in sales or profits, only 15 per cent to improvements in customer flow. A third of the sample estimated that more than half of their advertising expenditure was wasted; one even admitted: '75% is wasted, but I haven't the nerve to give it up completely'.

These findings suggested that much retail advertising has been prompted by the perceived need to match competitors' advertising, not by a scientific assessment of its cost-effectiveness as a marketing tool. In many cases, it is clear that increased expenditure on media advertising has not been accompanied by the necessary investment in performance evaluation research. The problems associated with advertising assessment have increased with the growth of theme or image-based advertising. The effects of this type of advertising are assumed to be longer-term and therefore more difficult to measure in terms of immediate sales response. This section will first look at some of the main approaches to evaluating advertising performances. Attention then turns to the assessment of advertising that incorporates specific product price reductions.

10.3.1 Evaluating advertising performance

There is no single method or technique that is most appropriate for the evaluation of all aspects of advertising performance. Some would argue that the overall cost-effectiveness of the advertising is, at the end of the day, the only relevant criterion, and that this is best assessed through the detailed analysis of sales/profit results and advertising costs. While this may be viable where the objective is simply to generate short-term sales response, the problems of isolating the effects of advertising on long-term sales and profits are far greater. The specific objectives of the advertisement or campaign must therefore guide the choice of method used to assess the extent to which these have been met. In the development of the campaign, techniques generally classified as 'pre-testing' can also be used to increase the probability that the advertisements achieve their

Table 10.6 Approaches to advertising assessment

Aspect of advertising to be assessed	Appropriateness of approach				
	Pre-testing	Day-after recall	Tracking	Area experiments	Sales analysis
Overall effectiveness	Tries	No	No	Yes	Yes
Meeting communication objectives	Yes	A little	A little	Possible	n.a.
Achievement of impact	Weak	Yes	Yes	Possible	n.a.
Diagnostic information about the ad.	Yes	Weak	Weak	Weak	n.a.
Difference between alternative ads.	Tries	Weak	Yes	Yes	Yes

Source: Twyman (1986).

objectives. Twyman (1986) provided a succinct review of general approaches to the monitoring of advertising performance. Table 10.6 summarizes the appropriateness of each of these for assessing specific aspects of the advertising.

Pre-testing Unlike all the forms of post-testing, pre-testing enables the advertiser to assess some aspects of the advertising before any media time or space is purchased; it therefore has the ability to avoid some expensive errors. Approaches include focus group sessions, at which shoppers are shown plans of the campaign in embryonic form or completed advertisements prior to broadcast or publication; alternatively, the plans can be exposed to larger samples of shoppers to obtain more quantitative assessments. Pre-testing methods can help to estimate the likelihood of attracting attention and the effects upon feelings and beliefs about the retailer. Alternative creative treatments or advertising formats can be compared and diagnostic information obtained. The main limitations of pre-testing are that the advertising is assessed in isolation and performance in the real market-place cannot be directly measured.

Day-after recall Tests of advertising recall shortly after the publication or broadcast provide a measure of impact *vis-à-vis* other current advertisements. Although recall tests measure consumers' propensity to remember the advertisement, there is some doubt as to whether recall is a good measure of advertising effectiveness (e.g. Perry and Perry 1976). A high level of attention and recall can be obtained, while not necessarily achieving the required influence upon shoppers' feelings and beliefs about the retailer. Day-after recall testing is less common in Europe than in the USA (Twyman 1986), although other recall tests are applied. For example, Marketing (1988) compared levels of spontaneous recall with levels of expenditure. In the latter part of 1987, Boots was the only retail advertiser to appear in the Adwatch top 20 'recall league', which was attributed to their pre-Christmas advertising burst. In view of the fact that 10 of the top 20 'expenditure league' were retailers, this suggests that most retail advertising does not score highly on this type of measure. The campaigns that achieved high recall tended to be strong on creativity and to use some special humorous or emotional approach, usually with a media mix biased towards television.

Advertising tracking   Some of the limitations of the short-term recall measures can be overcome with regular or continuous measurement of advertising awareness and attitudes towards the retailer. Some of the specific techniques available for this purpose have already been discussed in the context of image measurement in Chapter 5. Tracking studies have the advantage of recording changes over time, rather than levels of awareness/belief at a specific point in time. They also record the effects of the total advertising input and other market influences, yet can estimate the relative effects of specific advertisements or campaigns within the overall time period.

Area experimentation   This type of approach involves the administration of different advertising levels and/or content in different areas; this provides a good assessment of overall effectiveness and also enables comparisons to be made between different advertising treatments. Although essentially post-test measures, area experiments may precede the major campaign. For example, when seeking to shift their image from that of just a renter of televisions and videos, Granada tested various pilot campaigns in Grampian and Scottish regions (Ody 1987). The approach does however require careful experimental design to take account of all the factors that cannot be matched between areas. In the USA, 'Ad labs' have been established which carefully match sets of homes for their location, retail environment, exposure to other advertising, etc. (Twyman 1986).

Another variant upon area experimentation is 'split-run' testing. Mason and Mayer (1987) described the split-run facilities offered by some newspapers; different versions of an advertisement are given an identical position within the newspaper but are distributed to different sectors of the circulation. The more widespread use of cable television will provide increased opportunities for split-run testing, especially if the advertisements are designed to stimulate interactive cable or telephone response (see Chapter 2). Coupons also provide a convenient way of monitoring the effects of newspaper magazine or direct mail advertisements, using split-run or area experimentation. Chapman (1986) reported a field experiment in which the effects of different direct mail and coupon treatments were monitored at relatively low cost.

Sales analysis   In that sales are normally the ultimate objective of advertising, their analysis would appear to provide the strongest measure of advertising effectiveness. However, numerous other marketing inputs, competitor activities and changes in the market can also influence sales; the problems of isolating advertising effects are therefore considerable, even in the analysis of short-term effects. The development of point-of-sale scanners has increased the opportunities for monitoring short-term sales effects by providing timely and product-specific data, although the problems of monitoring longer-term and more general effects remain. Information derived from scanners and customer identification devices, such as store credit cards, can however assist in estimating the longer-term sales effects of a campaign targeted at specific customer segments.

Another fundamental weakness of the sales analysis approach is that only the overall relationship between advertising and sales is estimated. Unless supplemented with other research approaches, nothing may be learnt of the intermediary processes by which those additional sales may have been stimulated. Specifically, if the strengths and weaknesses of the advertisements are not isolated, the wrong elements may be developed or deleted as the campaign is evolved.

10.3.2   Advertising and price effects

Although price offers no longer dominate the content of mainstream retail advertising, they are still a very important element in many contexts. Most retailers of fast-moving consumer goods devote some of their advertising effort to traffic-building promotions, often funded by co-operative advertising money. Retailers of consumer durables also tend to revert to specific price claims, at least when sale times are being advertised. It is not the purpose of this section to review the legal or public policy issues relating to bargain offer claims; readers may wish to consult Brave (1983), Fulop (1988) and Department of Trade and Industry (1988) for such reviews. The purpose here is to look at some of the evidence relating to the effects of price advertising and the credibility of advertised price reductions.

Keiser and Krum (1976) investigated the effect and credibility of alternative price advertising systems for Right Guard deodorant. They found that advertisements containing two prices, i.e. an explicitly claimed price reduction, were more effective than single-price advertisements in persuading customers that the prices were lower than normal. Although most respondents believed the specific claim made in the advertisement, over two-thirds did not feel that newspaper advertisements in general were accurate or that they would influence their purchase decision.

A more elaborate methodology was utilized by Berkowitz and Walton (1980), who examined the effects on consumer price responses of various contextual influences of the advertisement. Among the significant findings were the effects of the exact semantics used to announce the price reduction, with a further interaction with the image of the advertising store. Their findings suggested that the exact wording of a price-oriented advertisement should be chosen with care and fitted to the trading position of the retailer, especially whether or not the retailer is perceived to be generally price-oriented. Monroe and Della Bitta (1981) examined consumer responses to eight different ways of presenting price reductions. They found that the presentation of the regular price and the money amount off was the most positively evaluated format; those showing the reduction in percentage terms were less well evaluated. Research by Bearden et al. (1984) suggested that the effects of including reference prices on consumers' intentions to purchase differed according to the product type advertised and its price level.

On the credibility of advertised price savings, Blair and Landon (1981) found that consumers generally do not accept reference prices at face value but still tend to attribute higher savings than if the reference prices were not present. This study was based upon electrical goods, which were also two of the three items in an earlier study by Fry and McDougall (1974). They found substantial distrust of reference prices but the credibility of the price claim in general was greatly affected by consumer perceptions of the stores involved. As noted by Keiser and Krum (1976), however, even when the price claim is believed, the customer is not necessarily significantly more likely to patronize the store.

Liefeld and Heslop (1985) studied reactions to five different price advertisement formats, three of which referred to a sale and the 'sale price'. They found that the mention of a sale reduced the credibility of the reference price:

This observation suggests that consumers are very suspicious of price claims made in a sale situation and discount their perceptions of the ordinary price by amounts which were in this case excessive, leading them to seriously understate the true ordinary selling prices.

The researchers concluded that the sale context is so over-used, and manufacturers' suggested list prices so rarely actually charged, that such claims are greatly discounted and distrusted.

Studies have been undertaken to assess the combined effects on sales of changes in advertising and retail prices, although these mainly adopt the manufacturer viewpoint. There is some disagreement as to whether advertising generally increases or decreases price sensitivity. Some argue that advertising creates a 'barrier to entry' within a market which inhibits entry by lower-cost operators (e.g. Vernon 1972). Others, such as Eskin (1975), have found that high advertising can create considerably greater price sensitivity. Wittink (1977) found support for the latter view, as did Eskin and Baron (1977) in relation to new products. Wittink explained the former view in terms of higher price and higher advertising being typical characteristics of successfully differentiated products, which is not necessarily indicative of advertising reducing price sensitivity. From a carefully controlled experiment involving the variation of advertising levels and retail prices, Prasad and Ring (1976) found that the nature of the interaction was heavily influenced by the message and the media of the advertisements.

Moriarty (1983) utilized point-of-sale scanner data relating to sales of an (unspecified) food product in five stores over a period of 92 weeks. Prices and advertising were not experimentally manipulated, although sufficient variation occurred in the prices and advertisements in three of the stores to allow detailed analysis in those cases. The interaction effects of price and advertising proved to be significant and negative, leading to the conclusion that the combined effect of the two marketing inputs is greater than the sum of the two effects used individually. Other studies of price/advertising effects include those of Nielsen (1983), who examined correlations between price and sales levels under different conditions of advertising. They found that a relationship could be established between sales and advertising/pricing combined; a considerable proportion of sales changes could be accounted for by price changes alone, unless the advertising by competitors reached a certain critical level.

In practice, retail advertising and pricing strategies are rarely conducted in isolation from other elements of the mix, especially display. Curhan (1974) investigated the effects of temporary changes in price, advertising, display space and display location upon the sales of fresh fruit and vegetables in supermarkets. The results varied considerably between individual products; advertising had the greatest influence upon the sales of higher-priced items within the 'less visible' product groups, such as cooking vegetables. For the more 'visible' products, such as salad vegetables and soft fruit, advertising had little direct effect, presumably because customers tend to 'shop' these departments.

Wilkinson et al. (1981, 1982) also investigated the effects of advertising, price reductions and display changes and found that, of the three variables, advertising generally achieved the least short-term effect. It should be noted however that Curhan (1974) and Wilkinson et al. (1981, 1982) were measuring short-term and product-specific sales effects. This does not take into account the longer-term effects of advertising on overall sales, as for example investigated by Doyle and Fenwick (1975), or the more general benefit to store image.

SUMMARY

For most major retailers, advertising provides the main channel of communication with existing and potential customers, outside the store itself. The specific objectives of advertising should be carefully defined: these may include various approaches to attracting new customers, increasing the expenditure of existing customers, building store traffic, increasing product sales or enhancing the store image. It is essential that all advertising and promotional activities be used as part of an overall strategy, not run in isolation or as a substitute for an adequate strategy.

Retailers continue to be among the major media advertisers in the UK, with an overall expenditure in 1987 of £441 million. Although this had grown by almost 50 per cent in the preceding five years, most of this growth was accounted for by cost inflation. Some retail categories, notably the grocery multiples and co-ops, have reduced expenditure in real terms, in part because of merger activity, shifts in the media mix and changes in overall strategy. Advertising tends to represent around 2 per cent or less of sales in most cases, although there are some exceptional expenditures of 5–10 per cent of sales.

Part of the high expenditure on advertising has been supported by manufacturers' advertising allowances, or 'vertical co-operative advertising'. For the largest retailers, these have tended to become just another discount, without which the manufacturer's products would not be promoted or maybe not even stocked. For small–medium-sized retailers, co-operative advertising can provide access to more powerful media, bring additional prestige and create profitable linkages to manufacturer campaigns. However, co-operative advertising has tended to give retail advertising an excessive product/price emphasis and often has led to the promotion of inappropriate products, in terms of the retailer's image and profitability.

Another consequence of excessive price emphasis was a certain sameness in retail advertising, with each company offering a similar set of offers in a similar format. The approach also tends to induce shopping around, whereas most retailers need to build loyalty. Obviously, not all retailers can offer the lowest prices, so attention needs to be shifted to more credible and sustainable areas of differentiation. Although many retailers continue to provide price/value reassurance within their campaigns, the major emphasis has turned to promoting other benefit areas, building longer-term store images and increased customer loyalty.

Because of the high cost and advertising 'clutter' in many established media, some retailers have become increasingly skilled at other forms of publicity. By creating or sponsoring newsworthy events, high attention and credibility can be achieved, as well as possibly media coverage at low cost. Social events, fashion shows and spectacular store openings are now among the ways of attracting publicity. Sponsorship of many different types has also been used, partly for the publicity benefits and partly in pursuit of personnel or welfare policies; sports sponsorship in particular has attracted major expenditure and interest.

Decisions on how much to spend on media advertising must be set within the retailer's promotional mix and overall strategic objectives. A number of approaches are adopted in setting advertising budgets, with varying degrees of merit. Some see a given percentage of sales as a rule of thumb, whereas others perceive a need to achieve a competitive parity in advertising expenditures. The more logical approach is to define the precise objectives, then determine the specific advertising tasks and costs required to achieve these.

Although many major retailers have extensive marketing departments, most use the services of one or more advertising agency. The agency can provide an outside perspective upon the characteristics of the market and the retailer's competitive position. Inputs can also be provided to strategic planning and in the formulation of advertising objectives. The agency also provides or obtains specialist creative and media planning services. The agency–retailer relationship is usually not long-term; only 29 per cent of retail accounts were held over a five-year period, the main reasons for leaving an agency being disappointing results, the need for new ideas, or poor service.

Determining the appropriate content and message of retail advertisements requires both creativity and a systematic appraisal of the company's strengths and weaknesses, both real and perceived. If an adequate volume and quality of consumer research data are available, computerized decision support systems have been developed which seek to maximize the advertising appeal to specific target groups. Detailed attention must also be paid to each precise element of the advertising content; the words, print faces, pictures, actors, etc., all communicate impressions of the retailer and store.

The choice of media types and specific media vehicles is very large indeed. Newspapers continue to attract the largest proportion of retail advertising expenditure; local newspapers in particular provide relatively good geographical selectivity and low wastage. Television provides high impact but, because of high costs and waste circulation, is being given less emphasis now by some retailers. Magazines have been adopted by some as major vehicles for image building campaigns; the vast range of specialist titles also achieves high selectivity. Direct mail, although expensive, has become an increasingly popular and effective means of communication, assisted by store credit records and other data files of addresses.

In planning the media mix, the advertiser must compare the costs of each available media vehicle, relative to the number of exposures and the impact achieved. Clearly, the number of effective exposures is not equal to the total circulation or audience. Similarly, the impact achieved in a given media vehicle depends upon the advertising message and characteristics of the target audience. In producing the detailed schedule of media use, the retailer may be influenced by strong seasonality in the sales of many product categories. A number of computer-based models have been evolved to assist in media mix and scheduling decisions.

In spite of their large expenditures on advertising, many retailers have not systematically monitored its effects. Changes in sales or store traffic may be caused by many other factors; rigorous experimental and/or statistical methods are therefore required to estimate the advertising effects. Prior to the campaign launch, pre-testing facilities can be used to minimize risk of failure; area experiments may then be used to test the effectiveness of alternative creative/media treatments. Campaign effectiveness can be fully measured only through a series of pre- and post-testing procedures.

The effectiveness of specific price claims in retail advertising remains an important issue in many contexts. Studies have shown that the credibility and effectiveness of price reductions depend upon the retailer's general reputation and the format used in the advertisement; specifically, there is evidence that the terms 'sale' and 'sale price' reduce the credibility of the stated savings. The evaluation of advertising and price effects on product sales is inevitably confounded by many other influences, notably product/brand type, display and other in-store variables.

REVIEW QUESTIONS

1. Taking a retail company of your choice, how should that company define its specific advertising objectives?
2. Explain why many retailers are among the major spenders on media advertising in the UK. Why do you think that media advertising expenditure, in real terms, has recently declined in some cases?
3. How would you evaluate the advantages and drawbacks of vertical co-operative advertising agreements if you were advising
   (a) an independent electrical goods retailer?
   (b) a large grocery chain?
4. 'Price as a platform can only ever be your tactical weapon—it can never be your strategy.' Discuss the validity of this statement in relation to the advertising emphasis of three different types of retailer.
5. Evelute some of the alternative approaches to attracting favourable publicity, other than by conventional advertising.
6. In establishing retail advertising budgets, compare the benefits and limitations of
   (a) the percentage of sales method.
   (b) the competitive parity method.
   (c) the objective and task method.
7. Describe the role of advertising agencies in relation to retail clients. If you were an account director in an agency, how would you set about attracting and retaining a major retail client?

8. Explain the concept of the 'identity prism'. How could this assist in determining the content of advertisements for
   (a) teenage fashion boutiques?
   (b) exclusive furniture stores?
9. Evaluate the strengths and limitations of (a) television and (b) newspapers as media for retail advertising. Why has the use of direct mail advertising increased in recent years?
10. Discuss the importance of seasonality in the scheduling of media advertising. Under what circumstances is a continuous or a concentrated schedule of advertising more appropriate?
11. Compare and contrast the following approaches to the assessment of advertising effectiveness:
    (a) pre-testing.
    (b) advertising recall tests.
    (c) area experimentation.
12. In what ways can the context and format of advertised price reductions affect
    (a) the credibility of the advertisement?
    (b) the consumers' purchase intentions?

REFERENCES

Admap (1987), 'The ADMAP press media race—1986', *Admap*, no. 260, 55–7.
Alexander, R. S. (1960), *Marketing Definitions: A Glossary of Marketing Terms*, American Marketing Association, Chicago.
Allaway, A., J. B. Mason and G. Brown (1987), 'An optimal decision support model for department-level promotion mix planning', *Journal of Retailing*, 63(3), 215–42.
Bearden, W. O., D. R. Lichtenstein and J. E. Teel (1984), 'Comparison price, coupon, and brand effects on consumer reactions to retail newspaper advertisements', *Journal of Retailing*, 60(2), 11–34.
Berkowitz, E. N. and J. R. Walton (1980), 'Contextual influences on consumer price responses: an experimental analysis, *Journal of Marketing Research*, 17(3), 349–58.
Berman, B. and J. R. Evans (1979), *Retail Management: a Strategic Approach*, Macmillan, New York.
Blair, E. A. and E. L. Landon (1981), 'The effects of reference prices in retail advertisements', *Journal of Marketing*, 45(2), 61–9.
Bolen, W. H. (1988), *Contemporary Retailing*, Prentice-Hall, Englewood Cliffs, NJ.
Bowen-Jones, C. (1987), 'Making a meal of ad. expenditure figures', *Marketing*, 12 February, 8.
Brave, J. (1983), *Law for Retailers*, Sweet & Maxwell, London.
Britton, N. (1988), 'Next puts its fashions on the screen', *Marketing*, 14 January, 1.
Carter, C. (1977), 'As quick as a price flash', *Campaign*, 18 November, 49–50.
Challiner, M. (1982), 'Where are we growing', in *JWT 81*, J. Walter Thompson, Manchester, pp. 12–13.
Chapman, R. G. (1986), 'Assessing the profitability of retailer couponing with a low-cost field experiment', *Journal of Retailing*, 62(1), 19–40.
Cohen, A. I. and A. L. Jones (1978), 'Brand marketing in the new retail environment', *Harvard Business Review*, 56(5), 141–8.
Coles, E. (1987), 'The quiet revolution', *British Business*, 9 January, 28–9.
Curhan, R. C. (1974), 'The effects of merchandising and temporary promotional activities on the sales of fresh fruit and vegetables in supermarkets', *Journal of Marketing Research*, 11(3), 286–94.
Curhan, R. C. and R. J. Kopp (1987/8), 'Obtaining retailer support for trade deals: key success factors', *Journal of Advertising Research*, 27(6), 51–60.
Davies, K., C. Gilligan and C. Sutton (1985), 'Structural changes in grocery retailing: the implications of competition', *International Journal of Physical Distribution & Materials Management*, 15(2), 1–48.
Department of Trade and Industry (1988), *Code of Practice for Traders on Price Indications*, DTI, London.
Douglas, T. (1988), 'Spotting 1987's big spenders', *Marketing Week*, 10(46), 15.
Doyle, P. and I. Fenwick (1975), 'An experimental design for measuring advertising payoff', *Operational Research Quarterly*, 26(4), 693–702.
Edwards, C. M. and C. F. Lebowitz (1981), *Retail Advertising and Sales Promotion*, Prentice-Hall, Englewood Cliffs, NJ.
Eskin, G. J. (1975), 'A case for test market experiments', *Journal of Advertising Research*, 15(2), 27–33.

Eskin, G. J. and P. H. Baron (1977), 'Effects of price and advertising in test-market experiments', *Journal of Marketing Research*, **14**(4), 499–508.

Feick, L. F. and L. L. Price (1987), 'The market maven: a diffuser of marketplace information', *Journal of Marketing*, **51**(1), 83–97.

Fry, J. N. and G. H. McDougall (1974), 'Consumer appraisal of retail price advertisements', *Journal of Marketing*, **38**(3), 64–74.

Fulop, C. (1987), 'The role of advertising in the retail marketing mix', *Fourth International Conference on Distribution*, CESCOM, Milan.

Fulop, C. (1988), 'Public policy and a marketing technique 1969–1986: comparative pricing and bargain offer claims' in E. Kaynak (ed.), *Transnational Retailing*, Walter de Gruyter, Berlin, pp. 197–207.

Gardner, M. P. and M. J. Houston (1986), 'The effects of verbal and visual components of retail communications', *Journal of Retailing*, **62**(1), 64–78.

Gofton, K. (1988), 'Hiring and firing', *Marketing*, 7 January, 31–2.

Green, P. E., V. Mahajan, S. M. Goldberg and P. K. Kedia (1984), 'A decision-support system for developing retail promotional strategy', *Journal of Retailing*, **59**(3), 116–43.

Guha, P. (1987), 'Cup that cheers for Littlewoods', *Marketing*, 28 May, 27.

Haight, W. (1976), *Retail Advertising: Management and Technique*, General Learning Press, Morristown, NJ.

Henry, H. (1988), 'The ADMAP press media race—1987', *Admap*, no. 271, 64–8.

Higie, R. A., L. F. Feick and L. L. Price (1987), 'Types and amount of word-of-mouth communications about retailers', *Journal of Retailing*, **63**(3), 260–78.

Jolson, M. A. (1979), 'How a retailer compared newspapers', *Journal of Advertising Research*, **19**(6), 29–32.

Jones, B. (1977), 'Retailing it just like it is', *Campaign*, 18 November, 40–1.

Kapferer, J.-N. (1986), 'Beyond positioning: retailer's identity', in *Retail Strategies for Profit and Growth*, ESOMAR, Amsterdam, pp. 167–75.

Kaufman, L. (1980), *Essentials of Advertising*, Harcourt, Brace Jovanovich, New York.

Keiser, S. K. and J. R. Krum (1976), 'Consumer perceptions of retail advertising with overstated price savings', *Journal of Retailing*, **52**(3), 27–36.

Kleimenhagen, A. K., D. G. Leeseberg and B. A. Eilers (1972), 'Consumer response to special promotions of regional shopping centres', *Journal of Retailing*, **48**(1), 22–9, 95.

Kotler, P. (1988), *Marketing Management: Analysis, Planning Implementation and Control*, Prentice-Hall, Englewood Cliffs, NJ.

Krugman, H. E. (1975), 'What makes advertising effective', *Harvard Business Review*, **53**(2), 96–103.

Liefeld, J. and L. A. Heslop (1985), 'Reference prices and deception in newspaper advertising', *Journal of Consumer Research*, **11**(4), 868–76.

Lynn, J. R. (1981), 'Newspaper ad. impact in nonmetropolitan markets', *Journal of Advertising Research*, **21**(4), 13–19.

Marketing (1988), 'Top 500 brands', *Marketing*, 25 February, 24–37.

Marketing Week (1985), 'Sainsbury in rethink on £3.5M. Saatchi business', *Marketing Week*, **7**(49), 14.

Mason, J. B. and M. L. Mayer (1987), *Modern Retailing: Theory and Practice*, Business Publications, Plano, Texas.

McEwan, F. (1987), 'Business sponsorship—marriage of convenience', *Financial Times*, 9 November, 15.

Miles, L. (1987), 'Sporting life', *Marketing*, 28 May, 26–8.

Mintel (1987), *Opportunities in Sponsorships*, Mintel, London.

Mintel (1988), 'Retail advertising—its place in the marketing mix', *Retail Intelligence*, **1**, 4.1–4.27.

Monroe, K. B. and A. J. Della Bitta (1981), 'The influence of comparative price advertisements on patronage behaviour', in R. F. Lusch and W. R. Darden (eds.), *Retail Patronage Theory 1981 Workshop Proceedings*, University of Oklahoma, Norman, Ok., pp. 20–6.

Moriarty, M. (1983), 'Feature advertising—price interaction effects in the retail environment', *Journal of Retailing*, **59**(2), 80–98.

Neill, R. (1980), 'The retailer speaks to the customer: the future for retail advertising', *Retail & Distribution Management*, **8**(4), 29–32.

Nielsen (1983), 'A price sensitivity study', *Nielsen Researcher*, **1**, 4–6.

Nielsen, J. (1974), 'How to use advertising effectively', *Retail & Distribution Management*, **2**(3), 26–9.

Ody, P. (1987), 'How effective is your advertising?' *Retail & Distribution Management*, **15**(1), 9–12, 60.

Otker, T. (1988), 'Exploitation: the key to sponsorship success', *European Research*, **16**(2), 77–86.

Perry, M. and A. Perry (1976), 'Recall: biased measure of media', *Journal of Advertising Research*, **16**(3), 21–5.

Poster Scene (1987), 'Posters make the advertising £ go further', *Poster Scene*, **2**, 22–3.

Prasad, V. K. and L. W. Ring (1976), 'Measuring sales effects of some marketing mix variables and their interactions', *Journal of Marketing Research*, **13**(4), 391–6.

Roberts, A. and S. Prentice (1978), 'Burst vs continuous advertising', *Admap*, no. 154, 178–82.

Rowney, P. (1986), 'The rise of the mail', *Marketing Week*, **9**(5), 51–2.

Sharman, H. (1987), 'Which brands spend what—and where', *Marketing Week*, **10**(17), 31–9.

Snoddy, R. (1988), 'Study into cost of TV adverts', *Financial Times*, 26 January, 6.

Soley, L. C. and W. L. James (1982), 'Estimating the readership of retail newspaper advertising', *Journal of Retailing*, **58**(3), 59–75.

Spitzer, H. and F. R. Schwartz (1982), *Inside Retail Sales Promotion and Advertising*, Harper & Row, New York.

Sponsorship News (1986), 'Car meetings: name three sponsors', *Sponsorship News*, December, 9.

Teel, J. E. and W. O. Bearden (1980), 'A media planning algorithm for retail advertisers', *Journal of Retailing*, **56**(4), 23–39.

Thorncroft, A. (1987), 'Hunt is on for imaginative tie-ups', *Financial Times*, 9 November, 17.

Turner, S. (1987), *Practical Sponsorship*, Kogan Page, London.

Twyman, A. (1986), 'Monitoring advertising performance: a canter round the field', *Admap*, no. 250, 131–5.

Vernon, J. M. (1972), *Market Structure and Industrial Performance: a Review of Statistical Findings*, Allyn and Bacon, Boston.

Walters, D. and D. White (1987), *Retail Marketing Management*, Macmillan, Basingstoke.

Ward, J. (1985), 'Retailers and advertising: who's changing who?' *Retail*, **3**(3), 8–9.

Warner, L. (1988), 'Sainsbury's tries a smile', *Marketing*, 17 March, 1.

Whitaker, J. (1983), 'To spend, or not to spend?' *Nielsen Researcher*, **2**, 2–15.

White, K. R., C. T. Anzalone and D. Barbour (1980), 'The effectiveness of shopper guides', *Journal of Advertising Research*, **20**(2), 17–24.

Wilkinson, J. B., J. B. Mason and C. H. Paksoy (1982), 'Assessing the impact of short-term supermarket strategy variables', *Journal of Marketing Research*, **19**(1), 72–86.

Wilkinson, J. B., C. H. Paksoy and J. B. Mason (1981), 'A demand analysis of newspaper advertising and changes in space allocation', *Journal of Retailing*, **57**(2), 30–48.

Wittink, D. R. (1977), 'Advertising increases sensitivity to price', *Journal of Advertising Research*, **17**(2), 39–42.

Wright, R. (1988), 'Measuring awareness of British football sponsorship', *European Research*, **16**(2), 104–9.

Yorke, D. A. and P. J. Kitchen (1985), 'Channel flickers and video speeders', *Journal of Advertising Research*, **25**(2), 21–5.

Young, R. F. and S. A. Greyser (1983), *Managing Co-operative Advertising: a Strategic Approach*, D.C. Heath, Lexington, Mass.

ELEVEN

THE SELLING ENVIRONMENT

INTRODUCTION

In all forms of store-based retailing, decisions relating to the design and arrangement of the store environment are now key elements of the retail market mix. In the 1960s, the spread of self-service retailing in many sectors emphasized the need to make the most cost-effective use of in-store selling space. The rapid development of large new stores from the 1970s drew attention to the need to consider the store selling environment as a whole, to ensure that the shopping experience is convenient and attractive. From the 1980s, there has been considerable emphasis upon store design, which has been used as a powerful weapon in the quest to achieve image differentiation.

This chapter considers each of these elements in creating the selling environment, starting with the overall design of stores, which could be seen as an extension of retail advertising and promotion. The concept of atmospherics is explored, as are elements of environmental psychology which are relevant to the design of the retail environment. Decisions regarding store layout and product display are then considered, including measures of display effectiveness. Attention then turns to the detailed allocation of display space, the concept of space elasticity, and systems for allocating space between categories and individual products. Finally, concepts and measures of unplanned purchasing are examined, this representing one of the main effects of a well designed selling environment. The focus is therefore upon the store itself and on its dual role of attracting customers and maximizing their purchases within the store. Personal selling is discussed in the next chapter within the overall context of retail service.

It is appropriate at this stage to comment on the term 'merchandising', in order to avoid ambiguities. To manufacturers, the scope of merchandising may be almost as wide as that of retailing itself. In the USA, retailers also tend to adopt a broad definition of the term; for example:

merchandising encompasses the areas of merchandise planning, merchandise resources, negotiating for merchandise, merchandise distribution and merchandise control. (Bolen 1988)

In the UK, retailers usually ascribe a more specific meaning to the term. Rogers (1985) lists the merchandise mix, space allocation and product placement as being the primary scope of merchandising. The role of 'merchandising managers' does however vary enormously between companies. Because of its many different definitions and connotations, the term 'merchandising' is used sparingly.

11.1 DESIGN AND ATMOSPHERE

In the last ten years there has been enormous investment by retailers and shopping centre developers in new store designs and refurbishments. Accordingly, a major new industry has developed, as design companies have shifted attention to the design of the retail selling environments. As yet, a strong conceptual framework for retail design has not been developed, although promising contributions have been made in the study of retail 'atmospherics'. This section first looks at the current role, scope and effectiveness of retail design, then considers some of the conceptual and empirical research findings that are relevant to this function.

11.1.1 Store design

The design function has become one of the most visible elements of retail positioning strategy. In the UK, the early trend-setters were considered to be George Davies, previously with the Next chain, and Terence Conran with Habitat. Very good store designs have of course existed for many years but, until relatively recently, the retail industry in general was characterized by rather dull and uniform selling environments. Now design has come to be recognized as a vital strategic function and is therefore receiving far more specialist attention. Mintel (1985) defined retail design as:

the visual result of a conceptual approach to store design and merchandising display. Its aim is to increase customer appeal as part of the retail marketing strategy.

Store design also plays a very direct role in affecting customers' in-store behaviour:

The designer must create a store that encourages the shopper, once inside, to lower his psychological defenses and become interested in the merchandise. If the customer is relaxed and interested, he may then ask a salesperson for assistance or take the time to evaluate the product himself and subsequently make the purchase. (Green 1986)

The demand for more exciting store designs is seen as being largely consumer-led. Expectations have been widened by increased travel, highly developed media and a greater diversity of leisure activities. There is also a growing need to establish some degree of individuality, which is particularly manifest in the purchasing of furniture and fashion goods. The selling environment should therefore make a positive statement about what the products can do to make the shopper a more interesting individual (Calcott 1980). The role of the retail designer has progressed from shopfitting to the provision of entertainment and inspiration to customers, thus creating added value in using the store (Mintel 1985).

Having defined the target customer segments, retail design can assist in focusing the store upon their needs, while also 'getting away from the curse of the average' (McFadyen 1981). Thomas (1987) pointed out that there are other reasons, good and not so good, for implementing design changes. Some retailers have refurbished stores simply because the competition has done so; others have tried design as a last resort when everything else has failed. Practical reasons may dictate the need for design changes, such as changing product assortments or the need to make better use of space. Whatever the motives, the use of design is unlikely to be successful unless it is integrated with merchandise policy, pricing, advertising and other elements of the strategic mix (Brown 1979).

The scope of a store design project depends upon the existing conditions and limitations, the marketing strategy of the retailer and, of course, the available budget. In the case of new stores and centres where few prior limitations exist, the potential scope of the design function is very

Table 11.1   Total visual merchandising process

Store environment design	Merchandise presentation	In-store customer communications	Consumer senses appeal
Store facade	Major trends	Signs	Sight
Decor	Store layout	Tickets	
Walls	Presentation	Product	Hearing
	methods	information	
Floors	Assortment		Smell
	organization	Graphics	Taste
Ceilings	Category		
Lighting	co-ordination	Sound	Touch
Atmosphere	Sample displays	Textures	Concept
Design integrity		Entertainment	—ideas
	Featuring	Education	—images
Fixtures	Lighting		
Communications	Colours	Active	
Heating &		promotions	
ventilation		Personal	
Services		services	
Interior		Cash points	
partitioning			
Modular			
systems			

Source: Management Horizons (UK) Ltd.

wide indeed. It could encompass all facets of internal and external design, fixtures, fittings and forms of communications with the customer. Table 11.1 summarizes the 'total visual merchandising process', as defined by Management Horizons (UK). In practice, a retailer may define a far more restricted design brief, although the designer should ensure that these elements are harmonized in order to avoid incongruity.

Readers may find numerous accounts of retail design projects within the pages of the practitioner journals and magazines. For example, Retail (1987) described the work of Landor Associates in redesigning the exclusive Dunhill Shop in the St James area of London. As part of the redesign, the entrance was moved to a corner position and made somewhat less intimidating to customers; overall, the store moved from a 'clubby' and traditional atmosphere to one of elegance and leisure. The new design for Greggs bakeries, developed by Crabtree Hall, is also described. Here again, attention was given to softening the entrance and removing the barrier that traditional shop doorways represent. In this case, it was achieved by a special counter which curves round in line with the store frontage. The Greggs redesign took care not to give the impression of moving up-market, as the company wished to retain its successful mass market position.

Designers of new stores in the UK are more restricted by planning regulations than their counterparts in some other countries (see Chapter 6). Some of the more bizarre and eye-catching store exteriors to be found in the USA cannot therefore be emulated. However, there has been a movement towards more distinctive and attractive exteriors, which can actually help in obtaining permission to build. The architects of Asda's Harrogate store set out to reflect the Edwardian character of the neighbourhood, using a design that incorporated gables and turrets, with decorative stone, slate and ironwork (Sharples 1986). The Homebase DIY warehouse at Catford adopts the theme of a Victorian greenhouse, with extensive use of plate glass and PVC domed roofs (Sharples 1985). Situated next to an existing pond, this offers an eye-catching design, elements of which have been copied in many other new store exteriors.

Design has also become a major competitive weapon for shopping centres, as they too seek new ways of establishing their competitive differentials. Marking (1986) described the additional problems involved in designing attractive and effective shopping centres:

In motivating consumers through a building, the desire for visual variety can play a large part. Retailers use it in the same way that classical gardens were designed—to provide surprise and delight: each new entrance reveals a new vista with its own special atmosphere and treasures beyond. Shopping centres have great trouble duplicating this come-on factor. Unexpectedness is rare because each floor or area is created to be a matching part of the whole complex.

Very large new centres, such as the Gateshead Metrocentre, have sought to overcome this problem by a diversity of materials and design within the different malls. Other older centres have sought to increase diversity within their refurbishment programmes.

The role of design consultants has now assumed major significance, as the majority of retailers have sought outside advice for at least some of their design projects. Mintel (1985) reported that, among 44 retailer companies, 34 had utilized design consultants. The fashion and consumer durables retailers had made the most extensive use of consultants, whereas the retailers of fast-moving consumer goods tended to rely more on in-house designers. Euromonitor (1987) estimated that there were around 40 design companies in the UK with overall turnovers in excess of £1 million. The four largest, in terms of their 1985 retail design income, were:

1. Fitch & Co. (£5.0 m)
2. Conran Design Group (£3.0 m)
3. Stewart McColl Associates (£3.5 m)
4. Allied International Designers (£3.0 m)

In that design consultants are understandably keen to communicate their benefits to the retail industry, many reviews and accounts of their work are published (e.g. Sharples 1983; Market Place 1986).

The majority of retailers feel that the design consultants understand the needs of their business (Mintel 1985), although some misunderstandings and mismatches have inevitably occurred. In such circumstances, the designer may claim that the brief was wrong, the retailer that the brief was not understood (Humphreys 1987). One reaction to this has been the preparation of far more comprehensive and explicit briefs, sometimes to the point of 'overbriefing' the consultants. Clearly, a close working relationship must exist if the retailer–designer partnership is going to be effective. There are some indications that larger retailers are starting to turn away from outside consultancies. A postal survey of 100 leading retailers showed that 70 per cent had used design companies in the last three years, and 64 per cent intended to use one in the next three years (Euromonitor 1987). There have also been reactions against design for its own sake:

design seems to be suffering from an attack of self-importance—it would appear to be an end in itself rather than a means to an end. (Retail & Distribution Management 1987).

the design revamp has been over-hyped and over-done—there are endless other opportunities for better retailing. (Thomas 1987)

Table 11.2 Success ratings of retail design

	Change of image (%)	Increasing store traffic (%)	Increasing average spend (%)
Better than expected	25	15	9
As expected	43	61	56
Not as good as expected	11	5	7
Don't know	14	14	23
Not an objective	7	5	5

N = 44 retailers

Source: Mintel (1985).

These comments reflect the new and entirely healthy scepticism towards the overselling of design. Without the necessary strategic thinking, design programmes have sometimes simply created a new type of uniformity, rather than the differentiation that was intended. In general, however, retailers claim to be satisfied with the results of retail design changes. Table 11.2 indicates the success ratings given by 44 retailers in the Mintel (1985) survey. The success of the design is rated in terms of change of image, increased store traffic and increasing spending in the store.

The costs of retail design programmes have now become a major concern. In the early stages of the design boom, Fitch (1981) was advocating the relative cheapness of new shop frontages and interiors, especially when compared with the costs of media advertising. In recent years, some retailers' design programmes have represented very major expenditures, for example a two-year programme costing £500 million for Marks & Spencer and a five-year, £60 million programme for British Home Stores (Mintel 1985). The life-cycle of a design has also become far shorter, especially in the fashion sector. A new design may last only three years; in the extreme case of a refurbishment for Burton's Top Shop, the new look lasted only 18 months (Thomas 1987).

The high costs of design programmes, coupled with doubts about the results in some cases, have brought a new emphasis upon cost/effectiveness in design. As in the early days of extensive television advertising by retailers, there was tendency to allocate large, 'me-too' budgets, without adequate consideration of strategic objectives. A more disciplined approach to retail design is now emerging, with more careful specifications by retailers, a higher proportion of in-house design work, and greater attention to cost control. Thomas (1987) cites an example in which the retailer sacked one design company and brought in a new team, reducing refurbishment costs from £250,000 to £100,000 per store unit.

11.2.2 Atmospherics in retailing

The high cost of retail design programmes and, in some cases, their lack of commercial success should underline the need for a scientific approach to the design of retail environments. In too many cases the designs have done no more than imitate others, have been based upon 'packaged concepts', or have simply been aesthetically pleasing. Some major design companies have developed research functions, but the science of 'atmospherics' is still in its infancy. Kotler (1973) defined atmospherics as:

the conscious designing of space to create certain effects in buyers. More specifically, atmospherics is the effort to design buying environments to produce specific emotional effects in the buyer that enhance his purchase probability.

He maintained that the atmosphere of a particular environment could be described in terms of the sensory channels through which the atmosphere is apprehended. The four main dimensions of atmosphere, in the retail context, are therefore:

1. Visual (sight)
   - Colour
   - Brightness
   - Size
   - Shapes
2. Aural (sound)
   - Volume
   - Pitch
3. Olfactory (smell)
   - Scent
   - Freshness
4. Tactile (touch)
   - Softness
   - Smoothness
   - Temperature

Each of these dimensions is likely to be incorporated within a store design, but the specific effects should be carefully monitored. For example, it has become common for supermarkets with in-store bakeries to arrange that the smell of fresh baked bread be apparent around the store entrance. In department stores, the aromas of the perfume counters, often situated in prime locations near entrances, are intended to create an elegant ambiance. The tactile dimension may be influenced by the choice of flooring materials, the texture of counters and displays, and the efficiency of the heating/air conditioning system. It is easy to assume the effects of these variables upon shopper behaviour, but far more rigorous testing is required.

A director of a large retail chain recently enquired about research into the effects of music upon shoppers. I was surprised to learn that the company had not based their use of music upon any systematic research, in spite of running some of the noisiest stores in the UK! Milliman (1982) studied the effects of music tempo upon shopper behaviour. Slow tempo music was found to reduce the pace of traffic flow in-store, compared with fast music or no music at all; the slow music also achieved the best effect upon sales volume. Milliman did however warn against excessive generalization of these findings, in that the study was limited to a supermarket setting. Companies such as Muzicord have now started to create 'bespoke' music tapes for specific retailers (Retail 1986). For example, the Laura Ashley tape includes classical orchestral and chamber music, to complement the image of gracious living. Richards give its customers a mix of light classical and cool jazz, while at Toys R Us, the children can shop to the sounds of Star Wars, the A-Team and pop music.

The visual dimension has been the subject of slightly more scientific investigation, particularly in relation to the use of colours. Bellizzi et al. (1983) undertook a laboratory-based experiment which indicated the effects of colours upon attraction to displays and upon store image. Warm colours would appear to be appropriate for store windows, for entrances, and for situations associated with unplanned purchases. On the other hand, where a more difficult and prolonged

Table 11.3 Effects of different colours in a retail store

Colour	Psychological effect	Temperature effect	Distance effect
Violet	Aggressive and tiring	Cold	Very close
Blue	Restful	Cold	Further away
Brown	Exciting	Neutral	Claustrophobic
Green	Very restful	Cold–neutral	Further away
Yellow	Exciting	Very warm	Close
Orange	Exciting	Very warm	Very close
Red	Very stimulating	Warm	Close

Source: Hayne (1981).

buying decision is usual, warm, tense colours may make shopping unpleasant and cause the shopping trip to be more rapidly terminated; cool colours may be more appropriate in such circumstances. The authors pointed out however that, because of the visual overstimulation in many shopping environments, reactions in stores will not exactly correspond with those observed in laboratory settings. The psychological, temperature and distance effects generally associated with different colours are summarized in Table 11.3.

The implications of colour for retailers are also discussed within a wide-ranging treatment of colour by Rossotti (1983). She noted that different colour schemes can be used to emphasize the uniqueness of departments but that the colour change between departments should not be too abrupt; otherwise customers may feel that they are being 'pushed' through the stores. Bright, primary colours are recommended to create a mood of excitement in the toy department, whereas neutral colours are likely to be more appropriate in the women's clothing departments to avoid clashing with the colourful merchandise. Rossotti also discusses the use of coloured lighting but warns that many clothing items will be returned to the store if the effect of the lighting differs significantly from that of normal home lighting. The technology of store lighting has responded to the demand for truer colour rendition, combined with the ability to highlight specific merchandise. In this context, the very compact, low-voltage tungsten halogen lights have gained great popularity, with no less than 1,750 of them in use within Debenhams' refurbished Oxford Street store (Sharples 1987).

The social psychology of store environments is now attracting increased academic attention. From a review of space effects upon behaviour, Markin *et al.* (1976) concluded:

Retail space, i.e., the proximate environment that surrounds the retail shopper, is never neutral. The retail store is a bundle of cues, messages and suggestions which communicate to shoppers. Retail store designers, planners and merchandisers shape space but that space in turn affects and shapes customer behaviour. The retail store is not an exact parallel to a Skinner box but it does create mood, activate intentions and generally affect customer reactions.

Another concept of relevance to the store environment is that of 'hedonic consumption'. Although not relating the concept specifically to retailing, Hirschman and Holbrook (1982) defined hedonic consumption as 'those facets of consumer behaviour that relate to the multisensory, fantasy and emotive aspects of product usage experience'. 'Multisensory' indicates the receipt of experience through multiple senses, such as sounds, scents and visual images. The hedonic perspective suggests that consumers not only respond to multisensory imagery from external stimuli but also generate multisensory images within themselves. These may represent historic imagery, recalling past events on the basis of the stimuli, or fantasy imagery, where an imaginary experience is constructed in the mind of the consumer.

The visual effects, aromas and sounds of a specialist delicatessen, for example, may evoke historic images of enjoyable foreign holidays. The multisensory stimuli of the boutique or the cosmetics department may be designed to evoke fantasy imagery of a rather different kind! The potential for store environments to stimulate historic and fantasy imagery have long been recognized, at least implicitly, but enormous scope exists for scientific investigation.

A useful conceptual framework for the study of atmospherics was suggested by Donovan and Rossiter (1982), based upon an environmental psychology approach. Their study suggested that: 'store atmosphere, engendered by the usual myriad of in-store variables, is represented psychologically by consumers in terms of two major emotional states—pleasure and arousal'. These two emotional states are held to be important mediators between in-store stimuli and shopper behaviour. Behavioural responses were classified into a series of approach or avoidance outcomes, including whether or not the shopper wished to stay in the store and whether or not a desire to explore the store was generated. The study concluded:

arousal, or store induced feelings of alertness and excitement, can increase time in the stores and also willingness to interact with sales personnel. In-store stimuli that induce arousal are fairly easy to identify and almost certainly include bright lighting and upbeat music.

inducement of arousal works positively only in store environments that are already pleasant; arousal inducement may have no influence (or even negative influence) in unpleasant store environments.

Donovan and Rossiter noted that the effects of atmospherics have frequently been underestimated in studies of shopper motivations and images. This is because the emotional states created are difficult to verbalize and, being transient, are difficult to recall when away from the stores. In view of the level of expenditure now being devoted to the design of store environments, there is a clear need to develop further research into the effects of atmospherics.

11.2 STORE LAYOUT AND DISPLAY

Having considered the effects of the overall store design and atmosphere on shopper behaviour, this section examines the more direct approaches to maximizing sales through the arrangement of the store environment. Through careful design of the store layout, a retailer can make the best use of available space and also manipulate traffic flow within the store to maximize exposure to the merchandise. Through the selective use of special displays, that exposure can be further increased to assist in the promotion of specific products or to provide an additional attraction to the stores as a whole. Displays also form an important part of the 'information environment' which should assist shoppers in their decision-making processes (Fletcher 1987).

11.2.1 Store layouts

Many different types of layout option are available to the retailers, and the choice is likely to be determined by market positioning, merchandise type, size of store, cost, and security considerations. Most layout patterns contain elements of one or more of the following:

1. *Grid pattern layout*   This is characterized by long rows of parallel fixtures, with straight aisles and little or no opportunity to pass between aisles, other than by going to the end of the aisle. Grid patterns are common in supermarkets and have also been adopted in some non-food

contexts, especially where there is a desire to convey an image of cheapness. The grid gives the maximum exposure to merchandise by encouraging circulation round the whole store. Little space is wasted, and it is usually economical to install and maintain (Lusch 1982). On the other hand, the overall effect can be rather dull, and shoppers may become alienated by having to walk down long aisles, if the concept is pursued to extremes.

2. *Free-flow layout*   Here the shopper is allowed considerably more freedom to move in any direction between fixtures, which are arranged in more irregular patterns. Many fashion stores use a free-flow layout, which encourages browsing and can be visually appealing. On the other hand, less intensive use is made of floorspace, costs are usually higher, and unless carefully co-ordinated the overall effect may be one of confusion.

3. *Boutique layout*   This is a variation of the free-flow layout, but the departments or sections are arranged in the form of individual speciality shops, targeted at specific market segments (Rosenbloom 1981). The boutique layout may be a result of using concessions (shops within shops), but its use is by no means confined to that situation. This layout does not usually offer an economical use of space but it does allow more complete orientation of design towards the target group.

Whatever system, or combination of systems, is adopted, the effects of the layout upon shopper circulation should be carefully evaluated. Rogers (1985) outlined the procedure adopted in tracking studies, starting with a diagram of the store or section of the store. The path taken through the store by a sample of customers is then observed and recorded on the diagram. In that a visible observer would probably affect the behaviour of shoppers, this form of tracking must be undertaken discreetly; in some studies, the store security cameras or slow running cinecameras have been used to avoid any distortion of in-store behaviour. Tracking can also be useful in observing shopper movements within shopping centres (Brown 1988).

Tracking studies can produce a great deal of information about circulation patterns, centres of attraction, congestion points and 'dead' areas of the store. A Progressive Grocer (1975) study within a 14-aisle supermarket found that 95 per cent of shoppers passed through the first aisle, only 58 per cent through the sixth. The study also identified the dominant directions of movement within each aisle; with this information, the most profitable items could be placed at the point in each section that most shoppers reached first. Buttle (1984a) reported increases in sales of 11 per cent, mostly attributable to layout changes following a tracking study.

In multi-level stores, it is a major challenge to stimulate circulation in the higher floors; cafés and other customer services are sometimes used as an attraction to these areas. There has been a great deal of investment by department stores in lifts and escalators that are both attractive and efficient, to try to lessen the perceived barriers between floors, but the costs can be formidable. Even in single-floor layouts, it is a considerable challenge to try to equalize traffic flow in all areas. An early Progressive Grocer (1960) study found that supermarket customers had a strong tendency to concentrate their time round the perimeters of stores. In a study of mental mapping of two supermarkets, Sommer and Aitkins (1982) found that the locations of items in peripheral aisles were recalled more frequently and accurately than those of items in central aisles.

The problem of low traffic in the central area of supermarkets was compounded by the tendency to place major centres of attraction, such as fresh foods and delicatessen, around the edge of the store. This was often justified on the grounds that chill/freezer cabinets could be serviced without disruption to customers and that heavy and frequency loading of cabinets could be achieved most efficiently. As single-level stores have become larger, it has been necessary to find ways of breaking the monotony of the central part of the layout, to improve both image and traffic flow. In large supermarkets it is now common for fresh foods and freezers to provide focal points in central parts of the store.

The placement of specific departments and product categories within the stores may be used to manipulate traffic flow. In many variety or department stores with food departments, these were situated centrally or in a basement area, in order to draw regular shoppers through the other departments.

A battery of supermarket layout techniques has been developed, many of which were discussed by Buttle (1984a, 1984b). For example, retailers often place high-demand items close to the entrance, in order to quickly overcome buyer inertia and inhibitions that the customer may have about spending money. Within the main gondola areas, high-demand items are placed at regular intervals in order to 'pull' the customer through the aisles. Sometimes these are alternated between the two sides of the aisle to create a 'bounce' pattern, as the customer moves from side to side, gaining maximum exposure to all the displays. 'Impulse' items are typically situated between these points, sometimes being complementary to the adjacent high-demand items, such as toppings situated near to the desserts.

With all layout techniques, a delicate balance must be struck between the manipulation of traffic flow and ensuring that the shopping experience is as convenient and enjoyable as possible. Some retailers have learnt this to their cost: displays blocking the aisles, product categories scattered around the stores and frequent, unnecessary changes to product locations are all likely to give the impression of a chaotic or, worse, a conniving store. Some retailers succeed in maintaining a convenient and orderly store, while still encouraging thorough traffic flow. Maybe the acid test should be the question, 'Am I inviting or am I forcing the customer to be in this part of the store?'

A similar balance of considerations must be applied to the width of aisles and the space allowed around checkouts or payment points. Wide aisles run the risk that shoppers will ignore the surrounding displays, but congestion inevitably loses sales (Buttle 1984a). In the layout of shopping centres, too, the problem exists of trying to maximize exposure to the store frontages without inducing the feeling in shoppers that the centre is dangerous or claustrophobic (Marking 1986).

The concept of 'retail crowding' is highly relevant to the design of layouts. Eroglu and Harrell (1986) found that customers' perceptions of density in a retail environment are affected by their motives, constraints and expectations. Density could be functional under some circumstances, for example where a low price image has attracted price-sensitive shopper segments. In this situation, the crowds actually reinforce the image and the decision to patronize the store. In an exclusive boutique, however, or where the convenience of shopping is of primary importance, crowding (or dysfunctional density) will deter shoppers. One problem is that crowding can vary enormously according to the time of day or day of the week. Under these circumstances, an increase in service staff and minor changes to displays and layout may be desirable to reduce perceptions of density at busy times.

11.2.2 Display techniques

This section considers the *way* in which merchandise is presented within stores; the amount of space allocated to each product and category is discussed in the following section. A distinction is usually drawn between 'normal' displays, which include every shelf or grouping of merchandise that is visible to the customers, and 'special' or 'off-shelf' displays. Special displays have tended to receive more attention both from retail management and from researchers; some of the studies of display effectiveness are considered here. It should be remembered, however, that the design of every area of display within the store exerts an influence upon product sales, the overall image of the store and the efficiency with which available space can be utilized. Rosenbloom (1981) identified several different approaches to display which represent developments upon the more basic styles of product presentation:

1. *Open displays*   These set out to create involvement by surrounding the shopper with merchandise, rather than distancing the shopper from the display. This approach is used extensively in department and fashion stores. The shopper is more likely to stop and touch the merchandise; the propensity to purchase then tends to increase.
2. *Theme displays*   The choice of themes is very wide, including local or national events, festivals, or specific international themes. Alternatively, the theme may be devised by the store, possibly to suit a particular season or an activity relevant to the clientele.
3. *Life-style displays*   In these, the presentation is likely to include pictures and other 'display props' designed to suggest the appropriateness of the store and the merchandise displayed to a specific target segment. These have been widely used in clothing retailing but are now being adopted in many other sectors (McFadyen 1985).
4. *Co-ordinated displays*   These follow the logic that items, if normally used together, should be displayed together. Clothing retailers therefore display co-ordinated outfits; furniture retailers such as Ikea create many complete room settings within their stores. This approach presents items within the best context; it tends to be more reassuring to customers and also stimulates sales of related items.
5. *Classification dominance displays*   These are designed to suggest that the retailer offers a great width or depth of assortment in a particular category of merchandise. This may be achieved by displaying together every size, colour or type of a specific product. Sports goods retailers sometimes use this approach, for example to suggest a very comprehensive range of tennis rackets.

Displays are not confined to the immediate selling areas of the store. For many years, department stores have practised the art of elaborate window displays, and, at the more basic level, windows are used extensively for price announcements by many discount stores. Although window displays can provide a powerful attraction to the store, they are now being given less emphasis in some retail contexts. One reason is that the more elaborate window displays can be expensive and require specialist skills if they are to be effective. Another is that designers often try to lessen the perceived barriers between the outside and inside of the store. An open view into the store or, in enclosed shopping malls, an entirely open frontage can achieve this. More attention is now being given to the total store's display potential. Walls or support pillars can be made more attractive and useful if adorned with displays relevant to the adjacent merchandise; similarly, high ceilings can offer scope for suspended display material, which may also help to create a more intimate and exciting atmosphere.

Display techniques appropriate to supermarket-type settings were discussed in detail by Buttle (1984a, 1984b). In some cases the most orderly displays do not achieve the best effects, at least not in terms of immediate product sales. In fact, 'starter-gaps' are sometimes left in newly constructed displays to suggest that the product is selling rapidly; there may also be some inhibition about disturbing orderly displays. Dump bins and cut case displays can also achieve the dual benefits of making products easy to pick up and also conveying the impression of bargains.

The objectives of 'off-shelf' displays were summarized by Buttle (1984a):

1. Meeting consumer demand—if normal shelf space does not allow sufficient stock to be displayed at peak season or during promotions

Table 11.4   Effectiveness of display locations

Location	Increase upon normal sales (%)
On back of store gondola end	110
Mid-aisle in front of checkouts	262
On front of store gondola end	153
At entrance to first aisle	363

Source: Dyer (1980), © Progressive Grocer 1980.

2. Creating consumer demand — by attracting consumers' attention in order to increase sales of high margin lines, bulk purchases or excess stock
3. Enhancing store image — by conveying impressions of bargain prices, exclusive merchandise or extensive assortments
4. Controlling traffic movement — acting either as barriers, to widen circulation, or as attractions to otherwise rather quiet areas of the store

Some research attention has been given to the short-term effectiveness of displays. Table 11.4 shows the effects achieved by displays positioned in four different types of location within the store (Dyer 1980). Clearly, those situated at the entrance of the first aisle tend to achieve considerably more effect. In a study of displays of a pharmacy product, Gagnon and Osterhaus (1985) also found that effectiveness varied significantly between different positions within the stores.

The measurement of display effects is made more complex by the fact that changes in display are usually accompanied by changes in price, advertising and/or space allocation. Characteristics of the product and its market are also likely to exert an influence upon the effects of display. Based upon eight product categories, Chevalier (1975a) investigated the effects of market growth, competitive structure, market share, price cuts and advertising-to-sales ratio upon the impact of display. Display proved to be most effective for mature products and for those product groups within which no one brand has a clear market advantage. The combination of display and a special price cut appeared to be especially effective where products had a close competitive structure and a low advertising-to-sales ratio.

Curhan (1974) tested the short-term effects on sales of four in-store variables, namely display space, display location, prices and advertising. In that the experiment involved four categories of fresh fruit and vegetables, the possible number of experimental treatments was very large indeed. To reduce these, each variable was tested at just two levels, i.e. 'normal' and 'featured'. A fractional factorial design (see for example Holland and Cravens 1973) was also used, which gives information on some, but not all, combinations of variables. Slow-selling items proved to be more responsive to display than fast-selling lines, and, in the case of soft fruit, higher-priced lines were more responsive. In most product areas, Curhan concluded that the impact of price reductions was not especially significant, although the items tested were not typical of supermarket products in general.

In a further multiple-factor experiment, Wilkinson *et al.* (1981, 1982) studied the short-term effects of price reductions, display alternatives and newspaper advertising on the sales of four supermarket products. Three display levels, three price levels and two advertising levels were incorporated within a factorial design which, with replication and alternating non-experimental weeks, was administered over an 80-week period. Wilkinson *et al.* concluded that:

Price reductions and changes in display appear to offer a greater opportunity for temporarily increasing unit sales of supermarket products than does newspaper advertising. (Wilkinson *et al.* 1981)

The effects of display and advertising upon the price–sales relationship for each product were also investigated, and the conclusion reached that:

The effect of increasing shelf space was negligible compared to the sales effect of building a special display. (Wilkinson *et al.* 1981)

This also underlines one of the problems in attempting to compare and generalize from the experimental studies conducted. The actual 'quality' and type of display changes administered varies considerably between the studies, and the distinction between display and in-store advertising becomes somewhat blurred.

The combined effects of display signs and price reductions were investigated by Woodside and Waddle (1975) in a rather smaller-scale experiment, which included two price levels, two price signs and one product (instant coffee). They found that the display sign without a price cut produced more additional sales than a 20 per cent price cut with no special display sign. When both treatments were applied, a synergism was found to exist in that additional sales greatly exceeded the sum of those produced by each treatment used independently.

The benefits of co-ordinated promotional strategies were also illustrated by Dickson (1974). He demonstrated significant sales benefits from relating in-store display signs to current television advertising. In a study based upon department store products, McKinnon *et al.* (1981) distinguished between the types of display sign used and their interactions with price. Signs that indicated both the price and some product benefits were more effective than 'price only' signs in stimulating sales when the price was reduced and were effective even at normal prices. Although many display signs, particularly in supermarkets, tend to be of the 'price only' type, considerable scope exists for combining price and benefit information.

Studies of display effects have concentrated mainly on the direct effects upon product sales: one reason for this is that many such studies have been motivated and/or sponsored by manufacturers. A major problem for the retailer in researching display effects is to measure the longer-term effects on store image and patronage. A store that contains many individual displays, each achieving improvements in short-term product sales, may actually be building an image of a rather uncoordinated or even chaotic environment, which may inhibit patronage in the longer term. Alternatively, the displays may be helping to reinforce an image of the store as an exciting environment or one with many bargains. These longer-term effects are more difficult to measure, but certainly should be a major consideration in display decisions.

11.3 ALLOCATING DISPLAY SPACE

With the continuing development of large new stores, it may be tempting to assume that the problems of allocating space are becoming less acute. In fact, this is far from true, and space remains a scarce and valuable resource for retailers. Consumers' demand for more choice, and extensive product developments to satisfy that demand, have ensured that space continues to be under pressure. Retailers' strategies of specialization and/or diversification have also created the need for more space to display deeper or wider product assortments.

11.3.1   Space elasticity

There has been a tendency in many approaches to space allocation to ignore the influence of space upon sales or, alternatively, to assume that it is equal across all products. This possibly stems from the artificial distinction that is often drawn between 'special' and 'normal' displays. Few people would expect all products to respond equally to special displays, yet it is sometimes assumed that this is the case with normal displays. A number of researchers have set out to challenge this assumption by demonstrating that 'space elasticity' differs considerably between products. Space elasticity has been defined as 'the ratio of relative change in unit sales to relative change in shelf space' (Curhan 1973).

Attempts to measure space elasticity have generally adopted either experimental or cross-sectional approaches. For reviews of in-store experimental approaches, readers may wish to consult Doyle and Gidengil (1977) or Lipstein (1981). Experimentation allows the manipulation of a real situation and the observation of the results, set against a control situation. The main difficulties are as follows:

1. The scope of the experiment is usually limited to a few products, stores and/or points in time.
2. Only the short-term results are usually observed, whereas space allocations also affect longer term images and patronage decisions.
3. It is difficult to exclude bias from the experiment, for example, the propensity of staff to keep displays unusually tidy when they are known to be under observation.

These problems are difficult to overcome, as retailers are understandably reluctant to risk major disruption of store operations and customer goodwill in order to co-operate with large-scale experiments. Cross-sectional approaches overcome these problems by statistically deriving the space–sales relationship from observations of space allocations and sales results in many different stores. The approach therefore permits the calculation of space elasticities for many, even all, products or categories within the assortment. The cross-sectional approaches unfortunately are not without their problems, notably the following:

1. The relationships are only inferred; it cannot therefore be firmly established that the space is the *cause* and the sales are the *effect*, as the reverse may be true.
2. The available sample of stores may be too heterogeneous for the space–sales records to be truly comparable.
3. The approach is effective only if a range of space allocations exists between the stores; if they are standardized, then it is not possible to judge the effects of different allocations.

Among the experimental approaches, two studies by Cox (1964, 1970) were undertaken within supermarkets and found different reactions to space among the products tested. In both experiments, just one of the four items tested showed a significant response to space changes, although the model used in the second study has been called into question (Peterson and Cagley 1973). Equivalent experiments have also been conducted in other retail settings. Kotzan and Evanson (1969), for example, found significant responses to increased space allocations for three of the four drug store products that they tested.

These experimental designs gave no indication of the extent of inter-brand or size substitution. In order to overcome this limitation, Chevalier (1975b) adopted a more comprehensive measurement system in a study in four supermarkets and concluded that only a modest proportion of sales increase resulted from substitution within the store; most of the increase was therefore assumed to be gained at the expense of other stores.

Most of these experimental designs have imposed rather artificial changes in space allocations and are necessarily limited to a few products. Frank and Massy (1970) attempted to overcome these constraints by using cross-sectional and time-series analysis; their study ran for 63 weeks and involved 30 supermarkets. Ultimately, the time-series analysis was abandoned, owing to lack of space variation over time. The cross-sectional analysis indicated that space elasticity may be greater in high-volume stores than in low-volume ones; the authors also found that little change in sales could be attributed to changes in shelf height, a result that would be challenged by many retailers.

Curhan (1972) set out to establish the effects of several independent variables upon space elasticity, based on a study of nearly 500 grocery products under actual operating conditions. The changes in space allocations were those suggested by store management and a computerized management information system. Elasticity proved to be higher for retailer brands than for manufacturer brands and, not surprisingly, higher for 'impulse' items. Unfortunately, from the regression analysis it proved possible to explain only a very small proportion of the variance in space elasticity. From a review of space elasticity studies, Curhan (1973) subsequently concluded that:

there is a small, positive relationship between shelf space and unit sales. This relationship, however, is uniform neither among products nor across stores or intra-store locations. A curvilinear model of declining marginal return probably holds; although for specific changes implemented, curvilinear, linear and indeterminate relationships are reported.

The likely existence of nonlinear space–sales relationships had previously been hypothesized by Brown and Tucker (1961). Writing at a time when products tended to be crudely dichotomized as being 'staple' or 'impulse', they suggested that there are at least three broad categories of response:

1. Unresponsive products—such as salt, for which increases in space would be unlikely to cause significant increases in sales
2. General use products—such as breakfast foods, for which the effects of increasing space are fairly strong from minimum levels but the point of diminishing returns is reached fairly quickly
3. Occasional purchase products—such as canned nuts, which are 'unlooked for' by most shoppers. Sales are likely to respond slowly to shelf space increases until the display is large enough to force its attention on the shopper, at which point the sales curve might rise steeply. This implies the existence of a step function or a threshold effect for some products.

It is intuitively reasonable to assume that space–sales relationships will frequently be nonlinear and that thresholds and/or diminishing returns will occur in many cases. There has however been some divergence between the theoretical and empirical work in this field (Leone and Schultz 1980). Having reviewed previous studies, Anderson (1979) stated:

the literature concerned with the conceptual development of brand demand as a function of display area shows a higher degree of consistency than does the empirical research done to test various functional specifications.

A major problem in the empirical work is to separate the relatively modest effects of space allocation changes from other more dramatic effects, such as those caused by changes in price, advertising and competitor activity.

Based upon a cross-sectional study of 57 product categories in over 100 supermarkets, McGoldrick and Thorpe (1977) used curve-fitting procedures to identify relationships between space and sales. In only 9 per cent of cases did a linear relationship provide the 'best fit'. Using

Table 11.5 Responsiveness of sales to space

Response levels	Product categories (examples)
Very low response	Butter
	Sugar
	Tea
	Cigarettes & tobacco
	Canned fruit
Low response	Margarine
	Flour
	Eggs
	Beer & ciders
	Canned fish
Average response	Dried fruit
	Bread & morning goods
	Dessert products
	Ready meals
	Cake mixes
High response	Detergents
	Fruit & vegetables
	Paper ware
	Cakes
	Wines
Very high response	Frozen foods
	Potato crisps
	Biscuits
	Toiletries
	Breakfast cereals

Source: McGoldrick and Thorpe (1977).

the equations derived from this procedure, a simple optimization process was undertaken which, within given boundaries, reallocated space between product categories. At each iteration, a very small proportion of space was added to the category that offered the best marginal return; the same proportion was then deducted from the category that showed the least reduction in sales. Table 11.5 shows examples of product categories which demonstrated high, average and low levels of responsiveness. After a large number of iterations, a solution was produced that suggested an increase in sales of 11.2 per cent. It was accepted, however, that logistical and other constraints would in some cases limit the scope for space allocation changes, thereby reducing the increase actually achieved.

11.3.2 Space allocation systems

Retailers face numerous space allocation decisions at various different levels, i.e. between departments, between product categories, and between individual items. Because these decisions are so numerous, there has been a tendency to rely upon relatively simple approaches which use readily available data. One doctrine frequently cited is that the space allocated should be directly proportional to the market share of each product. Buttle (1984b) points out that this approach does have some benefits for retailers, primarily, that the most efficient use is made of staff time. Some retailers describe this approach as the 'level rundown principle', denoting that the stocks of every item on display run down at approximately the same rate. In situations where the display areas carry all the stocks held by the store and where deliveries to the store are not frequent, the space allocation plan is likely to adopt the level rundown principle to some extent.

The manufacturers of leading brands are also enthusiastic advocates of the practice of relating space allocations to current market shares, as this helps to reinforce their market position and to exclude, or at least reduce, potential threats to their position. There are however several reasons why a retailer should not adhere to the principle of relating space allocations directly to sales:

1. It ignores the differential effects of display space in stimulating product sales (space elasticities).
2. Fast-moving lines and market leaders may not produce the best profit for the retailer.
3. Some speciality products may be excluded or may receive negligible display space.
4. Displays dominated by fast-moving lines can give the impression of a narrow and/or mundane assortment.
5. The progress and potential of new products may not be effectively exploited.

Some manufacturers have developed systems or models to assist retailers in their space allocation decisions. Inevitably, these are oriented towards the optimization of the manufacturer's sales/profits within the store, which may not contribute to the optimum result from the retailers viewpoint. Accordingly, the more sophisticated retailers have developed their own space allocation systems or utilized one of the 'packaged' systems available to assist in various store management decisions.

The most frequently utilized of these packaged systems are dominated by cost considerations, making little or no allowance for differential space elasticities. For example, the SLIM (Store Labour and Inventory Management) system suggested that space allocations be based upon rates of stock movement, thus reducing back-room inventories and minimizing handling costs. More recently, COSMOS (Computer Optimization and Simulation Modelling for Supermarkets) has been widely advocated. This incorporates the DPP (direct product profitability) of items, discussed in Chapter 5. The outputs of COSMOS include recommendations of space allocations, item locations, price changes and possible item deletions. Having reviewed these and other systems, Corstjens and Doyle (1981) were highly critical:

the drawback of all these systems stems from their failure to incorporate demand effects. Being limited to data normally on-hand to retailers they focus essentially on cost and static margin considerations. All have the unrealistic assumption that products have uniform space elasticities and that zero cross elasticities exist among products. As such, none can be considered seriously as optimisation models.

Corstjens and Doyle developed a model that recognized both the cost and the demand effects of space allocations. A particular feature of this model was the inclusion of cross-elasticities, in addition to space elasticities. The parameters of the model were estimated from a case study, which included 140 stores and five product groups; the cross-sectional approach was used to derive the elasticities. Table 11.6 shows the changes in percentage space allocations suggested by the model for small and for large stores within the chain. When the model was run without the inclusion of cross-elasticities, the implied profit improvement was $128,000 less across the 140 shops. The researchers concluded that:

Table 11.6 Model and existing space allocations

| | Small stores | | Large stores | |
Product	Model % space	Existing % space	Model % space	Existing % space
1	26	30	46	35
2	20	30	25	32
3	7	12	6	12
4	22	18	17	10
5	25	10	6	10
Profit ($)	37,680	31,436	46,530	45,011

Source: Reprinted by permission of M. Corstjens and P. Doyle, 'A model for optimiz-ing retail space allocations', *Management Science*, 27, 7, 1981, Copyright © 1981 The Institute of Management Sciences.

very significant profit improvements can be expected from an allocation procedure which optimally balances on the cost side product gross margins and handling costs and on the demand side space elasticities and cross elasticities among items in the store.

In a subsequent development of the model, Corstjens and Doyle (1983) highlighted the problem that most space allocation systems are based upon current, or past, sales and gross margins. This can produce a tendency to underestimate the value of early investment in new high-volume markets, a particular problem for high-technology, speciality retailers. For them, the consequences of being seen as 'left behind' are especially serious. A dynamic model was therefore proposed which recognized changing product life-cycles and consumer tastes. The effect of this was to encourage retailers to allocate more space to new products and divest more rapidly from declining ones.

Inevitably, as models become more comprehensive, they also tend to become more demanding of data and less readily understood by the majority of retail managers. In order to try to overcome both of these problems, a number of models have been suggested which require the input of management judgements. Singh and Cook (1986) suggested a decision support system that used a combination of 'hard' data and management judgements. Rinne *et al.* (1987) presented an approach to the allocation of space for departments within department stores. Again, manage-ment judgements provided an important input, and the model suggested both the specific location and the size for each department for each month. This approach to the construction and operation of space allocation models has the dual advantages of increasing management involvement and also reducing the need for extensive experimentation or cross-sectional study.

The spread of PoS computer systems is starting to increase the scope for day-to-day experimentation by retailers, potentially increasing the supply of 'hard' data for space allocation decisions. In that space is such a scarce and, frequently, expensive resource, there is obviously a strong incentive to optimize its utilization. It must be recognized, however, that the space allocation plan influences profits in a variety of ways, both short-term and long-term. Figure 11.1 illustrates two types of influence:

1. *Staff/cost influences* The space plan determines replenishment frequency, which directly affects costs. It also affects staff attitudes, especially if the staff are not effectively made aware of the rationale of the space plan. Negative staff attitudes or lack of adequate attention to the displays will lead to wrong allocations, untidy displays or lack of shelf stock, reducing overall sales.

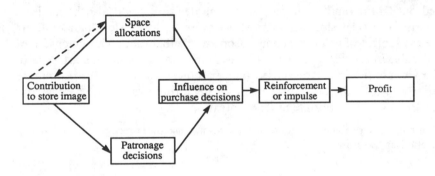

a) Staff/cost influences

b) Image/sales influences

Figure 11.1 Space allocation influences
Source: McGoldrick and Thorpe (1977).

2. *Image/sales influences* The space allocated exerts direct effects upon in-store decisions, either stimulating impulse purchases or reinforcing planned purchases. It also exerts a longer-term effect upon the consumer's image of the store, which in turn influences future patronage decisions.

Longer-term image influences are more difficult to measure but should be a major consideration within the space allocation plan. In the 1970s some supermarkets found that the direct product profitability of fresh fruit and vegetables, as they were then typically sold, was relatively low. Many therefore gave minimum attention to these sections, with most adverse consequences upon their image. The 1980s has seen a sharp increase in the attention given to fresh products, as these are highly instrumental in achieving image differentiation. The emphasis therefore turned to finding ways of selling fresh fruit and vegetables at a higher level of DPP. It does not of course necessarily follow that long-term and short-term effects are always in conflict. It must be recognized, however, that both types of effect exist and that an appropriate balance should be achieved in developing space allocation systems. As Sanghavi (1988) observed:

Too often, retailers think as suppliers and concentrate on what they want to sell, rather than on how they can best satisfy and serve customers. Most retailers listen to suppliers telling them what to stock, rather than listening to customers.

11.4   IMPULSE PURCHASING

A major objective in designing and arranging the retail environment is to maximize the extent of impulse or unplanned purchasing within the store. It is generally accepted that impulse purchasing has now become a prevalent feature of shopper behaviour in most retail settings. Clearly, the attributes of the retail environment are not the only factors that precipitate impulse purchasing; prices, product characteristics and packaging, point-of-purchase advertising and sales personnel can all contribute to the process. Impulse purchasing may therefore be regarded as a cumulative effect of the many in-store marketing variables.

Impulse purchasing has traditionally been defined in terms of the rapidity of the buying decision. For example, Davidson and Doody (1966) defined it as 'an unplanned, spur of the moment decision to purchase a product'. This is still the usual connotation of the term, although it does not strictly limit impulse purchasing to in-store decisions. For example, D'Antoni and Shenson (1973) pointed out that a rapid or impulsive buying decision could also be made at home, possibly in response to a television commercial. Conversely, a decision made entirely within the store may be the subject of extensive comparison and deliberation. This extension of the concept is of considerable interest to product manufacturers and to companies involved in direct selling. From the viewpoint of the store-based retailer, however, the essence of impulse purchasing is the location at which the decision is made. A definition proposed by Engel and Blackwell (1982) is therefore more appropriate in this context:

a buying action undertaken without a problem previously having been consciously recognised or a buying intention formed prior to entering the store.

11.4.1   Measures of unplanned purchasing

Although the concept of impulse purchasing is of immense importance in both retail and product marketing, it is not possible to form generalizations as to its extent. The available evidence spans a period of over forty years, but few of the published studies are truly comparable. This problem arises from inconsistency in the definitions used and from fundamental differences between the methods adopted in measuring impulse purchasing. With this necessary caveat, a useful summary of research findings, compiled by Cobb and Hoyer (1986), is presented in Table 11.7.

The series of studies undertaken by the du Pont company between 1945 and 1965 illustrated a general increase in the extent of impulse purchasing. This has been attributed both to changing customer characteristics and to changes in store environments. Time pressures arising from two-career families, geographical mobility and competing leisure-time opportunities reduce the opportunity for detailed pre-planning; increases in discretionary income may also reduce the inclination for such planning (Williams and Dardis 1972). The spread of self-service, increased product assortments and increased point-of-purchase promotion have also contributed to a tendency to transfer actual buying decisions to within the store. Cobb and Hoyer (1986) cited some evidence that impulse purchasing may have declined somewhat in the early 1980s, owing to recent recessionary conditions; the long-term trend, however, appears to remain upward.

Table 11.7 also illustrates that the extent of impulse purchasing differs very significantly between types of product and between retail settings. For example, Bellenger et al. (1978) found that 62 per cent of costume jewellery purchases in a department store were essentially unplanned,

Table 11.7 Incidence of unplanned purchasing by type of product and outlet: summary of findings

Source	Year	Type of product	Rate of unplanned purchasing (%)	Type of outlet	Rate of unplanned purchasing (%)
du Pont	1945	Grocery product		Grocery	38.2
	1949	categories			38.4
	1954				48.0
	1959				50.9
	1965				50.0
Clover	1950	n.a.	n.a.	19 types, incl.	
				Variety	60.5
				Grocery	26.0
				Service station	14.8
				Book	14.7
				Department	14.5
				Furniture	3.8
West	1951	14 categories, incl.			
		Candy	65.8	Grocery	43.5
		Bakery goods	70.1	Drug	26.6
		Cosmetics	41.8	Variety	41.5
		Jewellery	49.5	Department	33.6
		Wearing apparel	24.1		
Point-of purchase Advertising Institute	1963	50 categories, incl.		3 styles of drug stores:	
		Prescriptions	0.0	Clerk-assisting	11.0
		Camera supplies	10.0	Self-service	22.0
		Cosmetics	23.0	Super drug	30.0
		Candy	48.0		
Kollat and Willett	1967	64 grocery categories		Grocery	50.5
Williams and Dardis	1972	Women's outerwear	46.0	Speciality	33.0
		Women's underwear	30.0	Department	37.0
		Menswear	32.0	Discount/	
		Household textiles	24.0	variety	31.0
Prasad	1975	Various non-food categories		Department	39.3
				Discount	62.4
Bellenger, Robertson and Hirschman	1978	20 categories, incl.			
		Lingerie	27.0	Department	38.7
		Cosmetics	33.0		
		Men's apparel and furnishings	40.0		
		Bakery goods	50.0		
		Costume jewellery	62.0		

Source: Cobb and Hoyer (1986).

compared with only 27 per cent of women's lingerie purchases. In the study by Prasad (1975), 62.4 per cent of discount shoppers bought at least one item on an unplanned basis, compared with 39.3 per cent of department store shoppers.

Various researchers have suggested the factors that may contribute to impulse purchasing. Stern (1962) listed nine product-related factors:

Low price,
Marginal needs for item,
Mass distribution,
Self-service,
Mass advertising,
Prominent store display,
Short product life,
Small size or light weight,
Ease of storage.

On the basis of an empirical study, Kollat and Willett (1967) examined relationships between unplanned purchasing and four product-related factors, namely, purchase frequency, price, product advertising, and ease of storage. Among these, only purchase frequency was significantly related; products with a high purchase frequency tended to have a relatively low unplanned purchase percentage, and vice versa.

Kollat and Willett (1967) found no significant relationships between the propensity to make unplanned purchases and a series of economic, demographic and personality variables. The number of years that the shopping party had been married was however related, with couples married less than ten years demonstrating the lowest rate of unplanned purchasing. Following a subsequent empirical study, Prasad (1975) concluded:

the findings of the present study, along with those of past research which dealt with unplanned buying in supermarkets, point toward the hypothesis that unplanned buying may be more a function of situational variables (store-environment, product and trip-specific variables) than of shopper characteristics.

There is no general agreement on 'the best' way of measuring impulse purchasing. The problem is essentially to determine when and where the decision to purchase an item was formed. Every methodology used runs the risk of biasing the results in some way. Three main types of approach have been adopted:

1. Shoppers are asked what they intend to purchase on entering the store; actual purchases are then recorded as they leave the store. The difference between intentions and outcomes are deemed to be impulse purchases (e.g. du Pont 1965; Kollat and Willett 1967; Prasad 1975). One problem with this approach is that, having been asked to articulate their purchase intentions, shoppers may become more committed to fulfilling them (Pollay 1968). This would have the effect of reducing impulse purchasing. Furthermore, the shopper may be unable and/or unwilling to itemize all purchase intentions at the start of the shopping trip (Kollat and Willett 1969). An incomplete recording of intentions would then result in the overstatement of impulse purchasing, using this method.
2. Shoppers are questioned on leaving the store about the time and place of the purchase decision for specific item(s) bought (e.g. Bellenger *et al.* 1978; Deshpande and Krishnan 1980; McGoldrick 1982). The major problem with this approach is that respondents may tend to overstate their extent of pre-purchase planning, in order to appear rational and careful shoppers. The extent of impulses purchasing may therefore be under-recorded by this method.

3. Direct observation of shopper behaviour within this store (e.g. Wells and Lo Sciuto 1966; Davidson 1981; Cobb and Hoyer 1986). Unless undertaken very discreetly, however, this will almost certainly affect shopping behaviour. Direct observation may be a useful supplement to another methodology but cannot alone distinguish between planned and impulse purchases.

Some studies of impulse purchasing have dichotomized the recorded purchases into those that were planned or unplanned. In fact, there are various different levels of purchase planning, so it may be more appropriate to identify different degrees of impulse purchasing. Stern (1962) suggested four broad classifications of impulse purchasing:

1. Pure impulse—a novelty or escape-type purchase which breaks a normal buying pattern.
2. Reminder impulse buying—when a shopper sees an item and remembers that the stock at home is low, or recalls an advertisement or other information and a previous decision to buy
3. Suggestion impulse—when a shopper sees a product for the first time and visualizes a need for it; such purchases can be entirely rational or functional, unlike pure impulse purchases which are sparked by emotional appeal
4. Planned impulse—when a shopper enters the store with some specific purchases in mind but with the expectations and intention of making other purchases, depending on price specials, etc.

Stern's classification has however proved difficult to operationalize, particularly the distinction between categories 1 and 3. A more straightward classification system was adopted in a study by McGoldrick (1982), summarized in Table 11.8. This was based upon post-purchase interviews with 449 shoppers at six pharmacy stores. Their purchases were classified as follows:

1. Specifically planned purchases (57 per cent)—the need was recognized on entering the store and the shopper bought the exact item planned.
2. Generally planned purchases (23 per cent)—the need was recognized but the shopper decided in the store upon the item to satisfy the need.
3. Reminder purchases (13 per cent)—the shopper was reminded of the need by some influence within the store.
4. Entirely unplanned purchases (7 per cent)—the need had been recognized neither on entering the store nor prior to that.

Three of these categories therefore represent degrees of in-store decision-making, comprising 43 per cent of all the purchases. The results summarized in Table 11.7 would also suggest that rates of unplanned purchasing would be higher in many other types of retail store. The simple division of purchases into 'impulse' and 'planned' has inevitably tended to underestimate the effects of the store environment. From the retail marketing perspective, the identification of different levels of unplanned purchasing also provides the basis for a more thorough analysis of in-store effects.

SUMMARY

The retail store environment exerts an influence upon shopper behaviour at several different levels, including the overall design of the store, its atmosphere, the arrangement of its layout, the displays, and the allocation of space between departments and between products. At each of these levels, the decisions taken are likely to influence both the in-store purchasing behaviour of consumers and their longer-term patronage decisions. Store-based retailers therefore face numerous options and a complex network of decisions in attempting to achieve optimum results from the store environment.

Table 11.8   Extent of purchase planning

Product group	% of purchases that were:			
	Specifically planned	Generally planned	Reminder	Entirely unplanned
Toothpaste	45	32	21	2
Soap, shampoo, bath products	57	25	13	5
Cosmetics	54	25	7	14
Baby products	73	11	8	8
Medicines, surgical	77	14	8	1
Food and food drinks	40	26	22	12
Optical and photographic	76	12	12	0
Household, garden, electrical	48	26	13	13

Source: McGoldrick (1982).

Over the last ten years, retail design has become a very prominent element of retail marketing, as retailers have sought new forms of differentiation. The scope of design and refurbishment is very wide, potentially including most facets of the store's external and internal appearance. A major new retail design industry has developed, and most major retailers have employed consultants for at least part of their design programmes. However, concern has been expressed about the costs and the short life-cycles of some refurbishments. There is also a sharper realization that design changes are likely to be effective only if they are part of a co-ordinated marketing strategy.

More systematic attention is now being given to 'atmospherics', which describes the conscious designing of space to create certain effects on buyers. Visual, aural, olfactory and tactile dimensions may all be utilized to create a favourable atmosphere. Some evidence has emerged as to the effects of music tempo, colours and light on shoppers' perceptions and in-store behaviour. It is important that the effects induced by atmospherics be compatible with the type of store and shopping experience.

The design of the store layout contributes to the image created and can also be used to manipulate traffic flow. Many supermarkets use a grid pattern layout, which encourages circulation within all parts of the store. High-demand items are typically placed near the entrance, to initiate purchasing, and at appropriate points within each aisle. Free-flow or boutique-type layouts are usually favoured by department and fashion stores, making less intensive use of space but conveying an appropriate image. Tracking methods may be utilized to study shopper movements within the layout, identifying areas of congestion, areas of poor circulation, and centres of attraction within the store.

Special displays can provide interest and attraction, as well as stimulating the sales of the products featured. Displays may be centred around a specific theme or consumer life-style. Co-ordinated displays can link items that are normally used together, or classification-dominance displays can emphasize the strength of the assortment in a specific product category. The evaluation of a display should consider both long- and short-term effects; in many cases, the effects of the display must also be separated from the effects of changes in prices or advertising.

The growth of product assortments has increased the pressure to optimize the use of space in most retail settings. Various rules of thumb and computer-based 'packaged' systems have been developed for the allocation of space. These tend to be based primarily on logistical, cost and short-term profit considerations; sales effects have frequently been largely ignored. A new generation of space allocation models has started to emerge which also consider space elasticities. Space elasticity is a measure of the reaction of sales to changes in space allocated. Several experimental and cross-sectional approaches have been utilized to estimate space elasticity; some products are clearly more responsive than others to changes in space allocations.

The extent of impulse or unplanned purchasing has tended to increase, partly because of greater time pressures upon consumers but also because of more effective store environments. Studies of the extent of impulse purchasing have illustrated major differences between products and between retail store types. Various methodologies have been used to measure impulse purchasing; each has its limitations because of the problems in identifying the time and place of the purchase decision. Measures of unplanned purchasing do however provide valuable insights into the overall effects of in-store marketing variables.

REVIEW QUESTIONS

1. Account for the increased emphasis upon design in new store developments and refurbishments.
2. How would you ensure that your design programme for a chain of menswear stores is cost-effective? What criteria would you use to evaluate the success of the programme?
3. 'Atmospherics becomes a more relevant marketing tool as the number of competitive outlets increases.' Discuss.
4. What would be your specific objectives when selecting the in-store colour schemes and the background music for
   (a) a discount clothing store?
   (b) a department store?
5. Compare the advantages and disadvantages of
   (a) the 'grid pattern' layout,
   (b) the 'free-flow' layout.
6. What methods are available to track shoppers' movements within the store? How could such tracking studies contribute to the redesign of your store layout?
7. Compare the objectives and techniques of
   (a) life-style displays;
   (b) co-ordinated displays;
   (c) classification dominance displays.
8. How would you evaluate the effectiveness of special, off-shelf displays in a supermarket?
9. Define space elasticity. What approaches are available for the measurement of space elasticity, and what problems are likely to be encountered?
10. Discuss the advantages and limitations of space allocation systems based upon the 'level rundown' principle.
11. Define an impulse purchase. To what extent is the concept of impulse purchasing relevant to the design of the retail environment?
12. Compare and evaluate the alternative approaches to the measurement of impulse purchasing.

REFERENCES

Anderson, E. E. (1979), 'An analysis of retail display space: theory and methods', *Journal of Business*, **52**(1), 103–18.
Bellenger, D., D. Robertson and E. Hirschman (1978), 'Impulse buying varies by product', *Journal of Advertising Research*, **18**(6), 15–18.

Bellizzi, J. A., A. E. Crowley and R. W. Hasty (1983), 'The effects of color in store design', *Journal of Retailing*, **59**(1), 21–45.

Bolen, W. H. (1988), *Contemporary Retailing*, Prentice-Hall, Englewood Cliffs, NJ.

Brown, B. (1979), 'Using design as a strategic function', *Retail & Distribution Management*, **7**(5), 30–2.

Brown, S. (1988), 'Shopper movement in a planned shopping centre', *Retail & Distribution Management*, **16**(1), 30–4.

Brown, W. M. and W. T. Tucker (1961), 'Vanishing shelf space', *Atlanta Economic Review*, **9**, 9–16, 23.

Buttle, F. (1984a), 'Retail space allocation', *International Journal of Physical Distribution & Materials Management*, **14**(4), 3–23.

Buttle, F. (1984b), 'Merchandising', *European Journal of Marketing*, **18**(6/7), 104–23.

Calcott, D. (1980), 'Sell more and sell better with good design', *Retail & Distribution Management*, **8**(3), 45–7.

Chevalier, M. (1975a), 'Increase in sales due to in-store display', *Journal of Marketing Research*, **12**(4), 426–31.

Chevalier, M. (1975b), 'Substitution patterns as a result of display in the product category', *Journal of Retailing*, **50**(4), 65–72, 88.

Clover, V. T. (1950), 'Relative importance of impulse buying in retail stores', *Journal of Marketing*, **15**(1), 66–70.

Cobb, C. J. and W. D. Hoyer (1986), 'Planned versus impulse purchase behaviour', *Journal of Retailing*, **62**(4), 384–409.

Corstjens, M. and P. Doyle (1981), 'A model for optimizing retail space allocations', *Management Science*, **27**(7), 822–33.

Corstjens, M. and P. Doyle (1983), 'A dynamic model for strategically allocating retail space', *Journal of the Operational Research Society*, **34**(10), 943–51.

Cox, K. (1964), 'The responsiveness of food sales to shelf space changes in supermarkets', *Journal of Marketing Research*, **2**(2), 63–7.

Cox, K. (1970), 'The effect of shelf space upon sales of branded products', *Journal of Marketing Research*, **7**(1), 55–8.

Curhan, R. C. (1972), 'The relationship between shelf space and unit sales in supermarkets', *Journal of Marketing Research*, **9**(4), 406–12.

Curhan, R. C. (1973), 'Shelf space allocation and profit maximisation in mass retailing', *Journal of Marketing*, **37**(3), 54–60.

Curhan, R. C. (1974), 'The effects of merchandising and temporary promotional activities on the sales of fresh fruit and vegetables in supermarkets', *Journal of Marketing Research*, **11**(3), 286–94.

D'Antoni, J. S. and H. L. Shenson (1973), 'Impulse buying revisited: a behavioural typology', *Journal of Retailing*, **49**(1), 63–76.

Davidson, H. (1981), 'How and why shoppers buy', *Marketing*, 28 October, 18–20.

Davidson, W. R. and A. Doody (1966), *Retailing Management*, Ronald Press, New York.

Deshpande, R. and S. Krishnan (1980), 'Consumer impulse purchase and credit card usage: an empirical examination using the log linear model', in J. C. Olson (ed.), *Advances in Consumer Research*, Association for Consumer Research, Ann Arbor, Mich., pp. 792–5.

Dickson, J. P. (1974), 'Retail media co-ordination strategy', *Journal of Retailing*, **50**(2), 61–9.

Donovan, R. J. and J. R. Rossiter (1982), 'Store atmosphere: an environmental psychology approach', *Journal of Retailing*, **58**(1), 34–57.

Doyle, P. and B. Z. Gidengil (1977), 'A review of in-store experiments', *Journal of Retailing*, **53**(2), 47–62.

du Pont (1945, 1949, 1954, 1959, 1965), *Consumer Buying Habits Studies*, du Pont de Nemours, Wilmington, Del.

Dyer, L. W. (1980), 'In-store research at Publix', *Progressive Grocer*, **59**(12), 98–106.

Engel, J. and R. Blackwell (1982), *Consumer Behavior*, Dryden Press, Chicago.

Eroglu, S. and G. D. Harrell (1986), 'Retail crowding: theoretical and strategic implications', *Journal of Retailing*, **62**(4), 346–63.

Euromonitor (1987), 'Retail design and shopfitting', in *Retail Trade in the United Kingdom*, Euromonitor, London, pp. 261–70.

Fitch, R. (1981), 'The high street battle to reach a fickle public', *Campaign*, 6 November, 38–9.

Fletcher, K. (1987), 'Consumers' use and perceptions of retailer controlled information sources', *International Journal of Retailing*, **2**(3), 59–66.

Frank, R. E. and W. F. Massy (1970), 'Shelf position and space effects on sales', *Journal of Marketing Research*, **7**(1), 59–66.

Gagnon, J. P. and J. T. Osterhaus (1985), 'Effectiveness of floor displays on the sales of retail products', *Journal of Retailing*, **61**(1), 104–16.

Green, W. R. (1986), *The Retail Store: Design and Construction*, Van Nostrand Reinhold, New York.

Hayne, C. (1981), 'Light and colour', *Occupational Health*, **33**(4), 198–205.

Hirschman, E. C. and M. B. Holbrook (1982), 'Hedonic consumption: emerging concepts, methods and propositions', *Journal of Marketing*, **46**(3), 92–101.

Holland, C. W. and D. W. Cravens (1973), 'Fractional factorial experimental designs in marketing research', *Journal of Marketing Research*, **10**(3), 270–6.

Humphreys, F. (1987), 'Retail designers or designer retailers: who's briefing whom', *Retail*, **5**(2), 42–3.

Kollat, D. T. and R. P. Willett (1967), 'Consumer impulse purchasing behavior', *Journal of Marketing Research*, **4**(1), 21–31.

Kollat, D. T. and R. P. Willett (1969), 'Is impulse purchasing really a useful concept for marketing decisions?' *Journal of Marketing*, **33**(1), 79–83.

Kotler, P. (1973), 'Atmospherics as a marketing tool', *Journal of Retailing*, **49**(4), 48–64.

Kotzan, J. A. and R. V. Evanson (1969), 'Responsiveness of drug store sales to shelf space allocations', *Journal of Marketing Research*, **6**(4), 465–9.

Leone, R. P. and R. L. Schultz (1980), 'A study of marketing generalisations', *Journal of Marketing*, **44**(1), 10–18.

Lipstein, B. (1981), 'A review of retail store experiments', in R. W. Stampfl and E. C. Hirschman (eds.), *Theory in Retailing: Traditional and Nontraditional Sources*, American Marketing Association, Chicago, pp. 95–107.

Lusch, R. F. (1982), *The Management of Retail Enterprises*, Kent Publishing, Boston.

Market Place (1986), 'Design update', *Market Place*, **4**, 28–9.

Markin, R. J., C. M. Lillis and C. L. Narayana (1976), 'Social–psychological significance of store space', *Journal of Retailing*, **52**(1), 43–54, 94, 95.

Marking, G. (1986), 'Design for shopping', *Survey*, **3**(3), 9–11.

McFadyen, E. (1981), 'Getting away from the curse of the average', *Retail & Distribution Management*, **9**(4), 22–6.

McFadyen, E. (1985), 'How good merchandising has transformed the retail scene', *Retail & Distribution Management*, **13**(4), 16–21.

McGoldrick, P. J. (1982), 'How unplanned are impulse purchases?' *Retail & Distribution Management*, **10**(1), 27–32.

McGoldrick, P. J. and D. Thorpe (1977), *Shelf Space Allocation in Supermarkets*, RORU, Manchester Business School.

McKinnon, G. F., J. P. Kelly and E. D. Robinson (1981), 'Sales effects of point-of-purchase in-store signing', *Journal of Retailing*, **57**(2), 49–63.

Milliman, R. E. (1982), 'Using background music to affect the behavior of supermarket shoppers', *Journal of Marketing*, **46**(3), 86–91.

Mintel (1985), 'Retail design', *Mintel Retail Intelligence*, Summer, 91–110.

Peterson, R. A. and J. W. Cagley (1973), 'The effect of shelf space upon sales of branded products: an appraisal', *Journal of Marketing Research*, **10**(1), 103–4.

Point-of-Purchase Advertising Institute (1963), *Drugstore Brand Switching and Impulse Buying*, Point-of-Purchase Advertising Institute, New York.

Pollay, R. (1968), 'Customer impulse purchasing behavior: a re-examination', *Journal of Marketing Research*, **5**(3), 323–5.

Prasad, V. K. (1975), 'Unplanned buying in two retail settings', *Journal of Retailing*, **51**(3), 3–12.

Progressive Grocer (1960), 'Dillon study: how to build more profits into your special display programme', *Progressive Grocer*, **39**(1), 49–72.

Progressive Grocer (1975), 'Consumer behavior in a supermarket', *Progressive Grocer*, **54**(10), 36–59.

Retail (1986), 'Music while you shop', *Retail*, **3**(4), 36.

Retail (1987), 'Image making at Dunhill', *Retail*, **5**(1), 32–3.

Retail & Distribution Management (1987), 'Second thoughts about design', *Retail & Distribution Management*, **15**(1), 7.

Rinne, H., M. Guerts and J. P. Kelly (1987), 'An approach to allocating space to departments in a retail store', *International Journal of Retailing*, **2**(2), 27–41.

Rogers, D. (1985), 'Research tools for better merchandising', *Retail & Distribution Management*, **13**(6), 42–4.

Rosenbloom, B. (1981), *Retail Marketing*, Random House, New York.

Rossotti, H. (1983), *Colour*, Princeton University Press.

Sanghavi, N. (1988), 'Space management in shops: a new initiative', *Retail & Distribution Management*, **16**(1), 14–17.

Sharples, S. (1983), 'Retail designers in the '80s', *Retail & Distribution Management*, **11**(2), 42–5.

Sharples, S. (1985), 'DIY warehouse in disguise?' *Retail & Distribution Management*, **13**(4), 31–3.

Sharples, S. (1986), 'Asda's "gables" merging the old and new', *Retail & Distribution Management*, **14**(6), 22–3.

Sharples, S. (1987), 'Lighting up time: illumination in the retail environment', *Retail & Distribution Management*, **15**(3), 43–6.

Singh, M. G. and R. Cook (1986), 'RESOURCE-OPT: a decision support system for retail space and other allocation problems', in *Retail Strategies for Profit and Growth*, ESOMAR, Amsterdam, pp. 199–223.

Sommer, R. and S. Aitkens (1982), 'Mental mapping of two supermarkets', *Journal of Consumer Research*, **9**(2), 211–15.

Stern, H. (1962), 'The significance of impulse buying today', *Journal of Marketing*, **26**(2), 59–62.

Thomas, H. (1987), 'The design dilemma', *Marketing*, 5 November, 24–7.

Wells, W. D. and L. A. Lo Sciuto (1966), 'Direct observation of purchasing behavior', *Journal of Marketing Research*, **3**(3), 227–33.

West, C. J. (1951), 'Results of two years of study into impulse buying', *Journal of Marketing*, **15**(3), 362–3.

Wilkinson, J. B., J. B. Mason and C. H. Paksoy (1982), 'Assessing the impact of short-term supermarket strategy variables', *Journal of Marketing Research*, **19**(1), 72–86.

Wilkinson, J. B., C. H. Paksoy and J. B. Mason (1981), 'A demand analysis for newspaper advertising and changes in space allocation', *Journal of Retailing*, **57**(2), 30–48.

Williams, J. and R. Dardis (1972), 'Shopping behavior for soft goods and marketing strategies', *Journal of Retailing*, **48**(3), 32–41.

Woodside, A. G. and G. L. Waddle (1975), 'Sales effects of in-store advertising', *Journal of Advertising Research*, **15**(3), 29–34.

TWELVE

ELEMENTS OF RETAIL SERVICE

INTRODUCTION

It is appropriate that the concluding chapter of this book should be devoted to retail service, which has now become a major focus of many retailers' differentiation strategies. Retailing has always been a service industry, and, in the broadest sense, most aspects of the retailing mix represent a form of service to the consumer. For example, the buying and merchandising functions assemble and present an assortment to the consumer, at competitive prices; the location function seeks to ensure that this value and choice is conveniently accessible. This chapter adopts a more specific connotation of service, focusing upon personal service, financial services and other elements designed to reduce risks and make shopping easier, more efficient and more pleasant.

The potential scope of a retailer's service mix is very wide indeed. Within the domain of personal service, there is a great deal of opportunity to enhance the shopping experience through appropriate staff management and training. The efficiency, appearance, attitude, availability and product knowledge of store personnel are important issues for many shoppers. Among the financial services, the emergence of the store card and many other forms of credit have contributed both to transaction efficiency and to marketing effectiveness. Times of opening have also become an important form of differentiation, as retailers must increasingly cater for those unable to shop at 'normal' times. Some services aim to reduce the perceived risks of product purchases, such as changing rooms, favourable returns policies and extended warranties. Others aim to enhance convenience, such as free bagging and carry-out services.

It is essential that a retailer should develop an integrated service policy, based upon a clear understanding of the needs and preferences of the target segments. A service of great appeal to some types of shopper may convey altogether the wrong image for others. For example, the acceptance of credit cards for grocery purchases may be perceived as highly convenient, or as adding to cost; the provision of a service delicatessen may be regarded as adding to choice and human contact, or as an additional inconvenience and delay.

In a recent study by management consultants Ernst and Whinney, 98 per cent of senior retail managers interviewed felt that customer service should be a key factor within company strategy; however, only 35 per cent had considered a philosophy on customer care within their organization. Retailers have been criticized for adopting a piecemeal approach to the provision of services (e.g. Humble and Randell 1988), often simply copying the moves of rival companies. Although such reactions may sometimes be appropriate or even essential, they are obviously not the best route to the development of a co-ordinated or effectively differentiated service policy.

The service produced must be consistent with overall strategy and with the image that the company is seeking to portray (Hummel and Savitt 1988). In that most forms of service also add to retail costs, care must also be taken to ensure that the direct or indirect benefits outweigh these costs, and to determine the possible impact upon margins or prices.

12.1 PERSONAL SERVICE

Much of the evolution in retail outlets, discussed in Chapter 2, has involved increased levels of self-service and reduced levels of staffing. The supermarket represented the first major shift, and now self-service has spread into most retail sectors. This trend has obviously been fuelled by the desire to minimize wage costs, which in most cases are still the largest single category of retail costs. Although the quest for greater operational efficiency will continue, the realization has grown that services, including elements of personal service, are important means of achieving competitive advantage. An acute need therefore exists to differentiate clearly between those activities that represent avoidable costs and those that truly provide a service and an attraction to customers.

This section first considers the role of personal service in retailing, including evidence of consumer preferences between personal and self-service. Attention then turns to the personal selling function, including the various stages in the personal selling process. A detailed treatment of staff selection, motivation and training is beyond the scope of this text, although it must be appreciated that the effectiveness of the personnel and staff management functions in retailing are major determinants of the quality of personal service provided in the store.

12.1.1 The role of personal service

Even in retail settings dominated by self-service, the services provided by the store staff can exert a major influence upon patronage decisions and retail images. Teas (1981) cited several studies that have highlighted the importance of such service, although there are many research problems involved in trying to establish the relative importance of factors influencing store patronage, as discussed in Chapter 3. Studies that focus upon the service factors naturally tend to emphasize the importance of these, although there is good reason to believe that service is becoming an increasingly important area of differentiation between stores. Rainbow (1987) reported that staff politeness, presentability and knowledge of products were important to most shoppers in both specialized and convenience shopping. The attitude and availability of staff were also particularly important to customers when undertaking specialized shopping.

In all too many cases, the importance of service is most strongly conveyed through the complaints of customers. The Leo Burnett (1987) study, entitled *Are You Being Served?*, noted that the worst service appeared to be provided by some supermarkets, post offices, department stores, fast food outlets and shoe shops. The five complaints most frequently cited were:

1. Not enough tills at busy times (44%)
2. Queues (40%)
3. Staff who knew nothing about the goods (40%)
4. Paying for carrier bags (37%)
5. Staff who hover and pester you (31%)

The study also illustrated the acceptable trade-off between prices and services for many customers, with 70 per cent claiming that they would not mind if the goods were a little more expensive, if the service was particularly good; 91 per cent claimed that they would not go back somewhere if they got really bad service. Commenting on this report, Humble and Randell (1988) noted that most retailers do not encourage complaints, feeling that this would be to 'open up a can of worms'. This contrasts with practices elsewhere, where legitimate complaints are actively encouraged and are used as important diagnostic and marketing data.

Customers' attitudes to service were also reflected in the Euromonitor (1986) survey of nearly 3,000 grocery shoppers. When asked what they liked most about the store visited most often, 24 per cent mentioned the efficiency of checkout service, whereas hardly any mentioned friendly, helpful or polite personal service. This should not be interpreted as indicating that these factors are unimportant, rather that they do not tend to be well perceived. Rainbow (1987) found that 78 per cent of shoppers had been put off making purchases as the direct result of the attitude of a shop assistant.

There would appear to be major differences between countries in terms of the staff–customer relationship. For example, Williamson (1986) reported that customers tended to be treated as honoured guests within Japanese department stores. Each store has a motto, such as 'Sincerity with service', which is effectively instilled in all members of staff. In the USA, Sam Walton, chairman of the Wal-Mart discount chain, has established a vigorous staff motivation and customer care programme (Aldred 1989). To quote from the 'gospel according to Sam',

'I solemnly promise and declare that every customer that comes within 10 ft of me I will smile, look them in the eye and greet them, so help me Sam.'

Retailers in the UK are giving increased attention to staff training and motivation towards customer service. To assist this process, Tesco launched a competition to find the friendliest store among its branches. The winning store received £5,000 for a charity of its choice, plus a £50 bonus for each staff member. The DIY superstores have also found it necessary to improve customer service levels, this being a shopping situation in which customers have a particular need for information and advice (Davies *et al.* 1986). Most have established information points, although specialist information is still frequently unavailable. Wickes also makes 'fact-sheets' freely available within its stores to help to overcome this problem. The company has also now introduced better signage, glass-cutting, paint-mixing, roof rack loans, coffee shops and customer toilets into its upgraded stores. The commitment of Payless to improving customer service was reflected in the creation of a new, senior management post, designated Head of Customer Service.

Although many of the complaints about service have arisen, directly or indirectly, as a result of self-service and reduced staffing levels, it would be incorrect to assume that all customers would prefer to see a shift away from self-service. Across a range of different situations, Bateson (1985) found that many customers prefer self-service options, even when they are neither cheaper nor more convenient. Following a series of group interviews, scenarios were developed which sought to test consumer reactions to self-service and conventional service options, while keeping other factors constant. These included the following:

1. At the petrol station—attendant service versus self-service, assuming that prices and queue lengths are the same
2. At the bank—using an automatic teller machine (ATM) versus using the services of a bank clerk; again, queue lengths were standardized
3. At a fast food restaurant—self-service at the counter versus receiving waiter/waitress service at the table

Table 12.1 summarizes the proportions of respondents to a mail survey who would use the self-service alternative on some or all occasions in these three situations. In each case, around

Table 12.1 Use of self-service options

% of occasions respondents would use self-service option	Level of participation	% of respondents if at:		
		A petrol station	A bank	A fast food restaurant
0	None	31	22	13
1–39	Low	24	23	32
40–60	Medium	15	20	27
61–99	High	24	24	21
100	Full	6	11	7
N		659	731	735

Source: Bateson (1985).

30 per cent of respondents indicated that they would use the self-service option on more than 60 per cent of occasions, i.e. were classified as high or full participators. This propensity to opt for self-service also appeared to carry over between situations. A number of factors emerged as being relevant to the choice:

1. Time—some saw services as time-consuming.
2. Control—forms of conventional service may reduce the customer's feeling of control over the situation.
3. Effort—some forms of self-service increase the mental or physical effort required.
4. Dependence—many reacted against the need to depend on others to receive the service.
5. Efficiency—an important element in evaluating the benefit of services.
6. Human contact—different customers have different levels of need for human contact when receiving a service.
7. Risk—psycho-social and performance risks (Bauer 1960) were relevant to the choice of many cases.

The findings of this study confirmed that self-service is not always perceived negatively or as a withdrawal of services. Many facets of self-service were preferred by a significant proportion of consumers. This underlines the need to identify correctly those elements of service that are really important to consumers, as opposed to those that are simply the usual way of delivering the service. Whatever the balance between self- and assisted service, however, the attitude, manner and appearance of staff remain key elements of customers' store images.

12.1.2 Personal selling

Personal selling remains a very important element of the retail marketing mix in some sectors, especially where products are relatively complex, expensive and/or infrequently purchased. Even in predominantly self-service stores, well trained staff with high levels of product knowledge can be a major asset. For example, it was claimed that the sale of men's suits in Marks & Spencer doubled when selected assistants were specially trained in that product area (Sands 1987).

It is therefore surprising that the strategies and techniques of personal selling have received little attention recently within the retail marketing literature. Clarke (1983) noted that this tendency to underestimate the importance of personal selling also carries over into staff training:

Most staff training in department stores is geared to basic procedures (such as till operation, means of payment, paperwork systems) and formal rules, with relatively little attention paid to methods of selling.

Rogers (1988) stressed the importance of personal selling, particularly where expensive purchases are involved:

If there is one thing, above all others, that an intending purchaser really needs when about to spend a considerable sum of money on a product, it is a trained sales person.

The role of the retail salesperson has tended to be severely underestimated, in part because of the assumption that shoppers have been 'presold' through advertising, packaging and effective merchandising (Burstiner 1975/6). In that shoppers usually come to the retail salespersons, rather than vice versa, the latter have come to be regarded as just 'order-fillers' (Dubinsky and Mattson 1979). In fact, there are various different levels of personal selling in retailing, some of which are indeed routine but none the less important. James *et al.* (1981) suggested three broad categories of personal selling:

1. *Transaction processing*—for example, checkout cashiers. This level requires the least creative selling but is now the main form of staff–customer contact in many sectors. Staff performing such functions therefore need to be efficient, smart, helpful and friendly, as they carry a major responsibility for shoppers' images of the store.
2. *Routine selling*—for example, the sales assistants in department or discount stores who are involved in the selling of lower-cost, non-technical lines. The above characteristics, plus the ability to locate and describe the products efficiently, are the major requirements, although scope for suggestion selling frequently exists. Where point-of-sale computers are installed, these may prompt the suggestion selling by indicating related products that are available within the store.
3. *Creative selling*—where complex or expensive purchases are involved, the salesperson requires a high level of product knowledge and skill in the selling process. Some stores, for example those selling fitted furniture, use titles such as design/sales consultants to emphasize the specialist roles of those sales personnel. In theory, sadly not always in practice, they should be highly skilled in translating shoppers' needs into specific product and service solutions.

At the most creative level, the process of retail selling may be regarded as following a number of important steps. For a more detailed discussion of the selling process, readers may wish to consult a specialist text, such as Mills and Paul (1979) or Rogers (1988). In most settings, the main steps are as follows:

1. *Pre-customer contact* Before any contact is made with the customer, the salesperson needs to be fully informed of product features, benefits, options, prices, stock levels, delivery schedules, guarantees, returns policies, etc.:

A good salesperson possesses a fund of knowledge about the products, how they are made, how they are used, what they will do for their owners, and be able to justify the price being asked. (Rogers 1988)

If high-order selling activities are required, retailers clearly must be prepared to invest in relevant training and to accept that some degree of selling specialization is necessary, i.e. that mobility between product groups may be limited. In some situations, the salesperson may also be involved in prospecting for new customers, although this function is usually now centralized at store or company level.

2. *Opening the sale*   It is sometimes argued that more potential sales are lost at the initial contact stage than at any other. One problem is that many customers prefer to avoid engaging in discussion with sales staff when they are at the browsing or 'window-shopping' phase in their purchase decision (Fletcher 1987). A survey of the opening remarks used by 100 salespersons indicated that only 12 per cent opened with a truly positive selling effort (Bolen 1970). The usual clichés of 'May/can I help you?' were used by 77 per cent of the salespersons. In most cases, such opening lines simply get the reply 'no thank you, I'm just looking'; after that, the salesperson has little opportunity to continue the conversation. More positive openings can be achieved by asking the customer a question, for example about the colour or size that is being sought.

3. *Presentation of products*   Having successfully opened the conversation, the next phase involves the most effective presentation of the relevant products. Bolen (1988) stresses the importance of selling the user benefits, not just the product characteristics. The involvement of customers may also be increased by allowing them to use, try on or touch the products. A common error at the presentation stage is to confuse the customer with too great a product choice; a better strategy is to withdraw items that are obviously of less appeal, to reduce the decision to a manageable subset of the available choice.

4. *Handling objections*   As the sale progresses, it is likely that customers will express 'objections' about the potential purchase. The intention may be to delay the purchase decision, to seek reassurance from the salesperson, and/or to express strongly felt doubts. These typically relate to the product itself, the store, the after-sales service or the price. The salesperson must clearly identify the motive and the nature of the objection in order to respond appropriately. Engaging in a direct argument with the customer is rarely the most appropriate technique; obviously, the customer must be correctly informed and reassured, without giving offence.

5. *Closing the sale*   Even the most successful sales conversation usually requires a positive effort to close the sale effectively. A number of techniques have been suggested, which are summarized in Table 12.2. Whichever one is adopted, the timing is of crucial importance. Attempts to rush closure, possibly because other customers are waiting, may leave major objections outstanding; conversely, excessive delay in closure may leave the customer confused and weary of the process, therefore more inclined to postpone purchase.

Although these represent the main steps in personal selling, the process may continue beyond the closure of the specific sale. Scope for further suggestion selling exists in many situations, such as suggesting the accessories to accompany the purchase of a camera. If home delivery is involved, the salesperson should also monitor that promises are kept, otherwise complaints will quickly arise.

Any general summary of the selling process tends to underemphasize the importance of adaptation in personal selling. Every customer is different, as are his/her specific needs or wants. A retailer may seek to recruit salespersons with attributes similar to those of target customers (Churchill *et al.* 1975), but the need to adapt the selling approach remains strong. O'Shaughnessy (1971/2) depicted retail selling as an interpersonal influence process and outlined ways in which the selling strategy might be adapted to suit the customer's stage in the decision process. An important task of the salesperson is to establish the choice criteria of the specific customer and the extent to which these are defined; the selling strategy that best helps the customer to move towards a purchase decision can then be adopted. Such an approach requires an alert sensitivity and understanding of the customer's decision process; it is a long way from the standardized 'sales patter' so often encountered in personal selling.

Table 12.2   Techniques for closing sales

Technique	Example
Assumption	'Do you want this purchase charged to your account?'
Direct	'Do you want to purchase this?'
Limited choice	'Do you prefer the blue or the green?'
Special service	'Would you like me to gift-wrap it for you?'
Inducement	'We will include the batteries.'
Don't delay	'This is the last one in your size.'
Summary	The sales person summarizes the benefits of most appeal to the customer.
Silence	Simply wait, if the customer is close to a decision.

Source: Danny R. Arnold, Louis M. Capella and Garry D. Smith, *Strategic Retail Management*, Copyright © 1983, Addison-Wesley Publishing Co., Inc., Reading, Massachusetts. Adapted from Table 17.4 and reprinted with permission of the publisher.

12.2   FINANCIAL SERVICES

The ease with which customers can pay, both in terms of efficiency and available credit, has become an important influence upon store choice and transaction size. Retailers have a long history of providing credit for regular customers, a practice that became formalized into customer accounts, then into the present generation of store cards. For many years, credit tended to be associated with more expensive purchases; the spread of credit cards and the tendency towards fewer, larger shopping trips has brought credit usage into nearly all sectors of retailing. The development of 'own-brand' credit cards has also opened up many new marketing opportunities for retailers.

This section first examines the growth of credit cards and some characteristics of their usage in retail stores. The strategy of retail store cards is then considered, specifically the advantages, techniques and possible problems of operating a card system. The progression by some retailers from store cards into other forms of financial services is then briefly reviewed. Finally, attention turns to EFTPoS, the acronym for Electronic Funds Transfer at the Point of Sale. This is being developed as an alternative transaction mode, which could yield benefits for retailers and their customers.

12.2.1   The growth of credit cards

By 1988 it was estimated that the British held over 80 million financial plastic cards, of which nearly 30 million were credit cards (Frazer 1988). This represents a considerable rate of growth since the launch of the first bank credit card by Barclays in 1966. The holding of credit cards has proved particularly attractive in the UK; no other European country has a comparable number of cards on issue (Thomson 1988), and there is a greater reluctance to use credit to pay for minor purchases in some countries (Lafferty 1987). Even in the UK there is much scope for development, in that over half of men and about two-thirds of women still do not hold a credit card (Retail Business 1987a). This could be compared with the USA, where there are on average 7.2 cards per person, over half of which are retail credit cards (Market Place 1986).

Table 12.3 summarizes the growth since 1982 of bank-issued credit cards, which of course are just one source of credit for retail purchase. The combined number of Access and Visa accounts grew by 50 per cent over the four years to 1986, and the usage of the accounts, in terms of transactions, turnover and credit outstanding, also grew considerably. By comparison, retailer's

Table 12.3   Growth of bank-issued credit cards, 1982–1986

	1982	*1986*
Access/Visa cards issued (m)	14.6	21.9
Number of accounts (m)	12.0	18.0
Number of transactions (m)	218	451
Value of turnover (£m)	4,898	13,214
Credit outstanding (£m)	2,021	4,885
Credit per account (£)	168	271
Retail outlets accepting		
Access ('000)	190	270
Visa ('000)	192	258
Access business by sector	(%)	(%)
Clothing and footwear	11.3	10.6
Household and furniture	8.0	8.4
Consumer durables	13.5	13.4
General stores	14.4	11.9
Garages	22.3	18.1
Travel and entertainment	20.6	23.0
Miscellaneous	9.9	14.6
Total	100	100

Source: Retail Business (1987a).

'own-brand' credit cards had achieved more limited penetration but are growing very rapidly. Bliss (1988) estimated that the Burton, Marks & Spencer and House of Fraser cards had each achieved over 1.5 million accounts, with retail cards in general totalling over 10 million.

The number of retail outlets accepting Access and Visa cards has grown progressively, as few retailers are able to resist the demand for this mode of payment. In sectors where consumers have become accustomed to paying by credit card, only the strongest of multiple chains, such as Marks & Spencer and the John Lewis Partnership, have been able to refuse the major bank-issued credit cards. Supermarkets represent one major sector that has not traditionally accepted credit cards, although the situation is changing rapidly. Barclaycard found that their turnover in supermarkets increased by 132 per cent in 1986 (Retail Business 1987a). Access claim that 1,500 larger supermarkets now accept their card, although Sainsbury has resisted this trend (Walker 1988). The Dee Corporation has responded with the launch of its own card, making it the first supermarket group with a store card (Warner 1987).

Well before the recent boom in retail store cards, many retailers had gained experience in offering various types of credit facilities. Bliss (1979) described the three forms of credit offered by Debenhams:

1. *Option charge accounts*   Like bank credit cards, these provide the option of being used as a charge account, attracting no interest if the monthly account is paid within the specified period after the statement date.

2. *Budget accounts*   The customer establishes a monthly banker's order and is allowed credit of up to 24 times the basic monthly payment.
3. *Credit terms*   These are longer-term facilities, available over periods of up to three years, to assist major purchases. Such arrangements may include the incentive of zero interest if the account is settled within the first few months.

The credit formats of the new generation of store cards have become more standardized, although different names are used by the various retailers. For example, Next refer to their 'Option Account', Marks & Spencer to their 'Chargecard' and Sears simply to the 'Sears Card'. In each case, the card may be used as a charge card, interest-free, or payments may be spread over a longer period and interest incurred. The term 'credit card' tends to be avoided because of negative connotations and the more up-market/exclusive images of the well established charge cards, such as American Express and Diners Club.

One element that is certainly not standardized between the store cards is the rate of interest charged if the credit option is utilized. In general, the annual percentage rate (APR) of store cards tends to be higher than those of the main bank-issued cards. In a comparison published by the *Guardian* in 1988, only the John Lewis APR was lower at 19.5 compared with the 23.1 of both Access and Visa (Hunter 1988). At the other extreme, Dixon's APR was 39.8, closely followed by Rumbelows (39.2) and Comet (38.4). In all these cases, however, a lower APR applied if the customer agreed to establish a direct debit arrangement. Following adverse publicity about the high levels of interest applied by certain store cards, rates were reduced in some cases.

In that some retailers' APRs are more than double the level of others, it is clear that most consumers are insensitive to interest rates. The Save and Prosper financial services company had a disappointing response to its new Visa card, even with the lowest available APR at 17.4. According to the company's marketing director, 'there's a conventional wisdom in the financial services business that people are just interest rate insensitive—they simply don't care' (King 1988). In part, this insensitivity may reflect an optimism that the account can be settled in full each month, thereby making the APR irrelevant. Thomson (1988) reported that over half of credit card holders in the UK use their cards in this way. There is however also widespread ignorance as to the way in which interest is calculated; the National Consumer Council (1987) found that only 34 per cent of an interview sample knew the meaning of APR.

The particular characteristics of credit card users have made them an attractive target for retailers' promotional efforts. From a study of bank credit card users in department stores in the USA, Hirschman and Goldstucker (1978) found that they tended to have higher incomes, be active in community organizations, and play an important role in disseminating fashion information. Table 12.4 shows the percentages of specific age and social class groups that use various types of credit card in the UK. All have a distinctly up-market bias and lowest penetration among the over-54 age group (National Consumer Council 1987). Among credit card holders in general, the majority are male, but the reverse is true of store card holders; in fact, 62 per cent of Marks & Spencer charge card holders are female (Market Place 1986).

12.2.2   The store card strategy

An 'own-label' store card can offer numerous advantages and opportunities for retailers, if operated, promoted and utilized effectively. Michael Bliss, chief executive of House of Fraser's financial services, went as far as to claim that 'the store card could become the most powerful marketing tool there has ever been' (Johnson 1987). The main benefits of running a store card system are as follows:

Table 12.4 Profile of credit card users

		Percentages using			
Card(s)	Mastercard Access	Visa/ Barclaycard/ Trustcard	Shop/ store card	Other	None
Age range					
15–24	11	16	10	1	77
25–34	23	26	13	2	53
35–54	26	26	15	2	52
66 +	11	15	3	1	76
Social class					
ABC1	29	27	15	2	48
C2DE	10	16	6	—	74
Total	18	20	10	1	64

Source: National Consumer Council (1987).

1. Customer transaction sizes tend to be larger, with more unplanned purchasing.
2. Loyalty to the store increases and can be nurtured by improved communication and the feeling of exclusiveness.
3. Detailed information is gained about customer characteristics and spending patterns.
4. Direct mail can be targeted to appeal to specific customer types.
5. The effects of promotions can be more precisely monitored.
6. Other financial services can be developed and promoted.
7. Costs may be lower than those incurred by accepting bank-issued credit cards.

To an extent, customers who are able and inclined to obtain a retail card are also likely to have a higher spending propensity. The retail card can however reinforce this and help to ensure that a higher proportion of that spending is obtained by the specific retailer. Bliss (1979) had noted the American experience that credit customers tend to spend two or three times as much as cash customers.

Letino (1986) observed that people are less reserved when using a card; they do not feel the full financial constraints of spending, in that conventional money is not exchanged at the point of sale. An analogy was drawn with casinos, where the perceived risk is reduced by the use of plastic chips, rather than real money.

Whereas bank-issued credit cards have been promoted primarily as a convenient form of payment, store cards also attempt to convey the 'club concept'. They enable a special relationship to be developed between retailers and their best customers, encouraging further involvement and loyalty. Common 'privileges' for card holders include exclusive offers, special shopping evenings and previews of sale events (Bliss 1988). Marks & Spencer run Charge Card evenings outside normal opening hours, sometimes offering free wine and live music as additional attractions (Retail 1986).

Store cards enable retailers to know a great deal about their customers, offering the high-technology equivalent of the small retailer–loyal customer relationship. Although the bank-issued credit card companies also have much customer information on file, they are unable to disclose this to retailers. Store cards therefore provide an unprecedented insight into the cardholder's personal details, habits, tastes and spending patterns (Johnson 1987). The personal details disclosed on card application forms are used initially for credit-scoring, then for segmentation and target marketing. Such application forms are likely to obtain some or all of the following details:

- Full name and address
- Property ownership
- Type of residence
- Length of residence
- Age
- Number of children and their age(s)
- Marital status
- Occupation and employer
- Length of service
- Salary
- Previous occupation
- Occupation/salary of spouse
- Bank account(s) held
- Other credit/charge cards

Armed with such formidable arrays of data, there are numerous opportunities for precisely targeted direct mail advertising, possibly also including the most appropriate financial inducements (Johnson 1987). The data continue to accumulate as reactions of specific customers to specific types of offer can be monitored (Bliss 1988). In that monthly statements are sent to cardholders, selected advertising enclosures, or 'free-riders', can be enclosed at little extra cost (Worthington 1986). With detailed information on card-based transactions, personalized letters can also be produced to suggest appropriate supplementary purchases; however, care must be taken not to appear too intrusive of customers' privacy! The Burton group puts its customer data to particularly effective use; as customers of, for example, Top Shop reach the upper end of the targeted age range, they are mailed information about other stores in the group catering for their age group (Thompson 1988). It is likely that this approach to retailing and developing loyalty through each stage of customers' life-cycles will be extensively developed.

In view of these many advantages, it is not surprising that store cards are being very actively promoted. Bliss (1979) described in some detail the marketing of the Debenhams card, which included media advertising (principally in women's magazines), direct mail shots, in-store advertising and special displays. Staff training played a major part, as did an incentive scheme which rewarded a salesperson with £5 per five accounts established. Compared with the major bank-issued cards, retailers' expenditure on media advertising specifically in support of their card tends to be relatively modest (Retail Business 1987a). Many incentives are however offered, such as £5 off the first statement or, in the case of Marks & Spencer, a consumer competition with a first prize worth £3,000. The survey undertaken by the National Consumer Council (1987) found that 10 per cent of store card holders had been attracted by an introductory offer.

In evaluating the store card strategy, a retailer must also consider the costs and potential dangers. In theory, a well managed card can represent a cost saving, particularly when compared with the 1½–4 per cent charged by bank-issued credit cards on a £50 transaction (National Consumer Council 1987). The store card can also lead to more highly automated transactions, reducing clutter and congestion at the checkouts. However, not all the store cards have broken even (Bendall and Hayes 1987), and some of the major banks have found the provision of 'own-label' cards for retailers to be unprofitable. From the retailer's viewpoint, the overall evaluation of profitability must consider not only the 'hard' costs and savings but also the many other benefits in terms of improved marketing opportunities.

The skill and commitment of store card management will inevitably influence the cost-effectiveness of the strategy. Ognjenovic (1980) noted that many of the defensive, 'me-too' card schemes were not harnessing the full potential marketing benefits. W. Thompson (1988) pointed out:

The administration is complex—and expensive if not done properly. Credit scoring is a sensitive and thankless job which cannot be done without upsetting someone. The credit balances need to be financed and accounted carefully and it is easy to underestimate the care and work necessary to make the cards a fully integrated part of the retail operation.

The lax credit-scoring practices of some retailers were criticized by the National Consumer Council (1987). R. Thomson (1988) referred to the inadequate or non-existent assessment techniques of some retailers, which had brought credit cards in general a bad name, as well as leaving those retailers with more bad debts. The adverse publicity concerning interest rates and credit-scoring contributed to the decision of one major retailer to withdraw its store card, predicting that others might do the same (Hunter 1988).

12.2.3 Other financial services

The experience gained in operating store cards and credit systems could lead to more diversification into other financial services. One approach is to enter the general credit card business, with a card acceptable in a wide range of outlets. In the USA, Sears Roebuck has achieved excellent penetration with its 'Discover' card, having recruited 15 million cardholders in the first 18 months. The National Consumer Council (1987) observed that Marks & Spencer would have a sufficient customer base and marketing advantage to take a similar step. In Scotland, the 'Style' card, initially limited to the Goldberg chain, subsequently was accepted by many other companies; it became the largest credit card operation in Scotland, having achieved penetration of 15 per cent of households (Euromonitor 1987; Worthington 1987). Control of this card has been acquired now by the Royal Bank of Scotland, so the range of financial services offered to cardholders is likely to increase further.

Welbeck Financial Services Ltd, previously a subsidiary of Debenhams and now part of the Burton group, has diversified aggressively into other forms of financial service. Various forms of insurance product have been directly marketed, including hospital cash plans, term life insurance, accident plans and household insurance. Personal loans for cars and other major purchases have also been offered at advantageous rates (Bliss 1982). The company has also managed store cards for other retailers, for example, Wickes. Meanwhile, Debenhams/Burtons have tried 'Homecentres' property shops within some stores. 'Moneycentres', initially run as concessions, were also established on a trial basis, and the company is evolving this concept into a small chain of 'Debenhams Share Centres' (Bliss 1988). The House of Fraser group is giving more prominence to 'Harrods Trust' banking facilities within its Harrods store, which also offers stock market trading facilities. In addition, a Harrods Estate Agency operates in Park Lane.

The spectrum of financial services that a retailer can provide, either by direct marketing or within its branches, is therefore very wide and may include:

- In-store banking/ATMs
- Charge cards/credit facilities
- Credit protection plans

- Extended product warranties
- Mortgages
- Estate agencies
- Property insurance
- Life assurance
- Pensions
- Annuities
- Unit trusts and shares

Retailers have a number of natural advantages in diversifying into these areas. They tend to enjoy a friendlier and more approachable image than most of the major financial institutions, in spite of intensive efforts by the latter to overcome this problem. Retailers also tend to have more experience in fiercely competitive environments (Johnson 1987). Furthermore, the up-market profile and the high rate of house ownership among store card holders provides a very sound basis for the selling of many financial services (Market Place 1986).

There are of course dangers in treating financial services as just another product category. Retailers tend to feel that they have superior marketing skills to those of bankers, but financial services do represent a very fundamental diversification (Bendall and Hayes 1987). Another major issue is the role of the retail outlets; their quality and location must be appropriate to the financial services envisaged, and some services can be sold equally effectively by direct marketing. It seems likely that more retailers will acquire, or form partnerships with, financial institutions in order to develop the required expertise. Others will choose to take the pure retailing role and will become aggressive resellers of financial services bought from a wide range of institutions (Bliss 1988).

12.2.4   Electronic funds transfer

Systems for electronic funds transfer at the point of sale (EFTPoS) have now been developed in many countries. The term EFTPoS is applied to a wide range of services and systems (Frazer 1985), with different communication technologies, debit card characteristics, point-of-sale configurations and very different funding/charging agreements between retailers and financial institutions. A broad definition has been suggested by RMDP (1987), which defines EFTPoS systems as meeting the following criteria:

1. There is an electronic transfer of funds between the customer's account and the retailer's account.
2. The customer's authorization for payment is completed at the point of sale.
3. The system must process *debit* cards.

In fact, most EFTPoS systems accept credit cards, serving a dual purpose as a credit authorization terminal (Frazer 1988). Investment in EFTPoS systems is increasing rapidly in order to reduce the number of cash, credit and cheque transactions. In the UK, EFTPoS initially took the form of localized experimental schemes. In 1985, EftPos UK Ltd was formed by the major banks to co-ordinate the movement towards a national system (EftPos UK 1987). An inaugural service was established in three areas, involving eleven banks and three building societies. The extent to which retailers and financial institutions will enjoy the full, potential benefits of EFTPoS depends upon the success of the technologies employed, the agreements formed, and the scale of adoption by shoppers.

The initial EFTPoS schemes in the UK have mostly been based upon the relatively simple magnetic stripe debit cards. In that these contain only the basic customer identification information, they involve heavy use of telecommunications networks. In some other countries, notably France, the USA and Japan, the development emphasis has been on 'smart cards', incorporating their own microcomputer chip. These give a read-and-write memory facility, allowing the card itself to convey the updated account details and therefore largely eliminating the need for on-line authorization networks. The cost of the chip, once an inhibiting factor, soon fell from $8 to just $0.20 in the USA (Jones 1986). However, smart-card terminals are currently far more expensive than those required for magnetic stripe cards (Ody 1988).

The capabilities of the smart card are being further extended with the development of the 'super-smart card' (Walman 1986). These can incorporate a 64K microchip, compared with the 4–8K of earlier smart cards, and they can also incorporate a small key pad and display. In that authorization and transaction recording can be handled entirely within the card, they can be used in shops without full EFTPoS terminal equipment (Retail Business 1987b). The Midland Bank has experimented with smart cards at Loughborough (Ody 1988), and developments in super-smart cards may ultimately cause some rethinking on commitments to magnetic stripe cards.

In the UK, the attitudes of retailers towards EFTPoS have generally been ambivalent (McFadyen 1987). There are undoubtedly benefits to be derived for retailers, but these are usually seen as less substantial than the benefits for the financial institutions (Smith 1987). Consequently, there is among retailers an understandable reluctance to carry a major cost burden. The benefits of EFTPoS to retailers have been reviewed by Sparks (1984) and ICL (1987). These include:

- Faster transactions at checkouts
- Reduced paperwork and cash handling
- Faster and more secure payments
- Overriding of cheque guarantee limits
- Virtual elimination of credit risks

Some of these are also advantages for customers, therefore potentially representing an additional attraction to the store. EFTPoS transactions take around 22 seconds, compared with 40 seconds with cheques and 75 seconds with credit card vouchers (Mintel 1987). EFTPoS could provide savings of around 8p and 11p respectively, depending upon the specific system costs. It now costs J. Sainsbury over £4 million per year to process cheques; petrol retailers too are concerned about the costly growth of credit card usage (Muttram 1987). The benefits of EFTPoS *vis-à-vis* cash are less clear-cut; the chairman of the EFT Policy Committee of the UK Retail Consortium described the ideal world as 'paperless', not necessarily 'cashless' (Woodman 1987).

The system, if linked to PoS data capture, can also give more information about customers' buying patterns, providing the basis for closely targeted promotional activities (see Section 12.2.2). Retailers therefore have a considerable interest in the development of EFTPoS; but at what cost? In the UK, as in France and elsewhere, there has been a power struggle between the retailers and the banks (Freestone 1987). In general, the banks have tended to underestimate the power and determination of retailers with regard to the costing of EFTPoS (Heath 1987).

Although there has been much debate about the systems, benefits and costs of EFTPoS, relatively little is known about consumer responses; this is crucial to any marketing evaluation of EFTPoS as a service. From the USA, a study of early reactions to the Iowa Transfer System (Porter *et al.* 1979) indicated only 59 per cent awareness, in spite of the fact that all respondents had been sent a debit card. The study pointed to weaknesses in the marketing of the systems and illustrated that awareness and usage would not necessarily occur quickly or spontaneously. In contrast, a massive advertising and promotional campaign accompanied the launch of the national EFTPoS system in Singapore (Jones 1987).

Table 12.5   Main advantages and disadvantages of EFTPoS

	% of 'awares'	Social class % ABC1	χ^2 ($p =$)
Advantages			
Less use of cash	24.5	75.0	(.000)
Greater security	14.8	76.4	(.002)
Time-saving	10.4	78.0	(.002)
Convenient	8.4	78.7	(.004)
Wider choice of payment mode	7.2	65.2	(n.s.)
Know cash flow better	2.8	66.7	(n.s.)
Disadvantages			
Too easy to overspend	20.0	78.1	(.000)
Instant debiting	6.4	87.4	(.000)
Possible technical error	5.4	75.9	(.093)
Loss or fraud	5.3	75.0	(n.s.)
Possible loss of other payment modes	2.8	68.9	(n.s.)
Not universal	2.7	67.4	(n.s.)
All 'awares' ($N = 1,607$)	100	67.0	—

Source: Ironfield and McGoldrick (1988, p. 34).

The reactions of elderly consumers to scanners, ATMs and EFTPoS were studied by Ziethaml and Gilly (1987). Rather surprisingly, many of the elderly sample had enthusiastically adopted EFTPoS, convenience and safety being important among the reasons given. Retailer and consumer reactions to a combined EFTPoS and cheque authorization system in Houston were reported by Bennett (1988). It was found that the use of the system for cheque authorization vastly exceeded its use for EFTPoS. In this EFTPoS system, the customer's account was debited on the same day, which may have inhibited use in some cases.

Ironfield and McGoldrick (1988) examined the reactions of 3,000 consumers who had potentially been exposed to experimental EFTPoS schemes in the UK. Only 53 per cent of respondents were aware of EFTPoS, reflecting the limited coverage and promotion of the experimental systems. Similarly, usage was very low, at just 4.4 per cent of the sample. Awareness was strongly related to higher social class, younger age groups and the current use of cheques and credit cards. Table 12.5 summarizes the main advantages and disadvantages perceived by the 1,607 'aware' respondents; relationships of each response group with social class are also summarized. The greatest single advantage was 'less use of cash'; few of the users had actually reduced their use of credit cards. Fear of overspending, instant debiting, technical error, loss or fraud were the main disadvantages perceived. Retailers must clearly monitor consumer reactions to EFTPoS very closely to ensure that the system is perceived to be a useful service, rather than a source of anxiety or irritation.

12.3   OTHER ELEMENTS OF SERVICE

Having now examined the major elements of personal and financial services, the purpose of this final section is two-fold. First, the extension of shopping hours is considered as a means of widening the effective accessibility of retail stores; the strategy of extended opening hours is evaluated in terms of existing shopping patterns and consumer attitudes towards evening/ Sunday shopping. Second, the range of other service options is very briefly reviewed, illustrating the scope that exists for the expansion of services and the need for an integrated retail service strategy.

12.3.1   Extended opening hours

Retailing was not historically associated with short opening hours; in fact, the hours worked by shop-owners and assistants in previous generations were extraordinarily long. To an extent, the spread of shorter hours was associated with the growth of multiple stores, involving more employees and fewer independent shopkeepers. This brought greater pressure for more limited hours because of wage costs, legislation, union pressures and the expectation of a shorter working week. In many countries, the absurd situation was therefore reached that, with the exception of Saturdays, most shops were open only at times that many people were required to work. This situation demonstrated an assumption that much shopping could be undertaken by non-working members of the household and/or that many people were content to regard Saturday as their main shopping day.

Major changes in consumer life-styles have forced such assumptions to be challenged, notably the growth of two-career households and the demand for other leisure activities at weekends. Many retailers have therefore extended their evening opening hours, although the issue of Sunday opening remains a major topic of economic and political debate. Although reference is made to these issues, the focus within this section is upon hours as a retail marketing variable; Gripsrud and Horverak (1986) noted how little attention has been given to opening hours as a possible determinant of retail patronage. This is particularly surprising, in that extended hours can greatly increase the real accessibility of a store, possibly influencing the size/shape of its trading area and the profile of shoppers attracted to it.

Table 12.6 presents evidence of shopping trip times from the USA, where a larger proportion of supermarkets are open long hours. The importance of evening shopping to those in full-time employment is clearly illustrated, with some 41 per cent of them shopping between 5 and 9 pm. Similarly, 44 per cent of this group undertake their main grocery shopping on Saturday or Sunday, a proportion that would undoubtedly be higher if Sunday opening were allowed in all areas. It must also be recognized that grocery shopping is possibly not the most popular form of weekend shopping. In Scotland, where Sunday trading is permitted, Wm Low claim that Sunday opening is worthwhile only for superstores situated close to DIY centres or other popular sites (L'Aimable 1988).

Table 12.7 shows the grocery shopping times of a sample of nearly 3,000 UK shoppers. Certain trends are in common with those of the USA, notably the importance of evening and weekend shopping to those in full-time work. Grocery stores that are open every weekday evening are still in the minority in the UK, and openings beyond 8 pm are still uncommon. The same survey (Euromonitor 1986) also found that 33 per cent of respondents mentioned late opening as a factor especially liked about the store most frequently used; this factor was mentioned by 41 per cent of full-time workers. The particular appeal of evening shopping to younger age groups is illustrated by Table 12.7, which may suggest a time lag in changing

Table 12.6   Time and day of major supermarket trips—USA

	Shopper employed full-time (%)	Shopper not employed (%)	All (%)
Day			
Monday	7	11	9
Tuesday	11	18	12
Wednesday	5	16	12
Thursday	15	24	20
Friday	18	15	17
Saturday	34	13	24
Sunday	10	3	6
Time			
Morning (8.00–12.00)	25	52	40
Afternoon (12.00–17.00)	30	38	35
Evening (17.00–21.00)	41	10	22
Night (21.00–8.00)	4	0	3

Source: Progressive Grocer (1987, p. 42) © 1987 Progressive Grocer.

shopping habits.

In England and Wales there is a somewhat ambiguous body of legislation governing retailing on Sundays. A summary of relevant aspects of the 1950 Shops Act was provided by Clements (1987). As the law stands, only certain categories of goods can be sold on Sundays, including intoxicating liquors, cooked tripe and smokers' requisites! This has led to intriguing attempts to evade the law, such as the sale for £600 of a box of matches, plus a free suite of furniture. Attempts to achieve a major reform of Sunday opening restrictions were defeated in 1986, the strongest opposition being from some retailers, unions and religious groups.

In spite of the regulations much profitable retailing is undertaken on Sundays. In the words of a Home Office spokesman, the law 'has been discredited and widely flouted' (Britton 1987). The enforcement of the law is in the hands of local authorities, some of whom turn a 'blind eye' to Sunday traders. Even when fines are imposed, they are considered to be minimal compared with the benefits of opening: the maximum fine is £1,000 per offence; £500 is the average imposed (Clements 1987). The DIY warehouses are the most aggressive advocates of Sunday trading, their products being especially suitable for it. In a survey organized by the British Hardware Federation, it was found that 65 per cent of the DIY warehouses checked were open on a Sunday (Britton 1987). Including shops open both legally and illegally, it has been estimated that over 60 per cent of people in England and Wales buy some goods on Sundays (Euromonitor 1987).

A number of studies have sought to evaluate consumer attitudes to evening and/or Sunday shopping. In a survey for Mintel (1986), 55 per cent of housewives interviewed claimed that they would never use early morning or late night shopping facilities, but nearly 60 per cent would like to be able to shop on a Sunday. From studies in 1983 and 1985, Clements (1987) found no evidence of increasing demand for general Sunday trading but a considerable increase in demand for specific types of outlet to be open. The products most likely to be bought on Sunday appear

Table 12.7   Time of major grocery shopping trips—UK

| (N = 2,966) | Percentages shopping on: | | | |
	Any weekday morning	Any weekday afternoon	Any weekday evening	Weekends
Total	30	21	20	15
Sex				
Male	25	17	23	19
Female	34	23	18	14
Age				
16–24	15	24	29	20
25–34	20	21	28	18
35–44	25	19	26	16
45–54	27	18	23	19
55–64	38	20	11	18
65 +	54	22	3	6
Social class				
AB	25	19	23	15
C1	24	18	25	14
C2	26	22	24	17
DE	41	23	11	16
Working				
Full-time	10	16	34	23
Part-time	32	28	19	11
Non-working	42	22	11	12

Note: Rows do not total to 100 as 14% of respondents did not specify a particular time and day when they usually undertake their major grocery shopping trips.
Source: adapted from Euromonitor (1986).

to be DIY/decorating materials and garden products, although many other product categories were mentioned (Euromonitor 1987). Of respondents questioned, 23 per cent claimed that they would do their main food and grocery shopping on a Sunday, 54 per cent that they would do 'top-up' food shopping.

Interest in the Sunday trading debate has prompted a number of economic analyses of the effects of extended hours on the communities (e.g. Elliott and Levin 1987) or the retailers involved (e.g. Thurik 1987). The official Home Office enquiry, published before the major parliamentary debate, also contains very detailed estimates of retail costs and margins (Auld *et al.* 1984). Attempts to estimate the economic effects are however fraught with many difficulties (Moir 1987). Similarly, the demand for longer hours and Sunday retailing can be only partially assessed through surveys. Long-term experimentation is required, as major changes in shopping habits occur relatively slowly.

A retailer envisaging a major extension of hours must of course ensure that sufficient staffing and logistical support is available. The Progressive Grocer (1987) noted the particular importance of service departments to weekend grocery shoppers. Customer complaints inevitably arise if staff are unavailable, the fresh food is 'looking tired', shelves are depleted, or the store is less clean as a result of the long hours. Some retailers, however, are trading very effectively and profitably within extended hours. In spite of resistance within the industry, including some major retailers, it would seem inevitable that extended opening times will become an increasingly important marketing variable.

12.3.2 Planning the service mix

The total assortment of other services that a retailer may consider offering is almost without limit. Services range from the most basic, such as free parking or free carrier bags, to such specific services as engraving or gift-wrapping. The retailer can choose between offering free services, subsidized services or making them self-financing. The ideal service is obviously one that both offers an attraction to the store and is at least self-financing, although few meet this criterion. In most cases, the value of the service must be set against the costs and possible effects on margins/prices.

Expectations of other services appear to vary considerably between customer groups and between countries. It is probably true to say that most UK retailers are not high service providers, compared with their counterparts in the USA or some parts of Europe. Table 12.8 provides an analysis of the services offered by supermarkets in the USA, based upon the Progressive Grocer (1988) annual survey. It is interesting to note that bag-packing at the checkout is not even mentioned, being taken for granted in most cases. In over 80 per cent of cases, this extended to carry-out services to the car. Over the five years between 1982 and 1987, the service elements that had spread particularly rapidly were service delicatessens, service fish counters, pharmacies and service centres.

Some contrasts with Table 12.8 can be drawn from a survey of over 10,000 readers of Good Housekeeping magazine, reported in Super Marketing (1987). Among the services not provided that would be liked, bag-packing and carry-out to the car were ranked 2 and 5 in order of mentions. Bag-packing was provided automatically to only 23 per cent, and this was in a sample biased towards users of Sainsbury, Tesco, Waitrose and Safeway. Cash points (ATMs) were given rank 4 and the ability to use credit cards rank 7; Sunday opening was mentioned at rank 12. The facility most frequently requested (rank 1) was toilets, mentioned by 37 per cent. These represent a fairly high-cost service because of cleaning requirements and, if not sited carefully, may assist shoplifters. They are however increasingly demanded as part of the trend towards long shopping expeditions and greater family participation.

Service expectation and priorities are obviously very different in other retail sectors where greater perceived risks are involved in the product purchases; a number of service strategies can be applied to reduce risks and expedite the customer's purchase decision. The liberal returns policy operated by Marks & Spencer was more than just a substitute for changing room facilities, which they have since started to provide. With the freedom to return items, shoppers feel less inhibited in buying clothes, either for themselves or for other members of the household. Once the items are tried at home, the chances that they will be retained are far greater. The considerable cost of operating the returns departments is therefore well justified, and special fast-service returns facilities are often provided for store card holders.

The catalogue retailers also operate generous returns policies to overcome the risks of off-the-page purchasing. Both Argos and Littlewoods catalogue shops offer 16-day money-back guarantees if the customer is not fully satisfied. The operation of such policies obviously has implications for staff training, in that returns must be handled courteously and efficiently, while

Table 12.8   Services offered in supermarkets—USA

Services offered	Independents (%)	Chains (%)	Total (%)
Paper grocery bags	97	99	98
Carry-out services	85	80	82
Plastic grocery bags	65	81	74
Service delicatessen	63	70	67
Film processing service	44	75	61
Magazine reading centre	49	65	58
Scanning checkouts	48	62	56
Hot take-out food	45	53	49
Service centre	42	53	48
On-premise bake-off bakery	39	44	41
Movie cassette rental	34	42	38
Lottery tickets	37	36	36
Service meat	32	36	34
Service cheese	26	41	34
Self-service delicatessen	31	32	31
Service fish	17	32	25
On-premise scratch bakery	15	24	20
Salad bar	13	24	19
Video games	14	23	19
Catering	22	15	18
Pharmacy	6	23	15
ATMs	6	20	14
Sit-down eating	8	17	13
Banking centre	5	9	7

Source: Progressive Grocer (1988, p. 33) © 1988 Progressive Grocer.

checking that the product is in unspoilt condition. Extended warranties can also reduce the risks of purchasing items where some expensive repairs may be anticipated. For example, Comet has operated a five-year guarantee option, extending the legally required warranty for four years. Such warranties greatly assisted television retailers in weaning customers from the rental companies. Like store card services, extended warranties may be operated in-house or 'bought in' from an insurer, such as the Prudential. Extended warranties can be profitable, and staff may be trained to 'suggestion-sell' them.

The actual repair facilities may also be subcontracted or developed in-house. I know of one notable case, however, where the bad repair service provided by a contractor forced a retailer to withdraw from the sale of 'white goods', i.e. freezers, washing machines, etc. Home deliveries are another service that some retailers prefer to avoid, because of the high labour and vehicle costs involved. One extreme operation of this policy was a store selling large chest freezers with no delivery service or suggestions as to how delivery could be obtained! Most DIY warehouses have instituted home delivery services, for which a charge is usually made. In 1988 B & Q sought publicity and competitive advantage by offering free delivery, a strategy with major cost implications. Along with early morning openings, this move was designed particularly to attract trade customers, small builders, plumbers, etc., and amateurs making larger purchases (Retail 1988).

These few examples will have illustrated the range of services offered to enhance convenience, make shopping more interesting, or reduce purchase risks. However, a retailer must evaluate each service possibility with care and frequently re-evaluate those currently being offered. The following factors, adapted from Bolen (1988), may be taken into account in determining the types of service to offer:

1. Type of store—is it a discounter or a full-service department store?
2. Store status—is it a prestige store, where high service levels are expected, or one where basic services and lowest prices are anticipated?
3. Store size—will the volume of service utilization be sufficient in view of the store's size or turnover?
4. Type of products—are they heavy, bulky? Are the perceived risks high?
5. Competition—it is important to be aware of competitors' service propositions, not necessarily to follow them.
6. Promotional policy—will the opportunity be available to communicate effectively the service offering and attract new customers?
7. Location of store—free parking or home delivery, for example, may assume more importance if the store is less accessible; a cafeteria and children's play area may be more important if the store is out of town and remote from other such facilities.
8. Target market—different market segments have very different service priorities and attitudes towards paying for services, either directly or through higher prices.
9. Customer attitudes—is the service essential, expected or optional from the viewpoint of the target customers? Conversely, would the service be viewed as an unnecessary elaboration, catering for a minority and adding to prices?

The importance of relating customer service strategies to the needs and wants of target customer groups cannot be overemphasized. Having investigated the components of 'satisfaction-guaranteed' policies of some stores, Schmidt and Kernan (1985) found that different expectations of such a policy were held by different groups of customers. There is also a need to measure more objectively customers' perceptions of service quality, rather than relying on management judgement or on the analysis of complaints received. Parasuraman et al. (1988) examined the many components of service quality images and developed a scale (SERVQUAL) for tracking and comparing these images. The main image dimensions were considered to be:

- Tangibles—physical facilities, equipment and appearance of personnel
- Reliability—ability to perform the promised service dependably and accurately
- Responsiveness—willingness to help customers and provide prompt service
- Assurance—knowledge and courtesy of employees and their ability to inspire trust and confidence
- Empathy—caring, individualized attention for customers

Some of the more basic services, such as free car parking, become expected and could not easily be withdrawn by retailers. Other 'supplementary services' appear to go through a form of life-cycle, an appreciation of which may assist decisions to retain or withdraw the service (James et al. 1981):

1. Introduction—a new service is introduced, giving differential advantage to a specific retailer.
2. Duplication—if the service is popular and viable, it will be copied, to neutralize the competitive effect.
3. Stalemate—all retailers in the sector offer the service, so it becomes just an added cost; elimination of the service by just one retailer would however create differential disadvantage.
4. Institutionalization—over time, the service is taken for granted by consumers and becomes a basic part of the retail sector's offering.
5. Replacement—some services never disappear, whereas others may diminish in need and importance. Shopping patterns change, different market segments may be targeted, and some functions are taken over by other types of business. This may signal the need to delete, replace or institute/increase charges for a service currently offered.

Bates and Didion (1985) suggested a matrix approach to the development of service strategies. Each service should be evaluated according to whether its cost is high or low and whether its value to the customer is high or low. Low-cost, high-value services (patronage builders) are obviously attractive from the retailer's viewpoint; high-cost, low-value services (disappointers), on the other hand, are clear candidates for elimination. The evaluation of service cost-effectiveness is not an easy task, however, as a wide range of direct and indirect costs and benefits must be carefully weighed. The retailer must also judge the competitive advantage that is achieved and the congruence of the service with overall strategy and positioning.

SUMMARY

The range of services that can be offered by retailers is very wide, including forms of personal service, financial services and many others. In general, additional services set out to make shopping more interesting, more convenient or less worrying for the customers. Retailers are giving increased attention to services as a route to differential advantage, as it becomes increasingly difficult to obtain such advantage through superior locations, prices or assortments. Many of the most attractive target groups are also showing a greater willingness to pay for the right service mix.

The store staff is important in the provision of many forms of service; the quality of such services depends to a large part on effective selection, training, motivation and supervision. Store personnel are very instrumental in the formation of store images, and many customer complaints relate to the level or standard of personal service received. Retailers have been criticized for seeking to discourage or mollify complaints, rather than use them as important diagnostic and marketing information.

By no means all customers prefer personal service, when a satisfactory form of self-service is available instead. The assistance of sales staff, however, is especially important in purchasing items that are complex, expensive and/or infrequently purchased. Effective personal selling involves considerable skill in the application of appropriate techniques at each stage in the selling process. Many sales are lost through poor selling technique or through failure to adapt the product solution or message to the needs of the specific customer.

For a long time, retailers have offered a range of credit services to assist the purchasing of more expensive items. The increasing penetration of bank-issued credit cards and the trend towards larger shopping trips has brought the demand for credit into most sectors, including groceries. Customers are reluctant to carry large sums of money, and cheque transactions are particularly inconvenient. Younger and more up-market consumers are most likely to demand the facility to pay by credit card.

The provision of store cards has now become a major element of many retailers' marketing strategies. If managed properly, these can offer a lower-cost or profitable alternative to accepting bank-issued cards, partly because shoppers appear largely insensitive to different levels of interest rate. Their biggest advantage is the facility they provide to communicate directly with customers and to increase loyalty. Armed with valuable segmentation information about the card holders, a retailer has numerous opportunities to target direct mail and monitor response. Some retailers are also diversifying into other forms of financial services, including banking, personal loans, insurance, unit trusts and share-dealing.

EFTPoS (electronic funds transfer at the point of sale) is still in its infancy in the UK, but is likely to develop as a transaction mode through the 1990s. EFTPoS reduces time spent at the checkouts, and most systems can authorize either debit or credit transactions. EFTPoS offers advantages to retailers and a service to their customers, but this must be weighed against the costs involved and the possibility of annoying some customers if the system is not carefully implemented.

Among the other elements of the service mix, extended hours have now acquired much significance. The demand for shopping outside normal working hours has been stimulated by the increase in two-career households, family involvement in the shopping trip, the need/wish to use the family car for shopping, and other changes in life-styles. Over one-third of shoppers who work full-time now do their major supermarket shopping in the evening. There is evidence of significant demand for Sunday shopping, although this is still prohibited or severely restricted in many areas.

Given the vast choice of service options, a retailer must very carefully evaluate both the costs and the benefits, both direct and indirect, of providing a service. The appropriateness of a service is likely to depend upon the type, size, status and location of a store, the type of products sold, the services provided by competitors, and the target market and its attitudes towards the service. Many supplementary services display a form of life-cycle, whereby the differential advantage is lost as the service is copied, then eventually taken for granted. All existing services should be frequently re-evaluated in terms of their costs and real value to customers.

REVIEW QUESTIONS

1. What are the main factors that motivate retailers to offer additional services to their customers?
2. How should a large retail company organize its system to deal with customer complaints? Illustrate how this system could provide inputs to the determination of customer service strategy.
3. Is self-service simply a lack of service? Why do some consumers prefer to use self-service options, even when conventional service is offered at the same cost?
4. How would you define the role of personal service in:
    (a) a DIY warehouse?
    (b) a supermarket?
    (c) a high-fashion store?
5. What measures should salespersons in a computer shop take to improve their technique at each stage of the selling process?
6. Outline the alternative types of credit facility that a retailer could offer. Why do retailers in most sectors now accept bank-issued credit cards?
7. What are the main advantages and drawbacks of issuing the company's own store card?

8. With reference to specific retail companies of your choice, what scope exists for those companies to provide other forms of financial services?
9. What is an EFTPoS system? What advantages would a retailer expect to gain in adopting EFTPoS, and what problems may be encountered?
10. How would you evaluate the costs and the benefits of extending the hours of opening your store?
11. You are considering the option of providing bag-packing and carry-out services within a supermarket. What factors should you consider in reaching your decision?
12. Explain the concept of the service life-cycle. What are the implications of this cycle for retailers' service strategies?

REFERENCES

Aldred, G. (1989), Service with a sneer', *Retail*, **6**(4), 6–7.
Arnold, D. R., L. M. Capella and G. D. Smith (1983), *Strategic Retail Management*, Addison-Wesley, Reading, Mass.
Auld, R. *et al.* (1984), *The Shops Acts: Late Night and Sunday Opening: Report from Committee of Inquiry*, HMSO, London.
Bauer, R. A. (1960), 'Consumer behavior as risk taking', in R. S. Hancock (ed.), *Dynamic Marketing for a Changing World*, American Marketing Association, Chicago, pp. 389–98.
Bates, A. D. and J. G. Didion (1985), 'Special services can personalise retail environment', *Marketing News*, 12 April, 13.
Bateson, J. E. G. (1985), 'Self-service consumer: an exploratory study', *Journal of Retailing*, **61**(3), 49–76.
Bendall, A. and J. Hayes (1987), 'Retailers and bankers: will the marriage work?' *Retail*, **5**(1), 40–2.
Bennett, S. (1988), 'Draw your debit card, pardner', *Progressive Grocer*, **66**(1), 61–4.
Bliss, M. (1979), 'How Debenhams promoted the credit card', *Retail & Distribution Management*, **7**(1), 10–15.
Bliss, M. (1982), 'Diversification into private label credit cards for retailers', *Retail Control*, **51**(3), 2–8.
Bliss, M. (1988), 'The impact of retailers on financial services', *Long Range Planning*, **21**(1), 55–8.
Bolen, W. H. (1970), 'Customer contact: those first important words', *Department Store Management*, **33**(3), 25–6.
Bolen, W. H. (1988), *Contemporary Retailing*, Prentice-Hall, Englewood Cliffs, NJ.
Britton, N. (1987), 'Shop law open to debate—and Sunday trade', *Marketing*, 17 December.
Burstiner, I. (1975/6), 'Current personnel practices in department stores', *Journal of Retailing*, **51**(4), 3–13, 85–6.
Churchill, G. A., R. H. Collins and W. A. Strang (1975), 'Should retail salespersons be similar to their customers?' *Journal of Retailing*, **51**(3), 29–42, 79.
Clarke, E. D. (1983), 'The craft of selling in department stores', *Retail & Distribution Management*, **11**(1), 35–9.
Clements, M. A. (1987), 'Sunday trading: is partial deregulation the answer?' *Retail & Distribution Management*, **15**(2), 14–16.
Davies, K., C. T. Gilligan and C. J. Sutton (1986), 'The development of own label product strategies in grocery and DIY retailing in the United Kingdom', *International Journal of Retailing*, **1**(1), 7–19.
Dubinsky, A. J. and B. E. Mattson (1979), 'Consequences of role conflict and ambiguity experienced by retail salespeople', *Journal of Retailing*, **55**(4), 70–86.
EftPos UK (1987), *Business Service Specification for the EftPos UK Inaugural Service—Public Consultation Document*, EftPos UK, London.
Elliott, D. S. and S. L. Levin (1987), 'Estimating the economic impact of repealing laws prohibiting Sunday sales', *International Journal of Retailing*, **2**(1), 31–43.
Euromonitor (1986), *The Changing Face of Grocery Retailing*, Euromonitor, London.
Euromonitor (1987), *Retail Trade in the United Kingdom*, Euromonitor, London.
Fletcher, K. (1987), 'Consumers' use and perceptions of retailer-controlled information sources', *International Journal of Retailing*, **2**(3), 59–66.
Frazer, P. (1985), 'EFTPoS: issues and insights', *Journal of Retail Banking*, **7**(2), 1–8.
Frazer, P. (1988), 'The plastic card—the bank in your pocket', *Banking World*, **6**(3), 24–30.
Freestone, D. (1987), 'The Connect card debacle', *Retail & Distribution Management*, **15**(5), 19–20, 35.
Gripsrud, G. and O. Horverak (1986), 'Determinants of retail patronage: a "natural" experiment', *International Journal of Research in Marketing*, **3**(4), 263–72.
Heath, S. (1987), 'EFTPoS at the crossroads', *Banking Technology*, **4**(7/8), 14–18.
Hirschman, E. C. and J. L. Goldstucker (1978), 'Bank credit card usage in department stores: an empirical investigation', *Journal of Retailing*, **54**(2), 3–12, 93.

Humble, J. and D. Randell (1988), 'Service in retail', *Retail*, **5**(4), 39–41.

Hummel, J. W. and R. Savitt (1988), 'Integrating customer service and retail strategy', *International Journal of Retailing*, **3**(2), 5–21.

Hunter, T. (1988), 'Base instincts', *Guardian*, 16 April, 31.

ICL (1987), *Retailing Today*, ICL (UK), Slough.

Ironfield, C. E. and P. J. McGoldrick (1988), 'EFTPoS systems—determinants of shoppers' awareness and usage', *International Journal of Retailing*, **3**(4), 24–42.

James, D. L., B. J. Walker and M. J. Etzel (1981), *Retailing Today*, Harcourt Brace Jovanovich, New York.

Johnson, T. (1987), 'Flexing retail muscle with flexible friends', *Marketing Week*, **10**(36), 55–65.

Jones, D. (1986), 'The smart card comes in from the cold', *Banking Technology*, **2**(1), 30–1.

Jones, G. (1987), 'A pocketful of miracles', *Retail & Distribution Management*, **15**(4), 22–4.

King, D. (1988), 'Competition hots up for the card of your choice', *Times*, 16 May, 34.

Lafferty (1987), *People and Payments*, Lafferty Group, London.

L'Aimable, G. (1988), 'Scots "thumbs-down" to Sunday trading', *Super Marketing*, no. 816, 3.

Letino, J. (1986), 'Giving the consumer due credit', *Retail*, **4**(1), 39–40.

Leo Burnett (1987), *Are You Being Served?* Leo Burnett, London.

Market Place (1986), 'Who holds the plastic?', *Market Place*, **4**, 38–39.

McFadyen, E. (1987), 'Retailers' attitudes to EFTPoS', *Retail & Distribution Management*, **15**(4), 19–20.

Mills, K. H. and J. E. Paul (1979), *Successful Retail Sales*, Prentice-Hall, Englewood Cliffs, NJ.

Mintel (1986), *Retailing and the Shopper*, Mintel, London.

Mintel (1987), 'Electronic funds transfer at the point of sale', *Retail Intelligence*, **1**, 157–65.

Moir, C. B. (1987), 'Research difficulties in the analysis of Sunday trading', *International Journal of Retailing*, **2**(1), 3–21.

Muttram, J. (1987), 'Papering over the EFTPoS cracks?' *Super Marketing*, no. 767, 4–5.

National Consumer Council (1987), *Response to the Monopolies and Mergers Commission Inquiry into Credit Card Services*, NCC, London.

Ody, P. (1988), 'Joining the smart card set', *The Times*, 16 May, 38.

Ognjenovic, D. (1980), 'Is there a credit card in the house?' *Retail & Distribution Management*, **8**(2), 16–21.

O'Shaughnessy, J. (1971/2), 'Selling as an interpersonal influence process', *Journal of Retailing*, , **47**(4), 32–46.

Parasuraman, A., V. A. Zeithaml and L. L. Berry (1988), 'SERVQUAL: a multiple-item scale for measuring consumer perceptions of service quality', *Journal of Retailing*, **64**(1), 12–40.

Porter, T. C., R. A. Swerdlow and W. A. Staples (1979), 'Who uses bank debit cards?' *Business Horizons*, **22**(1), 75–83.

Progressive Grocer (1987), 'Consumers', 54th Annual Report, *Progressive Grocer*, **66**(4), pt. 2, 40–5.

Progressive Grocer (1988), 'The evolution of the supermarket', 55th Annual Report, *Progressive Grocer*, **67**(4), pt. 2, 33.

Rainbow, S. W. (1987), 'Your customers are not altogether happy', *Retail & Distribution Management*, **15**(4), 29–31.

Retail (1986), 'Metrocentre: the centre of attention', *Retail*, **4**(3), 5–6.

Retail (1988), 'The magnificent seven', *Retail*, **6**(1), 12–31.

Retail Business (1987a), 'Credit and charge cards', *Retail Business*, no. 356, 36–46.

Retail Business (1987b), 'Progress with EFTPoS', *Retail Business*, no. 352, 4–8.

Retail Review (1988), 'DIY majors on customer services drive', *Retail Review*, no. 142, 9.

RMDP (1987), *Using EFTPoS*, Retail Management Development Programme, Brighton.

Rogers, L. (1988), *Retail Selling: a Practical Guide for Sales Staff*, Kogan Page, London.

Sands, D. (1987), 'ICSC discuss the human face of retailing', *Retail & Distribution Management*, **15**(3), 36–8.

Schmidt, S. L. and J. B. Kernan (1985), 'The many meanings (and implications) of "satisfaction guaranteed"', *Journal of Retailing*, **61**(4), 89–108.

Smith, C. (1987), 'Will EFTPoS really help the retailers improve service at the checkout desk?' *EFTPoS International Bulletin*, May, 6–9.

Sparks, L. (1984), 'Electronic funds transfers at the point of sale—an overview', *University of Stirling Working Papers*, no. 8406.

Super Marketing (1987), 'Supermarket: what the customers think', *Super Marketing*, no. 771, 4–5.

Teas, R. K. (1982), 'Performance–reward instrumentalities and the motivation of retail salespeople', *Journal of Retailing*, **58**(3), 4–26.

Thompson, W. (1988), 'All credit to retailers', *Retail Technology*, **2**(3), 12–13.

Thomson, R. (1988), 'A nation in love with plastic money', *The Times*, 16 May, 32.

Thurik, A. R. (1987), 'Optimal trading hours in retailing', *International Journal of Retailing*, **2**(1), 22–30.

Walker, C. (1988), 'Access looks to a flexible future with food trade', *Super Marketing*, no. 807, 16.

Walman, B. (1986), 'What future for electronic payment systems?', *Retail & Distribution Management*, **14**(1), 6–8.

Warner, L. (1987), 'Dee to take on credit giants in "food on tick" battle', *Marketing*, 15 October, 1, 27.

Williamson, J. (1986), 'Department Stores in Japan', *Retail & Distribution Management*, **14**(4), 14–17.

Woodman, B. (1987), 'EFTPoS in the UK', *Proceedings of the EPoS87 with EFTPoS87 Conference*, RMDP, Brighton, Q1–Q24.

Worthington, S. (1986), 'Retailer credit cards and direct marketing—a question of synergy', *Journal of Marketing Management*, **2**(2), 125–31.

Worthington, S. (1987), 'Credit where credit's due!' *Retail & Distribution Management*, **15**(1), 36–7.

Zeithaml, V. A. and M. C. Gilly (1987), 'Characteristics affecting the acceptance of retailing technologies: a comparison of elderly and nonelderly consumers', *Journal of Retailing*, **63**(1), 49–68.

NAME INDEX

SUBJECT INDEX